Adolescent Romantic Relations and Sexual Behavior

Theory, Research, and Practical Implications

Adolescent Romantic Relations and Sexual Behavior

Theory, Research, and Practical Implications

Edited by

Paul Florsheim
University of Utah

LEA

LAWRENCE ERLBAUM ASSOCIATES, PUBLISHERS

2003   Mahwah, New Jersey   London

Lawrence Erlbaum Associates, Inc., Publishers
10 Industrial Avenue
Mahwah, NJ 07430

Cover design by Kathryn Houghtaling Lacey.
Cover photos by 17-year-old Alexander Uhlmann.
Photos used by permission of the photographer.

Library of Congress Cataloging-in-Publication Data

Adolescent romantic relations and sexual behavior : theory, research,
and practical implications / edited by Paul Florsheim
    p.   cm.
    Includes bibliographical references and index.
    ISBN 0-8058-3830-9
    1. Teenagers—United States—Sexual behavior. 2. Adolescent
psychology—United States. 3. Interpersonal relations—United States.
4. Interpersonal conflict—United States. I. Florsheim, Paul.

HQ27.A3634 2003
306.7'0835—dc21   SEP 1 5 2004   2003043897

Books published by Lawrence Erlbaum Associates are printed on acid-free paper,
and their bindings are chosen for strength and durability.

Printed in the United States of America
10 9 8 7 6 5 4 3 2 1

Contents

Introduction: Paul Florsheim   vii

Contributors   xv

Part I: NORMATIVE PERSPECTIVES ON ROMANTIC RELATIONS
AND SEXUAL BEHAVIOR AMONG ADOLESCENTS

1   The Role of Romantic Relationships in Adolescent Development   3
Wyndol Furman and Laura Shaffer

2   National Estimates of Adolescent Romantic Relationships   23
Karen Carver, Kara Joyner, and J. Richard Udry

3   Biological Influences on Adolescent Romantic and Sexual Behavior   57
Carolyn Tucker Halpern

4   Love Matters: Romantic Relationships Among Sexual-Minority   85
Adolescents
Lisa M. Diamond

5   Conflict and Negotiation in Adolescent Romantic Relationships   109
Shmuel Shulman

6   Attachment Styles and Adolescent Sexuality   137
*Jessica L. Tracy, Phillip R. Shaver, Austin W. Albino,
and M. Lynne Cooper*

Part II: PERSPECTIVES ON ROMANTIC AND SEXUAL BEHAVIOR
AMONG HIGH-RISK ADOLESCENTS

7   Psychopathology and Relational Dysfunction Among Adolescent   163
Couples: The Structural Analysis of Social Behavior as
an Organizing Framework
Trina Seefeldt, Paul Florsheim, and Lorna Smith Benjamin

8   When Love Hurts: Depression and Adolescent Romantic   185
Relationships
Deborah P. Welsh, Catherine M. Grello, and Melinda S. Harper

9   Child Maltreatment, Adolescent Dating, and Adolescent Dating   213
Violence
Christine Wekerle and Effie Avgoustis

10 The Development of Aggression in Young Male/Female Couples   243
Deborah M. Capaldi and Deborah Gorman-Smith

11 Health Behaviors and Reproductive Health Risk Within   279
Adolescent Sexual Dyads
J. Dennis Fortenberry

12 Romantic Relations Among Adolescent Parents   297
Paul Florsheim, David Moore, and Chuck Edgington

Part III: COMMENTARY AND SUMMARY

13 Are Adolescent Same-Sex Romantic Relationships on Our   325
Radar Screen?
Ritch C. Savin-Williams

14 A Marital Process Perspective of Adolescent Romantic   337
Relationships
Amber Tabares and John Gottman

15 The Joy of Romance: Healthy Adolescent Relationships as   355
an Educational Agenda
Bonnie Barber and Jacquelynne Eccles

16 Adolescent Romantic and Sexual Behavior: What We Know   387
and Where We Go From Here
Paul Florsheim

Author Index   387

Subject Index   407

Introduction

Paul Florsheim

At some point in our adult lives, most of us will feel compelled to say something useful to a young man or woman struggling with a romantic relationship. Perhaps this hypothetical youth falls for someone who looks (to us) like nothing but trouble, or things seem to be going too far too fast, or he or she is distraught following a bad fight or breakup. In these situations, it is difficult to know what to say. We are at a loss for words partly because we were once young and we know that in the realm of romance, wisdom and experience mean little to new initiates. Most of us made bad decisions in choosing romantic partners, and made mistakes about how we treated past loves. Yet, we know that we needed to live through and learn from these experiences and would have been unlikely to listen to advice offered by our elders.

We are also at a loss for words because we have only our own experiences to guide us. Although we have some ideas about what sorts of relationships are bad for adolescents, we recognize that the process of distinguishing between "healthy, normal, adaptive" and "unhealthy, abnormal, maladaptive" relationships is fraught with difficulties. Definitions of normal relations vary widely, depending on contextual norms, social constraints, cultural values, and developmental phases. Moreover, adolescents in relationships that appear healthy may experience a great deal of psychological distress when problems arise. Adolescents in relationships that seem troubling to us might feel happier than ever. These ironic twists make it difficult to offer useful guidance. How can we make sense of this?

While we know that there are no simple solutions to the difficulties posed by love and sex, it is nonetheless our responsibility to help youth in our care to sort though the issues and reflect upon their feelings. We need to provide a developmental context that helps adolescents make thoughtful, heartfelt decisions about love and sex. We need to help them acquire the tools they will need to build and maintain healthy relationships. First we need to identify those tools for ourselves.

Scholarship on adolescent romance is potentially helpful because it allows us to connect personal experiences with broader concepts and issues. It informs us about the range of experiences that are different from our own. It helps us to know and understand more than what we could ever hope to experience firsthand. The field is fortunate in that several prominent psychological theorists (Ainsworth, 1989; Bowlby, 1988; Blos, 1967; Erikson, 1968; Sullivan, 1953) have contributed a great deal to our current understanding of adolescent romance. However, until recently there has been very little research on adolescent romance, and even less on interventions designed to help adolescents develop healthy relationships (Brown, Feiring, & Furman, 1999).

It seems remarkable that developmental and clinical researchers have only just discovered the phenomenon of adolescent romance as a topic of serious scientific inquiry. This discovery may be related to the overwhelming evidence that adult romantic relationships are failing at alarming rate. Dramatic increases in the rates of divorce, out-of-wedlock childbirth, and relationship violence lead to questions about the developmental precursors of romantic love and commitment. What's wrong with love, and can it be fixed? This volume on adolescent romantic and sexual behavior is intended to address what I and others (Brown et al., 1999; Shulman & Kipnis, 2001) perceive as a serious gap in our understanding of adolescent development. As a clinical psychologist, I have tried to approach the topic of adolescent romance from an applied perspective.

The volume is divided into three parts. Part I focuses on romantic relations and sexual behavior from the perspective of normative adolescent development. None of the authors in this section actually attempts to define what constitutes a healthy adolescent relationship, but collectively they lay a conceptual framework and empirically based foundation for considering the issue. First and foremost, we need to understand the developmental context within which romantic relationships emerge. In chapter 1, Furman and Shaffer discuss the role of family and peer relations in laying an interpersonal foundation for the development of adolescent romantic relations. They then focus on how adolescent romantic and sexual relations can facilitate or inhibit the achievement of normative developmental tasks associated with adolescence, such as identity development, individuation from family of origin, and scholastic achievement.

Owing much to the work of sociologists and public health epidemiologists (Resnick et al., 1998; Sonenstein, Ku, Lindberg, Turner, & Pleck, 1998; Udry & Campbell, 1994), we have more information about the patterns of adolescent sexuality and birth control use than we know about the interpersonal and emotional contexts in which sexual behavior occurs. In chapter 2, Carver, Joyner, and Udry draw upon a nationally representative sample of adolescents to address basic questions about adolescent romance (as opposed to adolescent sexual behavior). When do adolescents begin dating? How stable are adolescent relationships? How do adolescent couples express their affection and commitment? To what extent are adolescent couples embedded within a larger social network of peers and family members? To complement the theoretical framework presented by Furman and Shaffer in chapter 1, the Carver, Joyner, and Udry chapter provides an empirically based framework that helps to anchor this section in the essential (but elusive) facts about adolescent romantic relations.

Most of the chapters in this volume focus on romantic and sexual behaviors as psychological phenomena. However, it is important to remember that we are biological organisms and that romantic and sexual behaviors are also biologically motivated. In chapter 3, which focuses on the biological bases of romantic behavior, Halpern addresses how biological changes that occur during adolescence affect the development of romantic behaviors, feelings, and interests. Somewhat unexpectedly in a chapter on the biological and neurochemical bases of romantic experiences, Halpern presents a fundamentally interactionist perspective, addressing several social issues relevant to the development of biological processes during adolescence.

In chapter 4, Diamond addresses the issue of same-sex romantic relationships from a normative developmental perspective. In a chapter that describes the diversity of experiences among sexual minority youth and charts some of the unexplored territory between distinctively "gay" and "straight" sexuality, Diamond debunks some prevalent and potentially harmful myths associated with sexual-minority youth. She also describes how the inclusion of same-sex attractions and behaviors into our understanding of adolescent development can help broaden our current understanding of sexuality.

Clinical psychologists tend to focus on conflict in close relationships as a risk factor for the development of clinically significant psychological problems, including depression and violence. Yet it seems that some form of conflict between romantic partners is as normal and expectable as the typical conflicts that occur among family members. This begs the question of how we might differentiate between adaptive and maladaptive modes of conflict between romantic partners. Moreover, what developmental function might "adaptive" conflicts serve? In chapter 5, Shulman examines the issue of conflict and conflict resolution among adolescent romantic partners, with case study illustrations of different conflict styles. Shulman builds the case that conflict is a normative feature of most romantic relations, and that having a healthy romantic relationship involves some degree of skill with conflict resolution.

In our effort to better understand the contexts in which sexual behaviors occur it is important that we not lose sight of individual psychological differences. Young individuals approach the developmental challenges posed by sexual intimacy with different sets of psychological resources. How successfully adolescents make the transition to becoming sexually active largely depends on their ability to self-regulate their behavior, and the emotional experiences associated with sexual encounters. Understanding these individual differences plays an important part in developing a framework for helping psychologically vulnerable adolescents successfully navigate this transition. In chapter 6, Tracy, Shaver, Albino, and Cooper apply Bowlby's theory of attachment relations to our current understanding of adolescent sexual behavior. This chapter marks an advance over purely descriptive approaches to the study of adolescent sexual behavior and presents some provocative findings relating attachment types to motivations and emotional experiences associated with sexual relationships.

The current research literature on marital relations provides ample evidence that when psychopathology occurs in one (or both) partner(s) the relationship is likely to suffer. Yet we know very little about how adolescent psychopathology or problem behavior affects the development of romantic and sexual relations. Part II of this volume focuses on romantic and sexual behavior among high-risk adolescents. In chapter 7, Seefeldt, Florsheim, and Benjamin focus on the importance of clarifying links between specific types of adolescent psychopathology and patterns of interpersonal processes within the context of romantic relationships. This chapter presents the Structural Analysis of Social Behavior (SASB) as a conceptual and methodological framework for differentiating between adaptive and dysfunctional romantic relationships among adolescents. While readers may find the SASB model complicated and difficult to grasp initially, the established clinical utility of this model makes it worth the effort (Benjamin, 1994, 1996).

It seems self-evident that some youth appear more vulnerable to interpersonal wounds than others. It is this group whom adults tend to worry about most as they enter puberty, become sexually active, and engage in romantic liaisons, because they appear to be more easily hurt and less quick to heal. In chapter 8, Welsh, Grello, and Harper address how adolescents who have a history of depression are particularly vulnerable to problems with romantic relations and that for some adolescents, the stress associated with romantic relations increases the risk for becoming depressed. In this chapter that focuses on the potentially "dark" side of adolescent romance, Welsh et al. provide a number of useful recommendations about how educators and public health professionals might address the link between adolescent depression (particularly in girls) and distress associated with romantic relationships.

There has been growing interest among researchers and clinicians in "cycles of abuse and victimization." Adolescent romantic relations appear to occupy

an important role in these cycles, because it is during adolescence that relational tendencies are either crystallized or transformed. In chapter 9, Wekerle
and Avgoustis review a body of research indicating that adolescents who have
a history of victimization (as children) are likely to become involved in violent
romantic relations, where they might become perpetrators, victims, or both.
Related to the issue of recurring patterns of violence, Capaldi and Gorman-
Smith (chapter 10) present data from two studies tracking the development of
aggressive, antisocial boys over a long period of time. This chapter identifies
links between childhood aggression, hostile attitudes toward women, and the
occurrence of violent behavior toward romantic partners. Their evidence suggests that aggressive boys are likely to become men who engage in violent
romantic relationships. They also found that these aggressive men tend to
find partners who are also aggressive, highlighting the transactional nature of
violence within close relationships. Both Capaldi and Gorman-Smith (chapter 10) and Wekerle and Avgoutis (chapter 9) make several very important
points regarding the development of preventive intervention programs focusing on adolescent romantic relationship as a window of opportunity for inter-
rupting the cycle of abuse and preventing the transmission of aggression from
one generation to the next.

In chapter 11, Fortenberry focuses on health-risk and health-protective
behaviors among a group of romantic dyads recruited from a Sexually Transmitted Disease (STD) clinic population. Starting with the hypothesis that
romantic partners are likely to have an influence on each other's risk and protective behaviors, Fortenberry demonstrates that risk status within sexual
dyads is highly correlated. The behavioral interdependence between partners
suggests the possibility that for certain types of problems (like sexually transmitted disease), preventive and treatment efforts that focus on the sexual dyad
as the "identified patient" might be more effective than traditional interventions that focus solely on the infected individual.

In chapter 12, Florsheim, Moore, and Edgington examine the romantic
relationships among pregnant teens and their partners, documenting that the
quality of relations between pregnant teens and their partners is relevant to
how successfully the young couple navigates the transition to parenthood. Furthermore, this chapter describes differences in the interpersonal behavior
functioning of couples who report low levels of relationship satisfaction,
underscoring the importance of helping young couples develop positive interpersonal skills that are likely to help them be supportive of each other across
the transition to parenthood.

Part III of this volume includes four chapters that summarize and comment
on the chapters included in Parts I and II, focusing on the implications for clinicians, educators and future researchers. In chapter 13, Savin Williams offers

a critical review of how well this volume addresses the issue of sexual orientation and provides a clear set of guidelines for avoiding heterocentricity in the study of romantic and sexual behavior. In Chapter 14, Taberes and Gottman draw upon the lessons learned from marital research to evaluate the contribution of this volume and offer conceptual and methodological guidance to future adolescent romance researchers. In chapter 15, Barber and Eccles address the educational implications of the chapters in this volume, focusing on the development of skill building and education programs and the provision of safe, open environments for addressing individual differences and gender-based inequities in romantic relations. Finally, in chapter 16, I take stock of where we are, as a field, with respect to (a) differentiating between healthy and dysfunctional adolescent romantic relations and (b) developing prevention and intervention programs for facilitating healthy romantic relationships among adolescents.

Although academic researchers have recently embraced the issue of adolescent romance (Collins, 2002), clinicians, educators, and policy makers are still unsure about how to work with adolescents on issues related to their romantic relations. When I initially contacted the authors who have contributed to this volume, I asked them to try to address some of the practical (e.g., clinical, educational, public health) issues related to their particular areas of expertise. Most of the authors accommodated this request thoughtfully, creatively, and cautiously. Together, the chapters in this volume make some progress toward bridging the gap between our theoretical and empirically based understanding of adolescent romantic relationships and our readiness to help adolescents successfully navigate the tumultuous waters of young love.

REFERENCES

Ainsworth, M. D. S. (1989). Attachments beyond infancy. *American Psychologist, 44*, 709–716.

Benjamin, L. S. (1994). SASB: A bridge between personality theory and clinical psychology. *Psychological Inquiry, 5*, 273–316.

Benjamin, L. S. (1996). A clinician-friendly version of the interpersonal circumplex: Structural Analysis of Social Behavior (SASB). *Journal of Personality Assessment, 66*, 248–266.

Blos, P. (1967) The second individuation process of adolescence. *The Psychoanalytic Study of the Child, 22*, 162–186.

Bowlby, J. (1988). *A Secure Base.* New York: Basic Books.

Brown, B. B., Furman, W., & Feiring, C. (1999). Missing the Love Boat: Why researchers have shied away from adolescent romance. In W. Furman & B. B. Brown (Eds.), *The development of romantic relationships in adolescence* (pp. 1–16). New York: Cambridge University Press.

Collins, W. A. (2002). *More than myth: The developmental significance of romantic relationships during adolescence.* Presidential Address delivered to the Society for Research on Adolescence, New Orleans, April 2002.

Erikson, E. H. (1968). *Identity: Youth and crisis.* New York: Norton.

Resnick, M. D., Bearman, P. S., Blum, R. W., Bauman, K. E., Harris, K. M., Jones, J., et al. (1998). Protecting adolescents from harm: Findings from the National Longitudinal Study of Adolescent Health. In R. E. Muuss & H. D. Porton (Eds.), *Adolescent behavior and society: A book of readings* (5th ed., pp. 376–395). New York: McGraw-Hill.

Shulman, S., & Kipnis, O. (2001). Adolescent romantic relationships: A look from the future. *Journal of Adolescence, 24,* 337–351.

Sonenstein, F. L., Ku, L., Lindberg, L. D., Turner, C. F, & Pleck, J. H. (1998). Changes in sexual behavior and condom use among teenaged males: 1988 to 1995. *American Journal of Public Health, 88,* 956–959.

Sullivan, H. S. (1953). *The interpersonal theory of psychiatry.* New York: Norton.

Udry, J. R., & Campbell, B. (1994). Getting started on sexual behavior. In Alice Rossi (Ed.), *Sexuality across the life course* (187–207). Chicago, IL: The University of Chicago Press.

Contributors

Austin W. Albino
Dept. of Psychology
University of Missouri–Columbia
Columbia, MO 65211

Effie Avgoustis
Behavioural Sciences Building
Psychology Department
York University
4700 Keele Street
Toronto, Ontario
M3J 1P3 Canada

Bonnie Barber
University of Arizona
Family and Consumer Sciences
1110 E. South Campus Dr.
Tucson, Arizona 85721–0033

Lorna Smith Benjamin
Department of Psychology
University of Utah
380 South 1530 East, Room 502
Salt Lake City, UT 84112

Deborah M. Capaldi
Oregon Social Learning Center
160 E. 4th Ave.
Eugene, OR 97401

Karen Carver
Indian Health Service
OPH/Statistics Program
801 Thompson Ave., Suite 120
Rockville, MD 20852

M. Lynne Cooper
Dept. of Psychology
University of Missouri–Columbia
Columbia, MO 65211

Lisa M. Diamond
Department of Psychology
University of Utah
380 South 1530 East, Room 502
Salt Lake City, UT 84112

Jacquelynne Eccles
University of Michigan
5201 Institute for Social Research
P.O. Box 1248
Ann Arbor, MI 48106

Chuck Edgington
Oklahoma State University
Department of Psychology
215 N. Murray
Stillwater, OK 74078–3064

J. Dennis Fortenberry
Indiana University School of Medicine
Department of Pediatrics
Riley Hospital for Children
Room 5900
702 Barnhill Drive
Indianapolis, IN 46202

Paul Florsheim
Department of Psychology
University of Utah
380 South 1530 East, Room 502
Salt Lake City, UT 84112

Wyndol Furman
Department of Psychology
University of Denver
Frontier Hall
Denver, CO 80208

Deborah Gorman-Smith
Institute for Juvenile Research
University of Illinois–Chicago
840 South Wood Street (M/C 747)
Chicago, IL 60612

John Gottman
Department of Psychology
Guthrie Hall
University of Washington
Box 351525
Seattle, WA 98195

Catherine M. Grello
Department of Psychology
Austin Peay Building
University of Tennessee
Knoxville, TN 37996–0900

Carolyn Tucker Halpern
Dept. of Maternal and Child Health
CB #7445, 427 Rosenau Hall
University of North Carolina
    at Chapel Hill
Chapel Hill, NC 27516

Melinda S. Harper
Department of Psychology
Austin Peay Building
University of Tennessee
Knoxville, TN 37996–0900

Kara Joyner
Department of Policy Analysis
    and Management
Cornell University
108 MVR Hall
Ithaca, NY 14853–4401

David Moore
Department of Psychology
University of Puget Sound
1500 N. Warner
Tacoma, WA 98416

Ritch C. Savin-Williams
Department of Human Development
Cornell University
Ithaca, NY 14853–4401

Trina Seefeldt
Department of Psychology
University of Utah
380 South 1530 East, Room 502
Salt Lake City, UT 84112

Laura Shaffer
Department of Psychology
University of Denver
Frontier Hall
Denver, CO 80208

Philip R. Shaver
Psychology Department
University of California
One Shields Avenue
Davis, CA 95616

Shmuel Shulman
Department of Psychology
Bar-Ilan University
Ramat-Gan 52900, Israel

Amber Tabares
Department of Psychology
Guthrie Hall
University of Washington
Box 351525
Seattle, WA 98195

Jessica L. Tracy
Department of Psychology
University of California, Davis
One Shields Avenue
Davis, CA 95616–8686

J. Richard Udry
Carolina Population Center
University of North Carolina
   at Chapel Hill
CB# 8120 University Square
Chapel Hill, NC 27516–3997

Christine Wekerle
Centre for Addiction
   and Mental Health
University of Toronto
250 College Street
Toronto, ON, Canada M5T 1R8

Deborah P. Welsh
Department of Psychology
Austin Peay Building
University of Tennessee
Knoxville, TN 37996–0900

I

NORMATIVE PERSPECTIVES ON ROMANTIC RELATIONS AND SEXUAL BEHAVIOR AMONG ADOLESCENTS

1

The Role of Romantic Relationships in Adolescent Development

Wyndol Furman
Laura Shaffer
University of Denver

Most of us would characterize our adolescent romantic relationships as short-lived and superficial. In some respects, this description is correct. Most adolescent relationships only last a few weeks or months; it is unlikely that these relationships have the depth and complexity that characterize long-term committed relationships.

At the same time, the characterization of these relationships as short and superficial is incomplete. These relationships are central in adolescents' lives. They are a major topic of conversation among adolescents (Eder, 1993; Thompson, 1994). Real or fantasized relationships are the most common cause of strong positive and strong negative emotions—more so than friendships, relationships with parents, or school (Wilson-Shockley, 1995). Moreover, adolescents are not the only ones who see these relationships as significant. The formation of romantic relationships is often thought to be one of the important developmental tasks of adolescence (Sullivan, 1953), and these relationships have significant implications for health and adjustment (Bouchey & Furman, in press).

Not only are adolescent romantic relationships significant in their own right, but the thesis of this chapter is that they play an important role in shaping the general course of development during adolescence. In particular, adolescents face a series of tasks that include (a) the development of an identity, (b) the transformation of family relationships, (c) the development of close relationships with peers, (d) the development of sexuality, and (e) scholastic achievement and career planning. In the sections that follow, we describe how romantic relationships may play a role in each of these key developmental tasks.

Three caveats are warranted. First, the research primarily has been conducted with heterosexual adolescents in Western cultures, and we know little about gay, lesbian, and bisexual relationships or romantic relationships in other cultures. Second, even the existing literature on Western heterosexual romantic relationships is limited. The question of what impact they have on development has received almost no attention. Thus, our comments are often speculative and will need to be tested empirically. Finally, the effects of romantic relationships vary from individual to individual. As will be seen repeatedly, the specific impact they have is likely to depend heavily on the nature of the particular experiences.

ROMANTIC RELATIONSHIPS
AND IDENTITY DEVELOPMENT

According to Erikson (1968), the key developmental task of adolescence is the development of identity. During early adolescence, there is a proliferation of self-representations that vary as a function of the social context (Harter, 1999). That is, early adolescents develop a sense of themselves with their mothers, fathers, friends, romantic partners, and others. Sometimes their different selves may contradict one another, but such contradictions are usually not acknowledged. In middle adolescence, they begin to recognize such seeming contradictions in their conceptions of themselves, and may be conflicted or confused. By late adolescence, many of them are able to integrate the seeming contradictions into a coherent picture.

Romantic experiences may play a role in the development of a sense of self or identity in two ways. First, adolescents develop distinct perceptions of themselves in the romantic arena. They do not simply have a concept of themselves with peers, but have different self-schemas of themselves with the general peer group, with close friends, and in romantic relationships (Connolly & Konarski, 1994; Gecas, 1972; Harter, 1988). Romantic self-concept is related to whether one has a romantic relationship and to the quality of that relationship (Connolly & Konarski, 1994; Kuttler, La Greca, & Prinstein, 1999), suggesting that romantic experiences may affect one's sense of self in the romantic domain. Thus, adolescents who have had positive experiences may think of themselves as attractive partners, whereas those who have had adverse romantic experiences may have little confidence in their ability to be appealing partners or have successful relationships.

Second, romantic experiences and romantic self-concept may also affect one's global self-esteem. This effect is poignantly expressed in one of our teen's reflections about her romantic experiences, including those with an abusive partner: "Hum, what have I gained? (6 sec. pause). I feel I haven't gained like a lot, but I feel like I lost a lot. I lost my self-respect. I don't respect myself. It's like I feel like I have no self-esteem, no self-control, no nothing." Consistent with her comments, romantic self-concept has been empirically found to be substantially related to self-worth (e.g., r's = .40 to .55; Harter, 1988, 1999). Romantic self-concept is also related to one's self-concept in other domains, particularly physical appearance and peer acceptance (Harter, 1988).

Although global self-esteem and perceived competence in various domains are fundamental aspects of self-representations, the concept of identity entails more than these. In the process of developing an identity, adolescents acquire moral and religious values, develop a political ideology, tentatively select and prepare for a career, and adopt a set of social roles, including gender roles (Waterman, 1985). Romantic relationships may facilitate the development of these facets of identity. For example, Erikson (1968) thought that adolescent love was an "attempt to arrive at a definition of one's identity by projecting one's diffused self-image on another and seeing it thus reflected and gradually clarified" (p. 132). On the other hand, sometimes romantic relationships may hinder the identity development process. For example, parenthood—a potential consequence of romantic involvement—is thought to have a detrimental effect on adolescents' normative exploration of identity because of the constant demands and responsibilities it entails (Coley & Chase-Lansdale, 1998). Unfortunately, we can only speculate about how romantic relationships may facilitate or hinder identity development, as we have little empirical data about the role they may play. We know that peers and friends influence adolescents' attitudes and behaviors (Kandel, 1978), but as yet the specific influence of romantic relationships or romantic partners simply has not been examined.

One particularly promising domain to study is gender-role identity. According to the gender intensification hypothesis, early adolescence is a period in which gender-related expectations become increasingly differentiated (Hill & Lynch, 1983). Girls are expected to adhere to feminine stereotypes of behavior, whereas boys are expected to adhere to masculine stereotypes. It is commonly thought that the emergence of dating may be one of the most powerful factors contributing to the intensification of conventional gender roles. Romantic partners, as well as other peers, may reinforce or punish different gender-related behaviors or roles; certainly adolescents are likely to act in ways that they think might make them more attractive to members of the other sex. Of course, different romantic partners are likely to have different expectations regarding gender roles, and one's own experiences in romantic relationships would be expected to affect one's concepts of gender roles (Feiring, 2000).

THE TRANSFORMATION
OF FAMILY RELATIONSHIPS

During adolescence, relationships with parents and other family members undergo significant changes. From middle childhood through adolescence, rates of parental support and interaction decrease (Csikszentmihalyi & Larson, 1984; Furman & Buhrmester, 1992; Larson & Richards, 1991; Laurson & Williams, 1997). Rates of conflict also decrease over the course of adolescence, although the intensity of the affect in the conflict appears to peak in middle adolescence (Laurson, Coy, & Collins, 1998).

These changes, however, do not usually reflect a detachment from parents, but instead a renegotiation and transformation of parent–child relationships. Most adolescents are able to become appropriately autonomous without severing the bonds with parents (Hill & Holmbeck, 1986). Similarly, most parents are gradually able to accept their children's individuality in the context of maintaining emotional ties (Youniss & Smollar, 1985). Thus, the process of transforming the relationship is a mutual one.

This process is not always a smooth one, however. Parents and adolescents have different expectations for each other (Collins, 1990, 1995). Such discrepancies in expectations periodically lead to conflicts, which in turn can lead to a realignment of expectations and eventually changes in the nature of the relationship.

Romantic relationships may play a role in these transformations of family relationships in several ways. At the most basic level, adolescents spend less time with family members and more time with the other sex or in romantic relationships as they grow older (Blyth, Hill, & Thiel, 1982; Darling, Dowdy, Van Horn, & Caldwell, 1999; Laursen & Williams, 1997; Richards, Crowe, Larson, & Swarr, 1998; Zimmer-Gembeck, 1999). Those who have romantic relationships spend less time with family members than those who are not currently involved with someone (Laursen & Williams, 1997).

Romantic relationships are also a common source of conflict and tension in the family (Laursen, 1995; Smetana, 1989). Adolescents and parents may disagree about curfews, choices of peers, and whether one may go to a party or social activity. Dating and romantic relationships are topics in which parents and adolescents have different expectations, and both are invested in exercising jurisdiction. Parents may want jurisdiction because of the risks associated with dating and sexual behavior, whereas adolescents want control over such personal issues. Thus, these topics are likely to lead to perturbations in the relationship, trigger discussion and re-examination of expectations, and contribute to the normative transformation of the decision making in these relationships. In other instances, however, it is not the romantic experiences that lead to normative changes in family relationships, but instead, conflicts with family members may lead some adolescents to seek out romantic relationships to escape family problems.

Empirical research is consistent with the idea that family conflicts and romantic relationships are linked. Students who are dating report more frequent and intense conflicts than non-daters (Dowdy & Kliewer, 1999). Those adolescents who are involved with a romantic partner at a young age also have higher rates of alcohol and drug use as well as lower levels of academic achievement (Aro & Taipale, 1987; Grinder, 1966). It appears that adolescents with interpersonal difficulties or familial problems may seek out romantic relationships earlier (Aro & Taipale, 1987; Pawlby, Mills, & Quinton, 1997), but it also seems possible that such early romantic relationships could lead to family discord or personal difficulties as well.

Even when dating is not a major source of conflict, parents may have ambivalent feelings about their children's romantic relationships (Bonini & Zani, cited in Zani, 1993). For example, mothers report being both joyful that their daughters are happy, and yet sometimes jealous and aware of the loss of an exclusive tie. Similarly, the satisfaction of seeing their sons mature can be counterbalanced by the realization that they are growing up and eventually leaving the household. Some fathers report being accepting of a romantic relationship, but concerned that their children may be torn between loyalty to a partner and to the family. A serious relationship can be seen as an intrusion or threat to the family. As yet, we do not know how such ambivalent feelings may impact family relationships, but it seems that they may very well lead to some rethinking or restructuring of the relationships between the parents and adolescents.

Although conflict and ambivalent feelings about romantic relationships may occur commonly, these should not be overstated. In popular stereotypes, adolescence is thought of as period of great strife between parents and peers, but in fact, peer and parental influences are typically synergistic (Hartup, 1983). We believe that the same synergism may be characteristic of romantic relationships and family relationships. For example, perceptions of parents' attitudes about "going steady" are associated with the likelihood of the adolescents actually having an exclusive relationship (Poffenberger, 1964). Although it is likely that this association stems partially from parents' control over their adolescents' dating behavior, it is also possible that adolescents' desires and romantic experiences will affect how their parents think about romantic relationships and what they will allow their offspring to do.

The links between supportive behavior in relationships with romantic partners and parents are complicated. As adolescents grow older, they are more likely to turn to a boyfriend or girlfriend for support (Buhrmester & Furman, 1987; Furman & Buhrmester, 1992; Youniss & Smollar, 1985). Moreover, they are less likely to seek support from their parents (Buhrmester & Furman, 1987; Furman & Buhrmester, 1992). The early phases of the transition from a parent as the primary attachment figure to a romantic partner may begin in adolescence, particularly in late adolescence (Furman & Wehner, 1994). Specifically, adolescents may begin to turn to their partners or peers for a safe haven, although their parents are likely to remain as their primary secure base (Hazan & Zeifman, 1994).

Interestingly, however, the amount of support in the two types of relationships at any particular age is positively correlated (Connolly & Johnson, 1996; Furman, 1999; Furman, Simon, Shaffer, & Bouchey, in press). Perhaps the ability to be supportive in one relationship carries over to the other relationship. Having a supportive romantic relationship (vs. just any romantic relationship) may also have a positive effect on one's general emotional state, which in turn may foster positive interactions in the home. Thus, although romantic relationships can be a source of strain on relationships with parents, they may have some positive effects on these relationships in other instances.

THE DEVELOPMENT OF CLOSE RELATIONSHIPS WITH PEERS

Concomitant with the changes in the family throughout adolescence are significant changes in peer relationships. On average, adolescents spend more than twice as much of their free time with peers than with their parents or other adults (Csikszentmihalyi & Larson, 1984). Over the course of adolescence, they increasingly turn to their peers for support as these relationships become more intimate in nature (Buhrmester & Furman, 1987; Furman & Buhrmester, 1992; Youniss & Smollar, 1985).

The importance of being part of a popular clique peaks in early adolescence, and declines in middle adolescence, as groups become more permeable and teens become members of multiple cliques (Gavin & Furman, 1989). Throughout adolescence, however, teens are categorized as being part of a crowd (Brown, 1990). Members of the same crowd are seen as having similar attitudes and beliefs, even though they may or may not interact directly with everyone who is seen as part of that crowd.

Adolescent romantic relationships may contribute to adolescents' peer relations in several ways. As the brief description of developmental changes indicates, adolescents spend increasing amounts of time with their peers, and these changes in the sheer frequency of interaction primarily occur in interactions with the other sex or in romantic relationships (Blyth et al., 1982; Laursen & Williams, 1997; Richards et al., 1998; Zimmer-Gembeck, 1999). One function such interactions serve is affiliation (Feiring, 1996; Furman, 1999; Roscoe, Diana, & Brooks, 1987; Skipper & Nass, 1966). These affiliative interactions are both stimulating and utilitarian in nature (Weiss, 1998). Such interchanges provide opportunities for reciprocal altruism, mutualism, and social play (Furman, 1999). Adolescents may develop their capacities to cooperate and co-construct a relationship. Moreover, the interactions are very rewarding in nature, as spending time with the other sex or having a romantic relationship is associated with positive emotionality (Neemann, Hubbard, & Masten, 1995; Richards et al., 1998).

The presence of such romantic relationships is also likely to influence the relationships one has with other peers. A boy/girlfriend becomes part of the adolescent's network and, in a significant minority of instances, remains part of the network even after the romantic element of the relationship has dissolved (Connolly, Furman, & Konarski, 2000). He or she may introduce the teen to other adolescents. If the relationship becomes more serious, the social networks of the two overlap more as mutual friendships develop (Milardo, 1982). In young adulthood, the networks usually become smaller as couples become more seriously involved and peripheral relations fade (see Surra, 1990). Even in adolescence, a romantic partner may vie with other peers for the person's attention (Laursen & Williams, 1997; Zimmer-Gembeck, 1999).

Just as the impact on family relationships varies, romantic relationships' effects on peer relations do also. For example, three different patterns of relations between the peer group and romantic relationships were identified by Ceroni et al. (cited in Zani, 1993) and by Zani, Altieri, and Signani (cited in Zani, 1993). In some cases the peer group became less salient as the romantic relationship was given priority. Sometimes, the choice between peers and romantic relationships was a source of conflict between the adolescent and the peers or partner. Finally, sometimes the peer group relations remained unchanged by the presence of the new relationship.

Romantic relationships can also affect one's standing in the peer group, as dating in Western cultures has traditionally served the functions of status grading and status achievement (Roscoe et al., 1987; Skipper & Nass, 1966). Dating a particularly attractive or popular person could improve one's popularity or reaffirm that one is popular. Consistent with this idea, high school students who received many positive nominations on a sociometric measure dated more frequently (Franzoi, Davis, & Vasquez-Suson, 1994).

Additionally, adolescents are likely to date those who share similar interests, attitudes, and values to theirs (Capaldi & Crosby, 1997). Their dating selections may reinforce the reputation they have or identify the crowd they are seen as being part of. That is, their peers are likely to think they are similar to the individuals they are dating.

Finally, although double standards of sexual behavior are much less striking than they used to be, ethnographic work suggests that having sexual inter-course can still enhance boys' status in the peer group, whereas it may jeopardize the status of girls in at least some peer groups (Eyre, Hoffman, & Millstein, 1998). Similarly, having a serious romantic relationship can lead to ridicule and jeopardize one's status in some peer groups where members of the other sex are simply seen as objects for sexual conquest (Alexander, 1990).

Up to this point, we have emphasized how romantic relationships may affect adolescents' peer relations in general. They also can affect friendships in particular. In fact, romantic relationships share many features with friendships (Furman, 1999), and could be thought of as a special form of friendship. Often a romantic partner becomes the best friend, displacing the old friend (Hendrick & Hendrick, 1993).

Regardless of whether romantic relationships do or do not displace a friendship, it seems likely that the experiences in friendships and romantic relationships may influence each other. Both forms of relationships entail intimate disclosure, support seeking and giving, and mutuality. The skills that these require appear likely to carry over from one type of relationship to the other. Ratings of support and negative interactions in friendships and in romantic relationships have usually been found to be related to one another, but not always (Connolly & Johnson, 1996: Furman, 1999; Furman et al., in press). It seems possible that the *ability* or *desire* to be supportive toward romantic partners and friends may be related to one another, but the *actual amount* of support in the two relationships may be less clearly related as friends and romantic partners may vie for the adolescent's attention. In other words, a teen may learn ways of being supportive from interacting with a boyfriend, but if she spends most of her time with him, she will not have many opportunities to be supportive of her friends. Consistent with the idea that the desire to be supportive or unsupportive may be related, adolescents' cognitive representations of romantic relationships and friendships are related to one another (Furman, 1999; Furman et al., in press). That is, teens who value intimacy and closeness and expect their romantic partners to be available and responsive are likely to have similar expectations for their friendships.

SEXUAL DEVELOPMENT

The development of sexuality is another key task in adolescence. As adolescents' bodies begin to mature in reproductive capacities, their sexual desires increase. Most adolescents begin to experiment with sexual behavior, and gradually develop some comfort with their sexuality. In a 1995 national survey, 83% of males and 70% of females had had sexual intercourse by the age of 19 (Abma & Sonenstein, 2001).

It almost seems unnecessary to say that romantic relationships play a key role in the development of sexuality. Certainly, sexual behavior often occurs in brief encounters, as adolescents "hook-up" with each other for an evening. Additionally, sexual behaviors, particularly mild forms of sexual behavior, commonly occur with friends with whom adolescents are not romantically involved (Shaffer, 2001; Shaffer & Furman, 2001). Nevertheless, casual or committed romantic relationships are primary contexts for sexual behavior and learning about sexuality. The majority of adolescents first have intercourse with someone they are going steady with or know well and like a lot (Abma, Chandra, Mosher, Peterson, & Piccinino, 1997; Rodgers, 1996). Moreover, most teenagers are selective about with whom they have intercourse. Forty-nine percent of sexually active 19-year-old girls and 30% of sexually active boys have had intercourse with one or two partners. Less than 20% of sexually active girls and 35% of sexually active boys have had 6 or more partners (Abma & Sonenstein, 2001).

Aside from the idea that romantic relationships are a primary context for the development of sexuality, we know remarkably little about the specific role these relationships play. In fact, we know more about the influence of peers and parents than about romantic partners. Yet, it is difficult to believe that the partner and the nature of the relationship do not play critical roles in determining sexual behavior and in determining what is learned from the experiences.

Some descriptive information exists on the characteristics of sexual partners. For example, 75% of girls' most recent heterosexual partners are at least a year older; 22% are 4 or more years older; in contrast, only 27% of boys' heterosexual partners are older, and 46% are at least a year younger (Abma & Sonenstein, 2001). Adolescents are also more likely to have sexual intercourse for the first time with someone who is already sexually active than someone who is not (Rodgers, 1996). Finally, the modal reason given for first having intercourse is to have the partner love them more (Rodgers, 1996). These findings suggest that the characteristics of the partner and one's feelings about the partner are critical determinants of sexual behavior, but we still know little about the particulars.

In part, the absence of information about the role of romantic relationships may reflect the field's focus on sexual intercourse, contraception, and pregnancy and their demographic correlates. The field has emphasized these components because of the significance they have for health. Yet, an understanding of adolescent sexuality requires a broader perspective (Welsh, Rostosky, &

Kawaguchi, 1999). Bukowski, Sippola, and Brender (1993) proposed that the development of a healthy sense of sexuality includes: (a) learning about intimacy through interaction with peers, (b) developing an understanding of personal roles and relationships, (c) revising one's body schema to changes in size, shape, and capability, (d) adjusting to erotic feelings and experiences and integrating them into one's life, (e) learning about social standards and practices regarding sexual expression, and (f) developing an understanding and appreciation of reproductive processes. We believe that one's romantic relationships are likely to be one of the primary, if not the primary context, for learning about most of those facets of sexuality. Romantic relationships provide a testing ground not only for the *how* of sexual behavior but also for the *what* and *when*. They provide a context in which adolescents discover what is attractive and arousing. Adolescents learn what they like in their partners and what partners tend to like. They learn to reconcile their sexual desires, their moral values, and their partners' desires.

Finally, a critical facet of sexual development is the establishment or solidification of sexual orientation. Much of the existing research on adolescent sexuality and romantic relationships has focused on heterosexual adolescents, but current estimates indicate that approximately 10% of youth in the U.S. will consider themselves gay, lesbian, or bisexual at some point in their lives (D'Augelli, 1988). Many sexual minority youth become aware of their same-gender attractions in early to mid-adolescence. The average age for first awareness of these feelings is approximately 13 for gay males (Remafedi, 1987) and 16 for lesbians (D'Augelli, Collins, & Hart, 1987). Few sexual minority youth enter into romantic liaisons with same-sex peers during adolescence because of the limited opportunities to do so (Sears, 1991). The majority, however, date heterosexually (Savin-Williams, 1996). Adolescents who are questioning their sexual orientation often find that these relationships help them determine or confirm their sexual preferences (Diamond, Savin-Williams, & Dubé, 1999).

SCHOLASTIC ACHIEVEMENT
AND CAREER PLANNING

Around the beginning of adolescence, students in the United States make a transition from elementary school to middle school or junior high. In middle adolescence, they move on to high school. Some continue on to colleges or vocational schools in late adolescence, whereas others complete their formal education when they graduate from high school, and still others drop out of middle school or high school. Similar educational transitions occur in other Western societies. What is common across Western cultures, at least, is that the emphasis on academic learning increases with age, and students begin to take increasingly different paths.

Friendships and peer groups can have either positive or negative effects on adolescents' academic involvement and achievement (Berndt & Keefe, 1995; Kindermann, McCollam, & Gibson, 1996). For example, those with supportive friends tend to become more involved in school, whereas those with more conflictual relationships become more disruptive (Berndt & Keefe, 1995). To date, however, we know less about the role that romantic relationships specifically may play.

As noted previously, early involvement in romantic relationships has been linked with poorer scholastic achievement (Grinder, 1966). In fact, romantic involvement and sexual behavior have been found to be negatively correlated with academic achievement throughout adolescence (Halpern, Joyner, Udry, & Suchindran, 2000; Neemann et al., 1995). Such associations could exist because those who are less academically oriented may be more likely to develop romantic relationships, or because romantic relationships may have an adverse effect on school achievement.

The time spent with a romantic partner could distract from schoolwork, but we suspect that any such effect may be highly dependent on the characteristics of the partner and the nature of the relationship, just as it is in the case of friendships (Berndt & Keefe, 1995). That is, some partners may detract from school, but others may promote achievement by studying together, helping with homework, encouraging achievement, or providing support. For example, an adolescent in one of our studies said, "It's really gotten me out of this big hole I used to be in. I used to go off and, I smoked weed a lot, drank a whole lot, I mean I used to love to party 24-7 and all that, and during this time, my grades just went down to like crap. . . . She's helped me actually get interested in school again, and be able to go off and just be actually be, I mean, she got me out of the rut. I mean I hardly drink. I don't smoke no more. I mean things like that. And just yesterday I mean, I won this award at our school." Once again, the nature of any such influence may be highly dependent on the particulars of the partner and the relationship.

Romantic partners may also influence career plans and aspirations. They can serve as comrades with whom to share ideas and dreams. They may encourage or discourage particular careers or educational plans. Developing a committed relationship, deciding to get married, or having a child is also likely to affect the plans for the future. For example, early parenthood has a strong negative effect on educational attainment (Coley & Chase-Lansdale, 1998). Adolescent parents may forego career dreams, because they no longer have time or financial resources to pursue the necessary training or education. Similarly, those who choose to commit to a romantic partner above all else may narrow their options for career opportunities. Thus, as with other domains of adolescent development, romantic relationships may have either benefits or drawbacks for career plans, depending on the particular circumstances.

CLINICAL AND EDUCATIONAL IMPLICATIONS

Our discussion of the role of romantic relationships in adolescent development has a number of implications for clinicians, educators, and parents. Perhaps the most obvious is how important romantic relationships can be in adolescents' lives. Not only are they central in the eyes of adolescents, but we have described the impact they may have on adolescent development.

Often, however, adults tend to downplay the significance of these relationships. Parents may tease their teens about a romantic relationship, or dismiss it as "only puppy love" and try to discourage them from getting too romantically involved as adolescents. In part, such reactions are understandable. Most adolescent relationships are not as serious or long-lasting as the ones that emerge in adulthood. Many adolescents may not really be prepared for making a long-term commitment to someone. Adolescent marriages are much more prone to divorce (Bramlett & Mosher, 2001). Romantic experiences entail a number of risks, such as pregnancy, sexual victimization, and violence. As valid as these parental concerns may be, however, they miss the point to some degree. Even if the relationships are relatively superficial, they are phenomologically quite important, and as we have suggested, may contribute to adolescent development. Thus, although parental monitoring of adolescent romantic experiences seems highly desirable, some sensitivity to the significance of the relationships for youth seems important as well. Disparaging or derogating a teen's relationship is not likely to be an effective parenting strategy.

The significance of these relationships for different aspects of development also means that parents and professionals may want to take them into account in understanding and treating adolescent problems. Problems in academic work or problems in family relationships could be linked to romantic experiences. For example, romantic break-ups are the most common trigger of the first episode of major depressive disorder, which would be likely to affect functioning in most domains of a teen's life (Monroe, Rhode, Seeley, & Lewinsohn, 1999).

In general, those working with adolescents would want to consider the role romantic experiences play in different aspects of development. For example, sex education programs may want to consider the role relationships play in sexual behavior, and not just focus on anatomy and contraceptive practices.

Similarly, because the romantic domain is an important one in identity development, clinicians working with adolescents who are struggling with identity issues may want to consider how these issues are enacted in relationships. Clinicians and parents should also be sensitive to the role romantic experiences may play in the process of redefining relationships with family members or peers.

Romantic experiences may provide adolescents opportunities to rethink who they are and who they want to be. Sullivan (1953) suggested that chumships—intimate preadolescent same-sex friendships—may serve as corrective emotional experiences. Perhaps some long-term, supportive romantic relationships could serve similar functions. Interestingly, middle adolescents' working models of romantic relationships are more likely to be secure than their models of relationships with parents (Furman et al., in press). At the very least, romantic experiences may be helpful to adolescents who have observed that their parents have an unhappy marriage. Such experiences may help them realize that they do not necessarily need to have such a relationship themselves. Adult support and guidance can be helpful in enabling corrective romantic experiences for adolescents.

Throughout this chapter, we have emphasized the marked individual differences in adolescent romantic relationships. It is not enough for a clinician to know that an adolescent has or has had a boyfriend. One would want to know about the characteristics of their relationships, as well as when they occurred and how long they lasted. An assessment of these relationships may also serve as a venue for exploring topics such as sexuality, control, aggression, or victimization.

Finally, just as we scientists know relatively little about adolescent romantic relationships, educators, clinicians, parents, and adolescents themselves are also likely to know little and could benefit from learning more about the topic. Our impression is that most parents and many professionals use their own experiences as an adolescent as one of their primary sources of data. If not their own experiences, they may rely on descriptions in the mass media. Either of these sources of information could be quite misleading, when we consider the individual differences in adolescents' experiences, and the historical changes in sexual behavior and romantic relationships. Our anecdotal impression is that most parents have little sense of the prevalence of sexual activity and typically overestimate how common sexual activity is. Cultural differences may also contribute to conceptions or misconceptions. Imagine how difficult it would be for immigrant parents to have some sense of whether their child's experiences in a new culture are normative or not. Adolescents, too, would be prone to assuming that their experiences or their friends' experiences are normative. Such assumptions could not only be inaccurate, but dangerous. Controlling behavior, coercive sexual behavior, or physical conflict may be more likely to be tolerated if a teen thought these occurred in most relationships.

FUTURE DIRECTIONS

Although we have tried to make the case that romantic relationships may influence the course of adolescent development, our evidence is quite limited. Not only has relatively little research been conducted on these relationships in adolescence, but also the existing work has been guided primarily by models in which these relationships are treated as outcomes. For example, most research, including our own, seems to implicitly be guided by the idea that friendships or family relationships affect romantic relationships. The studies, however, are all correlational, and in most cases, the data are gathered at one time point. Thus, it is at least theoretically possible that the causal influences are in the other direction, or in both directions.

The limitations in our data bases cannot be corrected by simply recognizing that correlation does not imply causation. In designing our research, we need to consider deliberately how romantic relationships may impact other adolescent relationships or facets of development. This point is nicely illustrated in the literature on parental reactions to dating relationships. Some studies suggested that parental support is associated with increased or continued involvement in a dating relationship (Lewis, 1972), whereas other work suggested that romantic relationships could be enhanced by parental interference—the Romeo and Juliet effect (Driscoll, Davis, & Lipetz, 1972). The issue here is not that the findings are contradictory, however, but that the work had only considered the idea that parents may shape their offsprings' romantic relationships. Little consideration was given to the idea that late adolescents may also be attempting to shape their parents' impressions of the relationship and thus, may modify their own interactions with their parents. Leslie, Huston, and Johnson (1986), however, found that the vast majority of late adolescents monitor the information they provide about their romantic relationships, and have made multiple efforts to influence their parents' opinions about the romantic relationships. The parents, too, had often communicated either approving or disapproving reactions. Thus, by considering the idea that the paths of influence may be bi-directional, the investigators provided a better understanding of the process than if they had simply tested a unidirectional model.

It is also important to remember that the effects of romantic experiences may not be salutary. We have focused mainly on how romantic relationships may contribute to the normative developmental tasks of adolescence, but there are risks as well. Approximately 20% to 25% of young women are victims of dating violence or aggression (Silverman, Raj, Mucci, & Hathaway, 2001; Wolfe & Feiring, 2000). Adolescent romantic break-ups are one of the strongest predictors of depression, multiple-victim killings, and suicidal attempts or completions (Brent et al., 1993; Fessenden, 2000; Joyner & Udry, 2000; Monroe et al., 1999). Most incidents of sexual victimization are perpetrated by a romantic partner (Flanagan & Furman, 2000). The sexual activity that commonly co-occurs with romantic involvement places adolescents at risk for sexually transmitted diseases or becoming pregnant.

Perhaps the critical point is that the impact of romantic experiences is likely to vary from individual to individual. In the various sections of this chapter, we have tried to emphasize how not only the existence of a romantic relationship, but the quality of that relationship or the timing of the involvement may determine what the outcome of the experience will be (see also Bouchey & Furman, in press). Similarly, the intensity of the relationship is likely to play a critical role as well. For example, the links with relationships with parents vary as a function of duration of the romantic relationship (Connolly & Johnson, 1996). The experiences of those adolescents who are married or have children also seems qualitatively different from those who are dating more casually. Finally, the characteristics of the partner will also influence the nature of the romantic experience and its impact.

The emphasis on the variability of romantic experiences points out the need to identify the critical processes that are responsible for any impact that romantic experiences have. It may not be the simple presence of a relationship, but instead certain features or experiences that occur within the relationship that determine the outcome. For example, the experience of romantic break-ups, rather than the simple presence of a romantic relationship, may trigger depressive episodes (Grello, Dickson, Welsh, Harper, & Wintersteen, 2001).

Finally, in order to understand the impact of romantic relationships, we will need to understand the context in which they occur. The nature of these experiences vary as a function of the social and cultural context in which they occur (Bouchey & Furman, in press; Simon, Bouchey, & Furman, 2000). Conversely, we need to separate out the specific influence of romantic experiences from related experiences. In several places in this chapter we pointed out how it had been shown that peer relationships in general had an impact on development, but as yet, nobody had examined the specific impact of romantic relationships. Although romantic relationships certainly share many features with other forms of peer relations, they also have some distinct features that may lead them to have a different impact than other peer relationships.

In summary, we have tried to discuss how romantic relationships may contribute to various facets of adolescent development, including the development of an identity, the transformation of family relationships, the development of close relationships with peers, the development of sexuality, and scholastic achievement and career planning. The evidence is consistent with the idea that romantic experiences may play a role in these various domains, but the evidence is still limited. It is clear that our work as scientists has just begun. It is hoped that this chapter contributes to the endeavor by delineating a series of questions that need to be addressed empirically.

ACKNOWLEDGMENTS

Preparation of this manuscript was supported by Grant 50106 from National Institute of Mental Health.

REFERENCES

Abma, J., Chandra, A., Mosher, W., Peterson, L., & Piccinino, L. (1997). Fertility, family planning, and women's health: New data from the 1995 National Survey of Family Growth. National Center for Health Statistics. *Vital Health Statistics, 23 (No. 19)*.

Abma, J. C., & Sonenstein, F. L. (2001). Sexual activity and contraceptive practices among teenagers in the United States, 1988 and 1995. National Center for Health Statistics. *Vital Health Statistics, 23 (No. 21)*

Aro, H., & Taipale, V. (1987). The impact of timing of puberty on psychosomatic symptoms among fourteen- to sixteen-year-old Finnish girls. *Child Development, 58*, 261–268.

Alexander, E. (1990). *Streetwise: Race, class, and change in an urban community*. Chicago: University of Chicago Press.

Berndt, T. J., & Keefe, K. (1995). Friends' influence on adolescents' adjustment to school. *Child Development, 66*, 1312–1329.

Blyth, D. A., Hill, J. P., & Thiel, K. S. (1982). Early adolescents' significant others: Grade and gender differences in perceived relationships with familial and nonfamilial adults and young people. *Journal of Youth and Adolescence, 11*, 425–449.

Bouchey, H. A., & Furman, W. (in press). Dating and romantic experiences in adolescence. In G. R. Adams & M. Berzonsky (Eds.), *The Blackwell handbook of adolescence*. Oxford, UK: Blackwell Publishers.

Bramlett, M. D., & Mosher, W. D. (2001). *First marriage dissolution, divorce and remarriage: United States* (Advance data from vital and health statistics, No. 323). Hyattsville, MD: National Center for Health Statistics.

Brent, D. A., Perper, J. A., Moritz, G., Baugher, M., Roth, C., Balach, L., & Schweers, J. (1993). Stressful life events, psychopathology, and adolescent suicide: A case control study. *Suicide and Life-Threatening Behavior, 23*, 179–187.

Brown, B. B. (1990). Peer groups and peer cultures. In S. S. Feldman & G. R. Elliott (Eds.), *At the threshold: The developing adolescent* (pp. 171–196). Cambridge, MA: Harvard University Press.

Buhrmester, D., & Furman, W. (1987). The development of companionship and intimacy. *Child Development, 58*, 1101–1113.

Bukowski, W. M., Sippola, L., & Brender, W. M. (1993). Where does sexuality come from? In H. E. Barbaree, W. L. Marshall, & D. R. Laws (Eds.), *The juvenile sex offender* (pp. 84–103). New York: Guilford.

Capaldi, D. M., & Crosby, L. (1997). Observed and reported psychological and physical aggression in young, at-risk couples. *Social Development, 5,* 184–206.

Coley, R. L., & Chase-Lansdale, P. L. (1998). Adolescent pregnancy and parenthood: Recent evidence and future directions. *American Psychologist, 53,* 152–166.

Collins, W. A. (1990). Parent-child relationships in the transition to adolescence: Continuity and change in interaction, affect, and cognition. In R. Montemayor, G. Adams, & T. Gullotta (Eds.), *From childhood to adolescence: A transitional period?* (pp. 85–106). Beverly Hills, CA: Sage.

Collins, W. A. (1995). Relationships and development: Family adaptation to individual change. In S. Shulman (Ed.), *Close relationships and socioemotional development* (pp. 128–154). New York: Academic Press.

Connolly, J. A., Furman, W., & Konarski, R. (2000). The role of peers in the emergence of heterosexual romantic relationships in adolescence. *Child Development, 71,* 1395–1408.

Connolly, J. A., & Johnson, A. M. (1996). Adolescents' romantic relationships and the structure and quality of their close interpersonal ties. *Personal Relationships, 3,* 185–195.

Connolly, J. A., & Konarski, R. (1994). Peer self-concept in adolescence: Analysis of factor structure and of associations with peer experience. *Journal of Research in Adolescence, 4,* 385–403.

Csikszentmihalyi, M., & Larson, R. (1984). *Being adolescent.* New York: Basic Books.

Darling, N., Dowdy, B. B., Van Horn, M. L., & Caldwell, L. L. (1999). Mixed-sex settings and the perception of competence. *Journal of Youth and Adolescence, 28,* 461–480.

D'Augelli, A. R. (1988). The adolescent closet: Promoting the development of the lesbian or gay male teenager. *The School Psychologist, 42,* 2–3.

D'Augelli, A. R., Collins, C., & Hart, M. M. (1987). Social support patterns of lesbian women in a rural helping network. *Journal of Rural Community Psychology, 8*(1), 12–22.

Diamond, L. M., Savin-Williams, R. C., & Dubé, E. M. (1999). Sex, dating, passionate friendships, and romance: Intimate peer relations among lesbian, gay, and bisexual adolescents. In W. Furman, B. B. Brown, & C. Feiring (Eds.), *The development of romantic relationships in adolescence* (pp. 175–210). Cambridge, UK: Cambridge University Press.

Dowdy, B. B., & Kliewer, W. (1999). Dating, parent–adolescent conflict, and behavioral autonomy. *Journal of Youth and Adolescence, 27,* 473–492.

Driscoll, R., Davis, K. E., & Lipetz, M. E. (1972). Parental inteference and romantic love: The Romeo and Juliet effect. *Journal of Personality and Social Psychology, 24,* 1–10.

Eder, D. (1993). "Go get ya a French!": Romantic and sexual teasing among adolescent girls. In D. Tannen (Ed.), *Gender and conversational interaction* (pp. 17–31). New York: Oxford University Press.

Erikson, E. H. (1968). *Identity, youth, and crisis.* New York: Norton.

Eyre, S. L., Hoffman, V., & Millstein, S. G. (1998). The gamesmanship of sex: A model based on African American adolescent accounts. *Medical Anthropology Quarterly, 12,* 467–489.

Feiring, C. (1996). Concepts of romance in 15-year-old adolescents. *Journal of Research on Adolescence, 6,* 181–200.

Feiring, C. (2000). Gender identity and the development of romantic relationships in adolescence. In W. Furman, B. B. Brown, & C. Feiring (Eds.), *The development of romantic relationships in adolescence* (pp. 175–210). Cambridge, UK: Cambridge University Press.

Fessenden, F. (2000, April 9). They threaten, seethe, and unhinge, then kill in quantity. *New York Times,* p. 1.

Flanagan, A. S., & Furman, W. C. (2000). Sexual victimization and perceptions of close relationships in adolescence. *Child Maltreatment, 5*, 350–359.

Franzoi, S. L., Davis, M. H., & Vasquez-Suson, K. A. (1994). Two social worlds: Social correlates and stability of adolescent status groups. *Journal of Personality and Social Psychology, 67*, 462–473.

Furman, W. (1999). Friends and lovers: The role of peer relationships in adolescent heterosexual romantic relationships. In W. A. Collins & B. Laursen (Eds.), *Relationships as developmental contexts: Minnesota Symposium on Child Development* (Vol. 30). Hillsdale, NJ: Lawrence Erlbaum Associates.

Furman, W., & Buhrmester, D. (1992). Age and sex differences in perceptions of networks of personal relationships. *Child Development, 63*, 103–115.

Furman, W., Simon, V. A., Shaffer, L., & Bouchey, H. A. (in press). Adolescents' working models and styles for relationships with parents, friends, and romantic partners. *Child Development.*

Furman, W., & Wehner, E. A. (1994). Romantic views: Toward a theory of adolescent romantic relationships. In R. Montemayor, G. R. Adams, & G. P. Gullota (Eds.), *Advances in adolescent development: Vol. 6. Relationships during adolescence* (pp. 168–175). Thousand Oaks, CA: Sage.

Gavin, L., & Furman, W. (1989). Age difference in adolescents' perceptions of their peer groups. *Developmental Psychology, 25*, 827–834.

Gecas, V. (1972). Parental behavior and contextual variations in adolescent self-esteem. *Sociometry, 35*, 332–345.

Grello, C. M., Dickson, J. W., Welsh, D. P., Harper, M. S., & Wintersteen, M. B. (2001, April). *Developmental trajectories of adolescent romantic relationships, sexual behaviors, and feelings of depression.* Poster presented at the meeting of the Society for Research in Child Development, Minneapolis, MN.

Grinder, R. E. (1966). Relations of social dating attractions to academic orientation and peer relations. *Journal of Educational Psychology, 57*, 27–34.

Halpern, C. T., Joyner, K., Udry, J. R., & Suchindran, C. (2000). Smart teens don't have sex (or kiss much either). *Journal of Adolescent Health, 26*, 213–225.

Harter, S. (1988). *Manual for the self-perception profile for adolescents.* Denver, CO: University of Denver.

Harter, S. (1999). *The construction of the self.* New York: Guilford Press.

Hartup, W. W. (1983). Peer relations. In P. H. Mussen (Series Ed.) & E. M. Hetherington (Vol. Ed.), *Handbook of child psychology: Vol. 4. Socialization, personality, and social development* (pp. 103–196). New York: Wiley.

Hazan, C., & Zeifman, D. (1994). Sex and the psychological tether. In K. Bartholomew & D. Perlman (Eds.), *Advances in personal relationships: Vol. 1. Attachment processes in adulthood* (pp. 151–180). London: Jessica Kingsley.

Hendrick, S. S., & Hendrick, C. (1993). Lovers as friends. *Journal of Social and Personal Relationships, 10*, 459–466.

Hill, J., & Holmbeck, G. (1986). Attachment and autonomy during adolescence. In G. Whitehurst (Ed.), *Annals of child development* (Vol. 3, pp. 145–189). Greenwich, CO: JAI Press.

Hill, J., & Lynch, M. T. (1983). The intensification of gender-related role expectations during early adolescence. In J. Brooks-Gunn & A. Peterson (Eds.), *Girls at puberty* (pp. 202–228). New York: Plenum.

Joyner, K., & Udry, J. R. (2000). You don't bring me anything but down: Adoescent romance and depression. *Journal of Health and Social Behavior, 41*, 369–391.

Kandel, D. B. (1978). Homophily, selection, and socialization in adolescent friendships. *American Journal of Sociology, 84,* 427–436.

Kindermann, T. A., McCollam, T. L., & Gibson, E., Jr. (1996). Peer networks and students' classroom engagement during childhood and adolescence. In J. Juvonen & K. R. Wentzel (Eds.), *Social motivation: Understanding children's school adjustment* (pp. 279–312). New York: Cambridge University Press.

Kuttler, A. F., La Greca, A. M., & Prinstein, M. J. (1999). Friendship qualities and social-emotional functioning of adolescents with close, cross-sex friendships. *Journal of Research on Adolescence, 9,* 339–366.

Larson, R., & Richards, M. H. (1991). Daily companionship in late childhood and early adolescence: Changing developmental contexts. *Child Development, 62,* 284–300.

Laursen, B. (1995). Conflict and social interaction in adolescent relationships. *Journal of Research in Adolescence, 5,* 55–70.

Laursen, B., Coy, K. C., & Collins, W. A. (1998). Reconsidering changes in parent–child conflict across adolescence. *Child Development, 69,* 817–832.

Laursen, B., & Williams, V. A. (1997). Perceptions of interdependence and closeness in family and peer relationships among adolescents with and without romantic partners. In S. Shulman & W. A. Collins (Eds.), *Romantic relationships in adolescence: Developmental perspectives: New directions for child development* (pp. 3–20). San Francisco: Jossey-Bass.

Leslie, L. A., Huston, T. L., & Johnson, M. P. (1986). Parental reactions to dating relationships: Do they make a difference? *Journal of Marriage and the Family, 48,* 57–66.

Lewis, R. (1972). A developmental framework for the analysis of premarital dyadic formation. *Family Process, 11,* 16–25.

Milardo, R. M. (1982). Friendship networks in developing relationships: Converging and diverging social environments. *Social Psychology Quarterly, 45,* 162–172.

Monroe, S. M., Rohde, P., Seeley, J. R., & Lewinsohn, P. M. (1999). Life events and depression in adolescence: Relationship loss as a prospective risk factor for first onset of major depressive disorder. *Journal of Abnormal Psychology, 108,* 606–614.

Neemann, J., Hubbard, J., & Masten, A. S. (1995). The changing importance of romantic relationship involvement to competence from late childhood to late adolescence. *Development and Psychopathology, 7,* 727–750.

Pawlby, S. J., Mills, A., & Quinton, D. (1997). Vulnerable adolescent girls: Opposite-sex relationships. *Journal of Child Psychology and Psychiatry, 38,* 909–920.

Poffenberger, T. (1964). Three papers on going steady. *The Family Coordinator, 13,* 7–13.

Remafedi, G. (1987). Homosexual youth: A challenge to contemporary society. *Journal of the American Medical Association, 258*(2), 221–225.

Richards, M. H., Crowe, P. A., Larson, R., & Swarr, A. (1998). Developmental patterns and gender differences in the experience of peer companionship during adolescence. *Child Development, 69,* 154–163.

Rodgers, J. L. (1996). Sexual transitions in adolescence. In J. A. Graber, J. Brooks-Gunn, & A. C. Peterson (Eds.), *Transitions through adolescence: Interpersonal domains and context* (pp. 85–110). Mahwah, NJ: Lawrence Erlbaum Associates.

Roscoe, B., Diana, M. S., & Brooks, R. H. (1987). Early, middle, and late adolescents' views on dating and factors influencing partner selection. *Adolescence, 22,* 59–68.

Savin-Williams, R. C. (1996). Dating and romantic relationships among gay, lesbian, and bisexual youths. In R. C. Savin-Williams & K. M. Cohen (Eds.), *The lives of lesbians, gays, and bisexuals: Children to adults* (pp. 166–180). Fort Worth, TX: Harcourt Brace.

Sears, J. T. (1991). *Growing up gay in the South: Race, gender, and journeys of the spirit.* New York: Harrington Park Press.

Shaffer, L. (2001). *Other-sex friendships: An unexamined context of adolescent sexual experience.* Unpublished doctoral thesis, University of Denver.

Shaffer, L., & Furman, W. (2001). *Other-sex friendships in adolescence: "Just friends?"* Unpublished manuscript, University of Denver.

Silverman, J. G., Raj, A., Mucci, L. A., & Hathaway, J. E. (2001). Dating violence against adolescent girls and associated substance use, unhealthy weight control, sexual risk behavior, pregnancy, and suicidality. *Journal of American Medical Association, 286,* 572–579.

Simon, V. A., Bouchey, H. A., & Furman, W. (2000). The social construction of of adolescents' representations of romantic relationships. In S. Larose & G. M. Tarabulsy (Eds.), *Attachment and development: Vol. 2. Adolescence.* Quebec: Les Presses de l'Universite du Quebec.

Skipper, J. K., & Nass, G. (1966). Dating behavior: A framework for analyses and an illustration. *Journal of Marriage and the Family, 28,* 412–420.

Smetana, J. G. (1989). Adolescents' and parents' reasoning about actual family conflict. *Child Development, 60,* 1052–1067.

Sullivan, H. S. (1953). *The interpersonal theory of psychiatry.* New York: W. W. Norton.

Surra, C. A. (1990). Research and theory on marital selection and premarital relationships in the 1980s. *Journal of Marriage and the Family, 52,* 844–865.

Thompson, S. (1994). Changing lives, changing genres: Teenage girls' narratives about sex and romance, 1978–1986. In A. S. Rossi (Ed.), *Sexuality across the life course* (pp. 209–232). Chicago: University of Chicago Press.

Waterman, A. S. (1985). Identity in the context of adolescent psychology. In A. S. Waterman (Ed.), *Identity in adolescence: Processes and contents* (pp. 5–24). San Francisco: Jossey-Bass.

Weiss, R. (1998). A taxonomy of relationships. *Journal of Social and Personal Relationships, 15,* 671–683.

Welsh, D. P., Rostosky, S. S., & Kawaguchi, M. C. (1999). A normative perspective of adolescent girls' developing sexuality. In C. B. Travis & J. S. White (Eds.), *Sexuality, society, and feminism: Psychological perspectives on women* (pp. 111–140). Washington, DC: American Psychological Association.

Wilson-Shockley, S. (1995). *Gender differences in adolescent depression: The contribution of negative affect.* Unpublished master's thesis, University of Illinois at Urbana-Champaign, Champaign.

Wolfe, D. A., & Feiring, C. (2000). Dating violence through the lens of adolescent romantic relationships. *Child Maltreatment, 5,* 360–363.

Youniss, J., & Smollar, J. (1985). *Adolescent relations with mothers, fathers, and friends.* Chicago: University of Chicago Press.

Zani, B. (1993). Dating and interpersonal relationships in adolescence. In S. Jackson & H. Rodriguez-Torne (Eds.), *Adolescence and its social worlds* (pp. 95–119). Hillsdale, NJ: Lawrence Erlbaum Associates.

Zimmer-Gembeck, M. J. (1999). Stability, change and individual differences in involvement with friends and romantic partners among adolescent females. *Journal of Youth and Adolescence, 28,* 419–438.

2

National Estimates
of Adolescent Romantic Relationships

Karen Carver
Indian Health Service

Kara Joyner
Cornell University

J. Richard Udry
University of North Carolina, Chapel Hill

Romantic relationships are a central concern not only to adolescents, but to researchers studying adolescence and the transition to young adulthood. After all, romantic relationships serve several important functions for youth. They are critical to relatedness and autonomy—developmental processes that are linked to secure attachment (Erikson, 1968; Hazan & Shaver, 1987). They also provide contexts for dating and sexual behavior (Collins & Sroufe, 1999; Sprecher, Barbee, & Schwartz, 1995), and facilitate mate sorting and selection (McDaniel, 1969), especially for youth who marry or cohabit early in the life course. The theoretical relevance of adolescent romantic relationships for explanations of pair bonding (i.e., attachment in intimate relationships) and family formation (e.g., childbearing, cohabitation, and marriage) is considerable.

Most of what we know about romantic relationships in adolescence is based on studies utilizing small samples from single schools or geographic regions. These studies have focused primarily on dating. Because many of these studies consider the impact of dating on psychological outcomes (e.g., psychosocial skill development, self-esteem, and identity) and behavioral outcomes (e.g., academic performance, delinquency, and eating disorders), they have generated meager and possibly biased descriptive information on romantic relationship behavior among adolescents (e.g., Cauffman & Steinberg, 1996; Joyner & Udry, 2000; McDonald & McKenney, 1994; Samet & Kelly, 1987; Simmons, Blyth, Van Cleave, & Bush, 1979; Smolak, Levine, & Gralen, 1993). Studies that have tangentially addressed adolescent romantic behavior using nationally representative samples limit their scope to sexual behavior, contraceptive use, pregnancy, and childbearing. Consequently, we know much about sexual and romantic behavior that is less typical of adolescents. We also know a great deal about behavior that occurs relatively later in sexual and romantic relationships—if it occurs at all.

In spite of having limited data on adolescent romantic relationships, a number of studies continue to speculate about their developmental significance. During puberty, adolescents become more interested in romantic relationships, and they become more attractive as romantic partners (Miller & Benson, 1999; Udry, 1988). In early and middle adolescence, when peer acceptance is most critical, adolescents use these relationships to enhance their peer group status (Brown, 1999), if not to validate their gender identity (Feiring, 1999a). Finally, as adolescents individuate from parents and peers, they seek companionship and intimacy from their romantic partners (Furman & Simon, 1999; Gray & Steinberg, 1999). Some of these studies suggest that these models of normative development obscure diversity in the romantic experiences of adolescents. These studies emphasize the role that social and economic factors play in structuring the timing and trajectories of romantic relationship behavior (Coates, 1999; Graber, Britto, & Brookes-Gunn, 1999). They suggest additionally that an exclusive focus on opposite-sex romantic relationships fails to adequately capture the experiences of sexual-minority youth (Diamond, Savin-Williams, & Dubé, 1999).

These studies suggest that the prevalence and characteristics of romantic relationships differs by age, to the extent that age is a proxy for developmental status. They also suggest that, at any given age, romantic relationship behavior varies considerably. However, these studies have failed to specify the parameters of these differences. Toward this end, this chapter provides national estimates of the prevalence and characteristics of adolescent romantic relationships using data from the National Longitudinal Study of Adolescent Health (Add Health).

This study addresses a number of questions critical to models of adolescent development. By late adolescence, what percent of adolescents experience a romantic relationship? How homogamous (as opposed to heterogamous) are the romantic relationships of adolescents? For instance, to what extent do romantic partners differ in age, sex, and race? How stable are romantic relationships? What kinds of behaviors typically occur within these relationships? How connected are these relationships to peer and parental relationships? And finally, how does romantic relationship behavior vary by the demographic characteristics of adolescents?

In the following section, we review studies concerning the romantic relationships of adolescents. Because few studies address this topic, we additionally review studies that consider romantic relationships among adults and friendship among adolescents. Based on this review, we posit expectations for how relationship qualities vary by the sex, age, and race of adolescents. Because studies typically focus on Whites, and rarely distinguish Asian and Hispanic adolescents, our expectations about racial differences are limited.

BACKGROUND

Romantic Relationship Experience

What percent of adolescents have experienced a romantic relationship? To our knowledge, previous studies have not addressed this specific question. Peripherally, a number of studies have concerned the development of close relationships with the opposite sex (e.g., friendships) in adolescence (Collins, 1997; Feiring, 1999b; Furman & Shaffer, 1999; Pawlby, Mills, & Quinton, 1997; Sharabany, Gershoni, & Hofman, 1981); the experience of romantic feelings in this period of the life course (Hill, Blakemore, & Drumm, 1997; Hatfield, Brinton, & Cornelius, 1989; Simon, Eder, & Evans, 1992); adolescent dating (Gargiulo, Attie, & Brooks-Gunn, 1987; Roscoe, Diana, & Brooks, 1987; Skipper & Nass, 1966); and first sexual intercourse (Joyner & Laumann, 2000; Sprecher et al., 1995). In fact, not until very recently has an academic book even focused on romantic relationships in adolescence (Furman, Brown, & Feiring, 1999).

Taken together, previous studies suggest that opposite-sex friendships, romantic, and sexual relationships all become more prevalent during adolescence, presumably because emotional and physical maturity increases in this period. Consequently, we expected that the prevalence of adolescent romantic relationships would increase with age. These studies also suggest that adolescent girls have more experience than adolescent boys with intimate relationships in general, due to their greater maturity. Besides, adolescent peer groups have long been shown to reinforce the importance of romantic relationships, particularly to girls (Coleman, 1961; Douvan & Adelson, 1966; Simon et al., 1992). This led us to expect that the percent distribution of romantic relationships would be slightly higher for girls (as compared to boys) at every age.

Research on adults has shown that African Americans are much less likely than Whites to ever marry (Bennett, Bloom, & Craig, 1989). However, differences in union formation between African Americans and Whites are found to be less dramatic when cohabiting relationships, as well as marriages, are included as unions (Raley, 1996). It is possible that the divergence in union formation may be first observed during adolescence. If this is the case, then the prevalence of romantic relationships for African American adolescents will be lower than that observed for Whites. Because studies on union formation among adults usually focus on marriage, descriptive information on romantic relationship prevalence offers potential insight into racial differences in romantic behavior in general.

Relationship Homogamy

How heterogamous are adolescent romantic relationships? For example, how common is it for adolescents to choose partners of a different race, partners who are relatively older or younger, or partners of the same sex? Again, little research addresses these questions specifically for adolescents. However, a good deal is known about the characteristics of adult partners that are typically *selected.* Adult romantic partners have a tendency to resemble one another on a variety of characteristics, including attractiveness (Feingold, 1988), education (Schoen & Wooldredge, 1989), race (Qian, 1997), religion (Glenn, 1982), and height (Spuhler, 1968).

Other research has emphasized the characteristics of mates individuals say they *prefer.* Typically, these studies find differences between the sexes in mate preference. Several studies, some of which are based on evolutionary theory, have shown that females value characteristics in males associated with the ability to acquire resources, such as social status; males value characteristics that signal reproductive capacity, such as physical attractiveness (Buss, 1989).

Age Differences.   Adolescents provide a unique context to test the latter part of this theory. Using age as a proxy for female reproductive capacity, Kenrick and colleagues found support for the idea that adolescent boys will prefer older partners up until the point the association between age and pubertal development diminishes (Kenrick, Gabrielidis, Keefe, & Cornelius, 1996). On the basis of their study, we generally expected that an examination of age differences between adolescent partners would mirror these findings. Specifically, younger boys would identify romantic partners who are older on average, and that older boys would identify younger partners on average. Girls would identify partners who are typically older on average. We had no reason to expect large variations in age differences between partners by race.

Interracial Relationships.   Previous research has suggested that the racial composition of schools conditions adolescents' chances of having a friend or romantic partner of a different race. More specifically, this research finds that adolescents are increasingly likely to have both opposite-sex and same-sex friends of a different race as the relative size of their racial group decreases.

Regardless of relative group size, adolescents are still more likely to pair up with someone of their own race than expected on the basis of random mating (Joyner & Kao, 2000). We expected to find a similar pattern of results.

Same-Sex Relationships. Because same-sex sexual relationships have been shown to be relatively rare in the adult population (Laumann, Gagnon, Michael, & Michaels, 1994), we expected the prevalence of same-sex romantic relationships to be low among adolescents. Previous studies suggest that same-sex sexual activity typically takes place outside the context of a romantic relationship. Furthermore, they suggest that sexual-minority youth may form romantic relationships with the opposite sex in adolescence to test or hide their sexual identity (Diamond et al., 1999).

Relationship Stability

How stable are the romantic relationships of adolescents? Relationship stability (or instability) is a key dimension of pair bonding in general. The stability of marriages and cohabiting unions has been fairly well established. It is estimated that if 1980 rates of divorce continue to hold, about half of all marriages will end in divorce (Cherlin, 1992). Cohabiting unions have been shown to be much less stable—only three out of five cohabiting relationships survive the first year (Bumpass & Sweet, 1989). However, since this estimate is based on the duration of the co-residential experience (excluding time spent in this relationship before co-residence), it represents a lower bound. The stability of romantic relationships, in general, is less well documented (for exceptions based on convenience samples, see Hill, Rubin, & Peplau, 1976; Simpson, 1987).

We assume that the romantic relationships of adolescents are less stable than the romantic relationships of young adults. As adolescents mature, they are better able to accomplish certain cognitive, affective, and behavioral tasks. For example, more mature adolescents are better able to see things through the eyes of another (cognitive), are more able to empathize with and sense another's feelings (affective), and work to communicate effectively (behavioral) (Paul & White, 1990).

Assuming the attainment of these skills makes adolescents better able to maintain a relationship, we predicted that relationship stability would increase as adolescents age. Assuming girls have more experience than boys with intimate relationships, we expected that the romantic relationships of adolescent girls would last longer, on average, than their similarly-aged male counterparts. We also expected this difference because girls tend to have older partners than boys. Since African American marriages are less stable than White marriages (Cherlin, 1992), romantic relationship stability was expected to be lower for African American adolescents than for White adolescents. Descriptive information on romantic relationship stability during adolescence may elucidate later racial differences in marital stability.

The Content of Romantic Relationships

Intimacy and Commitment. How committed and intimate are adolescent relationships? Intimacy is typically defined in terms of emotional closeness (Connolly & Goldberg, 1999; Furman & Simon, 1999). Three major types of commitment have been identified: personal, moral, and structural. Personal commitment refers to individuals' desire to stay in a relationship; moral commitment refers to their feelings of personal or moral commitment; and structural commitment refers to their feelings of being constrained in a relationship (Johnson, Caughlin, & Huston, 1999). While the first two types of commitment are a reflection of internal factors (e.g., couple identity and sense of obligation), the third type of commitment is an indication of external factors (e.g., alternatives and irretrievable investments).

Based on previous studies, we expected that both relationship intimacy and commitment would increase over the course of adolescence (Brown, 1999; Connolly & Goldberg, 1999). With respect to sex differences, there is evidence to suggest that girls are more intimate than boys, as mentioned earlier. However, previous studies suggest that adolescent boys and girls view commitment somewhat differently. When asked to write an essay defining the term *commitment,* boys were more likely to display moral commitment, showing a concern for following rules or living up to an explicit agreement; whereas girls tended to express personal commitment, viewing it from an emotional or affective standpoint (Galotti, Kozberg, & Appleman, 1990). We expected that girls would express higher levels of intimacy and commitment than boys. To the extent that relationship commitment, intimacy, and stability are all linked, we also expected that Whites would be more committed and intimate than African Americans.

Sexual Behavior. How prevalent are different acts of sexual behavior within adolescent romantic relationships? The specter of AIDS, and a focus on sexually transmitted diseases (STDs) and teenage childbearing has guaranteed that we know more about demographic differences in the sexual behavior of adolescents than we do about any other aspect of adolescent romantic relationships. Nationally representative data have demonstrated that the prevalence of sexual intercourse increases dramatically with age (Adams, Schoenborn, Moss, Warren, & Kann, 1995), and that at any given age females are less likely than males to have had intercourse (Miller & Benson, 1999). With respect to racial differences in sexual behavior, African American adolescents report first intercourse earlier than do Whites (Adams et al., 1995; Sonenstein, Ku, Lindberg, Turner, & Pleck, 1998).

Because we can examine other sexual behaviors besides sexual intercourse, we consider "petting" (touching each other under clothing) and "heavy petting" (touching each other's genitals) behaviors in our analyses. We assume that these behaviors are precursors to sexual intercourse. Consequently, we predicted that they would increase during adolescence. We had no compelling reason to expect sex and racial differences in these other behaviors.

Abuse. How common are verbal and physical abuse in adolescent romantic relationships? Although a number of nationally representative studies have documented the prevalence of sexual coercion in adolescence (e.g., Laumann et al., 1994), they have yet to reveal the prevalence of other types of abuse in relationships. Studies that have examined abuse in romantic relationships limit their scope to adults (for an exception based on a select sample, see Jezl, Molidor, & Wright, 1996). Because these studies fail to distinguish the type of abuse, we do not speculate about physical and verbal abuse in adolescent relationships (Johnson & Ferraro, 2000).

The Social Connectedness of Romantic Partnerships

How connected are romantic relationships to peer and parental relationships? Romantic relationships during adolescence are embedded in peer and friendship networks. Past research has shown that friend networks are fluid. As adolescents mature, their friend networks shift to include more members of the opposite sex than networks observed among younger adolescents (Dunphy, 1969). More gender heterogeneous networks provide additional opportunities for the formation of opposite-sex romantic pair bonds. Often, adolescents draw romantic partners from friendship networks. However, as romantic relationships become more intimate, romantic partners may withdraw from friend networks (Brown, 1999; Connolly & Johnson, 1996; Dunphy, 1969; Parks & Eggert, 1991).

Studies specifically addressing scripts for dating among undergraduates suggest that females are more likely than males to tell friends and family about a date; however, females and males are equally likely to meet friends and family (Rose & Frieze, 1989, 1993). Furthermore, studies concerning romantic involvement among the undergraduate population suggest that the majority of males and females reveal the existence of the relationship to friends and family (Baxter & Widenmann, 1993). It is difficult to extrapolate expectations from these studies because some of them do not quantify sex differences. Furthermore, differences by age and race are not highlighted in these studies.

METHODS

The National Longitudinal Study of Adolescent Health (Add Health)

We use data from the "core" Wave I and Wave II in-home samples of the National Longitudinal Study of Adolescent Health to examine the romantic relationships of a nationally representative group of U.S. adolescents. Add Health provides information for a group of adolescents who were in Grades 7 to 12 between September 1994 and April 1995 (Bearman, Jones, & Udry, 1997). Data were collected from students of 80 high schools (defined to contain an eleventh grade) that were randomly selected from a database of U.S. schools stratified on school size, region of the U.S., urbanicity (urban/suburban/rural), school type (public/private/religious), and racial mix. Schools were selected with a probability proportional to size. Seventy-nine percent of the schools contacted agreed to participate. If a school refused, another school within a similar cell for all the school strata characteristics was chosen and approached. Once a high school was recruited, feeder schools (defined to contain a seventh grade and to send their graduates to the recruited high school) were identified. Feeder schools were selected with a probability proportional to the number of students it contributed to the high school. Add Health includes 134 different schools in its main study. Schools varied in size from less than 100 students to more than 3,000 students (Bearman et al., 1997).

Various instruments were used to obtain data at a number of different points in time. The "in-school" instrument was administered during one 45- to 60-minute class period on one day during the 1994–95 school year (September 1994–April 1995). There was no makeup day for students not present on the day of administration. The in-school administration resulted in over 90,000 completed surveys. In most schools, well over 80% of all enrolled students participated in the in-school administration.

From a combined register of students listed on school rosters and students not on a roster who completed an in-school questionnaire, a random sample of 16,000 individuals was selected for a 90-minute in-home interview. Approximately 220 students from each school pair (high school and feeder school), irrespective of size, were selected to form this sample. We call this the "core" Wave I in-home sample to distinguish it from the "grand" sample which contains a number of over-samples originally identified from responses to the in-school instrument.

The Wave I in-home interviews were conducted between April and December, 1995, and were completed by 80% of those selected to participate. A computer-assisted personal interview was conducted for the majority of the in-home survey. For the sections of the interview containing sensitive questions (including the information gathered on romantic partners and romantic relationships), the respondent listened to pre-recorded questions through earphones and entered the answers directly into the laptop computer (audio-CASI). This technology minimizes the effects of interviewers (and others present during the interview) on responses. Approximately 1 year later, Wave II in-home interviews were conducted with all adolescents from Wave I except those who were in the twelfth grade at Wave I (and who were not a part of the genetic and disabled samples). These took place from April through August, 1996, and were completed by nearly 90% of the original Wave I in-home target population (Bearman et al., 1997).

Romantic Partner Data.   Romantic partners were identified on the Wave I in-home sample through the following method. Add Health first asked, "In the last 18 months—since [MONTH, YEAR]—have you had a special romantic relationship with anyone?" If the respondent answered "yes," the initials of these partners were recorded to be referenced by the CASI instrument. It was indicated to the respondent that the initials would be erased from the computer at the end of the section. If more than three partners were identified, the respondent was asked to reduce the list to three.

If the respondent answered "no," that they had not had a special romantic relationship with anyone, they were skipped to another section that asked, (a) "In the last 18 months, did you ever hold hands with someone who was not a member of your family?" (b) "In the last 18 months, did you ever kiss someone on the mouth who was not a member of your family?" (c) "In the last 18 months, did you ever tell someone who was not a member of your family that you liked or loved them?" and (d) "Did you do these things with the same person?" If they answered "yes" to all four questions, the reference person is considered a romantic partner. If the respondent indicated that more than one person qualified under this definition, they were asked to give the initials of the person they felt closest to at the time. We refer to these relationships as "liked" relationships for ease of communication, and distinguish them from romantic relationships in some of our analyses.

Once romantic relationship involvement was identified through either method, a series of questions were asked about the characteristics of partners and events in the relationship. Respondents who reported a romantic relationship had the opportunity to report about as many as three relationships. In contrast, respondents who had a "liked" relationship could only report on one.

In this study, we primarily use data from the "core" sample who completed the first in-home interview (N = 12,105). For various reasons (discussed later), we supplement these analyses with information obtained from Wave II "core" data. All analyses are weighted (with post-stratification) to adjust for differences in selection probabilities and response rates, and allow sample totals to serve as estimates of population totals (Tourangeau & Shin, 1998). While estimates are weighted, substantial differences from non-weighted results were not observed.

We distinguish adolescents by age and sex. We also divide respondents into five mutually exclusive racial groups: non-Hispanic White, African American, Hispanic, Asian, and Native American. To maintain consistency with other studies, we consider respondents who mark Hispanic to be Hispanic, regardless of their race (e.g., Laumann et al., 1994; Qian, 1997). We do not present results of statistical tests because we make multiple comparisons (i.e., ones by age, sex and, race), and because our large sample sizes enable us to obtain statistical significance for differences that are seemingly small.

RESULTS

Romantic Relationship Experience

What percent of adolescents experience a romantic relationship? Table 2.1 provides estimates of the percent of adolescents who had experienced a romantic relationship in the last 18 months. The second column shows the percent of adolescents who indicated they had a romantic relationship. From information presented in the first row, second column, we see that approximately 55% of all adolescents have experienced a romantic relationship. The third column shows the percent of adolescents who indicated they had a "liked" relationship. These adolescents did not directly report a romantic relationship, but displayed behaviors that others would consider to constitute a romantic relationship. Almost 10% of adolescents indicated that the relationship was of this second variety. Combining these two estimates, approximately 65% of adolescents in the "core" Wave I sample indicated that they had either type of romantic relationship experience in the last 18 months. The analyses in the following tables are based on these adolescents.

As generally expected, the percent of adolescents to report either type of relationship increases monotonically with age. Just over one third of adolescents age 12 have experienced a romantic relationship, whereas more than

TABLE 2.1

Percent of Adolescents Who Had Experienced a Romantic Relationship
in the Last 18 Months by Sex, Age, and Race
(National Longitudinal Study of Adolescent Health, Wave I, 1995)

	N	Romantic Relationship in Last 18 Months	"Liked" Relationship in Last 18 Months	No Relationship in Last 18 Months
Total	11,973	55.0	9.7	35.2
Age at Interview, by Sex				
Males	5,703	53.3	10.6	36.1
12 years	126	25.7	13.4	60.9
13 years	706	37.4	9.1	53.5
14 years	872	45.4	10.1	44.5
15 years	962	49.4	11.6	39.0
16 years	1,013	54.5	12.7	32.8
17 years	1,028	65.7	10.7	23.6
18 years	819	68.9	9.3	21.9
Females	6,270	56.7	8.8	34.4
12 years	187	26.9	3.4	69.7
13 years	837	34.2	7.3	58.5
14 years	986	43.2	12.3	44.6
15 years	1,066	56.2	10.3	33.4
16 years	1,088	63.6	8.5	28.0
17 years	1,099	74.2	7.8	17.9
18 years	888	76.1	7.6	16.3
Race, by Sex				
Males				
White	3,671	54.0	10.6	35.4
African American	1,030	53.9	12.3	33.7
Hispanic	693	52.5	11.2	36.3
Asian	243	39.2	3.2	57.6
Native American	57	56.3	6.1	37.6
Females				
White	3,970	59.8	8.2	31.9
African American	1,248	51.6	12.2	36.2
Hispanic	738	50.4	9.1	40.5
Asian	250	42.1	4.4	53.5
Native American	55	55.8	5.3	38.9

Note. Analyses are weighted with post-stratification.

four fifths of adolescents age 18 have relationship experience. In contrast, the percent of "liked" relationships stays relatively constant. Contrary to expectations, overall rates for boys and girls suggest that the sexes are equally likely to experience a romantic relationship (64% and 65%, respectively); however, boys are slightly more likely to indicate a "liked" relationship. A closer look at the sex difference by age indicates that relationship prevalence is slightly higher for girls who are 15 and older as compared to boys. Before age 15, boys generally report slightly higher rates of relationship experience than girls.

Turning to racial differences, Asian adolescents are notable for their much lower percents of relationship experience, including "liked" relationships. Less than half of these adolescents have experienced a romantic relationship. Whites, African and Native Americans, and Hispanics are relatively similar in terms of their experience with romantic relationships. Almost two fifths of these adolescents have relationship experience.

Relationship Homogamy

How homogamous are the romantic relationships of adolescents? Tables 2.2 and 2.3 present joint demographic characteristics of romantic partners by the age, sex, and race of the respondent. Specifically, we examine age differences between partners and the extent to which interracial relationships are common among this age group. Joint characteristics provide information about characteristics selected (and possibly preferred) in partners.

First, a methodological note: in order to calculate age differences between partners, the age at the beginning of the relationship is used. The age for the respondent is calculated from two pieces of information: the respondent's birth date and the beginning date of the union. The partner's age at the beginning of the relationship (but not at the time of the interview) was provided by the respondent who was directly asked how old his/her partner was when the relationship began. Given the potentially unreliable nature of such information, we first examine these temporal issues in a bit more detail.

The Difficulty of Positioning a Relationship in Time. From data not shown, it is important to note that over a quarter of all adolescents could not identify when the relationship began—indicating "don't know" as their response. In fact, a third of the boys and a fifth of the girls could not even tell us the *year* the relationship began. One possible explanation for such difficulty relates to the inaccuracy of using discrete information to describe a process—the process of relationship formation. How does one pinpoint exactly when a romantic relationship begins, especially if it begins as a friendship? Is it the first time you hold hands? Is it the first time you kiss? Is it when your partner first tells you that she or he loves you? Another straightforward explanation for the large number of "don't know" responses to this question is that it simply may be difficult to recall the date.

Analyses (not shown) suggest that age, sex, and race are important predictors of temporal uncertainty. Older adolescents are better able to date the beginning of a relationship. Younger boys have the most trouble (40% do not even report the year the relationship began) and older girls have the least difficulty (14% do not report the year). Race also appears to play a role, especially among boys. For instance, African American males appear to have the most difficulty (42%) as compared to White males (28%), Hispanic males (31%), and Asian males (34%). White females have the least difficulty (18% do not know the year the relationship began). Hispanic (27%), Asian (25%), and African American females (25%) report higher rates of uncertainty than White females. Thus, beginning date estimates are more likely to be accurate for Whites, girls, and older adolescents.

As might be expected, adolescents are more likely to report knowing the ending date of a relationship. The end date is a more recent event and thus, likely easier to remember. It is perhaps also more likely to be a discrete event than the events leading to the beginning of a romantic relationship. Overall, data indicate that approximately 15%–18% of adolescents do not know the month and/or year when the relationship ended. Boys and younger adolescents continue to express uncertainty about relationship ending dates. African American (24%) and Asian (14%) males are the most and least uncertain, respectively. Asian (12%) and Hispanic females (8%) are the most and least uncertain, respectively.

The potential bias inherent in the problem of positioning relationships in time affects two analyses in this chapter: the analyses of age differences and union stability. This problem affects the analysis of age differences because it is necessary to calculate both partners' ages at the beginning of the relationship. It also affects stability analyses, as beginning and ending dates provide a measure of relationship duration.

With respect to duration, we can think of reasons to expect bias toward both longer and shorter duration relationships. Add Health allowed for the collection of three romantic partnerships; and thus, relationship data are truncated for some adolescents. First-listed relationships are longer than second- and third-listed relationships (data not shown); therefore, truncation may cause shorter duration relationships to be under-represented. Also, shorter unions may be under-represented in general because their ephemeral nature may make them less likely to be reported. On the other hand, longer relationships may be under-represented because their beginning dates are further back in time and less likely to be remembered. In this case (because dates are missing), the entire observation is excluded from analysis.

Analytical decisions may also introduce bias because we have chosen to examine only first-listed relationships (typically of longer duration). We choose first-listed relationships based on the assumption that respondents listed more important relationships earlier in the nomination process (at the very least, they listed longer relationships). Despite such speculation, it is clear that such data are not missing at random. Data availability varies by a respondent's age, sex, and race. Older adolescents, girls in general, and White males (as compared to males from other racial groups) seem to be better able (or more willing to attempt) to position relationships in time.

Age Differences.   Despite potential biases due to missing temporal data, information on age differences can be illuminating for those partners who were more confidently able to date the relationship. Table 2.2 presents statistics on age differences between partners. These statistics provide clues about romantic relationship norms or partner preferences among adolescents. A positive mean age difference indicates that the partner is older than the respondent on average. Likewise, a negative mean age difference indicates that the average partner is younger than the average respondent. Results from Table 2.2 are likely least biased for older adolescents, for girls, and for non-African Americans because the dating of the beginning of the relationship is less problematic for these groups. Such information should be kept in mind as results are discussed.

TABLE 2.2
Mean Age Differences (Partner Age Minus Respondent Age)
Between Romantic Partners by Age, Sex, and Race
(National Longitudinal Study of Adolescent Health, Wave I, 1995)

	N	Mean Age Diff	Minimum	Q1	Median	Q3	Maximum
		MALES					
White Males	1,531	−0.018	−8	−1	0	1	13
13 years	107	0.537	−1	0	0	1	5
14 years	146	0.342	−2	0	0	1	5
15 years	235	0.187	−3	0	0	1	13
16 years	299	0.082	−3	−1	0	1	11
17 years	381	−0.194	−4	−1	0	1	5
18 years	300	−0.415	−8	−1	0	0	10

(Continued)

TABLE 2.2 *(Continued)*

	N	Mean Age Diff	Minimum	Q1	Median	Q3	Maximum
African American Males	355	0.182	−5	−1	0	1	7
13 years	29	1.245	−1	0	0	1	7
14 years	44	0.277	−2	0	0	1	5
15 years	48	0.413	−3	0	0	1	5
16 years	70	0.312	−2	−1	0	1	4
17 years	80	0.122	−4	−1	0	1	3
18 years	64	−0.438	−3	−1	−1	0	4
Hispanic Males	277	0.063	−5	−1	0	1	9
13 years	19	0.772	−1	0	1	1	4
14 years	34	0.734	−1	0	1	1	6
15 years	32	0.483	−2	−1	0	1	9
16 years	54	−0.015	−3	−1	0	1	3
17 years	57	−0.239	−3	−1	0	0	7
18 years	62	−0.376	−5	−1	0	1	5
FEMALES							
White Females	2,099	1.675	−3	0	1	3	25
13 years	139	1.349	−2	0	1	2	11
14 years	235	1.401	−2	0	1	2	13
15 years	354	1.701	−2	0	1.5	3	9
16 years	428	1.894	−3	0	2	3	21
17 years	488	1.611	−3	0	1	3	16
18 years	407	1.770	−3	0	1	3	25
African American Females	543	2.033	−8	0	2	3	16
13 years	29	2.591	−1	1	2	2	9
14 years	63	2.529	−6	1	2	3	13
15 years	89	2.338	−1	1	2	3	10
16 years	102	1.699	−2	1	1.5	2	9
17 years	132	1.696	−8	1	2	3	8
18 years	107	2.109	−2	0	1	3	16
Hispanic Females	315	1.984	−2	0	2	3	20
13 years	22	2.112	−1	0	2	2	6
14 years	29	2.171	−1	1	2	3	7
15 years	42	1.588	−2	0	2	3	7
16 years	59	2.108	0	1	2	3	8
17 years	73	2.291	−2	1	2	3	7
18 years	70	1.184	−2	0	1	2	20

Notes. Age differences are calculated at the time the relationship began for the first listed partner only. A positive mean age difference indicates that the partner is older than the respondent on average. A negative mean age difference indicates that the partner is younger than the respondent on average. Analysis is weighted with post-stratification.

As expected, from Table 2.2, we see that boys typically identify romantic partners who are on average older than they are—until they reach the age of 17 or 18. By late adolescence they tend to select younger partners. African American boys show a slightly more pronounced tendency for choosing older partners than other racial groups (mean age diff = 0.18 yrs, or roughly 2 months), and is particularly apparent at the youngest age group (mean age diff = 1.25, or roughly 15 months). African American boys also have the narrowest age difference range (being unlikely to pair up with girls more than 5 years younger, or more than 7 years older). White boys, on the other hand, have relationships with the broadest range of girls with respect to age (8 years younger to 13 years older). Hispanic boys appear to mirror White boys with respect to means and African American boys with respect to range. This greater variation on the part of African American and Hispanic boys could be an artifact of their smaller sample sizes.

Age patterns appear to be somewhat more striking and consistent for girls than boys. At all ages, girls pair up with boys who are on average older than they are. In no case did White girls pair up with boys (or at least *report* pairing with boys) who were more than 3 years younger. This tendency was even more pronounced among Hispanic girls, who never provided information about partners who were more than 2 years younger than were they. African American girls appear to be more lenient in their age norms, forming romantic relationships with boys of a greater variety of ages. Again, this could reflect their smaller numbers. Irrespective of whether these age differences are real or merely an artifact of respondents' willingness to report particular relationships, they tell us that age rules are important among adolescents.

Interracial Relationships. Table 2.3 presents information on the interracial relationships of adolescents. Because of the strong relationship between the racial composition of the school and the probability of engaging in an interracial relationship, we only present these data by the racial mix of the school. As predicted, Table 2.3 shows that as racial homogeneity increases (i.e., the percentage of one's school that is of the same racial background as the respondent), the probability of having an interracial relationship decreases. This pattern holds irrespective of the racial identification of the adolescent. It suggests that adolescents have less opportunity to form interracial relationships when nearly everyone in their school is of the same race.

These data also suggest that differences exist between racial groups in terms of their willingness to engage in interracial relationships. (For a more extensive consideration of this topic, see Joyner and Kao, 2000). In most school contexts, African Americans are the least likely to identify romantic partners of a different race, while Asians and Hispanics are the most likely to do so. Whites are

TABLE 2.3
Percentage of Interracial Relationships (Add Health, Wave I, 1995)
by the Relative Size of the Respondent's Racial Group in the School
(Add Health, In-School, 1994–95)

		Proportion of the School of Same Race				
		0–0.2	*0.2–0.4*	*0.4–0.6*	*0.6–0.8*	*0.8–1.0*
	N =	*747*	*1,104*	*809*	*2,095*	*2,397*
Race						
White		46.2	23.9	20.4	9.4	6.1
	(4,725)	(109)	(316)	(426)	(1,814)	(2,060)
African American		29.7	14.7	10.7	9.4	3.4
	(1,372)	(282)	(462)	(208)	(224)	(196)
Hispanic		68.5	43.8	21.5	12.9	6.1
	(784)	(234)	(230)	(121)	(58)	(141)
Asian		62.0	40.0	40.0	.	.
	(209)	(77)	(78)	(54)		
Sex						
Males		59.5	27.5	16.8	8.2	4.8
	(3,356)	(356)	(519)	(363)	(994)	(1,124)
Females		47.9	23.9	20.4	10.8	7.0
	(3,799)	(391)	(587)	(446)	(1,102)	(1,273)
Age at Interview						
12		64.5	44.0	14.9	15.4	2.6
	93	(15)	(16)	(14)	(24)	(24)
13		59.5	24.6	17.9	8.5	7.7
	609	(62)	(90)	(74)	(213)	(170)
14		61.8	26.1	22.0	10.1	5.1
	934	(95)	(155)	(115)	(289)	(280)
15		52.2	28.6	21.7	8.9	6.8
	1,176	(122)	(162)	(140)	(359)	(393)
16		52.5	24.5	16.1	11.1	6.1
	1,336	(146)	(199)	(147)	(385)	(459)
17		53.9	23.5	17.7	8.5	6.1
	1,550	(163)	(244)	(157)	(434)	(552)
18		49.6	26.0	16.4	9.4	5.0
	1,259	(116)	(202)	(135)	(339)	(467)
19		41.8	21.3	26.2	6.0	4.1
	168	(23)	(30)	(23)	(45)	(47)

Note. Sample sizes are in parentheses. Analyses are weighted with Wave I weights (with post-stratification).

more likely than African Americans, but less likely than Hispanics and Asians, to report interracial relationships.

In schools with less opportunity to pair up with a person of a similar race, boys are more likely than girls to nominate romantic partners of a different race. In contrast, girls are more likely to nominate different-race romantic partners than boys in schools with greater opportunity. The results in this table suggest additionally that adolescents prefer romantic partners of the same race. Even among adolescents whose racial group represents less than one fifth of their student body, the percent who forge relationships with a same-race partner is about one half. Age patterns are not readily apparent in these data.

It could be argued that the school context is a less important factor for relationships that occur outside of school; however, schools represent the racial mix of the communities in which they are embedded (data not shown). Besides, analyses (not shown) limited to school-based relationships reveal similar patterns.

Same-Sex Relationships. In Wave I, Add Health documented 191 respondents who nominated any same-sex romantic partner (data not shown). As we predicted, same-sex romantic relationships are rare. Of respondents who had reported any romantic relationship in the last 18 months, approximately 2.2% of boys and 3.5% of girls reported a same-sex romantic relationship.

As another indicator of same-sex romantic interest, Add Health asked all respondents about the extent to which they were romantically attracted to partners of each sex. Of those who had nominated a same-sex partner, not all indicated they were romantically attracted to a partner of the same sex. Of those who provided a same-sex nomination, approximately 18% of girls and 38% of boys also indicated a same-sex romantic attraction. Among all adolescents who had indicated a romantic relationship, approximately 6% of girls and 8% of boys indicated a same-sex romantic attraction.

A comparison of these figures suggests that the discrepancy between same-sex partner nominations and romantic attraction is less related to unreliable data (e.g., respondents made a mistake when entering the sex of the partner) than it is to the idea that "attraction" is weakly related to actual same-sex romantic relationships. Future research could partly address this issue by examining sexual relationships that involve partners of the same sex.

Stability of Relationships

How stable are adolescent romantic relationships? Table 2.4 provides life table estimates of relationship duration for those adolescents who felt confident enough to attempt to position the relationship in time. From the right-hand column in Table 2.4, we see that the median duration for an adolescent romantic relationship is nearly 14 months. As predicted, boys list relationships that are shorter in duration (12 months) than do girls (16 months). Furthermore, these patterns are age-dependent. Older adolescents typically report longer relationships. Respondents who were less than 14 at the time of interview reported durations of 5 months; 14–15-year-old adolescents reported relationships that are slightly longer (8 months); adolescents who were 16 and older reported relationships of almost 2 years in duration (21 months). In contrast to our expectations, African Americans appear to have more stable relationships than Whites or Hispanics. In fact, their relationships average over 2 years in

TABLE 2.4
Life Table Survival Estimates for First Listed Adolescent
Romantic Relationships by Sex, Age at Interview, and Race
(National Longitudinal Study of Adolescent Health, Wave I, 1995)

	Duration (Months)						Median Duration (Months)
	4	8	12	16	20	24	
Total	77	62	53	46	42	38	13.6
Sex							
Males	74	58	49	42	38	33	11.6
Females	79	65	56	50	45	42	15.9
Age at Interview							
<14	57	41	34	26	.	.	5.1
14–15	69	50	38	31	26	23	7.9
16+	82	69	61	55	51	46	20.5
Race							
White	74	59	50	43	39	35	11.8
African American	85	74	67	60	56	53	>24
Hispanic	81	66	57	48	42	36	14.5
Asian	77	60	47	.	.	.	11.0

Note. Adolescents had 5,188 relationships, of which 2,640 (50.9%) were censored. Females had 3,010 relationships, of which 1,628 (54.1%) were censored. Males had 2,178 relationships, of which 1,012 (46.5%) were censored. Adolescents who were less than 14 at time of interview had 390 relationships, of which 133 (34.1%) were censored. Adolescents who were 14–15 at time of interview had 1,372 relationships, of which 603 (44.0%) were censored. Adolescents who were 16 or older at time of interview had 3,424 relationships, of which 1,903 (55.6%) were censored. White adolescents had 3,543 relationships, of which 1,729 (48.8%) were censored. Black adolescents had 869 relationships, of which 529 (60.9%) were censored. Hispanic adolescents had 579 relationships, of which 294 (50.8 %) were censored. Asian adolescents had 145 relationships, of which 64 (44.1 %) were censored. Analyses are weighted with Wave I weights (with post-stratification).

duration. Whites and Asians reported shorter durations of nearly 12 months and 11 months, respectively. Hispanics fall between African Americans and Whites, reporting durations of 15 months on average.

Because of the difficulty with beginning and ending dates, Table 2.5 presents another analysis to triangulate results from Table 2.4. This second set of data compares adolescents who had current romantic relationships at Wave I which continued to Wave II. This analysis is generalizable only to romantic nominations that were directed toward individuals who were also in the same school (because in-school nominations can be linked across waves), whereas Table 2.4 presents results for all nominations (both in-school and out-of-school). The average length of time elapsed between the Wave I interview and the Wave II interview is 11 months. We observe no significant difference in the length of time between interviews between adolescents who remained in a relationship and those who did not.

Overall, results are similar between the two tables. Table 2.4 figures provide an estimate that 53% of adolescents had relationships that lasted at least 12 months. From Table 2.5, we see that 51% of adolescents had relationships that

TABLE 2.5

Percent of Adolescents With a Current Relationship at Wave I
Who Continued This Same Relationship to Wave II
(Includes Only In-School Nominations)

	N	Percent Who Continued
Total	947	51.0
Sex		
Males	453	43.7
Females	494	57.7
Age at Interview		
<14	85	21.2
14–15	357	48.7
16+	505	57.6
Race		
White	635	55.7
African American	181	35.9
Hispanic	94	48.9
Asian	21	57.1

Note. The average length of time elapsed between the Wave I interview and the Wave II interview is 11 months. No significant difference was observed between the length of time between interview for those who continued versus those who didn't continue. Analyses are weighted with Wave II weights (with post-stratification).

lasted at least 11 months. These figures agree fairly closely, as do figures for sex. Approximately 56% of relationships for girls lasted 12 months (Table 2.4) and 58% lasted 11 months (Table 2.5). Estimates for boys are also fairly close (49% from Table 2.4 and 44% from Table 2.5). Results differ, however, when compared for the age and race of the respondent. Very young respondents (< 14 yrs) show shorter durations in the second analysis (34% lasted 12 months from Table 2.4, and 21% lasted 11 months from Table 2.5). Fourteen- to 15-year-old adolescents, on the other hand, show longer durations in the second analysis (38% lasted 12 months from Table 2.4, and 49% lasted 11 months from Table 2.5). Rates for the oldest adolescents agree fairly closely (61% from Table 2.4, and 58% from Table 2.5).

One of the biggest notable differences between the two sets of results is that African American adolescents have relationships that are significantly shorter in duration when measured prospectively. Results from Table 2.4 show that approximately 67% of African American adolescents reported relationships that lasted at least 12 months. In Table 2.5, only 36% reported relationships that lasted at least 11 months. This rather large discrepancy was not completely unexpected given that African Americans also showed a high percent of "don't know" responses for temporal variables.

To summarize, these tables suggest that boys (to a relatively small degree) and African Americans (to a somewhat larger degree) provide less reliable information about relationship duration. In general, non-African American, older adolescents, and girls appear to be more reliable in the temporal dating of their relationships. The groups that have the highest levels of missing data on the temporal variables discussed previously also tend to be those with the largest discrepancies between results. It should be kept in mind, however, that the extent to which adolescents differ by whether they have in-school versus out-of-school romantic partners may affect the interpretation of these results. If in-school and out-of-school partnerships differ systematically in terms of relationship duration, the two analyses are less comparable.

Content of Relationships

Acts of Intimacy and Commitment. How committed and intimate are these relationships? Table 2.6 reports data that describe various acts of intimacy and commitment within romantic relationships. From previous work not reported here, we know that at least 30% of Wave I adolescents had difficulty using the audio-CASI program to answer questions specifically regarding the content of romantic relationships (Carver & Udry, 1997a). Therefore, when examining data on the content of romantic relationships, we use the more reliable Wave II data.

TABLE 2.6
Percent of Adolescents Who Reported Various Acts of Intimacy/Commitment
Within the Relationship, by Sex, Age, and Race
(National Longitudinal Study of Adolescent Health, Wave II, 1996)

	N	Thought of Yourselves as a Couple	Went Out Together Alone	Told One Another That You Loved Each Other	Gave Each Other Presents	Saw Less of Other Friends
Total	6,117	81.0	68.6	68.1	61.7	48.5
Age at Interview						
<14	182	80.8	37.6	68.0	42.4	26.4
14–15	1,762	80.5	55.7	66.5	54.8	38.7
16+	4,171	81.3	76.4	68.8	66.0	54.3
Age at Interview, by Sex						
Males	2,768	76.2	66.6	65.3	57.4	48.0
<14	74	78.2	44.2	77.3	40.4	26.6
14	327	79.3	50.6	64.3	45.7	35.3
15	436	72.1	59.0	65.3	53.7	42.7
16	543	75.9	66.9	62.1	54.8	43.8
17	664	75.9	73.1	64.7	63.6	55.3
18	513	79.6	77.2	67.8	65.5	59.1
19+	209	73.0	77.7	67.1	63.0	55.7
Females	3,349	85.6	70.5	70.6	65.8	48.9
<14	108	83.0	31.8	60.0	44.2	26.1
14	430	86.6	45.1	69.5	56.0	29.8
15	569	84.1	64.9	66.7	60.9	44.8
16	735	84.7	74.8	69.1	65.4	51.9
17	725	86.9	82.4	73.4	74.3	56.4
18	591	87.5	83.3	76.2	72.3	60.4
19+	191	81.4	79.4	71.6	70.1	52.6
Race						
Males						
White	1,805	79.3	70.0	66.5	58.2	48.9
African American	505	65.1	53.8	58.0	48.7	41.4
Hispanic	340	72.1	63.4	66.9	63.8	50.7
Asian	87	77.7	69.1	68.4	63.8	52.3
Females						
White	2,218	87.8	73.3	71.0	67.3	50.6
African American	644	78.9	60.6	68.8	58.7	41.3
Hispanic	358	80.6	66.8	70.0	64.6	50.9
Asian	97	81.9	66.8	71.9	67.5	38.1

Note. Analyses are constructed from Wave II data. Data are weighted with Wave II weights (with post-stratification).

From the first row in Table 2.6, we see that most romantically paired adolescents consider themselves a couple (81%), but are less likely to forego spending time with their other friends to spend time with their romantic interest (49%). They appear slightly less likely to give each other presents (62%) than to verbally express love for the other partner (68%) or to go out together alone (69%).

As expected, girls generally report more acts of intimacy and commitment than do boys. Girls (86%) are more likely than boys (76%) to report thinking of themselves as a couple, and to give each other gifts (66% vs. 57%). But, they are only slightly more likely to report verbal expressions of love (71% vs. 65%) and to report going out together alone (71% vs. 67%). It is interesting to note that such patterns do not hold for reports of seeing less of other friends to spend time with their partner. Girls and boys report similar levels on this particular dimension (48% and 49%, respectively).

A good deal of age variation exists with respect to acts of intimacy and commitment. As expected, younger adolescents are generally less committed and intimate overall. As adolescents age, they report more gift giving, more time spent alone with their partner, and less time spent with their other friends. However, both younger and older adolescents report similar levels of verbal expressions of love and thoughts about their "coupleness." Differences by race are consistent with our expectations. African Americans are generally less likely than Whites to report acts of intimacy and commitment.

Sexual Behavior. Just how sexual are romantic relationships? Table 2.7 reports various dimensions of sexual behavior within the context of a romantic relationship. Consistent with the notion that intercourse follows other behaviors, more "petting" (touching each other under clothing—57%) and "heavy petting" (touching each other's genitals—52%) is observed than actual sexual intercourse (41%). As expected, all these behaviors increase with age.

Girls report slightly higher engagement in these behaviors than do boys, and older adolescents report more engagement than younger adolescents. The biggest increase for both boys and girls occurs between ages 14 and 15 for petting and heavy petting behaviors. For girls, a significant increase in reports of sexual intercourse occurs between 16 and 17 years of age. For boys, this jump occurs between 18 and 19.

In contrast to our expectations, a higher percentage of girls than boys have had sexual intercourse in their relationships. This is probably due to the fact that girls are more likely than boys to have older partners. Keep in mind that these results are based on adolescents in romantic relationships, rather than adolescents as a whole. Also note that among adolescents who have intercourse, girls are more likely than boys to have it within the context of a romantic relationship (Sprecher et al., 1995).

TABLE 2.7
Percent of Adolescents Who Reported Various Dimensions
of Sexual Behavior Within the Relationship, by Sex, Age, and Race
(Add Health, Wave II, 1996)

	N	Touched Each Other Under Clothing	Touched Each Other's Genitals	Had Sexual Intercourse
Total	6,117	56.9	51.7	40.5
Age at Interview				
<14	182	27.8	19.9	7.6
14–15	1,762	41.7	35.6	23.2
16+	4,171	65.7	61.1	50.4
Age at Interview, by Sex				
Males	2,768	53.7	49.0	36.8
<14	74	30.8	19.4	8.4
14	327	27.0	23.0	13.2
15	436	45.6	39.3	24.3
16	543	51.1	48.2	35.3
17	664	63.0	57.7	44.9
18	513	69.1	64.9	51.2
19+	209	73.4	69.3	67.6
Females	3,349	59.9	54.4	44.0
<14	108	25.1	20.4	6.8
14	430	33.3	26.6	21.0
15	569	55.0	48.3	31.0
16	735	61.8	56.4	40.3
17	725	71.4	65.9	56.6
18	591	74.4	70.5	65.9
19+	191	73.6	69.0	72.5
Race, by Sex				
Males				
White	1,805	55.3	49.8	34.2
African American	505	50.7	47.5	46.9
Hispanic	340	47.8	45.1	39.9
Asian	87	48.6	42.5	22.7
Females				
White	2,218	62.8	57.6	43.7
African American	644	57.5	50.3	50.4
Hispanic	358	47.2	41.4	37.8
Asian	97	46.5	41.1	34.8

Note. Analyses are constructed from Wave II data. Data are weighted with Wave II weights (with post-stratification).

Consistent with previous research, African American boys and girls are the most likely to report having sexual intercourse. It was not expected that Asian girls (and especially, Asian boys) would report having the least amount. It is interesting to note that while African American adolescents report higher levels of sexual intercourse than Whites, they report comparatively lower levels of "petting" behaviors.

Abuse.   How abusive are adolescent romantic relationships? Table 2.8 presents various dimensions of abusive behavior within the relationship. Overall, the prevalence of abusive behavior ranges between 3% and 19%. For those adolescents who do report abusive behaviors within a relationship, they are most likely to report that a partner swore at them (19%) or insulted them in front of others (13%). More violent acts are less likely. However, pushing and shoving (8%) appears to be more likely than thrown objects (3%) or threats of violence (3%).

Overall, little difference is seen between reports of abusive behavior by the sex of the adolescent. Boys typically are equally likely to report abusive behaviors as are girls. However, girls do appear to report slightly more insults (15%

TABLE 2.8
Percent of Adolescents Who Reported Various Dimensions
of Abusive Behavior Within the Relationship, by Sex, Age, and Race
(Add Health, Wave II, 1996)

	N	Partner Insulted You in Front of Others	Partner Swore at You	Partner Threatened You With Violence	Partner Pushed or Shoved You	Partner Threw Something at You
Total	6,117	12.8	19.4	3.2	8.3	2.6
Sex						
Male	2,268	10.8	19.7	2.7	8.4	2.6
Female	3,349	14.6	19.2	3.7	8.1	2.7
Age at Interview						
<14	182	6.4	8.1	0.0	3.9	1.8
14–15	1,762	10.3	15.2	2.2	7.2	1.7
16+	4,171	14.3	22.0	3.9	9.0	3.2
Race/Ethnicity						
White	4,023	12.7	19.4	2.7	7.2	2.4
African American	1,149	11.5	17.4	4.5	12.8	3.4
Hispanic	698	15.0	21.0	4.0	8.2	3.4
Asian	184	11.6	24.7	3.9	11.7	2.1

Note. Analyses are constructed from Wave II data. Data are weighted with Wave II weights (with post-stratification).

TABLE 2.9
Percent of Adolescents Who Reported Various Dimensions
of Social Connectedness for the Relationship, by Sex, Age, and Race
(Add Health, Wave II, 1996)

	N	Told Other People You Were a Couple	Went Out Together in a Group	Met Your Partner's Parents
Total	6,117	78.7	72.9	68.7
Age at Interview				
<14	182	76.7	63.7	50.4
14–15	1,762	79.5	69.9	61.2
16+	4,171	78.4	74.9	73.3
Age at Interview, by Sex				
Males	2,768	73.7	68.3	65.5
<14	74	71.3	55.7	46.5
14	327	78.5	63.7	51.9
15	436	71.6	65.4	61.0
16	543	72.7	67.0	65.0
17	664	74.0	72.0	72.9
18	513	75.2	72.3	73.4
19+	209	69.5	71.8	67.8
Females	3,349	83.3	77.3	71.8
<14	108	81.4	70.7	53.9
14	430	84.7	70.3	59.7
15	569	83.1	78.0	68.9
16	735	82.6	75.9	73.7
17	725	83.4	81.0	76.9
18	591	85.7	81.9	80.1
19+	191	76.2	75.1	73.0
Race, by Sex				
Males				
White	1,805	77.2	73.4	70.1
African American	505	62.2	50.2	51.8
Hispanic	340	70.0	62.2	58.2
Asian	87	64.6	69.3	58.1
Females				
White	2,218	85.2	81.5	75.9
African American	644	78.7	58.1	62.5
Hispanic	358	78.6	76.2	60.9
Asian	97	72.3	76.6	61.6

Note. Analyses are constructed from Wave II data. Data are weighted with Wave II weights (with post-stratification).

vs. 11%) and violent threats (4% vs. 3%) than do boys. As adolescents age, reports of abusive behavior become more frequent across all dimensions of abuse, although this appears to taper off among 18-year-old adolescents (results not shown).

The Social Connectedness of Romantic Relationships

How connected are romantic relationships in adolescence? Table 2.9 presents various dimensions of social connectedness for romantic relationships. Approximately 70%–80% of all adolescents indicate that they had met their partner's parents, had told others that they were a couple, and had gone out together in a group.

Girls appear to be more connected than boys, with boys exhibiting slightly lower rates of all behaviors. Additionally, there appears to be some age dependency for the act of meeting your partner's parents (increases from 47% to 73%) and, to a lesser degree, going out together in a group (increases from 56% to 75%). Older adolescents are more likely to report both behaviors than are younger adolescents. Whites stand out in terms of significantly higher rates of connectedness on most dimensions. They appear to be most likely (78%) to go out together in a group. This same pattern holds for meeting the partner's parents (73% and 57%, respectively).

SUMMARY AND DISCUSSION

This study has provided estimates of the romantic relationship behavior of a nationally representative sample of adolescents. Its findings indicate that the majority of adolescents have engaged in a romantic relationship, underscoring the importance of these relationships for adolescents' lives. Still, roughly a fifth of adolescents age 18 did not report a romantic experience (at least in the past 18 months).

Relationship prevalence is higher for girls 15 and over than it is for similarly-aged boys. This may, to some degree, reflect the more rapid rates at which girls have been shown to develop intimate relationships in general. However, this would not explain the slightly higher relationship experience of boys (as compared to girls) before age 15. Of course, boys and girls may differ in their definitions of what constitutes a romantic relationship, as suggested later.

While African Americans are less likely than Whites to ever marry, this difference does not appear to be related to their likelihood of engaging in a relationship as an adolescent. African Americans were equally likely to report a romantic relationship as were Whites, Hispanics, and Native Americans. A number of studies suggest that African Americans are less likely to marry than Whites in part because they have fewer economic resources (e.g., Wilson, 1996). Since romantic relationships in adolescence presumably require less in the way of economic resources (i.e., money for dates and trendy clothing), racial differences are less prominent.

Interestingly, Asians are much less likely than other racial groups to have a romantic relationship. It is unfortunate that the heterogeneity of this group and the insufficiency of past research make it difficult to speculate about this difference. This difference could reflect the higher educational attainment or stronger family orientation on the part of some Asian ethnic groups (Portes & Rumbaut, 1996; Zhou & Bankston, 1998). Future research will be needed to more fully investigate this finding.

Previous work with Add Health has shown that a little more than half of all romantic relationships that occur inside the school are *not* reciprocally acknowledged by the other partner (Carver & Udry, 1997b). These findings are consistent with a retrospective study based on a sample of undergraduates. This sample reported a higher frequency of unrequited love experiences than requited love experiences, especially in early adolescence (Hill et al., 1997). The implications of these findings for rates of relationship experience are, at the present time, unclear. Rates of relationship experience could be adjusted downward with more stringent definitions of what constitutes a romantic relationship; we do not imply that a relationship that is not reciprocated is not a relationship. We simply note that the relationship may be interpreted differently by each of the partners. For example, one partner may think of the relationship as a special romantic relationship, and the other may think of it as a non-romantic friend relationship. Future research on romantic experiences among youth will need to consider differences in such definitions carefully.

Nevertheless, consistent differences were observed between the ages of romantic partners. Girls reported older partners, on average, at all ages. Younger boys tended to report romantic partners who were older, a finding which corroborates the findings of a previous study (Kenrick et al., 1996). Patterns observed among older boys were more consistent with adult male patterns (e.g., Laumann et al., 1994), with boys being more likely to report being in a romantic relationship with a younger girl. The consistency of these reports, even across race, generally supports the idea that there are strong age norms for what constitutes an "acceptable" romantic partner among adolescents.

Romantic relationships between same-sex partners were about 3%, but were similar in prevalence across race. Girls (3.5%) were slightly more likely than boys (2.2%) to report engaging in a same-sex romantic relationship. Of adolescents who nominated a same-sex romantic partner, only a minority reported a romantic *attraction* to a same-sex partner. Future research will be needed to address this incongruity.

Adolescents are shown to differ greatly in the likelihood of having an interracial romantic relationship depending on the racial composition of their schools. Adolescents are more likely to have a partner of a different race if they attend schools with fewer students of the same race. At the same time, they reveal a strong tendency to pair up with romantic partners of the same race. Presumably, this tendency reflects the possibility that adolescents draw their romantic partners from friendship networks that are racially segregated.

Generally speaking, older adolescents report having more stable, intimate, committed, and connected relationships than do younger adolescents. But they also report having more sexual and abusive relationships than younger adolescents. The fact that adolescents are at greater risk of contracting a sexually transmitted infection and becoming pregnant as they age, of course, is already documented by a number of studies. The fact that they are also increasingly at risk of experiencing abuse in their relationships has not been revealed by nationally representative studies. Future studies need to investigate factors that promote abuse in romantic relationships, and intervention programs need to target youth in abusive romantic relationships.

With respect to racial differences in relationship longevity, there is evidence to suggest that while African Americans engage in romantic relationships at levels similar to Whites, their relationships are shorter than those of Whites. Similarly, they also reported fewer acts of intimacy and commitment than Whites. Although African Americans are more likely than Whites to have sexual intercourse within a relationship, they are less likely than Whites to engage in "petting" behaviors.

While economic resources may not influence adolescents' chances of becoming romantically involved, they may have a bearing on the nature of their involvement. In economically depressed communities, becoming a parent early has a positive outcome precisely because other avenues to success are restricted to them, and because they do not expect to live very long (Anderson, 1990; Burton, Allison, & Obeidallah, 1995). Economically disadvantaged boys are said to view sexual conquests and the children that result from them as proof of manhood. Similary, girls are thought to view the child of an attractive yet unobtainable man as a "prize." As a consequence of this orientation, sex may be a more prominent feature of their relationships than commitment and intimacy, at least for boys.

Romantic relationships are an understudied dimension of many demographic processes. We have shown that these relationships are part of most adolescents' lives. Yet, adolescents' experiences with these relationships differ markedly by age, sex, and race. By simply describing these differences, our work may provide useful insight to studies that seek to model other behaviors of interest (e.g., adolescent pregnancy, childbearing, sexually transmitted disease prevalence, same-sex relationships, and later pair bonding).

ACKNOWLEDGMENTS

An earlier version of this chapter was presented at an NICHD-sponsored conference entitled, "The Ties That Bind: Perspectives on Marriage and Cohabitation." The authors wish to thank Alan Booth, Paul Florsheim, Sue Sprecher, and members of the Add Health staff for helpful comments on earlier versions of this chapter. This research is based on data from the Add Health project, a program project designed by J. Richard Udry (PI) and Peter Bearman, and funded by grant P01-HD31921 from the National Institute of Child Health and Human Development to the Carolina Population Center, University of North Carolina at Chapel Hill, with cooperative funding by the National Cancer Institute; the National Institute of Alcohol Abuse and Alcoholism; the National Institute on Deafness and Other Communication Disorders; the National Institute on Drug Abuse; the National Institute of General Medical Sciences; the National Institute of Mental Health; the National Institute of Nursing Research; the Office of AIDS Research, NIH; the Office of Behavioral and Social Sciences Research, NIH; the Office of the Director, NIH; the Office of Research on Women's Health, NIH; the Office of Population Affairs, DHHS; the National Center for Health Statistics, Centers for Disease Control and Prevention, DHHS; the Office of Minority Health, Office of Public Health and Science, DHHS; the Office of the Assistant Secretary for Planning and Evaluation, DHHS; and the National Science Foundation.

REFERENCES

Adams, P. F., Schoenborn, C. A., Moss, A. J., Warren, C. W., & Kann, L. (1995). Health Risk Behaviors Among Our Nation's Youth: United States, 1992. National Center for Health Statistics: *Vital and Health Statistics*, Series 10, No. 192.

Anderson, E. (1990). *Streetwise: Race, class and change in an urban community*. Chicago: University of Chicago Press.

Baxter, L. A., & Widenmann, S. (1993). Revealing and not revealing the status of romantic relationships to social networks. *Journal of Social and Personal Relationships, 10*, 321–337.

Bearman, P. S., Jones, J., & Udry, J. R. (1997). The national longitudinal study of adolescent health: Research design. Available online: http://www.cpc.unc.edu/projects/addhealth/design.html

Bennett, N. G., Bloom, D. E., & Craig, P. H. (1989). The divergence of Black and White marriage patterns. *American Journal of Sociology, 95*, 692–722.

Brown, B. B. (1999). You're going out with who? Peer group influences on adolescent romantic relationships. In W. Furman, B. B. Brown, & C. Feiring (Eds.), *The development of romantic relationships in adolescence* (pp. 291–329). Cambridge, UK: Cambridge University Press.

Bumpass, L. L., & Sweet, J. A. (1989). National estimates of cohabitation. *Demography, 26*(4), 615–625.

Burton, L. M., Allison, K. W., & Obeidallah, D. (1995). Social context and adolescence: Perspectives on development among inner-city African-American teens. In L. J. Crockett & A. C. Crouter (Eds.), *Pathways through adolescence and individual development in relation to social context* (pp. 119–138). Mahwah, NJ: Lawrence Erlbaum Associates.

Buss, D. M. (1989). Sex differences in human mate preferences: Evolutionary hypotheses tested in 37 cultures. *Behavioral and Brain Sciences, 12,* 1–49.

Cauffman, E., & Steinberg, L. (1996). Interactive effects of menarcheal status and dating on dieting and disordered eating among adolescent girls. *Developmental Psychology, 32,* 631–635.

Carver, K. P., & Udry, J. R. (1997a, August). *The reliability of partners' reports of the content of adolescent romantic relationships.* Paper presented at the meeting of the American Sociological Association, Toronto, Ontario, Canada.

Carver, K. P., & Udry, J. R. (1997b, March). *Reciprocity in the identification of adolescent romantic partners.* Paper presented at the meeting of the Population Association of America, Washington, DC.

Cherlin, A. J. (1992). *Marriage, divorce and remarriage.* Cambridge, MA: Harvard University Press.

Coates, D. L. (1999). The cultured and culturing aspects of romantic experience in adolescence. In W. Furman, B. B. Brown, & C. Feiring (Eds.), *The development of romantic relationships in adolescence* (pp. 330–363). Cambridge, UK: Cambridge University Press.

Coleman, J. (1961). *The adolescent society: The social life of a teenager and its impact on education.* New York: The Free Press of Glencoe.

Collins, W. A. (1997). Relationships and development during adolescence: Interpersonal adaptation to individual change. *Personal Relationships, 4*(1), 1–14.

Collins, W. A., & Sroufe, L. A. (1999). Capacity for intimate relationships: A developmental construction. In W. Furman, B. B. Brown, & C. Feiring (Eds.), *The development of romantic relationships in adolescence* (pp. 125–147). Cambridge, UK: Cambridge University Press.

Connolly, J., & Goldberg, A. (1999). Romantic relationships in adolescence: The role of friends and peers in their emergence and development. In W. Furman, B. B. Brown, & C. Feiring (Eds.), *The development of romantic relationships in adolescence* (pp. 266–290). Cambridge, UK: Cambridge University Press.

Connolly, J. A., & Johnson, A. M. (1996). Adolescents' romantic relationships and the structure and quality of their close interpersonal ties. *Personal Relationships 3,* 185–195.

Diamond, L. M., Savin-Williams, R. C., & Dubé, E. M. (1999). Sex, dating, passionate friendships, and romance: Intimate peer relations among lesbian, gay, and bisexual adolescents. In W. Furman, B. B. Brown, & C. Feiring (Eds.), *The development of romantic relationships in adolescence* (pp. 175–210). Cambridge, UK: Cambridge University Press.

Douvan, E., & Adelson, J. (1966). *The adolescent experience.* New York: John Wiley & Sons.

Dunphy, D. C. (1969). *Cliques, crowds, and gangs.* Melbourne: Chesire.

Erikson, E. H. (1968). *Identity: Youth and crisis.* New York: Norton.

Feingold, A. (1988). Matching for attractiveness in romantic partners and same-sex friends: A meta-analysis and theoretical critique. *Psychological Bulletin, 104*(2), 226–235.

Feiring, C. (1999a). Gender identity and the development of romantic relationships in adolescence. In W. Furman, B. B. Brown, & C. Feiring (Eds.), *The development of romantic relationships in adolescence* (pp. 211–232). Cambridge, UK: Cambridge University Press.

Feiring, C. (1999b). Other-sex friendship networks and the development of romantic relationships in adolescence. *Journal of Youth and Adolescence, 28*(4), 495–512.

Furman, W., Brown, B. B., & Feiring, C. (Eds.). (1999). *The development of romantic relationships in adolescence.* Cambridge, UK: Cambridge University Press.

Furman, W., & Shaffer, L. A. (1999). The story of adolescence: The emergence of other-sex relationships. *Journal of Youth and Adolescence, 28*(4), 513–522.

Furman, W., & Simon, V. A. (1999). Cognitive representations of adolescent romantic relationships. In W. Furman, B. B. Brown, & C. Feiring (Eds.), *The development of romantic relationships in adolescence* (pp. 75–98). Cambridge, UK: Cambridge University Press.

Galotti, K. M., Kozberg, S. F., & Appleman, D. (1990). Younger and older adolescents' thinking about commitments. *Journal of Experimental Child Psychology, 50*(3), 324–339.

Gargiulo, J., Attie, I., & Brooks-Gunn, J. (1987). Girls' dating behavior as a function of social context and maturation. *Developmental Psychology, 23,* 730–737.

Glenn, N. D. (1982). Interreligious marriage in the United States: Patterns and recent trends. *Journal of Marriage and the Family, 44,* 555–566.

Graber, J. A., Britto, P. R., & Brooks-Gunn, J. (1999). What's love got to do with it? Adolescents' and young adults' beliefs about sexual and romantic relationships. In W. Furman, B. B. Brown, & C. Feiring (Eds.), *The development of romantic relationships in adolescence* (pp. 364–395). Cambridge, UK: Cambridge University Press.

Gray, M. R., & Steinberg, L. (1999). Adolescent romance and the parent–child relationship: A contextual perspective. In W. Furman, B. B. Brown, & C. Feiring (Eds.), *The development of romantic relationships in adolescence* (pp. 235–265). Cambridge, UK: Cambridge University Press.

Hatfield, E., Brinton, C., & Cornelius, J. (1989). Passionate love and anxiety in young adolescents. *Motivation and Emotion, 13*(4), 271–289.

Hazan, C., & Shaver, P. (1987). Romantic love conceptualized as an attachment process. *Journal of Personality and Social Psychology, 52*(3), 511–524.

Hill, C. A., Blakemore, J. E. O., & Drumm, P. (1997). Mutual and unrequited love in adolescence and adulthood. *Personal Relationships, 4*(1), 15–23.

Hill, C. T., Rubin, Z., & Peplau, L. A. (1976). Breakups before marriage: The end of 103 affairs. *Journal of Social Issues, 32*(1), 147–168.

Jezl, D. R., Molidor, C. E., & Wright, T. L. (1996). Physical, sexual and psychological abuse in high school dating relationships: Prevalence rates and self-esteem issues. *Child and Adolescent Social Work Journal, 13,* 69–87.

Johnson, M. P., Caughlin, J. P., & Huston, T. L. (1999). The tripartite nature of marital commitment: Personal, moral, and structural reasons to stay married. *Journal of Marriage and the Family, 61*(1), 160–177.

Johnson, M. P., & Ferraro, K. J. (2000). Research on domestic violence in the 1990s: Making distinctions. *Journal of Marriage and the Family, 62*(4), 948–963.

Joyner, K., & Kao, G. (2000). School racial composition and adolescent racial homophily. *Social Science Quarterly, 81*(3), 810–825.

Joyner, K., & Laumann, E. O. (2000). Teenage sex and the sexual revolution. In E. O. Laumann & R. T. Michael (Eds.), *Sex, love, and health in America: Private choices and public policy* (pp. 41–71). Chicago: University of Chicago Press.

Joyner, K., & Udry, J. R. (2000). You don't bring me anything but down: Adolescent romance and depression. *Journal of Health and Social Behavior, 41*(4), 369–391.

Kenrick, D. T., Gabrielidis, C., Keefe, R. C., & Cornelius, J. S. (1996). Adolescents' age preferences for dating partners: Support for an evolutionary model of life-history strategies. *Child Development, 67,* 1499–1511.

Laumann, E. O., Gagnon, J. H., Michael, R. T., & Michaels, S. (1994). *The social organization of sexuality.* Chicago: University of Chicago Press.

McDaniel, C. O., Jr. (1969). Dating roles and reasons for dating. *Journal of Marriage and the Family, 31,* 97–107.

McDonald, D. L., & McKenney, J. P. (1994). Steady dating and self-esteem in high school students. *Journal of Adolescence, 17,* 557–564.

Miller, B. C., & Benson, B. (1999). Romantic and sexual relationship development during adolescence. In W. Furman, B. B. Brown, & C. Feiring (Eds.), *The development of romantic relationships in adolescence* (pp. 99–121). Cambridge, UK: Cambridge University Press.

Parks, M. R., & Eggert, L. L. (1991). The role of social context in the dynamics of personal relationships (W. H. Jones & D. Perlman, Eds). In *Advances in personal relationships: A research annual* (pp. 1–34). London: Jessica Kingsley Publishers.

Paul, E. L., & White, K. M. (1990). The development of intimate relationships in late adolescence. *Adolescence, 98,* 375–400.

Pawlby, S. J., Mills, A., & Quinton, D. (1997). Vulnerable adolescent girls: Opposite-sex relationships. *The Journal of Child Psychology and Psychiatry and Allied Disciplines, 38,* 909–920.

Portes, A., & Rumbaut, R. G. (1996). *Immigrant America.* Berkeley: University of California Press.

Qian, Z. (1997). Breaking the racial barriers: Variations in interracial marriage between 1980 and 1990. *Demography, 34,* 263–276.

Raley, R. K. (1996). A shortage of marriageable men? A note on the role of cohabitation in Black–White differences in marriage rates. *American Sociological Review, 61,* 973–983.

Roscoe, B., Diana, M. S., & Brooks, R. H. (1987). Early, middle, and late adolescents' views on dating and factors influencing partner selection. *Adolescence, 22,* 59–68.

Rose, S., & Frieze, I. H. (1989). Young singles' scripts for a first date. *Gender & Society, 3*(2), 258–268.

Rose, S., & Frieze, I. H. (1993). Young singles' contemporary dating scripts. *Sex Roles: A Journal of Research, 28*(9/10), 499–509.

Samet, N., & Kelly, E. W. (1987). The relationship of steady dating to self-esteem and sex role identity among adolescents. *Adolescence, 22,* 231–245.

Schoen, R., & Wooldredge, J. (1989). Marriage choices in North Carolina and Virginia, 1969–71 and 1979–81. *Journal of Marriage and the Family, 51,* 465–481.

Sharabany, R., Gershoni, R., & Hofman, J. E. (1981). Girlfriend, boyfriend: Age and sex differences in intimate friendship. *Developmental Psychology, 17*(6), 800–808.

Simon, R. W., Eder, D., & Evans, C. (1992). The development of feeling norms underlying romantic love among adolescent females. *Social Psychology Quarterly, 55,* 29–46.

Simmons, R. G., Blyth, D. A., Van Cleave, E. F., & Bush, D. M. (1979). Entry into early adolescence: The impact of school structure, puberty, and early dating on self-esteem. *American Sociological Review, 44,* 948–967.

Simpson, J. A. (1987). The dissolution of romantic relationships: Factors involved in relationship stability and emotional distress. *Journal of Personality and Social Psychology, 53,* 683–692.

Skipper, J. K., & Nass, G. (1966). Dating behavior: A framework for analysis and an illustration. *Journal of Marriage and the Family, 28*(4), 412–420.

Smolak, L., Levine, M. P., & Gralen, S. (1993). The impact of puberty and dating on eating problems among middle school girls. *Journal of Youth and Adolescence, 22,* 355–368.

Sonenstein, F. L., Ku, L., Lindberg, L. D., Turner, C. F., & Pleck, J. H. (1998). Changes in sexual behavior and condom use among teenaged males: 1988 to 1995. *American Journal of Public Health, 88*(6), 956–959.

Sprecher, S., Barbee, A., & Schwartz, P. (1995). Was it good for you, too? *Journal of Sex Research, 32*(1), 3–15.

Spuhler, J. N. (1968). Assortative mating with respect to physical characteristics. *Eugenics Quarterly, 15,* 128–140.

Tourangeau, R., & Shin, H. (1998). *National longitudinal study of adolescent health: Grand sample weight documentation.* Chicago, IL: National Opinion Research Center.

Udry, J. R. (1988). Biological predispositions and social control in adolescent sexual behavior. *American Sociological Review, 53*(5), 709–722.

Wilson, W. J. (1996). *When work disappears: The world of the new urban poor.* New York: Alfred A. Knopf.

Zhou, M., & Bankston, C. L. (1998). *Growing up American: How Vietnamese children adapt to life in the United States.* New York: Russell Sage Foundation.

3

Biological Influences on Adolescent Romantic and Sexual Behavior

Carolyn Tucker Halpern
University of North Carolina, Chapel Hill

Establishing romantic relationships and initiating sexual activity are key developmental tasks during adolescence and early adulthood. These transitions have important emotional-affective dimensions, but they also rest on the biological changes of puberty, which eventually culminate in sexual maturity. Beyond the obvious functional implications for sexuality and reproduction, biological concepts and processes historically have been central to developmental theory and are at the core of the concept of change (e.g., Harris, 1957). Some classic biologically based theories (e.g., Freudian models) reflect predetermined epigenetic models of development in which biology is viewed as driving development, and unidirectional structural and functional development is assumed (Gottlieb, 1998). Although these models are compatible with what Petersen and Taylor (1980) labeled "direct effects" models, in which the physiological changes of puberty, for example, may directly affect adolescent interests or behavior, they are not synonymous, as "direct effects" do not necessarily imply unidirectional action.

Much of contemporary developmental theory emphasizes the probabilistic and bidirectional nature of structural and functional change. In developmental frameworks that have been called "developmental systems," "developmental contextual," or "dynamic interactionism" (Gottlieb, 1998; Lerner, 1986; Magnusson & Cairns, 1996), it is assumed that the sequences and outcomes of development are probabilistically determined by the coactional operations of biological, psychological, and social/contextual factors and events (Gottlieb, 1998). In a developmental systems approach, individual development is conceptualized as having multiple interacting levels with bidirectional influences (Gottlieb, 1991). Biological factors, such as genetic and hormonal activity, are part of the developmental system, as are contextual factors such as romantic partners, peer groups, and parenting practices. Thus, not only do biological factors contribute to higher level psychological development, for example, but emotional and cognitive processes may alter biological processes. Bidirectional and interactional processes that cross major levels of activity (e.g., genetic activity, interpersonal behavior, social context) are fundamental to this conceptualization, and the paths linking causes and effects may not be obvious. Models labeled "mediated effects" models by Petersen and Taylor (1980), in which physical processes and psychological/behavioral processes are linked through complex causal chains of intervening or mediating variables, are compatible with this perspective, although a mediated effects model does not necessarily imply bidirectional effects or coaction.

This chapter provides an overview of biological contributions to adolescent romance and sexuality. Although the focus is on the "biological level" of the developmental system, interactive and coactional effects are assumed and illustrated where possible. When biological factors are excluded from models of adolescent sexual development, it is tacitly assumed that adolescents who have different predispositions, or who are at different stages of biological development, will seek out similar peer groups or social contexts, and will behave similarly when they are exposed to the same social determinants of sexual behavior. Yet we know, for example, that adolescents who reach puberty early are likely to date and become sexually active earlier, are more likely to be accepted and influenced by older adolescents, and experience expectations of more mature behavior from adults (Simmons & Blyth, 1987; Stattin & Magnusson, 1990). There is also evidence that the effects of biological or dispositional factors may be more pronounced during periods of transition and discontinuity, or in situations of ambiguity and novelty, such as those likely to be encountered during adolescence (Caspi & Moffitt, 1991; Udry, 1988). Conversely, biological models that exclude psychosocial and contextual factors fail to account for environmental influences on biological factors, and important moderating effects on behavioral outcomes are missed. Relatively little work has been done in applying biological concepts to the developmental processes of adolescent romance, to noncoital sexual behavior, or to same-sex sexual experiences during adolescence. Therefore, most of the discussion in this chapter centers on coital behavior, particularly the transition to first sex, as this transition has received the lion's share of research attention. Behaviors such as dating, which appear to be associated largely with age-graded norms (Dornbusch et al., 1981; Gargiulo, Attie, Brooks-Gunn, & Warren, 1987), are not systematically examined here. This chapter is intended to be illustrative rather than comprehensive, and covers three broad biological dimensions that have implications for adolescent sexuality: pubertal timing, pubertal hormonal changes, and genetics. These dimensions reflect the bulk of past work and promising future directions for biosocial research.

PUBERTY

The physical and physiological changes of puberty are definitive features of adolescence. These changes are profound, extend over multiple years, and occur in domains that are both visible and invisible to peers, parents, and other adults. The full range of physical mechanisms and feedback systems that produce pubertal maturation, including its initiation, are complex and not fully understood, but center on the neuroendocrine system, primarily the reactivation of the hypothalamic-pituitary-gonadal axis and the hypothalamic-pituitary-adrenal axis. These endocrine systems are operative during the fetal period and shortly after birth, but drop back to low levels of activity during childhood.

Testosterone (T), the most potent androgen or "male" hormone, is at low (< 100 ng/dl in serum) and relatively constant levels during childhood for both females and males. In male puberty, levels of testosterone increase 10- to 20-fold from prepubertal to adult levels (Faiman & Winter, 1974; Knorr, Bidlingmaier, Butenandt, Fendel, & Ehrt-Wehle, 1974; Lee, Jaffe, & Midgley, 1974). For some individuals this rise may occur in the relatively brief period of a year or less, and usually occurs in conjunction with a growth spurt. For females, T levels approximately double during puberty, but the changes typically occur over multiple years. The largest increases occur before menarche, the first menstrual period, with more gradual change thereafter. Although the magnitude and pace of these changes are less than those seen in males, experimental data from animal models suggest that females may be behaviorally sensitive to T levels to which males do not respond. For example, the effects of exogenous prenatal androgen injections on the genitalia and postnatal behavior of female rhesus monkeys are sensitive to the dose, duration, and timing of injections during gestation (Wallen, 1996). Early large doses affect genitalia and later behavior; the effects of later (i.e., second trimester) and smaller doses are limited to behavior. Analyses of the limited human data sets that are available to address this point have produced results that are consistent with findings from animal models. For example, females exposed in utero to relatively higher T levels during the second trimester evidence more masculine qualities as adults (Udry, 2000). Although a parallel test has not been conducted in human males, it is unlikely that differences in T exposure of the same, relatively small magnitude would yield obvious and significant behavioral differences. Measurable differences between males and females in circulating estradiol, the most active gonadal estrogen, are not detectable before about 7 or 8 years of age. However, by about age 10, circulating estradiol levels in females are about double those in males.

During the prenatal period, hormone effects are considered to be "organizational," in that they are influencing the development and structure of the brain. During puberty and thereafter, hormonal effects are considered to be "activational," in that they may play a role in gene activation to produce neurotransmitters, activate neural structures that were prenatally influenced by hormones, or affect peripheral processes such as sensitivity of parts of the body to touch or pain. Some activational effects may, in fact, depend on earlier organizational effects (Beach, 1975). For example, Udry (2000) has demonstrated significant interactions between the "organizational" effects of second trimester prenatal androgen exposure and the "activational" effects of adult androgen levels in their contributions to gendered behavior. These findings suggested that with greater levels of prenatal androgen exposure, adult androgen levels are less strongly related to adult gendered behavior.

Most of the principal changes of puberty are the result of changes in these steroid hormones, and others secreted by the adrenal gland. These physical changes are not detailed here, but include a growth spurt, which at its peak velocity is about twice the growth rate of childhood, development of the gonads (ovaries and testes), development of secondary sex characteristics (e.g., breasts, beard growth), changes in body composition (e.g., quantity and distribution of fat, muscle growth), and further development of body systems such as the circulatory and respiratory systems. For boys there is relatively greater muscle growth; for girls, there is a significant accumulation of body fat. Many of these changes yield the male and female form distinctions that publicly signify sexual readiness.

During adolescence there is also continued brain maturation and growth of brain structures such as the corpus callosum, the parietal and temporal lobes, and the frontal lobes, with a second wave of overproduction of gray matter (Giedd et al., 1999). The frontal lobes, the seat of executive functions such as self-control, judgment, and emotional regulation that have implications for sexual decision making, show the greatest change between puberty and the young adult years. There is refinement in brain structure and function as new neuronal connections (synaptic and axonal) that are unused are pruned back or eliminated. There may be selective survival of functionally meaningful neuronal connections, partly based on experience (Keshavan & Hogarty, 1999). The excess of synapses during childhood and early adolescence may compensate for early brain injuries. During adolescence and young adulthood there is also continuing myelination of areas of the cortex. It has been suggested that this later myelination may contribute to emotional maturity (Benes, 1989).

BIOSOCIAL APPROACHES TO ADOLESCENT ROMANCE AND SEXUALITY

Despite the centrality of physical change to adolescent development, particularly sexual development, there was little research incorporating pubertal processes or biological measures until the late 1970s and the 1980s. Exceptions are the classic longitudinal studies conducted at the University of California at Berkeley in the 1920s and 1930s (e.g., Oakland Growth Study, Berkeley Guidance Study) and the Fels Longitudinal Studies. (See Eichorn, 1963, Clausen, 1975, and Livson & Peskin, 1980, for reviews.) This omission is probably due largely to the sensitivity of the private aspects of pubertal development and sexual behavior, the intrusiveness of obtaining physiological measures and physical assessments, and technical limitations in assessments of some types of biological markers such as hormones. Most work has focused on observable morphological changes. However, with advances in the technology of hormone measurement, studies explicitly examining hormone levels and associations with mood and sexual behavior began to be conducted in the 1980s.

Pubertal Timing and Morphological Change

Although the general sequence of pubertal development is similar across individuals, there is great individual variation in the timing and rate of pubertal change. The process of accommodating to the physical changes themselves, and to the variation in their timing and pace, may have important implications for behavior and emotional adjustment, and therefore for adolescent romance and sexuality. How a given adolescent navigates the accommodation process will vary according to characteristics of the individual (e.g., cognitive style, prior history of behavior adjustment problems) and his or her social context (e.g., norms, composition of friendship groups). The presence of a romantic partner, and characteristics of the interpersonal dynamics with that partner, may serve an especially important role in pubertal accommodation, yet little is known about how accommodation proceeds in the context of the particular composition of adolescent couples.

In considering the implications of pubertal accommodation for adolescent sexuality, it is important from a theoretical standpoint to distinguish the concepts of pubertal status and pubertal timing. Status is an indicator of the degree of maturation completed; timing is a relative concept indicating maturational status relative to other adolescents of the same or similar age, or relative to some expected level of development (see Brooks-Gunn, Petersen, & Eichorn, 1985; Steinberg, 1987). Depending on the underlying processes and behaviors of interest, these two concepts may have differential relevance. For example, timing may be more closely linked to psychological processes and status to biological processes. It is also important to separate these two concepts from chronological age; when age and indicators of pubertal development are simultaneously included in analyses, age can be conceptualized as a generalized proxy for age-graded norms and social controls.

Despite the conceptual differences between timing and status, the constructs often have not been explicitly distinguished, separately measured, and simultaneously included in empirical work. However, a number of studies have demonstrated significant associations between pubertal status and/or timing and the initiation of sexual activity (Flannery, Rowe, & Gulley, 1993; Halpern, Udry, Campbell, & Suchindran, 1993; Meyer-Bahlburg et al., 1985; Stattin & Magnusson, 1990; Udry, 1979; Udry & Billy, 1987; Westney, Jenkins, & Benjamin, 1983; Zabin, Smith, Hirsch, & Hardy, 1986; Zelnick, Kantner, & Ford, 1981). When demonstrated, findings consistently indicate that early timing, or more advanced pubertal status, is associated with earlier sexual activity. However, patterns of associations can vary according to demographic characteristics of adolescents, the particular sexual behavior examined, and contextual variables such as gender composition of the school attended (Caspi, 1995). Further, patterns of variations are not necessarily consistent across studies. For example, Zabin et al. (1986) found that ages at menarche or first wet dream were associated with age at first intercourse among Black male and female adolescents in an inner-city sample, with earlier pubertal timing indicating earlier sexual activity. In a different cross-sectional study based on Black and White adolescents from a broader range of socioeconomic backgrounds, pubertal maturation predicted coital transition for Black females, but with chronological age controlled, was not significantly associated with coital transition for White males or females (Udry & Billy, 1987). (Parallel analyses for Black males could not be conducted due to the small number of virgins at Time 1.) A later cross-sectional study in this research line that incorporated hormone measures did find associations between pubertal status and first sex for White males at the zero order (Udry, Billy, Morris, Groff, & Raj, 1985).

In longitudinal analyses of about 100 boys followed over 3 years from early to mid-adolescence, Halpern et al. (1993) demonstrated significant zero-order associations between a multidimensional measure of pubertal timing and both noncoital activity and coital transition for White males. Boys of the same chronological age who were more physically mature had more noncoital experience, and were more likely to have made the transition to first coitus. However, when testosterone measures were added to these models, associations between sexual behavior and pubertal timing became nonsignificant. This result was consistent with the idea that hormones may make contributions to behavior that do not operate exclusively through socially mediated processes associated with observable physical change. Parallel panel analyses of a sample of about 200 Black and White females failed to show an association between pubertal status and sexual behavior (Halpern, Udry, & Suchindran, 1997). However, the absence of a bivariate link in this latter study of females may be due partly to the relatively advanced levels of pubertal maturation in the sample (all girls were post-menarcheal at study entry). Using different outcome measures, Cairns and Cairns (1994) found no association between early pubertal timing and early marriage or teen parenthood in their longitudinal sample.

One of three models is typically used in social/psychological interpretations of pubertal timing effects: a stage termination model, a goodness of fit model, and a deviance or "off-time" model (Brooks-Gunn et al., 1985). The models have somewhat different implications for hypotheses about adolescent sexual behavior and adjustment. Briefly, the stage termination model suggests that early puberty does not allow the adolescent enough time to complete prior developmental tasks before the onset of puberty and new developmental pressures; this model would predict that early-maturing adolescents are at the greatest risk for adjustment problems, including early sexual activity. The goodness-of-fit model centers on how well the adolescent's pubertal timing and status allow him or her to fit into their sociocultural context. If adult features are valued, the later maturer will be at greater risk; if child-like features are valued, the later maturer would benefit. Finally, the deviance model is probably the most commonly used in research. This model indicates that early- and late-maturing adolescents visibly differ from their peers at a time when conformity is important. Because girls, on average, begin pubertal development earlier than boys, early-maturing girls and late-maturing boys are predicted to be at greatest risk for adjustment problems, and in the case of early maturers, early transition into behaviors that may symbolize adulthood, such as sexual activity.

The deviance model centers on the fact that many components of pubertal change are public, or visible to parents, peers, and potential romantic/sex partners. These observable physical changes signal impending sexual maturity, and imply concomitant maturation of attitudes, capabilities, and behavior. Adolescents who look more physically mature will be more likely to be perceived by others, and to see themselves, as attractive and appropriate romantic and sexual partners. Appearance can therefore change the adolescent's social context and opportunities or pressures for romantic and sexual activity, by opening up possibilities for dating and for socializing with older adolescents who are engaging in more advanced behaviors. For example, in Stattin and Magnusson's (1990) work on 1,300 Swedish children, girls who reached menarche at or before age 11 showed more sexual activity, along with other indicators of deviant behavior, than did average or later maturing girls. These patterns appeared to be based on the mediating mechanism of affiliation with older males during early adolescence. This is one of the few studies that has explicitly examined mediating mechanisms for timing effects, and the potential impact of pubertal timing for aspects of romance and sexuality beyond mid-adolescence. Although some associations were time-limited to adolescence, even in adulthood early maturing girls were more likely to have married earlier and to have had more children. A few other studies have also found similar implications of early pubertal timing for later fertility (Borgerhoff-Mulder, 1989; Udry & Cliquet, 1982).

To illustrate the potential for bidirectional relationships, it should be noted that contextual factors have been associated with pubertal timing. For example, life-event stress, father absence, emotionally distant mother–daughter relationships, depression, and exposure to greater family conflict have been empirically associated with an earlier age at menarche (Graber, Brooks-Gunn, & Warren, 1995; Moffitt, Caspi, Silva, & Belsky, 1992; Steinberg, 1988; Surbey, 1990). However, the mechanisms underlying these links are unclear, and some would argue, at odds with historical evidence and evolutionary theory (e.g., MacDonald, 1997; Miller, 1994).

Often studies that include pubertal timing or status as predictors of adolescent sexual activity stop short of examining the biological and social processes that underlie associations with sexual behavior. The physical changes of puberty are accompanied by heightened romantic and sexual interest, partially due to the underlying hormonal changes to be discussed later. Pubertal accommodation also entails a heightened concern with physical appearance. Sex-linked differences in criteria of attractiveness may have differential implications for dating and sexual opportunities for adolescent boys and girls. Adolescent boys gain muscle and tend to lose body fat during puberty, a change that is consistent with idealized adult male images. Girls, in contrast, accumulate body fat and begin to physically diverge from the ultra-slim female ideal that predominates popular media. In this cultural context, the coincidence of fat gain and increased interest in dating and having a boyfriend can have important implications for weight concerns and dieting behavior. Using longitudinal data, Halpern, Udry, Campbell, and Suchindran (1999) empirically demonstrated the implications of pubertal differences in body fat for dating and sexual activity among White adolescent girls and Black adolescent girls of higher socioeconomic status. More fat was associated with a significantly lower likelihood of dating; in fact, girls who were below average in fat had significantly higher odds of dating than did girls of average body fat levels. Further, although pubertal timing was associated with dating, sexual activity, and dieting/weight concerns, differences in the probabilities of these behaviors were much more strongly linked to body fat than to pubertal timing or status when considered together in the same model. This pattern suggests that body fat is one important mediating mechanism through which pubertal timing or status effects on sexual activity operate.

Hormonal Contributions to Sexuality

Links between pubertal status and romantic/sexual interest and activity may reflect social processes such as those described already, and they may reflect more direct hormonal contributions beyond the role of hormone-induced physical maturation. In one of the earliest studies examining the correlates of pubertal change, Stone and Barker (1939) illustrated the differences in interest in "boys" and "personal adornment" that characterize pre- versus post-menarcheal girls of the same chronological age and social status. Based on 1,000 girls from two junior high schools in Berkeley, California, more of the post-menarcheal girls showed the "more mature" sex-linked interest. This early work is suggestive of the contributions that hormonal change may make to maturation of sexual and romantic interests.

Later Udry and his collaborators began to systematically examine how physical and social processes surrounding pubertal change contributed to adolescent sexual interest and behavior, and were among the first to explicitly examine lay assumptions about the contributions of pubertal hormonal changes to adolescent sexual interest and behavior in non-clinical samples. The series of studied initiated by Udry in the late 1970s attempted to fill in the theoretical gaps relevant to motivation and physical change that characterize many sociological approaches to adolescent sexuality. Commonly used sociological frameworks such as Social Control theory (Hirschi, 1969) simply assume motivation for sexual behavior (Udry, 1988). Empirical research derived from these perspectives therefore focuses on those aspects of the adolescent's immediate environment that might facilitate or inhibit sexual behavior, and omits factors, such as developmental changes in hormone levels or pubertal status, which could contribute to individual differences in sexual interest or motivation, and to differential exposure and reaction to social contexts.

In a cross-sectional study of typically developing adolescents that incorporated hormone measures, strong associations between free (biologically active) testosterone (T) levels and multiple indices of sexual behavior were detected.

Based on about 100 males and 100 females in the eighth, ninth, and tenth grades, this study used a single T measure from serum and a one-time, self-administered questionnaire that tapped pubertal status and cumulative sexual experiences (Udry et al., 1985; Udry, Talbert, & Morris, 1986). Controlling for age and multiple aspects of pubertal development, almost half of the variance in a composite Sexuality Factor score that included ideation and partnered and non-partnered behavior was accounted for by T alone for males, suggesting direct, powerful contributions of T to adolescent male sexuality (Udry et al., 1985; Udry, 1988). Serum T was also an important predictor of sexual ideation and motivation for adolescent females, but did not predict partnered sexual behavior. However, social factors, of lesser importance in male models, loomed much larger in models of female sexuality, and important interactions between hormone levels and social factors were identified (Udry et al., 1986; Udry, 1988). For example, participation in sports moderated the association between T and sexual behavior for girls. Among girls who did not participate in sports, T was strongly associated with the Sexuality Factor. Among girls who did participate in sports, T was unrelated to Sexuality, even though the mean T level for this group of girls was actually higher. Father presence was also an important moderator of biological associations. Girls who did not have a father in the home showed a strong association between T and Sexuality; the relationship was suppressed among girls who did have a father in the home (Udry, 1988). These cross-sectional patterns were consistent with the animal literature and with hypothesized biosocial interactions. The sex differences in biosocial patterns were interpreted as a function of the traditionally stronger social sanctions applied to early female sexual activity in U.S. culture.

In the cross-sectional study just described, serum hormone measures were collected in conjunction with retrospective reports of sexual activity. A better test of the developmental processes implied in that work requires a longitudinal design, in which the same adolescents are followed over time and their physical and behavioral changes are monitored from pre- to post-pubertal time points. Such a design allows for investigation of whether prior hormone levels are associated with subsequent sexual activity; varying time lags between hormonal and behavioral changes could also be explored.

Udry and collaborators implemented this basic design for 100 White males and 200 Black and White females. Multiple measures of T levels were collected via blood (semiannual) and saliva (weekly or monthly) samples, semiannual assessments of physical growth and changes in secondary sex characteristics were made, and weekly or monthly reports of sexual ideation, interest, and behavior were collected over 3- and 2-year periods for males and females, respectively. Sex hormone binding globulin (SHBG), a protein that binds T molecules, thereby rendering them biologically inactive, was also measured semiannually in plasma. In these panel studies, T levels and, more importantly, changes in T and SHBG were associated with between-individual differences in levels of sexual experience and with within-individual changes in sexual activity over time. These associations persisted when factors like age and pubertal status were controlled. The findings indicated that during the early and middle adolescent years, males and females with higher T levels were more likely to initiate sexual intercourse. Analyses examining within-individual change demonstrated that increases in T were associated with an increased likelihood of sexual transition, and for boys, increases in noncoital sexual activity (Halpern, Udry, & Suchindran, 1997, 1998).

In addition to direct associations between hormones and sexual behavior, biosocial interactions were detected that were consistent with those seen earlier in the cross-sectional data, and that reaffirmed the importance of simultaneously considering both biological and social factors in the same models of adolescent sexuality. Again using the framework of Social Control Theory mentioned earlier, higher T can be conceptualized as a proxy for greater sexual motivation, and more frequent attendance at religious services as a protective contextual factor or "social control." As previously noted, contributions of biological factors to behavior should be more evident in novel situations or when social controls are weak or absent. This theoretically predicted pattern was supported in the transitions to intercourse over time in the longitudinal study of males. By study completion at age 16, almost three quarters of males who had been high in T at study entry 3 years earlier and who never or infrequently attended religious services (i.e., high in sexual motivation, low in a social control or contextual protective factor) had had sexual intercourse. In contrast, only 12% of males who had been low in T at study entry and who attended religious services frequently (low sexual motivation, high social control/protection) had had sexual intercourse by age 16 (Halpern, Udry, Campbell, Suchindran, & Mason, 1994). In contrast to findings for measures of behavior and sexual motivation, attitudinal variables (e.g., approval of premarital sex) were associated with religious attendance, but not T. This pattern is consistent with a theoretical model in which T levels are conceptualized as contributing to differences in motivation, and opinions or attitudes are more strongly linked to learning experiences like exposure to religious teachings.

In these panel studies, associations between hormones and sexual behavior, as well as identified biosocial interactions, were consistent with theoretical prediction, and suggested that pubertal increases in testosterone meaningfully contribute to the timing of sexual initiation during adolescence for both males and females, and to the frequency of sexual experiences. Analyses supported interpretations of both direct biological contributions and socially mediated paths through pubertal timing and status. However, there were inconsistencies across this series of studies that illustrate the need for further research and more complex, multilevel modeling of factors contributing to adolescent sexuality. For example, the large effect sizes seen in the original cross-sectional study (i.e., T alone accounted for almost half of the variance in the males' Sexuality Factor Scores) were not replicated in the later longitudinal work, where variance accounted for in sexual measures was more on the order of 5% to 10%. In addition, the significant association between T and sexual behavior demonstrated for males in the panel study was evident for salivary, but not plasma, T measures collected from the same males. Significant associations between T and sexual transition for females were based on plasma T; salivary T levels in samples collected from females proved to be too low for adequate reliability in measurement. Finally, although the same measures were used across studies, the important theoretical path between T and sexual interest/motivation, a link that had been empirically supported in cross-sectional data, was not fully replicated in the later longitudinal study. Although a variety of potential explanations for the differences in results between the cross-sectional and longitudinal work and for differential behavioral correlates according to specimen type was explored (see Halpern et al., 1998, or Halpern & Udry, 1999, for a summary), a satisfying explanation was not identified. Given that a panel design provided a better test of the question of whether pubertal changes in androgens contribute to subsequent changes in sexual interest and activity, the more modest findings yielded by the longitudinal studies probably merit more confidence.

In summary, these findings support a model of hormonal contributions to adolescent sexuality. However, they also suggest that hormonal contributions, considered outside the context of other social and psychological factors, are relatively modest. Further, the complexity of processes linking the biological and behavioral levels of the developmental system lessens the likelihood of replicating relatively simple associations across different study designs. Just as the effects of social factors may vary, depending on the developmental status of the adolescent, the influence of biological factors may also vary, depending on the total context of the individual. These facets will be differentially captured across studies, and conclusions may vary accordingly. High testosterone, like any other single risk factor, does not necessarily result in early or more sexual activity. However, as illustrated with even relatively simple multilevel biosocial models incorporating the timing of the pubertal rise in testosterone (T) and attendance at religious services, the combined influences of biological and contextual factors can mean a *much* higher or lower risk of early sexual activity.

Because many pubertal changes occur within a relatively short time frame, normal puberty can be conceptualized as a "natural experiment" that involves endogenous increases ("administrations") of T. The series of studies conducted by Udry and colleagues capitalized on this "natural experiment" by monitoring pre- to post-pubertal hormonal changes and examining concurrent and lagged changes in sexual interest and behavior in non-clinical samples of adolescents. In contrast, Finkelstein et al. (1998) used a randomized, double blind, placebo-controlled cross-over clinical trial to investigate the effects of exogenously administered estrogen and testosterone on the sexual interest and behavior of a clinical sample of hypogonadal adolescents who were 10 to 19 years old. Although hormone administration was associated with increases in sexual activity for both boys and girls, significant effects were limited to a small number of the behaviors examined (nocturnal emission and sexual touching for boys; necking for girls). Thus, the positive findings were supportive of a model specifying hormones as making a necessary contribution to adolescent sexuality, and suggest, consistent with the animal literature and literature based on hypogonadal adult males, that there is a threshold below which sexual response will not appear. However, increases in sex steroids do not appear to be sufficient for sexual behavior. Consistent with coactional processes specified in a developmental systems framework, consideration of both biological and social factors is required for a more complete accounting of adolescent sexual development.

To move forward in our understanding of adolescent romance and sexuality, work incorporating hormonal measures will need to expand the "outcome" behaviors of interest and tackle more fully elaborated specifications of additive and interactive processes linking biological, psychological, and social factors. Regarding the first point, little work has been conducted on the ways in which between-individual hormonal differences or within-individual hormonal change may contribute to the developmental progression of romantic relationships. Research literature based on adults indicates that certain styles of personality, temperament, and interpersonal interaction influence the quality of relationships and the satisfaction of individuals within the relationship. Differences in temperament or mood, which may be linked to hormonal change or to genetic factors such as those discussed hereafter, and related childhood experiences may influence how adolescents learn about and "practice" romantic relationships. For example, anxious or depressed adolescents may over-anticipate negative relationship outcomes, fixate on unimportant details, or focus attention on themselves to the neglect of their partner (Clore, Schwarz, & Conway, 1994). Temperament characteristics associated with an increased likelihood of childhood rejection experiences may lead to a "rejection sensitive" interpersonal style (Downey, Bonica, & Rincon, 1999) by which adolescents readily, and perhaps mistakenly, expect or perceive rejection by their partner. Such a style may lead ultimately to coercive behavior patterns, or alternatively to tolerance of abuse or acquiescence to pressures for unwanted sexual activity or deviance behavior in order to lessen the likelihood of rejection (Downey et al., 1999).

Beyond the neglect of romance, per se, examination of sexual outcomes has typically been limited to the transition to first sex. Further biosocial examination of romantic and noncoital sexual behavior, and of sexual risk-taking behaviors that put adolescents at risk for contracting STDs, including HIV, would be useful. As an example, work examining physiological reactivity to novelty, as indicated by serial measures of the "stress hormone" cortisol in response to experimentally produced novel or stressful situations, has demonstrated an association between reactivity and condom use in late adolescent/ young adult males. Males classified as physiological reactors (versus nonreactors) reported less consistent condom use, controlling for availability of a steady partner (Halpern, Campbell, Agnew, Thompson, & Udry, 2002). Because condom use is an interdependent behavior that requires cooperation between partners, factors such as interpersonal confidence, self-assertiveness, and anticipated affective reactions of the partner can influence rates of condom use (Agnew, 1998, 1999; Helweg-Larsen & Collins, 1994; Pendergrast, DuRant, & Gaillard, 1992). Taken together, these findings suggest the importance of simultaneously considering trait-like variables that may have their origins in both biology and experience (e.g., reactivity to novelty), developmental histories, and the immediate situational context (e.g., the potentially uncomfortable situation of partner discussion and/or negotiation) as contributors to adolescents' romantic and sexual decisions.

A related and complementary direction for future research is to examine biological elements when the adolescent is "placed" in the context of his or her romantic partner, and the couple is, in turn, placed in other broader social contexts. As has been demonstrated in studies of pubertal timing effects, such contextually based analyses may be helpful in understanding the empirical inconsistencies between T associations with sexual behavior and sexual motivation. For example, whether, and under what circumstances, adolescents' sexual activity may be driven more by their partner's preferences than by their own intrinsic sexual interest.

Genetic Contributions

There is increasing interest in exploring the role of genetic factors in cognitive and socio-emotional development, and behavior. Relatively little work has been published to date related to adolescent health and social development and, by extension, romantic and sexual behavior patterns. Currently available literature reflects primarily population-based behavioral genetic analytic strategies.[1] Behavior genetic analyses model the joint contributions of genetic biological factors and social/environmental factors to variance in behavior. Using sampling designs that include individuals who have varying degrees of genetic relatedness (e.g., identical twins, fraternal twins, full siblings, adopted siblings, etc.) and whose shared environment is known or assumed, these analyses statistically decompose behavioral variation in a population into that which may be attributed to additive and non-additive genetic sources, shared environment, nonshared environment, gene–environment interactions, and error variance.

Using behavioral genetic analyses, several studies have reported genetic contributions to the age at first coitus (Dunne et al., 1997; Martin, Eaves, & Eysenck, 1977; Miller et al., 1999; Rodgers, Rowe, & Buster, 1999), fertility expectations (Rodgers & Doughty, 2000), and childbearing motivation (Pasta & Miller, 2000). To illustrate, Rodgers et al. (1999) applied a linking algorithm to kinship data from the National Longitudinal Survey of Youth (NLSY) in order to conduct a behavioral genetic analysis of age at first intercourse. They used a DeFries & Fulker (1985) multiple regression analysis, which uses kinship pairs with multiple levels of relatedness to estimate genetic and shared environmental influences. Their findings suggested genetic influences for Whites, but not Blacks, and that a very early or very late transition to coital behavior may be more influenced by genetic factors. However, the findings underscored the importance of non-shared environmental factors (e.g., friends and acquaintances) in determining the timing of sexual transition, and the potential importance of secular changes (e.g., in use of birth control) in influencing the additive genetic variance identified in any given behavior genetic analysis (Rodgers et al., 1999).

A similar environmental emphasis is evident in analyses based on adult twin data, in which results suggest that genetic contributions to romantic love styles (e.g., value love, passion, and intimacy; value companionship and affection, avoid commitment) are relatively minimal, with more of the variation accounted for by shared and/or unique environmental experiences (Waller & Shaver, 1994). This finding is in contrast to a few other studies that have found associations between genetic factors and love attitudes and/or personality characteristics that may play significant roles in couple satisfaction and relationship duration (Bouchard, Lykken, McGue, & Segal, 1990; Hendrick & Hendrick, 1992). There are also findings suggesting genetic contributions to various types of sexual behavior, such as interest in casual sex (Bailey, Kirk,

---

[1]However, see the volume edited by Rodgers, Rowe, and Miller (2000) for multidisciplinary population and molecular perspectives on genetic influences on sexual behavior, fertility, and reproduction.

Zhu, Dunner, & Martin, 2000) or the timing of first sexual intercourse, as noted earlier.

Although behavior genetic analyses have played an important role in documenting potential genetic contributions to adolescent romantic and sexual behavior, the approach does relatively little to help us understand the individual developmental processes that underlie romantic and sexual behavior patterns. To address this limitation, there are ongoing efforts to refine structural equation modeling techniques that decompose shared environmental variance and allow the incorporation of specific hypothesized factors (e.g., parental warmth) and social/contextual processes. However, to paraphrase Udry (2000), behavioral genetic analysis aims to tell us whether variance in a phenotypic outcome within a population is associated with variation in genes in that population. If there is no association, one conclusion is that the same genes are associated with that outcome for all individuals. Such an approach, therefore, does not address explanations of individual development. Further, because behavior genetic analyses assume it is possible to isolate "genetic causes" and "environmental causes," and therefore possible to simply partition variance sources (Gottlieb, 1995), they are philosophically at odds with a developmental systems model. Behavior genetic models cannot currently capture statistically the interactional and coactional processes that are at the heart of developmental approaches. In a developmental systems framework, genetic contributions to behavior are explicitly conceptualized as probabilistic, not deterministic. Therefore, genetic variations may change the likelihood that a given behavior occurs, but they do not cause the behavior directly. Similarly, experience and context may change gene expression or the timing of expression. It is the interactions of genetic probabilities with experience and context that ultimately yield complex aspects of personality and behavior (Gottlieb, 1998). The cause of development is not "in" the genes or "in" the environment. Rather, it is the coaction between factors within and across levels of the developmental system that makes development happen (Gottlieb & Halpern, 2002). This does not, however, mean that the roles of particular genes in sexual development processes cannot be specified, and molecular genetic approaches hold promise for the identification of specific genes that are part of these coactional processes.

Possibilities in Molecular Genetics—Dopamine.   There has been an explosion of work in the field of molecular genetics, and a subsequent call for more active collaborations between developmental scientists and geneticists (Plomin & Rutter, 1998; Reiss, 1997). Such collaborative efforts would maximize the contributions of both fields to our understanding of adolescent health and social development, and increasing numbers of investigations based on nonclinical human populations are appearing in the literature. Although there are a number of behavior genetic publications that examine various facets of adolescent development (e.g., Reiss, Neiderhiser, Hetherington, & Plomin, 2000; Jacobson & Rowe, 1999), no work in molecular genetics to date has dealt explicitly with human adolescent romantic and sexual behavior. Yet there are interesting possibilities, such as exploring associations with candidate genes for various neurotransmitters, that are within the reach of today's technology.

When specific genes occur in more than one form (alleles) and yield functional protein polymorphisms, they may contribute to meaningful differences between individuals. Dopamine (DA) is one of the most important catecholamine neurotransmitters in the brain, and is thought to generally act to "arouse and activate motivational systems" (Miller et al., 1999). Animal models indicate that dopamine is facilitative of sexual activity (Hull et al., 1999). Dopamine is one of the most studied neurotransmitters because of its ligand-binding properties and its location in limbic brain areas (Gelernter et al., 1997). The mesolimbic system is thought to be key to general activation, appetitive behavior, and reinforcement (Hull et al., 1999), and so may be activated in conjunction with behaviors such as sex and substance use. Dopamine also has peripheral functions, such as moderating hormone secretion. There are two classes of dopamine receptors, D1-like (D1 and D5) and D2-like (D2, D3, and D4). The dopamine D4 receptor gene (DRD4) has a high number of expressed polymorphisms, or normal variations, in humans. The alleles with four repeats (DRD4*4R—60% to 64% of humans), seven repeats (DRD4*7R—14% to 21% of humans), and two repeats (DRD4*2R—8% to 10% of humans) are the most common (Chang, Kidd, Livak, Pakstis, & Kidd, 1996; Missale, Nash, Robinson, Jaber, & Caron, 1998). The seven repeat variant of D4 has been of special interest in studies of behavior because it (versus lower repeat numbers of the 48 base-pair repeat in exon III) appears to confer functional differences (Van Tol et al., 1992).

Although not centered on adolescents, there have been numerous studies exploring the links between variations in DRD4 and the personality trait of novelty seeking, a trait that may have significant implications for adolescent romantic styles, sexuality, and sexual risk taking. In Cloninger's (1987; Cloninger, Svrakic, & Przybeck, 1993) tridimensional Biosocial Theory of Personality, novelty seeking is conceptualized as a heritable tendency toward excitement in response to novel stimuli or cues for possible reward; it was hypothesized to be associated with dopaminergic activity because of the behavior-activating effects of dopamine. Novelty seeking reflects impulsive, exploratory, or sensation-seeking behavior, and overlaps with Zuckerman's (1979) construct of sensation seeking, also conceptualized as a relatively stable personality dimension with a biological foundation. Higher levels of sensation seeking have been associated with earlier sexual initiation and greater levels of sexual activity among adolescents and young adults (Halpern et al., 2002). These links suggest that normal variation in dopamine receptors may be distally associated with tendencies toward novelty or sensation seeking. In conjunction with particular developmental histories and/or social contexts, such personality tendencies may ultimately translate into important differences in romantic styles and sexual behavior patterns.

More than a dozen studies have looked at the relationship between DRD4 polymorphisms and novelty seeking. Findings are split in terms of detecting an association. Based on studies of unselected samples of adults, individuals with one or two long DRD4 alleles have been found to have significantly higher novelty-seeking scores than individuals with short alleles (Benjamin, Patterson, Greenberg, Murphy, & Hamer, 1996; Ebstein et al., 1996; Ebstein, Nemanov, Klotz, Gritsendo, & Belmaker, 1997; Ekelund, Lichtermann, Jarvelin, & Peltonen, 1999; Noble et al., 1998, Ono et al., 1997; Tomitaka et al., 1999). In some studies that included both male and female respondents (e.g., Ebstein, Nemanov, et al., 1997; Ono et al., 1997), associations were found only for women.

Other studies, however, have failed to find bivariate relationships between DRD4 and novelty seeking in samples of unrelated individuals (e.g., Gelernter et al., 1997; Jonsson et al., 1997; Malhotra et al., 1996; Poston et al., 1998; Sullivan et al., 1998; Vandenbergh, Zonderman, Wang, Uhl, & Costa, 1997) and in linkage studies (e.g., Hill, Zezza, Wipprecht, Locke, & Neiswanger, 1999). Some investigators have suggested that an association between DRD4*7R and novelty seeking might only be evident in the context of other specific genetic and environmental factors (Gelernter et al., 1997). However, much of the research to date has examined only bivariate relationships, and these coactional possibilities have not been explored. The argument that context must be considered is consistent with biological arguments proposed by Comings (1998) for polygenic inheritance and with the developmental systems perspective: genotypes or other single biological components do not result directly in phenotypes, and therefore the contribution of genetic polymorphisms will not necessarily map directly or obviously onto complex personality or behavioral outcomes. One might hypothesize that links between dopamine polymorphisms, novelty seeking, and sexual behavior patterns in adolescents are more likely to be evident, or perhaps to take a certain form, in particular family contexts. For example, in the context of limited parenting skills or permissive, uninvolved parenting, an adolescent's tendency toward novelty seeking may be less likely to be channeled in constructive directions, such as enthusiasm for reading or travel, or the pursuit of athletic excellence, and more likely to lead to early sexual experimentation or the exploration of deviant behaviors such as substance use or delinquent activity.

Work has been done in adult humans to examine the relationship between polymorphisms in three dopamine receptor genes and the timing of first sex, yielding findings that are consistent with animal models. Using a sample of about 400 non-Hispanic White adults, Miller et al. (1999) examined the association between genotype grouping variables, constructed on the basis of polymorphisms in three dopamine receptor genes (D1, D2, D4), and self-reported age at first sex. Variations in DRD4 were unrelated to the timing of sexual initiation in bivariate analyses. However, in both bivariate analysis and in regression models controlling for 10 psychosocial predictors representing personality dimensions, early family experience, adolescent experience (e.g., father presence, high school grades), and developmental pace, a variation in the DRD2 gene was found to be associated with a later age of first sex and increased the variance accounted for in the model from .19 to .24, or by about 23%. Use of an interaction term between D1 and D2 further increased the variance accounted for (compared to the psychosocial only model) to .31. As in earlier examples, these findings suggest that the inclusion of indicators from multiple levels of the developmental system may yield a better account of differences in the timing of sexual transition. Unfortunately, interactions between genotype groups and contextual variables were not examined for their combined associations with age at first sex.

Serotonin as a Moderator of Dopaminergic Effects. In contrast to the sexually facilitative effects of dopamine, the effects of another neurotransmitter, serotonin, are regarded as inhibitory. Reduced serotonergic transmission may contribute to decreased impulse control. Empirical support for links between serotonergic transmission and personality characteristics that have theoretical implications for sexual behavior have been reported for human adults. Ebstein, Segman, et al. (1997) examined an amino acid substitution (cysteine to serine) in a serotonin receptor. They found that the less common allele is associated with decreased reward dependence and persistence as measured by Cloninger's Tridimensional Personality Questionnaire (TPQ; Cloninger, 1987; Cloninger, Przybeck, & Svrakic, 1991). In Cloninger's personality model, reward dependence is conceptualized as a theoretically heritable tendency to behave in ways that elicit social approval and succor. However, this characteristic was originally hypothesized to be associated with norepinephrine, and a third dimension, harm avoidance, was hypothesized to be associated with serotonin.

In addition to the serotonin/reward-dependence link, in the Ebstein, Segman, et al. (1997) analyses, there was a significant statistical interaction between dopamine and serotonin polymorphisms in association with reward dependence. Respondents who had both the long repeat DRD4 (i.e., the allele associated with novelty seeking) and the amino acid substitution in the serotonin receptor allele had reward dependence scores that were more than two standard deviations lower than other allele combinations. Ebstein, Segman, et al. (1997) suggested that serotonergic neurons that synapse on mesolimbic dopamine neurons may regulate reward-dependence behavior by modulating dopamine transmission. Although these results are based on a small sample size, and do not map exactly onto the original theoretical model, they suggest interesting possibilities for the investigation of adolescent sexual activity, particularly for testing hypotheses in a developmental systems framework with other individual and contextual factors taken into consideration. For example, individuals who have the long DRD4 repeat should be higher in novelty seeking, and those who have the serotonin amino acid (serine) substitution should be more likely to be lower in reward dependence. According to Cloninger's Biosocial Theory of Personality, this particular combination of high novelty seeking and low reward dependence should yield a higher likelihood of opportunistic and unconventional behavior. Unconventionality is predictive of problem behavior during adolescence (Jessor, 1991), suggesting that, other things being equal, individuals with these polymorphic combinations may be more likely to be sexual adventurers.

These possibilities, as well as selected findings and speculations discussed earlier, are illustrated in Fig. 3.1. Polymorphisms in neurotransmitter receptors

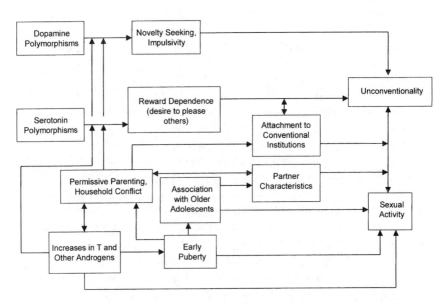

FIG. 3.1.   Illustrative biosocial paths in adolescent sexual activity.

or transporters may be linked to personality traits such as novelty seeking or a desire to please others. These traits, in turn, may be linked to a higher order construct of "unconventionality." However, the paths linking differences in genetic structures (i.e., different alleles) and gene expression with personality may be moderated by other biological factors and multiple types of experience over time. In this illustration, factors in the family context are posited as moderators. Although not indicated in the diagram for purposes of simplicity, personality characteristics like novelty seeking may also be associated with social contexts, such as association with older adolescents, which may in turn affect patterns of sexual activity through multiple pathways. Increases in T and other hormones may also affect gene expression, as well as various interpersonal processes (e.g., household conflict, association with older peers) through multiple mechanisms such as changes in interests, mood fluctuation, or the morphological changes of puberty. How unconventionality relates to different possible patterns of sexual behavior may depend on multiple factors, including hormone levels and pubertal timing, as well as the moderating effects of partner characteristics, relationship dynamics, and attachment to conventional institutions like schools and organized religion. In theory, all of these paths are potentially bidirectional, although that possibility has only been noted in a few instances in the figure.

IMPLICATIONS

As noted at the start of this chapter, most biosocial analysis of adolescent sexuality has been limited to the transition to first sex, with relatively little attention given to applying biological concepts to developmental and interpersonal processes of adolescent romance, noncoital sexual behavior, or same-sex sexual experiences. Expanding research efforts into these topic areas would advance our understanding of the broader developmental tasks of establishing romantic and sexual intimacy. Most work to date has documented relatively modest biological effects on adolescent sexuality, with the variance accounted for in regression models typically ranging from 3% to 5%, occasionally higher. This modest relationship is not surprising, given the multitude of other factors—and the coaction between factors at the same and different levels of the developmental system—that are not usually considered.

Investigation of biological contributions to adolescent romance and sexuality, and the potential implications for public policy, may be worrisome to some. Such investigations may raise the unsavory spectrum of "biology-driven policy," with possibilities such as use of testosterone inhibitors or genetic engineering. Such simplistic, exclusively biological "interventions" clearly raise ethical issues, and are not the logical outcome of biopsychosocial investigations of adolescent sexual development. Although complex and challenging to systematically apply in research and practice, a developmental systems view calls for policy, prevention, and intervention to be driven by the same multifaceted considerations that drive developmental research. Because sexual development is driven by the coaction of biological and social process, efforts to enhance adolescent development and prevent excessive sexual risk taking must, as would be indicated by more traditional psychological and sociological models, focus on social and contextual factors that are modifiable and clearly within the purview of public health.

Udry has suggested that we think of policies as "independent variables in macro-models of social change" (Udry, 1995a, p. 354). All behavior is influenced by biological and social/contextual contributions, at both the individual and the population level.

> Changing social arrangements can bring about changes in the level of effect of biological variables, even though the biology of the population is not changed. ... [Because restrictive norms can suppress biologically based predispositions] social process, and therefore social policy, can and does produce secular change. (Udry, 1995a, p. 354)

Although the number and patterns of specific causes are still unclear, decreases in the prevalence of early adolescent sexual transitions over the past decade illustrate how the same constellation of biological predispositions play out differently in the context of changing social conditions, such as concerns about STDs and HIV. Because biological contributions are always operating in league with social factors, social environment is key to changing the level or distribution of behavior patterns in a population.

The biological dimensions discussed in this chapter entail bidirectional effects within and across levels of the developmental system. For example, genes direct endocrine glands to produce hormones, and hormones activate genes that code for the production of proteins in the form of neurotransmitters, and so on, that ultimately contribute to behavior (Udry, 1995b). Behavior, in turn, may alter levels of hormones and gene expression. Adolescent romantic and sexual behavior therefore represents complex biosocial interactions of biological variation and probabilities with potentially modifiable social and environmental factors. Prevention and intervention programs that are not informed by comprehensive developmental analysis, and that do not approach the adolescent and his or her environment as an integrated, multi-level developmental system, are unlikely to yield enduring successes in the promotion of healthy psychosexual development and sexual lifestyles.

REFERENCES

Agnew, C. R. (1998). Modal versus individually-derived beliefs about condom use: Measuring the cognitive underpinnings of the theory of reasoned action. *Psychology and Health, 13,* 271–287.

Agnew, C. R. (1999). Power over interdependent behavior within the dyad: Who decides what a couple does? In L. J. Severy & W. B. Miller (Eds.), *Advances in population: Psychosocial perspectives* (Vol. 3, pp. 163–188). London: Jessica Kingsley.

Bailey, J. M., Kirk, K. M., Zhu, G., Dunner, M. P., & Martin, N. G. (2000). Do individual differences in sociosexuality represent genetic or environmentally contingent strategies? Evidence from the Australian twin registry. *Journal of Personality and Social Psychology, 78,* 537–545.

Beach, F. A. (1975). Behavioral endocrinology: An emerging discipline. *American Scientist, 63,* 178–187.

Benes, F. M. (1989). Myelination of corticalhippocampal relays during later adolescence. *Schizophrenia Bulletin, 15,* 585–593.

Benjamin, J., Li, L., Patterson, C., Greenberg, B. D., Murphy, D. L., & Hamer, D. H. (1996). Population and familial association between the D4 dopamine receptor gene and measures of novelty seeking. *Nature Genetics, 12,* 81–84.

Borgerhoff-Mulder M. (1989). Menarche, menopause and reproduction in the Kipsigis of Kenya. *Journal of Biosocial Science, 21,* 179–192.

Bouchard, T. J., Jr., Lykken, D. T., McGue, M., & Segal, N. L. (1990). Sources of human psychological differences: The Minnesota Study of Twins Reared Apart. *Science, 250,* 223–228.

Brooks-Gunn, J., Petersen, A. C., & Eichorn, D. (1985). The study of maturational timing effects in adolescence. *Journal of Youth and Adolescence, 14,* 149–161.

Cairns, R. B., & Cairns, B. D. (1994). *Lifelines and risks: Pathways of youth in our time.* New York: Cambridge University Press.

Caspi, A. (1995). Puberty and the gender organization of schools: How biology and social context shape adolescent experience. In L. J. Crockett & A. C. Crouter (Eds.), *Pathways through adolescence: Individual development in relation to social contexts. The Penn State series on child and adolescent development* (pp. 57–74). Hillsdale, NJ: Lawrence Erlbaum Associates.

Caspi, A., & Moffitt, T. (1991). Individual differences are accentuated during periods of social change: The sample case of girls at puberty. *Journal of Personality and Social Psychology, 61,* 157–168.

Chang, F. M., Kidd, J. R., Livak, K. J., Pakstis, A. J., & Kidd, K. K. (1996). The world-wide distribution of allele frequencies at the human dopamine D4 receptor locus. *Human Genetics, 98,* 91–101.

Clausen, J. A. (1975). The social meaning of different physical and sexual maturation. In S. E. Dragastin & G. H. Elder (Eds.), *Adolescence in the life cycle* (pp. 25–47). Washington, DC: John Wiley and Sons.

Cloninger, C. R. (1987). A systematic method for clinical description and classification of personality variants. *Archives of General Psychiatry, 44,* 573–588.

Cloninger, C. R., Przybeck, T. R., & Svrakic, D. M. (1991). The Tridimensional Personality Questionnaire: U.S. normative data. *Psychological Reports, 69,* 1047–1057.

Cloninger, C. R., Svrakic, D. M., & Przybeck, T. R. (1993). A psychobiological model of temperament and character. *Archives of General Psychiatry, 50,* 975–990.

Clore, G. L., Schwarz, N., & Conway, M. (1994). Affective causes and consequences of social information processing. In R. S. Wyer & T. K. Srull (Eds.), *Handbook of social cognition* (2nd ed., pp. 323–417). Hillsdale, NJ: Lawrence Erlbaum Associates.

Comings, D. E. (1998). Why different rules are required for polygenic inheritance: Lessons from studies of the DRD2 gene. *Alcohol, 16,* 61–70.

DeFries, J. C., & Fulker, D. W. (1985). Multiple regression analysis of twin data. *Behavior Genetics, 15,* 467–473.

Dornbusch, S. M., Carlsmith, J. M., Gross, R. T., Martin, J. A., Jennings, D., Rosenberg, A., & Duke, P. (1981). Sexual development, age, and dating: A comparison of biological and social influences upon one set of behaviors. *Child Development, 52,* 179–185.

Downey, G., Bonica, C., & Rincon, C. (1999). Rejection sensitivity and adolescent romantic relationships. In W. Furman, B. B. Brown, & C. Feiring (Eds.), *The development of romantic relationships* (pp. 148–174). Cambridge: Cambridge University Press.

Dunne, M. P., Martin, N. G., Statham, D. J., Slutske, W. S., Dinwiddie, S. H., Bucholz, K. K., Madden, P. A. F., & Heath, A. C. (1997). Genetic and environmental contributions to variance in age at first sexual intercourse. *Psychological Science, 8,* 211–216.

Ebstein, R. P., Nemanov, L., Klotz, I., Gritsendo, I., & Belmaker, R. H. (1997). Additional evidence for an association between the dopamine D4 receptor (D4DR) exon III repeat polymorphism and the human trait of novelty seeking. *Molecular Psychiatry, 2,* 472–477.

Ebstein, R. P., Novick, O., Umansky, R., Priel, B., Osher, Y., Blaine, D., Bennett, E. R., Nemanov, L., Katz, M., & Belmaker, R. H. (1996). Dopamine D4 receptor (D4DR) exon III polymorphism associated with the human personality trait of novelty seeking. *Nature Genetics, 12,* 78–80.

Ebstein, R. P., Segman, R., Benjamin, J., Osher, Y., Nemanov, L., & Belmaker, R. H. (1997). 5-HT2c (HTR2C) serotonin receptor gene polymorphism associated with the human personality trait of reward dependence: Interaction with dopamine D4 receptor (D4DR) and Dopamine D3 (D3DR) polymorphisms. *American Journal of Medical Genetics (Neuropsychiatric Genetics), 74,* 65–72.

Eichorn, D. H. (1963). Biological correlates of behavior. In H. Stevenson (Ed.), *Yearbook of the National Society for the Study of Education, 63, Part 1* (pp. 4–61). Chicago: University of Chicago Press.

Ekelund, J., Lichtermann, D., Jarvelin, M. R., & Peltonen, L. (1999). Association between novelty seeking and the Type 4 dopamine receptor gene in a large Finnish cohort sample. *American Journal of Psychiatry, 156,* 1453–1459.

Faiman, C., & Winter, J. S. D. (1974). Gonadotropins and sex hormone patterns in puberty: Clinical data. In M. M. Grumbach, G. D. Grave, & F. F. Mayer (Eds.), *Control of the onset of puberty* (pp. 32–61). New York: Wiley.

Finkelstein, J. W., Susman, E. J., Chinchilli, V. M., D'arcangelo M. R., Kunselman, S. J., Schwab, J., Demers, L. M., Liben, L. S., & Kulin, H. E. (1998). Effects of estrogen or testosterone on self-reported sexual responses and behaviors in hypogonadal adolescents. *Journal of Clinical Endocrinology and Metabolism, 83,* 2281–2285.

Flannery, D. J., Rowe, D. C., & Gulley, B. L. (1993). Impact of pubertal status, timing, and age on adolescent sexual experience and delinquency. *Journal of Adolescent Research, 8,* 21–40.

Gargiulo, J., Attie, I., Brooks-Gunn, J., & Warren, M. (1987). Girls' dating behavior as a function of social context and maturation. *Developmental Psychology, 23,* 730–737.

Gelernter, J., Kranzler, H., Coccaro, E., Siever, L., New, A., & Mulgrew, C. L. (1997). D4 dopamine-receptor (DRD4) alleles and novelty seeking in substance-dependent, personality-disorder, and control subjects. *American Journal of Human Genetics, 61,* 1144–1152.

Giedd J. N., Blumenthal J., Jeffries N. O., Castellanos, F. X., Liu, H., Zijdenbos, A., Paus, T.,

Evans, A. C., & Rapoport, J. L. (1999). Brain development during childhood and adolescence: a longitudinal MRI study [letter]. *Nature Neuroscience, 2*(10), 861–863.

Gottlieb, G. (1991). Experiential canalization of behavior development: Theory. *Developmental Psychology, 27*, 4–13.

Gottlieb, G. (1995). Some conceptual deficiencies in "developmental" behavior genetics. *Human Development, 38*, 131–141.

Gottlieb, G. (1998). Normally occurring environmental and behavioral influences on gene activity: From central dogma to probabilistic epigenesis. *Psychological Review, 105*, 792–802.

Gottlieb, G., & Halpern, C. T. (2002). A relational view of causality in normal and abnormal development. *Development and Psychopathology, 14*, 421–435.

Graber, J., Brooks-Gunn, J., & Warren, M. (1995). The antecedents of menarcheal age. *Child Development, 66*, 346–359.

Halpern, C. T., Campbell, B., Agnew, C. R., Thompson, V., & Udry, J. R. (2002). Associations between stress reactivity and sexual and non-sexual risk-taking in young adult human males. *Hormones and Behavior, 42*, 387–398.

Halpern, C. T., & Udry, J. R. (1999). Pubertal changes in testosterone and implications for adolescent sexuality. In L. J. Severy & W. B. Miller (Eds.), *Advances in population: Psychosocial perspectives* (pp. 127–162). London: Jessica Kingsley Publishers.

Halpern, C. T., Udry, J. R., Campbell, B., & Suchindran, C. (1993). Testosterone and pubertal development as predictors of sexual activity: A panel analysis of adolescent males. *Psychosomatic Medicine, 55*, 436–447.

Halpern, C. T., Udry, J. R., Campbell, B., & Suchindran, C. (1999). Effects of body fat on weight concerns, dating, and sexual activity: A longitudinal analysis of Black and White adolescent girls. *Developmental Psychology, 35*, 721–736.

Halpern, C. T., Udry, J. R., Campbell, B., Suchindran, C., & Mason, G. A. (1994). Testosterone and religiosity as predictors of sexual attitudes and activity among adolescent males: A biosocial model. *Journal of Biosocial Science, 26*, 217–234.

Halpern, C. T., Udry, J. R., & Suchindran, C. (1997). Testosterone predicts initiation of coitus in adolescent females. *Psychosomatic Medicine, 59*, 161–171.

Halpern, C. T., Udry, J. R., & Suchindran, C. (1998). Monthly measures of salivary testosterone predict sexual activity in adolescent males. *Archives of Sexual Behavior, 27*, 445–465.

Harris, D. B. (1957). *The concept of development.* Minneapolis: University of Minnesota Press.

Helweg-Larsen, M., & Collins, B. E. (1994). The UCLA Multidimensional Condom Attitudes Scale: Documenting the complex determinants of condom use in college students. *Health Psychology, 13*, 224–237.

Hendrick, S. S., & Hendrick, C. (1992). *Romantic love.* Newbury Park, CA: Sage.

Hill, S. Y., Zezza, N., Wipprecht, G., Locke, J., & Neiswanger, K. (1999). Personality traits and dopamine receptors (D2 and D4): Linkage studies in families of alcoholics. *American Journal of Medical Genetics, 88*, 634–641.

Hirschi, R. (1969). *Causes of delinquency.* Berkeley, CA: University of California Press.

Hull, E. M., Lorrain, D. S., Du, V., Matuszewich, L., Lumley, L. A., Putnam, S. K., & Moses, J. (1999). Hormone-neurotransmitter interactions in the control of sexual behavior. *Behavioral Brain Research, 105*, 105–116.

Jacobson, K. C., & Rowe, D. C. (1999). Genetic and environmental influences on the relationship between family connectedness, school connectedness, and adolescent depressed mood: Sex differences. *Developmental Psychology, 35*, 926–939.

Jessor, R. (1991). Risk behavior in adolescence: A psychosocial framework for understanding and action. *Journal of Adolescent Health, 12*, 597–605.

Jonsson, E. G., Nothen, M. M., Gustavsson, J. P., Neidt, H., Brene, S., Tylee, A., Propping, P., & Sedvall, G. C. (1997). Lack of evidence for allelic association between personality traits and dopamine D4 receptor gene polymorphism. *American Journal of Psychiatry, 154,* 697–699.

Keshavan, M. S., & Hogarty, G. E. (1999). Brain maturational processes and delayed onset in schizophrenia. *Development and Psychopathology, 11,* 525–543.

Knorr, D., Bidlingmaier, F., Butenandt, O., Fendel, H., & Ehrt-Wehle, R. (1974). Plasma testosterone in male puberty. *Acta Endocrinologica, 75,* 181–194.

Lee, P. A., Jaffe, R. B., & Midgley, A. R. (1974). Serum gonadotropin, testosterone, and prolactin concentrations throughout puberty in boys: A longitudinal study. *Journal of Clinical Endocrinology and Metabolism, 39,* 664–672.

Lerner, R. M. (1986). *Concepts and theories of human development* (2nd ed.). New York: Random House.

Livson, N., & Peskin, H. (1980). Perspectives on adolescence from longitudinal research. In J. Adelson (Ed.), *Handbook of adolescent psychology* (pp. 47–98). New York: John Wiley and Sons.

MacDonald, K. (1997). Life history theory and human reproductive behavior: Environmental/contextual influences and heritable variation. *Human Nature, 8,* 327–360.

Magnusson, D., & Cairns, R. B. (1996). Developmental science: Toward a unified framework. In R. B. Cairns, G. H. Elder, Jr., & E. J. Costello (Eds.), *Developmental science* (pp. 7–30). New York: Cambridge University Press.

Malhotra, A. K., Virkkunen, M. , Rooney, W., Eggert, W., Linnoila, M., & Goldman, D. (1996). The association between the dopamine D4 receptor (D4DR) 16 amino acid repeat polymorphism and Novelty Seeking. *Molecular Psychiatry, 1,* 388–391.

Martin, N. G., Eaves, L. J. , & Eysenck, H. J. (1977). Genetical, environmental, and personality factors influencing the age of first sexual intercourse in twins. *Journal of Biosocial Science, 9,* 91–97.

Meyer-Bahlburg, H. F. L., Ehrhardt, A. A., Bell, J. J., Cohen, S. F., Healey, J. M., Feldman, J. F., Morishima, A., Baker, S. W., & New, M. I. (1985). Idiopathic precocious puberty in girls: Psychosexual development. *Journal of Youth and Adolescence, 14,* 339–353.

Miller, E. (1994). Optimal adjustment of mating effort to environmental conditions. *Mankind Quarterly, 34,* 294–316.

Miller, W. B., Pasta, D. J., Macmurray, J., Chiu, C., Wu, H., and Comings, D. E. (1999). Dopamine receptor genes are associated with age at first sexual intercourse. *Journal of Biosocial Science, 31,* 43–54.

Missale, C., Nash, S. R., Robinson, S. W., Jaber, M., & Caron, M. G. (1998). Dopamine receptors: From structure to function. *Physiological Reviews, 78,* 189–225.

Moffitt, T., Caspi, A., Silva, P., & Belsky, J. (1992). Childhood experience and the onset of menarche: A test of a sociobiological model. *Child Development, 63,* 47–58.

Noble, E. P., Ozkaragoz, T. Z., Ritchie, T. L., Zhang, X., Belin, T. R., & Sparkes, R. S. (1998). D2 and D4 dopamine receptor polymorphisms and personality. *American Journal of Medical Genetics (Neuropsychiatric Genetics), 81,* 257–267.

Ono, Y., Manki, H. , Yoshimura, K., Muramatsu, T., Mizushima, H., Higuchi, S., Yagi, G., Kanba, S., & Asai, M. (1997). Association between dopamine D4 receptor (D4DR) exon III polymorphism and Novelty Seeking in Japanese subjects. *American Journal of Medical Genetics, 74,* 501–503.

Pasta, D. J., & Miller, W. B. (2000). A heritability study of childbearing motivation. In J. L. Rodgers, D. C. Rowe, & W. B. Miller (Eds.), *Genetic influences on human fertility and sexuality: Theoretical and empirical contributions from the biological and behavioral sciences* (pp. 107–120). Boston: Kluwer Academic Publishers.

Pendergrast, R. A., DuRant, R. H., and Gaillard, G. L. (1992). Attitudinal and behavioral corre-lates of condom use in urban adolescent males. *Journal of Adolescent Health, 13*, 133–139.

Petersen, A. C., & Taylor, B. (1980). The biological approach to adolescence: Biological change and psychological adaptation. In J. Adelson (Ed.), *Handbook of adolescent psychology* (pp. 117–155). New York: John Wiley.

Plomin, R., & Rutter, M. (1998). Child development, molecular genetics, and what to do with genes once they are found. *Child Development, 69*, 1223–1242.

Poston, W. S., Ericsson, M., Linder, J., Haddock, C. K., Hanis, C. L., Nilsson, T., Astrom, M., & Foreyt, J. P. (1998). D4 dopamine receptor gene exon III polymorphism and obesity risk. *Eating & Weight Disorders: EWD, 3*, 71–77.

Reiss, D. (1997). Mechanisms linking genetic and social influences in adolescent development: Beginning a collaborative search. *Current Directions in Psychological Science, 6*, 100–105.

Reiss, D., Neiderhiser, J. M., Hetherington, E. M., & Plomin, R. (2000). *The relationship code: Deciphering genetic and social influences on adolescent development.* Cambridge, MA: Harvard University Press.

Rodgers, J. L., & Doughty, D. (2000). Genetic and environmental influences on fertility expecta-tions and outcomes using NLSY kinship data. In J. L. Rodgers, D. C. Rowe, & W. B. Miller (Eds.), *Genetic influences on human fertility and sexuality: Theoretical and empirical contributions from the biological and behavioral sciences* (pp. 85–105). Boston: Kluwer Academic Publishers.

Rodgers, J. L., Rowe, D. C., & Buster, M. (1999). Nature, nurture and first sexual intercourse in the USA: Fitting behavioral genetic models to NLSY kinship data. *Journal of Biosocial Science, 31*, 29–41.

Rodgers, J. L., Rowe, D. C., & Miller, W. B. (2000). *Genetic influences on human fertility and sex-uality: Theoretical and empirical contributions from the biological and behavioral sciences.* Boston: Kluwer Academic Publishers.

Simmons, R. G., & Blyth, D. A. (1987). *Moving into adolescence: The impact of pubertal change and school context.* New York: Aldine De Gruyter.

Stattin, H., & Magnusson, D. (1990). *Pubertal maturation in female development.* Hillsdale, NJ: Lawrence Erlbaum Associates.

Steinberg, L. (1987). Impact of puberty on family relations: Effects of pubertal status and puber-tal timing. *Developmental Psychology, 23*, 451–460.

Steinberg, L. (1988). Reciprocal relation between parent–child distance and pubertal matura-tion. *Developmental Psychology, 24*, 122–128.

Stone, C. P., & Barker, R. C. (1939). The attitudes and interests of pre-menarcheal and post-menarcheal girls. *Journal of Genetic Psychology, 54*, 27–71.

Sullivan, P. F., Fifield, W. J., Kennedy, M. A., Mulder, R. T., Sellman, J. D., & Joyce, P. R. (1998). No association between novelty seeking and the type 4 dopamine receptor (DRD4) in two New Zealand samples. *American Journal of Psychiatry, 155*, 98–101.

Surbey, M. (1990). Family composition, stress, and human menarche. In F. Bercovitch & T. Zei-gler (Eds.), *The socioendocrinology of primate reproduction* (pp. 11–32). New York: Liss.

Tomitaka, M., Tomitaka, S., Otuka, Y., Kim, K., Matuki, H., Sakamoto, K., & Tanaka, A. (1999). Association between novelty seeking and dopamine receptor D4 (DRD4) Exon III polymorphism in Japanese subject. *American Journal of Medical Genetics (Neuropsychiatric Genetics), 88*, 469–471.

Udry, J. R. (1979). Age at menarche, at first intercourse, and at first pregnancy. *Journal of Biolog-ical Science, 11*, 411–433.

Udry, J. R. (1988). Biological predispositions and social control in adolescent sexual behavior. *American Sociological Review, 53*, 709–722.

84 HALPERN

Udry, J. R. (1995a). Policy and ethical implications of biosocial research. *Population Research and Policy Review, 14*, 347–357.

Udry, J. R. (1995b). Sociology and biology: What biology do sociologists need to know? *Social Forces, 73*, 1267–1278.

Udry, J. R. (2000). Biological limits of gender construction. *American Sociological Review, 65*, 443–457.

Udry, J. R., & Billy, J. O. G. (1987). Initiation of coitus in early adolescence. *American Sociological Review, 52*, 841–855.

Udry, J. R., Billy, J. O. G., Morris, N. M., Groff, T. R. , & Raj, M. H. (1985). Serum androgenic hormones motivate sexual behavior in adolescent boys. *Fertility and Sterility, 43*, 90–94.

Udry, J. R., & Cliquet, R. L. (1982). A cross-cultural examination of the relationship between ages at menarche, marriage, and first birth. *Demography, 19*, 53–63.

Udry, J. R., Talbert, L. M., & Morris, N. M. (1986). Biosocial foundations for adolescent female sexuality. *Demography, 23*, 217–230.

Vandenbergh, D. J., Zonderman, A. B. , Wang, J., Uhl, G. R., & Costa, Jr., P. T. (1997). No association between novelty seeking and dopamine D4 receptor (D4DR) exon III seven repeat alleles in Baltimore Longitudinal Study of Aging Participants. *Molecular Psychiatry, 2*, 417–419.

Van Tol, H. H. M., Caren, M. W., Guan, H. C., Ohara, K., Bunzow, J. R., Civelli, O., Kennedy, J., Seeman, P., Niznik, H. B., & Jovanovic, V. (1992). Multiple dopamine D4 receptor variants in the human population. *Nature, 358*, 149–152.

Wallen, K. (1996). Nature needs nurture: The interaction of hormones and social influences on the development of behavioral sex differences in rhesus monkeys. *Hormones and Behavior, 30*, 364–378.

Waller, J. G., & Shaver, P. R. (1994). The importance of nongenetic influences on romantic love styles: A twin-family study. *Psychological Science, 5*, 268–274.

Westney, O. E., Jenkins, R. R., & Benjamin, C. (1983). Socioesexual development of preadolescents. In J. Brooks-Gunn & J. Peterson (Eds.), *Girls at puberty* (pp. 273–300). New York: Plenum.

Zabin, L. S., Smith, E. A., Hirsch, M. B., & Hardy, J. B. (1986). Ages of physical maturation and first intercourse in Black teenage males and females. *Demography, 23*, 595–605.

Zelnick, M., Kantner, J., & Ford, K. (1981). *Sex and pregnancy in adolescence.* Beverly Hills: Sage Publications.

Zuckerman, M. (1979). *Sensation-seeking: Beyond the optimal level of arousal.* New York: Wiley.

4

Love Matters: Romantic Relationships Among Sexual-Minority Adolescents

Lisa M. Diamond
University of Utah

Research on sexual-minority (i.e., nonheterosexual) youths has exploded in the past 10 years, but this research has been fairly lopsided in its emphasis. Disproportionate attention has been paid to these youths' suicidality, verbal and physical victimization, and risk behaviors (particularly unsafe sex and substance use), whereas more normative features of their development have received little attention. Reflecting this fact, there has been scant research on the quality and developmental significance of sexual-minority youths' romantic experiences. Although the unique dynamics of lesbian, gay, and bisexual *adults'* romantic relationships have been extensively studied (Gray & Isensee, 1996; James & Murphy, 1998; Kurdek, 1994, 1998; Peplau, Cochran, & Mays, 1997; Peplau, Veniegas, & Campbell, 1996), this has not been true for sexual-minority youths (for exceptions see Diamond, Savin-Williams, & Dubé, 1999; Savin-Williams, 1996a, 1998).

This hampers the efforts of clinicians, educators, and policy makers to promote the well-being of sexual-minority youths. As this and other recent volumes have demonstrated (Furman, Brown, & Feiring, 1999), romantic relationships are key sites for numerous developmental transitions that take place during the adolescent years. Healthy, developmentally appropriate relationships not only provide adolescents with social support and companionship, but allow them to establish core social competencies that will help them sustain nurturing, intimate ties over the life span. Considering the extra challenges faced by sexual-minority youths—stigma, discrimination, victimization, potential familial rejection—the successful maintenance of such ties may be particularly important for their mental health.

Yet advocates for sexual-minority youth have been strangely silent on the topic of same-sex adolescent romance. This collective silence reflects widespread disagreement over how best to handle issues of adolescent sexual orientation. Despite the fact that social acceptance of same-sex sexuality has increased dramatically over the past 20 years, many parents and educators continue to argue that adolescents with same-sex attractions should be discouraged from expressing those attractions. Some even advocate "reparative" therapy for sexual-minority youth aimed at extinguishing their same-sex sexual desires and reinforcing heterosexual behavior.

In order to avoid inflaming opposition from such individuals, advocates for sexual-minority youths often adopt a "hands-off" approach to these youths' intimate relationships, instead devoting the bulk of their attention to "safe" issues such as suicide, family rejection, physical victimization, drug abuse, and unsafe sex. After all, even if society disagrees on whether youths with same-sex attractions should be permitted to act on those attractions, it generally agrees that they should not face outright harm. Yet as a result of this myopic strategy, sexual-minority youths receive little or no guidance on how to form and keep healthy same-sex romances, and many report notable frustration that even their most supportive counselors and teachers typically clam up when youths want to discuss romantic relationships (Owens, 1998).

Clinicians, educators, and service providers can no longer afford to ignore this issue. The average sexual-minority youth spends far more time ruminating about love and romance than about suicide, hate crimes, or homelessness, and they currently have nowhere to turn with their concerns. One study (D'Augelli, 1991) found that sexual-minority youths rated the termination of a current romance as their second most troubling problem, topped only by disclosure of their sexual orientation to parents. Yet sexual-minority youths are far more likely to receive sensitive information and guidance about the latter problem than about the former. The lack of attention to sexual-minority youths' romantic relationships also underestimates the considerable influence such relationships can have on their well-being. Sexual-minority youths often describe their first positive same-sex relationship as dramatically transforming their self-esteem and self-confidence (Savin-Williams, 1998), whereas their romantic *difficulties* are associated with higher rates of truancy, depression, and substance use (Anderson, 1995; Mercier & Berger, 1989; Savin-Williams, 1994).

Advocates for sexual-minority youths can play an important role in promoting their healthy development by helping them navigate the challenges of flirting, dating, falling in love, and breaking up with their peers. Toward this end, this chapter reviews the unique features of sexual-minority youths' romantic experiences and their social-developmental implications. Emphasis is placed on the diversity of sexual-minority youths' intimate ties, critical gender differences in relationship patterns and processes, and how educators, clinicians, and service providers can best support these youths' relational development.

THE ROMANTIC LANDSCAPE
OF SEXUAL-MINORITY ADOLESCENTS

It is impossible to describe the typical sexual-minority romance because there is no such thing as a typical sexual-minority adolescent. Although the media frequently depict generalized prototypes of these youths, such prototypes belie the tremendous diversity of this population. For example, it is commonly thought that most sexual-minority youths quietly struggle with same-sex attractions in childhood, shy away from heterosexual dating, and gradually realize that they are gay or lesbian in mid- to late-adolescence. Although many youths follow this linear trajectory, many deviate from it as well. For example, many youths have no childhood memories of same-sex attractions, and undergo more abrupt realizations of their same-sex sexuality during late adolescence (Diamond, 1998; Diamond & Savin-Williams, 2000; Savin-Williams, 1998).

Also, sexual-minority youths are typically described as "gay and lesbian youths," with the implicit presumption that they all experience *exclusive* same-sex attractions. Yet research using a random, representative study of American youths has found that the majority of adolescents with same-sex attractions also experience some degree of other-sex attractions (French, Story, Remafedi, Resnick, & Blum, 1996; Garofalo, Wolf, Wissow, Woods, & Goodman, 1999), as is the case among American adults (Laumann, Gagnon, Michael, & Michaels, 1994). Importantly, this does not suggest that these youths are *equally* attracted to the same sex and the other sex, or that the quality of these attractions is identical. Rather, it demonstrates that most sexual-minority youths contend with mixed (and sometimes perplexing) patterns of attractions for same-sex and other-sex partners. This is a critical point to consider when interpreting these youths' motives for past, current, and future relationships and the quality of their relationship experiences.

Finally, although it is commonly assumed that adolescents who sexually desire the same sex also (and always) fall in love with the same sex, it is not always quite this simple. Sexual and emotional attractions are often notably discordant, in both adolescence and adulthood (Savin-Williams, 1998; Weinberg, Williams, & Pryor, 1994). For example, some youths claim that their same-sex attractions are purely physical, whereas others claim that their same-sex feelings have more to do with emotional attachment (Savin-Williams, 1998). Attractions for other-sex partners show similar variability. One gay male adolescent interviewed by Savin-Williams (1998) described sex with his former girlfriend as "satisfying physically, but not emotionally," while another claimed that despite his emotional attachment to a former girlfriend, "physically I didn't want her" (p. 110). It is difficult to interpret the overall relevance of these variations because we know little about the specific relationship between the sexual and affectional components of sexual orientation, and whether they undergo independent or interconnected development during adolescence. Adolescent sexual maturation is usually studied independently of emotional development (with a few notable exceptions, such as Steinberg, 1988), and consequently we cannot say when and how adolescents start perceiving connections between their sexual desires and their emotional longings. Similarly, we cannot say when and how adolescents perceive and experience *distinctions* between their most intimate platonic friendships and their newly developing romantic ties.

Notably, these three aspects of same-sex sexuality—diverse patterns of initial expression, the prevalence of bisexual attractions, and frequent discordance between sexual and affectional feelings—may appear to challenge contemporary models of sexual orientation. Prevailing models generally suggest that sexual orientation is a basic, genetically based predisposition (Bailey & Pillard, 1995; Bailey, Pillard, Neale, & Agyei, 1993; Bem, 1996; Ellis, 1996; Ellis & Ebertz, 1997; Gladue, 1993; Green, 1993), and many have inferred on this basis that same-sex desires are inherently exclusive, longitudinally stable, and impervious to situational influences. Yet although these inferences are intuitively appealing, they lack both a theoretical and an empirical basis. Plenty of basic, genetically influenced traits (such as temperament) show diverse patterns of expression in different individuals, in different contexts, and at different stages of life, whereas plenty of consciously adopted behavior patterns (such as vegetarianism) show remarkable stability, internal consistency, and resistance to outside influence over the life course.

Thus, diversity in individuals' experiences of same-sex sexuality should not be misinterpreted as evidence for *or* against a trait-based conceptualization of same-sex sexuality. Rather, individuals' interpersonal relationships, sociocultural environments, and even personal ideologies may render same-sex and other-sex attractions differentially salient in different situations and at different ages (see especially Fine, 1988; Tolman, 1994), regardless of how long a particular individual has experienced these attractions, how exclusive they are, and whether they are coded in the genes. In fact, the potential for fluidity in sexual attractions may *itself* be a biologically based trait that varies in both sexual-minority and nonheterosexual individuals (Baumeister, 2000; Diamond, 2003).

Clearly, same-sex sexuality is a substantially more complex and heterogeneous phenomenon than the conventional wisdom typically suggests. Given this complexity, it is extremely difficult to interpret the immediate and long-term significance of different *relationship* patterns among sexual-minority youths. Whether and with whom a youth pursues (and enjoys!) physically and/or emotionally intimate ties with same-sex and/or other-sex partners depends on multiple factors: his or her underlying pattern of attractions, the experiential quality of these attractions, how he or she interprets the relationship between sexual and affectional desires, his or her needs and perceived opportunities for physical and emotional intimacy with different partners, his or her prior history of intimate relationships, and his or her interpretations of these experiences.

The end result is a remarkably complex fabric of romantic possibilities. For example, whereas some sexual-minority youths forego all forms of same-sex intimacy altogether, others elect to maintain conventional romantic relationships with other-sex partners while pursuing exclusively sexual same-sex contacts in secret (Savin-Williams, 1998). Others show the opposite pattern, pursuing casual sex with other-sex partners while developing more substantive romantic bonds with same-sex partners. Some youths develop altogether unique constellations of intimate relationships that violate conventional notions of "friendship" and "romance," such as nonsexual friendships that contain the emotional passion, devotion, possessiveness, and exclusivity typically associated with romantic ties (Diamond, 2000). These and other possibilities are reviewed in more detail elsewhere (Diamond et al., 1999). The main point is that in order to adequately address the relational concerns of sexual-minority youths, we cannot simply extrapolate from research on heterosexual youths and switch the gender labels. Rather, we must take into account the full range of variation in sexual-minority youths' sexual and affectional desires for same-sex and other-sex partners, and the corresponding variation in the number, type, and quality of their intimate relationships.

DO SEXUAL-MINORITY YOUTHS *NEED* ROMANTIC RELATIONSHIPS?

Some sexual-minority youths, of course, have no romantic relationships whatsoever during their teen years. Given the stigma associated with same-sex sexuality and the difficulty most sexual-minority have finding potential partners, it is not surprising that sexual-minority youths are less likely than their heterosexual counterparts to have *any* romantic relationships during their teenage years (Diamond & Dubé, 2002). Is this problematic, in and of itself? After all, one might argue that learning to accept one's sexual identity, receiving reliable social support from friends and family members, and feeling safe from verbal and physical harassment are more pressing and important issues. If a youth ends up delaying his first romance until age 25, is this really cause for concern?

It might be, depending on the circumstances. The total absence of romantic experience could be a trivial matter for one youth, whereas for another it could indicate potential deficits in social competence, social support, self-esteem, and identity development. In order to determine whether this is so, we must consider exactly why a particular youth lacks romantic experience. Most notably, is it by choice or circumstance? Some youths intentionally avoid romantic relationships in order to control and perhaps suppress their same-sex desires. Others fully accept their same-sex desires, but feel compelled to hide them from friends and family members by eschewing any hint of same-sex intimacy. Alternatively, an openly-identified gay, lesbian, or bisexual adolescent might have supportive and accepting friends and family members, but little contact with sexual-minority peers that he/she can potentially date. Another youth might have plenty of sexual-minority peers, and yet none of them may find *her* attractive.

These different scenarios have different consequences for a youth's sense of self-esteem, self-efficacy, normalcy, and attractiveness. For this reason, it is impossible to state categorically that sexual-minority youths who forego romantic relationships during adolescence face psychological risks. Instead, we must consider the underlying circumstances, the youth's current needs for intimacy and social support, and his/her overall psychological adjustment. This is precisely why clinicians, educators, and service providers must create safe contexts for sexual-minority youths to discuss their relationship histories and relationship concerns. Allowing a youth to voice his frustrations about finding romantic partners—or to reveal why he has stopped looking for the time being—can reveal important facets of his personality, self-concept, and social context that impinge on his social functioning.

It is also important to note that even if a youth's lack of romantic experience has fairly innocuous origins (such as lack of access to sexual-minority peers), it might generate its own set of social-developmental problems over time. Although plenty of adolescents successfully traverse their teenage years without boyfriends or girlfriends, romantic relationships can nonetheless play powerful roles in validating a youth's sense of self-worth, helping him or her to master interpersonal skills related to intimacy, and providing emotional support and security (Brown, 1999; Connolly & Johnson, 1996; Furman & Wehner, 1994, 1997; Miller & Benson, 1999). The importance of these factors may be heightened for sexual-minority adolescents. Because of the stigmatization of same-sex sexuality, many sexual-minority youths have trouble maintaining close, supportive ties with friends and family members (Anderson, 1987; D'Augelli & Hershberger, 1993). In such cases, the emotional intimacy and support of a romantic relationship may be particularly valuable. For some adolescents, a romantic partner is the only person who knows and accepts their sexual orientation, making that person an indispensable social resource.

Healthy same-sex romances can also serve as powerful sources of validation for youths' nascent sexual identities, allowing them to "road test" their private thoughts and fantasies in real-life encounters. Many youths are reluctant to make *any* conclusions about their sexual orientation until they have had a chance to experience a full-fledged same-sex love affair. This is particularly true for women, many of whom continue to view their sexual identity label as dependent on their current romantic relationship well into adulthood (Blumstein & Schwartz, 1977; Esterberg, 1994). Among many sexual-minority youths, a successful same-sex romance can be a turning point in their identity development that prompts them not only to accept and embrace their sexual orientation, but to disclose it to close friends and family (Cohen & Savin-Williams, 1996; Savin-Williams, 1996a). Thus, although same-sex relationships are by no means preconditions for healthy sexual identity development, they can speed and smooth this process considerably.

Romance and Socioemotional Development

Romantic relationships are also important for the normative socialization opportunities they offer sexual-minority youths. As Brown (1999) noted, adolescents master critical skills related to patience, mutuality, commitment, trust, and emotion regulation in the course of progressing from superficial dating relationships to more serious romantic bonds. Skills regarding emotion regulation are particularly important for positive adjustment. Although adolescence is no longer thought to be necessarily turbulent, these years can nonetheless be emotionally intense (Larson, Csikszentmihalyi, & Graef, 1980), and much of this heightened emotionality is directly attributable to romantic entanglements (Larson & Richards, 1994). Some of the most important skills adolescents gain by participating in romantic relationships involve the effective management of this heightened emotionality: learning to identify exactly what they are feeling, why they are feeling this way, and what action they can/should take in response (Larson, Clore, & Wood, 1999).

Of course, these are lifelong tasks, but adolescent romantic relationships allow youths to wrestle with a wider and more complex range of feeling states than are typically experienced in other contexts. During a single relationship, youths might veer from the euphoria, preoccupation, and hypersensitivity of early infatuation to the security and vulnerability of long-term affection to the despair and panic of conflict and dissolution. Perhaps one of the most important lessons adolescents learn through romantic participation is that these strong feelings are normal, manageable, and transitory. Similarly, youths learn to use these feelings as sources of important information regarding the underlying dynamics of a particular interaction. As Larson et al. (1999) pointed out, youths caught in the throes of intense anxiety or jealousy regarding a particular partner may come to ask themselves, "What was going on the last time I felt this way? What did I do about it? Did it work?" Gaining the ability to step back from powerful, distracting emotions and make responsible decisions is a critical social-developmental task, and romantic relationships are an important context in which it is practiced and eventually mastered.

Just as important, but less often discussed, is the role that romantic participation plays in structuring youths' *non-romantic* relationships. As researchers have increasingly acknowledged (see especially Brown, 1999; Eder, 1993), a key component of many adolescents' romantic experiences is the process of *discussing* their crushes, dates, and break-ups with peers. Conversations focus on "who likes whom," how to safely signal interest to potential partners, what social and sexual behaviors are typical at different stages of a relationship, how to interpret the partner's verbal and nonverbal cues, how to advance the relationship, and how to end it. In addition to providing a supplementary source of romantic socialization, such interchanges are often uniquely pleasurable for youths, allowing them to feel a sense of solidarity with their peers, to voice and hopefully alleviate secret anxieties, and to have their euphoria and excitement validated and affirmed.

This might be particularly important for sexual-minority youths, many of whom have felt chronically excluded from these heady exchanges in the past. Participating in the dramatic give-and-take of romantic gossip can allow these youths to feel, perhaps for the first time, like typical teenagers. Also, the romantic socialization provided by such interchanges takes on special importance for sexual-minority youths given that the conventional social scripts structuring heterosexual romance do not translate easily to same-sex contexts (Klinkenberg & Rose, 1994). For this reason, many adult sexual minorities who eschewed same-sex relationships in adolescence claim that when they finally start having such relationships in adulthood, they suddenly feel like awkward adolescents all over again, flustered and uncertain about the rules and expectations for same-sex dating. Who pays? Who drives? Should you avoid using public restrooms at the same time? Sexual-minority youths who have their first same-sex romances during adolescence have the chance to talk, argue, and giggle about these unexpected dilemmas at a time in their lives when it is developmentally appropriate and even enjoyable to do so.

THE ROLE OF OTHER-SEX RELATIONSHIPS

Although many sexual-minority youths fail to form same-sex romantic relationships in adolescence, this does not mean that they traverse their adolescent years without any romantic experience whatsoever. Rather, the majority of sexual-minority youths participate in *other-sex* relationships at some point during their teenage years (reviewed in Diamond et al., 1999). These other-sex romantic relationships take a variety of forms. Some are fairly minor dating interactions that occur before the youth has recognized his/her same-sex attractions. Others are serious romantic bonds that may even involve tentative discussions of marriage. Some youths only pursue these relationships before self-identifying as lesbian, gay, or bisexual, whereas others continue to do so afterwards.

Sexual-minority adolescents' motives for pursuing other-sex relationships vary widely. Obviously, there are powerful normative pressures on adolescents to participate in other-sex dating. Middle to late adolescence is a period during which youths are particularly preoccupied with fitting in, gaining popularity, and achieving status (Coleman, 1961; Eder, 1985), and those who have already started to feel ominously "different" because of their nascent same-sex attractions might seek to reassure themselves of their heterosexuality *and* their social standing by participating in other-sex relationships. Others may simply be going along with what all their peers are doing, never stopping to ask how satisfied they are by these relationships.

Nonetheless, it is a mistake to assume that all sexual-minority youths' other-sex relationships are intrinsically false and unsatisfying. As noted earlier, the majority of sexual-minority youths report experiencing other-sex attractions as well as same-sex attractions (French et al., 1996; Garofalo et al., 1999), and such youths are often authentically interested in and satisfied by their other-sex relationships (Diamond, 1998; Savin-Williams, 1998). Notably, other-sex romances are more common among female than male sexual-minority youth (D'Augelli & Hershberger, 1993; Sears, 1991), and this might be attributable to the fact that women are more likely than men to report experiencing bisexual attractions (Laumann et al., 1994). Of course, it might also reflect the fact that gender-differentiated norms for adolescent behavior often make it more difficult for young women than young men to avoid *unwanted* other-sex relationships (Weinberg et al., 1994).

Even if the youth is not strongly attracted to his/her other-sex partner, other-sex relationships can provide important social-developmental benefits. The adolescent might derive considerable social support and companionship from the romance, and may experience numerous powerful emotions (devotion, commitment, jealousy, dependence, security) that render it developmentally significant. These relationships may also facilitate the sexual questioning process; some youths report that it was a concerned, sensitive other-sex partner that first gently asked them whether they might be attracted to the same sex, and gave them the support and confidence to realistically consider the possibility. Thus, sexual-minority youths' other-sex relationships should not be

dismissed as inherently inauthentic or unimportant. As with same-sex relationships, no assumptions can be made about their immediate and long-term
implications without careful examination of the circumstances and motives
structuring these ties.

RELATIONSHIP QUALITY

Of course, not every romantic relationship is validating, affirming, and supportive. The extent to which a sexual-minority youth's romantic relationship
will foster positive development depends on the quality of the relationship.
"Relationship quality" is obviously a broad construct that can encompass every-
thing from pleasurable companionship to sexual compatibility to trustworthi-
ness. Perhaps the most relevant dimensions of relationship quality for adolescent social development are intimacy and emotional support. In other words,
does the youth feel that he can safely share his deepest worries, hopes, and
dreams with his partner, and does he feel that his partner is a reliable source of
emotional sustenance?

There are clearly multiple factors that influence the degree of intimacy and
support in an adolescent relationship, such as relationships length, partners'
respective behavioral styles, and interpersonal skills. These factors show as
much variation among sexual-minority youths as among heterosexual youths,
and thus one finds just as much variation in the quality of same-sex as other-
sex relationships during adolescence. Nonetheless, there are several unique
facets of sexual-minority experience that can exert a distinctive press on the
quality of same-sex romantic relationships.

One such facet concerns childhood experiences. A youth's mastery of the
multiple interpersonal skills necessary to maintain a positive, mutually supportive, intimate romantic relationship is directly related to the quality of
his/her childhood and early adolescent peer interactions (Masten et al., 1995;
Neemann, Hubbard, & Masten, 1995). For sexual-minority youths who
became aware of their "differentness" from the other kids at an early age
(Savin-Williams, 1996b), these formative peer interactions may already have
been notably strained. The same is true for sexual-minority youths who were
highly gender-atypical as children, many of whom were stigmatized and
ostracized long before they became consciously aware of their same-sex
attractions. To the extent that such youths face difficulties maintaining positive childhood and early adolescent peer relationships, they might be at increased risk for developing deficits in social competence that compromise the
quality of their romantic relationships in late adolescence and early adulthood.

Male sexual-minority youths appear to be at greater risk for developing such deficits than female sexual-minority youths, for a number of reasons. First, girls are more consistently channeled into intimate dyadic interchanges with peers during childhood than young boys, and as a result they are quicker to master the interpersonal skills that are relevant to establishing and maintaining romantic intimacy (Buhrmester & Prager, 1995). Second, male sexual-minority youths are more likely than their female counterparts to experience early awareness of their same-sex attractions, early feelings of "differentness," and early gender atypicality (reviewed in Diamond, 1998), and gender atypicality carries far less negative social consequences for young girls than for young boys (Fagot, 1977). Consequently, male sexual-minority youths are more likely to undergo the early stigmatization and ostracization that might impair their childhood peer interactions and, by extension, their later romantic relationships.

Gender-Composition Effects

Gender also influences the quality of sexual-minority youths' romantic relationships via the gender-composition of the dyad—that is, whether it contains two males, two females, or one of each. Although many simplistically assume that one partner in a same-sex relationship plays "the feminine role" and the other plays "the masculine role," this is rarely the case. Rather, *both* partners typically conform to standard gender-differentiated behavioral styles. As a result, normative gender differences in relationship behavior appear to be magnified in same-sex relationships (Klinkenberg & Rose, 1994; Kurdek, 1994; Peplau, 1982). For example, male–male couples typically place greater emphasis than do female–female couples on sexual activity and physical attractiveness, whereas female–female couples place greater emphasis than do male–male couples on emotional bonding and verbal disclosure (Cimbalo & Novell, 1993; Feingold, 1990; Nardi, 1992). These findings are consistent with the voluminous body of research on differences between heterosexual men's and women's orientations toward sexual versus emotional intimacy (reviewed in Regan, 1998).

Although very little research has been conducted on the quality of sexual-minority *adolescents'* romantic relationships, extant findings have detected the same general pattern (Diamond & Dubé, 1998). When sexual-minority youths were asked to report on the most significant romance they had ever had, male–male relationships were described as typically beginning as sexual liaisons and subsequently progressing to romantic involvement. In contrast, female–female relationships typically began as close friendships, progressed to romantic involvement, and *then* incorporated sexual activity. Furthermore, male–male relationships contained significantly lower levels of interpersonal closeness, emotional attachment, and emotional support than either female–female relationships or female–male relationships. Notably, this mirrors findings from research on adolescent and adult friendships demonstrating higher levels of expressive intimacy, mutual closeness, and social support in female–female than male–male friendships (Barth & Kinder, 1988; Buhrke & Fuqua, 1987; Buhrmester & Prager, 1995; Reis, Senchak, & Solomon, 1985; Rose, 1985).

As noted previously, girls tend to develop the interpersonal skills relevant for intimate interactions at earlier ages than do boys (Buhrmester & Prager, 1995), such that by the time they reach adolescence, girls show more consistent capacities to establish and maintain close friendships characterized by intimate disclosure and emotional support than do their male counterparts (Berndt, 1982; Buhrmester & Furman, 1987; Camarena, Sarigiani, & Petersen, 1990; Sharabany, Gershoni, & Hofman, 1981). The same dynamics may explain the aforementioned differences in the quality of youths' male–male and female–female romantic relationships. Importantly, participation in *other-sex* romantic relationships is a common route through which male heterosexual youths "catch up" to their female counterparts in developing motivations and skills for intimate interpersonal interactions (Connolly & Johnson, 1996; Mark & Alper, 1985). In other words, it is often through being "drawn out" by their girlfriends that male youths come to develop a greater capacity for and comfort with such interactions. Sexual-minority male youths who choose not to pursue substantive heterosexual romances forego such "training" opportunities, potentially delaying their mastery of the skills necessary for sustaining significant intimate ties.

Of course, this is not the case for all male sexual-minority youths. It is no more appropriate to assume that male–male adolescent romances are uniformly superficial than it is to assume that female–female adolescent romances are uniformly deep and meaningful. As noted earlier, relationship quality is influenced by multiple factors, all of which vary within as well as between genders and sexual orientations. Furthermore, with respect to sexual-minority male youths' "training opportunities" for interpersonal intimacy, it bears noting that male sexual-minority youths are more likely than their heterosexual counterparts to have large numbers of female friends and to nominate women as their best friends (Diamond & Dubé, 2002; Diamond & Lucas, 2001). These intimate other-sex friendships likely provide many of the same opportunities to develop interpersonal skills as do heterosexual romances, perhaps compensating for any deficits male sexual-minority youths might otherwise incur by failing to participate in other-sex romantic relationships.

The extent to which the quality of sexual-minority youths' adolescent relationships presages the quality of their adult relationships is unknown. Thus, it is not clear that male sexual minority youths who emphasize sexual over emotional intimacy during their teenage years will have difficulty developing more emotionally intimate and supportive relationships in the future. However, support for this possibility comes from one study which found that lower levels of closeness and intimacy within male–male versus male–female adult couples were attributable to the fact that participants in the male–male couples had poorer relationship skills, lower relationship expectations, and were more likely than the heterosexual couples to have begun their relationship as a sexual involvement (Dubé, 2000). Future research should expand on these findings by exploring whether these differences in relationship skills, expectations, and initiation patterns are in fact meaningfully related to men's *adolescent* experiences of closeness and intimacy with male versus female peers.

Another important direction for future research concerns the relative importance of other-sex versus same-sex peer relationships for the social development of *female* youths. Although the research reviewed previously suggests that relationships with females are "better" for the development of intimacy skills than relationships with males, intimacy is obviously only one aspect of relationship quality. In fact, many have argued that the psychological literature on close relationships has inadvertently adopted a female-biased definition of—and emphasis on—intimacy that does not do service to men's unique relationship skills (reviewed in Prager, 1995). Thus, it is possible that relationships with *males* serve unique and important socialization functions for adolescent *females* that are worthy of substantive attention when considering the social-developmental trajectories of sexual-minority versus heterosexual women.

Overall, extant findings regarding gender differences in relationship patterns demonstrate the importance of giving sexual-minority youths opportunities to talk with adults about their experiences and expectations regarding intimate relationships. Many sexual-minority male youths complain that "guys just want sex," and that they would prefer to develop more committed, emotionally intimate relationships if only they could find partners who wanted the same thing. Yet many of these very youths will admit in the next breath that they have never openly expressed their desires for such a relationship with potential romantic partners. As with many heterosexual men, they often fear that expressing such desires makes them appear weak and unmasculine— characterizations that are particularly stinging for sexual-minority male youths who are routinely viewed as "sissies" by the culture at large. In order to help sexual-minority youths find and keep the types of relationships they want, we should make them aware of their own assumptions regarding "what men/women want" and prompt them to question normative ideals about masculinity and femininity.

FROM RESEARCH TO PRACTICE:
RECOMMENDATIONS
FOR YOUTH ADVOCATES

Appreciating Sexual Diversity

Perhaps the most important recommendation for clinicians, educators, policy makers, and service providers is to resist making assumptions about the sexual and romantic interests of *all* the youths they work with, whether they have disclosed same-sex attractions or not. In the "dark ages" of adolescent research, youths were uniformly presumed heterosexual, and the very existence of sexual-minority adolescents was never acknowledged. This is no longer the case, and the very presence of this chapter in the current volume demonstrates the extent to which youth advocates have become aware of the special needs and experiences of sexual-minority adolescents.

Yet too often these needs and experiences are drastically oversimplified. This is particularly true with regard to the exclusivity of sexual-minority youths' attractions and romantic behavior. Most discussions of sexual-minority adolescents are framed as discussions of "gay and lesbian" adolescents, despite the fact that the majority of sexual-minority adolescents have bisexual attractions or behavior. The presumption of exclusive same-sex sexuality among sexual-minority adolescents is detrimental to efforts to understand the challenges they face, provide them with pertinent, accurate, and useful information about sex and romance, and develop educational and social policies that meet their needs.

For example, some youths with bisexual attractions find that after struggling to gain tenuous acceptance of their same-sex sexuality from parents, friends, teachers, and counselors, they face confusion, anger, and disdain if they express interest in an other-sex peer. Notably, much of this disdain often comes from their gay and lesbian friends, many of whom have inherited a distinct distrust of bisexual individuals from the adult gay and lesbian community. Thus, youths with bisexual attractions often find, ironically, that participating in a "socially desirable" heterosexual romance suddenly garners them *more* scorn and anger than did their same-sex romances. Their gay and lesbian peers might accuse them of "selling out" and trying to pass as heterosexual. Their parents may claim that their other-sex attractions prove that their same-sex attractions were a phase, or that they can "give up" their same-sex interests if they so desire.

Given that many bisexual adolescents are themselves confused about the relative strength and intensity of their same-sex and other-sex attractions, these claims and accusations can be perplexing and hurtful. For this reason, it is critically important that those who work with sexual-minority youth understand the incredible diversity of the sexual-minority population and communicate this diversity to the youths themselves. It is common for youths with ambiguous, late-appearing, or bisexual attractions to feel abnormal by both heterosexual and gay/lesbian standards, leaving them doubly confused and isolated. These youths need to be reassured that such inconsistencies and ambiguities are common among sexual-minority youths, and need to be given safe spaces to discuss their feelings and relationship experiences.

This is particularly important for sexual-minority women, who appear more likely than men to experience ambiguous, late-appearing, or bisexual attractions during adolescence, and who are more likely to first become aware of their feelings in the context of a specific emotionally intimate relationship (reviewed in Diamond & Savin-Williams, 2000). For many such women, questions about sexual identity are not "yes" or "no" questions about basic desires, but more complicated questions about what types of intimate ties they want and expect to achieve with male versus female partners. For example, some women may experience equally strong physical desires for men as for women, but may pursue female partners because they find the emotional quality of their same-sex relationships to be more compelling. This highlights the important role that specific relationships can play in shaping how youths envision their current and future identity.

Responding to Questioning or Heterosexually Identified Youths

Not all youths who experience same-sex desires or relationships in adolescence will continue to do so in adulthood. Just as other-sex desires and relationships in adolescence do not constitute proof of a heterosexual orientation, same-sex desires and relationships in adolescence do not constitute proof of a lesbian/gay/bisexual sexual orientation. Many heterosexual adults report having participated in unexpected same-sex encounters in adolescence, often when unusually close same-sex friendships spilled over into sexual contact (a pattern more common among women than men) or simply in the context of sexual experimentation (a pattern more common among men than women). Heterosexual youths with these experiences often wonder whether they are gay, lesbian, or bisexual, and unfortunately there is no way for an adult advocate to definitively answer that question.

Such cases create somewhat of a quandary for clinicians, educators, and service providers. Youths who dismiss their same-sex experiences as experimental, insignificant, and unrelated to sexual identity might be making a truthful and accurate assessment, or they might be unhealthfully denying their same-sex sexuality. Although it is important for adult advocates to avoid over-interpreting same-sex behavior and prematurely categorizing the youth's sexual identity, it is also important to prompt youths to honestly reflect on the nature of their same-sex feelings and determine their personal relevance. Allowing youths to unilaterally dismiss the significance of same-sex feelings out of defensiveness or fear can only impede this process. Thus, advocates must walk a careful line between "taking a youth's word for it" and prodding the youth to dig deeper for potentially hidden truths. Because there is no bona fide way to separate "true" sexual minorities from curious heterosexuals, the best strategy is for supportive adults to serve as nonjudgmental sounding boards so that youths can reflect openly and honestly about the quality and personal relevance of their experiences in a safe, pressure-free environment. Counselors and educators might also remind youths that no single romantic experience can "prove" one's true sexual identity, and no single relationship (no matter how positive) can be counted on to put a definitive end to the sexual questioning process.

Importantly, successful resolution of the questioning process may not, in fact, entail adoption of a lesbian, gay, bisexual, *or* heterosexual identity. Whereas older research on sexual identity development suggested that the adoption of a clear-cut identity label was fundamental to healthy sexual iden-tity development (Cass, 1979; Troiden, 1989), there is now more widespread acknowledgment that embracing and accepting one's sexuality need not entail categorizing and naming it (Diamond & Savin-Williams, 2000). Many youths feel limited by sexual identity labels, or feel that none of the existing labels accurately describes the way they see their sexuality. Reluctance to adopt a sex-ual identity label is particularly common among youths with attractions to both sexes, those who have only experienced same-sex attractions for one specific person, and those who feel that they "fall in love with the person and not the gender" (Blumstein & Schwartz, 1990; Golden, 1987; Savin-Williams, 1998, in press). Given that women are disproportionately repre-sented in these groups, it is not surprising that female sexual minorities are more likely to eschew conventional sexual identity labels than male sexual minorities (Laumann et al., 1994; Savin-Williams & Diamond, 2000).

Thus, clinicians and educators should avoid making assumptions about a youth's "real" identity or his/her motives for rejecting *or* adopting an identity label without carefully attending to his/her reasons and reasoning. There is no single pathway for healthy sexual identity development, and no prototypical outcome. Youths with different peer environments, different families, different ethnic and cultural backgrounds, and different personalities face markedly different options and constraints in crafting healthy identities and relationships. Educators and clinicians should therefore help youths weigh these multiple options rather than prescribing one particular goal.

The Importance of Sexual-Minority Peer Groups

Perhaps the best way to assist sexual-minority youths in forming and keeping nurturing romantic relationships is to assist them in forming and keeping supportive networks of sexual-minority peers. For the average sexual-minority youth, the most salient distinguishing feature of her day-to-day life, in comparison to heterosexual youths, is the simple fact that her peers do not share her sexual orientation. They cannot be considered potential romantic partners; they cannot be safely flirted with; they cannot be asked for advice on the peculiarities of same-sex dating; they do not fully understand or relate to her most private feelings. Given that heterosexual romantic relationships typically develop out of existing friendship networks (Connolly & Johnson, 1996), sexual-minority youths with no sexual-minority peers are at a distinct disadvantage when it comes to finding same-sex romantic partners, gaining support for their relationships, and participating in the larger processes of romantic socialization that occur in peer contexts.

For this reason, same-age sexual-minority peer groups are often critically important for sexual-minority youths' relational development, and many sexual-minority youths claim that the only thing they want more than a romantic relationship is a sexual-minority friend that they can *talk to* about romantic relationships. It is often exceedingly difficult for youths to find such friends, particularly if they live in isolated, rural environments where there are few openly identified sexual minorities and perhaps no openly identified sexual-minority youths. Those who live in larger cities are more fortunate, as lesbian/gay/bisexual community centers in most urban environments sponsor regular youth programming, ranging from chaperoned recreational activities to structured support groups. In some areas, local high schools even sponsor "gay/straight alliances" where sexual-minority youths can meet other sexual-minority peers as well as supportive and accepting heterosexual peers.

For many youths, these opportunities to socialize with other sexual-minority peers are highly prized, evidenced by the fact that some will gladly spend an hour and a half on public transportation simply to attend youth meetings. Their enthusiasm for such groups highlights the fact that fostering these youths' well-being involves more than reassuring them that they are normal and helping them deal with social stigma. It involves giving them the chance to experience the full range of seemingly mundane interpersonal rituals associated with "normal" adolescence, from passing messages about "who likes whom" to primping in the bathroom during a double date to crying with friends over being dumped. Same-age sexual-minority peer groups make such experiences possible, and thus a key priority for policy makers should be to increase the availability and accessibility of sexual-minority youth programs. A corresponding priority for educators and clinicians should be to make youths aware of these programs and encourage them to attend. Although some adults have expressed concerns that sexual-minority youth groups place inordinate emphasis on youths' sexual identities, exactly the opposite appears to be true. Many youths claim that the most distinctive thing about hanging out with sexual-minority peers is the fact that sexual identity is suddenly "no big deal," and they can finally think and talk about something *else* for a change.

CONCLUSION

Most sexual-minority youths expect that they will have no opportunity to experience a same-sex romance during their high school years (Savin-Williams, 1998), but given the increased availability of opportunities for sexual-minority peers to socialize with one another, more and more of these youths are able to do so. These experiences (as well as the *lack* of such experiences) can have profound influences on how youths perceive their sexual-minority identity, how they cope with the stressors of social stigma, and how they view their future options for intimate experiences. Thus, both researchers who study sexual-minority youths and advocates who work with them should begin devoting systematic attention to these youths' relationship experiences, expectations, and struggles. With all the attention paid to sexual-minority youths' risks for suicide, parental rejection, and peer victimization, it is easy to forget that the defining characteristic of these youths is their desire for intimate same-sex ties. Helping them find and maintain these ties in the most positive, healthful way possible should be a priority for all those seeking to promote their well-being.

REFERENCES

Anderson, D. (1987). Family and peer relations of gay adolescents. *Adolescent Psychiatry, 14,* 162–178.

Anderson, D. A. (1995). Lesbian and gay adolescents: Social and developmental considerations. In G. Unks (Ed.), *The gay teen: Educational practice and theory for lesbian, gay, and bisexual adolescents* (pp. 17–30). New York: Routledge.

Bailey, J. M., & Pillard, R. C. (1995). Genetics of human sexual orientation. *Annual Review of Sex Research, 6,* 126–150.

Bailey, J. M., Pillard, R. C., Neale, M. C., & Agyei, Y. (1993). Heritable factors influence sexual orientation in women. *Archives of General Psychiatry, 50,* 217–223.

Barth, R. J., & Kinder, B. N. (1988). A theoretical analysis of sex differences in same-sex friendships. *Sex Roles, 19,* 349–363.

Baumeister, R. F. (2000). Gender differences in erotic plasticity: The female sex drive as socially flexible and responsive. *Psychological Bulletin, 126,* 247–374.

Bem, D. J. (1996). Exotic becomes erotic: A developmental theory of sexual orientation. *Psychological Review, 103,* 320–335.

Berndt, T. J. (1982). The features and effects of friendship in early adolescence. *Child Development, 53,* 1447–1460.

Blumstein, P., & Schwartz, P. (1977). Bisexuality: Some social psychological issues. *Journal of Social Issues, 33,* 30–45.

Blumstein, P., & Schwartz, P. (1990). Intimate relationships and the creation of sexuality. In D. P. McWhirter, S. A. Sanders, & J. M. Reinisch (Eds.), *Homosexuality/heterosexuality: Concepts of sexual orientation* (pp. 307–320). New York: Oxford University Press.

Brown, B. B. (1999). "You're going out with *who?*" Peer group influences on adolescent romantic relationships. In W. Furman, B. Brown, & C. Feiring (Eds.), *The development of romantic relationships during adolescence* (pp. 291–329). New York: Cambridge University Press.

Buhrke, R. A., & Fuqua, D. R. (1987). Sex differences in same- and cross-sex supportive relationships. *Sex Roles, 17,* 339–352.

Buhrmester, D., & Furman, W. (1987). The development of companionship and intimacy. *Child Development, 58,* 1101–1113.

Buhrmester, D., & Prager, K. (1995). Patterns and functions of self-disclosure during childhood and adolescence. In K. J. Rotenberg (Ed.), *Disclosure processes in children and adolescents* (pp. 10–56). New York: Cambridge University Press.

Camarena, P. M., Sarigiani, P. A., & Petersen, A. C. (1990). Gender-specific pathways to intimacy in early adolescence. *Journal of Youth and Adolescence, 19,* 19–32.

Cass, V. (1979). Homosexual identity formation: A theoretical model. *Journal of Homosexuality, 4,* 219–235.

Cimbalo, R. S., & Novell, D. O. (1993). Sex differences in romantic love attitudes among college students. *Psychological Reports, 73,* 15–18.

Cohen, K. M., & Savin-Williams, R. C. (1996). Developmental perspectives on coming out to self and others. In R. C. Savin-Williams & K. M. Cohen (Eds.), *The lives of lesbians, gays, and bisexuals: Children to adults* (pp. 113–151). Fort Worth, TX: Harcourt Brace.

Coleman, J. S. (1961). *The adolescent society.* New York: The Free Press.

Connolly, J. A., & Johnson, A. M. (1996). Adolescents' romantic relationships and the structure and quality of their close interpersonal ties. *Personal Relationships, 3,* 185–195.

D'Augelli, A. R. (1991). Gay men in college: Identity processes and adaptations. *Journal of College Student Development, 32,* 140–146.

D'Augelli, A. R., & Hershberger, S. L. (1993). Lesbian, gay, and bisexual youth in community settings: Personal challenges and mental health problems. *American Journal of Community Psychology, 21,* 421–448.

Diamond, L., Savin-Williams, R. C., & Dubé, E. M. (1999). Sex, dating, passionate friendships, and romance: Intimate peer relations among lesbian, gay, and bisexual adolescents. In W. Furman, B. Brown, & C. Feiring (Eds.), *The development of relationships during adolescence* (pp. 175–210). New York: Cambridge University Press.

Diamond, L. M. (1998). Development of sexual orientation among adolescent and young adult women. *Developmental Psychology, 34,* 1085–1095.

Diamond, L. M. (2000). Passionate friendships among adolescent sexual-minority women. *Journal of Research on Adolescence, 10,* 191–209.

Diamond, L. M. (2003). What does sexual orientation orient? A biobehavioral model distinguishing romantic love and sexual desire. *Psychological Review, 110,* 173–192.

Diamond, L. M., & Dubé, E. M. (1998, May). *What's sexual orientation got to do with it? Intimacy and attachment in the romantic relationships of sexual-minority and heterosexual youth.* Paper presented at the meeting of the International Network on Personal Relationships, Norman, OK.

Diamond, L. M., & Dubé, E. M. (2002). Friendship and attachment among heterosexual and sexual-minority youths: Does the gender of your friend matter? *Journal of Youth and Adolescence, 31,* 155–166.

Diamond, L. M., & Lucas, S. (2001, July). *Support, commitment, and loss in the friendships and romantic relationships of sexual-minority youth.* Paper presented at the meeting of the International Network on Personal Relationships, Prescott, AZ.

Diamond, L. M., & Savin-Williams, R. C. (2000). Explaining diversity in the development of same-sex sexuality among young women. *Journal of Social Issues, 56,* 297–313.

Dubé, E. M. (2000). Same- and cross-gender romantic relationships: Mediating variables between female presence and relationship quality (Doctoral dissertation, Cornell University, 1990). *Dissertation Abstracts International, 60*(8-B), 4273.

Eder, D. (1985). The cycle of popularity: Interpersonal relations among female adolescents. *Sociology of Education, 58,* 154–165.

Eder, D. (1993). "Go get ya a French!": Romantic and sexual teasing among adolescent girls. In D. Tannen (Ed.), *Gender and conversational interaction* (pp. 17–31). New York: Oxford University Press.

Ellis, L. (1996). The role of perinatal factors in determining sexual orientation. In R. C. Savin-Williams & K. M. Cohen (Eds.), *The lives of lesbians, gays, and bisexuals: Children to adults* (pp. 35–70). Fort Worth, TX: Harcourt Brace.

Ellis, L., & Ebertz, L. (Eds.). (1997). *Sexual orientation: Toward biological understanding.* Westport, CT: Greenwood Publishing Group.

Esterberg, K. G. (1994). Being a lesbian and being in love: Constructing identities through relationships. *Journal of Gay and Lesbian Social Services, 1,* 57–82.

Fagot, B. I. (1977). Consequences of moderate cross-gender behavior in preschool children. *Child Development, 48,* 902–907.

Feingold, A. (1990). Gender differences in effects of physical attractiveness on romantic attraction: A comparison across five research paradigms. *Journal of Personality and Social Psychology, 59,* 981–993.

Fine, M. (1988). Sexuality, schooling, and adolescent females: The missing discourse of desire. *Harvard Educational Review, 58,* 29–53.

French, S. A., Story, M., Remafedi, G., Resnick, M. D., & Blum, R. W. (1996). Sexual orientation and prevalence of body dissatisfaction and eating disordered behaviors: A population-based study of adolescents. *International Journal of Eating Disorders, 19,* 119–126.

Furman, W., Brown, B., & Feiring, C. (Eds.). (1999). *The development of relationships during adolescence.* New York: Cambridge University Press.

Furman, W., & Wehner, E. A. (1994). Romantic views: Toward a theory of adolescent romantic relationships. In R. Montemayor, G. R. Adams, & T. P. Gullotta (Eds.), *Personal relationships during adolescence* (pp. 168–195). Thousand Oaks, CA: Sage.

Furman, W., & Wehner, E. A. (1997). Adolescent romantic relationships: A developmental perspective. In S. Shulman & W. A. Collins (Eds.), *Romantic relationships in adolescence: Developmental perspectives* (pp. 21–36). San Francisco: Jossey-Bass.

Garofalo, R., Wolf, R. C., Wissow, L. S., Woods, E. R., & Goodman, E. (1999). Sexual orientation and risk of suicide attempts among a representative sample of youth. *Archives of Pediatrics and Adolescent Medicine, 153,* 487–493.

Gladue, B. A. (1993). The psychobiology of sexual orientation. In M. Haug, R. E. Whalen, C. Aron, & K. L. Olsen (Eds.), *The development of sex differences and similarities in behavior* (pp. 437–455). Dordrecht, the Netherlands: Kluwer.

Golden, C. (1987). Diversity and variability in women's sexual identities. In Boston Lesbian Psychologies Collective (Ed.), *Lesbian psychologies: Explorations and challenges* (pp. 19–34). Urbana: University of Illinois Press.

Gray, D., & Isensee, R. (1996). Balancing autonomy and intimacy in lesbian and gay relationships. In C. J. Alexander (Ed.), *Gay and lesbian mental health: A sourcebook for practitioners* (pp. 95–114). New York: Harrington Park Press/Haworth Press.

Green, R. (1993). On homosexual orientation as an immutable characteristic. In M. Wolinsky & K. Sherrill (Eds.), *Gays and the military* (pp. 56–83). Princeton, NJ: Princeton University Press.

James, S. E., & Murphy, B. C. (1998). Gay and lesbian relationships in a changing social context. In C. J. Patterson & A. R. D'Augelli (Eds.), *Lesbian, gay, and bisexual identities in families: Psychological perspectives* (pp. 99–121). New York: Oxford University Press.

Klinkenberg, D., & Rose, S. (1994). Dating scripts of gay men and lesbians. *Journal of Homosexuality, 26,* 23–35.

Kurdek, L. A. (1994). The nature and correlates of relationship quality in gay, lesbian, and heterosexual cohabiting couples: A test of the individual difference, interdependence, and discrepancy models. In B. Greene & G. M. Herek (Eds.), *Lesbian and gay psychology* (pp. 133–155). Thousand Oaks: Sage.

Kurdek, L. A. (1998). Relationship outcomes and their predictors: Longitudinal evidence from heterosexual married, gay cohabiting, and lesbian cohabiting couples. *Journal of Marriage and the Family, 60,* 553–568.

Larson, R., Csikszentmihalyi, M., & Graef, R. (1980). Mood variability and the psychosocial adjustment of adolescents. *Journal of Youth and Adolescence, 9,* 469–490.

Larson, R., & Richards, M. (1994). *Divergent realities: The emotional lives of mothers, fathers, and adolescents.* New York: Basic Books.

Larson, R. W., Clore, G. L., & Wood, G. A. (1999). The emotions of romantic relationships: Do they wreak havoc on adolescents? In W. Furman, B. Brown, & C. Feiring (Eds.), *The development of romantic relationships during adolescence* (pp. 19–49). New York: Cambridge University Press.

Laumann, E. O., Gagnon, J. H., Michael, R. T., & Michaels, F. (1994). *The social organization of sexuality: Sexual practices in the United States.* Chicago: University of Chicago Press.

Mark, E. W., & Alper, T. G. (1985). Women, men, and intimacy motivation. *Psychology of Women Quarterly, 9,* 81–88.

Masten, A. S., Coatsworth, J. D., Neemann, J., Gest, S. D., Tellegen, A., & Garmezy, N. (1995). The structure and coherence of competence from childhood through adolescence. *Child Development, 66,* 1635–1659.

Mercier, L. R., & Berger, R. M. (1989). Social service it needs of lesbian and gay adolescents: Telling in their way. In P. Allen-Meares & C. Shapiro (Eds.), *Adolescent sexuality: New challenges for social work* (pp. 75–95). New York: Haworth Press.

Miller, B. C., & Benson, B. (1999). Romantic and sexual relationship development during adolescence. In W. Furman, B. Brown, & C. Feiring (Eds.), *The development of romantic relationships during adolescence* (pp. 99–121). New York: Cambridge University Press.

Nardi, P. M. (1992). That's what friends are for: Friends as family in the gay and lesbian community. In K. Plummer (Ed.), *Modern homosexualities: Fragments of lesbian and gay experience* (pp. 108–120). London: Routledge.

Neemann, J., Hubbard, J., & Masten, A. S. (1995). The changing importance of romantic relationship involvement to competence from late childhood to late adolescence. *Development and Psychopathology, 7,* 727–750.

Owens, R. E. (1998). *Queer kids: The challenges and promise for lesbian, gay, and bisexual youth.* New York: The Haworth Press.

Peplau, L. A. (1982). Research on homosexual couples: An overview. *Journal of Homosexuality, 8,* 3–8.

Peplau, L. A., Cochran, S. D., & Mays, V. M. (1997). A national survey of the intimate relationships of African American lesbians and gay men: A look at commitment, satisfaction, sexual behavior, and HIV disease. In B. Green (Ed.), *Ethnic and cultural diversity among lesbians and gay men. Psychological perspectives on lesbian and gay issues* (pp. 11–38). Thousand Oaks, CA: Sage.

Peplau, L. A., Veniegas, R. C., & Campbell, S. M. (1996). Lesbian and gay relationships. In R. C. Savin-Williams & K. M. Cohen (Eds.), *The lives of lesbians, gays, and bisexuals: Children to adults* (pp. 250–273). Fort Worth, TX: Harcourt Brace.

Prager, K. (1995). *The psychology of intimacy.* New York: Guilford.

Regan, P. C. (1998). Of lust and love: Beliefs about the role of sexual desire in romantic relationships. *Personal Relationships, 5,* 139–157.

Reis, H. T., Senchak, M., & Solomon, B. (1985). Sex differences in the intimacy of social interaction: Further examination of potential explanations. *Journal of Personality and Social Psychology, 48,* 1204–1217.

Rose, S. M. (1985). Same and cross-sex friendships and the psychology of homosociality. *Sex Roles, 12,* 63–74.

Savin-Williams, R. C. (1994). Verbal and physical abuse as stressors in the lives of lesbian, gay male, and bisexual youths: Associations with school problems, running away, substance abuse, prostitution, and suicide. *Journal of Consulting and Clinical Psychology, 62,* 261–269.

Savin-Williams, R. C. (1996a). Dating and romantic relationships among gay, lesbian, and bisexual youths, *The lives of lesbians, gays, and bisexuals: Children to adults* (pp. 166–180). Fort Worth, TX: Harcourt Brace.

Savin-Williams, R. C. (1996b). Memories of childhood and early adolescent sexual feelings among gay and bisexual boys: A narrative approach. In R. C. Savin-Williams & K. M. Cohen (Eds.), *The lives of lesbians, gays, and bisexuals: Children to adults* (pp. 94–109). Fort Worth, TX: Harcourt Brace.

Savin-Williams, R. C. (1998). *". . . And then I became gay": Young men's stories.* New York: Routledge.

Savin-Williams, R. C. (in press). *". . . And then I kissed her": Young women's stories.* New York: Routledge.

Savin-Williams, R. C., & Diamond, L. M. (2000). Sexual identity trajectories among sexual-minority youths: Gender comparisons. *Archives of Sexual Behavior, 29,* 419–440.

Sears, J. T. (1991). *Growing up gay in the South: Race, gender, and journeys of the spirit.* New York: Harrington Park Press.

Sharabany, R., Gershoni, R., & Hofman, J. E. (1981). Girlfriend, boyfriend: Age and sex differences in intimate friendships. *Developmental Psychology, 17,* 800–808.

Steinberg, L. (1988). Reciprocal relation between parent–child distance and pubertal maturation. *Developmental Psychology, 24,* 122–128.

Tolman, D. L. (1994). Doing desire: Adolescent girls' struggles for/with sexuality. *Gender and Society, 8,* 324–342.

Troiden, R. R. (1989). The formation of homosexual identities. *Journal of Homosexuality, 17,* 43–73.

Weinberg, M. S., Williams, C. J., & Pryor, D. W. (1994). *Dual attraction: Understanding bisexuality.* New York: Oxford University Press.

5

Conflict and Negotiation
in Adolescent Romantic Relationships

Shmuel Shulman
Bar-Ilan University

Love and romantic relationships are usually described in terms of connectedness, relatedness, bondedness, or the yearning for intimacy (Sternberg, 1998). Adolescent romantic relationships have also been described to consist of affiliation, intimacy, care, and support that increase with age (Connolly, Craig, Goldberg, & Pepler, 1999; Feiring, 1996; Shulman & Scharf, 2000a). Moreover, adolescent romance is romanticized and has been described in terms like *absolutes,* and *idealism* (Fischer & Alapack, 1987), and a sense of *endless love* (Gray & Steinberg, 1999). However, common experience shows that conflicts and disagreements are also integral to family and romantic relationships. Anger, envy, and contempt color all relationships. "To speak of relational connection is not to imply seamless harmony or warm fuzziness"; conflict is an integral part of or even a form of relationship (Josselson, 1992, p. 267).

The aim of this chapter is to understand the role of conflict in adolescent romantic relationships. The basic premise is that partners express and use their resentment and anger both to dissolve a relationship and as a way to change the nature and course of a relationship in order to meet one's own needs within the relationship. Thus, the need for commitment and exclusivity with a romantic partner should not be disconnected from the impetus for individuality and separate views. Conceptually, the central premise of this chapter is that emotional closeness and individuality are two central axes of a close relationship in general and a romantic relationship in particular, and that the balance between the two will determine the nature and quality of the romantic relationship and how disagreements or conflicts will be perceived and resolved. Moreover, disagreements and conflicts are inevitable and integral to the balance of a relationship and its evolvement over time.

In order to demonstrate this, first, developmental and systemic issues related to the understanding of disagreements, conflicts, and negotiation in parent–adolescent, relationships with peers, and family relationships are reviewed. Second, functions and ways of expressing conflict and negotiation in adolescent romantic relationships are discussed. Third, models for understanding adaptive and maladaptive modes of coping with disagreements as outlined in the literature on adolescent development and marital relationships are formulated. Case examples highlighting constructive and nonconstructive strategies for coping with conflict in adolescent romantic relationships is then presented. The presentation of case examples is followed by the discussion of the issues related to the failure of some adolescents to develop adaptive conflict resolution strategies in their romantic relationships. Finally, implications for practice and clinical intervention are described.

DEVELOPMENTAL AND SYSTEMIC ISSUES IN UNDERSTANDING CONFLICT AND NEGOTIATION

The unavoidable conflict between the motivation of maintaining the relationship and the sense of closeness, and expression of individual needs and preferences is evident among romantic partners. There is evidence that friends and romantic partners are aware of the dangers posed by conflict. Across adolescence, poorly managed conflicts are increasingly regarded as forces that threaten close relationships (Selman, 1980). For this reason, friends and romantic partners handle conflicts in ways that minimize potential disruption of the relationship and may use conflicts to repair inequity between partners. Negotiation has been described as the most common method of resolving conflict, whereas coercion occurs infrequently (see Collins & Laursen, 1994, for review). Due to the dearth of studies on conflict management and resolution in adolescent romantic relationships, developmental and systemic issues are presented and discussed in order to learn more about disagreements and conflicts in close relationships. In particular, this chapter draws from the developmental literature on parent–adolescent relationships, and adolescent friendships, as well as the literature on family systems.

Developmental Issues in Adolescents' Conflicts With Parents and Peers

Closeness and individuality or relatedness and autonomy are also central processes in the psychological development of adolescents (Allen, Hauser, Bell, & O'Connor, 1994; Blatt & Blass, 1990, Connolly & Goldberg, 1999). Developmental theorists refer to relatedness as those processes that underlie interactions with other persons which are conducted in a warm, close, and mutually fulfilling manner. During adolescence, although relatedness with parents is negotiated (Collins, 1995), parents are among those closest to the adolescent. In addition, developmental maturation leads to intensification of the sense of relatedness with friends (Furman & Buhrmester, 1992; Sullivan, 1953), and to the establishment of significant romantic relationships.

Individuality, or autonomy, has been defined in terms of separation, referring to adolescent desires to weaken dependency on parents and achieve independence from parental influence (Blos, 1967). Yet autonomy is also the ability to take more responsibility for one's actions (Blos, 1967) and the capacity for self-determination and expression of appropriate self-reliance (Hill & Holmbeck, 1986). Thus, autonomy is the ability to think or act independently, and to insist on personal choices or values while maintaining a close relationship with the significant other, whether this means parents or peers. Despite the positive connotation of the emphasis on autonomy within a close relationship, it may lead to disagreements and conflicts with significant others.

The management of conflicting needs and disagreements has been extensively studied and demonstrated in parent–adolescent interactions and relationships, revealing how disagreements are successfully or unsuccessfully negotiated among family members. The emergence of adolescent strivings for autonomy and self-assertion is accompanied by transformations in family relations that require parents and adolescents to renegotiate their relationships and negotiate different views (Collins, 1995; Smetana, 1989). Grotevant and Cooper (1985) recorded interactions between parents and adolescents while discussing a joint task. Interactions were analyzed in terms reflecting four characteristics of family communication and relationships:

1. Awareness of one's point of view and responsibility for communicating it clearly.
2. Expressions of difference in views between self and the other.
3. Responsiveness and openness to others' ideas.
4. Sensitivity and respect in relating to others.

These terms reflect the extent to which individuals are comfortable with expressing themselves while interacting with others, and whether others' views are listened to and respected. Hauser et al. (1984) differentiated between enabling and constraining interactions between parents and their children. *Enabling* pertains to parental respect and support of adolescent ideas, whereas *constraining* refers to parents being either indifferent or judgmental toward their adolescents.

Adolescent friendships are also organized around intimacy (Hartup, 1993). Friends display mutual empathy, love, and security (Sullivan, 1953) and share

important feelings and information (Reis & Shaver, 1988). Through rewarding exchanges, friends strongly influence the thoughts, feelings, and behaviors
of one another (Laursen, 1993). In circumstances that do not allow equal distribution of rewards, mutual opposition and conflict may emerge (Hartup,
1983), even in relationships that might have been perceived as close (Shantz,
1987). Few friends are able to avoid disagreements, for disputes are an inevitable part of all close relationships. The mere presence of conflict, therefore,
reveals less about the quality of a relationship than the way in which it is han-
dled (Perry, Perry, & Kennedy, 1992). Conflict management is a particularly
important barometer of relationship functioning, because friends are both
invested in the rewards of affiliation and free to discontinue interconnections
perceived to be disadvantageous. The fact that adolescents adopt more concil-
iatory management strategies with friends than with nonfriends (Caplan,
Bennetto, & Weissberg, 1991) suggests that adolescents are aware that interests of self and other must be addressed and negotiated within a sustained
relationship.

Systemic Perspectives in Understanding Adolescents' Conflicts With Significant Others

The balance between self and other is a basic premise of human existence
wherein individuals either "set others at distance" or "enter into relations with
others" (Buber, 1955). Karpel (1976) developed a theoretical framework for
the possible balances between the poles of self and others. For example, individuals may enter into a relationship even though they are ambivalent about
the relationship and the other. Partners may "maintain contact by establishing
a pattern in which one partner keeps up a facade of distance, while the other
pursues" (p. 74). In another relationship mode, partners may establish "fusion,"
a state in which an individual gives up personal responsibility for the sake of
preserving the relationship. In a mature relationship, the poles of self and other
are integrated in such a way that they nourish and foster each other. Ideally,
partners respond to the other as a whole and separate person and not merely as
a part of their own experience or personal needs. Under such circumstances,
the dialogue between partners provides an optimal context for individuation.
Above all, partners feel free to express their disagreement and insist on being
listened to and respected.

The dialectic of closeness versus separateness is central in the discussion and
description of family systems. According to Wynne and colleagues (Wynne,
Rycoff, Day, & Hirsch, 1958; Wynne, 1970), human contact fulfills a basic
need for affection and warmth. In addition, family members strive to fulfill
their own goals and to differentiate the self from others. Family relationships

that balance these forces are referred to as "true mutuality" (Wynne et al., 1958). Relationships that emphasize closeness and warmth at the expense of individuality are referred to as "pseudomutual" (Wynne et al., 1958), suggesting that family members show a facade of unity that in fact conceals unexpressed dissatisfaction. Families that emphasize individuality at the expense of closeness are referred to as "pseudohostile" (Wynne, 1970). In these families, anger and resentment among family members keeps them together, and hate is the mechanism that maintains the relationship (Josselson, 1992).

The studies and conceptualizations emerging from the developmental and family systems literature show that disagreements between family members or friends (Laursen, 1993) provide an opportunity for partners to define the relationship, distinguishing areas of agreement from disagreement (Hartup, 1992). In addition, discussion and negotiation in response to conflict may foster positive adaptive outcomes among friends. Disagreements provide unique opportunities to improve communication and enhance interpersonal understanding, which may strengthen the social skills of participants (Schultz & Selman, 1989) and monitor behavior in conflictual exchanges to avoid undesirable consequences. Moreover, under conditions where a sincere concern for the partner combined with respect for one's own uniqueness exists, the capacity to incorporate the partner's experience may lead to collaboration for mutual interest (Selman, 1990). Yet there are conditions where partners are unable to acknowledge disagreements or to discuss them, which in turn result in imbalanced relationships.

FUNCTION AND WAYS OF EXPRESSING CONFLICT AND NEGOTIATION IN ADOLESCENT ROMANTIC RELATIONSHIPS

Romantic partners, like family members or friends, cannot avoid the emergence of individual needs and preferences within a relationship—which must be addressed—if they wish their relationship to continue. Research on young adult romantic partners suggests that variations in the balance of needs and wishes of each partner and the level of commitment to the relationship produce three types of relationships: genuine intimacy, merger, and pseudointimacy (Orlofsky, 1976). *Genuine intimacy* is characterized by depth of roles presented by each partner, where each partner is at ease presenting here or his needs, wishes, and preferences, and this presentation is combined with mutual commitment to the relationship. *Merger* describes a relationship that lacks balance and free expression. Partners are not comfortable presenting their own wishes and give up their individuality for the sake of the partner and maintenance of the relationship. *Pseudointimate* relationships offer room to explore individuality, but little commitment to the relationship. Partners do not attend to the needs of the other or of the relationship.

Shulman, Levy-Shiff, Kedem, and Alon (1997) described how adolescent partners approach the dialectic of closeness and individuality. In this study, adolescent romantic partners were observed while working on a joint task in which partners could either cooperate or work individually. In the majority of dyads, romantic partners cooperated in an optimal manner that reflected a clear sense of closeness combined with respect for ideas suggested by the other. Moreover, partners did not try to impose their own ideas on one another. Among other dyads, partners tended not to cooperate when the other raised an idea different than theirs. In some cases, one partner tried to impose his or her own ideas on the other. Needless to say, the sense of closeness among these dyads was lower that among those who showed capability in balancing cooperation and individual ideas.

The Orlofsky (1976) and Shulman et al. (1997) studies show that romantic partners may employ different modes to balance self and other needs and to address their disagreements and conflicts of interest. When disagreements are acknowledged and negotiated, the chance that they will escalate into severe conflicts is low. However, when partners are not capable of balancing opposing needs or expectations, conflicts may emerge and intensify over time. The "merger" mode of relatedness suggests that there are circumstances in which both partners, or at least one of them, gives up their own preferences for the sake of maintaining the relationship. In this case, the relationship is not immediately confronted with conflict, but its health and longevity is questionable (Wynne, 1970). In this vein, adolescent romantic relationships resemble those of adults.

However, balancing between needs of self and other is more complicated among adolescent romantic partners. Unlike adult partners, whose romantic relationships are supposed primarily to provide care and support, among adolescents, romantic partners may serve also as companions and friends (Furman & Simon, 1999) or just for showing peers that they have a romantic partner. As a result, adolescent partners may become involved in romantic relationships for different reasons. A girl may be expecting a close and intimate relationship, whereas a boy is more interested in enhancing his social status by having a girlfriend. In addition to fulfillment of affiliative needs, sexual attraction is also a quite a prominent factor in adolescent romantic relationships. The need to coordinate self and other needs while considering sexual processes might be a more complicated task (Furman & Wehner, 1994). The inexperience of coordinating various needs and wishes may result in a series of relationships that are often quite different from one another. One relationship might be described as supportive, and another as problem-ridden or even abusive (Furman & Simon, 1999).

In many cases, adolescents' romantic encounters do not develop into sustained relationships (Brown, Feiring, & Furman, 1999). Conceptually, this raises the question of whether or when romantic attractions and interactions can be conceptualized and assessed in terms of relationships (Brown et al., 1999). Hinde (1997) distinguished between interactions and relationships, whereby interactions are *encounters* between two persons that are not sustained, and *relationships* involve "interchanges over an extended period of time" (p. 37). It can be assumed that the balancing of self and other needs are different in interactions and relationships. For example, collaboration for mutual interest (Selman, 1990) is relevant in a lasting relationship and less relevant in an interaction that is not sustained.

Adolescent romance may take different forms, and it is questionable which form can be considered a relationship. Connolly and Goldberg (1999) described sequential stages in adolescent romantic relationship. In the *initial infatuation* stage, physical attraction and passion are the prominent features. Attraction is directed toward a particular person but may not be accompanied by actual interaction.

Only at the later stages of adolescence do relationships (a) become long-term, (b) combine attraction, intimacy, and care, (c) feature partners who are committed to each other, and (d) resemble, to some extent, marital relationships. In their earlier phases, romantic relationships are predicated on principles of social exchange (Laursen & Bukowski, 1997). As relationships grow more committed, interdependence declines and the needs and expectations of each person surface. In sustained romantic relationships—*intimate and committed romantic relationships*—partners must address the possible conflicting needs of the dyad and of each partner and arrive at some balance between the two, as outlined in the previous section.

Though romantic attractions as well as a less committed encounter with a member of the other gender are probably less governed by systemic perspectives, possible different wishes of the players in the encounter cannot be ignored. One person might be more interested in the interaction than the other, and this imbalance must be addressed in a "relationship" that has not yet evolved. This notion suggests that in committed as well as "precommitted" romantic relationships, adolescents face dilemmas of balancing conflicting needs of self and the other. How do adolescents deal with the emergence of conflicting needs, a dilemma central to any relationship, in the romantic encounter? How does an adolescent deal with the "other" when it is not clear whether the relationship exists in reality?

Larson, Clore, and Wood (1999) proposed that emotions may serve the individual under such circumstances. Negative emotions such as anger, jealousy, and contempt may have the role of mobilizing the individual to protect threatened romantic attachments to discourage undesirable attachments (p. 22). These negative feelings are helpful in the interpretation of events. One day the adolescent in love may feel wrong about her romantic feelings or encounters. The next day she concludes that her partner was wrong for her anyway. Negative emotions can also be experienced when adolescents' actual feelings do not conform to what they think they are supposed to feel (Simon, Eder, & Evans, 1992). Thus, emotions may be expressed or enacted to help the individual to assess an interaction before it has evolved into a lasting relationship. However, since it is not clear to what extent individuals are aware of their emotional reactions, it is not clear how these emotions might help in future romantic interactions.

An additional source of disagreements and questioning of the balance between adolescent partners might be attributed to the differences between genders. Feminist theories assert that due to distinct socialization processes, there are differences in the way males and females understand and behave in close relationships (Brown & Gilligan, 1992). Females, who throughout their development are expected to stay connected in meaningful ways (Papp, 1989), are thus thought to be more capable of expressing higher levels of intimacy, and perceiving their romantic interactions from a perspective that focuses on emotional closeness and connectedness. Females are twice as likely to be described as the more involved couple member (Felmlee, 1994). Males, in contrast, perceive interactions from a more competitive and power-oriented perspective. Studies of married couples show that the majority of couples are not disparate, with men using more power and being more direct in their interaction as compared to women (Steil, 1994). For this reason, every relationship possibly consists, in fact, of two relationships—hers and his, each experienced differently, with different consequences for the two partners, leading to disagreements and different preferred solutions.

Galliher, Rostosky, Welsh, and Kawaguchi (1999) examined the balance of power in late adolescent romantic dyads. The majority of couples endorsed some traditional gender roles in dating behavior (such as males driving or paying during a date), and males were more likely to describe themselves as dominant in decision making about important matters. However, in the majority of couples, neither partner was concerned about being too dependent in the relationship, and in many areas such as winning arguments, imbalances were likely to favor the females. When females and males were asked to reflect on self and partner's behavior during an interaction, a clear difference between the two genders emerged (Welsh, Galliher, Kawaguchi, & Rostosky, 1999). Females were more sensitive to issues of power in their interactions. Females saw their boyfriends trying harder to persuade them to accept their opinion, but conceding more to their girlfriends. The males, in contrast, did not experience themselves as trying to persuade their girlfriends, nor as conceding to their girlfriends.

These results show that power does not appear to be a major gender-linked issue among adolescent dating couples, although females are, to some extent, more concerned that males have an inclination to control them. Power imbalances described in married couples in adulthood possibly develop later, when relationships are involuntary (Laursen & Jensen-Campbell, 1999), as males grow more confident in the romantic relationship domain, and economic disparities and dependencies come more into play (Welsh et al., 1999).

Nevertheless, it is important to note that females' concern with power was more evident among females in non-egalitarian couples (Galliher et al., 1999). The findings of Shulman and colleagues (1997) are also in line with this trend. Whereas among interdependent couples, females and males were similar on indices of closeness and mutual respect, among disengaged couples males reported less similarity to their partner and less respect for her. We do not know whether, among couples who are unable to resolve gender-linked power issues, there is a higher tendency to develop imbalanced relationships, or whether among partners who are unable to balance closeness and individuality, the consolidation of a disengaged relationship pattern also brings to the surface gender-linked power issues.

There is, however, one aspect where gender issues are relevant. Sexuality seems to be emphasized among contemporary adolescents, but its integration with aspects of mutual commitment develops during later stages of adolescence (Furman & Simon, 1999). For this reason, partners may be less comfortable and competent in discussing and negotiating sexual issues. This may result in behaviors where one partner "gives in" to the other's sexual advances, hoping to gain greater intimacy while not necessarily wanting to have sex. In these situations, usually it is the female partner that gives in. De Gaston, Jensen, and Weed (1995) reported that many adolescent females wished they had waited to have sex. Thus, where romantic relationships are usually mutual and consensual, sexual relationships are sometimes not (Miller & Benson, 1999), and may reflect an imbalanced interaction.

Thus, disagreements between romantic partners are inevitable. Contingent upon their developmental age or the stage of the relationship, adolescents express their disagreements in various levels; indirectly—through emotions, or directly through verbal responses or behaviors. These disagreements serve for expression of, and insisting on, individual needs within the relationship and are the mechanism that will determine in which direction the relationship will proceed. It is important to understand that under conditions where a sustained relationship has not yet developed, it is more difficult to be aware of the imbalance in the interaction, which may be expressed more on the level of emotions. It addition, we do not know whether girls are capable of coping openly with possible inequalities in their romantic relationships as boys do.

MODELS FOR UNDERSTANDING ADAPTIVE AND MALADAPTIVE STRATEGIES FOR COPING WITH CONFLICT IN CLOSE RELATIONSHIPS

A review of the literature on parent–adolescent relationships and the literature on conflict resolution behavior among married couples provides several examples and models for coping with conflicts in close relationships. In line with the focus of this chapter, an adaptive strategy would represent respect for balance between the needs of the individual and that of the dyad. In contrast, a maladaptive strategy would represent disrespect for the needs of an individual within the relationship, or a deterioration of the relationship.

Allen, Hauser, Bell, and O'Connor (1994) elaborated on the negotiations between family members and described parental behaviors that encourage individuals to think autonomously, as well as maintain and support the relationship. These co-concurrent behaviors, termed as *autonomy* and *relatedness,* were defined with regard to the challenge parents face when interacting with their adolescents. Autonomy-exhibiting behaviors were defined as negotiating a difference of opinions, reflecting independence of thought, and self-determination in social interaction. Relatedness-exhibiting behaviors were defined as reflecting interest, involvement, and validation of the other's thoughts and feelings. Such behaviors represent an adaptive mode of coping with a disagreement in the family. In contrast, inhibiting autonomy and relatedness might also co-occur. Inhibiting autonomy may include behaviors that make it difficult for family members to discuss their own reasons for their position within the conflict. This may consist of overpersonalizing a disagreement, recanting a position without appearing to have been persuaded the position is wrong (thus ending the discussion), or pressuring another member of the family to agree without making any rational arguments. Inhibiting relatedness consists of hostile behavior toward a family member, or rude interruptions (Allen et al., 1994, p. 183). Such behaviors represent a maladaptive mode of coping with a disagreement in the family. Exposure to adaptive modes of interactions and coping with disagreements was found to facilitate the adolescent's exploration of differences with the parents. Moreover, the establishment of a balanced partnership between parents and adolescents supported adolescents' establishing autonomy without sacrificing relatedness (Kobak, Cole, Fleming, Ferenz-Gillies, & Gamble, 1993). A study by Rubinstein and Feldman (1993) shows more specifically how the quality of the relationship with parents predicted, over a period of 4 years, adolescents' modes of coping with a conflict in the family. Arriving at a compromise, which reflects the ability to perceive one's needs within the connection to and awareness of the others, was predicted from experiencing a supportive family. Attack and avoidance, which are said to reflect relative inability to coordinate one's own and others' needs and preferences and a sense of helplessness in negotiating with others, was predicted from inconsistent parenting or an unsupportive family.

Though family members remain the greatest source of conflict across adolescence, interviews suggest that adolescent friends are also involved in fights and arguments (Berndt & Perry, 1986). Even so, most friends meet the challenge successfully: Adolescent conflict with friends is characterized by less coercion, negative affect, and detrimental outcomes than that with family members or acquaintances (Caplan et al., 1991; Laursen, 1993). Adolescents' employment of constructive negotiation strategies, as performed within their families, is related also to the quality of their friendships. Friends that were observed to balance the needs of the individual and the needs of the partner and to be supportive of each other reported to assume more responsibility for their behavior, to be less angry, and to work toward a compromise. In contrast, friends who were observed to pursue personal goals at the expense of relationship goals, reported that they more often blamed their partners, got upset, and were as likely to use other tactics like power assertion to resolve disputes as they are to compromise (Shulman & Laursen, 2002).

The literature on conflict resolution behavior describes several behaviors designed to minimize conflicts. These behaviors include: compromise, distraction, overt anger, seeking social support, and avoidance (Creasey, Kershaw, & Boston, 1999; Reese-Weber & Bartle-Haring, 1998; Feldman, & Gowen, 1998). Research on married couples demonstrates that avoidance in marital conflicts or responding with anger or hostility is unlikely to produce positive marital outcomes. In contrast, negotiation that is not accompanied by negative affect or attempts to control or dominate enables couples to successfully manage the inevitable differences and conflicts that arise in marital life (Leonard & Roberts, 1998).

Rusbult's theory of the accommodation process further elaborates the concept of conflict resolution behaviors (Rusbult, Bissonnette, Arriaga, & Cox, 1998). The theory proposes four major reactions to relationship dissatisfaction:

1. Exit—separating, abusing the partner, screaming at the partner and threatening to leave.
2. Voice—discussing the problem, changing oneself to solve the problem, seeking advice.
3. Loyalty—reacting positively in face of criticism or disagreement with the hope for improvement of the relationship.
4. Neglect—refusing to cope with the problem or ignoring the partner.

These categories reflect constructive versus destructive responses in managing problems in a relationship. Individuals may be tempted to engage in behaviors that promote self-interest. However, a healthy relationship will develop when partners are willing to accommodate and adopt constructive approaches.

The literature on the developmental course of marital dysfunction provides an important insight to the role of conflict in the life of a couple. Based on a series of longitudinal studies, Gottman (1991) found that functional responses to conflict were beneficial to the marriage in the long run even if they were upsetting at the time of the conflict. Gottman described a number of positive and negative behaviors characteristic during conflict among couples. Though conflict is an unpleasant experience, when partners are able to present their issues and their spouses are able to listen, the conflict may carry with it new opportunities for the couple. In contrast, when conflict is accompanied by negative affect, partners probably feel emotionally detached, and the chance for resolution of the conflict is not high (Gottman & Levenson, 2000). In particular, when partners became defensive during disagreement (like blaming the other, "You always . . ."), criticizing, showing contempt, and avoiding the other, marriages were likely to dissolve in the long run. A typical scenario of a conflict may then look as follows: In response to a wife's complaints, her husband may withdraw as a listener (stonewalling), not move his face, and avoid eye contact. She may try to re-engage her husband, but in response to his continuous withdrawal she will express more criticism and disgust. As a consequence, both may withdraw, their lives becoming increasingly parallel (as opposed to intertwined), leading to the deterioration of the marriage over time. Heavey, Christensen, and Malamuth (1996) described a similar pattern. The wife started the interaction with a demand, and the husband reacted by withdrawal; the marital satisfaction was subjected to decline. Wives' being agreeable and compliant was no guarantee for marital stability over time, either (Gottman, 1991), pointing to the importance of conflict resolution that adheres to the needs of both partners. Couples who are characterized as adaptive are not free of disagreements and conflicts. Yet, what is typical for these couples is that during a disagreement husbands do not display more negative affect (Gottman & Levenson, 1999). The ability to incorporate positive affect within the conflict supports the attainment of an adaptive solution.

Conflict resolution behaviors are thus a powerful marker of differences between relationships. Interactions within the family and with close friends can provide the necessary forum for critical social experiences for coping with conflicts. In coping with disagreements, romantic partners must choose between constructive solutions that maintain the relationship by addressing the needs of both partners, and destructive solutions that advance outcomes for one partner at the expense of the other. Couples may also avoid the conflict, which in turn may lead to the deterioration of the relationship. These are also instances when conflicts may be resolved without any specific verbal problem behavior (Leonard & Roberts, 1998). Instead, couples may become aware of differences with their partner and learn to respect different views and wishes. However, in some cases, the tendency to avoid arguments and coercion may also lead to disengagement (Laursen, 1993). Thus, a conflict-free relationship may cover for a tendency to suppress conflicts at the expense of one partner, and a relationship that may appear healthy may then deteriorate over time.

CASE EXAMPLES HIGHLIGHTING CONSTRUCTIVE AND DESTRUCTIVE STRATEGIES FOR COPING WITH CONFLICT IN ADOLESCENT ROMANTIC RELATIONSHIPS

Vignettes of how romantic partners deal with an emerging disagreement or conflict demonstrate possible varieties of successful and unsuccessful negotiation strategies. The vignettes cited in this section are taken from a study where romantic partners were asked to indicate separately the level of conflict (on a scale from 0 to 100) between them on a list of topics, such as the amount of time spent together, friends, jealousy, sex, hobbies, money, and so on. The highest revealed disagreement was presented to the partners and they were asked to discuss the different ratings and arrive at an agreement (Shulman & Scharf, 2000b).

Case 1: Disagreement About Hobbies — Basketball
(Female rated level of conflict — 80,
male rated level of conflict — 20)

F: Should we try to solve this disagreement?
M: I am very sensitive about this issue, probably too sensitive. I am crazy about basketball, so we have a lot of arguments. I must admit that I am too glued to it.

There are many fights. She says that basketball is more important to me that she is, and she feels jealous.

F: Not jealous. Sometimes I want to smash the TV on a night there is a game (laughter). I see basketball, playing or watching as a hobby, but the amount of time it demands, little time is left for us together.

M: This is what I said. I'm too much into basketball.

F: It's not too critical, and it is in the background of our relationship, but *we talk about it.*

M: I mentioned it . . . it is an issue, this is something we discuss and deal with quite often.

F: Yet, I don't think that we have too many difficult conflicts. OK, I bring it up when it bothers me, it causes some problems but this is not something you have to cope with otherwise. . . . I think he's very much into it and I think we try to arrive at some middle ground. There are ups and downs, and today I don't see it as a problem as [I did] in the past.

M: So do you think the conflict is an 80?

F: I think we have more conflicts on this issue than on other issues. So 80 is how I see it.

M: I don't think it is 80. This bothers us from time to time. *Each of us has to learn to insist on what he likes.* We learn how to accept something that somebody doesn't like. That's life.

Inspection of the discussion shows that the partners acknowledge the fact that they are in conflict about the boy's fascination with basketball. They distinguish areas of agreement from disagreement (Hartup, 1992) and even feel comfortable expressing disappointment or anger, "smashing the TV" (Bradbury, Cohan, & Karney, 1998). Conflict does not undermine constructive communication. On the contrary, conflict is understood as the mechanism that allows each partner to learn and to respect the different views of the other. Consequently, conflict fosters expressions of self-preference as an integral part of the relationship, and contributes to its evolution.

Case 2: Disagreement About Jealousy (Female rated level of conflict—11, male rated level of conflict—0)

M: Jealousy, did I rate it 0? That's a mistake (laughter). No, I probably didn't see it well. Jealousy is not 0.

Interviewer: So what is your rating?

M: It's 15 or 20. Something like that.

F: You have to take a second test.

M: I didn't see it well, I did it too quickly.

Interviewer: So let's take another disagreement. With regard to friends, you [the girl] indicated 1, and you [the boy] indicated 10.

M: Did I write 10 or 5?

Interviewer: 10

M: Oh, 10.

F: It's probably a question of a different way of rating.

M: Yeah, it's a . . .

F: I said 1 because I meant [the conflict is about] one friend.

M: Yes, she wrote 1, as if, no, and I meant 10 percent, like she [the friend] is out of ten friends and I don't like one of her ten friends.

F: We agree about which friend he does not like.

M: We agree on most of the (Girl laughs), on most we agree . . .

F: of the conflicts.

This couple is very cautious of expressing disagreement. They hardly allow themselves to express that they do not agree on something. When a disagreement is revealed, they try to conceal it. It is difficult for them to set up the conflict discussion, recalling the conflict-avoider couples (Gottman, 1993). Absurd justifications are raised in order to avoid a sense of disagreement. The partners clearly do not try to understand the perception of the other. Moreover, the partners do not allow themselves to express self-preferences and to discuss their relationship. The emphasis on presenting a joint facade surpasses separate wishes.

Case 3: Disagreement About Friends (Female rated level of conflict — 20, male rated level of conflict — 50)

F: I have a feeling that we are different on most of the issues. OK, I don't see it as a problem that the people he likes to hang out with are of no interest to me. That's . . . that's the problem (laughs).

M: I think it's a problem for us, I mean not a critical problem, but it deserves a 50.

F: Fine, OK, we can rate it higher. I don't know if I see it as a problem but as another difference between us. It is how things are, what can I do?

M: What's about me?

F: Do you have a problem with my friends?

M: Of course.

F: What's the problem?

M: Do you want to hear about it now?

F: Yes.

M: I have a problem with M. and with C.

F: You don't have a problem with M.

M: (laughs and coughs)

F: OK, I have more a problem with your friends, they do not interest me, they're boring and I don't like them.

M: We should go to a psychologist.

In contrast to the couple presented in Case 2, these partners are aware of their conflict. Yet when a problem is mentioned by one partner, the other does not respect the partner's feeling or point of view. The discussion reveals disrespect for the other, expressing it in a belittling manner, as well as not being willing to accept that her friends are a problem for her boyfriend (Gottman & Levenson, 2000). It is evident that the discussion does not lead the couple to new ground, and they remain with the sense that their point of view is not accepted.

Conceptually, these different modes of dealing with an agreement recall family typologies presented by Reiss (1981), couple typologies (Fitzpatrick, 1988; Gottman, 1993), and applied by Shulman in the study of adolescent close friendships (Shulman & Knafo, 1997). In the first type, termed *environment-sensitive* or *interdependent*, when a problem is presented to family members or close friends, each member is aware of the need to explore the possible information to solve the problem. They also make full use of one another to achieve the best solution. They react objectively and are free to accept or reject solutions proposed by one another. The solution is not arrived at immediately, but rather at the end of a process of mutual evaluation of available information. There is no pressure to accept a solution suggested by either member. Ideas or suggestions raised by each member help clarify the problem, and attempts are made to reach an optimal solution. The ultimate solution balances individual perceptions and each partners' contribution. In this type of relationship, both dyadic and individual needs are respected.

In the second type, termed *consensus-sensitive*, family members or partners strive for cohesion and complete agreement. Each partner is sensitive to the opinions of the other and tries not to express ideas that may clash with or hurt the other. To remain united and work cooperatively, family members tend to arrive at solutions while refraining from disagreement. An emphasis on cohesion prevents partners from examining the views of family members, so that the agreement reached is not always the most effective. In this type of relationship, individual inclinations are suppressed in favor of closeness.

In the third type, termed *distance-sensitive* or *disengaged*, family members use joint discussion as an arena for expressing independence from one another. Accepting a partner's opinion is seen as evidence of weakness. Each partner barely relates to or respects ideas or information provided by the other. In this type of relationship, cooperation is scarcely an aim, as partners prefer to demonstrate separateness.

This typology raises a major question: What brings partners to act in different modes when confronting disagreement? Studies have examined more with the description of conflict management styles but inquired less about the reasons or antecedents of employing specific conflict management styles. Moreover, adolescent romantic relationships are voluntary in nature (Laursen & Jensen-Campbell, 1999), raising the question of why partners do not terminate a relationship when they are unable to express their views or wishes or where conflicts are not resolved.

ISSUES RELATED TO THE FAILURE TO DEVELOP ADAPTIVE CONFLICT RESOLUTION STRATEGIES

Individuals may approach each other with different expectations when entering into a romantic relationship. Expectations may be based on personal beliefs, such as that others can be turned to in time of stress, or on previous relational experiences within the family, with friends, or with a romantic partner. In this respect, individual characteristics or previous experience may affect how an individual will interact with a romantic partner, what kind of a relationship will develop, and how conflicts will be perceived and resolved.

Individual Characteristics

The attachment theory has been widely used to provide an explanation for both current behavior and conflict management skills in adolescent romantic relationships (Furman & Wehener, 1997; Furman & Simon, 1999; Creasey et al., 1999). Through participation in salient relationships with caregivers, basic expectations and attitudes concerning social partners' behavior are internalized. In addition, an individual may come to anticipate the implications of his or her expectations on the partner's behavior (Sroufe & Fleeson, 1986). Assuming continuity in interpersonal adaptations over time, the individual projects inner representations of relationships onto future social contacts, leading to a repetition and confirmation of expected patterns of behavior. In the spirit of attachment theory, individual differences in relationship expectations have been documented (Main, 1996): *secure*—comfortably relying on others for emotional support and viewing oneself as a viable attachment figure for the other; *avoidant-dismissing*—has difficulties in trusting others or relying on them, is emotionally distant; and *anxious/preoccupied*—preoccupied whether or not they rely on others, but feels that reliance on others is vital.

In order to develop an intimate and close romantic relationship, one must first be oriented to values and seek closeness. In addition, one must be able to share emotional experiences freely, and be able to tolerate, or even embrace, the intense emotions that are central in a close relationship. Finally, one must have the capacity for mutual reciprocity, sensitivity to the feelings of the other, and a sincere concern for the well-being of the other. A number of studies found that late adolescents with secure attachment representations were more likely to be involved in an exclusive romantic relationship (Furman & Wehner, 1997), to indicate higher levels of intimacy in their romantic relationships (Bartholomew & Horowitz, 1991), and to have a better relationship quality (Simpson, 1990) than individuals with insecure representations. Several other studies investigated the association between attachment measures and conflict management behaviors among married couples. Kobak and Hazan (1991) found that individuals with secure attachment representations were more supportive and less rejecting of their spouses during joint interactions. Simpson, Rholes, and Phillips (1996) were able to predict a higher level of conflict management difficulties with romantic partners during a problem-solving task among individuals with insecure representations as compared to individuals with secure representations.

Results of a recent study by Creasey et al. (1999) on a cohort of late adolescents offer a clearer answer to the question of which adolescent will employ a specific conflict management pattern. In this study, adolescents' ambivalent and avoidant attachment representations were assessed in addition to how they coped with interpersonal conflict with a romantic partner. The more ambivalent and avoidant adolescents described being engaged in conflicts with romantic partners that are marked with general negativity. Quarrels between these partners involved behaviors such as nagging, whining, defensiveness, and complaining. In addition, results predicted specific conflict management techniques. Highly ambivalent individuals were more likely to report getting into disagreements that involved angry, out-of-control arguments. Highly avoidant individuals, in contrast, tended more to withdraw when facing a conflict with their partner. Ambivalent and avoidant reactions to conflict with a romantic partner may reflect how these individuals perceive the relationship. Individuals with ambivalent representations place a high emphasis on the relationship; it is difficult for them when their partner does not respond to their point of view and they react with anger and hostility to provoke guilt from the partner and to restore the sense of closeness. Individuals with avoidant representations are more likely to devalue intimacy, and act in an emotionally distant manner. A conflict is thus a good excuse for them to distance from their partner (Creasey et al., 1999, pp. 538–539).

Downey also suggested that expectations influence adolescent romantic relationships, elaborating specifically on the role of expectations of attaining acceptance and avoiding rejection (see Downey, Bonica, & Rincon, 1999). Building on social cognitive approaches as well as on the attachment theory, Downey proposed that an adolescent who has developed defensive expectations of rejection as a result of having experienced rejection, initially from parents and subsequently from peers, will more anxiously or angrily expect rejection, readily perceive, and react intensely to rejection. Downey termed such individuals *rejection sensitive*. An adolescent may enter a romantic relationship hopeful that it will repair the rejection experienced in a previous relationship and provide a new experience of acceptance. However, defensive expectations of rejection will make the adolescent hypervigilant for signs of rejection, such as the partner's being inattentive, disagreeing on something, or being friendly to a potential rival. Under such circumstances, the capacity to discuss disagreements or to resolve conflict in a balanced manner is, of course, minimal. Moreover, the perceived rejection resulting from a disagreement can prompt intense affective and behavioral reactions, including hostility, despondence, withdrawal, or inappropriate efforts to gain acceptance. The overreaction by a rejection-sensitive individual might be diminished once the partner initiates a calm discussion of the disagreement, focusing on understanding what prompted the overreaction. It is more common to find the partner seeking to control the situation either through coercion or compliance. Coercion involves acts of aggression, regulating the partner's life to keep him or her dependent on the relationship, or threats of self-harm to keep the partner in the relationship. Compliance involves submission to the wishes or demands of the partner or tolerating abusive behavior.

In a study by Downey, Freitas, Michaelis, and Khouri (1998), a daily diary study of naturally occurring conflict in dating couples revealed that when rejection-sensitive women felt rejected, they tended to report having a conflict with their partner the next day. During the conflict they behaved in a hostile manner. The following day, the relationship satisfaction and commitment of high rejection-sensitive women's partners' declined, reflecting that the conflict was not resolved successfully. Discussion of conflict with a woman low in rejection sensitivity was observed to lead to a reduction in anger and resentment by their partners.

Seiffge-Krenke (1997) investigated how healthy and diabetic adolescents balance intimacy and conflict in their romantic relationships. Results of this longitudinal study, conducted over a period of 4 years, revealed that diabetic adolescents expected their partners to be good listeners and to show understanding, and perceived the partner as providing a sense of security. Conflicts were attributed to a lack of sufficient attention from partners. Overall, diabetic adolescents reported a lower level of conflict in their romantic relationships as compared to their healthy counterparts. Healthy adolescents were more capable of being involved in a relationship where intimacy and conflict co-existed.

To summarize, unrealistic expectations either for "over-availability" or unavailability of others may lead individuals to difficulties in negotiating issues of self and others in their romantic relationships. Unresolved conflicts may lead to dissolution of a relationship, establishment of a distant relationship with low expectations from the partner, or to compliance and giving up the welfare of one partner.

Previous Experience

Conflict management is not new to the adolescent romantic partner. Adolescents have had to resolve conflicts with their parents and friends and have been exposed to parental conflicts and negotiations. Previous experience may thus serve as a model, and adolescents may imitate those behaviors in their own conflicts (Bandura, 1986). Collins and Sroufe (1999) reported that parent–child conflict resolution scores at age 13 were significant predictors of overall quality of romantic relationships and conflict resolution at ages 20–21. Emerging from a systems perspective, Reese-Weber and Bartle-Haring (1998) investigated how conflict resolution styles between one family dyad are related to other family dyads, and how these relate to conflict resolution styles that adolescents exhibit in their romantic relationships. The parent–adolescent resolution style was related to the attack and avoidant styles in the romantic relationships. In addition, the relationship between interparent and romantic resolution styles was mediated through the parent–adolescent resolution styles. The sibling relationship was also significantly related to conflict resolution in romantic relationships.

Furman and Wehner (1997) have pointed to the importance of the interaction experience for the quality of a romantic relationship. Through involvement in a relationship one must learn how to interact with a partner. Studies in social exchange theory suggest that mutually beneficial exchanges promote future cooperation as participants learn to rely on one another for rewards (Kelly et al., 1983). Furman and Wehener (1997) found that college women in exclusive relationships were more secure and less preoccupied in their romantic styles than those who had dated more casually. In spite of the fact that previous experience shapes later behavior, adolescents may underscore the importance of a previous romantic relationship. Adolescents may see some of their previous romance as a "mistake," as something that should be unlearned (Furman & Simon, 1999, p. 86). However, as research and clinical material shows, previous patterns of interaction are repeated in future relationships and in particular under conditions of stress (Sroufe & Fleeson, 1986).

Partners' Interdependence: Systemic Perspectives

The ideas presented thus far, influenced by attachment theory, implicate individual-level factors in accounting for the course of a relationship. It is important to also consider dyad-level processes. Hinde (1997) has indicated that a lasting relationship involves interchanges over an extended period of time. When interactions are sustained, the current interaction may be affected by partners' interactions in the past, and by expectations of how the specific partner will behave in the future. Sensitivity to rejection may diminish when a partner is capable of initiating a calm discussion (Downey et al., 1999). However, as family systems theories have suggested, selection of a partner is not made by chance. Individuals have a tendency to select partners similar to them on levels of differentiation between self and other (Bowen, 1976). Adolescents were also found to establish close friendships with those who had a similar attachment history as their own (Shulman, Elicker, & Sroufe, 1994). Under such circumstances, partners may each develop unrealistic expectations that may maintain or even intensify rejection expectations. Thus, both partners share the responsibility for how the relationship will evolve.

IMPLICATIONS FOR PRACTICE AND CLINICAL INTERVENTION

This chapter provides a conceptual framework for the understanding of disagreements and conflicts in adolescent romantic relationships. Based on systemic approaches, the contention of this chapter is that the way adolescent couples understand and cope with disagreements and conflicts may serve as a "relational diagnosis" for understanding the dynamics of the romantic bond. When adolescent romantic partners are incapable of using disagreement as a grounds for personal and mutual growth, relationships may take different forms. It is reasonable to assume that continued conflicts will lead to the breakup of an adolescent romantic relationship as the costs of the voluntary relationship surpasses its benefits (Laursen & Jensen-Campbell, 1999). Yet other imbalanced relational patterns may persist. There are relational patterns where partners avoid conflict either by joint leveling or denying of conflicts (see verbatim Case 2), or when one partner coerces the other to submit to his or her point of view. Such relationship patterns are the forerunners of family pathologies.

Another less-adaptive type of romantic relationship might be when partners oscillate between fights and conciliation, revealing a pattern of romanticized relatedness followed by repeated fights, combined with an inherent inability to arrive at a balanced relationship or to separate (Bowen, 1976, Wynne, 1984).

To an outside observer, a close, committed, and "conflict free" relationship may look like at the expression of *endless love* romanticized by adolescents and to some extent by adults. In my clinical experience, I witnessed a 16-year-old girl referred to therapy due to fatigue and breathing problems. We learned that the girl's 18-year-old boyfriend was about to join the army and the girl felt she could not continue living without him. Their relationship had lasted for more than 2 years. The boy was described as a caring person ready to help the girl in every aspect of her life. Of course, he was the center of her life and she said that she hardly felt any wish to have close friends. Our impression was that this couple resembled Bowen's (1976) description of an "undifferentitated ego mass" looking among adolescents like Romeo and Juliet, and perhaps not raising any concern. Cases where one partner uses coercive strategies to cause the other to submit (see Downey et al., 1999) are not easy to detect, because the couple may show a facade of a very close relationship (see Case 3). Though cases of unstable relatedness are easier to detect, partners are less ready to listen to an outsider's opinion due to their inability to separate from one another.

It is important to raise the awareness of parents, school counselors, and mental health professionals about unhealthy relationships that can be found among adolescent romantic partners. In particular, it is important to notice how adolescent partners approach disagreements, how they resolve them, and whether they respect each other's points of view while coping with the conflict. Moreover, pacific and full-of-love relationships may hide an overly dependent relationship or a condition where one partner controls the other.

Due to the shorter duration of adolescent romantic relationships, there is less of a chance that adolescents will apply for or be referred to therapy as a couple. More commonly, one partner will be in therapy and the nature of her or his romantic relationship will emerge in the therapeutic sessions. First, it will be helpful to help the adolescent to become more aware of the dynamics of the relationship in which she or he is involved; what are the roles played by both partners in the relationship, and whether the relationship respects the needs of each partner, or is tuned more for the benefit of one partner at the expense of the other. As in individual therapy, it is then important to uncover the reasons that an individual enters into an imbalanced relationship. Understanding their inner models of relationship, exploring, for example, the origins for their sensitivity to rejection (that may lead to overdependence on a partner) could become a significant phase in the therapeutic process. Exploring past romantic experiences and how conflicts were managed could be an additional avenue for understanding how the adolescent approaches romance and the role he or she adopts in these relationships. A better understanding of each partner's role in the relationship may help young people to correct and to avoid repeating previous difficult experiences, and in particular how to cope with disagreements in the relationship.

Clinicians and professionals working with adolescents should also be more aware about two groups of adolescents: young adolescents and females. As outlined in this chapter, the ability to negotiate differences represents the ability to take the perspective of the other (Selman, 1980). For this reason, disagreements are probably more difficult for younger adolescents. Previous research showed that early romantic involvement has negative consequences. Young adolescents probably become involved in relationships that may interfere with the pursuit of their developmental tasks at the expense of maintaining the relationship (Neemann, Hubbard, & Masten, 1993). Due to gender roles in our society, girls might tend more willingly to give up their position, while being in conflict with their partner. This tendency may result in some cases in a relationship that shows less respect for the girl's views or wishes. In particular, such a relationship can result in not fully consented sex, which many girls later regret (de Gaston et al., 1995).

Disagreements and modes of negotiation can provide an insight into the difficulties young people may have with their romantic partners. Yet, it is important to remember that disagreements and conflicts are integral to adolescent family, peer, and romantic relationships. Moreover, previous studies showed that adolescent romantic partners prefer negotiation over coercive conflict management (Laursen, 1993). Therefore, in the majority of cases, conflict is more likely to improve the relationship.

REFERENCES

Allen, P. A., Hauser, S. T., Bell, K. L., & O'Connor, T. G. (1994). Longitudinal assessment of autonomy and relatedness in adolescent–family interactions as predictors of adolescent ego development and self esteem. *Child Development, 65,* 179–194.

Bandura, A. (1986). *Social foundations of thought and action.* Englewood Cliffs, NJ: Prentice-Hall.

Bartholomew, K., & Horowitz, L. (1991). Attachment styles among young adults: A test of a four-category model. *Journal of Personality and Social Psychology, 61,* 226–244.

Berndt, T. J., & Perry, T. B. (1986). Children's perceptions of friendships as supportive relationships. *Developmental Psychology, 22,* 640–648.

Blatt, S. J, & Blass, R. B. (1990). Attachment and separateness: A dialectic model of the products and processes of development throughout the life cycle. *The Psychoanalytic Study of the Child, 45,* 107–127.

Blos, P. (1967). The second individuation process in adolescence. *The Psychoanalytic Study of the Child, 22,* 162–186.

Bowen, M. (1976). Theory in the practice of psychotherapy. In P. J. Guerin (Ed.), *Family therapy, theory and practice* (pp. 65–90). New York: Gardner Press.

Bradbury, T. N., Cohan, C. L., & Karney, B. R. (1998). Optimizing longitudinal research for understanding and preventing marital dysfunction. In T. N. Bradbury (Ed.), *The developmental course of marital dysfunction* (pp. 279–311). New York: Cambridge University Press.

Brown, B. B., Feiring, C., & Furman, W. (1999). Missing the love boat: Why researchers have shied away from adolescent romance. In W. Furman, B. B. Brown, & C. Feiring (Eds.), *The development of romantic relationships in adolescence* (pp. 1–18). Cambridge, UK: Cambridge University Press.

Brown, L. M., & Gilligan, C. (1992). *Meetings at the crossroads: Women's psychology and girls' development.* Cambridge, MA: Harvard University Press.

Buber, M. (1955). *Between man and man.* Boston: Beacon Press.

Caplan, M., Bennetto, L., & Weissberg, R. P. (1991). The role of interpersonal context in the assessment of social problem-solving skills. *Journal of Applied Developmental Psychology, 12,* 103–114.

Collins, W. A. (1995). Relationships and development: Family adaptation to individual change. In S. Shulman (Ed.), *Close relationships and socioemotional development* (pp. 128–154). Norwood, NJ: Ablex.

Collins, W. A,. & Laursen, B. (1994). Interpersonal conflict during adolescence. *Psychological Bulletin, 115,* 197–207.

Collins, W. A., & Sroufe, L. A. (1999). Capacity for intimate relationships a developmental construction. In W. Furman, B. B. Brown, & C. Feiring (Eds.), *The development of romantic relationships in adolescence* (pp. 125–147). Cambridge, UK: Cambridge University Press.

Connolly, J., Craig, W., Goldberg, A., & Pepler, D. (1999). Conceptions of cross-sex friendships and romantic relationships in early adolescence. *Journal of Youth and Adolescence, 28,* 481–494.

Connolly, J., & Goldberg, A. (1999). Romantic relationships in adolescence: The role of friends and peers in their emergence and development. In W. Furman, B. B. Brown, & C. Feiring (Eds.), *The development of romantic relationships in adolescence* (pp. 266–290). Cambridge, UK: Cambridge University Press.

Creasey, G., Kershaw, K., & Boston, A., (1999). Conflict management with friends and romantic partners: The role of attachment and negative mood regulation expectations. *Journal of Youth and Adolescence, 28,* 523–543.

de Gaston, J. F., Jensen, L., & Weed, S. (1995). A closer look at adolescent sexual activity. *Journal of Youth and Adolescence, 24,* 465–479.

Downey, G., Bonica, C., & Rincon, C. (1999). Rejection sensitivity and adolescent romantic relationships. In W. Furman, B. B. Brown, & C. Feiring (Eds.), *The development of romantic relationships in adolescence* (pp. 148–174). Cambridge, UK: Cambridge University Press.

Downey, G., Freitas, A., Michaelis, B., & Khouri, H. (1998). The self fulfilling prophecy in close relationships: Do rejection sensitive women get rejected by their partners? *Journal of Personality and Social Psychology, 75,* 545–560.

Feiring, C. (1996). Concepts of romance in fifteen year old adolescents, *Journal of Research on Adolescence, 6,* 181–200.

Feldman, S. S., & Gowen, L. K. (1998). Conflict resolution in romantic relationships in high school students. *Journal of Youth and Adolescence, 27,* 691–717.

Fischer, C. T., & Alapack, R. A. (1987). A phenomenological approach to adolescence. In L. van Hassellt (Ed.), *Handbook of adolescence psychology* (pp. 91–109). New York: Wiley.

Felmlee, D. H. (1994). Who is on top? Power in romantic relationships. *Sex Roles, 31,* 275–295.

Fitzpatrick, M. A. (1988). *Between husbands and wives: Communication in marriage.* Newbury Park, CA: Sage.

Furman, W., & Buhrmester, D. (1992). Age and sex differences in perceptions of networks of personal relationships. *Child Development, 63,* 103–115

Furman, W., & Simon, V. A. (1999). Cognitive representations of adolescent romantic relationships. In W. Furman, B. B. Brown, & C. Feiring (Eds.), *The development of romantic relationships in adolescence* (pp. 75–98). Cambridge, UK: Cambridge University Press.

Furman, W., & Wehner, E. A. (1994). Romantic views: Toward a theory of adolescent romantic relationships. In R. Montemayor (Ed.), *Advances in adolescent development: Vol. 3. Relationships in adolescence* (pp. 168–195). Beverly Hills, CA: Sage.

Furman, W., & Wehner, E. A. (1997). Adolescent romantic relationships: A developmental perspective. In S. Shulman & W. A. Collins (Eds.), *Romantic relationships in adolescence: Developmental perspectives* (pp. 21–36). San Francisco: Jossey-Bass.

Galliher, R. V., Rostosky, S. S., Welsh, D. P., & Kawaguchi, M. C. (1999). Power and psychological well-being in late adolescent romantic relationships. *Sex Roles, 40,* 689–710.

Gottman, J. M. (1991). Predicting the longitudinal course of marriages. *Journal of Marital and Family Therapy, 17,* 3–7.

Gottman, J. M. (1993). The roles of conflict engagement, and avoidance in marital interaction: A longitudinal view of five types of couples. *Journal of Consulting and Clinical Psychology, 61,* 6–15.

Gottman, J. M., & Levenson, R. W. (1999). Rebound from marital conflict and divorce prediction. *Family Process, 38,* 287–292.

Gottman, J. M., & Levenson, R. W. (2000). The timing of divorce: Predicting when a couple will divorce over a 14-year period. *Journal of Marriage and the Family, 62,* 737–745.

Gray, M. R., & Steinberg, L. (1999). Adolescent romance and parent-child relationship: A contextual perspective. In W. Furman, B. B. Brown, & C. Feiring (Eds.), *The development of romantic relationships in adolescence* (pp. 235–265). New York: Cambridge University Press.

Grotevant, H. D., & Cooper, C. R. (1985). Patterns of interactions in family relationships and the development of identity exploration in adolescence. *Child Development, 56,* 415–428.

Hartup, W. W. (1983). Peer relations. In E. M. Hetherington (Ed.), *Handbook of child psychology: Vol. 4. Socialization, personality and social development* (pp. 103–196). New York: Wiley.

Hartup, W. W. (1992). Conflict and friendship relations. In C. U. Shantz & W. W. Hartup (Eds.), *Conflict in child and adolescent development.* New York: Cambridge University Press.

Hartup, W. W. (1993). Adolescents and their friends. In B. Laursen (Ed.), *Friendships in adolescence* (pp. 3–22). San Francisco: Jossey-Bass.

Hauser, S. T., Powers, S. I., Noam, G. G., Jacobson, A. M., Weiss, B., & Follansbee, D. J. (1984). Familial contexts and adolescent ego development. *Child Development, 55,* 195–213.

Heavey, C. L., Christensen, A., & Malamuth, N. M. (1996). The longitudinal impact of demand and withdrawal during marital conflict. *Journal of Consulting and Clinical Psychology, 63,* 797–801.

Hill, J., & Holmbeck, G. N. (1986). Attachment and autonomy during adolescence. In G. Whitehurst (Ed.), *Annals of child development* (Vol. 3, pp. 207–223). Greenwich, CT: GAI.

Hinde, R. A. (1997). *Relationships a dialectical perspective.* Hove, East Sussex: Psychology Press.

Josselson, J. (1992). *The space between us, exploring the dimensions of human relationships.* San Francisco: Jossey-Bass.

Karpel, M. (1976). Individuation: From fusion to dialogue. *Family Process, 15,* 65–82.

Kelly, H. H., Bercheid, E., Christensen, A., Harvey, J. H., Huston, T. L., Levinger, G., McClintock, E., Peplau, L. A., & Peterson, D. R. (1983). *Close relationships.* New York: Freeman.

Kobak, R., Cole, H. E., Ferenz-Gillies, R., Fleming, W. S., & Gamble, W. (1993). Attachment and emotion regulation during mother–teen problem solving: A control theory analysis. *Child Development, 64,* 231–245.

Kobak, R., & Hazan, C. (1991). Attachment in marriage: Effects of security and accuracy of working models. *Journal of Personality and Social Psychology, 60,* 861–869.

Larson, R. W., Clore, G. L., & Wood, G. A., (1999). The emotions of romantic relationships: Do they wreak havoc on adolescents? In W. Furman, B. B. Brown, & C. Feiring (Eds.), *The development of romantic relationships in adolescence* (pp. 19–49). Cambridge, UK: Cambridge University Press.

Laursen, B. (1993). The perceived impact of conflict on adolescent relationships. *Merrill-Palmer Quarterly, 39,* 535–550.

Laursen, B., & Bukowski, W. M. (1997). A developmental guide to the organization of close relationships. *International Journal of Behavioral Development, 21,* 747–770.

Laursen, B., & Jensen-Campbell, L. A. (1999). The nature and functions of social exchange in adolescent romantic relationships. In W. Furman, B. B. Brown, & C. Feiring (Eds.), *The development of romantic relationships in adolescence* (pp. 50–74). New York: Cambridge University Press.

Leonard, K. H., & Roberts, L. J. (1998). Marital aggression, quality, and stability in the first year of marriage: Findings from the Buffalo newlywed study. In T. N. Bradbury (Ed.), *The developmental course of marital dysfunction* (pp. 44–73). New York: Cambridge University Press.

Main, M. (1996). Introduction to the special section on attachment and psychopathology: 2. Overview of the field of attachment. *Journal of Consulting and Clinical Psychology, 64,* 237–243.

Miller, B. C., & Benson, B. (1999). Romantic and sexual relationships development during adolescence. In W. Furman, B. B. Brown, & C. Feiring (Eds.), *The development of romantic relationships in adolescence* (pp. 99–124). Cambridge, UK: Cambridge University Press.

Neemann, J., Hubbard, J., & Masten, A. S. (1993). The changing importance of romantic relationship involvement to competence from late childhood to late adolescence. *Development and Psychopathology, 7,* 727–750.

Orlofsky, J. L. (1976). Intimacy status: Relationships to interpersonal perceptions. *Journal of Youth and Adolescence, 5,* 73–88.

Papp, P. (1989). The godfather. In M. Walters, B. Carter, P. Papp, & O. Silverstein (Eds.), *The invisible web: Gender patterns in family relationships* (pp. 229–246). New York: Guilford Press.

Perry, D. G., Perry, L. C., & Kennedy, E. (1992). Conflict and the development of antisocial behavior. In C. U. Shantz & W. W. Hartup (Eds.), *Conflict in child and adolescent development.* New York: Cambridge University Press.

Reis, H. T., & Shaver, P. (1988). Intimacy as an interpersonal process. In S. Duck (Ed.), *Handbook of personal relationships: Theory, relationships, and intervention* (pp. 367–389). Chichester: Wiley.

Reiss, D. (1981). *The family's construction of reality.* Cambridge, MA: Harvard University Press.

Reese-Weber, M., & Bartle–Haring, S. (1998). Conflict resolution styles in family subsystems and adolescent romantic relationships. *Journal of Youth and Adolescence, 27,* 735–752.

Rubinstein, J. L., & Feldman, S. S. (1993). Conflict resolution behavior in adolescent boys: Antecedents and adaptational correlates. *Journal of Research on Adolescence, 3,* 41–66.

Rusbult, C. E., Bissonnette, V. L., Arriaga, X. B., & Cox, C. l. (1998). Accommodation processes during the early years of marriage. In T. N. Bradbury (Ed.), *The developmental course of marital dysfunction* (pp. 74–113). New York: Cambridge University Press.

Schultz, L. H., & Selman, R. L. (1989). Bridging the gap between interpersonal thought and action in early adolescence: The role of psychodynamic processes. *Development and Psychopathology, 1,* 133–152.

Seiffge-Krenke, I. (1997). The capacity to balance intimacy and conflict: Differences in romantic between healthy and diabetic adolescents. In S. Shulman & W. A. Collins (Eds.), *Romantic relationships in adolescence: Developmental perspectives* (pp. 53–68). San Francisco: Jossey-Bass.

Selman, R. L. (1980). *The growth of interpersonal understanding: Developmental and clinical analyses.* New York: Academic Press.

Selman, R. L. (1990). Fostering intimacy and autonomy. In W. Damon (Ed.), *Child development today and tomorrow* (pp. 409–435). San Francisco: Jossey Bass.

Shantz, C. U. (1987). Conflict between children. *Child Development, 58,* 283–305.

Shulman, S., Elicker, J., & Sroufe, L. A. (1994). Stages of friendship growth in preadolescence as related to attachment history. *Journal of Social and Personal Relationships, 11,* 341–362.

Shulman S., & Knafo, D. (1997). Balancing closeness and individuality in adolescent close relationships. *International Journal of Behavioral Development, 21,* 687–702.

Shulman, S., & Laursen, B. (2002). Adolescent perceptions of conflict in interdependent and disengaged friendships. *Journal of Adolescent Research, 12,* 353–372.

Shulman, S., Levy-Shiff, R., Kedem, P., & Alon, E. (1997). Intimate relationships among adolescent romantic partners and same-sex friends: Individual and systemic perspectives. In S. Shulman & W. A. Collins (Eds.), *Romantic relationships in adolescence: Developmental perspectives* (pp. 37–51). San Francisco: Jossey-Bass.

Shulman, S., & Scharf, M. (2000a). Adolescent romantic behaviors and perceptions: Age-related differences and links with family and peer relationships. *Journal of Research on Adolescence, 10,* 99–118.

Shulman, S., & Scharf, M. (2000b, March). *Adolescent romantic relationships: A look from the future.* Paper presented at the eighth biennial meeting of the Society for Research on Adolescence, Chicago.

Simon, R. W., Eder, D., & Evans, C. (1992). The development of feeling norms underlying romantic love among adolescent females. *Social Psychology Quarterly, 55,* 29–46.

Simpson, J. A. (1990). Influence of attachment styles on romantic relationships. *Journal of Personality and Social Psychology, 59,* 971–980.

Simpson, J. A., Rholes, W. S., & Phillips, D. (1996). Conflict in close relationships: An attachment perspective. *Journal of Personality and Social Psychology, 71,* 899–914.

Smetana, J. G. (1989). Adolescents' and parents' reasoning about actual family conflicts. *Child Development, 60,* 1052–1067.

Sroufe, L. A., & Fleeson, J. (1986). Attachment and the construction of relationships. In W. W. Hartup & Z. Rubin (Eds.), *Relationships and development* (pp. 57–71). Hillsdale, NJ: Lawrence Erlbaum Associates.

Steil, J. M. (1994). Equality and entitlement in marriage: Benefits and barriers. In M. J. Lerner & G. Mikula (Eds.), *Entitlement and the affectional bond: Justice in close relationships* (pp. 229–258). New York: Plenum Press.

Sternberg, R. J. (1998). *Cupid's arrow, the course of love through time.* New York: Cambridge University Press

Sullivan, H. S. (1953). *The interpersonal theory of psychiatry.* New York: Norton.

Welsh, D. P., Galliher, R. V., Kawaguchi, M. C., & Rostosky, S. S. (1999). Discrepancies in adolescent romantic couples' and observers' perceptions of couple interaction and their relationship to depressive symptoms. *Journal of Youth and Adolescence, 28,* 645–666.

Wynne, L. C. (1970). Communication disorders and the quest for relatedness in families of schizophrenics. *American Journal of Psychoanalysis, 30,* 100–114.

Wynne, L. C. (1984). The epigenesis of relational systems: A model for understanding family development. *Family Process, 23,* 297–318.

Wynne, L. C., Rycoff, I., Day. J., & Hirsch, S. (1958). Pseudomutuality in families of schizophrenics. *Psychiatry, 1,* 205–250.

6

Attachment Styles and Adolescent Sexuality

Jessica L. Tracy
Phillip R. Shaver
University of California, Davis

Austin W. Albino
M. Lynne Cooper
University of Missouri, Columbia

For many adolescents, the teen years are a time of intense challenge and change, even though theorists continue to argue about the applicability of the German phrase *stürm und drang* ("storm and stress"; Hall, 1904) to adolescence (e.g., Arnett, 1999; Offer & Schonert-Reichl, 1992). According to Arnett (1999), adolescence is the developmental period during which individuals are most likely to face the triple strain of conflict with parents, severe mood swings, and a propensity toward risk-taking. For many adolescents, romantic relationships are an important source of extreme feelings, both positive and negative (Larson & Asmussen, 1991). The typical adolescent is moving away from parents as primary attachment figures, relying more on the opinions and support of peers, and—whether consciously or not—moving toward a time when his or her primary attachment figure will be a lover or spouse rather than a parent (Hazan & Zeifman, 1994, 1999). Adolescents typically experience emotional turmoil in connection with romantic relationships—those they have, those that go awry, and those they fantasize (Larson, Clore, & Wood, 1999).

Across adolescence, the time spent with peers in general and opposite-sex peers in particular increases substantially, and the time spent with family members decreases proportionally—by 60% from fifth to twelfth grade (Larson, Richards, Moneta, Holmbeck, & Duckett, 1996; Sharabany, Gershoni, & Hofman, 1981). In addition, teens begin to use each other as sources of support and intimacy as well as amusement and entertainment (Furman & Wehner, 1994; Hazan & Zeifman, 1994). This change is part of the gradual, documented shift of primary attachment from parents to peers (Fraley & Davis, 1997; Trinke & Bartholomew, 1997).

Adolescence is also an important period for self-definition and identity formation (Block & Robins, 1993; Dusek & Flaherty, 1981; Erikson, 1968; Harter, 1998). When older adults look back over their lives, adolescence and young adulthood are the periods most densely packed with self-defining memories, many of which were emotionally charged when acquired and still evoke strong emotions when recalled (McAdams, 1988; Rubin, Rahhal, & Poon, 1998; Thorne, 2000). Early romantic and sexual experiences are likely to be among those memories, because they are novel, personally and socially significant, dangerous in real and imagined ways, and the foundation for later sexual and mating experiences. They can contribute to an adolescent's developing identity and growing sense of competence, or inflict painful feelings of humiliation that damage self-esteem. They can provide what Bowlby (1969/1982) called a safe haven and a secure base—the major provisions of a secure attachment relationship—or make a teenager feel that safety and security are precarious and perhaps unattainable. When a romantic relationship works, it can help partners figure out who they are and whom they wish to be, heighten positive emotion and boost self-esteem, and provide training in intimacy and mutual affirmation that contribute favorably to subsequent relationships (Larson et al., 1999).

Clearly, not everyone experiences adolescence or adolescent relationships in the same way. There are differences related to gender, personality, and social history. One potentially important variable is attachment style, an individual-difference construct that includes conscious and unconscious beliefs and feelings about the self and close relationship partners. These beliefs and feelings are theorized to stem from previous experiences in close relationships with parents, caregivers, siblings, and peers. In studies of adults (mostly college students), individual differences in attachment style have been associated with a host of relationship behaviors and outcomes (see reviews by Feeney, 1999; Shaver & Clark, 1994; Shaver & Hazan, 1993). Until recently, however, similar studies had not been conducted with adolescents, whose self-concepts are less likely than those of adults to possess tightly interwoven attachment and sexual components, and who are less likely to be autonomous from parents.

In the present chapter we use data from a large, representative study of adolescents in one American city to explore the possibility that differences in attachment style are related to sexual behavior that occurs in the context of fledgling romantic relationships. We begin by providing a brief overview of research on intrapsychic and interpersonal processes associated with attachment style in college-age and older samples. We then use these previous studies as a source of hypotheses about ways in which attachment style in adolescence might be related to sexual behaviors and experiences. Next, we test the hypotheses and discuss implications of the results for research on adolescent sexuality and romantic relationships, and for possible interventions to help insecure adolescents navigate the difficult passage from childhood to adulthood relationships.

THEORY AND RESEARCH
ON ADULT ATTACHMENT

Attachment theory was proposed by Bowlby (1973, 1980, 1969/1982) in a series of volumes entitled *Attachment and Loss,* and operationalized in a series of studies by Ainsworth and her colleagues (Ainsworth, Blehar, Waters, & Wall, 1978). At the heart of the theory is an innate set of psychological processes that Bowlby and Ainsworth called the *attachment behavioral system.* Especially during infancy, this neurobehavioral system, which humans share with other primates, is—especially under conditions of real or imagined threat —vigilant concerning the availability and sensitivity of a protective other whom the theory calls an attachment figure. If a young child's attachment figure proves to be generally available, sensitive, and responsive to the child's signals of distress (i.e., proves to be a safe haven in times of distress and a secure base from which to explore one's capacities and environment when distress is absent), the child develops secure "working models" of self and attachment figures and generally enjoys a psychological state called *felt security* (Sroufe & Waters, 1977). In contrast, if a child's attachment figure is either inconsistently available or consistently unavailable psychologically, the child develops nonoptimal, insecure working models of self and/or attachment figures that adversely affect subsequent close relationships.

Ainsworth et al. (1978) identified three major patterns of infant–caregiver attachment, which they called *secure, anxious* (or insecure/ambivalent or insecure/resistant), and *avoidant* (or insecure/avoidant). Classification of infants at ages 12 to 18 months proved to be predictive of a wide range of social and emotional developments months and years later (see, e.g., Weinfield, Sroufe, Egeland, & Carlson, 1999, for a review). In 1987, Hazan and Shaver proposed that attachment theory be extended to the realm of adolescent and adult romantic/sexual relationships. These authors created a simple self-report measure of attachment style that asked adolescent and adult respondents which of three descriptions of feelings and behavior in romantic relationships was most similar to their own. The three descriptions, labeled *secure, anxious,* and *avoidant,* were extrapolated from Ainsworth et al.'s (1978) descriptions of the three major patterns of infant–caregiver attachment. This measure proved to be related in theoretically predictable ways to cognitive models of self and relationship partners, feelings of confidence versus insecurity in romantic relationships, relational behavior (e.g., intimacy, provision of support, constructive communication and handling of conflict), relationship stability, and reactions to breakups.

Specifically, avoidant adults tend to be relatively uninterested in romantic relationships (Shaver & Brennan, 1992), have a higher breakup rate than secure adults (Hazan & Shaver, 1987; Kirkpatrick & Davis, 1994; Shaver & Brennan, 1992), and grieve less following a breakup (Simpson, 1990). Conversely, anxious adults tend to be obsessed with romantic partners and suffer from extreme jealousy (Carnelley, Pietromonaco, & Jaffe, 1996; Collins, 1996; Hazan & Shaver, 1987), which in the case of anxious men can lead to abusive behavior (Dutton, Saunders, Starzomski, & Bartholomew, 1994). Like avoidance, anxious attachment is also related to a high breakup rate. Secure adults tend to be highly invested in relationships and to have long, stable ones characterized by trust, friendship, and frequent positive emotions (Collins & Read, 1990; Hazan & Shaver, 1987; Kirkpatrick & Davis, 1994; Simpson, 1990).

Overall, it appears that Bowlby's characterization of the attachment behavioral system applies well to adults. Fraley and Shaver (1998) unobtrusively observed adult couples in waiting areas at airports and coded their contact-seeking behavior before learning whether both partners were boarding a plane together or were about to separate. Contact seeking was much more intense in couples who subsequently separated. Moreover, avoidant individuals (identified with a brief questionnaire) expressed less distress than nonavoidant individuals, and more anxious individuals felt more upset about separation. Mikulincer, Gillath, and Shaver (2002) found in a series of experiments involving college student participants that subliminal presentation of threat words, such as "failure" and "separation," automatically caused the names of participants' attachment figures to become mentally accessible. In other words, mental representations of attachment figures were automatically activated under threatening conditions. Interestingly, more anxious individuals exhibited chronic activation of mental representations of attachment figures even under relatively nonthreatening conditions, and more avoidant individuals exhibited *inhibition* of attachment figures' names when the subliminal threat word was attachment-related ("separation"), but not when the word was "failure." Such studies show that simple self-report measures of attachment style are associated with theoretically predictable differences in social behavior and unconscious mental processes.

There have been relatively few studies of attachment style and sexual behavior, but in an early study of adults, Hazan, Zeifman, and Middleton (1994) found that attachment security was related to enjoyment of a variety of sexual activities, including mutual initiation of sexual activity and enjoyment of physical contact, usually in the context of a long-term relationship. Attachment anxiety was related to anxiety about sexual attractiveness and acceptability—an extension of anxious individuals' general concern with rejection and abandonment—and was also related to greater liking for the affectionate and intimate aspects of sexuality than for the genital aspects. Attachment avoidance was related to dislike of much of sexuality, especially the affectionate and intimate aspects. Fraley, Davis, and Shaver (1998) obtained similar results in studies aimed primarily at understanding avoidant attachment. Avoidance was related negatively to holding hands, mutual gazing, cuddling, feeling comfortable when held, and verbally expressing love for one's partner during sex. Avoidance has also been found, however, to be positively associated in adulthood with more accepting attitudes toward casual sex (Feeney, Noller, & Patty, 1993) and more frequent "one-night stands" (Brennan & Shaver, 1995; Hazan et al., 1994).

We can summarize these preliminary investigations by saying that reactions to sexual intimacy are part and parcel of attachment patterns. Attachment security is conducive to intimacy; sharing; considerate communication; and openness to sexual exploration. Attachment anxiety includes deep, general concerns about rejection and abandonment which are easily imported into sexual situations. Similarly, attachment avoidance interferes with intimate, relaxed sexuality because sex inherently calls for physical closeness and psychological intimacy, a major source of discomfort for avoidant individuals.

HYPOTHESES CONCERNING ATTACHMENT STYLES, RELATIONSHIPS, AND SEX IN ADOLESCENCE

Based on the extensive literature concerning attachment styles and close relationships, and on the still scanty literature on attachment styles and sexuality in adulthood, we proposed three broad hypotheses for the research summarized in this chapter.

Hypothesis 1

Anxious adolescents' sexual and dating behaviors in romantic relationships should reflect their prevalent concerns about rejection and abandonment. Anxious teens are likely to allow themselves to become quickly involved in sexual encounters in order to feel close to their partners and (especially in the case of anxious girls, who may believe that sex is important to their male partners) to avoid being abandoned. Anxious adolescents can be expected to fall in love easily (as happens with anxious adults; Hazan & Shaver, 1987) and view sex as a means of expressing love. Unfortunately, they are unlikely to experience positive emotions during their sexual experiences because of the nagging concern that their partners will find them deficient and reject or abandon them. Thus, despite having passionate feelings for their partners, anxious adolescents may find sexual encounters more troubling than pleasurable. Furthermore, they may look to alcohol and drugs to reduce anxiety about sexual encounters.

Hypothesis 2

Avoidant adolescents' sexual and dating behaviors should reflect their discomfort with intimacy and unwillingness or inability to form close bonds with others. Their sexual discomfort may be manifested psychologically as erotophobia and behaviorally as reluctance to enter romantic/sexual relationships. When they do choose to have sex, perhaps mostly for extrinsic reasons (e.g., to comply with peer pressure to lose their virginity), avoidant adolescents will likely experience intrapsychic tensions that make intimacy and positive emotions other than sexual arousal difficult to obtain. Their discomfort may be so great that they experience negative rather than positive emotions during sex, and they may use alcohol and drugs to help themselves relax. Their avoidant tendencies may have benefits as well as liabilities, making it easy for them to downplay the importance of romantic/sexual relationships and experiences and thereby avoid becoming overly invested in relationships that are unlikely to last.

Hypothesis 3

Secure adolescents' sexual and dating behaviors in romantic relationships will reflect their underlying positive views of self and other and their resultant capacity to feel comfortable with intimacy. They may experience some anxiety in these situations, as is natural for any teenager participating in new, psychologically significant activities, but their fears are likely to be realistic rather than neurotic. Secure adolescents should also be able to acknowledge their sexual drives; they should be less erotophobic and less likely to display aggression or to become the victims of aggression in sexual relationships. Their comfort with intimacy and their ability to engage in intimate, considerate communication with partners may allow them to have sexual intercourse within the context of semi-committed, relatively long relationships. Secure adolescents should experience positive emotions in their sexual encounters and obtain a sense of increased competence and esteem from them. They should feel connected to their partners and be motivated to have sex at least partially by a desire to express feelings of love.

BACKGROUND AND METHODS
OF THE STUDY

Sample and Procedure

The analyses reported in this chapter were based on a subset of 2,011 adolescents aged 13 to 19 residing in Buffalo, New York, in 1989–1990 who participated in a larger study of psychosocial factors affecting health risk behavior (see Cooper, Peirce, & Huselid, 1994; Cooper, Shaver, & Collins, 1998, for details). Adolescents in this subsample (all but 41 of the original sample) completed the attachment style measure (described later). Random-digit-dial techniques were used to identify study participants, and telephone exchanges concentrated in primarily Black neighborhoods were over-sampled to yield a final sample that was 48% White, 44% Black, and 8% other racial groups (mostly Hispanic- and Asian-American). Boys and girls were represented in roughly equal numbers, and respondents were fairly evenly distributed across the 13 to 19 age range, with a mean of 16.7 years.

Face-to-face interviews were conducted by 30 professionally trained interviewers using a structured interview schedule. Interviewers and respondents were always matched on sex and, when possible, race (about 75% of the cases). Average interview length was 2 hours, and respondents were paid $25 for participating. The interview contained both interviewer-administered and self-administered portions. Sexual behavior and attitudes were assessed using interviewer-administration of less threatening questions and private, self-administration of more sensitive questions. Respondents were provided with simply worded definitions of sexual behavior to ensure a common understanding of key terms.

Measures

Attachment Style. Attachment style was measured in two ways using a slightly modified version of Hazan and Shaver's (1987, 1990) questionnaire, the only self-report measure available when the study was designed. Each respondent was first asked whether he or she had ever been involved in a serious romantic relationship. If the answer was yes (75% of the sample), the respondent was asked to answer the attachment questions with respect to experiences during those relationships. If the answer was no, the respondent was asked to imagine what his or her experiences *would* be like in such relationships. Respondents read each of three attachment-style descriptions and rated how self-characteristic each style was on a 7-point Likert-type scale (which produced three quantitative ratings). They were then asked to choose which of the three styles was most self-descriptive (a categorical measure). The three answer alternatives were worded as follows:

- *Avoidant.* I am somewhat uncomfortable being close to others; I find it difficult to trust them completely, difficult to allow myself to depend on them. I am nervous when anyone gets too close, and often, love partners want me to be more intimate than I feel comfortable being.
- *Anxious-Ambivalent.* I find that others are reluctant to get as close as I would like. I often worry that my partner doesn't really love me or won't want to stay with me. I want to get very close to my partner, and this sometimes scares people away.
- *Secure.* I find it relatively easy to get close to others and am comfortable depending on them. I don't often worry about being abandoned or about someone getting too close to me.

The construct validity of both the categorical and quantitative measures has been established in scores of studies published since 1987 (see Feeney, 1999, and Shaver & Clark, 1994, for reviews). In the present study, a procedure used by Mikulincer and others (e.g., Mikulincer, Florian, & Tolmacz, 1990) was used to distinguish consistent from inconsistent responders. Inconsistent respondents (20% of the sample) were excluded from further analyses because their highest Likert rating failed to correspond to the attachment style chosen as most self-characteristic (see Cooper et al., 1998, for a detailed comparison of consistent and inconsistent respondents).

Dating and Relationship Experiences.   Four aspects of dating and relationship experience were assessed. Respondents were asked whether they currently had a boy- or girlfriend, or were dating someone seriously.[1] Answers were scored 0 = No; 1 = Yes. They were also asked to indicate the number of times they had ever been involved in a serious romantic relationship (defined as a

---

[1]The respondents were also asked about sexual orientation, using a 5-point continuous scale where 1 = completely heterosexual and 5 = completely homosexual. Only 5% of the sample labeled themselves anything other than completely heterosexual (4% mostly heterosexual, 0.8% equally attracted to males and females; less than 0.5% either mostly or completely homosexual). Nevertheless, sexual orientation was significantly related to attachment style. Insecure adolescents were slightly more likely than secure adolescents to describe themselves as homosexual (means were 1.09 for avoidants, 1.08 for anxious, and 1.03 for secure respondents; eta squared = .01). In no case, however, did controlling for sexual orientation change the substantive conclusions of our analyses. Moreover, in several cases the results became stronger after controlling for sexual orientation, suggesting that in these instances sexual orientation slightly suppressed the relationship between attachment style and sexual variables. For the purposes of the present chapter, we decided not to present detailed analyses involving sexual orientation.

"relationship in which you had very strong feelings for the other person and saw only this person or mainly this person"), and the number of times they had been "in love." Finally, those who had ever been on a date (85%) were asked how often they had been on a date in the past 6 months. Answers were scored on a 0 (not at all) to 4 (3 or more times/week) scale. Number of dating partners in the past 6 months was also assessed, but did not differ significantly across attachment groups.

General Sexual Experience. Respondents were asked whether they had ever had sexual intercourse. Virgins (36%) were asked to complete a series of questions about any sexual experiences they may have had, ranging from kissing to petting above the waist and below the waist and oral sex. These data were used to create an ordinal scale that ranged from 0 = no contact whatsoever to 4 = oral sex. This rank-ordering of behaviors can be justified in terms of its relation to a well-known development sequence of sexual experiences leading up to intercourse (see Miller, Christopherson, & King, 1993). Non-virgins were asked to indicate how often they had had intercourse in the past 6 months on a 1 (not at all) to 5 (3 or more times/week) scale. Finally, male respondents were asked whether they had ever used verbal or physical force to make a woman or a girl do something sexual or have intercourse when she didn't want to, and female respondents were asked parallel questions about their male partners' use of verbal or physical force against them. From these questions, the following ordinal scale was formed: 0 = no verbal or physical force ever used; 1 = use of threats or verbal coercion only; 2 = use of physical force (with or without verbal coercion) to engage in some sexual behavior *other than intercourse;* 3 = use of physical force (with or without verbal coercion) to engage in intercourse. (See Cooper et al., 1998, for analyses of attachment styles in relation to other aspects of sexual experience.)

Experiences on Specific Occasions of Intercourse. Sexually experienced respondents were asked a series of questions regarding three discrete occasions of intercourse: (a) their first intercourse experience; (b) their last intercourse experience; and (c) their first sexual experience with their most recent partner, if they had intercourse more than once with that partner. Depending on each individual's idiosyncratic sexual history, he or she might have experienced one, two, or all three of these sexual events. Thus, valid *ns* vary across occasions. For each kind of occasion respondents had experienced, they were asked about their reasons for having sex, the emotions they recall experiencing, and their substance use on that occasion.

Motives for having sex were assessed by five items asking respondents to rate on a 1 (not at all) to 5 (extremely) scale how important each of the following reasons was on that specific occasion: (a) expressing love for your partner; (b) having a good time; (c) proving that you were attractive or desirable; (d) being carried away by the excitement of it all; and (e) fear that your partner would leave you or not like you anymore. For first intercourse, respondents also rated the extent to which a desire to lose their virginity motivated intercourse. However, because attachment style differences were not consistently observed for the second, third, and fourth reasons, only data for expressing love, fear of partner rejection, and losing virginity are discussed in the present chapter.

Emotions experienced during sex were assessed by an adjective checklist. A count of the number of negative (including *nervous, scared, worried, frustrated, angry, disgusted, guilty, sad, jealous, rejected, bored, uneasy, vulnerable, confused, lonely, disappointed, insecure,* and *self-conscious*) and positive (including *excited, powerful, affectionate, happy, aroused, contented, mature, proud, passionate, confident, calm, hopeful, interested,* and *caring*) emotion words were analyzed separately. A subset of positive words assessing feelings of passion, love, and arousal were also examined. Alphas for the negative and positive emotion words, respectively, ranged from .72 to .76, and from .34 to .63, across the three occasions. Coefficient alphas for the more homogeneous subset of passion words ranged from .53 to .59 across the three occasions.

Substance use was measured by two items asking whether the respondent had consumed any alcohol prior to or during intercourse, or smoked marijuana or used any other drugs prior to or during intercourse. These data were used to create a dichotomy in which 0 = no alcohol, marijuana, or other drugs and 1 = any substance consumed. Use of alcohol or drugs by the respondent's partner was also assessed using a single item scored in the same manner (0 = none, 1 = any). Finally, respondents were asked to rate the degree of intoxication they felt on that occasion on a 1 (not at all high) to 4 (extremely high) scale. In addition, respondents who had sex in the past 6 months were asked to report how often they were drunk or very, very high when they had intercourse. Responses ranged from 1 (none of the time) to 5 (every time/nearly every time), and comprised a scale representing frequency of intoxication during sex.

Two kinds of *situation perceptions* were assessed about each occasion or situation. Respondents answered two questions about how important that particular sexual situation was to them and how much they cared about how it turned out. The two items formed a reliable composite across all three situations (alphas ranged from .63 to .71). Respondents also answered three questions about their confidence in their ability to handle the situation, including the amount of perceived control in the situation, how much they doubted their ability to handle the situation (reverse scored), and overall how confident they felt in that situation. These items also formed a reliable composite scale across the three situations (alphas ranged from .68 to .72).

Psychological Attitudes Toward Sex.   Three measures of psychological attitudes toward sex were included. The Erotophobia subscale by Fisher, Byrne, and White (1983) assesses attitudes and feelings about sexual topics (alpha = .73). Need for sex was measured with five items developed for the present study to assess the importance of being and feeling sexual. Items were rated on a 5-point scale ranging from 1 = not at all to 5 = extremely (e.g., "In general, how important is sex to you?"; alpha = .84). Sexual competence was assessed with six items developed for the present study in which respondents rated the degree of confidence (on a 6-point scale) they felt in their ability to be a responsive and caring lover and to get their sexual needs met (alpha = .77).

TESTS OF THE HYPOTHESES

The hypotheses were tested by a series of covariance analyses in which attachment style was treated as a three-category independent variable, with gender and age controlled. The tables included in the present chapter contain covariate-adjusted means for each variable broken down by attachment style, statistical significance levels, and amount of variance accounted for (eta squared). Interactions of attachment style with both age (coded as a three-level variable [13 to 14; 15 to 17; 18 to 19]) and gender were tested in an additional series of analyses where attachment style, gender, and age group were all treated as factors. Although we chose not to show interactions in the tables, we will mention interactions involving gender and age when they arise.

The upper half of Table 6.1 displays results concerning dating and romantic relationships. Avoidant adolescents were least likely ever to have had a date or to be currently involved in a romantic relationship; they had participated in the fewest serious relationships and had been in love the fewest number of times. Anxious adolescents had been in love the most times. Among adolescents who had ever been on a date, secures reported the most frequent dating during the previous six months, which was partly, but not completely, a consequence of their being more likely to be in a long-term relationship. Thus, as expected, the secure attachment style was associated with frequent dating and participation in romantic relationships. Furthermore, anxious adolescents reported almost equally high rates of dating and higher rates of being in love, supporting previous findings that adolescents high in anxiety are more likely than others to experience what they interpret as passionate love, possibly beginning as early as age 12 (Hatfield, Brinton, & Cornelius, 1989).

The lower half of Table 6.1 summarizes results for various sexual experience variables: ever having intercourse, amount of sexual experience for those who had not had intercourse, frequency of intercourse during the 6 months prior to

TABLE 6.1
Experience with Dating, Relationships, and Sex

Dating and Relationship Variables	Attachment Style			
	Secure	Anxious	Avoidant	Eta Squared
Ever had a date	.87$_a$ (.34)	.87$_a$ (.33)	.79$_b$ (.42)	.010**
Currently in relationship	.62$_a$ (.49)	.60$_a$ (.49)	.46$_b$ (.50)	.017***
Number times in serious relationship	1.39$_a$ (1.18)	1.48$_a$ (1.14)	1.23$_b$ (1.18)	.006*
Number times in love	1.02$_a$ (1.01)	1.15$_b$ (1.04)	.90$_c$ (1.12)	.006**
Of those who have ever been on date				
Frequency of dating, past 6 months	2.61$_a$ (1.08)	2.36$_b$ (1.15)	2.33$_b$ (1.15)	.014***

Sexual Experience Variables	Secure	Anxious	Avoidant	Eta Squared
Ever had intercourse	66%$_a$ (.47)	69%$_a$ (.46)	52%$_b$ (.50)	.022**
Sexual experience; virgins only	.88$_a$ (1.40)	.83$_a$ (1.44)	.57$_b$ (1.21)	.011*
Frequency of intercourse, past 6 months	2.06$_a$ (1.06)	1.94$_a$ (1.08)	1.81$_b$ (1.04)	.007*
Sexual aggression	.32$_a$ (.76)	.43$_b$ (.90)	.44$_b$ (.96)	.005*

Note. Values in parentheses are standard deviations. Means and percentages with a common letter subscript are not significantly different at the p level specified.
*$p < .05$. **$p < .01$. ***$p < .001$.

assessment, and (in the case of girls) experiencing or (for boys) perpetrating sexual aggression. As previously reported (Cooper et al., 1998), avoidant adolescents were the least likely ever to have had sexual intercourse (52% vs. 66% and 69% for secure and anxious adolescents) and, among virgins, they reported the least sexual experience. Among girls in particular, anxiously attached adolescents had the most sexual experience, whereas among boys, securely attached adolescents had the most experience. In the younger age groups, anxiously attached individuals had more sexual experience, but among older adolescents, secure individuals did. Secure and anxious adolescents, as compared with avoidant adolescents, also reported greater frequency of intercourse during the 6 months prior to assessment, but there were no significant differences in the number of partners reported among the three groups during this period. Finally, secure adolescents (of both genders) were less likely than insecure adolescents to report perpetration of or victimization by sexual aggression. (This latter finding is compatible with the research on older samples by Dutton et al., 1994, showing that men's attachment insecurity is associated with abusive behavior.) Thus, as predicted, avoidant adolescents had the least sexual experience and secure adolescents were least likely to have been involved in sexual aggression.

The upper half of Table 6.2 presents results concerning motives for having sex on three different occasions of intercourse (the first time ever, the first time with the most recent partner, and the most recent time with the most recent partner). Attachment style was related to motives for having sex at all three

TABLE 6.2
Motives For and Emotions During Sex

| Motives for Having Sex | Attachment Style | | | |
	Secure	Anxious	Avoidant	Eta Squared
First time				
Fear partner leaving	1.59$_a$ (.98)	1.94$_b$ (1.28)	1.69$_a$ (1.08)	.019***
To express love	3.09 (1.33)	3.15 (1.36)	3.04 (1.31)	.001
To lose virginity	2.72$_a$ (1.45)	2.88$_{ab}$ (1.55)	3.05$_b$ (1.60)	.007*
First time with most recent partner				
Fear partner leaving	1.40$_a$ (.84)	1.60$_b$ (1.09)	1.45$_a$ (.93)	.008*
To express love	3.26$_a$ (1.25)	3.24$_a$ (1.37)	2.86$_b$ (1.38)	.013**
Most recent sex				
Fear partner leaving	1.21$_a$ (.65)	1.43$_b$ (.93)	1.27$_a$ (.79)	.014**
To express love	3.91$_a$ (1.06)	3.91$_a$ (1.17)	3.60$_b$ (1.26)	.011*
Emotions experienced during sex	Secure	Anxious	Avoidant	Eta Squared
First Time				
Negative	.31$_a$ (.19)	.36$_b$ (.21)	.35$_b$ (.20)	.020***
Positive overall	.48 (.27)	.46 (.26)	.46 (.29)	.001
Passionate	.64 (.52)	.58 (.50)	.62 (.53)	.003
First time with most recent partner				
Negative	.17$_a$ (.16)	.23$_b$ (.19)	.24$_b$ (.21)	.034***
Positive overall	.59$_a$ (.24)	.54$_{ab}$ (.30)	.53$_b$ (.29)	.009*
Passionate	.75$_a$ (.54)	.65$_b$ (.56)	.66$_{ab}$ (.53)	.008*
Most recent sex				
Negative	.06$_a$ (.10)	.11$_b$ (.18)	.13$_b$ (.18)	.043***
Positive overall	.68$_a$ (.22)	.65$_{ab}$ (.26)	.62$_b$ (.27)	.009*
Passionate	1.03$_a$ (.58)	.89$_b$ (.59)	.92$_{ab}$ (.59)	.012*

Note. Values in parentheses are standard deviations. Means and percentages with a common letter subscript are not significantly different at the *p* level specified.
*$p < .05$. **$p < .01$. ***$p < .001$.

time points. On the first occasion of sexual intercourse, especially for girls, anxious attachment was associated with having sex because of fear of losing one's partner. Especially in the middle age group (15- to 17-year-olds), avoidant attachment was related to having sex in order to lose one's virginity. The association between anxious attachment and having sex to hold onto one's partner, especially among girls, recurred the first and last times respondents had sex with their most recent partner. At those two time points, a new motive also became relevant: Both anxious and secure adolescents, more than their avoidant peers, had sex to express love for their partner. Thus, as expected, anxious attachment was associated with having sex to avoid abandonment, especially among girls; secure and anxious attachment were associated with having sex to express love; and avoidant attachment was related, at first intercourse, to having sex to lose one's virginity.

The lower half of Table 6.2 presents results concerning emotions experienced during sex on each of the three occasions. At each time point, secure adolescents experienced fewer negative emotions than did anxious and avoidant adolescents. There was no relation between attachment style and positive or passionate emotions at the time of first intercourse, but at both the first and the most recent times with the most recent partner, secure adolescents experienced more positive and passionate emotions than anxious or avoidant adolescents. Somewhat surprisingly, given their propensity for falling in passionate love, anxious adolescents experienced the fewest passionate emotions during sex on both of these occasions, whereas avoidant adolescents experienced the fewest positive emotions at these times. The findings tended to hold across gender, although regardless of attachment style, girls experienced more negative and fewer positive emotions than boys at all three time points. In addition, negative emotions decreased and positive emotions increased across the three points, suggesting that adolescents in this study became more comfortable emotionally as they accumulated sexual experience.

Overall, as expected, attachment style was related to emotions experienced during sexual episodes, with secure adolescents seeming to enjoy sex significantly more than their anxious and avoidant peers. Furthermore, anxious adolescents were unable to experience passionate emotions during sex, possibly because of their fear and fear-related motives for having sex. Avoidant adolescents were particularly unable to experience positive emotions other than passion (by which they may have meant sexual arousal) during sex, perhaps because they were uncomfortable with intimacy or their partners' wish that they express intimacy. These findings are particularly interesting in light of attachment-style differences in motives for having sex: Anxious adolescents have sex to feel or express love for their partner, yet their fears about closeness prevent them from actually experiencing passion-related emotions during sexual encounters. Avoidant adolescents have sex to lose their virginity without much desire for interpersonal intimacy.

Table 6.3 presents results concerning substance use prior to sex the first time and the first time with the most recent partner. (There were no significant differences for last sex, most likely owing to the low base rates of substance use reported across all attachment groups.) It is important to examine these findings while statistically controlling for more general drug and alcohol use, so that the effect of attachment style on substance use during sexual experiences can be distinguished from the significant effect of attachment style on overall substance use (Cooper et al., 1998). With this control in place, avoidant adolescents were most likely to have consumed alcohol and been intoxicated at both times, and secure adolescents were the least likely to drink at either time. This distinction between avoidant and secure adolescents (with anxious adolescents falling in between the two groups on both occasions) also applied to partners' substance use. (In many cases, both members of a couple used drugs or alcohol; the correlation between self's and partner's substance use was .81 at first intercourse, .78 on the first occasion with the most recent partner, and .70 on the last occasion.) In general, as expected, insecure attachment was related

TABLE 6.3
Substance Use During Sex Controlling for Overall Use

| Substance Use Variables | Attachment Style | | | Eta Squared |
	Secure	Anxious	Avoidant	
First time				
Substance use	9%$_a$ (.30)	13%$_{ab}$ (.34)	17%$_b$ (.37)	.009*
Intoxicated	10%$_a$ (.38)	16%$_{ab}$ (.47)	19%$_b$ (.49)	.008*
Partner substance use	11%$_a$ (.32)	13%$_{ab}$ (.34)	20%$_b$ (.40)	.009*
First time with most recent partner				
Substance use	15%$_a$ (.37)	23%$_b$ (.43)	30%$_b$ (.46)	.022***
Intoxicated	20%$_a$ (.52)	26%$_{ab}$ (.58)	36%$_b$ (.62)	.011*
Partner substance use	17%$_a$ (.37)	22%$_{ab}$ (.42)	28%$_b$ (.45)	.011*
Last six months				
Frequency of intoxication during sex	.22$_a$ (.50)	.33$_b$ (.71)	.35$_b$ (.69)	.011*

Note. Values in parentheses are standard deviations. In addition to the usual demographic covariates, all variables concerning substance use in sexual situations were controlled for more general alcohol use. Means and percentages with a common letter subscript are not significantly different at the p level specified.

*$p < .05$. **$p < .01$. ***$p < .001$.

to alcohol, drug, and overall substance use prior to first-time sex with a particular partner, suggesting a lack of self-confidence or the presence of worries about closeness or rejection. We tested this interpretation by re-estimating the relationship between attachment style and substance use prior to sex, controlling for efficacy in sexual situations. We found that sexual efficacy mediated the effect of attachment style on substance use at first sex, but not at the first sex with the most recent partner.

Table 6.4 displays results concerning how adolescents viewed themselves in each of the situations in which they had intercourse and the importance with which they imbued those situations. On all three occasions, secure adolescents felt more efficacious (more confident of their ability to "control and handle the situation") than either anxious or avoidant adolescents. Avoidant adolescents felt less efficacious and also rated the situation as less important than did secure and anxious adolescents. (The difference in reported importance of the situation occurred only for first intercourse with the most recent partner.)

Table 6.5 shows the results concerning more general sex-related psychological variables: erotophobia, sex drive, and perceived sexual competence (overall, not just in one situation). Insecurely attached adolescents, especially the anxious ones, were likely to be erotophobic. This effect was qualified, however, by both sexual experience and age. Among nonvirgins, anxiously attached adolescents were the most erotophobic, but among virgins, avoidant adolescents were the most erotophobic. This difference suggests that, for younger adoles-

TABLE 6.4
Situation Assessment During Sex

| Situation Variables | Attachment Style | | | |
	Secure	Anxious	Avoidant	Eta Squared
First time				
Sexual efficacy	3.19_a (.61)	3.02_b (.60)	3.00_b (.64)	.022***
Importance	3.33 (.72)	3.35 (.78)	3.36 (.73)	.000
First time with most recent partner				
Sexual efficacy	3.56_a (.48)	3.44_b (.49)	3.33_b (.64)	.028***
Importance	3.37_a (.67)	3.42_a (.63)	3.20_b (.86)	.011*
Most recent sex				
Sexual efficacy	3.75_a (.38)	3.58_b (.50)	3.63_b (.47)	.030***
Importance	3.46 (.61)	3.44 (.67)	3.36 (.73)	.003

Note. Values in parentheses are standard deviations. Means and percentages with a common letter subscript are not significantly different at the p level specified.
*$p < .05$. **$p < .01$. ***$p < .001$.

TABLE 6.5
Sex-Related Psychological Variables

Psychological Variables	Attachment Style			Eta Squared
	Secure	Anxious	Avoidant	
Erotophobia	2.32_a (.99)	3.50_b (1.02)	3.50_b (1.04)	.012***
Sex drive	2.92_a (.94)	2.95_a (.97)	2.76_b (.94)	.006**
Sexual competence	5.09_a (.73)	4.95_b (.79)	4.78_c (.87)	.025***
Non-virgins only				
Erotophobia	3.12_a (.92)	3.34_b (1.04)	3.23_{ab} (.99)	.011**
Virgins only				
Erotophobia	3.61_a (1.03)	3.70_a (.94)	3.97_b (.98)	.026**

Note. Values in parentheses are standard deviations. Means and percentages with a common letter subscript are not significantly different at the p level specified.
*$p < .05$. **$p < .01$. ***$p < .001$.

cents at least, avoidant individuals' sexual fears may be linked to lack of experience (i.e., to being virgins), whereas anxious adolescents' fears may be linked to over-investment and fear of rejection in sexual relationships once they start having them. In the oldest age group (18 to 19 years), secure adolescents were the most erotophobic of those who had not yet had intercourse, suggesting that although they possessed generally positive models of self and others, they were fearful specifically about sex and this fear had kept them from engaging in it.

Turning to the other sex-related psychological variables, avoidant adolescents reported a lower sex drive than the other two groups and felt the least sexually competent. Secure adolescents reported the highest levels of sexual drive and competence. In summary, as expected, the secure attachment style was associated with a more positive psychological profile regarding sexuality and sexual experiences than those displayed by adolescents with insecure attachment styles.

IMPLICATIONS, LIMITATIONS, AND FUTURE DIRECTIONS

Overall, the results corroborated predictions based on attachment theory and research. As predicted, anxious adolescents' dating and sexual experiences were strongly colored by fears of rejection and abandonment. They fell in love often, perhaps in response to a partner merely showing positive interest in them, and had sex more frequently at a young age, but were prevented from enjoying it by the fear of rejection or abandonment. This predicted pattern was especially evident among girls. Furthermore, anxious individuals were prone to use alcohol and drugs to reduce anxiety about sexual interactions.

The findings regarding the anxious attachment style help to illuminate the results of a recent study by Joyner and Udry (2000), which showed that teenagers in love, especially younger teens and girls, were at higher risk than their peers for depression and alcohol problems. The authors made what may have been a mistake in attributing these adolescent difficulties to the detrimental effects of adolescents' involvement in romantic relationships rather than to individual differences in the kinds of relationships teenagers get into. Our results suggest that an anxious attachment style contributes to early adolescent girls' desire for a romantic relationship, and that their feelings and behaviors within their ill-fated relationships contribute to depression and alcohol use.

Also as predicted, avoidant adolescents' sexual and dating profiles reflected their discomfort with intimacy and unwillingness or inability to form close bonds with others. These adolescents were relatively erotophobic, motivated to have intercourse by a desire to lose their virginity rather than to get closely involved emotionally with another person, relatively low in perceived sex drive, less sexually active than their anxious and secure peers, and less confident of their sexual competence. They were the most likely of the three groups to use alcohol and drugs to quell their sexual fears. It is interesting to note that attachment-related avoidance, which begins in early adolescence with sexual fear and relatively low sexual drive and low frequency of intercourse, can later in life become associated with non-intimate and uncommitted but not necessarily infrequent sexual encounters (Fraley et al., 1998).

As expected, secure adolescents' sexual and dating experiences coincided with their positive views of self (including sexual competence), positive views of partners, and comfort with interpersonal intimacy. These adolescents were less erotophobic, more love-oriented, more likely to be involved in a relationship, less likely to display sexual aggression or become the victims of sexual aggression, less likely to use drugs or alcohol in sexual situations, and likely to experience more positive and fewer negative emotions during sex.

The results suggest that it is misleading to draw general conclusions about romantic relationships and sexual involvement during adolescence. Adolescents with a secure attachment style, most of whom probably had a good relationship with one or both parents or other attachment figures, are likely to be involved in what, for their age, are relatively serious and supportive relationships. They tend to have enjoyable sexual experiences and, presumably, are learning something valuable about intimacy, communication, compromise, and reliance on a peer as a potential attachment figure. Avoidant and anxious adolescents who engage in sexual intercourse may do so in less favorable contexts. Our conclusion is similar to the one reached a number of years ago by Shedler and Block (1990), who found that adolescents who experimented with marijuana without becoming dependent on it were better adjusted psychologically than either those who abstained completely or those who became heavy drug users. Exploration of sexuality is a normative feature of adolescence which need not end in heartbreak or addiction.

If we were to create interventions or educational programs for *secure* adolescents, these programs might not need to do much more than provide information about safe sex, good relationship skills, and the availability and advisability of counseling for the confusion and hurt feelings that can arise in any romantic or sexual relationship. In contrast, interventions for *insecure* adolescents would need to be tailored to the nature of different individuals' underlying difficulties. Avoidant teenagers need both relational skills training, focused on the nature and importance of communication and intimacy, and drug and alcohol counseling. Their problems are likely to go unnoticed in early adolescence, because avoidant teens may seem not to have trouble with sexuality (in early adolescence, they may not be engaging in sex). Their problems may be quite serious later on, however, and may affect not only themselves but also their relationship partners, who may be hurt by their lack of caring and intimacy. Anxious teenagers, especially girls, might benefit from counseling that deals with the healthy and unhealthy goals of relationships, and the important differences between love, sex, and security. Attachment-anxious adolescents may also need the kinds of clinical help that foster more general self-esteem and good judgment.

Although our preliminary findings could prove useful in designing interventions related to adolescent romance and sexuality, several limitations should be noted. First, the measure of attachment used in our study has been revised both theoretically and psychometrically in recent years. Shortly after our data were collected, Bartholomew and Horowitz (1991) proposed that Hazan and Shaver's (1987) three-category typology of attachment styles be elaborated to include a distinction between two kinds of avoidance: fearful and dismissing. They also suggested that the resulting four attachment styles be viewed as quadrants in a two-dimensional space defined by the positivity or negativity of internal working models of self and relationship partners. Their suggestions led to a proliferation of self-report measures, reviewed and factor-analyzed by Brennan, Clark, and Shaver (1998), which can be efficiently summarized in terms of two dimensions: anxiety and avoidance. Brennan et al. (1998) created two highly reliable multi-item scales to measure the two dimensions, and Fraley, Waller, and Brennan (2000) showed how the two scales could be improved based on item-response-theory statistics. Future studies of attachment and adolescent sexuality should make use of these more precise measures, which will almost certainly yield stronger associations among theoretically related variables.

Several conceptual issues regarding attachment in adolescence need clarification. We still do not know the extent to which attachment style, in adolescence and as measured here or with the Brennan et al. (1998) scales, is a stable feature of an individual's personality or a changeable feature of the person anchored in a set of current close relationships. Furthermore, we do not know how much a person's security influences the course of his or her romantic/sexual relationships compared with how much such relationships influence the person. Studies with adults suggest bi-directional causality (Kirkpatrick & Hazan, 1994; Shaver & Brennan, 1992.)

We also do not know the extent to which adolescent romantic relationships are actually *attachment* relationships rather than, say, forms of friendship (for a discussion of some of the distinctions, see Furman & Wehner, 1997, and Mikulincer & Selinger, 2001). Research to date (e.g., Fraley & Davis, 1997; Furman & Wehner, 1997; Hazan & Zeifman, 1999; Trinke & Bartholomew, 1997) suggests that romantic partners *are* primary attachment figures for some adolescents but not for all, and that the occurrence of genuine attachment to romantic partners increases with age and with a person's degree of attachment security. Regardless of how this important theoretical issue is ultimately resolved by empirical research, our results clearly indicate that attachment styles as we measured them are associated in adolescence with theoretically predictable patterns of relationship-related sexual motives, feelings, and behaviors. We hope our preliminary findings will pave the way for further research and effective interventions informed by attachment theory.

REFERENCES

Ainsworth, M. D. S., Blehar, M., Waters, E., & Wall, S. (1978). *Patterns of attachment: A psychological study of the strange situation.* Hillsdale, NJ: Lawrence Erlbaum Associates.

Arnett, J. J. (1999). Adolescent storm and stress, reconsidered. *American Psychologist, 54,* 317–326.

Bartholomew, K., & Horowitz, L. (1991). Attachment styles among young adults: A test of a four-category model. *Journal of Personality and Social Psychology, 61,* 226–244.

Block, J., & Robins, R. W. (1993). A longitudinal study of consistency and change in self-esteem from early adolescence to early adulthood. *Child Development, 64,* 909–923.

Bowlby, J. (1973). *Attachment and loss: Vol. 2. Separation: Anxiety and anger.* New York: Basic Books.

Bowlby, J. (1980). *Attachment and loss: Vol. 3. Loss: Sadness and depression.* New York: Basic Books.

Bowlby, J. (1982). *Attachment and loss: Vol. 1. Attachment* (rev. ed.; original edition published in 1969). New York: Basic Books.

Brennan, K. A., Clark, C. L., & Shaver, P. R. (1998). Self-report measurement of adult romantic attachment: An integrative overview. In J. A. Simpson & W. S. Rholes (Eds.), *Attachment theory and close relationships* (pp. 46–76). New York: Guilford Press.

Brennan, K. A., & Shaver, P. R. (1995). Dimensions of adult attachment, affect regulation, and romantic relationship functioning. *Personality and Social Psychology Bulletin, 21,* 267–283.

Carnelley, K. B., Pietromonaco, P. R., & Jaffe, K. (1996). Attachment, caregiving, and relationship functioning in couples: Effects of self and partner. *Personal Relationships, 3,* 257–277.

Collins, N. L. (1996). Working models of attachment: Implications for explanation, emotion, and behavior. *Journal of Personality and Social Psychology, 71,* 810–832.

Collins, N. L., & Read, S. J. (1990). Adult attachment, working models, and relationship quality in dating couples. *Journal of Personality and Social Psychology, 58,* 644–663.

Cooper, M. L., Peirce, R. S., & Huselid, R. F. (1994). Substance use and sexual risk taking among Black adolescents and White adolescents. *Health Psychology, 13,* 251–262.

Cooper, M. L., Shaver, P. R., & Collins, N. L. (1998). Attachment styles, emotion regulation, and adjustment in adolescence. *Journal of Personality and Social Psychology, 74,* 1380–1397.

Dusek, J. B., & Flaherty, J. F. (1981). The development of the self-concept during the adolescent years. *Monographs of the Society for Research in Child Development, 67,* 1–61.

Dutton, D. G., Saunders, K., Starzomski, A., & Bartholomew, K. (1994). Intimacy-anger and insecure attachment as precursors of abuse in intimate relationships. *Journal of Applied Social Psychology, 24,* 1367–1386.

Erikson, E. H. (1968). *Identity: Youth and crisis.* New York: Norton.

Feeney, J. A. (1999). Adult romantic attachment and couple relationships. In J. Cassidy & P. R. Shaver (Eds.), *Handbook of attachment: Theory, research, and clinical applications* (pp. 355–377). New York: Guilford.

Feeney, J. A., Noller, P., & Patty, J. (1993). Adolescents' interactions with the opposite sex: Influence of attachment style and gender. *Journal of Adolescence, 16,* 169–186.

Fisher, W. A., Byrne, D., & White, L. A. (1983). Emotional barriers to contraception. In D. Byrne & W. A. Fisher (Eds.), *Adolescents, sex, and contraception* (pp. 207–239). Hillsdale, NJ: Lawrence Erlbaum Associates.

Fraley, R. C., & Davis, K. E. (1997). Attachment formation and transfer in young adults' close friendships and romantic relationships. *Personal Relationships, 4,* 131–144.

Fraley, R. C., Davis, K. E., & Shaver, P. R. (1998). Dismissing-avoidance and the defensive organization of emotion, cognition, and behavior. In J. A. Simpson & W. S. Rholes (Eds.), *Attachment theory and close relationships* (pp. 249–279). New York: Guilford Press.

Fraley, R. C., & Shaver, P. R. (1998). Airport separations: A naturalistic study of adult attachment dynamics in separating couples. *Journal of Personality and Social Psychology, 75,* 1198–1212.

Fraley, R. C., Waller, N. G., & Brennan, K. A. (2000). An item response theory analysis of self-report measures of adult attachment. *Journal of Personality and Social Psychology, 78,* 350–365.

Furman, W., & Wehner, E. A. (1994). Romantic views: Toward a theory of adolescent romantic relationships. In R. Montemayor (Ed.), *Advances in adolescent development: Vol. 3. Relationships in adolescence* (pp. 168–195). Thousand Oaks, CA: Sage Publications.

Furman, W., & Wehner, E. A. (1997). Adolescent romantic relationships: A developmental perspective. In S. Shulman & W. A. Collins (Eds.), *Romantic relationships in adolescence: Developmental perspectives* (pp. 21–36). San Francisco: Jossey-Bass.

Hall, G. S. (1904). *Adolescence: Its psychology and its relation to physiology, anthropology, sociology, sex, crime, religion, and education* (Vols. 1 & 2). Englewood Cliffs, NJ: Prentice-Hall.

Harter, S. (1998). The development of self-representations. In W. Damon (Ed.) & N. Eisenberg (Vol. Ed.), *Handbook of child psychology* (5th ed., Vol. 3: Social, Emotional, and Personality Development; pp. 553–617). New York: Wiley.

Hatfield, E., Brinton, C., & Cornelius, J. (1989). Passionate love and anxiety in young adolescents. *Motivation and Emotion, 13,* 271–289.

Hazan, C., & Shaver, P. R. (1987). Romantic love conceptualized as an attachment process. *Journal of Personality and Social Psychology, 52,* 511–524.

Hazan, C., & Shaver, P. R. (1990). Love and work: An attachment-theoretical perspective. *Journal of Personality and Social Psychology, 59,* 270–280.

Hazan, C., & Zeifman, D. (1994). Sex and the psychological tether. In K. Bartholomew & D. Perlman (Eds.), *Advances in personal relationships: Vol. 5. Attachment processes in adulthood* (pp. 151–177). London: Jessica Kingsley.

Hazan, C., & Zeifman, D. (1999). Pair bonds as attachments: Evaluating the evidence. In J. Cassidy & P. R. Shaver (Eds.), *Handbook of attachment: Theory, research, and clinical applications* (pp. 336–354). New York: Guilford.

Hazan, C., Zeifman, D., & Middleton, K. (1994, July). *Adult romantic attachment, affection, and sex.* Paper presented at the Seventh International Conference on Personal Relationships, Groningen, The Netherlands.

Joyner, K., & Udry, J. R. (2000). You don't bring me anything but down: Adolescent romance and depression. *Journal of Health and Social Behavior, 41,* 369–391.

Kirkpatrick, L. A., & Davis, K. E. (1994). Attachment style, gender, and relationship stability: A longitudinal analysis. *Journal of Personality and Social Psychology, 66,* 502–512.

Kirkpatrick, L. A., & Hazan, C. (1994). Attachment styles and close relationships: A four-year prospective study. *Personal Relationships, 1,* 123–142.

Larson, R., & Asmussen, L. (1991). Anger, worry, and hurt in early adolescence: An enlarging world of negative emotions. In M. E. Colten & S. Gore (Eds.), *Adolescent stress: Causes and consequences* (pp. 21–41). New York: Aldine de Gruyter.

Larson, R. W., Clore, G. L., & Wood, G. A. (1999). The emotions of romantic relationships: Do they wreak havoc on adolescents? In W. Furman, B. B. Brown, & C. Feiring (Eds.), *The development of romantic relationships in adolescence* (pp. 19–49). Cambridge, UK: Cambridge University Press.

Larson, R., Richards, M. H., Moneta, G., Holmbeck, G., & Duckett, E. (1996). Changes in adolescents' daily interactions with their families from ages 10 to 18: Disengagement and transformation. *Child Development, 32,* 744–754.

McAdams, D. P. (1988). *Power, intimacy, and the life story: Personological inquiries into identity.* New York: Guilford Press.

Mikulincer, M., Florian, V., & Tolmacz, R. (1990). Attachment styles and fear of personal death: A case study of affect regulation. *Journal of Personality and Social Psychology, 58,* 273–280.

Mikulincer, M., Gillath, O., & Shaver, P. R. (2002). Activation of the attachment system in adulthood: Threat-related primes increase the accessibility of mental representations of attachment figures. *Journal of Personality and Social Psychology, 83,* 881–895.

Mikulincer, M., & Selinger, M. (2001). The interplay between attachment and affiliation systems in adolescents' same-sex friendships: The role of attachment style. *Journal of Social and Personal Relationships, 18,* 81–106.

Miller, B. C., Christopherson, C. R., & King, P. K. (1993). Sexual behavior in adolescence. In T. P. Gullota, G. R. Adams, & R. Montemayor (Eds.), *Adolescent sexuality* (pp. 57–76). Newbury Park, CA: Sage.

Offer, D., & Schonert-Reichl, K. A. (1992). Debunking the myths of adolescence: Findings from recent research. *Journal of the American Academy of Child and Adolescent Psychiatry, 31,* 1003–1014.

Rubin, D. C., Rahhal, T. A., & Poon, L. W. (1998). Things learned in early adulthood are remembered best. *Memory and Cognition, 26,* 3–19.

Sharabany, R., Gershoni, R., & Hofman, J. E. (1981). Girlfriend, boyfriend: Age and sex differences in intimate friendship. *Developmental Psychology, 17,* 800–808.

Shaver, P. R., & Brennan, K. A. (1992). Attachment styles and the "Big Five" personality traits: Their connections with each other and with romantic relationship outcomes. *Personality and Social Psychology Bulletin, 18,* 536–545.

Shaver, P. R., & Clark, C. L. (1994). The psychodynamics of adult romantic attachment. In J. M. Masling & R. F. Bornstein (Eds.), *Empirical perspectives on object relations theory* (pp. 105–156). Washington DC: American Psychological Association.

Shaver, P. R., & Hazan, C. (1993). Adult romantic attachment: Theory and evidence. In D. Perlman & W. Jones (Eds.), *Advances in personal relationships* (Vol. 4, pp. 29–70). London: Jessica Kingsley.

Shedler, J., & Block, J. (1990). Adolescent drug use and psychological health: A longitudinal inquiry. *American Psychologist, 45,* 612–630.

Simpson, J. A. (1990). Influence of attachment styles on romantic relationships. *Journal of Personality and Social Psychology, 59,* 971–980.

Sroufe, L. A., & Waters, E. (1977). Heart rate as a convergent measure in clinical and developmental research. *Merrill-Palmer Quarterly, 23,* 3–27.

Thorne, A. (2000). Personal memory telling and personality development. *Personality and Social Psychology Review, 4,* 45–56.

Trinke, S. J., & Bartholomew, K. (1997). Hierarchies of attachment relationships in young adulthood. *Journal of Social and Personal Relationships, 14,* 603–625.

Weinfield, N. S., Sroufe, L. A., Egeland, B., & Carlson, E. A. (1999). The nature of individual differences in infant–caregiver attachment. In J. Cassidy & P. R. Shaver (Eds.), *Handbook of attachment: Theory, research, and clinical applications* (pp. 68–88). New York: Guilford.

II

PERSPECTIVES ON ROMANTIC AND SEXUAL BEHAVIOR AMONG HIGH-RISK ADOLESCENTS

7

Psychopathology and Relational Dysfunction Among Adolescent Couples: The Structural Analysis of Social Behavior as an Organizing Framework

Trina Seefeldt
Paul Florsheim
Lorna Smith Benjamin
University of Utah

When two people enter into a romantic relationship, they are usually seeking some measure of intimacy. Based on the principles of attachment theory, it is safe to assume that most romantic couples—even those who are psychologically impaired—engage in high rates of affiliative behavior (Hazan & Shaver, 1994; Tracy, Shaver, Albino, & Cooper, chap. 6, this volume). The warm expression of fondness and caring (security-seeking behavior) is a critical component of most romantic liaisons, at least in the courtship phase of engagement. However, for adolescents who are just beginning the process of learning about and engaging in intimate relationships these experiences can be especially bittersweet: In addition to expressing warmth and care, romantic partners can become demanding, attacking, jealous, and neglecting. The ups and downs of having a romantic relationship (or even an infatuation) will affect the emotional state of most adolescents. Conversely, the psychological health of an adolescent is likely to influence the quality of his or her romantic relationships.

In addition to coping with the normal stressors of learning new social roles, renegotiating family relations, and engaging in intimate relationships, a substantial number of adolescents have serious psychological problems that can undermine the normal course of interpersonal developmental processes (Levitt, Selman, & Richmond, 1991). Compared to children, adolescents are much more likely to be diagnosed with psychological disorders such as depression (Birmaher et al., 1996), alcohol and other substance abuse (Substance Abuse and Mental Health Services Administration Report, 2001), and eating disorders (Association of Anorexia Nervosa and Associated Disorders, 2000). For example, the rate of depression among adolescents is much higher than the rate among prepubescent children (approximately 8% in adolescents, compared to approximately 3% in children; Birmaher et al., 1996).

The prevalence of psychological disorders among adolescents is relevant to adolescent romantic and sexual behavior because it seems likely that adolescents diagnosed with psychological disorders would be at increased risk for engaging in dysfunctional romantic relationships. As clinically oriented developmental researchers begin to investigate the romantic relations of high risk adolescents, there is an emergent need for a conceptual model that will help discriminate among the relational risks associated with different types of psychological disorders. To illustrate, imagine you stop at a coffee shop that is a hangout for local high school students. You sit down next to a young couple, Jim and Rose, who are playfully recalling their day spent in different classes, filling each other in on the antics of their peers. Suddenly, the conversation grows more tense and uncomfortable:

Jim: So, what do you want to do tonight?
Rose: Oh, I can't get together with you tonight because I promised Rita, Deb and Kara that we'd have a girls' night out.
Jim: (whiny tone of voice) What? When did this happen?
Rose: Oh Jim, I told you a few days ago!
Jim: Well, but why can't I go with you? What am I supposed to do all by myself?
Rose: I don't know. It's just one night, Jim. I don't see my friends all that often and I'd really like to catch up with them.
Jim: Oh, so now you care more about your friends than you do about me? . . . You can't go! You can't do this to me!
Rose: (irritated) Well, I'm sorry, but I'm going. I'm sure you'll find something else to do.
Jim: (with a hurt look on his face) Well, I guess I'm the loser.
Rose: Jim, look, I'm not doing this to hurt you. I like spending time with you. After tonight we'll spend the whole weekend together.

Listening to this conversation, you cannot help but develop some hypotheses about the long-term prognosis of this relationship and the psychological profile of Jim. Unfortunately, there has been very little research to guide you in your efforts to identify links between the interpersonal processes of adolescent romantic partners and their individual psychological processes.

The goal of this chapter is to present the Structural Analysis of Social Behavior (SASB; Benjamin, 1974) as a conceptual framework and methodology for clarifying critical links between psychopathology and relational dysfunction among couples in general and adolescent couples in particular. As we describe in more detail later, the SASB is a method for describing interpersonal processes at a high level of specificity that can be used to generate an interpersonal profile for a particular individual, dyad, or group. In the first section of this chapter, we describe the SASB model and illustrate the utility of SASB for systematically describing relational patterns among both adolescent and adult couples. In the second section we discuss developmental issues related to how psychological disorders may affect the intimate relationships of adolescents. Thirdly, we focus on the case of depression to illustrate how the SASB-based coding system can help delineate specific relational patterns associated with subcategories of psychological disorders. In conclusion, we address the need to develop programs designed to facilitate positive relationship skills among specific groups of at-risk adolescents, who seem particularly prone to engage in dysfunctional and psychologically harmful romantic relationships.

THE STRUCTURAL ANALYSIS
OF SOCIAL BEHAVIOR

The SASB is a circumplex-based model of interpersonal and intrapsychic processes developed by Benjamin (1974). Like other circumplex models of personality and behavior (Kiesler, 1983; Leary, 1957; Schaefer, 1965) the SASB model is based on two orthogonal dimensions of behavior: affiliation and interdependence. Like earlier models, the horizontal axis of the SASB model (affiliation) represents the degree of hostility or warmth of a given psychological process (e.g., a kiss would typically be considered high in affiliation; a slap would be high in hostility.) However, the vertical axis of the SASB model differs from earlier models: Benjamin took Schaefer's vertical dimension of "control/emancipate" and Leary's vertical dimension of "dominate/submit" and combined them into one model. The vertical axis of the SASB model (interdependence) represents both the degree of enmeshment (controlling or submitting) and autonomy (granting or taking) of a given psychological process (e.g., a command would be considered high in control; the refusal to obey a command would be high in autonomy taking; soliciting approval would be highly submissive). This combining process necessitated expanding the earlier single-circumplex models into three circumplexes (Focus on Other, Focus on Self, and Intrapsychic Focus).

As illustrated in Fig. 7.1, the SASB model consists of three interpersonal foci or circumplex surfaces (i.e., Focus on Other, Focus on Self, and Intrapsychic Focus), each of which is based on the same configuration of the two orthogonal dimensions (affiliation and interdependence) described previously.

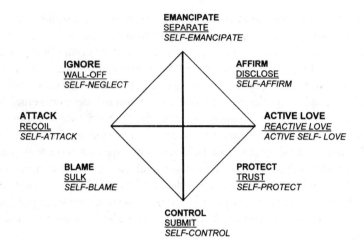

FIG. 7.1. The simplified SASB cluster model. From L. S. Benjamin, 1996, *Interpersonal Diagnosis and Treatment of Personality Disorder* (2nd ed.), New York: Guilford Press. Reprinted by permission.

The first SASB circumplex surface (Focus on Other, in **bold**) describes transitive actions that are directed outward toward, for, or about another individual. The second surface (Focus on Self, <u>underlined</u>) describes behaviors that are generally reactive to another person and/or about the self. The third surface (Introject, in *italics*) describes actions directed by the self toward the self. Introjective actions may represent the internalization of behaviors directed toward the self by important others (such as attachment figures). The cluster codes in capital letters in Fig. 7.1 provide a shorthand description of interpersonal processes based on the combination of focus, affiliation, and interdependence.

The SASB system is well suited for describing couples' interactions in three important ways. First, the circumplex structure of SASB helps the clinical researcher to systematically describe the behavior of romantic partners. This generally involves two steps which, with practice, become relatively easy to follow. The first step is to map a particular behavior onto the model by assigning a cluster code. This involves (a) deciding whether the behavior is self-focused, other-focused, or both self- and other-focused; (b) determining its degree of interdependence on a scale ranging from highly enmeshed to highly differentiated; and (c) determining the degree of affiliation on a scale ranging from extremely hostile to extremely warm. Based on these three decisions, a specific categorical code can be assigned to any given behavior. These categorical interpersonal "cluster" codes differentiate between various combinations of hostility, warmth, control, autonomy, and submissiveness.

To illustrate how the SASB model is used to describe behavior in terms of focus, affiliation, and interdependence (i.e., Step 1), we return to the previous conversation between Jim and Rose. Generally, this interaction is characterized by Jim's tendency to control Rose by sulking and expressing dejection, and Rose's tendency to assert and nurture (reassure) Jim. More specifically, Jim's statement to Rose, "You can't go," would be considered "Other-focused" because he is attending to her behavior. On the affiliation dimension, his behavior would be given a neutral rating depending on his tone and affect. On the interdependence dimension Jim's behavior would receive a high rating. In summary, his behavior would be cluster coded as **CONTROL**.

Rose's statement, "I'm going," would be considered self-focused because she is attending to her own behavior. It would also be coded as neutral on the affiliative dimension and low on the interdependence dimension. In summary, Rose's statement would be cluster coded as SEPARATE.

Jim's response, "I guess I'm the loser," would be coded on the Intrapsychic Focus because it is self-evaluative, reflecting Jim's feelings about himself. On the affiliation dimension, the statement would receive a rating of moderate hostility, and on the interdependence dimension it would receive a rating of moderate control. Thus, this behavior would be cluster coded as *SELF BLAME*. This behavior would also receive a code on the Self Focus circumplex because the statement is highly reactive to Rose's declaration of autonomy. More specifically, the behavior—paraphrased as a "poor me" statement—would be considered moderately submissive and moderately hostile and cluster coded as SULK.

The second step in describing interpersonal processes involves identifying the pattern of interaction between the partners. Based on the analysis of a SASB-coded interaction, an exchange can be described as complementary, similar, or antithetical. Complementary processes occur when one partner's behavior complements the behavior of the other. For example, if one partner were to blame the other ("You're an hour late!"), a complementary response would be to provide a whiny apology ("I'm *sorrry*"). A similar process occurs when one partner responds to the other "in kind." In the example just given, blame would be matched with blame: "Chill out; you're so uptight!" Antithetical processes are the opposite of complementary processes. For example, an antithetical response to the previous statement ("You're so uptight") would be assertive/autonomous ("I don't think I'm uptight, I'm just upset about waiting").

The second aspect of SASB that makes it useful in the study of couples' relationships is that a particular interpersonal behavior can be assigned up to three codes, thus allowing for a very precise description of that behavior. People often communicate two or more messages in the same breath. For example, a young woman might say to her boyfriend, "Do whatever you want." This may look like it is autonomy-giving, but when it is said in a blaming, belittling tone, the message takes on a different meaning altogether. With SASB, both parts of the message are coded. In this example, the woman's statement would probably be given the code **EMANCIPATE** (for the autonomy-giving part) and **BLAME** (for the hostile-control aspect).

The flexibility of the SASB model allows coders (or clinicians) to describe subtle complexities of interpersonal interactions. In some circumstances, complex messages can be problematic because they simultaneously express two incompatible or contradictory pieces of information. In the preceding example, it is unclear whether the boyfriend should respond to the freeing or the blaming part of his girlfriend's statement. Often, individuals will respond to complex messages in a complementary way, so that in the example given, the boyfriend might respond by saying in a whiny way, "Fine, I will then!" and storming out of the house (his codes would thus likely be SEPARATE and SULK). This example demonstrates how complex communications can often create an atmosphere of confusion, misunderstanding, and distrust in interpersonal relationships. This concept is explored further hereafter as we discuss previous research on individuals with psychological disorders and their interpersonal/romantic relations.

The third aspect of the SASB model that is relevant to the study of psychopathology and relational dysfunction is that it can help the clinical researcher distinguish between distinct forms of negative (hostile) and positive (warm) interpersonal behavior. Much of the previous research on psychopathology and relational process has been oriented toward documenting that the occurrence of psychopathology is associated with negative or hostile interpersonal processes (e.g., Johnson & Jacob, 1997; McCabe & Gotlib, 1993). While these findings are useful, in order to develop models for treating couples struggling to cope with particular disorders, it may be necessary to clearly distinguish between specific types of hostility associated with particular types of psychopathology. In addition, we believe that some forms of psychopathology involve complex combinations of friendliness and hostility.

We know that hostility can be expressed in many different ways. How to help a young man respond constructively to his partner's hostility is likely to vary depending on *how* that hostility is conveyed and whether her pattern of hostile engagement is associated with a specific disorder. The SASB model is able to systematically distinguish between different types of negative and positive behaviors, allowing clinical researchers to more clearly delineate and articulate the interpersonal correlates of specific types of psychopathology. For example, SASB codes in the "disrupted attachment" group include **BLAME**, SULK, **ATTACK**, RECOIL, **IGNORE**, and WALL OFF (the corresponding

Intrapsychic codes, shown on the left-hand side of the model in Fig. 7.1, would be *SELF-BLAME, SELF-ATTACK,* and *SELF-NEGLECT*). Simply stating that a couple with psychological dysfunction exhibits more negative behaviors than control couples misses the fact that hostility can come in several distinct "flavors." Knowing which "flavor" of hostility is present at different times in a couple's interactions can aid researchers and clinicians to help these couples work on different ways of responding.

The descriptive power of the SASB model is useful for identifying links between couples' behavior and psychopathology, because tracking interpersonal processes can be confusing and disorienting. Having a clear set of interpersonal coordinates and guidelines for mapping these processes allows the clinical researcher to maintain his or her bearings and systematically organize his or her perceptions.

To further illustrate how SASB can be used to systematically differentiate interpersonal patterns of interaction, we will use SASB to code the five couple types Gottman (1993) identified in his landmark study of marriage and conflict resolution. In this study, Gottman identified three types of "stable couples" and two types of "unstable couples." These two groups differ in their frequency of serious discussions about divorce and/or occurrence of divorce. The "stable couples" included *validators,* who tended to show mild negative emotion regarding the discussion of a conflict, but also were apt to validate and support their spouse's viewpoint; *volatiles,* who showed a great deal of both positive and negative emotion; and *avoiders,* who showed little emotion, either positive or negative, and tended to avoid discussion of the conflict except on a very superficial and vague level. The "unstable couples" included the *hostile* couples, who tended to show much negative emotion and defensiveness; and *hostile/detached* couples, who tended to be emotionally detached from one another, but the little emotion they showed was mostly negative.

All these types of couples can be "mapped" onto the SASB circumplex. For example, validators tend to support their spouse's viewpoint, which would be coded as **AFFIRM** on the circumplex. They might also show some negativity when discussing a conflict, which would likely be coded as either **BLAME** or SULK, but these negative exchanges would not be sustained. Although similar to validators, volatiles show a lot of both positive and negative emotion. They would receive high rates of both the affiliative and disaffiliative cluster codes. Avoiders would receive high rates of autonomy codes (both focus on self and other) and low rates of **BLAME** codes because they avoid engaging in direct conflict. Hostile couples would engage in high rates of behavior represented on the disaffiliative side of the circumplex (particularly **BLAME** and SULK) and very few scores on the affiliative side of the SASB circumplex. Hostile-detached couples would engage in high rates of **IGNORE** and WALL-OFF behaviors. They would also engage in relatively low rates of controlling and submissive behaviors.

ADOLESCENT ROMANCE
AND PSYCHOPATHOLOGY
IN A DEVELOPMENTAL CONTEXT

There is a substantial body of research on married couples indicating that the occurrence of psychological problems in one or both partners is linked—negatively—to the quality their romantic relationship (Gottman, 1993; Johnson & Jacob, 1997; Kowalik & Gotlib, 1987; McCabe & Gotlib, 1993). Generally, this research indicates that compared to psychologically healthy couples, psychologically disordered couples engage in less warm/affiliative behavior and more hostile/disaffiliative behaviors. Not surprisingly, psychologically "disordered" couples have also been found to be less satisfied with their relationships and their partners than normal "control" couples.

Although there has been very little research investigating links between psychological problems and adolescent romantic relationships, in recent years the results of several studies have underscored the importance of this line of inquiry. For example, Andrews, Foster, Capaldi, and Hops (2000) found that young men and women who had a history of antisocial behavior during adolescence were at increased risk for engaging in physical violence toward their romantic partners as adults. Related to these findings, Florsheim, Moore, Zollinger, MacDonald, and Sumida (1999) found that adolescent fathers who had a history of conduct disorder were more likely to report relationship problems with their coparenting partners than fathers without such a history. Given the prevalence of antisocial behavior among adolescent boys and the high rate of violence among adult partners (Andrews et al., 2000; O'Leary, Malone, & Tyree, 1994; Wolfe, Wekerle, Reitzel-Jaffe, & Lefebvre, 1998), the links between adolescent behavior problems and developmental origins of relational violence should be explored in greater depth.

There is also some evidence that romantic relationship problems can contribute to the development of psychological dysfunction. For example, Monroe, Rhode, Seeley, and Lewinsohn (1999) found evidence that the breakup of a romantic relationship is a significant risk factor for the onset of depression among adolescents. Monroe et al. (1999) suggest that while it does not make sense to consider relationship breakups as a causal factor in depression, breakups may increase an adolescent's level of vulnerability for becoming depressed and may tip adolescents who are already vulnerable into a depressive episode. Generally, these findings suggest that adolescent romantic relationships can indeed affect an adolescent's psychological well being and may be an important target for preventive-intervention efforts (Kaczmarek & Backlund, 1991; also see Welsh, Grello, & Harper, chap. 8, this volume).

Before proceeding to the next section, in which we use the SASB model to describe interpersonal processes associated with two variants of depression, it is important to note that much of the research on psychopathology and interpersonal behavior is based on adult couples. The lack of clinical research on adolescent romantic relationships requires that we look to the adult literature as a point of departure for developing a better understanding of links between adolescent psychopathology and romantic relations. However, it is important to underscore the point that findings based on adult couples will not necessarily generalize to adolescent couples because adolescents, as a group, are different from adults both with respect to the quality of their romantic relationships and nature of their psychopathology.

First, the nature of psychopathology can be different for adolescents and adults. Most notably, many adolescents struggle with specific developmental issues (puberty, family conflict, peer pressure) directly related to the occurrence of psychological dysfunction (Dishion, Capaldi, Spracklen, & Li, 1995; Reicher, 1993). Also, because adolescents are changing very rapidly in response to new developmental challenges, they are more likely than adults to experience transient psychological difficulties. Psychological problems tend to be less entrenched in adolescents than in adults and as such, the interpersonal correlates of psychopathology among adolescents tend to be more fluid and open to the influence of significant others.

Second, although most adolescents have learned to negotiate friendships with same sex peers, they are still in the process of learning how to "be" in a romantic relationship. This may influence the variability of a teenager's behavior within any given relationship and across different romantic liaisons. Adolescents are thought to be in the process of "trying out" different relational roles and discovering/formulating their social identities (Erikson, 1968). As such, their interpersonal functioning is expected to be relatively fluid and less predictable. Thus, the patterns observed among distinct groups of adult couples may be less generally applicable to adolescent couples, and it is for this reason that future research should focus specifically on adolescent couples.

Third, adolescent romantic relationships tend to be shorter in duration than adult relationships (Carver, Joyner, & Udry, chap. 2, this volume), and adolescents tend to enter romantic relationships with a different set of expectations. Adolescents are less likely to seek long-term commitment or assess their partner in terms of his or her qualities as a lifelong mate (Jackson, 1993). Therefore, it is unlikely that an adolescent will seek couples therapy. Thus,

it may be more expedient to address links between psychopathology and dysfunctional romantic relationships through individual therapy or the development of psychoeducational programs designed to help adolescents identify
dysfunctional patterns and learn healthy interpersonal skills. These ideas are
further elaborated in the last section of this chapter.

Finally, there are important cognitive-developmental differences between
younger and older adolescents that may dramatically influence the quality of
romantic relations (Neemann, Hubbard, & Masten, 1995). Younger adolescents may be more egocentric, less able to read their partner's interpersonal
cues, and less able to understand their partner's requests for reassurance and
support. Or, even if they are able to understand, they may not be at a level
where they can competently handle the situation. Also, because adolescents
are still in the throes of developing a coherent identity, they may have more
difficulty articulating their feelings clearly and coherently. Thus, they may
be more prone to engage in complex communications reflecting their ambivalence about autonomy and intimacy.

THE SASB MODEL APPLIED:
DEPRESSION AND ADOLESCENT ROMANCE

Developmental psychopathologists have documented that there are many different ways to become depressed, antisocial, anxious, and so on, and that the
intrapersonal and interpersonal correlates of psychopathology vary greatly
within any particular category of disorder (Benjamin, 1996; Kagan, 1997;
Sroufe, 1997). For example, several clinical theorists have suggested that there
are at least two distinct types of depression (and probably more), each based on
different interpersonal histories and characterized by different interpersonal
needs, wishes, and fears (Blatt & Homann, 1992; Haslam & Beck, 1994).
Some depressed individuals seek protection and nurturance from others, and
behave in ways intended to elicit sympathy or force others to take care of them.
Other depressives are characteristically more irritable, self-critical, preoccupied with achievement, and generally more isolative and avoidant of relationships (Blatt & Zuroff, 1992; Haslam & Beck, 1994).

The vast heterogeneity among and within psychological disorders with
respect to their relational correlates poses a practical problem for researchers
and clinicians: How can we move beyond the general observation that psychologically disordered individuals tend to engage in more hostile relationships
toward an understanding of the more specific links between psychological disturbance and relational dysfunction? In this section we focus on the inter-

personal processes associated with depression to illustrate the utility of SASB model for delineating specific modes of relational dysfunction associated with specific types of psychological disorder.

Because the current DSM system of diagnosis focuses on the *intra*personal aspects of psychopathology, the relational correlates of psychopathology have not been well researched (Kaslow & Robison, 1996). Although almost all diagnoses make some reference to a disruption in social functioning, the specific nature of this dysfunction is rarely well articulated. For example, the DSM currently defines depression in terms of the following symptoms: depressed or sad mood, anhedonia, self-blaming and self-critical behaviors, low self-esteem, pessimism, guilty feelings, and vegetative symptoms (American Psychiatric Association, 1999). This definition is intended to be highly flexible, allowing for a high degree of diagnostic heterogeneity. Indeed, it is widely acknowledged that there are several distinct variants of depression and therefore there may be a variety of ways in which depressive symptoms might influence interpersonal functioning.

Dependent/Anaclitic/Sociotropic Depression

Blatt and colleagues have described a type of depression (which they refer to as anaclitic depression) characterized by feelings of helplessness, weakness, and feelings of being unloved. Blatt (1974) hypothesized that anaclitically depressed individuals are likely to have experienced their parents as abandoning and/or neglectful. As such, anaclitically depressed individuals are governed by powerful wishes to be soothed and cared for by others, and have difficulty tolerating delay of these actions. Because their sense of well-being is dependent on a continual supply of love and assurance, they often seem needy or clingy. Moreover, they may be conflict avoidant within the context of close relationships due to an overriding fear of abandonment or lost affection. Coming from a somewhat different theoretical perspective, Beck and colleagues (Clark & Beck, 1989; Haslam & Beck, 1994) have used the term *sociotropic* to describe a type of depression that is very similar to Blatt's *anaclitic* depression. According to Haslam and Beck (1994), sociotropic depression is likely to occur in individuals who are particularly sensitive to rejection or abandonment by others. This type of depression is often a reaction to perceived or actual loss of an important social relationship. Perpetually confronted with the fear of loss, sociotropic depressives tend to be care-seekers and preoccupied with maintaining attachments.

Consistent with Blatt's and Beck's theories of depression, Coyne (1976) has suggested that the excessive dependency needs of depressed individuals will affect their interactions with family members, including their partners. Coyne theorized that depressive symptoms represent a call for reassurance and support from family members (spouse, parents, or children). However, the nature of depression is such that even if family members respond positively to these requests, the intense need of the depressed person is likely to feel unmet, and the requests will continue and perhaps become more forceful. Coyne suggests that at this point, family members may begin to feel overburdened and resentful of the depressive's demands, but also may feel guilty. As such, family members are unlikely to express their anger directly. Rather, they may offer help in a way that combines both positive and negative affect. The depressed person is then likely to feel insecure and more needy than before. This cycle continues until either the family member or the depressed person disengages or withdraws.

Autonomous/Introjective/Self-Critical Depression

Clinical theorists have also identified a second major substrate of depression that has been alternately referred to variously as *autonomous, introjective*, or *self-critical* depression (Blatt, 1974; Beck, Epstein, & Harrison, 1983). Blatt (1974) theorized that autonomously depressed individuals experienced their parents as excessively demanding and critical. In other words, these individuals are prone to feel that nothing was ever good enough or that parental love was entirely contingent on performance. This type of depression is characterized by feelings of "unloveable-ness" (vs. feeling unloved), shame, guilt, and unworthiness. These individuals tend to hold overly high expectations and ideals for themselves and therefore are under constant self-scrutiny and self-blame. They often feel helpless about acquiring approval from others, yet fear disapproval and punishment. Based on the perception of others as critical and demanding, they tend to be more isolative and avoidant of close relationships.

According to Clark and Beck (1989), autonomous depression is triggered by events involving defeat or failure, which are perceived as losses to self-determination, independence, competence, or control. Depression that occurs in response to a perceived failure is typically characterized by self-blame and shame and an increased desire to be left alone (Clark & Beck, 1989). Based on a particular set of interpersonal expectations, autonomously depressed individuals may select a partner who also has high expectations for them and/or is very achievement-oriented. However, according to Clark and Beck, when a real or perceived failure occurs, the depressed person is likely to become more isolative and feel worthless and unlovable. Autonomously depressed individuals are often loath to seek reassurance and support from important others when they become acutely distressed, as they are very afraid of being blamed or punished.[1]

Empirical Findings of Differences in Subtypes of Depression

There is some evidence in support of the idea that these two distinct types of depression are associated with different patterns of romantic relations (Ayduk, Downey, & Kim, 2001; Beck et al., 1983; Benazon, 2000; Blatt, 1974; Joiner, Alfano, & Metalsky, 1992). For example, Lynch, Robins, and Morse (2001) investigated the romantic relationships of depressed psychiatric patients. Patients who reported having a romantic relationship of 6 months or longer were administered measures of sociotropy/autonomy and relationship functioning. Results indicated that patients whose depression was colored by high levels of sociotropy tended to engage in higher levels of demanding behavior while their partners were perceived as more withdrawing. Conversely, patients whose depression was colored by high levels of autonomy seeking tended to become withdrawn, while their partners were perceived as more demanding. This research lends further support to the premise that particular types of psychopathology will be associated with distinct forms of relationship dysfunction. Further, results are consistent with the SASB predictive principle of antithesis (i.e., the opposite of complementarity: a complementary behavior to demandingness would be submission, and the opposite of submission would be autonomy-taking or perhaps hostile withdrawal).

Moreover, there is some research that suggests that these particular forms of depression and their associated interpersonal styles can become self-fulfilling prophecies (Benazon, 2000; Downey, Freitas, Michaelis, & Khouri, 1998). For example, Benazon (2000) investigated the marital interactions of 89 couples in which at least one spouse was undergoing treatment for depression. Consistent with Coyne's theoretic propositions, it was found that depressed patients who engaged in high rates of reassurance seeking (from their spouse) were more likely to be described unfavorably (by their spouse) across several dimensions, including intellectual ability, emotional stability, and physical attractiveness. The relationship between reassurance seeking and negative appraisals remained significant after controlling for associated variables, such as spouse's mood and marital distress. Benazon (2000) suggests that the tendency among some depressed patients to express high levels of relationship insecurity and to

---

[1] Other theoreticians focus on helplessness (Seligman, 1973) and/or unpredictability (Mineka, 1979) as correlates of depression. These subtypes may converge with Beck's autonomous depression. Further consideration of how to classify subtypes of depression that have interpersonal antecedents is beyond the present scope of this chapter.

constantly seek reassurance can have the unintended consequence of annoying and alienating their partners and reinforcing their insecurity.

Case Illustrations

The interpersonal characteristics associated with these two types of depression can be coded and differentiated using the SASB model. Building on the theories of Blatt, Beck and colleagues, we theorized that the primary interpersonal wish of the dependently depressed person is to be **PROTECTED** and the primary interpersonal fear is to be **IGNORED**. As such, it seems likely that a dependently depressed person would engage with a romantic partner in a helpless and needy manner (TRUST plus SUBMIT or SULK). As may be seen in the Simplified Cluster model, TRUST is the complementary response to **PROTECT**, which is theorized to be the primary interpersonal wish of the dependently depressed individual. If reassurance is not sufficient, dependently depressed individuals may behave in ways designed to "force" their partners to provide caring and support through guilt induction. In SASB language, this would be coded as a complex combination of submission and control (e.g., TRUST plus **CONTROL**, SULK plus **CONTROL**, or TRUST plus **BLAME**). Depending on the personality structure to the caregiver, the response is likely to be a complex mix of resentment and support (SULK plus **PROTECT**: "Alright already, I will take care of you") or a mix of disengagement and support (**IGNORE** plus **PROTECT**; "I tell you what, I'll take care of you as soon as I finish filing my nails"). Eventually the caregiver is likely to become more fully disengaged (**IGNORE** or WALL OFF). The hypothetical case of Jim and Rose presented at the beginning of the chapter illustrates the SASB-based conceptualization of how dependent depression might typically influence the romantic liaison between two adolescents.

> When Rose first met Jim, one of the things that she found attractive was that he seemed so vulnerable and sweet. He seemed to need a lot of help, and she enjoyed looking out for him. However, once they began dating Jim very quickly moved their relationship to higher level of intensity by constantly seeking to be with Rose. He often told her that he loved her and wanted to spend all his time with her. Although Rose responded to Jim's love, she also began feeling somewhat overwhelmed by his needs and made some effort to diminish the intensity of their involvement by spending time with her family and friends. However, these efforts were perceived by Jim as threats of abandonment and were met with tears, self-recrimination, and subtle blame. Rose felt guilty and coerced into taking care of Jim. Although she was fond of him, Rose felt herself becoming more and more drained by their relationship. She began to make excuses to avoid contact with Jim and eventually broke off the relationship.

In this hypothetical example, the relationship is first characterized by a complementary interpersonal process. Jim uses a combination of **CONTROL** plus <u>TRUST</u> and Rose responds with a combination of **PROTECT** plus <u>SUBMIT</u>. With time Rose becomes weary of Jim's needy demands and begins to respond antithetically. At first, she tries to assert her independence while being sensitive to his needs (<u>SEPARATE</u> plus **PROTECT**), but eventually she feels compelled to **IGNORE** Jim's increasingly hostile demands for nurturance.

In contrast to the case of Jim, and again following the theories of Blatt (1974) and of Beck and colleagues (1983), the autonomously depressed person's internal experience might be characterized by self-criticism, unrealistically high expectations, and a chronic sense of disappointment. Feelings of unworthiness and unloveable-ness would probably be coded on the introject surface of the SASB model as *SELF-BLAMING* or *SELF-ATTACKING*. The tendency to hold unreasonably high expectations for themselves would be coded as *SELF-CONTROL*. In SASB terms, the primary fears of introjectively depressed individuals would be SASB coded as **ATTACK** and **BLAME**. The primary wish for approval by others would be SASB coded as **AFFIRM**. Finally, these individuals would likely be SASB coded as inclined to <u>WALL-OFF</u> from others, which is nearly opposite of what individuals with dependent depression are thought to do when they are feeling down. The following hypothetical vignette illustrates what the autonomous depression pattern might look like in an adolescent romantic relationship:

> Polly grew up in a family with very high expectations for achievement, but with low levels of support when any of the children failed to meet those expectations. If Polly received an A in school, her parents acted as though it was expected: anything lower was totally unacceptable. Throughout most of high school, Polly was too busy to date. However, during her senior year, she met Scott in AP English. They both excelled in school, and they would often study together and compare grades after tests. Getting good grades made Polly feel temporarily valued. However, when she felt she had not met the expectations she had set for herself, Polly would become self-critical and would feel unworthy to be dating Scott. Whenever anything went wrong in their relationship, Polly blamed herself. Scott liked Polly and tried to be comforting and reassuring when she got down on herself. However, Scott was usually unable to lift Polly's spirits. When she was feeling down, she preferred to be by herself. Sometimes, she would not talk to him for days. If pursued, she would express the fear that he was thinking badly of her or regretting their relationship.

In this case example, the dominant pattern is antithetical. That is, when Polly becomes depressed and disengaged (*SELF-BLAME* and <u>WALL-OFF</u>), Scott attempts to comfort her (**PROTECT**). Scott's effort to care for Polly heightens her performance anxiety and her sense of failure in meeting expectations. Her response is to become more fearful of Scott's disapproval (SULK) and more prone to WALL-OFF. The bleak interpersonal profile of Jim and Polly's relationship raises the important question of whether anything could be done to help facilitate a more positive interpersonal development of these and similar cases.

SASB as a Tool for Clinicians

In addition to being a useful model for describing patterns of behavior, SASB is also a useful prescriptive tool that can help guide interventions designed to facilitate change among psychologically impaired couples. That is, after a particular interpersonal problem has been identified and described (in SASB language), the principles of the SASB model can be used to help develop a treatment plan that directly addresses the problem. As indicated previously, a primary tenet of SASB is that once problematic interpersonal patterns have been clearly delineated and mapped onto the SASB circumplex, the therapist is in a better position to help a couple create more adaptive solutions to their particular interpersonal dilemma.

In the hypothetical case of Jim, the therapist might focus on helping him recognize that when he tries to force others to provide the love and support he craves, his efforts backfire and drive others away, leaving him feeling more isolated and rejected. The therapist might address Jim's dependency by (a) helping him to become more self-soothing, and (b) helping him balance his own need for care and reassurance with his partner's need for autonomy. This approach may not save his relationship with Rose, but it may help him to become less clingy with future partners.

In the case of Polly, a therapist may want to focus on her tendency to be self-demanding. The goal might be to render this process less hostile, shifting from *SELF-BLAME* to *SELF-CONTROL* and eventually to *SELF-PROTECT* and *SELF-AFFIRM*. Therapy might also be oriented toward helping Polly learn to be more open to the support of others, focusing on her relationship with Scott as a vehicle for facilitating change. Finally, the therapist could help Scott learn to respond to Polly's self-criticism by resisting the tendency to comfort, which seems to backfire. Rather he should allow her to take the space she needs (EMANCIPATE) while also DISCLOSING his feeling about her and AFFIRMING her positive qualities.

IMPLICATIONS

This chapter is based on two fundamental premises. First, specific types of psychological dysfunction are associated with specific interpersonal processes and problems. Second, there is an emergent need for a systematic approach in both research and therapeutic situations to assess the links between psychopathology and interpersonal process within the context of adolescent romantic relations. We believe that romantic relationships among adolescents often play an important developmental role either by diminishing the influence of previous negative events on developmental outcomes or by contributing new problems to the developmental process. A systematic approach to the study of psychopathology and romantic relations will help clarify how different types of psychopathology can influence a couple's relationship and perhaps how interpersonal relations may influence the development of psychopathology.

Although we have focused on depression as a point of reference, the SASB model can be used to delineate the interpersonal correlates of other types of psychopathology. Benjamin (1996) has applied the SASB model to each of the DSM personality disorders, and used it to help make differential diagnoses and develop hypotheses about prototypic interpersonal histories and associated treatment recommendations for each disorder. For example, despite a notable lack of research on antisocial or conduct disordered couples, we can generate some working hypotheses regarding the romantic relationships of antisocial individuals based on our current understanding of the phenomenology of the disorder (how antisocial individuals tend to experience and engage with others). Specifically, it seems that conduct disordered adolescents are likely to be highly controlling or demeaning toward their partners, while ignoring of their partner's needs (**CONTROL, BLAME, IGNORE**). However, conduct-disordered youth tend to combine or alternate these hostile behaviors with expressions of **ACTIVE LOVE** and **PROTECTION**, keeping their partners hooked into believing they really care, deep down. Because antisocial youth are fearful of being controlled by others, they are also likely to engage in high rates of <u>WALLING-OFF</u> behavior, such as not showing up when they were asked.

The utility of the SASB model for clearly delineating specific types of interpersonal processes is also potentially useful in the development of preventive-intervention programs designed to facilitate the development of positive relationship skills among particular groups of at-risk youth. For many adolescents, couples treatment is either impractical or unnecessary because many adolescent romantic liaisons are expectedly transient. When serious problems arise within the context of an adolescent romance, splitting up is often the most expedient and developmentally appropriate solution. However, relationship-focused programs could help provide individuals with the tools to prevent the occurrence of psychologically harmful behavior in relationships, including psychological and physical abuse. Such programs could also facilitate the development of interpersonal skills among groups of adolescents who are known to have social skill deficits, including seriously depressed and conduct disordered youth. This could have significant preventative value.

There is some evidence that education-based programs designed to prevent violent behavior among teenagers have been successful. For example, Foshee et al. (1998) developed a school-based program targeting the prevention of violence among adolescent couples by teaching relationship skills and addressing beliefs about relationship violence. Adolescents who participated in this Safe Dates program reported fewer incidents of psychological abuse and violence in their relationships at follow-up compared to a control group that received no prevention. The success of this program and others like it (Wekerle & Wolfe, 1999) may be related to the fact that problems related to romance and dating are highly salient to most adolescents, even those who tend to be resistant to intervention.

A SASB based program designed to delineate highly specific patterns of interpersonal behavior associated with particular psychological problems or disorders could target adolescents in juvenile detention facilities, substance abuse clinics, and residential or hospital settings. Like the Safe Dates program, the goal of such a prevention-intervention program could be to help adolescents recognize maladaptive relationship patterns and practice more adaptive interpersonal strategies. For example, a program designed to target depressed youth might (a) demonstrate how some common cognitive distortions associated with depression tend to have a negative impact on romantic relationships and (b) teach interpersonal strategies that can help break the link between a maladaptive set of relational expectations and the development of self-defeating relationship patterns. Helping depressed adolescents to become more aware of their own interpersonal processes, to learn to recognize problems in their relationships, and to practice techniques for extricating the themselves from toxic interpersonal encounters could help reduce the persistence of depression into adulthood.

Learning to successfully negotiate intimacy and autonomy within a romantic relationship is a major developmental milestone for adolescents. When stressors such as depression, substance abuse, or other psychopathologies are added to the mix, many adolescents can have an exceedingly difficult time finding and/or maintaining a healthy, developmentally appropriate relationship. Conversely, it may also happen that for some adolescents, involvement in a romantic relationship can exacerbate or ameliorate deficits in psychological and interpersonal functioning. Although adolescent relationships and psychopathologies may be similar in some ways to those of adults, there are also important differences due to developmental level which make it crucial that researchers not merely adapt adult findings to teens, but investigate adolescent relationships in their own right. In this chapter, we have attempted to delineate some ways in which psychopathology and interpersonal functioning can interact to affect the romantic relationships of adolescents, and have made some suggestions as to how this information may be used by clinicians involved with this population. However, we recognize that research and clinical work in this area are yet in their beginning stages, and the lack of empirical research that has been done reflects this state of affairs. Therefore, it is our hope that this chapter can be used as a stepping stone for further, more fine-grained research which, ultimately, may help guide adolescents along a path of better psychological and interpersonal functioning.

REFERENCES

American Psychiatric Association. (1994). *Diagnostic and statistical manual of mental disorders* (4th ed.). Washington, DC: Author.

Andrews, J. A., Foster, S. L, Capaldi, D., & Hops, H. (2000). Adolescent and family predictors of physical aggression, communication, and satisfaction in young adult couples: A prospective analysis. *Journal of Consulting and Clinical Psychology, 68,* 195–208.

Association of Anorexia Nervosa and Associated Disorders. (2000). Ten-year study. Results outlined in *Eating Disorder Education Organization,* www.edeo.org/edinfo/factstats.htm.

Ayduk, O., Downey, G., & Kim, M. (2001). Rejection sensitivity and depressive symptoms in women. *Personality & Social Psychology Bulletin, 27,* 868–877.

Beck, A. T., Epstein, N., & Harrison, R. (1983). Cognitions, attitudes and personality dimensions in depression. *British Journal of Cognitive Psychotherapy, 1,* 1–16.

Benazon, N. R. (2000). Predicting negative spousal attitudes toward depressed persons: A test of Coyne's interpersonal model. *Journal of Abnormal Psychology, 109,* 550–554.

Benjamin, L. S. (1974). Structural analysis of social behavior. *Psychological Review, 81,* 392–425.

Benjamin, L. S. (1996). *Interpersonal diagnosis and treatment of personality disorders* (2nd ed.). New York: Guilford Press.

Birmaher, B., Ryan, N. D., Williamson, D. E., Brent, D. A., Kaufman, J., Dahl, R. E., Perel, J., & Nelson, B. (1996) Childhood and adolescent depression: A review of the past 10 years. Part I. *Journal of the American Academy of Child and Adolescent Psychiatry, 35,* 1427–1439.

Blatt, S. J. (1974). Levels of object representation in anaclitic and introjective depression. *Psychoanalytic Study of the Child, 29,* 7–157.

Blatt, S. J., & Homann, E. (1992). Parent–child interaction in the etiology of dependent and self-critical depression. *Clinical Psychology Review, 12,* 47–91.

Blatt, S. J., & Zuroff, D. C. (1992). Interpersonal relatedness and self-definition: Two prototypes for depression. *Clinical Psychology Review, 12,* 527–562.

Clark, D. A., & Beck, A. T. (1989). Cognitive theory and therapy of anxiety and depression. In P. C. Kendall & D. Watson (Eds.), *Anxiety and depression: Distinctive and overlapping features* (pp. 379–411). New York: Academic Press.

Coyne, J. C. (1976). Toward an interactional description of depression. *Psychiatry, 39,* 28–40.

Dishion, T. J., Capaldi, D., Spracklen, K. M., & Li, F. (1995). Peer ecology of male adolescent drug use. *Development and Psychopathology, 7,* 803–824.

Downey, G., Freitas, A. L., Michaelis, B., & Khouri, H. (1998). The self-fulfilling prophecy in close relationships: Rejection sensitivity and rejection by romantic partners. *Journal of Personality and Social Psychology, 75,* 545–560.

Florsheim, P., Moore, D., Zollinger, L., MacDonald, J., & Sumida, E. (1999). The transition to parenthood among adolescent fathers and their partners: Does antisocial behavior predict problems in parenting? *Applied Developmental Science, 3,* 178–191.

Foshee, V., Bauman, K. E., Arriaga, X. B., Helms, R. W., Koch, G. G., & Linder, G. F. (1998). An evaluation of safe dates, an adolescent dating violence prevention program. *American Journal of Public Health, 88,* 45–50

Gottman, J. M. (1993). The roles of conflict engagement, escalation, and avoidance in marital interaction: A longitudinal view of five types of couples. *Journal of Consulting and Clinical Psychology, 61,* 6–15.

Haslam, N., & Beck, A. T. (1994). Subtyping major depression: A taxometric analysis. *Journal of Abnormal Psychology, 103,* 686–692.

Hazan, C., & Shaver, P. R. (1994). Attachment as an organizational framework for research on close relationships. *Psychological Inquiry, 5,* 1–22.

Jackson, S. (1993). Social behaviour in adolescence: The analysis of social interaction sequences. In S. Jackson & H. Rodriguez-Tome (Eds.), *Adolescence and its social worlds* (pp. 15–45). Hillsdale, NJ: Lawrence Erlbaum Associates.

Johnson, S. L., & Jacob, T. (1997). Marital interactions of depressed men and women. *Journal of Consulting and Clinical Psychology, 65,* 15–23.

Joiner, T. E., Alfano, M. S., & Metalsky, G. I. (1992). When depression breeds contempt: Reassurance seeking, self-esteem, and rejection of depressed college students by their roommates. *Journal of Abnormal Psychology, 101,* 165–173.

Kaczmarek, M. G., & Backlund, B. A. (1991). Disenfranchised grief: The loss of an adolescent romantic relationship. *Adolescence, 26,* 253–259.

Kagan, J. (1997). Conceptualizing psychopathology: The importance of development profiles. *Development & Psychopathology, 9,* 321–334.

Kaslow, F., & Robison, J. A. (1996). Long-term satisfying marriages: Perceptions of contributing factors. *American Journal of Family Therapy, 24,* 153–170.

Kiesler, D. J. (1983). The 1982 Interpersonal Circle: A taxonomy for complementarity in human transactions. *Psychological Review, 90,* 185–214.

Kowalik, D. L., & Gotlib, I. H. (1987). Depression and marital interaction: Concordance between intent and perception of communication. *Journal of Abnormal Psychology, 96,* 127–134.

Leary, T. (1957). *Interpersonal diagnosis of personality.* New York: Ronald Press.

Levitt, M. Z., Selman, R. L., & Richmond, J. B. (1991). The psychosocial foundations of early adolescents' high-risk behavior: Implications for research and practice. *Journal of Research on Adolescence, 1,* 349–378.

Lynch, T. R., Robins, C. J., & Morse, J. Q. (2001). Couple functioning in depression: The roles of sociotropy and autonomy. *Journal of Clinical Psychology, 57,* 93–103.

McCabe, S. B., & Gotlib, I. H. (1993). Interactions of couples with and without a depressed spouse: Self-report and observations of problem-solving situations. *Journal of Social and Personal Relationships, 10,* 589–599.

Mineka, S. (1979). The role of fear in theories of avoidance learning, flooding, and extinction. *Psychological Bulletin, 85,* 1376–1400.

Monroe, S. M., Rhode, P., Seeley, J. R., & Lewinsohn, P. M. (1999). Life events and depression in adolescence: Relationship loss as a prospective risk factor for first onset of major depressive disorder. *Journal of Abnormal Psychology, 108,* 606–614.

Neemann, J., Hubbard, J., & Masten, A. S. (1995). The changing importance of romantic relationship involvement to competence from late childhood to late adolescence. *Development and Psychopathology, 7,* 727–750.

O'Leary, K. D., Malone, J., & Tyree, A. (1994). Physical aggression in early marriage: Prerelationship and relationship effects. *Journal of Consulting and Clinical Psychology, 62,* 594–602.

Reicher, H. (1993). Family and peer relations and social-emotional problems in adolescence. *Studia Psychologica, 35,* 403–408.

Schaefer, E. S. (1965). Configurational analysis of children's reports of parent behavior. *Journal of Consulting Psychology, 29,* 552–557.

Seligman, M. E. (1973). Fall into helplessness. *Psychology Today, 7,* 43–48.

Sroufe, L. A. (1997). Psychopathology as an outcome of development. *Development and Psychopathology, 9,* 251–268.

Substance Abuse and Mental Health Services Report. (2001). Results from the 2001 National Household Survey on Drug Abuse. Retrieved December 28, 2002, from http://www.samhsa .gov/oas/nhsda/2k1nhsda/vol1/chapter2.htm#2.age

Wekerle, C., & Wolfe, D. A. (1999). Dating violence in mid-adolescence: Theory, significance, and emerging prevention initiatives. *Clinical Psychology Review, 19,* 435–456.

Wolfe, D. A., Wekerle, C., Reitzel-Jaffe, D., & Lefebvre, L. (1998). Factors associated with abusive relationships among maltreated and non maltreated youth. *Development and Psychopathology, 10,* 61–85.

8

When Love Hurts: Depression and Adolescent Romantic Relationships

Deborah P. Welsh
Catherine M. Grello
Melinda S. Harper
University of Tennessee

The pervasiveness of depression along with the extremely serious psychological, social, and economic consequences it wreaks in our society makes it one of the most pressing mental health concerns of our time (Cicchetti & Toth, 1998). Depression in adolescents is associated with detrimental consequences, including social impairment in family, peer, and romantic relationships, academic problems, suicide, and risk for future depressive episodes (see Compas, Connor, & Hinden, 1998). Adolescence, particularly early to middle adolescence, is considered the pivotal time period during which overall rates of depression rise and gender differences in depressive symptoms emerge (Compas et al., 1998; Leadbeater, Blatt, & Quinlan, 1995; Nolen-Hoeksema & Girgus, 1994). Interestingly, this is also the time during which adolescents typically begin romantic relationships. Although romantic relationships clearly play a normative, healthful role in adolescent development for most adolescents (as described in the majority of chapters in this volume), this chapter focuses on the dark side of adolescent romance. That is, we examine when romantic relationships may be detrimental to adolescent development and may be associated with the rise of depressive symptomatology as well as with the gender difference in depression that emerges during adolescence.

In this chapter we first present the dominant theoretical models explaining the etiology of adolescent depression and current theoretical models of adolescent romantic relationships. We attempt to integrate these perspectives in an effort to explain the link between romantic relationships and depressive symptomatology in adolescents. Our integrative model posits that a variety of individual characteristics may place certain adolescents at risk for developing depressive symptoms when exposed to the stressors inherent in romantic relationships. Second, we examine some of these stressors or challenges associated with different developmental stages of adolescents' romantic relationships. Finally, we discuss practical implications for program planning, health education, and clinical intervention.

MODELS OF ADOLESCENT DEPRESSION

Most contemporary models of adolescent depression are multifaceted and include cognitive, interpersonal, socio-cultural, and biological components. One cognitive component that has received considerable recent interest and empirical support in etiological models of depression pertains to the ways in which individuals cope with distressing feelings (Nolen-Hoeksema, 1994; Nolen-Hoeksema & Girgus, 1994). Some people respond to distressing feelings with a passive, ruminative style of coping that tends to promote further depressive symptoms while others use more active, distracting types of strategies that are more effective in interfering with the positive feedback cycle of depressive symptoms. Girls and women are more likely to ruminate in response to depressive feelings, while boys and men are more likely to use the more active, and adaptive, coping styles (Nolen-Hoeksema, 1994). Nolen-Hoeksema and Girgus (1994) have argued that the gender difference in depression that first emerges in adolescence results from the risk factors that girls carry even before adolescence, particularly their tendency toward a ruminative coping style, in conjunction with the increased challenges faced during early adolescence. We argue later in this chapter that the challenge of mastering the new domain of developing and maintaining sexual/romantic relationships is the most prominent new hurdle experienced by adolescents.

Global interpersonal styles have also been suggested as an important component in developmental models of depression. Leadbeater and colleagues (1995) posited a model for the development of internalizing disorders that emphasizes the role of interpersonal vulnerability. Interpersonally vulnerable individuals are preoccupied with the affection of others, with feelings of loneliness and helplessness, fear abandonment, desire intense closeness, and they have difficulty in expressing anger overtly. Leadbeater and her colleagues suggested that when individuals with this pattern of interpersonal vulnerability experience stressful events involving other people, intense feelings of interpersonal vulnerability are potentiated, and internalizing psychological disorders result. Once again, the role of adolescent romantic relationships is likely to serve as one of the most significant stressors for adolescents in this etiological model of depression.

Specific styles of interpersonal coping have also been implicated in the development of depression in adolescents (Powers, 2000; Powers, Pollack,

Nascimento, & Sachar, 1998; Powers & Welsh, 1999). Powers' biopsycho-social model posits that the dramatic rise in gender differences in depression during late adolescence can be partially explained by gender-related difficulties in interpersonal behavioral coping. She suggested that difficulties in achieving individuation within parent–adolescent relationships may be reflected in later romantic relationships. These differences are manifested in maladaptive inter-personal behaviors that maintain and increase depressive symptoms in adoles-cents by exacerbating physiological stress responses to interpersonal conflict. Physiological hyperreactivity to interpersonal stress acts as a mediator of mal-adaptive behavioral coping to depressive symptoms. Thus, the model posits that the ways in which adolescents cope behaviorally with interpersonal con-flict is related to their depressive symptoms. Two types of gender-related ineffective interpersonal coping—"agitated submission" and "passive submis-sion"—are hypothesized to predict depression in adolescents. Depressed girls tend to perceive their interpersonal coping as both highly conflictual and highly submissive (Powers & Welsh, 1999). This style, wherein girls engage in interpersonal conflict but give up and concede to others, is hypothesized to be positively reinforced by others with whom they are in close relationships because it conforms to cultural stereotypes of feminine behavior and because it maintains a close and active connection between romantic partners. In con-trast, boys with higher levels of depressive symptoms exhibit a behavioral pat-tern that is highly submissive, but low in conflict and more distancing (Powers et al., 1998). This behavioral coping pattern runs counter to cultural expec-tations for males and is thus expected to be negatively reinforced by others. There is some evidence that the mothers of adolescents perceive the behaviors of depressed daughters positively and the behaviors of depressed sons nega-tively (Powers et al., 1998). Therefore, the differential pattern of behavior and reinforcement is hypothesized to be a significant contributor to the gender differences in adolescent depression.

Adolescent romantic relationships play a significant role in these three models of adolescent depression. They provide the context in which precipi-tating ineffective cognitive coping strategies (e.g., rumination), potentiating feelings of interpersonal vulnerability, and/or ineffective behavioral coping are likely to manifest and be maintained.

MODELS OF ADOLESCENT ROMANTIC RELATIONSHIPS

Contemporary developmental models of adolescent romantic relationships tend to be situated within an attachment theoretical framework (e.g., Collins & Sroufe, 2000; Downey, Bonica, & Rincon, 2000; Furman & Wehner, 1994,

1997), which suggests that individual's internal representations of relationships are developed from past relationship experiences and influence the nature of one's current and future relationships throughout the lifespan (Bowlby, 1969). These models take a developmental continuity perspective in suggesting that the quality of early parent–child relationships is internalized and that the internal representations of those early relationships impact adolescents' current romantic relationships by influencing how adolescents' interact with their dating partners as well as how adolescents' interpret their dating partners' and their own behaviors and intentions.

The importance of examining individual couple members' subjective understanding (or interpretation) of their interactions is integral to each of these models of romantic relationship development. Collins and his colleagues (Collins & Sroufe, 2000; Collins, Hennighausen, Schmit, & Sroufe, 1997) integrated attachment theory, intimacy theory, and empirical investigations of childrens' and adolescents' relationships. Central to their conceptualization of the development of adolescents' romantic relationships is their belief that "children form expectations concerning themselves in the environment based on salient relationship experiences in earlier life. These expectations guide encounters with the environment and *interpretations* of experience" (Collins et al., 1997, p. 70). Collins and Sroufe (2000) referred to these individual differences in interpretation as cognitive biases, and they posited that these biases are related to individual differences in attachment history.

Furman and Wehner (1994, 1997) also proposed a developmental theory of adolescent romantic relationships that builds upon attachment theory. A fundamental component of their theoretical model is the concept of "views," which refers to the preconceptions, beliefs, and expectations held by individuals about particular types of relationships. Furman and Wehner postulated that individual couple members' views of romantic relationships influence their patterns of interaction in their romantic relationships as well as the way they *interpret* the interactions that occur within those relationships. Thus, two members of the same dating couple may be involved in the same interaction and, due to differences in their views of romantic relationships, may interpret and respond to that interaction very differently. Furman and Wehner (1994, 1997) conceptualized individuals' views of romantic relationships as either *secure, dismissing,* or *preoccupied* in nature, similar to the categorization scheme used by attachment theorists. They asserted that individuals' views of romantic relationships are affected by romantic experiences and, in turn, affect adolescents' perceptions of their romantic experiences. Therefore, a correlation is expected between individuals' views of romantic relationships and their perceptions of the interaction occurring in their romantic relationships. In fact, empirical evidence using a video-recall procedure to understand adolescent dating couples' subjective understanding of their own videotaped interactions revealed significant differences in couple members' perceptions of their own and their dating partners' behaviors in their conversations. Moreover, these discrepancies were related to symptoms of depression in the adolescents (Welsh, Galliher, Kawaguchi, & Rostosky, 1999) and to the quality of their romantic relationships (Galliher, Welsh, Rostosky, & Kawaguchi, in press).

Downey and her colleagues suggested that one of the key ways in which internal working models of past relationships influence adolescents' current romantic relationships is via their impact on expectations of attaining acceptance and avoiding rejection (Downey et al., 2000; Downey & Feldman, 1996; Feldman & Downey, 1994). They have described adolescents who have developed anxious or angry expectations of rejection as a result of a history of experiencing rejection from parents, peers, and romantic partners. These "rejection-sensitive" individuals possess a cognitive-affective processing system that becomes activated in social situations where rejection is possible, and influence the interpretation and course of their interactions in ways that confirm and maintain their rejection expectations. One way rejection-sensitive individuals may try to avoid rejection is by exercising self-silencing behaviors, including the suppression of their opinions, thus submerging their individual identity within the context of the romantic relationship. In our current project of high-school-aged adolescents, the Study of Tennessee Adolescent Romantic Relationships (STARR), we found that girls who reported the greatest loss of their sense of self in their romantic relationships were significantly more likely to report depressive symptoms when compared to all other adolescents (Harper, Welsh, & Grello, 2002). Interestingly, adolescent boys were twice as likely as girls to lose their sense of self in their romantic relationships. However, losing their sense of self in their romantic relationships did not seem to be problematic for the adolescent boys in the sample. There was no correlation between loss of self and depressive symptoms in boys.

In summary, these recent models of romantic relationship development highlight the importance of understanding the lenses that individual adolescents bring to their romantic relationships and the ways in which these lenses impact couple members' own perceptions of their interpersonal relationships and interactions. These models predict that individual qualities that adolescent couple members bring to their romantic relationships (i.e., their beliefs and expectations of relationships formed from their prior experiences of relationships) will be related to the nature of their current romantic relationships, their interactions within the context of these current romantic relationships, and their subjective understanding of these interactions. In a cyclical and self-fulfilling manner, adolescents' subjective understanding of their interactions impacts the nature of their interactions with their romantic partners which, in a recursive loop, further impacts their subjective understanding of those interactions.

Although these models were formulated to understand the normative development of adolescent romantic relationships, they have clear implications for the development of depression, especially when integrated with the models of depression discussed previously. For example, adolescents who transition to romantic relationships with insecure models of relationships and are highly sensitive to relational rejection will be likely to interpret their partners' behaviors in more negative ways, which will result with these individuals responding to their partners in less effective ways, such as self-silencing. The interactional patterns within these relationships may resemble the "agitated submissive" interpersonal coping style posited by Powers (2000), in which girls experience their boyfriends as being overly conflictual due to their insecure view of relationships. They may respond to the perceived conflict in a submissive way in order to maintain the relationship. The lack of instrumentality and assertiveness they experience within the interaction further perpetuates their insecure models of romantic relationships and their expectations of rejection. Furthermore, even though most adolescent romantic relationships tend to be brief (Feiring, 1996), rather than viewing the end of romantic relationships as a normative event, adolescents with insecure models of relationships will be likely to interpret the breakup of their romantic relationships as additional evidence of their inability to maintain enduring close, positive relationships, which activates their interpersonal vulnerability (Leadbeater et al., 1995) and serves as a precipitant of depression. A ruminative cognitive style may further exacerbate their depressive feelings (Nolen-Hoeksema, 1994).

DEVELOPMENTAL CONSIDERATIONS
OF ROMANTIC RELATIONSHIPS

It is important to consider the developmental timing of romantic relationships in understanding their role as either a stressor or as a context for health or pathology. We begin with the premise that the ability to initiate and maintain romantic relationships is a normative process that proceeds along a developmental trajectory. Straying far from the normative developmental trajectory may be associated with psychological distress. For example, a monogamous long-term romantic relationship may be appropriate and growth-facilitating for late adolescents, but might be inappropriate and symptomatic of pathology in early adolescents. In this section we present theories and empirical evidence about the developmental timing of romantic relationships.

In a classic study, Dunphy (1963) interviewed and observed relationship development in a sample of 303 adolescents between ages 13 and 21. Based on his data, he proposed a stage theory that began with same-sex chumships (or isolated uni-sex cliques) in early adolescence, progressed to single-gendered cliques interacting in mixed-gender group settings in middle adolescence, followed by group dating in which romantic couples see each other in group settings, and finally culminating in intimate dyadic pairings in late adolescence. Although Dunphy's research was conducted almost 40 years ago in Australia, his stage theory based on that data has received recent empirical support (Connolly, Furman & Konarski, 2000; Feiring, 1996).

Erikson (1968) postulated that premature involvement in long-term romantic relationships may interfere with one's identity development. He asserted that adolescents who prematurely initiate romantic relationships do not experience "true intimacy" with each other; rather, they experience "pseudo-intimacy." Directing energy into a pseudointimate relationship may inhibit the development of individual identity, which Erikson believed was a prerequisite for experiencing true intimacy. Thus, committed dyadic dating too early may reflect identity foreclosure and would, therefore, be associated with poorer psychological adjustment. In support of Erikson's thesis, long-term romantic relationships in early and middle adolescents have been associated with subsequent emotional and academic problems (Connolly & Williams, 2000; Downey & Bonica, 1997), whereas they have been associated with increased psychological well-being in late adolescents (Niederjohn, Welsh, & Kawaguchi, 1998).

Sullivan (1953) proposed an alternative model that hypothesized that intimacy development *precedes* the development of a coherent sense of identity. Sullivan felt that intimacy development occurred in the context of same-sex chumships in early adolescence and in opposite-sex romantic peer relationships in late adolescence. Research in support of this notion has shown that boys and girls who have experienced genuine intimacy within a close friendship have an experiential basis for establishing intimacy with a romantic partner (Connolly & Goldberg, 1999). Sullivan's model posits that identity development does not become the primary task until late adolescence. Empirical investigations of these differing perspectives have not provided clear support for either position (Dyk & Adams, 1990; Levitz-Jones & Orlofsky, 1985). Rather, it appears that there are individual differences in rates and order of identity and intimacy development. It has been suggested that gender may play a role in the developmental progression, with Sullivan's ideas being more applicable to the development of girls and Erikson's views more appropriate for boys' development (Dyk & Adams, 1990). This controversy clearly has implications for the study of the connection between adolescent romantic relationships and adolescent functioning and mental health, as well as for the developmental nature of these connections. Specifically, Erikson's theory suggests that long-term committed romantic relationships in middle adolescence should be associated with poorer developmental functioning. Sullivan's theory does not predict this connection. Both theories, however, predict that long-term committed relationships will be associated with healthier functioning in late adolescence.

In summary, we have argued that the similar timing between the increase in rates of depression, the emergence of gender differences in depression, and the onset of adolescent romantic relationships is probably not coincidental. Rather, theoretical and empirical evidence suggest that adolescent dating relationships may serve as a stressor facilitating depression, an interpersonal context in which maladaptive coping styles develop and are maintained, as well as a context in which symptoms of psychological distress become manifest. Our integrative model posits that a variety of individual characteristics may place certain adolescents at risk for developing depressive symptoms when exposed to the stressors inherent in romantic relationships. Some of the key individual characteristics differentiating deleterious romantic relationships from healthy normative development include gender (female), a ruminative cognitive style of coping, an interpersonally vulnerable style, an agitated submissive (girls) or passive submissive (boys) pattern of interpersonal behavioral coping, an insecure internal working model of relationships, rejection sensitivity, self-silencing behavior, and developmental level (e.g., premature commitment, premature transition to sexual intercourse). We argue that these elements gleaned from theories of depression and theories of romantic relationship development fit together to provide a framework for understanding the intersection between adolescents' romantic relationships and the emergence of adolescent depressive symptoms (see Fig. 8.1). We turn now to a discussion of the literature on specific aspects of romantic relationships that are particularly problematic for adolescents who, for the reasons we've just discussed, may be more vulnerable to the developmental challenges of romantic relationships.

STRESSORS ASSOCIATED WITH THE ROMANTIC RELATIONSHIP CONTEXT

Romantic relationships are the most affectively charged domain for adolescents, and, thus, are the single largest source of stress for adolescents (Larson, Clore, & Wood, 1999; Larson & Asmussen, 1991). Larson and his colleagues conducted a series of beeper studies in which they beeped adolescents at random times during their day to understand more about adolescents' daily expe-

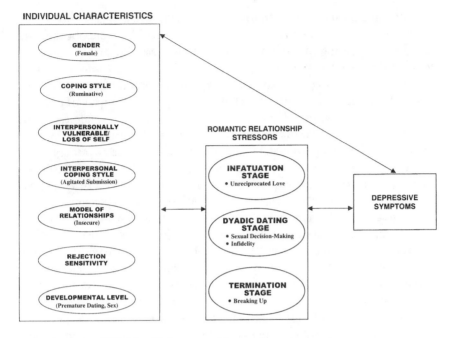

FIG. 8.1.   Pathways to adolescent depressive symptoms.

riences. The researchers asked adolescents to explain what was going on when they reported experiencing strong feelings connected with their various daily experiences. In a high school sample, they discovered that girls attributed 34% of their strong emotions to real and fantasized romantic relationships and boys attributed 25% of their strong emotions to romantic relationships (Wilson-Shockley, 1995). The suggestion that romantic relationships accounted for between a quarter and a third of all middle teens' strong emotional states was quite impressive and far greater than any other single domain including school, family, or same-sex peer relationships which accounted, respectively, for 13%, 9%, and 8% of adolescents' strong emotions. Although the majority of these strong emotions attributed to romantic relationships were positive, a substantial minority (42%) were negative, including feelings of depression. In another sample, they found that adolescents who were involved with a romantic partner during the week of data collection reported wider daily emotional swings than those who were not (Larson, Csikszentmihalyi, & Graef, 1980).

In a recent empirical investigation of over 12,000 nationally representative adolescents between 12 and 17 years of age, Joyner and Udry (2000) examined the association between change in depressive symptoms over a 1-year period and involvement in a romantic relationship. They found that adolescents who became romantically involved during the year between data collection points showed more depressive symptoms than adolescents who were not romantically involved during the year. Although both males and females showed this tendency, younger females experienced larger increases in depressive symptoms than males in response to romantic involvement. Joyner and Udry (2000) suggested that females are more vulnerable to the detrimental impact of romantic relationships. Romantic relationships are a new domain for adolescents in which they must struggle to gain competence. It is probably not surprising that they occupy a disproportionately large portion of adolescents' thoughts and create more stress (both positive and negative) than any other domain. These studies provide strong and compelling empirical data to suggest that aspects of romantic relationships are stressful and related to depression in adolescents.

Adolescent romantic relationships have three developmental stages. There are different challenges associated with each stage of relationship development. In the first stage, *infatuation,* adolescents are concerned with whether or not the object of their attraction reciprocates their interest. Unreciprocated love can be stressful for adolescents. If the interest is reciprocated, adolescents may move to the second stage of romantic relationships, *the dyadic dating stage.* The process of negotiating sexual behaviors and the potential consequences of those behaviors occur during this stage and can be stressful for some adolescents. One of the culturally endorsed assumptions of dyadic dating relationships is exclusivity. Thus, another difficult event that often arises during the dyadic phase of adolescents' romantic relationships occurs when a member of the couple violates this assumption and engages in an emotional or physical interaction with another potential dating partner. The dyadic dating stage typically evolves into the final stage of adolescent romantic relationships, *the termination stage.* Sometimes, the dyadic dating stage may culminate in a long-term, committed relationship or marriage, in which case the couple does not go through the termination stage. In the following sections, we examine these specific struggles associated with each of the developmental stages of adolescent dating: infatuation (stressor = unreciprocated love), dyadic dating stage (stressors = sexual behavior decision-making and infidelity), and the termination stage (stressor = breaking-up).

INFATUATION STAGE

Unreciprocated Love

Adolescents are clearly capable of experiencing romantic love. However, quite frequently, these feelings are one-sided and unreciprocated (Baumeister, Wotman, & Stillwell, 1993; Downey & Bonica, 1997; Hatfield, Schmitz, Cornelius, & Rapson, 1988). The feelings of love for another can exist even when the adolescent has rarely or never spoken to the admired one (Montgomery & Sorell, 1998). Their desire can continue for this admired person even when the admired individual shows no interest in return. Fantasy can be strong, as many adolescents believe that the admired one returns the same feelings of admiration (Montgomery & Sorell, 1998). When the fantasy is potent, adolescents frequently misinterpret signals from the admired individual. These misinterpretations can increase the adolescents' vulnerability to disappointment when the adolescent eventually discovers that the individual does not return the admiration (Hatfield, 1988).

Although adolescents typically report positive feelings during the pursuit of a relationship, when the rejection from unreciprocated adolescent love occurs, the rejected adolescent frequently reports decreased self-esteem and despair, increased humiliation and feelings of inferiority, and decreased feelings of desirability and attractiveness (Baumeister et al., 1993). These negative emotions are reportedly devastating and often enduring, as the adolescent not only has to deal with the personal rejection but the abandonment of the fantasy (Hatfield, 1988). Individuals who enter an unrequited love relationship who are rejection sensitive, have insecure attachment models, tend to ruminate, are interpersonally vulnerable, or have agitated submissive interpersonal patterns of interaction would be expected to be particularly prone to depressive symptoms following the rejection of an unreciprocated love relationship.

DYADIC DATING STAGE

Sexual Decision Making

Sexual behaviors are an important aspect of adolescents' romantic relationships. In fact, the incorporation of sexuality into relationships is the primary element that distinguishes romantic relationships from adolescents' other close relationships (Furman & Wehner, 1994; Hatfied & Rapson, 1987). Sexual intercourse, the primary and almost exclusive sexual behavior examined by researchers, has become a statistically normative behavior among adolescents (Graber, Britto, & Brooks-Gunn, 2000; Graber, Brooks-Gunn, & Galen, 1998). Almost a quarter of 14-year-olds, 30% of 15-year-olds, 42% of 16-year-olds, 59% of 17-year-olds, and 71% of 18-year-olds report having engaged in sexual intercourse (Alan Guttmacher Institute, 1994). In a nationally representative sample of over 6,000 adolescents in Grades 7–12, 33% of virgin adolescents reported engaging in intercourse for the first time within the first

2 months of a romantic relationship. Adolescents who had previously engaged in sexual intercourse progressed to intercourse more quickly in subsequent relationships, with 73% of sexually experienced adolescents engaging in intercourse within the first 2 months after beginning a new romantic relationship (Grello, Dickson, Welsh, & Wintersteen, 2000). Sexual activity is clearly prevalent in adolescent romantic relationships. The decision about what sexual activities should and will occur within the context of any given adolescent's romantic relationships and the sequella of those decisions, however, are often associated with a great deal of turmoil.

Adolescents report that peer pressure is one of the strongest motivations for engaging in sexual behavior (Cullari & Mikus, 1990; Koch, 1988), and peer group rejection or acceptance of sexual intercourse is very much related to adolescents' decisions to abstain or transition to sexual intercourse (Bearman & Bruckner, 1999; Graber, Brooks-Gunn, & Petersen, 1996). The decision to have sexual intercourse is experienced differently by adolescent males and females, with females experiencing first intercourse significantly more negatively than males (Koch, 1988; Weis, 1998). It is likely that adolescents who are more vulnerable to depression, particularly interpersonally vulnerable adolescents and less securely attached or rejection sensitive adolescents, are especially susceptible to the power of peer pressure. In addition, these high-risk adolescents may look to sexuality to compensate for poor past relationships (Whitbeck, Hoyt, Miller, & Kao, 1992). Attachment style has been empirically associated with adolescent sexual behavior (see Allen & Land, 1999). Not surprisingly, insecurely attached adolescents are more sexually promiscuous, have sex more frequently, and engage in sexual behaviors at an earlier age (Feeney & Noller, 1990; Hazen & Shaver, 1987; O'Beirne & Allen, 1996).

Adolescents often have a difficult time refusing unwanted sexual activity. In one study of college undergraduates, 46% of females and 62% of males reported having engaged in unwanted sexual intercourse (Muehlenhard & Cook, 1988). Peer pressure and general societal expectations, particularly for men, make it difficult for adolescents to refuse unwanted sexual experiences (Muehlanhard & Cook, 1988; Zimmerman, Sprecher, Langer, & Holloway, 1995). Although males experience greater social pressure to desire and engage in sexual intercourse, and report engaging in unwanted sexual intercourse more frequently than females, the negative impact appears greater for females (Zimmerman et al., 1995).

Sexual behaviors have been strongly linked with depression, especially in adolescent females. A powerful constellation of behaviors has been identified in adolescent females that includes sexual intercourse, alcohol, smoking, low self-esteem, depression, and suicide attempts (Adcock, Nagy, & Simpson, 1991; Harvey & Sprigner, 1995; Jessor, Costa, Jessor, & Donovan, 1983; Jessor

& Jessor, 1975; Whitbeck et al., 1992). This link is strongest in younger adolescents, suggesting that sexual intercourse may be a clearer marker of psychological distress when it occurs early or off-time rather than when it occurs at a more normative time. In support of this idea, O'Beirne and Allen (1996) found that insecure attachment styles were not related to whether a sample of at-risk 16-year-old adolescents had begun to have sexual intercourse, but were related to early sexual debut. Additionally, Crockett and her colleagues (Crockett, Bingham, Chopak, & Vicary, 1996) found that adolescents who transitioned to sexual intercourse "on time" had positive peer relationships and high academic involvement, whereas both males and females who transitioned early demonstrated significantly more problem behaviors than those who transitioned in middle adolescence. Interestingly, adolescents who transitioned in late adolescence had poor peer relationships. Similarly, Tubman, Windle, and Windle (1996) found evidence that premature sexual debut was associated with depression and that late transition to intercourse was associated with decreased self-esteem and poor social relationships. Grello and her colleagues examined a nationally representative sample of 2,377 adolescents who had never dated nor had ever had sexual intercourse and were followed up a year later (Grello, Welsh, Dickson, & Harper, 2002). They found adolescents who showed more depressive symptoms at Time 1 were more likely to enter sexual and dating relationships a year later and this transition further exacerbated their pre-existing depressive symptoms. Young adolescent females who engaged in sexual intercourse in both casual and dating relationships showed the highest levels of depressive symptoms both before and after becoming sexually active. These results suggest that promiscuity may be a marker, rather than a cause, of depressive symptoms in adolescents (Grello et al., 2001).

In an earlier project from our lab, we observed and interviewed 61 middle- to late-adolescent heterosexual couples in an intensive study of their communication processes, their relational and psychological functioning, and their sexual behavior. We found that distinct sexual behaviors were related in very different ways to the couple members' individual and relational functioning. Specifically, we found that the more affectionate sexual behaviors of hand-holding, kissing, and light petting were associated with more committed and more intimate relationships (Rostosky, Galliher, Welsh, & Kawaguchi, 2000; Rostosky, Welsh, Kawaguchi, & Vickerman, 1999). Whether or not couples were engaging in sexual intercourse was not related to their individual or relational functioning. However, sexual intercourse was associated with couple members' perceptions of higher levels of interpersonal conflict in their video-taped conversations (Rostosky et al., 2000). Additionally, we found that couple members' experience of having power or control in their sexual decision making was related to psychological well-being in the adolescent females. Female couple members who felt that they had less voice than their boyfriends in decisions about sex reported lower self-esteem (Galliher, Rostosky, Welsh, & Kawaguchi, 1999). These findings suggest that sexual behaviors and decision-making are related to adolescents' mental health.

In summary, sexual behaviors are associated with depressive symptoms in what is probably a bi-directional or cyclic fashion. That is, depressed adolescents are more likely to engage in sexual behaviors, specifically sexual intercourse, and these behaviors are likely to further exacerbate adolescents' depression. However, it is important to keep in mind that most of the literature on adolescent sexuality has operated from a deficit model, in which sexual behaviors (intercourse) are assumed to be a marker or symptom of psychological distress in adolescents. Thus, research operating from this deficit paradigm has focused on comparing adolescents who have had sexual intercourse with those who have not. This sort of investigation prevents an understanding of the diversity of adolescents' experiences about their sexuality. Further, by focusing exclusively on heterosexual intercourse as the definition of sexuality, the current research literature fails to capture the diversity of sexual behaviors experienced by heterosexual as well as gay and lesbian adolescents and the mental health implications of these behaviors. It is important for future research in this area to explore adolescent sexuality from a normative, developmental position that allows us to understand the meanings that adolescents ascribe to sexual behaviors and to their decisions about whether to engage in particular sexual activities. This approach will allow researchers to differentiate the adolescents for whom sexual behavior is symptomatic of psychological disturbance from those for whom sexual behavior is associated with healthy, developmentally appropriate exploration (Welsh, Rostosky, & Kawaguchi, 2000; Wilcox, 1999).

Infidelity

Heterosexual adolescents' romantic relationships are typically characterized by mutual expectations for emotional and sexual fidelity (Feldman & Cauffman, 1999a; Alan Guttmacher Institute, 1994; Sheppard, Nelson, & Andreoli-Mathie, 1995). This expectation is not universally held among gay adolescent males, however, as many hold more permissive attitudes regarding exclusivity within dyadic romantic relationships (Blasband & Peplau, 1985; Savin-Williams, 1998). Investigations of heterosexual adolescents' attitudes toward sexual betrayal reveal very low tolerance of infidelity from both males and females (Feldman & Cauffman, 1999b). Adolescents typically define infidelity in terms of sexual behaviors, especially petting and intercourse. Females have a broader definition of infidelity, as they are more likely to include non-intercourse behaviors indicative of emotional involvement in their meaning of romantic betrayal. Males tend to have a narrow definition of infidelity and typically identify only sexual intercourse with someone other than one's partner as being unfaithful (Roscoe, Cavanaugh, & Kennedy, 1988). Although both male and female adolescents report disapproval in their attitudes toward sexual betrayal, females report stronger disapproval than males (Feldman & Cauffman, 1999b; Seal, Agostinelli, & Hannett, 1994). However, there are relatively few gender differences in the actual incidence of sexual betrayal (Feldman & Cauffman, 1999b; Seal et al., 1994).

In spite of strong personal as well as cultural heterosexual prescriptions for exclusive dyadic romantic relationships, extra-dyadic romantic involvement is extremely common during adolescence among heterosexual and gay youth (Feldman & Cauffman, 1999b; Hansen, 1987; Savin-Williams, 1998). The majority of late adolescents report having been in a romantic relationship where either their partner or they had engaged in petting or intercourse with a third partner during their relationship (Feldman & Cauffman, 1999b; Roscoe et al., 1988; Hansen, 1987). In an early adolescent sample of sixth graders, suspicion of a partner's unfaithfulness was the main cause of conflict in romantic relationships (Downey & Bonica, 1997).

Feldman and Cauffman (1999a, 1999b) argued that the extremely high degree of sexual betrayal identified among adolescent romantic couples in spite of strong personal attitudes and cultural prescriptions about the unacceptability of infidelity may stem from competing and conflicting developmental demands of adolescence. Two of the most important developmental tasks of adolescence include identity development and intimacy development. Adolescents' search for identity is facilitated by exploration, including multiple romantic partners. To the extent that the perception of oneself as sexually and socially desirable is important to adolescents' developing identities, opportunities for greater sexual experiences that promote positive self-image will be difficult to resist. These developmental needs conflict, however, with adolescents' need to develop the capacity to maintain intimate, committed, enduring relationships. The high incidence of infidelity as well as the conflicting positive and negative emotions experienced by the betrayer may stem from these contradictory developmental demands (Feldman & Cauffman, 1999a; 1999b).

Unfaithfulness in a romantic relationship can be particularly devastating to adolescents who value exclusivity as they experience the violation as a loss of trust and loyalty in addition to the loss of the romantic partner (Feldman & Cauffman, 1999b). Adolescents express the belief that when a partner cheats, the relationship is irreparably damaged (Hansen, 1987). Most adolescent romantic relationships do not survive infidelity and are typically terminated once the transgression is exposed, and both partners appear to experience a range of negative emotions (Feldman & Cauffman, 1999a). Feldman and Cauffman (1999a) examined the emotional responses of late adolescents to extra-dyadic relationships. In their sample, the unfaithful adolescent often reported feelings of confusion and guilt, however they also reported positive emotions such as excitement. The aggrieved partner reported strong negative emotions including anger, sadness, and depression. Some also expressed feeling inadequate and guilty and blamed themselves for their partner's unfaithfulness. Those who were cheated on stated that their immediate reactions following the revelation of infidelity by their partner ranged from avoidance of the issue to obvious emotional distress with crying, withdrawal, anger, and aggression being reported. However, after the initial emotional response, aggrieved females were more tolerant and forgiving of their partners and less likely to withdraw or become violent to their partner than aggrieved males (Feldman & Cauffman, 1999a).

The guilt and confusion over violating one's personal values along with the feelings of excitement experienced in conjunction with the infidelity may lead certain unfaithful adolescents toward depression. Likewise, the loss of trust, loss of relationship, and the feelings of personal undesirableness experienced by the partner cheated on can also initiate a negative spiral of depression in vulnerable youth. The potential deleterious effects of infidelity may be less serious for gay male adolescents who may not hold the strong value about the wrongfulness of the behavior. Thus, the aspect of betrayal may not be as salient (Savin-Williams, 1998).

TERMINATION STAGE

Breaking Up

Breaking up with a romantic partner is common as adolescents will typically experience a series of brief but emotionally intense relationships (Feiring, 1996; Frazier & Cook, 1993; Montgomery & Sorell, 1998). The termination of these emotionally intense relationships is often traumatic for heterosexual as well as for gay and lesbian adolescents and clearly amplifies an adolescent's vulnerability for depression (Bell & Weinberg, 1978; Kaczmarek, Backlund, & Biemer, 1990; Mearns, 1991). Gay, lesbian, and heterosexual couples have not been found to differ in either their reasons for dissolving a relationship or on the levels of distress caused by the breakup (Kurdek, 1997). Several investigations have found that females are especially susceptible to depressive symptomatology immediately following the dissolution of a romantic relationship (Mearns, 1991; Monroe, Rohde, Seeley, & Lewinsohn, 1999).

Most studies have found that initial distress following the breakup of a romantic relationship is high and then subsides as time passes (Sprecher, Felmlee, Metts, Fehr, & Vanni, 1998). However, for some adolescents, especially female adolescents, the pain can endure. In a prospective investigation, Monroe et al. (1999) examined the relationship between the recent breakup of a romantic relationship and the onset of the first episode of Major Depressive Disorder (MDD) in 1,470 adolescents (mean age = 16.6 years). They found that the recent dissolution of a romantic relationship significantly increased the risk of onset of the first episode of MDD in their sample. Approximately 50% of the adolescents who met the diagnostic criteria for MDD had experienced the breakup of a romantic relationship within the preceding 12 months. For those with a prior history of depression, experiencing the recent breakup of a romantic relationship increased the likelihood of a subsequent episode of MDD. Depression was found to occur more frequently for girls even when other predictors of adolescent depression were controlled. Interestingly, while the majority of research provides evidence of intense initial distress (e.g., Sprecher et al., 1998), symptoms of MDD emerged on average 8 months following the termination of the relationship (Monroe et al., 1999) suggesting that while it is normal to feel a great deal of sadness immediately following the breakup of a romantic relationship, serious problems of depression result when adolescents are unable to move forward after the initial period of sorrow.

Mearns (1991) also found evidence linking clinical depression with recent romantic relationship dissolution, particularly for females, and explored a potential mechanism mediating this relationship. In support of cognitive theories of depression (Nolen-Hoeksema, 1994; Nolen-Hoeksema & Girgus, 1994), males and females used different cognitive styles of coping with the termination of their romantic relationships, and these coping strategies were associated with emotional outcomes. Males were more likely to cope with the termination of their romantic relationships using more active coping strategies in which they were proactive, had the ability to evaluate the problems in the relationship and to examine the larger picture, whereas females were more likely to use avoidant strategies that were more passive and ruminative in nature. Individuals who used proactive coping strategies experienced less intense emotional distress than those who relied on avoidant coping strategies.

Another explanation for the gender difference in the impact of romantic relationship termination may be a consequence of the intensity of emotion, commitment, and investment in the relationship. Although males report falling in love more frequently and at younger ages than females, females report experiencing more commitment and more passionate feelings towards their partners (Eaton, Mitchell, & Jolley, 1991; Hatfield, 1988; Hatfield, Brinton, & Cornelius, 1989). Studies have consistently demonstrated that increased commitment leads to increased relationship investment (Bui, Peplau, & Hill, 1996; Rusbult, 1980; Rusbult & Bunk, 1993). Other studies have found that the intensity of distress following the dissolution of a romantic relationship is dependent on the amount of investment the individual had in the relationship (Fine & Sacher, 1997; Frazier & Cook, 1993; Simpson, 1987; Sprecher, 1994). Thus, females' tendency to be more committed and have more investment in their romantic relationships, possibly in conjunction with their greater tendency to use less adaptive cognitive and interpersonal coping strategies, may contribute to the greater incidence of depression they experience following the termination of their romantic relationships.

There is evidence that the impact of relationship termination may depend on who initiates the breakup as well as the availability of alternative resources and social support. The partner who initiates the termination of the relationship suffers less initial emotional distress following the breakup than the aggrieved partner (Frazier & Cook, 1993). The initiator of a desired breakup has more control over the breakup and therefore, has had more time to mentally prepare for the loss of the relationship. The initiator of a desired breakup is also likely to be the less committed member of the couple and is more likely to have alternative options. The partner who feels responsible for the problems that led up to the breakup, especially when this partner is female, often experiences strong distress along with guilt and self-blame following the relationship termination (Sprecher, 1994). Psychological distress following relationship dissolution subsides when adolescents begin new romantic relationships (Simpson, 1987; Sprecher et al., 1998). This may stem from the increased self-esteem adolescents experience as a result of feeling renewed desirability, from the reparation of adolescents' fragile developing sense of personal identity which may be located within a relational domain, or from the resumption of day-to-day interactions, goals, and plans that were interrupted by the breakup. Social support in general facilitates recovery and adjustment following romantic relationship dissolution in the long run, although social support does little to relieve the initial distress of breaking up (Frazier & Cook, 1993).

IMPLICATIONS FOR PROGRAM PLANNING, HEALTH EDUCATION, AND CLINICAL INTERVENTION

Taken together, the available theoretical and empirical evidence supports a link between adolescent romantic relationships and the development of depressive symptomatology. Programs and policies designed to address the profound problem of adolescent depression should target adolescent romantic relationships as a key component. Intervention/prevention strategies need to be designed at multiple levels of influence including interventions focused on impacting adolescents directly as well as programs aimed at influencing those who work with and care for adolescents.

Large-scale depression prevention programs need to be developed and implemented in schools, church youth groups, and extracurricular youth groups (e.g., Girl Scouts, Girls and Boys Clubs). School-based health education is probably optimal for the mass dissemination of this sort of program. School-based health education curriculum should promote healthy relationship behaviors as well as teach positive coping strategies. While school-based health education programs frequently discuss abstinence and the consequences of sexual behavior, very few address normative romantic relationship development. Self-efficacy and an understanding of interpersonal needs may help adolescents prepare for future intimate relationships. Small group discussions can provide adolescents with a forum to share their experiences, both the highs and the lows of romance, as well as discussions of what love is and an understanding of healthy relationships. Rather than focusing only on the prevention of sexual behaviors, adolescents can benefit from learning proactive behaviors that promote positive emotional and physical health. The curriculum for these professionally facilitated groups of adolescents should focus on adolescents' romantic relationships, paying particular attention to the especially challenging aspects of romantic relationships (including unreciprocated love, sexuality, infidelity, and breaking up), and emphasizing specific adolescent-generated examples of adaptive and maladaptive strategies of coping with these specific relational challenges. The adaptive value of more proactive coping strategies and the destructiveness of ruminative coping strategies, for example, can be covered in response to relational challenges. Adolescents might also practice using more assertive, direct interpersonal communication patterns through role-playing or other techniques. Furthermore, these patterns might be contrasted with more maladaptive submissive communication patterns permitting adolescents to witness the less effective communication and coping styles in a more concrete forum. This sort of curriculum focused on health promotion would, optimally, fit within the curriculum of current health education programs. Alternatively, it could be condensed into a workshop format and presented to adolescents in schools or other youth-oriented organizations by trained professionals in the way that the recent APA Youth Violence Prevention Program, "Warning Signs" has been successfully administered (American Psychological Association, 1999).

Programs aimed at educating parents, teachers, and others who work with adolescents also need to be developed and enacted. Parents and others who work with adolescents need to be familiar with the symptoms of depression in order to make earlier referrals for professional services. They need to take the affective swings that adolescents regularly experience in relation to their romantic relationships seriously. Adults view adolescents' romantic relationship through very different lenses than do adolescents themselves. For example, adults understand the ephemeral nature of adolescents' romantic relationships and may minimize adolescents' affective experiences in well-intentioned attempts to reduce depressive symptoms. Phrases such as "There are many fish in the sea" or "You are better off without him" in response to the breakup of a romantic relationship tend to exacerbate rather than reduce depressive symptoms as the adolescent feels devalued and misunderstood (Kaczmarek & Backlund, 1991; LaGrand, 1989). It is important for adults to acknowledge their understanding of the magnitude of adolescents' pain surrounding romantic relationship challenges. In addition, however, it is important for adults to encourage adolescents to utilize active strategies for coping with their feelings. It would also be useful for adults to be aware of the interpersonal behavioral patterns associated with depression (e.g., agitated submission) in order to try not to reinforce these patterns of interaction in their daughters and female students, in particular. Finally, adults should be informed about the research on the developmental nature of adolescent romantic relationships. They need to know that dating and sexual activity in early adolescence is associated with depression and also that dating and certain sexual activities in late adolescence are not. This sort of curriculum might best be implemented in a workshop format in the context of PTA associations, church groups, and teacher in-service programs.

Screening programs for identifying adolescents who are at risk for depression can also be developed. These programs would administer measures to assess and identify adolescents who rely heavily on ruminative cognitive coping strategies, are very dependent (or interpersonally vulnerable) in their relationships, utilize agitated-submissive behavioral patterns for coping with interpersonal conflict, and possess insecure internal representations of relationships. Individuals identified by these screenings could be selectively offered early intervention programs (like those described earlier) if administering the programs to all adolescents is not considered feasible (although widespread implementation would be more desirable). Additionally, high-risk adolescents could be monitored more closely, especially during periods of relational (or other) stressful challenges. They could be referred during these challenging periods for professional intervention.

When an adolescent requires professional intervention, the clinician should help the adolescent examine his or her history of attachment with family, peers, and romantic partners as well as the ways in which he or she copes with interpersonal challenges. Although the vast majority of research operating from an attachment framework has emphasized how early infant–caregiver relationships are internalized and determine essentially stable personality characteristics, recent researchers are returning to Bowlby's (1969) previously neglected claim that attachment is a relational construct and that current relationships continue to be the major factor in whether an adolescent is in a secure or insecure state (Kobak, 1999). Furman and Wehner (1997) emphasized that adolescents may hold different views or internal representations of different types of relationships (e.g., parent–child, friend, romantic partner). In order for these internal representations to be effective, they must be open to changes that reflect experience. This theoretical possibility allows an opening for clinicians to help intervene in helping adolescents to construct more coherent, useful understandings of their relationships (see Slade, 1999 for more clinical detail).

CONCLUSION

We have argued for a link between developmental models of depression and developmental models of adolescent romantic relationships. We have provided theoretical and empirical evidence that suggests that certain cognitive and interpersonal strategies utilized by some adolescents, particularly female adolescents, along with insecure internal representations of interpersonal relationships put these adolescents at risk for developing depressive symptoms during their adolescent years. This risk may be expressed in the form of depression when these at-risk adolescents are faced with certain relational challenges common to adolescents as they learn to develop and maintain mature romantic relationships. We have recommended that depression prevention and intervention programs incorporate developmental theories and findings regarding adolescent romantic relationships with interpersonal and cognitive theories of depression in an attempt to change the ways in which adolescents interact within their romantic relationships, how they view their relationships, and how they cope with the challenging aspects of those relationships in order to promote healthier individual and relational functioning.

ACKNOWLEDGMENT

This chapter was supported by Grant RO1-HD39931 from the National Institute of Child Health and Human Development.

REFERENCES

Adcock, A. G., Nagy, S., & Simpson, J. A. (1991). Selected risk factors in adolescent suicide attempts. *Adolescence, 26*(104), 815–826.

Alan Guttmacher Institute. (1994). *Sex and America's teenagers.* Washington, DC: Author.

Allen, J. P., & Land, D. (1999). Attachment in adolescence. In J. Cassidy & P. R. Shaver (Eds.), *Handbook of attachment: Theory, research, and clinical applications* (pp. 319–335). New York: Guilford Press.

American Psychological Association. (1999). *Warning signs: A youth anti-violence initiative.* Washington, DC: Author.

Baumeister, R. F., Wotman, S. R., & Stillwell, A. M. (1993). Unrequited love: On heartbreak, anger, guilt, scriptlessness, and humiliation. *Journal of Personality and Social Psychology, 64*(3), 377–394.

Bearman, P., & Bruckner, H. (1999). Peer effects on adolescent sexual debut and pregnancy: An analysis of a national survey of adolescent girls. In *Peer potential: Making the most of how teens influence each other.* Washington, DC: The National Campaign to Prevent Teen Pregnancy.

Bell, A., & Weinberg, M. S. (1978). *Homosexualities: A study of diversity among men and women.* New York: Simon & Schuster.

Blasband, D., & Peplau, L. A. (1985). Sexual exclusivity versus openness in gay male couples. *Archives of Sexual Behavior, 14,* 395–412.

Bowlby, J. (1969). *Attachment and loss: Vol. 1. Attachment.* New York: Basic Books.

Bui, K. T., Peplau, L. A., & Hill, C. T. (1996). Testing the model of relationship commitment and stability in a 15-year study of heterosexual couples. *Personality and Social Psychology Bulletin, 22*(12), 1244–1257.

Cicchetti, D., & Toth, S. L. (1998). The development of depression in children and adolescents. *American Psychologist, 53,* 221–241.

Collins, W. A., & Sroufe, L. A. (2000). Capacity for intimate relationships: A developmental construction. In W. Furman, B. Brown, & C. Feiring (Eds.), *Contemporary perspectives on adolescent romantic relationships* (pp. 125–147). Cambridge, UK: Cambridge University Press.

Collins, W. A., Hennighausen, K. C., Schmit, D. T., & Sroufe, L. A. (1997). Developmental precursors of romantic relationships: A longitudinal analysis. In S. Shulman & W. A. Collins (Eds.), *New directions for child development: Romantic relationships in adolescence: Developmental perspectives* (pp. 21–36). San Francisco: Jossey-Bass.

Compas, B. E., Connor, J. K., & Hinden, B. R. (1998). New perspectives on depression during adolescence. In R. Jessor (Ed.), *New perspectives on adolescent risk behavior* (pp. 319–362). New York: Cambridge University Press.

Connolly, J., Furman, W., & Konarski, R. (2000). The role of peers in the emergence of heterosexual romantic relationships in adolescence. *Child Development, 71,* 1395–1408.

Connolly, J., & Goldberg, A. (1999). Romantic relationships in adolescence: The role of friends and peers in their emergence and development. In W. Furman, B. Brown, & C. Feiring (Eds.), *Contemporary perspectives on adolescent romantic relationships* (pp. 266–290). Cambridge, UK: Cambridge University Press.

Connolly, J., & Williams, T. (2000, April). *Psychosocial adaptation of precocious daters in early adolescence.* Paper presented at the biennial meeting of the Society for Research on Adolescence, Chicago, IL.

Crockett, L. J., Bingham, C. R., Chopak, J. S., & Vicary, J. R. (1996). Timing of first intercourse: The role of social control, social learning, and problem behavior. *Journal of Youth and Adolescence, 25*(1), 89–111.

Cullari, S., & Mikus, R. (1990). Correlates of adolescent sexual behavior. *Psychological Reports, 66,* 1179–1184.

Downey, G., & Bonica, C. (1997, April). Characteristics of early adolescent dating relationships. In D. P. Welsh & G. Downey (Co-Chairs), *Romantic relationships and adolescent adjustment.* Symposium conducted at the biennial meeting of the Society for Research in Child Development, Washington, DC.

Downey, G., Bonica, C., & Rincon, C. (2000). Rejection sensitivity and adolescent romantic relationships. In W. Furman, B. B. Brown, & C. Feiring (Eds.), *The development of romantic relationships in adolescence* (pp. 148–174). Cambridge, UK: Cambridge University Press.

Downey, G., & Feldman, S. (1996). Implications of rejection sensitivity for intimate relationships. *Journal of Personality and Social Psychology, 70,* 1327–1343.

Dunphy, D. C. (1963). The social structure of urban adolescent peer groups. *Sociometry, 26,* 230–246.

Dyk, P., & Adams, G. (1990). Identity and intimacy: An initial investigation of three theoretical models using cross-lag panel correlations. *Journal of Youth and Adolescence, 19,* 91–110.

Eaton, Y. M., Mitchell, M. L., & Jolley, J. M. (1991). Gender differences in the development of relationships during late adolescence. *Adolescence, 26*(103), 565–568.

Erikson, E. H. (1968). *Identity: Youth and crisis.* New York: W. W. Norton.

Feeney, J. A., & Noller, P. (1990). Attachment style as a predictor of adult romantic relationships. *Journal of Personality and Social Psychology, 58,* 281–291.

Feiring, C. (1996). Concepts of romance in 15-year-old adolescents. *Journal of Research on Adolescence, 6*(2), 181–200.

Feldman, S. S., & Cauffman, E. (1999a). Sexual betrayal among late adolescents: Perspectives of the perpetrator and the aggrieved. *Journal of Youth and Adolescence, 28*(2), 235–258.

Feldman, S. S., & Cauffman, E. (1999b). Your cheatin' heart: Attitudes, behaviors, and correlates of sexual betrayal in late adolescents. *Journal of Research on Adolescence, 9*(3), 227–252.

Feldman, S., & Downey, G. (1994). Rejection sensitivity as a mediator of the impact of childhood exposure to family violence on adult attachment behavior. *Development and Psychopathology, 6,* 231–247.

Fine, M. A., & Sacher, J. A. (1997). Predictors of distress following relationship termination among dating couples. *Journal of Social and Clinical Psychology, 16*(4), 381–388.

Frazier, P. A., & Cook, S. W. (1993). Correlates of distress following heterosexual relationship dissolution. *Journal of Social and Personal Relationships, 10,* 55–67.

Furman, W., & Wehner, E. A. (1994). Romantic views: Toward a theory of adolescent romantic relationships. In R. Montemayor, G. R. Adams, & T. P. Gullotta (Eds.), *Personal relationships during adolescence* (pp. 168–195). Thousand Oaks, CA: Sage.

Furman, W., & Wehner, E. A. (1997). Adolescent romantic relationships: A developmental perspective. In S. Shulman & W. A. Collins (Eds.), *New directions for child development: Romantic relationships in adolescence: Developmental perspectives* (pp. 21–36). San Franciso: Jossey-Bass.

Galliher, R. V., Rostosky, S. S., Welsh, D. P., & Kawaguchi, M. C. (1999). Power and psychological well-being in late adolescent romantic relationships. *Sex Roles, 40,* 689–710.

Galliher, R. V., Welsh, D. P., Rostosky, S. S., & Kawaguchi, M. C. (in press). Interaction and relationship quality in late adolescent romantic couples. *Journal of Social and Personal Relationships.*

Graber, J. A., Britto, P. R., & Brooks-Gunn, J. (2000). What's love got to do with it? Adolescents' and young adults' beliefs about sexual and romantic relationships. In W. Furman, B. B. Brown, & C. Feiring (Eds.), *The development of romantic relationships in adolescence* (pp. 364–395). Cambridge, UK: Cambridge University Press.

Graber, J. A., Brooks-Gunn, J., & Galen, B. R. (1998). Betwixt and between: Sexuality in the context of adolescent transitions. In R. Jessor (Ed.), *New perspectives in adolescent risk behavior* (pp. 270–316). Cambridge, UK: Cambridge University Press.

Graber, J. A., Brooks-Gunn, J., & Petersen, A. C. (1996). Adolescent transitions in context. In J. A. Graber, J. Brooks-Gunn, & A. C. Petersen (Eds.), *Transitions through adolescence: Interpersonal domains and context* (pp. 369–383). Mahwah, NJ: Lawrence Erlbaum Associates.

Grello, C. M., Dickson, J. W., Welsh, D. P., & Wintersteen, M. B. (2000, April). Adolescent romantic relationships: When do they begin having sex? Poster presented at the 16th Biennial meeting of the Conference on Human Development, Memphis, TN.

Grello, C. M., Welsh, D. P., Dickson, J. W., &, Harper, M. S. (2002). *Depressive sumptoms and the transition to dating relationships and sexual behavior in adolescents.* Manuscript submitted for publication.

Hansen, G. L. (1987). Extradyadic relations during courtship. *Journal of Sex Research, 23*, 382–390.

Harper, M. S., Welsh, D. P., & Grello, T. (2002, April). Silencing the self: Depressive symptoms and the loss of self in adolescent romantic relationships. In D. P. Welsh (Chair), *When love hurts: Adolescent romantic relationships and depressive symptoms.* Symposium conducted at the biennial meeting of the Society for Research on Adolescence, New Orleans, LA.

Harvey, S. M., & Sprigner, C. (1995). Factors associated with sexual behavior among adolescents: A multivariate analysis. *Adolescence, 30*(118), 253–264.

Hatfield, E. (1988). Passionate and compassionate love. In R. J. Sternberg & M. L. Barnes (Eds.), *The psychology of love* (pp. 191–217). New Haven, CT: Yale University Press.

Hatfield, E., Brinton, C., & Cornelius, J. (1989). Passionate love and anxiety in young adolescents. *Motivation and Emotion, 13(4)*, 271–289.

Hatfield, E., Schmitz, E., Cornelius, J., & Rapson, R. L. (1988). Passionate love: How early does it begin? *Journal of Psychology and Human Sexuality, 1*, 35–51.

Hatfield, E., & Rapson, R. L. (1987). Passionate love/sexual desire: Can the same paradigm explain both? *Archives of Sexual Behavior, 16*, 259–278.

Hazen, C., & Shaver, P. (1987). Romantic love conceptualized as an attachment process. *Journal of Personality and Social Psychology, 52*, 502–511.

Jessor, R., Costa, F., Jessor, S., & Donovan, J. E. (1983). Time of first intercourse: A prospective study. *Journal of Personality and Social Psychology, 44*, 608–626.

Jessor, R., & Jessor, S. (1975). Transition from virginity to nonvirginity among youth: A social-psychological study over time. *Developmental Psychology, 11*, 473–484.

Joyner, K., & Udry, R. (2000). You don't bring me anything but down: Adolescent romance and depression. *Journal of Health and Social Behavior, 41*, 369–391.

Kaczmarek, M. G., & Backlund, B. A. (1991). Disenfranchised grief: The loss of an adolescent romantic relationship. *Adolescence, 26*(102), 253–259.

Kaczmarek, P., Backlund, B., & Biemer, P. (1990). The dynamics of ending a romantic relationship: An emipirical assessment of grief in college students. *Journal of College Student Development, 31*, 319–324.

Kobak, R. (1999). The emotional dynamics of disruptions in attachment relationships: Implications for theory, research, and clinical intervention. In J. Cassidy & P. R. Shaver (Eds.), *Handbook of attachment: Theory, research, and clinical applications* (pp. 21–43). New York: Guilford Press.

Koch, P. B. (1988). The relationship of first intercourse to later sexual functioning concerns of adolescents. *Journal of Adolescent Research, 3*(3/4), 345–362.

Kurdek, L. A. (1997). The link between facets of neuroticism and dimensions of relationship commitment: Evidence from gay, lesbian, and heterosexual couples. *Journal of Family Psychology, 11,* 503–514.

LaGrand, L. E. (1989). Youth and the disenfranchised breakup. In K. J. Doka (Ed.), *Disenfranchised grief: Recognizing the hidden sorrow* (pp. 173–185). Lexington, MA: Lexington Books.

Larson, R. W., & Asmussen, L. (1991). Anger, worry, and hurt in early adolescence: An enlarging world of negative emotions. In M.E. Colten & S. Gore (Eds.), *Adolescent stress: Causes and consequences* (pp. 21–41). New York: Aldine de Gruyter.

Larson, R. W., Clore, G. L., & Wood, G. A. (1999). The emotions of romantic relationships: Do they wreak havoc on adolescents? In W. Furman, B. Brown, & C. Feiring (Eds.), *The development of romantic relationships in adolescence* (pp. 19–49). Cambridge, UK: Cambridge University Press.

Larson, R. W., Csikszentmihalyi, M., & Graef, R. (1980). Mood variability and the psychosocial adjustment of adolescents. *Journal of Youth and Adolescence, 9,* 469–490.

Leadbeater, B. J., Blatt, S. J., & Quinlan, D. M. (1995). Gender-linked vulnerabilities to depressive symptoms, stress, and problem behaviors in adolescents. *Journal of Research on Adolescence, 5,* 1–29.

Levitz-Jones, E., & Orlofsky, J. (1985). Separation-individuation and intimacy capacity in college women. *Journal of Personality and Social Psychology, 49,* 156–169.

Mearns, J. (1991). Coping with a breakup: Negative mood regulation expectancies and depression following the end of a romantic relationship. *Journal of Personality and Social Psychology, 60*(2), 327–334.

Monroe, S. M., Rohde, P., Seeley, J. R., & Lewinsohn, P. M. (1999). Life events and depression in adolescence: Relationship loss as a prospective risk factor for the onset of major depressive disorder. *Journal of Abnormal Psychology, 108*(4), 606–614.

Montgomery, M. J., & Sorell, G. T. (1998). Love and dating experience in early and middle adolescence: Grade and gender comparisons. *Journal of Adolescence, 21,* 677–689.

Muehlenhard, C. L., & Cook, S. W. (1988). Men's self-reports of unwanted sexual activity. *Journal of Sex Research, 24,* 58–72.

Niederjohn, D. M., Welsh, D. P., & Kawaguchi, M. C. (1998, August). *Late adolescence: A period of transition in intimate dating relationships.* Poster presented at the annual meeting of the American Psychological Association, San Francisco, CA.

Nolen-Hoeksema, S. (1994). An interactive model for the emergence of gender differences indepression in adolescence. *Journal of Research on Adolescence, 4,* 519–534.

Nolen-Hoeksema, S., & Girgus, J. S. (1994). The emergence of gender differences in depression during adolescence. *Psychological Bulletin, 115,* 424–443.

O'Beirne, H. A., & Allen, J. P. (1996, March). *Adolescent sexual behavior: Individual, peer, and family correlates.* Paper presented at the biennial meeting of the Society for Research on Adolescence, Boston.

Powers, S. I. (2000). *Test of a biopsychosocial model of adolescent depression.* Funded NIMH grant proposal.

Powers, S. I., Pollack, K., Nascimento, E., & Sachar, T. (1998, February). *Family interaction and gender differences in adolescent internalizing and externalizing symptoms.* Paper presented at the biennial meeting of the Society for Research in Adolescence, San Diego, CA.

Powers, S. I., & Welsh, D. P. (1999). Mother–daughter interactions and adolescents girls' depression. In M. Cox & J. Brooks-Gunn (Eds.), *Conflict and cohesion in families: Causes and consequences.* Mahwah, NJ: Lawrence Erlbaum Associates.

Roscoe, B., Cavanaugh, L. E., & Kennedy, D. R. (1988). Dating infidelity: Behaviors, reasons, and consequences. *Adolescence, 23*(89), 35–43.

Rostosky, S. S., Galliher, R. V., Welsh, D. P., & Kawaguchi, M. C. (2000). Sexual behaviors and relationship qualities in late adolescent couples. *Journal of Adolescence, 23,* 583–597.

Rostosky, S. S., Welsh, D. P., Kawaguchi, M. C., & Vickerman, R. C. (1999). Commitment and sexual behaviors in adolescent dating couples. In W. Jones & J. Adams (Eds.), *Handbook of interpersonal commitment and relationship stability* (pp. 323–338). New York: Plenum.

Rusbult, C. E. (1980). Commitment and satisfaction in romantic associations: A test of the investment model. *Journal of Experimental Social Psychology, 16*(2), 172–186.

Rusbult, C. E., & Bunk, B. P. (1993). Commitment processes in close relationships: An interdependence analysis. *Journal of Social and Personal Relationships, 10*(2), 175–204.

Savin-Williams, R. C. (1998). *And then I became gay.* New York: Rutledge.

Seal, D. W., Agostinelli, G., & Hannett, C. A. (1994). Extradydadic romantic involvement: Moderating effects of sociosexuality and gender. *Sex Roles, 31*(1/2), 1–22.

Sheppard, W., Nelson, E., & Andreoli-Mathie, V. (1995). Dating relationships and infidelity: Attitudes and behavior. *Journal of Sex and Marital Therapy, 21,* 202–212.

Slade, A. (1999). Attachment theory and research: Implications for the theory and practice of individual psychotherapy with adults. In J. Cassidy & P. R. Shaver (Eds.), *Handbook of attachment: Theory, research, and clinical applications* (pp. 575–594). New York: Guilford Press.

Simpson, J. A. (1987). The dissolution of romantic relationships: Factors involved in relationship stability and emotional distress. *Journal of Personality and Social Psychology, 53*(4), 683–692.

Sprecher, S. (1994). Two sides to the breakup of dating relationships. *Personal Relationships, 1,* 199–222.

Sprecher, S., Felmlee, D., Metts, S., Fehr, B., & Vanni, D. (1998). Factors associated with distress following the breakup of a close relationship. *Journal of Social and Personal Relationships, 15*(6), 791–809.

Sullivan, H. S. (1953). *The interpersonal theory of psychiatry.* New York: Norton.

Tubman, J. G., Windle, M., & Windle, R. C. (1996). The onset and cross-temporal patterning of sexual intercourse in middle adolescence: Prospective relation with behavioral and emotional problems. *Child Development, 67,* 327–343.

Weis, D. L. (1998). Interpersonal heterosexual behaviors: Adolescent sexuality. In P. B. Koch & D. L. Weis (Eds.), *Sexuality in America: Understanding our sexual values and behavior.* New York: Continuum.

Welsh, D. P., Galliher, R. V., Kawaguchi, M. C., & Rostosky, S. S. (1999). Discrepancies in adolescent romantic couples' and observers' perceptions of couple interaction and their relationship to mental health. *Journal of Youth and Adolescence, 28,* 645–666.

Welsh, D. P., Rostosky, S. S., & Kawaguchi, M.C. (2000). A normative perspective of adolescent girls' developing sexuality. In C. B. Travis & J. S. White (Eds.), *Sexuality, society, and feminism: Psychological perspectives on women* (pp. 111–140). Washington, DC: American Psychological Association.

Whitbeck, I. B., Hoyt, D. R., Miller, M., & Kao, M. (1992). Parental support, depressed affect, and sexual experience among adolescents. *Youth and Society, 24*(2), 166–177.

Wilcox, B. L. (1999). Sexual obsessions: Public policy and adolescent girls. In N. Johnson, M. Roberts, & Worrell, J. (Eds.), *Beyond appearance: A new look at adolescent girls* (pp. 333–354). Washington, DC: American Psychological Association.

Wilson-Shockley, S. (1995). *Gender differences in adolescent depression: The contribution of negative affect.* Unpublished master's thesis, University of Illinois at Urbana-Champaign.

Zimmerman, R. S., Sprecher, S., Langer, L. M., & Holloway, C. (1995). Adolescents' perceived ability to say "No" to unwanted sex. *Journal of Adolescent Research, 10*(3), 383–399.

9

Child Maltreatment, Adolescent Dating, and Adolescent Dating Violence

Christine Wekerle
Centre for Addiction and Mental Health
University of Toronto

Effie Avgoustis
York University

Adolescent dating is becoming less of a mystery to researchers. While still an emergent area, the normative context of dating is described by a general pattern where most youth are thought to move from the smaller same-sex cliques of middle childhood to larger mixed-sex crowds of early to mid-adolescence, to heterosexual coupling of mid- to late adolescence (Connolly, Furman, & Konarski, 2000). Given that there is no epidemiological work on adolescent dating patterns over the course of adolescence, there may be substantial variation within age groups and between genders, ranging from dating abstinence to exclusive partnering. In their peerships, teens are seeking to fulfill an increasing number of needs, including recreation, status-seeking, affiliation, support, and emotional, physical, and sexual intimacy (Feiring & Furman, 2000; Furman & Wehner, 1994, 1997). Adolescents develop heterosocial skills through observational learning and direct reinforcement from their peer groups (Hansen, Christopher, & Nangle, 1992).

Romantic relationships, for many youth, are initiated in early- to mid-adolescence (Krajewski, Rybarik, Dosch, & Gilmore, 1996), as their social networks come to include a larger number of opposite-sex friends (Feiring & Lewis, 1991; Connolly, Craig, Goldberg, & Pepler, 1999; Connolly et al., 2000). A survey conducted by the Henry J. Kaiser Family Foundation and *YM* magazine (1999) found that while the majority of 13- to 14-year-olds surveyed reported they had begun dating, romantic behaviors were largely limited to kissing, with only 4% identifying intercourse. By age 17 to 18 years, 52% of the youth reported dating relationships as including intercourse. Interestingly, while most of the 13- to 18-year-old youth surveyed ($N = 650$) had a romantic relationship, only 19% self-identified as having had a "serious" partnership, which was dominantly reflected by exclusivity, rather than the onset of intercourse or a feeling of "being in love." It is suggested that these more serious romantic relationships are typically found in late adolescence and are functionally distinct in that they have greater levels of caregiving and commitment (Paul & White, 1990). The adolescent romantic relationship, where the partner is the preferred attachment figure, having supplanted the parent in the attachment hierarchy, is suggested as a central feature under stable or committed relationships (Furman & Wehner, 1994). Ainsworth (1989) identified four key components of an attachment relationship. Applied to the adolescent romantic relationship, the youth should display proximity-seeking towards their partner (e.g., much physical togetherness), more exploratory behavior when in the presence of their partner (e.g., greater risk taking behavior in their company), seeking out the partner for protection or comfort when in a situation of threat (e.g., handling problems with parents) and protest reactions to an involuntary separation (e.g., breaking up). However, it remains an empirical question whether, when, and why an attachment relationship may form earlier than expected in adolescence. As well, it is of interest how well integrated the attachment system becomes with the sexual/reproductive system.

Clinically, we have recently been involved with a 16-year-old female who has a history with child protective services. She reported to us her most recent partnership with a boy 3 years her senior, whom she conceptualized as her "boyfriend." Very sadly, this 2½-week relationship ended with her rape. This brief, but affectively intense, relationship may have borne similarities to her earlier attachment relationships, raising the issue as to whether adolescents approach their romantic relationships in a manner consistent with the attachment models they have generated from their earlier caregiving experiences. Also, it suggests a possibility that maltreated youth may differ from their non-maltreated counterparts in their approach to and the function of their close relationships. For the maltreated youth, romantic relationships may mark an area of greater developmental challenge. Because of unmet basic needs for love, belongingness, and protection within the caregiving context, it has been speculated that the maltreated youth may be at risk for showing an accelerate push towards dating (i.e., early age of onset), as well as prematurely transferring priority attachment from caregivers to their partners (i.e., form an attachment relationship earlier) (Mueller & Silverman, 1989).

This chapter first overviews child maltreatment and the importance of trauma to interpersonal functioning. We then review the literature on normative dating, including such factors as age of onset of dating, duration of dating relationship, and age of onset of sexual intercourse. As such normative understandings are considered, the relevant empirical work on child maltreatment is presented. Next, we discuss the problem of dating violence and subsequently consider empirical work on child maltreatment history as a risk factor. Finally, we examine associated contexts for dating violence, especially substance abuse, and consider its relation to child maltreatment. Given that the literature on adolescent interpersonal outcomes for maltreated youth is in its early stages, discussion of the issues that the maltreated youth may face are provided as a means of mapping out future research needs.

CHILD MALTREATMENT
AND INTERPERSONAL FUNCTIONING

Child maltreatment is a point of sadness across our human history. It creates a substantial burden of suffering such that its costs to individuals and families, to health care, legal, education, and other systems identify child maltreatment as an urgent public health issue (see Wekerle & Wall, 2002). Child maltreatment has been defined as "physical or emotional injury, sexual abuse or exploitation, or maltreatment of a child under the age of eighteen by a person in a position of responsibility, trust, or power" (The World Health Organization [WHO], 1999). Physical maltreatment refers to behaviors such as striking, shaking, and scalding, which leave some evidence of physical injury (e.g., bruising, bleeding, burns). Sexual abuse ranges from adult-to-child exposure (of body, pornography etc.) to more invasive assaults such as fondling, oral sex, and penetration. Neglect represents a range of acts of omission, including failure to provide the child with basic health care, nutrition, education, and protection from danger and injury. Emotional abuse includes such behaviors as verbal and emotional assaults (e.g., rejection, ridicule, isolation), as well as inappropriate confinement (e.g., physical restraint); it is commonly thought to coincide with other forms of abuse (Wekerle & Wolfe, 1996).

Close to three million children are identified by child protective services (CPS) as abuse and neglect victims in the United States, either substantiated or indicated (i.e., reasonable grounds, but insufficient evidence for prosecution) (U.S. Department of Health and Human Services [USDHHS], 2001). The national rate of maltreatment was 15 child victims per 1,000 children in the population. Neglect emerged as the most prevalent form (52% of children). Neglect is predominantly committed by adult females (69%). Victimization decreases with child age, with the majority of victims under age 8, and with similar proportions of male and female children. To a lesser extent than neglect, are physical abuse (23%) and sexual abuse (14%). While similar proportions of males and females are represented in both the perpetrators and victims of physical abuse, males predominantly perpetrate sexual abuse (82%), with females being predominantly victimized (77%). Emotional abuse is a rarer cause for reporting (approximately 6% of cases).

When considering risk factors, it appears that it is the accumulation of risk factors, rather than a single stressor, that is the more potent predictor of serious emotional and behavioral problems (e.g., Rutter, 1989, Seifer & Sameroff, 1987). Such a cumulative risk model acknowledges that multiple negative experiences may engender a reinforcement of maladaptive coping. The constellation of risk factors may be conceptualized as either additive (each stressor makes a unique contribution; see Garmezy, Masten, & Tellegen, 1984), multiplicative (one stressor potentiates the other; see Rutter 1989), or developmentally activated (critical experience at particular developmental juncture alters the trajectory of development; see Rutter, 1989, 1996). With regard to forming dating relationships, child maltreatment history may function as an additive risk factor (individual types or total trauma, e.g., Herman, 1992), a multiplicative risk factor (different types of maltreatment, e.g., McGee, Wolfe, & Wilson, 1997), as well as one that is developmentally activated by the transition in adolescence to forming romantic relationships (e.g., Earls, Cairns, & Mercy, 1993). To date, there is insufficient work with child protective services samples of adolescents and maltreated youth in the community to suggest *the way* in which child maltreatment impairs adolescent interpersonal functioning. We have, however, begun to accumulate knowledge on the range of negative outcomes for maltreated youth with regard to adolescent romantic relationships, largely based on studies of community samples of youth.

Child maltreatment has been associated with an array of negative sequelae including aggression, delinquency, depression, substance abuse, suicidal ideation, running away, promiscuity, early pregnancy, and revictimization (e.g., Beitchman, Zucker, Hood, Da Costa, & Akman, 1991; Beitchman et al., 1992; Kolko, 1996; Wekerle & Wolfe, 1996; Widom, 1989, 1998). For example, Wolfe, Wekerle, Reitzel-Jaffe, and Lefebvre (1998) divided a school-based sample of 15-year-olds into maltreated and non-maltreated based on youth self-report. Maltreatment was defined as: (a) repeated (i.e., youth indicated a frequency of "sometimes" or "a lot"), and (b) one or more experiences of severe physical abuse (i.e., "kicked, bit or punched"; "choked, burned or scalded"; "threatened with severe harm"; "physically attacked in some way") or sexual abuse (i.e., "threatened to have sex"; "touched the sexual parts of your body"; "tried to have sex or sexually attacked"). Compared to their non-maltreated counterparts ($n = 277$), maltreated youth ($n = 132$) reported more hostility and interpersonal sensitivity (e.g., self-depreciation, feelings of uneasiness), lower problem-solving self-efficacy, higher self- and teacher ratings on peer aggression. No significant differences were observed on positive peer behavior. Maltreated youth, while they may not be at a disadvantage for exhibiting prosocial behavior, would appear to struggle with aggression toward others and compromised self-functioning.

One important issue to consider is whether child maltreatment sets the stage for adolescent atypical dating patterns, including involvement in dating violence. From both a social learning theory (SLT; Bandura, 1977; O'Leary, 1988; O'Leary, Malone, Masten, & Tyree, 1994; Wall & McKee, 2002) and an attachment theory (Bowlby 1969, 1973, 1979, 1980; Crittenden, 1997; Crittenden & Claussen, 2002) perspective on relationship violence, childhood experiences that pair intimacy with either observed or experienced aggression may exert an influence on subsequent close relationships through one's schema for reinforced behaviors (e.g., self-efficacy, outcome expectancies) or working model for close relationships (e.g., inner working models of the self, the other, and of the relationship). While attachment theory asserts that both sides of a relationship would be learned and, hence, both victim and victimizer roles would be in a maltreated child's behavioral repertoire (e.g., Wekerle & Wolfe, 1998), social learning theory articulates the perpetrator role more clearly than that of the victim, as acquiring victim behaviors would suggest either positive or negative reinforcement was observed or experienced (Wall & McKee, 2002). SLT would suggest that there is something that is being reinforced in the victim for this behavior pattern to be repeated or maintained. Such a functional relationship, though, would seem very difficult to discern, although a negative self-view as victim may be reinforced and reinforcing (i.e., role or model-consistent information) to persons conditioned in this way. Also, the very fact of being in a relationship, even though it is an abusive one, may be reinforcing to the victim; this may be of particular relevance to the adolescent for whom partnership status may imply secondary gains of greater peer acceptance.

In the case of witnessing domestic violence, modelling of the observed aggression is suggested by SLT and the role of such relevant SLT factors as identification with the parent/perpetrator are not typically addressed in the context of child maltreatment and subsequent interpersonal aggression. One recent exception is a study of undergraduates that found that students who witnessed only their same-sex parent perpetrate physical marital aggression were at increased risk for perpetrating physical aggression in their dating relationship (Jankowski, Leitenberg, Henning, & Coffey, 1999). It was also noted that there was no increased risk for dating violence perpetration when the youth witnessed only their opposite-sex parent perpetrate aggression. No same-sex modeling effects were found for dating violence victimization; witnessing bi-directional marital violence increased the risk for receiving aggression from a dating partner.

Whether a direct or indirect exposure to parental aggression occurs, aggression is a viable, and perhaps preferred, behavioral option that may be learned. While based on female college students, Murphy and Blumenthal (2000) found support that interpersonal problems with dominance, intrusiveness, and vindictiveness fully mediated the association between childhood exposure to family violence and aggressive dating relationships (i.e., both aggression by partner and aggression by self indicated intimate aggression). These authors suggested that instead of acquiring a tendency to repeat specific forms of aggression (e.g., those specifically witnessed), the acquisition of a more generalized tendency toward domineering and controling behavior may occur (i.e., a broad response set).

In the case of attachment theory, given that unmet dependency needs that exist in the maltreated child, where there may also be a fear of injury, loss, or abandonment, the stimulation of dependency needs may create an intrapersonal distress state (e.g., panic and preoccupation with the other; suppression of anxiety and avoidance of the other) that would be expected to invoke the attachment system. In the next sections, we consider normative dating patterns and the relevant literature on child maltreatment and then adolescent dating violence, considering child maltreatment as a risk factor.

NORMATIVE ADOLESCENT DATING

Hansen et al. (1992) discussed the importance of heterosocial interaction to adolescent development. Peerships may assist youth, for example, with establishing support systems, sexual attitudes, social values, and improving or maintaining self-esteem. Dating relationships may additionally promote interpersonal competence, enhancement of status in the peer group, experimentation with sex-role behaviors and sexual activity, and mate selection. These authors identified relevant social learning mechanisms in heterosocial competence (e.g., date initiation) as exposure to appropriate social skill models, consequences associated with the youth's social behavior (e.g., reinforcement, punishment, extinction), exposure to and participation in peer social activity, and cognitive factors (e.g., self-statements, attributions). These authors discussed that dating-related problems (e.g., heterosocial anxiety) may be a function of the transition to a new social role and, therefore, may be transitory. It would seem that most youth do move through the dating process with low levels of distress; it is also suggested that maltreated youth are among those more likely to encounter problems while negotiating the transition to romantic relationships.

AGE OF DATING ONSET AND DURATION
OF DATING RELATIONSHIPS

Feiring has reported a number of studies based on a longitudinal project that was initiated in infancy with Caucasian, middle-class families. In one report ($N = 117$), Feiring (1996) found that most (88%) 15-year-old youth reported that they had begun dating, with fewer (21%) reporting a current partnership at the time of the interview. This is consistent with other research that most 14- to 15-year-olds have initiated dating (e.g., Connolly & Johnson, 1996). The average length of relationship was about 4 months, with 8% of teens reporting a relationship of 1 year or longer. Frequent contact was noted with an average of over 5 days of both in-person and phone contact across the week. In this sample, dating occurred more in a group than in a couples-only context, with girls reporting a greater number of group context dates than boys. Finally, this study found that positive personality traits (e.g., nice, outgoing) and physical attractiveness were the most frequently reported likes about the dating partner, for both males and females. Feiring characterized the dating patterns of these 15-year-olds as "short-term fascination" given the high frequency contact within the week. It was not clear, however, from the data whether this contact was facilitated by attendance in the same school.

Feiring (1999) also considered the duration of romantic relationships and found an increase over time, with an average length of 3.8 months at age 15 to an average of 9.3 months at age 18. The longest duration of partnerships was reported by girls who had a larger number of opposite-sex friends. It remains to be determined what implications are associated with these gender differences, whether the quality of partnerships are dominantly positive or are associated with other positive factors. For example, in an earlier report on this sample (Feiring & Lewis, 1991), it was found that, for girls at age 13, as the number of and daily contact with opposite-sex friends increased, self-perceived academic competence decreased. Thus, greater interest in and time commitment to opposite-sex friends may be an indicator of at least transitory problems.

Early romantic involvement has been associated with a greater risk, including courtship violence (Makepeace, 1986) and other antisocial indicators (Neemann, Hubbard, & Masten, 1995). However, as is evident from the work just mentioned, age of dating onset alone may be insufficient as a predictor of adolescent problems; complex relationships may exist that would include the time involvement and commitment to the relationship, the duration of partnership, the number of opposite-sex friends, as well as other factors such as the onset of sexual intercourse in the dating relationship, the age of the dating partner, and the function of the dating relationship.

With regard to age of onset, duration, number of opposite-sex friends, and time involvement, unfortunately, there is little work specifically on child protective services samples or community youth who are elevated in terms of maltreatment experiences. For example, one recent study on dating and dating violence by Jonson-Reid and Bivens (1999) was conducted on youth in the foster care system ($N = 85$). These authors included questions regarding experiences of both perpetration and victimization in dating relationships (i.e., sexual coercion, physical abuse, threats of self-harm, verbal abuse), in addition to asking youth to report the number of lifetime dating partners. Similar prevalence rates on dating violence were found in this sample of foster care youth as compared to other high school survey (e.g., Smith & Williams, 1992). The results showed that the number of partners, if greater than three, were associated with a greater likelihood of being victimized by a dating partner for female, but not for male, foster care adolescents. Of the foster care youth who reported dating violence, 73% either continued to stay in the same abusive relationship or began new relationships that also included abuse. These authors found that a majority of the foster care youth were in mutually violent relationships, having reported both perpetration and victimization experiences. One important outstanding issue, though, is the age of the dating partners that maltreated youth select and/or are selected by. In a community survey of Grade 8 and 9 students ($N = 1,405$), Foshee et al. (1996) reported that 72% of youth reported to have begun dating; 75% of girls reported dating boys older than Grade 9, and 75% of the boys reported dating girls younger than Grade 8. It would be important to know whether maltreated youth are at greater risk for negative dating outcomes when, for instance, there is a dramatic age difference (e.g., males dating younger females; females dating older males). Clearly, these basic data on dating demographics, as well as the quality of the relationship, remain important questions to address in maltreated youth.

ONSET OF SEXUAL INTERCOURSE IN DATING

As noted earlier, the survey by the Henry J. Kaiser Family Foundation and *YM* magazine (1999) found intercourse among 13- to 14-year-olds to be a rare phenomenon (4%), as compared to 17- to 18-year-olds (52%). One important issue that has been generally neglected in this early work on dating is ethnic and cultural differences. The major U.S. epidemiological survey for adolescent youth risk behaviors—the Youth Risk Behavior Surveillance, which in 2001 sampled over 13,000 youth across 50 states—found that Black youth reported significantly higher rates of sexual intercourse before age 13 than did their Caucasian and Hispanic counterparts. Black youth reported the highest level of forced sexual intercourse, although this query was not restricted to dating relationships (Centers for Disease Control and Prevention, 2002). Early onset of sexual intercourse has been found to be linked with a greater number of sexual partners and lack of condom use among adolescents (e.g., Shrier, Emans, Woods, & DuRant, 1996).

It has been suggested that one long-term implication of early victimization is the increased likelihood of engagement in higher risk situations and a greater array of risky behaviors, where some of these risk behaviors may represent revictimization experiences for the maltreated youth (Wekerle et al., 2001; Wekerle & Wolfe, 1998). In a study of pregnant or parenting adolescent females, Jacoby, Gorenflo, Wunderlich, and Eyler (1999) found that age at first pregnancy was predicted by family-of-origin risk factors (drinking problem; physical abuse) and individual risk factors (early age of intoxication, early age of first wanted sexual experience). Similarly, familial and partner violence were predictive of rapid repeat pregnancy among low-income adolescent females (Kellogg, Hoffman, & Taylor, 1999). Further, younger age at first unwanted sexual experience predicted earlier entry into wanted sexual experience. As with other risk behaviors, such as adolescent substance abuse, early entry into sexual intercourse may be a marker of a more negative developmental trajectory.

Developmental researchers have incorporated biological variables in the study of risky sexual behaviors; for example, early onset of puberty has been associated with early sexual intercourse (e.g., Capaldi, Crosby, & Stoolmiller, 1996; Rosenthal, Smith, & de Visser, 1999) and teen pregnancy (e.g, Capaldi et al., 1996). It would be important for studies of maltreated early adolescents to include such biopsychosocial variables as well in attempting to understand dating and related outcomes. Taken together, these studies suggest an association between family-of-origin maltreatment and both risky sexual practices (e.g., sex leading to pregnancy) and desired sexual activity among adolescents, although much more work needs to be conducted to adequately examine maltreated youth who have not been "captured" by formal systems, like child welfare or foster care.

FUNCTION OF DATING RELATIONSHIP

Feiring (1999) reported another study 92 teens' peerships at ages 9, 13, and 18 years. A greater number of same-sex friends, as compared to other-sex friends, were maintained at each time point. By age 13, girls had larger friendship networks than boys, which was also true at age 18. Overall, 13-year-olds who reported a greater number of other-sex friends were more likely to describe their romantic relationships at age 15 in affiliative terms (e.g., self-disclosure, support, as compared to social status). Feiring suggests that greater exposure to and experience with other-sex friends may provide more opportunities and motivation for romantic pairings. However, in a study of dominantly Caucasian, two-parent youth age 10 to 13 years (N = 1,755), Connolly et al. (1999) found that early adolescents were more likely to report passion (i.e., infatuation, physical contact) and commitment (i.e., companionship) as features of romantic relationships, and affiliation as related to cross-sex friendships. These authors concluded that youth, in Grades 5 though 8, possess distinct conceptualizations of cross-sex friendships and cross-sex romantic relationships, although experience with dating was infrequent.

These studies do highlight that greater work is needed to better understand the needs and conceptualizations youth hold about heterosexual peerships and partnerships and, importantly, how these are transformed across adolescence as youth begin to accumulate experience with dating. Importantly, the quality of the dating experience and the predictive value of the first romantic relationship may contribute to youth's conceptualization of a relationship. These research questions remain to be applied to the context of maltreatment. For maltreated youth, the experience of a highly supportive and caring early partnership may create a window of opportunity for positive change regarding the youth's relationship representations. When a maltreated youth encounters a dating relationship that bears much similarity to abusive caregiving, without direct intervention, such a window for change may become lessened. Like normative dating, dating violence is a recent area of inquiry, with empirical work first emerging in the last two decades (e.g., Bethke & DeJoy, 1993; Makepeace, 1986; O'Keefe, Brockopp, & Chew, 1986; Roscoe & Callahan, 1985) and larger-scale surveys occurring in the mid- to late 1990s (e.g., Centers for Disease Control, 2000). Presently, there is no longitudinal studies of adolescent dating that captures onset of dating violence in either normative or maltreated youth populations.

ADOLESCENT DATING VIOLENCE

In a recent review of dating violence among high school and college youth, Lewis and Fremouw (2001) noted the definitional ambiguity of the term *dating violence*. These authors adopted a definition that solely reflects the use or threat of physical aggression, either force or restraint, with the intention to cause harm. In college studies, date rape is often investigated separately from dating aggression, which is more narrowly defined as *physical aggression* (Wood & Sher, 2002), which is lamentable since verbal aggression and sexual coercion that includes behaviors other than intercourse are relevant. Adolescent dating violence studies have queried the broader range of abusive behaviors, although such acts as forced intercourse or assault with a weapon seem to have very low base rates.

The percent of youth reporting dating violence varies widely among high school surveys, with most studies finding rates of 10% to 25% reporting physically aggressive and sexually coercive behaviors; when verbal or psychological aggression items are included, the majority of youth surveyed report some experience either as a victim or perpetrator (Wekerle & Wolfe, 1999). As discussed later, most of these single population surveys do not take into account a wide array of relevant factors such as socioeconomic status, ethnic, cultural, and gender differences, initiation and consequence of violence, as well as sampling both perpetration and victimization. The only epidemiological data that provides a broad sampling on demographic factors is the Centers for Disease Control and Prevention (CDC) Youth Risk Behavior Surveillance Survey (2002) which, in 1999, added a single dating violence question tapping intentional physical aggression, not perpetration, nor sexual and verbal/psychological aggression. In querying whether a youth had been "hit, slapped, or physically hurt on purpose by a boyfriend or girlfriend," 9.5% of youth positively endorsed this item. In this CDC survey, where U.S. youth from 50 states were sampled, the endorsement on this item ranged from a low of 6% to a high of 18.1%, and no gender differences were noted. While a minority of U.S. youth report self-perceived intentional aggression from a dating partner, this prevalence estimate translates into a substantial number of youth about whom our education and health delivery systems need to be concerned.

To date, adolescent relationships appear to be mutually violent, with both males and females inflicting and sustaining aggression (Avery-Leaf, Cascardi, O'Leary, & Cano, 1997; Gray & Foshee, 1997), although the meaning of this finding is unclear. O'Keefe (1997) found that while both males and females state that they use violence because of anger, males reported engaging in violence as a desire to control their partners, whereas females used it in self-defense. Unlike their adult counterparts, non-cohabiting adolescent partners may not differ as dramatically in size and strength, their partnership is not financial, as in the case of support for housing and children, and they may be occupied in the same daily activities (i.e., attending school).

Although research in the 1980s began to focus on adolescent dating violence, these studies often did not address gender effects (e.g., Henton, Cate, Koval, Lloyd, & Christopher, 1983; Roscoe & Kelsey, 1986; Burcky, Reuterman, & Kopsky, 1988). For example, these studies either included both males and females and did not explore gender differences (Henton et al., 1983) or focused solely on females (Burcky et al., 1988). Often only male-to-female violence was investigated without addressing female-to-male dating violence (Roscoe & Callahan, 1985). More recent studies have explored gender differences in adolescent dating behavior by looking specifically at a wide variety of dating violence behaviors (i.e., physical, sexual, emotional coercion), as well as including both perpetration and victimization experiences.

Molidor and Tolman (1998) found that while overall rates of violence were similar for males and females, gender differences were observed in types of violence experienced. In this study, females reported sustaining more severe physical violence (e.g., punched, forced sexual activity), whereas males were more likely to report sustaining more moderate forms of violence (e.g., slapped, pinched, scratched). Similarly, Cascardi, Avery-Leaf, O'Leary, and Smith-Slep (1999) found that females were more likely to be victimized by their partners with more severe behaviors (e.g., forced sexual activity, punching), whereas male victimization tended to include mild-to-moderate forms of violence (e.g., pinching, slapping, scratching, and/or kicking). When considering perpetration, O'Keefe (1997) noted that females were more likely to inflict slapping, kicking, biting, or hitting with a fist or object, whereas males were more likely to inflict forced sexual activity on their partners. However, one study found that high school females experienced more severe physical violence than boys, and females were more emotionally affected by their injuries (Cascardi et al.,1999). Further, both males and females reported that males more often initiate the violent incident (Molidor & Tolman, 1998; O'Keefe, 1997). For females, specifically, victimization appears to be related to a greater number of dating partners, poor academic performance, and frequency of dating (Bergman, 1992).

Looking specifically at sexual violence in adolescent relationships, Poitras and Lavoie (1995) found that in a sample of 644 adolescents between 15 and 19 years old, almost half of the girls had experienced unwanted sexual contact including kissing, petting, and fondling, whereas less than 10% of the boys reported this. The rate for boys was twice as high for perpetrating this unwanted sexual contact. It may be that in adolescent relationships males and females are both perpetrators and victims of dating violence, however, this may differ by type of violence and also by the context (meaning, motivation, and consequence) of this violence. The consistent finding of these studies, though, is that females are dominantly the victims of sexual coercion in dating partnerships, not males.

When looking at victimization in this sample, for males, inflicting dating violence was a significant predictor in their sustaining violence (O'Keefe &

Treister, 1998). That mutually violent relationships may be a result of female self-defense is supported by the findings that females tend to respond to physical aggression or sexual coercion by trying to fight back, therefore male report of violence sustained may be their partners' acts of self-defense (Molidor & Tolman, 1998). Interestingly, for females, a number of predictors of their victimization emerged, including: inflicting violence, justification of male–female violence, not being as satisfied as their partners in the relationship, more serious relationships, and more dating partners (O'Keefe & Treister, 1998).

Gender differences continue to be apparent when considering the consequences of violence. For example, in a recent study by Jackson and colleagues (Jackson, Cram, & Seymour, 2000) investigating the emotional impact of violence with adolescents 16 to 20 years old, males were more likely than females to report not feeling bothered by or feeling okay after a violent incident. In this study, as in others, males were more likely to respond to the abuse with laughter and females to respond with fear (O'Keefe & Treister, 1998). This suggests that males either accept the use of violence in their relationships or they do not experience the behavior as abusive. Other studies support the notion that males have a greater acceptance and tolerance for violence in dating relationships (Bookwala, Frieze, Smith, & Ryan, 1992). With respect to the physical consequences of dating violence, not surprisingly, females are significantly more likely to report receiving bruises and needing medical attention (Foshee, 1996). Foshee (1996) reported that while females reported more perpetration of violence than males, they also reported receiving significantly more injuries (e.g., bruise, a burn, a cut or a broken bone) than males. Males are also more likely to report that their relationships improved or stayed the same after experiencing violence whereas females were more likely to report that their relationships worsened after a severe violent incident (Molidor & Tolman, 1998). In general, the violence is not destructive to adolescent relationships, and adolescents continue to date their partner after the abusive incident (Gray & Foshee, 1997; Henton et al., 1983).

Although theorizing about dating violence is premature, models proposed in other arenas may be applicable. For example, Wekerle and Wolfe (1999) discussed a social learning model of coercive escalation that may describe the process in violent teen couples. In this model of coercive escalation, adolescent dating partners may initiate mild forms of violence (e.g., verbal insult) that each partner matches in kind and aggression, therefore having a greater potential to become violent or physically injurious. As the spiral escalates, threats that are not carried out fail to extinguish the previous aggression of the interactant. Aggression may also be met with humor or attempts at positive physical engagement (e.g., forced affection) and, hence, positively reinforced. While no study has tracked dating interactional sequences over time (i.e., conditional probabilities), limited data do suggest that gender-based reinforcement patterns may exist. For example, one study of high school youth found that girls reported their use of aggression as most typically "expressive" (i.e., feeling angry, frustrated), whereas boys reported their use of aggression as often "playful" (Scott, Wekerle, & Wolfe, 1997). In a similar vein, Cascardi et al. (1999) reported that in responding to their "worst" incident of violence, adolescent males typically reported that they "laughed it off," whereas females reported responses of crying (40%), fighting back (36%), running away (11%), and obeying their partner (12%). Unfortunately, these data are not available for youth with and without a history of maltreatment. An early study by Main and George (1985) showed maltreated toddlers to be inappropriate responders to another's distress, failing to show appropriate concern and instead responding with anger or aversion. It would be of interest, for example, to understand whether maltreated males initially respond with inappropriate affect, which may later move into an anger state given persistent girlfriend distress.

Another relevant theoretical model, as noted previously, is attachment theory, which has been utilized to explain adolescent dating violence. Crittenden and Claussen (2002) and Lyons-Ruth and Jacobvitz (1999) presented an attachment perspective on relationship violence that is relevant to both child maltreatment and teen dating violence, notably in terms of the intergenerational transmission of relational patterns. "Violence in intimate relationships can be one . . . in which great intensity of positive longing, anger, and fear may be combined with a lack of felt security, lapses in attention, dysfluent communication, and unregulated arousal" (Lyons-Ruth & Jacobvitz, 1999, p. 542). A main relational theme is the power imbalance where there is a helpless (victim) versus hostile/controlling (victimizer) dyadic dichotomy in relationship roles. Maltreated youth would be expected to show a greater likelihood of regulation difficulties with fearful arousal. The greater the need of one interactant to regulate such arousal, the more skewed the relational polarity becomes. The controlling behavior may emerge as aggression or more subtle mechanisms as withdrawal, self-preoccupation, and making the other feel guilty. An individual, though, may activate either victim or victimizer roles sequentially or simultaneously (i.e., the victimizer perceiving himself/herself to be the victim). Relevant to the latter, a recent study (Wekerle et al., 2001) compared teens who positively endorsed the same childhood history of maltreatment item (e.g., "I was molested"), but varied on their endorsement of a global self-descriptor item (e.g., "I was sexually abused") that may tap perceptions of their maltreatment experiences. Findings from a child protective services sample of adolescents indicated that for females, a self-conceptualization as a victim of emotional, physical, and/or sexual abuse interacted with child maltreatment to predicting victimization from a dating partner. Where the female teen increasingly endorsed self-descriptor statements, at higher levels of maltreatment, there was heightened risk for victimization. For adolescent males, there was a significant interaction between self-labeling and maltreatment in predicting perpetration of dating violence. As males increasingly endorsed self-descriptor statements, at higher levels of maltreatment, there was a heightened risk for perpetrating violence toward their dating partner. In this study, regarding one-self as a victim of child maltreatment produced a gender-specific patterning in results, predicting female victimization and male perpetration. Greater work into how maltreated youth conceptualize or re-conceptualize their maltreatment experiences, as well as their self-definition, may be a relevant area for future inquiry into romantic relationship functioning.

Limited work has been done to date that considers the association between child maltreatment and teen dating violence, and no work has been prospective in nature. Most work has been conducted on community high school youth, where child welfare status has not been typically queried. Further, the range of child maltreatment types (sexual, physical, emotional abuse, neglect, witnessing domestic violence) has not been typically assessed, with several studies focusing exclusively on witnessing interparental aggression, even though it overlaps substantially with direct physical aggression toward the child (Appel & Holden, 1998). Wekerle and Wolfe (1998), in a single school sample, found that total child maltreatment (combined physical, sexual, and witnessing interparental violence) was a consistent predictor of victimization for teen relationship partners, but only predicted perpetration in males.

Other studies have found mixed results. Smith and Williams (1992) operationalized child abuse as any of: forced sex with parent, "punched hard" by parent, had an object thrown at them by parent, and/or had been threatened with a weapon by a parent. High school students ($N = 1,240$) who reported parental abuse were more likely to report "light" (e.g., swore, damaged personal property), "moderate" (e.g., slapped, kicked, choked), and/or "severe" (e.g., forced sex, threaten with weapon) aggression towards their dating partner. Also, abused youth were more likely to report having ended a dating relationship because of violence, more likely to continue dating a person who acted violently, and more likely to have a dating relationship end because of the youth's perpetration toward a dating partner. It should be noted that in another study of high school students ($N = 939$), neither experiencing physical aggression from parents nor witnessing physical aggression between parents, considered as separate predictors, predicted victimization in dating relationships (O'Keefe & Treister, 1998). Carlson (1990), in a sample of at-risk youth (residential treatment or youth shelter), found that those youth who reported witnessing parental violence were not more likely to be in the category of having ever "hit, slapped, pushed, or punched" their dating partner or received such behavior.

Thus, different results regarding child maltreatment emerge, depending on the operationalization of child maltreatment and teen dating violence. However, in most studies, an association between child maltreatment and adolescent dating violence has been found; however, clearly, not all maltreated youth go on to aggressive partnerships. One area of interest in understanding those youth at risk has been adolescent attachment style.

Two studies have examined the association among child maltreatment, adolescent self-perceived attachment style, and dating violence. Wekerle and Wolfe (1998) found that, for females, avoidant attachment style (low tolerance for closeness) predicted both abusiveness and victimization in teen partnerships. For males, child maltreatment interacted with avoidant attachment to predict male abusiveness; males who were high on avoidance and maltreatment represented the highest risk group. Also for males, child maltreatment interacted with anxious-ambivalent attachment (desperation for greater closeness) in predicting male's reports of being victimized by their relational partner; males who were high on maltreatment and on anxious-ambivalent attachment style were those at most risk. Because this study combined heterosexual close peerships and partnerships, a relevant concern is whether similar findings would occur when only dating relationships were considered.

In another sample of high school dating youth ($N = 372$), Avgoustis and Wekerle (2001) considered the association of childhood maltreatment and violence in both dating relationships and peer relationships separately, with adolescent attachment style as a moderator in this relationship. Emotional neglect (e.g., not feeling loved) was found to be a significant predictor above and beyond other forms of maltreatment (i.e., physical abuse, emotional abuse and physical neglect) of adolescent aggression. In predicting dating violence, emotional neglect was related to increased risk of being a victim in females, and of being a perpetrator in males, beyond the contribution of other forms of maltreatment. In a similar fashion, emotional neglect significantly predicted males' aggressive behavior towards peers (not partners). In exploring the contribution of attachment style as a moderator of the emotional neglect and dating violence relationship, a high-risk group was identified. Mid-adolescent females who currently perceive their relationship style as avoidant and who had high emotional neglect scores were more likely to be victims of physical and emotional abuse from their dating partners. In a similar vein, highly avoidant, emotionally neglected males emerged as at-risk for dating violence, being more likely to be offenders of dating physical, sexual, and emotional abuse towards their dating partner. These studies suggest that child maltreatment measured broadly is a risk factor for adolescent dating violence, whereby victimization among females and perpetration among males may be of greater likelihood among maltreated youth. Further, the relative neglect of neglect in the child maltreatment literature highlights the potential importance of emotional neglect to adolescent relationship functioning.

ALCOHOL AND OTHER DRUG USE

Alcohol has been noted as the drug of courtship and relationship difficulties (Zucker et al., 1997). Substance use is the norm in adolescence, an exemplar of developmentally appropriate curiosity and risk taking (Baumrind & Moselle, 1985), with secondary gains including bolstering self-confidence, initiative-taking, stress tolerance, and peer acceptance (Baumrind, 1987). For some youth, notably those with elevated trauma-induced symptomatology, substance use comes to hold functional value in reducing negative affective states (e.g., post-traumatic distress symptomatology, depression, anxiety), as well as increasing positive affective states (e.g., sociability, interest, euphoria) (Stewart, 1996). Thus, one set of youth that may be vulnerable to a functional use of substances are those with a maltreatment history.

The bulk of the empirical work on adolescent substance use to date has focused on child sexual abuse, rather than a broader spectrum of maltreatment history (e.g., physical and emotional neglect, emotional abuse, witnessing domestic violence). Consistently, an association between maltreatment and adolescent substance abuse has been found. For example, Clark, Lesnick, and Hegedus (1997) found that teens who reported alcohol abuse or dependence were 6–12 times more likely to have a history of childhood physical abuse, and 18–21 times more likely to have a history of sexual abuse. Using self-report with a large sample of students in Grades 7 through 12 ($N = 36,000$), females endorsing a sexual abuse item were more likely to report weekly use of tobacco, alcohol, and marijuana than randomly selected females who did not endorse the sexual abuse item. A number of other dangerous behaviors differentiated these young girls (average age of about 15 years), including suicidal thoughts and suicide attempts, binge-eating and dieting, sexual intercourse and pregnancy (Chandy, Blum, & Resnick, 1996b). When comparing sexually abused males to females, males reported greater substance use before and during school, greater weekly alcohol and marijuana use, and more binge-drinking episodes (5 or more drinks/occasion) than females (Chandy, Blum, & Resnick, 1996a). Similar results on the greater deleterious effects of sexual abuse on male versus female youth, with respect to alcohol and drug use, was found in a Netherlands school study (Garnefski & Arends, 1998). Further, being physically abused, in addition to experiencing sexual abuse, increased the likelihood of binge drinking (Luster & Small, 1997) and multiple substance use (Harrison, Fulkerson, & Beebe, 1997) in large statewide school surveys.

Few studies on child maltreatment history and substance use/abuse have also considered teen dating violence. While the possible link between adolescent dating violence and the use of alcohol and drugs has been acknowledged (Burcky et al., 1988), little empirical research on this overlap among junior and high school students has been reported. Research on behavioral intentions, though, would indicate that an overlap between substance use/abuse and dating violence likely exists. High school surveys find that youth, especially males, endorse the view that drug or alcohol intoxication is justifiable grounds for forced sex (USDHHS, 1992). One study of adolescent females ($N = 670$) found that sexual molestation on dates ranged from 5.9% (Grade 8) to 14.0% (Grade 11); sexual victimization (which combined child maltreatment with dating violence) was predictive of use of alcohol and different classes of drugs (e.g., marijuana, hallucinogens, inhalants, amphetamines; Watts & Ellis, 1993). We first consider some theoretical underpinnings to this association and subsequently examine the limited empirical work to date.

When trauma is relationship-based, as with child maltreatment, the whole enterprise of close relationships may be fear-ridden. That is, a recognized relationship (e.g., father–daughter, partner–partner, etc.) has been established as a setting event where physical proximity is paired with threat, danger, and harm. Consequently, substances may be employed to initiate, negotiate, maintain, and tolerate interpersonal closeness. Substance abuse, then, may function as either an avoidance strategy (reduce intimacy needs) or an engagement strategy (facilitate interactions). Thus, substance use may be used functionally to support dating behavior and may facilitate dating violence when judgment is impaired, contributing to either victimization or victimizing, or when inhibitions to behaving aggressively are weakened by intoxication. As avoidance tools, substances have been likened to attachment objects, in their constant physical proximity, presence during distress, and perceived ability to effect comfort (Covington & Surrey, 1997). Thus, substance use may be used functionally following negative dating experiences, including date rape and dating violence, as a means of tension reduction and withdrawal from further dating interactions.

Serving *engagement* purposes, substance use has been noted to support sexual relations, especially among females, where there may be a link to a history of sexual abuse (Wilsnack, Klassen, Schur, & Wilsnack, 1991). This finding has been labeled *cognitive* or *subjective* sexual arousal, as it stands in contrast to the reduced physiological arousal (i.e., suppression of blood flow) found with alcohol consumption (Wilsnack, Plaud, Wilsnack, & Klassen, 1997). The association between imbibing alcohol and sexual readiness, though, applies to both males and females. In a national survey of adults (age 21 and older), both men and women expected alcohol to promote sexuality and emotional intimacy (Wilsnack et al., 1997). Males reported greater alcohol effects regarding feelings of emotional closeness, sexual pleasure, sexual assertiveness, and being less particular in the choice of partners than did females. Whether this applies to or is even amplified in adolescents is unclear.

Given that relationship violence, including child maltreatment and teen dating violence, may distort the victim's self-perception as worthless, loathsome, helpless, unloveable, and so on (Briere, 1997), substance abuse may function as a self-destructive behavior, resonating with and reinforcing the negative self-concept. Elements of this self-dysfunction may overlap with antisocial tendencies. Work with problem teens has found self-derogation to be a significant mediating variable in the relationship between child victimization and teen illicit drug use (Dembo et al., 1989). Similarly, from a statewide student survey that queried reasons for use, substance-using physical and/or sexual abuse victims were more likely to endorse using because it is illegal than did non-maltreated, substance-using youth (Harrison et al., 1997).

Lundberg-Love and Geffner's (1989) model of date rape may apply to the sexual, physical, and emotional coercion in teen partnerships, which overlaps with Finkelhor and Browne's (1988) model of sexual abuse of children. These authors advance four pre-conditions for perpetration of sexual violence to occur:

1. The motivation, or inclination, to abuse must be present (e.g., power and control needs).
2. Internal inhibitions must be overcome (e.g., prior perpetration, attitudinal acceptance of violence).
3. There must be an opportunity for perpetration (e.g., being on a date, date location) and external impediments must be overcome (e.g., use of substances).
4. Factors that undermine the victim's resistance to abuse must be present (e.g., history of victimization, victim's substance abuse).

Alcohol intoxication of either relationship partner has been consistently linked with physical and sexual aggression in adults (for a review, see Wekerle & Wall, 2002) and college youth (for a review, see Wood & Sher, 2002). For example, Abbey, McAuslan, and Ross (1998) found that male consumption of alcohol is related to misperception of the female's sexual intent, which in turn relates to sexual assault of the dating partner. These authors added that alcohol may promote intimate abuse through behavioral disinhibition (i.e., becoming more aggressive) and psychological disinhibition (i.e., becoming less empathic). It is suggested that alcohol contributes to victimization by impairing the assessment of and response to personal risk (Fromme, D'Amico, & Katz,

1999), as well as by signaling vulnerability to exploitation to a predatory partner (Abbey et al., 1998). It is also possible that consumption may be a consequence of intimate violence. Indeed, the majority of teens who binge drink reported that they drink when they are upset (U.S. Dept. of Health and Human Services, 1991).

As noted, some work has considered maltreatment, substance use/abuse, and aggression between dating partners. A study of high school students by O'Keefe (1997) found that alcohol and drug use (frequency of use during past year of alcohol, marijuana, and other drugs) was a significant predictor of aggression towards a dating partner for both males and females. In this study, parent–child violence, defined as physical abuse only, was not a significant predictor; witnessing interparental physical violence was a significant predictor of inflicting dating violence only for males. In addition to considering perpetration of dating violence, Wekerle, Hawkins, and Wolfe (2002) considered dating violence victimization, along with child maltreatment history, in predicting adolescent substance use. High school youth ($N = 302$) in Grades 9 and 10 completed questions on typical weekly use of alcohol and street (nonprescription) drugs, maltreatment experiences while growing up, and conflict in their close adolescent heterosexual relationships over the past 6 months. Child maltreatment, a composite score across physical, sexual, and emotional abuse, and adolescent dating/close relationship aggression, both in terms of perpetration and victimization, were used to predict adolescent use of alcohol, heavy use of alcohol (more than 5 drinks/week), and use of illicit "street" drugs. For males, child maltreatment was a significant predictor of alcohol use (1 to 5 drinks/week) in adolescence, while neither dating violence perpetration nor victimization scores were significant predictors beyond the contribution of child maltreatment history. Child maltreatment did not predict illicit drug use among males. For females, child maltreatment was a significant predictor and remained so even after dating violence was entered. However, the experience of teen dating violence carried dramatically more predictive weight than child maltreatment. Receiving physical, sexual, or verbal abuse from one's partner made it 11.40 times more likely that alcohol use existed, and 5.82 times more likely that consumption was "heavy" (more than 5 drinks per week). Further, females who emitted verbally abusive behaviors toward their dating partners had nearly a 20-fold increase for using alcohol, and over a 7-fold increase for heavy use. Both victim and offender dating experiences made a significant contribution to differentiating female, but not male, abstainers from drug users. Females who reported being a victim of abuse/blame from their dating partner, as well as being a perpetrator of abuse/coercion and/or negative communication towards their dating partner, were 7 to 22 times more likely to be drug users than abstainers.

Although making such a distinction should be approached with caution, in the Wekerle et al. (2002) study, being a victim of physical, sexual, and verbal coercion in dating had twice the likelihood as did directing verbal abuse and negative communication to the partner. This may reflect a situation where the female illicit drug user is more likely to become associated with a dangerous partner. Given the high likelihood associated with female verbal and sexual coercion towards partner, the possibility is raised that females who utilize street drugs may be at greater risk of being involved in relationships where female lower-level violence, like slapping, is reciprocated. As being a victim was comparable to being an offender when comparing the likelihood estimates of alcohol heavy use, this drug use result may be related to then to polysubstance use, whereby more varied substances may be accessed to cope with victim-related stress. Indeed, when considering those females who reported using street drugs, 96% reported also using alcohol (44% fell into the heavy use category). An important question, not available in the data, would be the consumption patterns of the partners of these females.

SUMMARY

This review of the literature to date on adolescent dating violence suggests that further research in this area is warranted. The majority of the research has dominantly considered the youth rather than the dating couple as the source of data for dating violence victimization and perpetration and, clearly, more work needs to explore couple dynamics by questioning and observing both members in a relationship over time and in more natural observational settings (e.g., party scenario). Given the prevalence of teen dating violence and the understanding that such behaviors have not crystallized into a pattern of intimate relationships, further empirical work is encouraged on the development of dating violence over time, both in terms of the entry into and the exit from an involvement in an aggressive and coercive couple.

It would seem that identifying the at-risk teens would urge our efforts to assist them in a proactive and positive way to prevent the initiation of aggressive interactions which would develop into a violent dynamic in later romantic relationships. A main risk factor considered to date is a history of childhood maltreatment. Because adolescence is a time of developmental shift, with greater movement towards peers as romantic partners, it represents a prime window of opportunity to understand early warning signs of problematic dating and to intervene proactively prior to the crystallization of victim–victimizer relationship style across romantic partnerings. Indeed, the entry into romantic relationships may precipitate a resurgence of maltreatment-related post-traumatic stress symptomatology as situational characteristics that bear similarity to the abuse situation, both specifically (e.g., a specific sex act like fondling) and generally (e.g., close physical proximity, intense affect, sexual arousal) may be present in the current relationship experiences with a partner. Without intervention, youth may be at-risk of re-enacting abusive scenarios and may be ill-equipped to negotiate physical and sexual intimacy given a lack of effortful processing and decision-making regarding likes and dislikes, boundaries of risk-taking, expectations for a partner and relationships, and so forth. Thus, the youth may be vulnerable to more automatic cognitive processes and reflexive responding, rather than effortful ones supporting reflective responding. The concomitant communication and problem-solving skills to support a youth's decisions around violence in intimate relationships may also be lacking.

Although intervention is not discussed presently, it should be noted that the parallel effort to intervene proactively to promote dating health and reduce the likelihood of dating violence in an empirically demonstrated way was initiated in the 1990s (for a review of prevention programs, see Wekerle & Wolfe, 1999). As one example of empirically validated prevention programming for youth with a history of maltreatment, the Youth Relationships Project (YRP; Wolfe et al., 1996; Wolfe, Wekerle, & Scott, 1997) is an 18-week coeducational, curriculum-based competency and empowerment-based intervention. A male and female trained facilitator team, typically social service professionals, lead a group of 10 to 20 youth, aged 14 to 17 years, in weekly, 2-hour sessions devoted to understanding violence in relationships and conceptualizations of a healthy intimate relationship, relationship-related skill development (e.g., active listening, empathy, assertive communication, problem-solving), and social action (e.g., knowledge of community agencies, mastery at accessing help, and antiviolence advocacy). Pittman and Wolfe (2002) overviewed the YRP and program evaluation, which found that child protective services youth who received the YRP reported less victimization and victimizing in dating relationships, less trauma symptomatology and a trend toward less general hostility toward others over a 2-year follow-up period, as compared to child protective services youth receiving regular services. Such prevention programming on a developmentally sensitive issue like romantic relationships with youth who are at-risk but not yet emitting a crystallized pattern of partner violence in their early experiences with dating is a viable option for altering their relationship trajectories. A search for effective prevention is hopeful, as it demonstrates that the problematic ways of relating that may have been learned in the maltreating environment have the potential to be unlearned in the dating arena. As clinicians, educators, and concerned stakeholders in our youth, supporting the movement toward healthy romantic relationships and breaking the cycle of violence is a most worthwhile and achievable goal.

ACKNOWLEDGMENTS

This work was supported by a New Investigator Fellowship from the Ontario Mental Health Foundation, and research grants from the Canadian Institutes for Health Research and the Social Sciences and Humanities Research Council to the first author.

REFERENCES

Abbey, A., McAuslan, P., & Ross, L. T. (1998). Sexual assault perpetration by college men: The role of alcohol, misperception of sexual intent, and sexual beliefs and experiences. *Journal of Social and Clinical Psychology, 17,* 167–195.

Ainsworth, M. D. S. (1989). Attachments beyond infancy. *American Psychologist, 44,* 709–716.

The Alan Guttmacher Institute. (1994). *Sex and America's teenagers,* New York: Author.

Appel, A. E., & Holden, G. W. (1998). The co-occurrence of spouse and physical child abuse: A review and appraisal. *Journal of Family Psychology, 12*(4), 578–599.

Avery-Leaf, S., Cascardi, M., O'Leary, K. D., & Cano, A. (1997). Efficacy of a dating violence prevention program on attitudes justifying aggression. *Journal of Adolescent Health, 21*(1), 11–17.

Avgoustis, E., & Wekerle, C. (200, April). *The importance of childhood emotional neglect in predicting adolescent interpersonal functioning.* Poster session presented at the biennial meeting of the Society for Research in Child Development, Minneapolis, MN.

Bandura, A. (1977). *Social learning theory.* New York, Prentice-Hall.

Baumrind, D. A. (1987). Developmental perspective on adolescent risk taking in contemporary America. *New Directions for Child Development, 37,* 93–125.

Baumrind, D. A., & Moselle, K. A. (1985). A developmental perspective on adolescent drug abuse. *Advances in Alcohol and Substance Abuse, 4,* 41–67.

Beitchman, J. H., Zucker, K. J., Hood, J. E., Da Costa, G. A., & Akman, D. (1991). A review of the short-term effects of child sexual abuse. *Child Abuse and Neglect, 15,* 537–556.

Beitchman, J. H., Zucker, K. J., Hood, J. E., Da Costa, G. A., Akman, D., & Cassavia, E. (1992). A review of the long-term effects of child sexual abuse. *Child Abuse and Neglect, 16,* 101–118.

Bergman, L. (1992). Dating violence among high school students. *Social Work, 37,* 21–27.

Bethke, T. M., & DeJoy, D. M. (1993). An experimental study of factors influencing the acceptability of dating violence. *Journal of Interpersonal Violence, 8,* 36–51.

Bookwala, J., Frieze, I. H., Smith, C., & Ryan, K. (1992). Predictors of dating violence: A multivariate analysis. *Violence and Victims, 7,* 297–311.

Bowlby, J. (1969). *Attachment and Loss.* New York: Basic Books.

Bowlby, J. (1973). *Attachment and loss: Vol. 2. Separation, anxiety, and anger.* New York: Basic Books.

Bowlby, J. (1979). *The making and breaking of affectional bonds.* London: Tavistock.

Bowlby, J. (1980). *Attachment and loss: Vol. 3. Loss: Sadness and depression.* New York: Basic Books.

Briere, J. (1997). Treating adults severely abused as children: The self-trauma model. In D. A. Wolfe, R. J. McMahon, & R. DeV. Peters (Eds.), *Child abuse: New directions in prevention and treatment across the lifespan* (pp. 177–204). Thousand Oaks, CA: Sage.

Burcky, W., Reuterman, N., & Kopsky, S. (1988). Dating violence among high school students. *The School Counselor, 35,* 353–358.

Capaldi, D. M., Crosby, L., & Stoolmiller, M. (1996). Predicting the timing of first sexual intercourse for at-risk adolescent males. *Child Development, 67*(2), 344–359.

Carlson, B. E. (1990). Adolescent observers of marital violence. *Journal of Family Violence, 5*(4), 285–299.

Cascardi, M., Avery-Leaf, S., O'Leary, K. D., & Smith-Slep, A.-M. (1999). Factor structure and convergent validity of the Conflict Tactics Scale in high school students. *Psychological Assessment, 11,* 546–555.

Centers for Disease Control and Prevention. (June 21, 2002). Youth Risk Behavior Surveillance—United States, 2001. *Morbidity and Mortality Weekly Report, 51*(5504), 1–64.

Chandy, J. M., Blum, R. W., & Resnick, M. D. (1996a). Gender-specific outcomes for sexually abused adolescents. *Child Abuse and Neglect, 20,* 1219–1231.

Chandy, J. M., Blum, R. W., & Resnick, M. D. (1996b). Female adolescents with a history of sexual abuse. *Journal of Interpersonal Violence, 11,* 503–518.

Clark, D. B., Lesnick, L., & Hegedus, A. M. (1997). Traumas and other life events in adolescents with alcohol use and dependence. *Journal of the American Academy of Child and Adolescent Psychiatry, 36,* 1744–1751.

Connolly, J., Craig, W., Goldberg, A., & Pepler, D. (1999). Conceptions of cross-sex friendships and romantic relationships in early adolescence. *Journal of Youth and Adolescence, 28,* 481–495.

Connolly, J., Furman, W., & Konarski, R. (2000). The role of peers in the emergence of heterosexual romantic relationships. *Child Development, 71,* 1395–1408.

Connolly, J. A., & Johnson, A. M. (1996). Adolescents' romantic relationships and the structure and quality of their interpersonal ties. *Personal Relationships, 3,* 185–195.

Covington, S. S., & Surrey, J. L. (1997). The relational model of women's psychological development: Implications for substance abuse. In R. W. Wilsnack & S. C. Wilsnack (Eds.), *Gender and alcohol: Individual and social perspectives* (pp. 335–351). Piscataway, NJ: Rutgers Center of Alcohol Studies.

Crittenden, P. (1997). Toward an integrative theory of trauma: A dynamic-maturation approach. In D. Cicchetti & S. L. Toth (Eds.), *Developmental perspectives on trauma: Theory, research, and intervention. Rochester symposium on developmental psychology, Vol. 8* (pp. 33–84). Rochester, NY: University of Rochester Press.

Crittenden, P., & Claussen, A. (2002). Developmental psychopathology perspectives on substance abuse and relationship violence. In C. Wekerle & A.-M. Wall (Eds.), *The violence and addiction equation: Theoretical and clinical issues in substance abuse and relationship violence* (pp. 44–63). New York: Brunner-Routledge.

Dembo, R. M., Williams, L., LaVoie, L., Berry, E., Getreu, A., Wish, E. D., Schmeidler, J., & Washburn, M. (1989). Physical abuse, sexual victimization, and illicit drug use: Replication of a structural analysis among a new sample of high-risk youths. *Violence & Victims, 4(2),* 121–138.

Earls, F., Cairns, R. B., & Mercy, J. A. (1993). The control of violence and the promotion of nonviolence in adolescents. In S. G. Millstein, A. C. Peterson, & E. O. Nightingale (Eds.), *Promoting the health of adolescents: New directions for the 21st century* (pp. 285–304). New Oxford: Oxford University Press.

Feiring, C. (1999). Friendship networks and the development of romantic relationships in adolescence. *Journal of Youth & Adolescence, 28*(4), 495–512.

Feiring, C., & Furman, W. (2000). When love is just a four letter word: Victimization and romantic relationships in adolescence. *Child Maltreatment, 5*(4), 293–298.

Feiring, C. (1996). Concept of romance in 15-year-old adolescents. *Journal of Research on Adolescence, 6*(2), 181–200.

Feiring, C., & Lewis, M. (1991). The transition from middle childhood to early adolescence: Sex differences in the social network and perceived self-competence. *Sex Roles, 24,* 489–509.

Finkelhor, D., & Browne, A. (1988). Assessing the long-term impact of child sexual abuse: A review and conceptualization. In L. Walker (Ed.), *Handbook on sexual abuse of children* (pp. 55–71). New York: Springer.

Foshee, V. A. (1996). Gender differences in adolescent dating abuse prevalence, types, and injuries. *Health Education Research, 11,* 275–286.

Foshee, V. A., Linder, G. F., Bauman, K. E., Langwick, S. A., Arriaga, X. B., Heath, J. L., McMahon, P. M., & Bangdiwala, S. (1996). The Safe Dates project: Theoretical bases, evaluation design, and selected baseline findings. *American Journal of Preventive Medicine, 12,* 39–47.

Fromme, K., D'Amico, E. J., & Katz, E. C. (1999). Intoxicated sexual risk taking: An expectancy or cognitive impairment explanation? *Journal of Studies on Alcohol, 60,* 54–63.

Furman, W., & Wehner, E. A. (1994). Romantic views: Toward a theory of adolescent romantic relationships. In R. Montemayor, G. R. Adams, & G. P. Gullota (Eds.), *Advances in adolescent development: Volume 6. Relationships during adolescence* (pp. 168–195). Thousand Oaks, CA: Sage.

Furman, W., & Wehner, E. A. (1997). Adolescent romantic relationships: A developmental perspective. In S. Shulman & W. A. Collins (Eds.), *New directions for child development: Adolescent romantic relationships* (pp. 21–36). San Francisco: Jossey-Bass.

Garmezy, N., Masten, A. S., & Tellegen, A. (1984). The study of stress and competence in children: A building block for developmental psychopathology. *Child Development, 55*(1), 97–111.

Garnefski, N., & Arends, E. (1998). Sexual abuse and adolescent maladjustment: Differences between male and female victims. *Journal of Adolescence, 21,* 99–107.

Gray, H. M., & Foshee, V. (1997). Adolescent dating violence. Differences between one-sided and mutually violent profiles. *Journal of Interpersonal Violence, 12,* 126–141.

Hansen, D. J., Christopher, J. S., & Nangle, D. (1992). Adolescent heterosocial interactions and dating. In C. Van Hassalt & M. Hersen (Eds.), *Handbook of social development: A lifespan perspective* (pp. 347–370). New York: Plenum Press.

Harrison, P. A., Fulkerson, J. A., & Beebe, T. J. (1997). Multiple substance use among adolescent physical and sexual abuse victims. *Child Abuse and Neglect, 21*(6), 529–539.

Henry J. Kaiser Family Foundation and *YM* magazine. (1999). *1998 National Survey of Teens: Teens talk about dating, intimacy, and their sexual experiences.* Menlo Park, CA: Kaiser Family Foundation.

Henton, J., Cate, R., Koval, J., Lloyd, S., & Christopher, S. (1983). Romance and violence in dating relationships. *Journal of Family Issues, 4,* 467–482.

Herman, J. L. (1992). *Trauma and recovery: The aftermath of violence—From domestic abuse to political terror.* New York: Basic Books.

Jacoby, M., Gorenflo, D., Wunderlich, C., Eyler, & A. E. (1999). Rapid repeat pregnancy and experiences of interpersonal violence among low-income adolescents. *American Journal of Preventive Medicine, 16,* 318–321.

Jackson, S. M., Cram, F., & Seymour, F. W. (2000). Violence and sexual coercion in high school students' dating relationships. *Journal of Family Violence, 15*(1), 23–36.

Jankowski, M. K., Leitenberg, H., Henning, K., & Coffey, P. (1999). Intergenerational transmission of dating aggression as a function of witnessing only same sex parents vs. opposite sex parents vs. both parents as perpetrators of domestic violence. *Journal of Family Violence, 14,* 267–279.

Jonson-Reid, M., & Bivens, L. (1999). Foster youth and dating violence. *Journal of Interpersonal Violence, 14*(12), 1249–1262.

Kellogg, N. D., Hoffman, T. J., & Taylor, E. R. (1999). Early sexual experiences among pregnant and parenting adolescents. *Adolescence, 34,* 293–303.

Kolko, D. J. (1996). Child physical abuse. In J. Briere, L. Berliner, J. A. Bulkley, C. Jenny, & T. Reid (Eds.), *The APSAC handbook on child maltreatment* (pp. 21–50). Thousand Oaks, CA: Sage Publications.

Krajewski, S. S., Rybarik, M. F., Dosch, M. F., & Gilmore, G. D. (1996). Results of a curriculum intervention with seventh graders regarding violence in relationships. *Journal of Family Violence, 11,* 93–112.

Lewis, S. F., & Fremouw, W. (2001). Dating violence: A critical review of the literature. *Clinical Psychology, 21,* 105–127.

Lundberg-Love, P., & Geffner, R. (1989). Date rape: Prevalence, risk factors, and a proposed model. In M. A. Pirog-Good & J. E. Stets (Eds.), *Violence in dating relationships: Emerging social issues* (pp. 169–184). New York: Praeger Publishers.

Luster, T., & Small, S. A. (1997). Sexual abuse history and problems in adolescence: Exploring the effects of moderating variables. *Journal of Marriage and the Family, 59,* 131–142.

Lyons-Ruth, K., & Jacobvitz, D. (1999). Attachment disorganization: Unresolved loss, relational violence, and lapses in behavioral and attentional strategies. In J. Cassidy & P. R. Shaver (Eds.), *Handbook of attachment: Theory, research, and clinical applications* (pp. 520–554). New York: Guilford Press.

Makepeace, J. M. (1986). Gender differences in courtship violence victimization. *Family Relations, 35,* 383–388.

Main, M., & George, C. (1985). Responses of abused and disadvantaged toddlers to distress in age mates: A study in the day care setting. *Developmental Psychopathology, 6,* 121–143.

McGee, R. A., Wolfe, D. A., & Wilson, S. K. (1997). Multiple maltreatment experiences and adolescent behavior problems: Adolescents' perspectives. *Development and Psychopathology, 9*(1), 131–149.

Molidor, C., & Tolman, R. M. (1998). Gender and contextual factors in adolescent dating violence. *Violence Against Women, 4*(2), 180–194.

Mueller, E., & Silverman, N. (1989). Peer relations in malreated children. In D. Cicchetti & V. Carlson (Eds.), *Child maltreatment: Theory and research on the causes and consequences of child abuse and neglect* (pp. 529–578). Cambridge: Cambridge University Press.

Murphy, C. M., & Blumenthal, D. R. (2000). The mediating influence of interpersonal problems on the intergenerational transmission of relationship aggression. *Personal Relationships, 7,* 203–218.

Neemann, J., Hubbard, J., & Masten, A. (1995). The changing importance of romantic relationship involvement to competence from late childhood to late adolescence. *Development and Psychopathology: Special Issue. Developmental processes in peer relations and psychopathology, 7*(4), 727–750.

O'Keefe, M. (1997). Predictors of dating violence among high school students. *Journal of Interpersonal Violence, 12*(4), 546–568.

O'Keefe, M., & Treister, L. (1998). Victims of dating violence among high school students: Are the predictors different for males and females? *Violence Against Women, 4*(2), 195–223.

O'Keeffe, N. K., Brockopp, K., & Chew, E. (1986). Teen dating violence. *Social Work, 31*(6), 465–468.

O'Leary, K. D. (1988). Pysical aggression between spouses: A social learning theory perspective. In V. B. Hasselt & R. L. Morrison (Eds.), *Handbook of family violence* (pp. 31–55). New York: Plenum Press.

O' Leary, K. D., Malone, J., Masten, J., & Tyree, A. (1994). Physical aggression in early marriage: Prerelationship and relationship effects. *Journal of Consulting and Clinical Psychology, 62,* 594–602.

Paul, E. L., & White, K. M. (1990). The development of intimate relationships in late adolescence. *Adolescence, 25,* 375–399.

Pittman, A.-L., & Wolfe, D. A. (2002). Bridging the gap: Prevention of adolescent risk behaviors and development of healthy nonviolent dating relationships. In C. Wekerle & A.-M. Wall (Eds.), *The violence and addiction equation: Theoretical and clinical issues in substance abuse and relationship violence* (pp. 304–323). New York: Brunner-Routledge.

Poitras, M., & Lavoie, F. (1995). A study of the prevalence of sexual coercion in adolescent heterosexual dating relationships in a Quebec sample. *Violence and Victims, 10,* 299–313.

Roscoe, B., & Callahan, J. E. (1985). Adolescents' self-report of violence in families and dating relations. *Adolescence, 20*(79), 545–553.

Roscoe, B., & Kelsey, T. (1986). Dating violence among high school students. *Psychology, 23,* 53–59.

Rosenthal, D. A., Smith, A. M., & de Visser, R. (1999). Personal and social factors influencing age at first sexual intercourse. *Archives of Sexual Behavior, 28,* 319–333.

Rutter, M. (1989). Intergenerational continuities and discontinuities in serious parenting difficulties. In C. Dante & V. Carlson (Eds.), *Child maltreatment: Theory and research on the causes and consequences of child abuse and neglect* (pp. 317–348). New York: Cambridge University Press.

Rutter, M. (1996). Transitions and turning points in developmental psychopathology. *International Journal of Behavioral Development, 19,* 603–626.

Scott, K. L., Wekerle, C., & Wolfe, D. A. (1997, April). *Considered sex differences in youth's self-reports of violence and their implications for the development of violent relationships.* Poster presented at the biennial meeting of the Society for Research in Child Development, Washington, DC.

Seifer, R., & Sameroff, A. J. (1987). Multiple determinants of risk and invulnerability. In E. J. Anthony, B. Cohler, & J. Bertram (Eds.), *The invulnerable child* (pp. 51–69). New York: Guilford Press.

Shrier, L. A., Emans, S. J., Woods, E. R., & DuRant, R. H. (1996). The association of sexual risk behaviors and problem drug behaviors in high school students. *Journal of Adolescent Health, 20,* 377–383.

Smith, J. P., & Williams, J. G. (1992). From abusive household to dating violence. *Journal of Family Violence, 2,* 153–165.

Stewart, S. H. (1996). Alcohol abuse in individuals exposed to trauma: A critical review. *Psychological Bulletin, 120,* 83–112.

Taylor-Seehafer, M., & Rew, L. (2000). Risky behavior among adolescent women. *Journal of the Society of Pediatric Nurses, 5,* 15–25.

U.S. Department of Health and Human Services. (1991). Alcohol and other drug use among high school students: United States, 1990, *Morbidity and Mortality Weekly Report (MMWR), 11/91* Washington, DC: U.S. Government Printing Office.

U.S. Department of Health and Human Services. (2001). *Child maltreatment 1999: Reports from the states to the National Child Abuse and Neglect Data System.* Washington, DC: U.S. Government Printing Office.

240 WEKERLE AND AVGOUSTIS

U.S. Department of Health and Human Services, Office of the Inspector General. (1992). *Youth and alcohol: Dangerous and deadly consequences.* Washington, DC: U.S. Government Printing Office.

Wall, A-M., & McKee, S. A. (2002). Cognitive social-learning models of substance abuse and relationship violence. In C. Wekerle & A.-M. Wall (Eds.), *The violence and addiction equation: Theoretical and clinical issues in substance abuse and relationship violence* (pp. 123–152). New York: Brunner-Routledge.

Watts, W. D., & Ellis, A. M. Sexual abuse and drinking and drug use: Implications for prevention. *Journal of Drug Education, 23*(2), 183–200.

Wekerle, C., & Wall, A.-M. (2002). The overlap between intimate violence and substance abuse. In C. Wekerle & A.-M. Wall (Eds.), *The violence and addiction equation: Theoretical and clinical issues in substance abuse and relationship violence.* New York: Brunner-Routledge.

Wekerle, C., Hawkins, D. L., & Wolfe, D. A. (2002). *Child maltreatment and dating violence: Risk factors for adolescent and street drug use.* Manuscript submitted for publication.

Wekerle, C., & Wolfe, D. A. (1996). Child maltreatment. In E. Mash & R. A. Barkley (Eds.), *Child psychopathology* (pp. 492–537). New York: Guilford Press.

Wekerle, C., & Wolfe, D. A. (1998). The role of child maltreatment and attachment style in adolescent relationship violence. *Development and Psychopathology, 10,* 571–586.

Wekerle, C., & Wolfe, D. A. (1999). Dating violence in mid-adolescence: Theory significance, and emerging prevention initiatives. *Clinical Psychology Review, 19,* 435–456.

Wekerle, C., Wolfe, D. A., Hawkins, D. L., Pittman, A.-L., Glickman, A., & Lovald, B. E. (2001). The value and contribution of youth self-reported maltreatment history to adolescent dating violence: Testing a trauma mediational model. *Development and Psychopathology, 13,* 847–871.

Widom, C. (1989). Does violence beget violence? A critical review of the literature. *Psychological Bulletin, 106*(1), 3–28.

Widom, C. (1998). Childhood victimization: Early adversity and subsequent psychopathology. In B. P. Dohrenwend (Ed.), *Adversity, stress, and psychopathology* (pp. 81–95). New York: Oxford University Press.

Wilsnack, S. C., Plaud, J. J., Wilsnack, R. W., & Klassen, A. D. (1997). Sexuality, gender, and alcohol use. In R. W. Wilsnack & S. C. Wilsnack (Eds.), *Gender and alcohol: Individual and social perspectives* (pp. 250–288). Piscataway, NJ: Rutgers Center of Alcohol Studies.

Wilsnack, S. C., Klassen, A. D., Schur, B. E., & Wilsnack, R. W. (1991). Predicting onset and chronicity of women's problem drinking: A five-year longitudinal analysis. *American Journal of Public Health, 81*(3), 305–318.

Wolfe, D. A., Wekerle, C., Reitzel-Jaffe, D., & Lefebvre, D. L. (1998). Factors associated with abusive relationships among maltreated and nonmaltreated youth. *Development and Psychopathology, 10*(1), 61–85.

Wolfe, D. A., Wekerle, C., & Scott, K. (1997). *Alternatives to violence: Empowering youth to promote non-violence.* Thousand Oaks, CA: Sage Publications.

Wolfe, D. A., Wekerle, C., Gough, R., Reitzel-Jaffe, D., Grasley, C., Pittman, A., Lefebvre, L., & Stumpf, J. (1996). *The youth relationship manual: A group approach with adolescents for the prevention of woman abuse and the promotion of healthy relationships.* Thousand Oaks, CA: Sage Publications.

Wood, M. D., & Sher, K. J. (2002). Sexual assault and relationship violence among college students: Examining the role of alcohol and other drugs. In C. Wekerle & A.-M. Wall (Eds.), *The violence and addiction equation: Theoretical and clinical issues in substance abuse and relationship violence* (pp. 169–193). New York: Brunner-Routledge.

World Health Organization. (1999, March). *Report of the consultation on child abuse prevention.* WHO, Geneva: Author.

Zucker, R. A., Davies, W. H., Kincaid, S. B. Fitzgerald, H. E., & Reider, E. E. (1997). Conceptualizing and scaling the developmental structure of behavior disorder: The Lifetime Alcohol Problems Score as an example. *Development and Psychopathology, 9*(2), 453–471.

10

The Development of Aggression in Young Male/Female Couples

Deborah M. Capaldi
Oregon Social Learning Center

Deborah Gorman-Smith
University of Illinois at Chicago

Physical aggression in adolescent relationships is a relatively new field of research, with empirical work beginning only in the early 1980s. As with many other mental health issues in childhood or adolescence, research in this area has primarily been a downward extension of research conducted with adults. Much of the focus of work with adults has been based on feminist theories of partner violence. A commonly held belief was that women stayed in violent relationships because of factors that made it difficult for them to leave, such as economic dependence and having children (Straus, 1976). It therefore came as a surprise to the domestic violence field when studies found relatively high rates of physical aggression toward a partner occurring among adolescent dating couples. Prevalence rates of perpetration or victimization among adolescents range from 20% to 60% (Bergman, 1992; Foshee et al., 1996; Jaffe, Sudermann, & Reitzel, 1992; Jezl, Molidor, & Wright, 1996). Furthermore, the prevalence of physical aggression toward a partner has been found to be highest at young ages and to decrease with time (Gelles & Straus, 1988; McLaughlin, Leonard, & Senchak, 1992). As a result of these startling findings, questions immediately arose regarding the nature and extent of the problem. Some of the questions researchers have recently attempted to address include: the degree to which such aggression is related to later marital aggression; why dating couples engage in physically aggressive behavior; the seriousness of the aggression; and the predictors, associated risk factors, and future outcomes of such aggression. We attempt to address these issues in this chapter by presenting an early life-span developmental-contextual model focusing on family-of-origin processes, the development of antisocial behavior, peer deviancy training, and individual–environment interactions. The model includes processes associated with trajectories that involve adjustment failures, including failure in the key area of intimate relationships. Aggression toward a partner in adolescence is set within the context of theory and findings related to such aggression in adulthood, because these behaviors are considered to be phenomenologically similar. The theoretical approach is based on prior work with our longitudinal studies of at-risk community samples spanning childhood to young adulthood.

In this chapter, estimates of the prevalence of physical aggression in dating relationships are presented, followed by a brief review of the main theories of aggression toward a partner. Second, definitions of aggression toward a partner and issues in the study of aggression toward a partner in adolescence are presented. Third, the two longitudinal studies of adolescent development and aggression toward a partner conducted by the authors and colleagues (Oregon Youth Study; OYS, and Chicago Youth Development Study; CYDS) are briefly described, and the findings that began to emerge in the last 5 years from developmental studies, including our own, regarding aggression toward a partner are presented. The highly controversial issue of gender and aggression toward a partner is addressed. Prevention implications are discussed. Aggression within same-sex adolescent couples is not within the scope of this chapter. Very little research has addressed such aggression for adolescents. For discussion and review of this issue in adult couples, see Burke and Follingstad (1999) and West (1998).

PREVALENCE RATES

Carlson (1987) reviewed rates of physical aggression among dating couples for high school and college students, generally, as reported on the Conflict Tactics Scale (Straus, 1990). Rates for less serious acts (e.g., slapping) were quite variable and ranged between 13% and 61% (Cate, Henton, Koval, Christopher, & Lloyd, 1982; Henton, Cate, Koval, Lloyd, & Christopher, 1983; Laner & Thompson, 1982; Makepeace, 1981). The most serious types of aggression, such as threatening with or using a weapon, were much less common with prevalence rates ranging from 1% to 4% (Henton et al., 1983; Laner & Thompson, 1982; Makepeace, 1981). The prevalence of aggression toward a partner appears to be higher in late adolescence through young adulthood than in mid-adolescence (Sugarman & Hotaling, 1989).

Moffitt and Caspi (1999) compared the findings of three studies with large samples for rates of physical aggression in late adolescence and young adulthood (under 25 years of age): two U.S. studies with data collection in the mid-1980s, namely, the National Family Violence Survey (NFVS; Fagan &

Browne, 1994), the National Youth Survey (NYS; Elliott, Huizinga, & Morse, 1985), and 1993–94 findings from their study with a New Zealand sample. Across these studies, perpetration rates ranged from about 36% to 50% for women and 25% to 40% for men, somewhat higher than in college samples. In summary, findings across these reviews indicate surprisingly high prevalence rates of physical aggression among young couples.

BIDIRECTIONAL AGGRESSION

Aggression between adolescent partners is often bidirectional or mutual (Capaldi & Crosby, 1997; Gray & Foshee, 1997). Of adolescent dating couples showing any physical aggression toward a partner, reported rates of bidirectional aggression are as high as 59% to 71% (Capaldi & Crosby, 1997; Gray & Foshee, 1997; Henton et al., 1983). Most often the partners in mutually aggressive couples report approximately equal frequency and severity of physical aggression perpetrated and sustained (Gray & Foshee, 1997; Henton et al., 1983) and that both partners were equally responsible for initiating the behavior (Henton et al., 1983). These couples also report sustaining and initiating greater amounts of physical aggression, more types of physical aggression, and more injuries than those who report unidirectional physical aggression in their relationship. Individuals participating in bidirectional aggression are also more likely to be involved in physical aggression across relationships.

PHYSICAL AGGRESSION IN DATING, COHABITING, AND MARRIED COUPLES

A key developmental feature of relationships in adolescence and young adulthood is that of change, including transition to new relationships and, on average, to more committed relationships. Prevalence rates for physical aggression have been found to vary by type of relationship. Cohabiting couples show substantially higher rates of aggression toward a partner than married or dating couples (Stets & Straus, 1990). However, the difference between cohabiting and married couples was much smaller once age was considered, because cohabiting couples are younger on average than married couples. Moffitt and Caspi (1999) reported rates of physical aggression that were about twice as high in married or cohabiting couples as in dating couples, with rates for dating couples of 21%. It may be that length of relationship is a key factor related to higher rates of physical aggression in cohabiting and married couples. Capaldi, Shortt, and Crosby (in press) found that length of relationship accounted for increases in physical aggression toward a partner from late adolescence to young adulthood.

THEORIES OF AGGRESSION
TOWARD A PARTNER

There are three major theoretical perspectives regarding aggression toward a partner: feminist theory, theories relating to mutual couple conflict, and theories relating to intergenerational transmission.

Feminist and Couple Conflict Theories

Most of clinical practice, as well as much research in the area of partner violence, is based in feminist theory and writings. The feminist perspective is that aggression and violence toward a partner is rooted in a culture of patriarchy and oppression that keeps men in power through subjugation of women (Dobash & Dobash, 1979; Kurz, 1993; D. Martin, 1976; Walker, 1984). Aggression or "battering" is a method of control by men, and thus is instrumental behavior. Therefore, men are seen as perpetrators and women as victims. A central tenet of this perspective is that all men are potentially violent and controlling toward women. Predictions based on feminist theory are that physical aggression toward a partner will be almost exclusively by men, unless in self-defense.

The issue of male and female participation in aggression toward a partner continues to be the most contentious issue in the area of domestic violence research. The issue has centered around contrasts between researchers with a feminist theoretical perspective and researchers characterized as family violence researchers, who view physical aggression in couples as often due to mutual conflict (Feld & Straus, 1989; Straus & Gelles, 1986) but also frequently embrace the view that feminist theories explain part of the variance in men's physical aggression toward women (Straus, 1993, 1994).

Evidence for the view that a tradition of male dominance in *Western* society includes support for men's physical aggression toward women in modern times is rather sparse. Very often, an 18th-century British "rule of thumb" law by which a husband was allowed to beat his wife with a stick no bigger around than his thumb is referenced as validating male violence toward women (Kelly, 1994). In fact, such a law was never in existence, and the judge's suggestion was considered so outlandish that he was lampooned in the press. There were no British statutes allowing husbands' physical aggression toward their wives. In fact, the English legal commentator Blackstone wrote that, as early as the 17th century, use of physical force against a wife, claimed as justified by civil law, was questioned, and a court comment in 1659 stated, "If a husband beat his wife, she can bind him to his good conduct before a Justice of the Peace, or she can sue him in the Spiritual Court, to be divorced by reason of cruelty" (as quoted in Kelly, 1994). Evidence of a direct relationship between structural patriarchy and wife assault is mixed (Dutton, 1994; Straus, 1994).

Archer (2000) conducted a meta-analysis of sex differences in aggression between male–female partners. In a categorical analysis by age, values were found to be in the direction of a higher prevalence of female than male physical aggression for the younger age group (14–22 years of age), and a higher prevalence of aggression for men than women in the older age group (23–49 years of age). Archer (2000) also examined sex differences in injuries. Studies with samples at younger ages (14–22 years of age) were associated with almost equal injury rates, whereas studies using older age samples found higher rates of infliction of injuries by men, but still with a significant proportion of injuries sustained by men.

A key aspect of an adequate theory of aggression toward a partner is that it should be able to explain individual differences in participation in aggression or violence toward a partner, because the majority of men are not physically aggressive toward their partners. In fact, there are several socio-contextual and developmental factors that can explain individual differences in aggression toward a partner, including functioning within the family of origin, history of abuse, and antisocial behavior (Capaldi & Clark, 1998; Magdol et al., 1997; Simons & Johnson, 1998) and assortative partnering by antisocial behavior and deprssive symptoms (Kim & Capaldi, 2003).

A second aspect of couples aggression that is a challenge to theorists is to explain women's physical aggression toward a partner that is not in self-defense. There is increasing evidence to suggest that not all female aggression toward a partner is in self-defense (Archer, 2000; Henton et al., 1983). In fact, there are some data to suggest that late adolescent and young adult women may initiate aggression toward their partners more often than men (Capaldi & Crosby, 1997; Capaldi & Owen, 2001).

Intergenerational Transmission

The intergenerational transmission paradigm has predominated in social learning explanations of aggression toward a partner in adults for almost 20 years. At least two processes in the family of origin may be associated with later aggression toward a partner. Aggression between parents may be observed and directly modeled for later relationships with partners (Rosenbaum & O'Leary, 1981; Stets, 1991; Straus, Gelles, & Steinmetz, 1980). Violence between parents may legitimize later violence against intimate partners (Kalmus, 1984). Second, physical abuse toward the children themselves may teach them that aggression is a tactic to use in family relationships. Thus, these children are likely to behave aggressively toward both their spouse *and* their children when they grow up (Straus et al., 1980).

However, many people who experienced or witnessed violence as children do not go on to commit violence against an intimate partner (Kalmus, 1984; Malone, O'Leary, & Tyree, 1989; Straus et al., 1980; Widom, 1989). This has led to a call for examining the mediating mechanisms by which aggression in the family of origin is associated with later aggression in adult relationships (Egeland, 1993; Kaufman & Zigler, 1993). Early tests of intergenerational models, with or without mediating processes, have been weak because most published studies used retrospective assessment of aggression in the family of origin (e.g., Doumas, Margolin, & John, 1994; Lackey & Williams, 1995; B. Martin, 1990; Simons, Wu, Johnson, & Conger, 1995).

DEVELOPMENTAL-INTERACTIONAL MODEL OF AGGRESSION TOWARD A PARTNER

We propose a developmental-contextual model whereby aggression toward a partner is examined within a life-span, individual-environment interaction framework (Capaldi, DeGarmo, Patterson, & Forgatch, 2002; Capaldi & Shortt, in press). From this perspective, social learning in the family of origin, along with individual differences in temperament, contribute to the development of coercive and aggressive strategies in social interactions and to the development of antisocial behavior. In this model, the direct treatment of the child by the parent is viewed as more central to the development of aggression than witnessing aggression between the parents (Capaldi & Clark, 1998). That is, it is the parents' behavior toward the child that has a direct relation to the child's behavior. Social learning of aggressive strategies may then be continued in the deviant-peer group, by a process conceptualized as deviancy training, involving reinforcement for antisocial behavior as well as learning of new forms of antisocial behavior (Dishion, Spracklen, Andrews, & Patterson, 1996). The combination of individual characteristics or risk factors in interaction with key influential individuals continues in the intimate romantic relationships, when the most proximal and important environmental factors affecting individual behavior are the characteristics and behaviors of the romantic partner. Thus, if the young woman is higher in antisocial behavior, this also may increase the risk for aggression in the relationship. The risk may be particularly high when both partners show higher levels of antisocial behavior. The frequency of such partnerings are higher than would be predicted by chance. Significant levels of assortative partnering by antisocial behavior have been found for OYS as well as other studies (Capaldi & Crosby, 1997; Krueger, Moffitt, Caspi, Bleske, & Silva, 1998; Merikangas, 1982). Conversely, a continuing association with a socially skilled partner may be associated with stability in nonaggressive behavior.

The young couple's relationship also is affected by contextual factors, such as the male partner's continued engagement in the deviant-peer group or stressors such as school failure and unemployment.

We hypothesize that the main social learning mechanisms involved in the intergenerational transmission of aggression involve unskilled parenting, especially ineffective and coercive discipline practices and low levels of parental monitoring, and reinforcement of aggression by antisocial peers. We posit that the majority of aggression in couples, including dating couples, is due to a combination of the development of antisocial and aggressive behavior in childhood and adolescence and to the use of nonconstructive problem-solving strategies, including learned coercive and psychologically aggressive behaviors that result in couple conflict and escalation to physical aggression. Later in the chapter, we review the empirical data supporting this theoretical model.

DEFINITIONAL AND METHODOLOGICAL ISSUES

The research on aggression among adolescent and young adult couples is plagued by a number of methodological issues and challenges that make it difficult to discern the nature, extent, and etiology of such aggression. A major issue has been the differing use of terms throughout the literature. The terms *aggression, abuse, violence,* and *battering* seem to be used interchangeably, despite the fact that the meanings of these terms vary considerably. There is also considerable variation in the types of behaviors included across studies. Many studies limit the focus to acts of physical aggression. A few studies limit behaviors to those that cause "bodily harm or injury" (Burcky, Reuterman, & Kopsky, 1988). Some researchers have also examined threat of violence (Sugarman & Hotaling, 1989) and verbal or psychological aggression (Capaldi & Crosby, 1997; Symons, Groer, Kepler-Youngblood, & Slater, 1994). Still others provide little information to discern exactly what is being measured.

Clearer conceptualization and methodological definition of types of aggression, specifically physical and psychological aggression, as well as further conceptualization of the consequences of aggression, would advance understanding in this field. Archer (1994, 2000) and Heyman, Slep, Capaldi, Eddy, and Stoolmiller (1999) recommend that the *impacts* or consequences of physical aggression be considered separately from the *acts,* avoiding the assumption that all physical aggression has the same degree of damaging consequences for all individuals. The impacts of aggression include such psychological consequences as fear and depression, as well as physical injury (Capaldi & Owen, 2001; Dutton & Painter, 1993; Gelles & Harrop, 1989). In summary, to increase understanding of aggression in adolescent couples, greater conceptual clarity along with examination of frequency, severity, and the impacts of aggression are required.

A second limitation in studies attempting to understand aggression in young couples is related to sampling. The majority of studies have been conducted using convenience samples, making it difficult to assess the nature and extent of any potential bias in findings and the generalizability of the findings. Many studies involve surveys of youth in school, thus excluding youth who are no longer attending school or are absent on the day of the survey. This may lead to underestimation of the prevalence of physical aggression (Roscoe & Kelsey, 1986). Until recently, surprisingly few studies have been longitudinal or have taken a developmental approach to the topic.

A major controversy in the study of physical aggression toward a partner has been the issue of measurement. By far the most widely used instrument for assessing physical aggression in couples is the Conflict Tactics Scale (CTS; Straus, 1990), on which respondents are asked to report the extent to which they have used various types of aggression during an argument or disagreement with their partner. Reliance on the CTS as the sole measure of physical aggression has been criticized, particularly for the lack of attention to the context and consequences of the physical aggression (Dobash, Dobash, Wilson, & Daly, 1992; White, Smith, Koss, & Figueredo, 2000). There is no way to determine whether or how much the behavior was in self-defense. Critics argue that most of women's reported aggression toward partner is likely to be in self-defense, rather than initiated by the woman. Similarly, it has been argued that the consequences of aggression toward women are much more severe; women suffer more serious injuries as a result of the males' aggression (Cantos, Neidig, & O'Leary, 1994). Prior versions of the CTS did not allow for any measurement of injuries sustained. Additional issues included the lack of a comprehensive list of the types of aggression that could be perpetrated and the scaling of the CTS. The scaling of the CTS involves aggregating across all of the items and does not weight items based on severity. Thus, critics argued that even if women report greater use of aggression on the CTS, it is likely that women use less severe forms of aggression. Despite these criticisms, the Conflict Tactics Scale is the most widely used instrument to measure aggression toward a partner.

Few studies have obtained information from both partners or used alternative assessment methodologies, such as observations. Reliance on self-reports may be particularly problematic in trying to understand the issue of men as victims of aggression. There are some data to suggest that men may be less likely to report being the victim of aggression or violence by partner, owing to social stigma for men victims (Jezl et al., 1996). Data from the CYDS (Gorman-Smith, Tolan, & Henry, 1997) suggest this may be the case. Of the partner pairs interviewed at 18–21 years of age, 28% of the young men reported that their partners had been physically aggressive in the relationship. Among those same partners, 47% of the women reported they had been physically aggressive toward their partner.

In part as a response to these criticisms, some researchers have started to obtain observational measures of aggression toward a partner, as well as more comprehensive self- and partner reports. Because self-reports of interactive behaviors have considerable limitations and biases, observation of behavior has been used to provide important additional information in family studies (Patterson & Forgatch, 1995; Patterson, Reid, & Dishion, 1992). Studies of adult couples rely heavily on observations of problem-solving interactions in order to understand the nature of conflict and aggression in couples (e.g., Cordova, Jacobson, Gottman, Rushe, & Cox, 1993; Margolin, John, & Gleberman, 1988). Findings regarding observations of aggression for young couples are reported later in the chapter.

THE OREGON YOUTH STUDY AND THE CHICAGO YOUTH DEVELOPMENT STUDY

The OYS and the CYDS are both longitudinal studies of males who were considered at increased risk for delinquency. Both samples were followed from childhood through young adulthood, and starting in late adolescence, their aggressive behavior with female partners was examined.

Oregon Youth Study

The OYS sample is a community-based sample recruited from schools with a higher-than-usual incidence of delinquency in the neighborhood for a medium-sized metropolitan area. All fourth-grade boys were invited to participate, and the recruitment rate was 74% (Capaldi & Patterson, 1987). The sampling design was such that the boys would have an elevated risk for delinquency, but the majority did not have conduct problems in Grade 4. The sample was 90% White, and the parents were 75% lower and working class. Yearly assessments were collected through young adulthood, including data from multiple sources (e.g., the boy, both parents, teachers, school and official records, peers, romantic partners) and observational data of family, peer, and romantic partner interactions as well as interview and questionnaire data. Participation rates in late adolescence and young adulthood averaged about 98%, or a sample size of around 200 (Capaldi, Chamberlain, Fetrow, & Wilson, 1997). In the juvenile period (prior to 18 years of age) about half of the boys were arrested one or more times, with 20% having five or more arrests. Forty-nine percent graduated from high school with their class.

In late adolescence (17–18 years of age), the young men were invited to participate in an assessment with a romantic partner. Fifty-eight percent participated within a 3-year period (Time 1, late adolescence; mean age for the young men was 18 years of age).[1] A further assessment was collected at about age 21 years (Time 2, young adulthood), with a 77% participation rate. Findings presented in this chapter are for the subset of OYS males who participated at Time 1 or Time 2 with a romantic partner. In late adolescence, at an average age of around 18 years, 31% of the young men with partners and 36% of their female partners had engaged in physical aggression toward a partner in the past year (Capaldi & Crosby, 1997). In addition to physical aggression, measures of psychological aggression were obtained. The term *psychological aggression* refers to acting in an offensive or degrading manner toward another, usually verbally. This behavior, sometimes termed *emotional abuse,* is usually present in violent couples and has been reported by many physically abused women to have a more severe impact than the physical abuse (Follingstad, Rutledge, Berg, Hause, & Polek, 1990).

Measurement of aggression for OYS in late adolescence included both partners' reports of psychological and physical aggression, including both their own and their partner's behaviors, as well as coded behavior and coder ratings of a problem-solving interaction between the young couple where they discussed issues of conflict selected from a couples' issues checklist (Capaldi & Clark, 1998; Capaldi & Crosby, 1997). Observed aggression was found to be significantly associated with reported aggression, and the correlation between physical and psychological aggression toward a partner in late adolescence was .60 for the young men and .55 for the young women ($p < .001$).

Chicago Youth Development Study

The CYDS is a longitudinal study of the development of serious delinquency. Like the OYS, the study applies a multilevel, multiwave assessment strategy to

---

[1]The primary reason for nonparticipation at each time point was that the young man was not in a romantic relationship.

evaluate interactions between individual, family, peer, community, and social factors affecting boys' involvement in antisocial behavior.

Boys were initially recruited from Grades 5 and 7 of 17 Chicago Public Schools, located in communities in Chicago with above average rates of poverty for the city. The median poverty rate for the sample was 34.6%, which is at the 67th percentile for Chicago. The student populations of the targeted schools and communities were predominately minority, with most having over 97% African American and Latino enrollment. Sampling permitted equal likelihood of Latino and African American enrollment.

After obtaining parental permission, 92% of the population of fifth- and seventh-grade boys were screened using the Achenbach Teacher Rating Form (TRF; Achenbach, 1991). Fifty percent of the boys selected were considered at "high risk" for development of serious aggression on the basis of teacher ratings. These youth were selected from the top third of the original screening sample (above the 90th percentile using national norms). After this categorization, subjects were randomly selected from the remainder of those screened. Seventy-five percent of the eligible participants completed interviews in the first wave ($N = 341$).

Yearly assessments were completed through young adulthood, including data from multiple sources (e.g., the boy, both caregivers, teachers, school and official records, and romantic partners). Observations of family interactions were also obtained. Participation rates in late adolescence and young adulthood were 85%.

As of late adolescence, 74% of the sample reported involvement in at least some minor delinquent behavior over time (i.e., occurring over multiple waves). Forty percent reported involvement in serious and/or violent offending over multiple waves. Among those with partners in late adolescence or young adulthood, 31% reported perpetrating minor or severe physical violence toward their partners. Eight-two percent reported verbal or psychological aggression.

Intergenerational Models

Capaldi and Clark (1998) assessed prospective mediational models of the association between family-of-origin factors and later psychological and physical aggression toward female partners for the OYS sample. Prediction was compared for two family process constructs: parental dyadic aggression and unskilled parenting. Parenting (supervision and discipline) and parents' dyadic aggression (both parent's reports on the CTS and observations of negative exchanges) were assessed three times in childhood and early adolescence (Grades 4, 6, and 8), boys' antisocial behavior (parent and teacher reports,

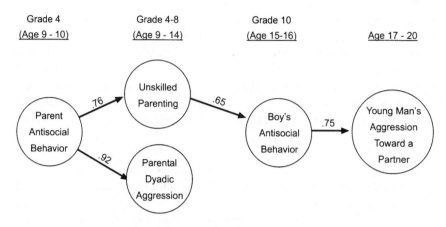

FIG. 10.1.   Findings for the hypothesized mediated intergenerational model aggression toward a partner.

arrest records, self-report delinquency) was assessed in midadolescence, and aggression toward a partner was assessed in late adolescence (average age of 18 years). Measurement of physical and psychological aggression toward a partner was already described.

Correlations indicated a significant association of aggression toward a partner in late adolescence with prior exposure to unskilled parenting, but not with prior exposure to parental dyadic aggression. Findings for the hypothesized developmental model are shown in Fig. 10.1. Parents with high levels of antisocial behavior were very likely to be aggressive toward their partners and to use poor discipline and supervision with their children. Unskilled parenting showed a stronger association with the boy's antisocial behavior in midadolescence than did parental dyadic aggression. Finally, the boy's antisocial behavior was a strong predictor of his later aggression toward a partner. The association between unskilled parenting and later aggression toward a partner was fully mediated by the development of antisocial behavior in adolescence. Findings indicated a significant association between antisocial behavior and aggression toward a partner across two generations.

Simons and Johnson (1998) had similar findings of the association of poor parenting, antisocial behavior, and aggression toward a partner for an adult sample, with the associations being found for both men and women. The association of antisocial behavior in childhood and adolescence and later physical aggression toward a partner in adolescence and young adulthood also has been found in recent prospective studies of young women's aggression toward a partner (Andrews, Foster, Capaldi, & Hops, 2000; Giordano, Millhollin, Cernkovich, Pugh, & Rudolph, 1999; Magdol et al., 1997).

Two tests of intergenerational models were completed using data from the CYDS. First, following a similar model as used by Capaldi and colleagues, the longitudinal relations (over six waves of data collection) between mother's antisocial behavior (historical and current at Waves 1 and 2), parenting practices (discipline and monitoring, Wave 3), son's general antisocial behavior (Wave 4), and son's participation in violence on the street and violence as part of a romantic relationship at ages 15–19 years (combined Waves 5 and 6) were evaluated (Gorman-Smith, Tolan, & Henry, 2003). This model did not include any measure of parental partner violence. Similar to findings from the OYS, we found a significant association between mother's antisocial behavior and parenting practices, with greater antisocial behavior related to poorer parenting. Unskilled parenting was related to son's delinquent involvement, and son's delinquency was related to later violence on the street. However, there was not a relation between son's delinquency and son's report of partner violence, although there was a significant relation between son's violence on the street and partner violence. We found both direct and indirect paths from mother's antisocial behavior to son's violence. These findings may represent a difference in developmental context and violence involvement, with partner violence related more specifically to involvement in other violence, rather than to nonviolent antisocial behavior (e.g., property crimes). Both OYS and CYDS did converge, however, in finding an association between parental antisocial behavior, poor parenting practices, the son's antisocial or violent behavior, and aggression toward a partner.

A second model test using the CYDS addressed the specific relations between parental partner violence, parenting, and youth involvement in violence (Tolan, Gorman-Smith & Henry, in press). The relation of maternal (primary caregiver) self-reported partner violence, including both perpetration and victimization, to youth involvement in street violence and the relative increase of youth violence over time, was examined. We hypothesized that the association of mother's partner violence involvement and youth violence would be mediated by parenting practices (discipline and monitoring) and parental harshness. Findings indicated that mother's violence victimization did not directly predict youth violence, nor did it predict parenting practices. However, violence perpetration did relate to youth violence. This association was mediated by parental harshness and monitoring, with greater violence perpetration related to increased harshness and less monitoring. Overall, these results seem to implicate maternal partner violence perpetration as a critical risk factor for youth violence, and parental harshness and low monitoring as the processes through which much of its impact occurs.

These findings suggest that the impact of parental partner violence is mediated through the effects on parenting (Simons et al., 1995). An important finding here is the role of maternal perpetration in impacting risk. If maternal violence overshadows maternal victimization in affecting risk, this does not mean that maternal victimization is not an important issue in its own right. However, it may mean that interventions, particularly family-oriented prevention programs, should broaden any focus on partner conflict and violence to consider both partners' perpetration as detrimental to the children.

These findings on the role of unskilled parenting in the prediction of both antisocial behavior and later aggression toward a partner suggest that researchers and practitioners in the area of domestic violence have overemphasized the role of witnessing aggression between parents and underestimated the role of unskilled parenting in intergenerational transmission. This situation likely arose in part because of an overemphasis on examining risk factors in isolation, rather than the *processes* by which risk factors are associated with outcomes. Furthermore, the importance of both maternal antisocial behavior and aggressive behavior within the family has been barely recognized.

Peer Process and Aggression Toward a Partner

To date, there is little research on the specific processes within the adolescent-peer group that potentially contribute to the values, beliefs, and interaction patterns underlying aggressive behavior with female, intimate partners. Collins, Maccoby, Steinberg, Hetherington, and Bornstein (2000) pointed to the importance of developmental models that consider the roles of peers as well as parenting in socialization. Capaldi, Dishion, Stoolmiller, and Yoerger (2001) expanded on the Capaldi and Clark (1998) model of the contribution of family-of-origin process to later aggression toward a partner and on the work of Dishion and colleagues (Dishion, Andrews, & Crosby, 1995; Dishion, Patterson, & Griesler, 1994; Dishion et al., 1996) on peer deviancy training, by examining the contribution of peer process to later aggression toward a partner. Capaldi, Dishion, et al. (2001) posited that, from a life-span perspective regarding the role of relationships in social development, parenting contributes to basic levels of socialization, leading in turn to selection into adolescent-peer groups, which then play a role in establishing and maintaining prosocial or antisocial developmental trajectories. Adolescence is a critical period for the influence of peers, with respect to establishing norms, values, and behaviors that account for subsequent individual differences in adjustment. Dishion et al. (1994, 1995) examined the process whereby antisocial behavior can form the basis for adolescent friendships. Their observations of discussions between adolescent males and their friends indicated that reinforcement of rule-breaking talk occurred for some of the dyads, and predicted various problematic outcomes, such as escalations in drug use (Dishion et al., 1996).

Capaldi, Dishion, et al. (2001) predicted that hostile talk about women with antisocial male peers would make a unique contribution to the prediction of later aggression toward a partner, over and above the prediction from prior antisocial behavior. It was hypothesized that association with *antisocial* peers would predict hostile talk about women during male-peer interactions, and that these misogynous discussions would be mostly mutual. It was posited that expression of such hostility by a member of the dyad indicates that they feel that such talk is allowed within that friendship, indicating support for aggressive and derogatory behavior with women in later intimate relationships.

Developmental Model of Hostile Talk About Women With Deviant Peers

Deviant-peer association was assessed in early adolescence (13–14 years of age) by teacher, parent, and self-reports. Hostile talk about women was assessed by coder ratings from a peer interaction task with a chosen male friend conducted when the OYS male was 17–18 years of age. As part of the task, the pair was asked to discuss for 5 minutes what they liked and disliked about the girls they knew. Coders rated 7 items regarding the derogatory and aggressive nature of the comments by each of the boys. Aggression toward a partner was assessed at Time 2 (approximately 21 years of age). The standardized path coefficients for the hypothesized model with observed hostile talk assessed as a latent variable (i.e., with conservative correction for reliability of this single measure construct) are shown in Fig. 10.2. All paths shown in Fig. 10.2 were significant at the .05 level.

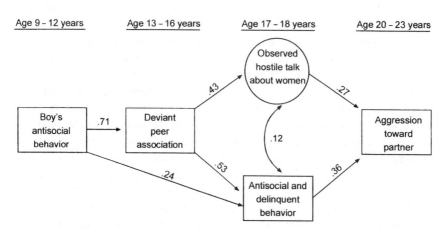

FIG. 10.2. Developmental model of deviant peer process, hostility toward women, and aggression toward a partner.

A close developmental association was found between antisocial behavior and deviant-peer association, such that boyhood antisocial behavior predicted adolescent deviant-peer association, and both of these constructs predicted late adolescent antisocial behavior. Adolescent deviant-peer association significantly predicted observed hostile talk about girls and women with a friend in late adolescence. Finally, both late adolescent antisocial behavior and such hostile talk predicted aggression toward a partner an average of 3 years later, in young adulthood.

Findings from the hypothesized model and from alternative model tests indicated that deviant-peer association and reinforcement of aggression toward women with such peers was clearly part of the developmental process associated with later aggression toward a partner. The findings are consistent with the view that aggression toward women tends to be part of a deviant socialization process rather than a normative process. The findings suggest that friendships between antisocial male adolescents are likely to include mutual hostile talk about women that may then undermine the quality of intimate relationships with women. Consistent with a social interactional view of development, the interactions of antisocial males predicted the young men's approach to conflict in romantic relationships.

Assortative Partnering

It follows from the findings from developmental studies indicating the association of childhood antisocial behavior and later aggression toward a partner for both young men and women, that if both partners show higher levels of antisocial behavior, the couple may be at heightened risk for aggression in their relationship. Aggressive characteristics of the partner may tend to support aggressive characteristics of the individual. The individual–environment interaction perspective leads to the prediction of assortative partnering by antisocial behavior via two processes: first, by *active* selection of environments (e.g., an adolescent boy who likes to "party" is likely to meet adolescent girls with the same social preferences at such activities and is likely to choose such girls to date); second, prior adjustment failures and engagement in conduct problem-related behaviors leads to unintended *restriction* of environmental options (e.g., an adolescent who drops out of high school may not attend a 4-year college and is unlikely to date a young woman attending such a college).

For the OYS sample, we examined an additive risk model, whereby it was posited that additional variance in aggression toward a partner in young adulthood would be explained by the young woman's antisocial behavior. The interaction term was also entered to examine the hypothesis that risk for aggression would be heightened if both partners showed higher levels of antisocial behavior. Antisocial behavior was assessed by multiple indicators in young adulthood for each partner, including criminal activities. Aggression outcomes examined at approximately 21 years of age included both physical and psychological aggression for the young men and women, respectively, as well as overall aggression constructs for each partner and a dyadic aggression score. Individually, both the young men's and young women's antisocial behavior was significantly associated with all of these outcomes. Findings generally indicated support for the additive model. With the antisocial behavior scores of each partner entered in the regression models, *both* partners' levels of antisocial behavior were significantly predictive of the young man's total aggression scores, but only the young woman's antisocial behavior was predictive of her total aggression score. The dyadic aggression construct score was predicted by both the young man's and the young woman's antisocial behavior. A significant interaction effect was found, in that the woman's physical aggression a toward partner was predicted by her own antisocial behavior *and* by the interaction of the couple's antisocial behavior measures. There was a stronger association between her antisocial behavior and her physical aggression toward a partner when his antisocial behavior score was above the mean. These findings indicate that assortative partnering by antisocial behavior indicates heightened risk for aggression toward a partner due both to the additive and interactive effects of both partner's engagement in antisocial and generally aggressive behaviors. They also indicate the importance of a dyadic theory of aggression in romantic relationships. Kim and Capaldi (2003) are extending this work by examining assortative partnering by both antisocial behavior and depressed symptoms and the effects on couples' aggression.

Clustering of Relationship Characteristics

The majority of research that has been conducted on patterns of violent relationships has focused on defining typologies of male batterers, with little attention being paid to the partner's role in the relationship (Gottman et al., 1995; Holtzworth-Munroe & Stuart, 1994; Margolin et al., 1988). Aspects of abuse other than physical violence, such as psychological aggression and other aspects of relationship quality that may be aversive (Follingstad et al., 1990), are rarely considered.

Using the CYDS data, we identified clusters of relationships based on self- and partner reports of seven relationship variables: (a and b) physical aggression (by self and by partner), (c and d) psychological aggression (by self and by partner), (e) support/intimacy, (f) extent of criticism by partner, and (g) antisocial behavior (Gorman-Smith, Tolan, & Henry, 2003b). Hierarchical and nonhierarchical cluster solutions were constructed. We identified a three-cluster solution as the best fit to the data. Couples in the first (and largest) cluster, named "good relationships" (66%), were characterized by the highest levels of support/intimacy and the lowest levels of all negative behaviors, including aggression and antisocial and critical behaviors. Couples in the second cluster, "generally abusive relationships," (7%) had high levels of physical and psychological aggression by both self and partner, as well as high levels of antisocial and critical behavior. Surprisingly, couples in this cluster did not differ from the first cluster in their descriptions of positive features of their relationships. The third cluster, "psychologically abusive relationships," (27%) contained couples with lower levels of physical aggression, high levels of psychological aggression, and high levels of antisocial and critical behaviors. This group had the lowest levels of support/intimacy.

Logistic regression models were conducted to predict the odds of involvement in each of the three relationship clusters from family background and delinquency patterns. Because longitudinal data were available only for the young men, we ran these models separately by gender. We found that young men involved in serious and violent delinquent behavior were less likely to be in good relationships and at increased risk for generally abusive relationships. Young men reporting a history of abuse in their families of origin were also more likely to be in each of the abusive types of relationships. Young men from the highest functioning families were more likely to be in good relationships and less likely to be in the generally abusive and psychologically abusive clusters.

With the cross-sectional data for the young women, we evaluated the relation between current delinquency and family functioning and pattern of relationships. Delinquency was related to increased risk for membership in both the generally abusive and psychologically abusive relationship clusters. A history of abuse was also related to involvement in generally abusive relationships. There was no relation between any of the other family variables and relationship pattern for girls. These findings regarding assortative partnering and clusters of relationship characteristics indicate that young couples who may be particularly at risk for aggression and abuse in their relationships are those where *both* the young man and young woman are higher in antisocial behavior and were from abusive or poorly functioning families of origin.

Frequent Physical Aggression, Injury, and Fear

Johnson (1995) attempted to explain the discrepant findings from feminist and family violence research by positing two theoretically different kinds of violence in couples, namely, *common couple violence* and *patriarchal terrorism*. He posited that common couple violence is due to conflicts between partners that are poorly managed and occasionally escalate to minor violence and, more rarely, to serious violence. He speculates that such violence is more likely to be mutual, of lower frequency, and less likely to persist. Johnson posits that patriarchal terrorism is patterned male violence against women, and he argues that such violence is likely to be much more frequent, persistent, and almost exclusively to be perpetrated by men.

Capaldi and Owen (2001) examined the association of *frequent* physical aggression with the impacts of injury and fear and conducted gender comparisons for these constructs for the OYS sample in young adulthood (at approximately 21 years of age). It was hypothesized that, contrary to Johnson's (1995) thesis that frequent physical aggression in romantic relationships is a male-only phenomenon, such aggression in couples would be bidirectional. Evidence of predominantly male physical aggression comes from shelter samples and media-recruited samples screened for male physical aggression toward a partner. As Kellam (1990) pointed out, such samples come from unknown total populations and entail selection bias in the sampling, because those who volunteer or seek help may show important differences from those with similar problems who do not seek such help. This has been found to be the case for samples seeking help for psychological problems (Greenley & Mechanic, 1976; Greenley, Mechanic, & Clearly, 1987).

Bidirectionality of Frequent Physical Aggression

Less than $\frac{1}{10}$ of 1% ($n = 4$) of respondents to the 1985 National Family Violence Survey (Straus, 1990) showed frequencies of physical aggression as high as mean levels for shelter samples. This may be because such individuals tend not to respond to the survey (Straus, 1990). Capaldi and Owen (2001) hypothesized that there would be a considerably higher proportion of individuals showing high frequencies of physical aggression among the young OYS couples than in large-scale survey samples. This was predicted because the OYS sample was selected as at risk for delinquency and aggression, and also because physical aggression toward a partner is more frequent at younger ages. In addition, the higher-risk young men did not self-select out of the sample by refusing participation. Secondly, it was hypothesized that frequently aggressive individuals would be likely to have a partner who was also frequently aggressive and, thus, that such behavior would be likely to be bidirectional, or mutual.

For the subset of the OYS young men who were assessed with their female romantic partners in young adulthood, a cut-off score of 19 or more acts of physical aggression toward a partner in the past year identified a group with a mean number of aggressive acts of one or more per week (in the range of shelter samples). By either partner's report, 9% of the young men and 13% of the

TABLE 10.1
Bidirectionality of Frequent Physical Aggression Toward a Partner
and Mean Frequencies of Physical Aggression Toward a Partner
in the Past Year

Physical Aggression in Young Men	Physical Aggression in Young Women	
	High	Low or None
High		
n	13	2
%	8	1
Mean frequency (men)	59	52
Mean frequency (women)	65	7
Low or none		
n	8	136
%	5	86
Mean frequency (men)	4	1
Mean frequency (women)	70	2

young women were in this frequent group. Bidirectionality of frequent physical aggression for the young adult subset of 159 young men and their women partners is shown in Table 10.1. Frequent physical aggression was significantly likely to be bidirectional in couples—the proportion of such couples was six times higher than expected by chance.

Gender Differences in Injury Rates

Capaldi and Owen (2001) also examined gender differences in the prevalence of injuries. It was hypothesized that when all injuries were considered, rather than only more severe injuries or those requiring medical attention, there would not be large discrepancies in the number of injuries between the young men and young women. However, it was predicted that women would show higher rates of injuries and more severe injuries than men, due predominantly to males' generally higher levels of antisocial and violent behaviors (Blumstein, Cohen, Roth, & Visher, 1986) and greater size and strength (Felson, 1996). It was predicted that the high-frequency couples would be more likely to sustain injuries.

Injury was defined as being hurt by partner judged to be on purpose or due to aggression. Thirteen percent of the young men and 9% of the young women indicated that they had been hurt at least once, with 4% of the young men and 3% of the young women indicating that they had been hurt five or more times. Injury was also likely to be mutual, at three times higher than expected by chance. The prevalence of injuries for young men and women in the sample was not significantly different. The most common injury for the young men was being cut or bleeding and for the young women was bruising. Descriptions of injury occasions indicated aggressive attacks by partners of both sexes. However, the three most severe injuries were to women. The probability of an injury was surprisingly low, in that even when the partner was frequently physically aggressive, with an average of over one occasion of physical aggression toward a partner per week, the probability of any injury was only .40 for the young women and .19 for the young men. Given the high frequency of physical aggression, this would suggest that in the majority of cases both young men and young women keep their aggression within certain bounds—it appears that they must actually be trying not to physically hurt the partner, at least to the extent of causing bruising, cuts, or abrasions. This would suggest that such aggression is rule governed to some degree. Perhaps these young people do not want physically to hurt the person for whom they have affection and are aware that injuring their partner will step over the bounds of what is permissible and run the risk of ending the relationship.

This view of aggression as rule governed is supported by the fact that our impression, so far, from police reports of arrests for aggression toward a partner and from reports of the young men and women in the study after a breakup, is that severe violent events are more likely to occur once a separation is underway. This could be because the norms governing acceptable behavior in an intimate relationship tend to break down during a separation, and stress levels are very high. If these conjectures are correct, that would help to explain why surveys of intact couples find extremely low injury rates (Stets & Straus, 1990) and why women in shelters, who may be more likely to enter a shelter during a relationship breakdown, may have recently experienced more severe violence and injury.

The association of frequent physical aggression and injury was also examined. Findings indicated that a young woman had a six times higher likelihood of being hurt if her partner was frequently aggressive, but the young man did not have a significantly higher chance of being hurt if his female partner was frequently aggressive. This finding may indicate that frequently physically aggressive women are less severely physically aggressive than frequently aggressive men. This seems to indicate that being hurt as a consequence of his partner's physical aggression may be more random for young men than for young women.

Female Perpetration and Her Own Risk for Injury

A finding with major implications for prevention programs was that if the young woman was frequently aggressive toward her partner, she herself had a three times greater likelihood of injury and also had a higher probability of more frequent and severe injuries. This frequent aggression is unlikely to be in self-defense. In late adolescence, the female partners of the OYS young men were observed to use physical aggression toward their partners at two to three times the rate of the young men (Capaldi & Crosby, 1997). Furthermore, the necessity of self-defense seems an unlikely explanation for such behavior, especially when the rate of hurt and injury is very low. This finding is in keeping with the prior findings for the present sample that the young woman's physical aggression was strongly predictive of her partner's future physical aggression (Capaldi, Shortt, & Crosby, in press). The present findings are in keeping with the contention of Straus and colleagues that physical aggression toward a partner by women is an important problem, because it may put them in danger of retaliation by their partners that could result in injury (Feld & Straus, 1989; Straus, 1999).

Physical Aggression and Fear

It has been posited that one of the major differences between male and female physical aggression is seen in the impact of fear. Jacobson et al. (1994) posited that there is gender asymmetry in fear of partner, with men's violence provoking more fear in women than vice versa, and that this is a major factor in the differential impact of violence by a partner for men and women. Jacobson et al. argued that if the function of male physical aggression is control of the partner, then only the woman should experience and express fear during arguments. Capaldi and Owen (2001) examined gender differences in the impact of fear, and the association of fear with having a frequently aggressive partner and with having sustained an injury for the OYS sample. It was predicted that due to mutual fighting and aggression, and the expectation that some young men would experience injuries (as turned out to be the case), they would show some degree of fear of partner's behavior. However, it was expected that due to the size and weight differential between young men and women, and men's higher levels of antisocial behavior as well as women's greater likelihood of injury, young women would be more likely to be frightened by their partner's behaviors than would men.

Findings for distributions on a self-report item regarding whether the young men and women (at an average of 21 years of age) were sometimes frightened by their partner's behavior, along with associations with frequent aggression and injury, are shown in Table 10.2. There was no significant difference in mean levels for young men and young women on their ratings of how true it was that they were sometimes frightened by their partner's behavior. Correlations indicated that the association between the young man being in the

TABLE 10.2
Association of Partner's Frightening Behavior, Frequent Physical Aggression,
and Injury

| | Sometimes Frightened by Partner's Behavior | | | | | | | |
| | Not at All True | | Hardly True | | Somewhat True | | Mostly or Very True | |
Reports	%	n	%	n	%	n	%	n
Women's (n = 159)								
Full sample	54	86	29	46	10	16	7	11
With a frequently aggressive male partner	13	2	40	6	27	4	20	3
With young woman reporting any injury by partner	14	2	36	5	36	5	14	2
Men's (n = 158)								
Full sample	58	92	30	47	9	15	3	4
With a frequently aggressive female partner	38	8	43	9	14	3	5	1
With man reporting any injury by partner	33	7	38	8	29	6	0	0

frequently aggressive group and his partner's report of how fearful she felt was significant ($r = .29$, $p < .001$), and approached significance for the young woman being in the frequently aggressive group and her male partner being fearful ($r = .14$, $p < .10$). The associations of reports of being fearful of a partner with having sustained any injury were examined next. The correlations were significant both for the young women and young men ($r = .24$, $p < .01$; $r = .20$, $p < .05$, respectively). Proportions reporting any injury by each category of the frightened item are shown in Table 10.2. Those young women and men who reported that it was somewhat, mostly, or very true that their partner sometimes acted in a way that frightened them were over 13 and 4 times as likely (respectively) to report that they had been injured by their partner than those who responded that it was "not at all true" that they felt frightened.

These findings indicate, as predicted, that young men as well as young women experience negative impacts of aggression in the form of injuries and fear. Overall, the prevalence of frequent physical aggression by women and of injury and fear for men was surprisingly high. These findings are consistent with a model of assortative partnering by antisocial behavior and of mutual couple conflict and aggression. The findings also indicate that the negative impact of women's physical aggression on men is substantial.

Interpretation of Physical Aggression in Young Couples

Even assuming mutual conflict, the findings regarding physical aggression for these young couples are a challenge to interpret. Viewing of the couples' problem-solving interactions for the OYS sample suggested that physical aggression may be a complex form of intimate communication that is related to proximal factors such as irritability, impulsivity, attention seeking, sexual ownership display, and sexual signaling and arousal. It also shows parallels to rough-and-tumble play between family members (Maccoby, 1980). It appeared that physical aggression was often a privileged liberty allowed to the romantic partner, especially in the case of the young men's tolerance of female physical aggression. Perhaps physical aggression plays some role in breaking down distance and awkwardness for some young couples and helps establish physical intimacy. However, the potential for escalation in severity of physical aggression during heated altercations for couples with a very physical interaction style would appear to be a strong risk.

Stability and Change in Aggression Toward a Partner Over Time

Studies of physical aggression toward a partner in adolescence have mainly been confined to cross-sectional designs; thus, little is known about the important issue of desistance and persistence in aggression toward a partner at this developmental stage. Samples ranging from cohabiting or newlywed young adults (Aldarondo, 1996; Mihalic, Elliott, & Menard, 1994; O'Leary et al., 1989) to the NFVS including a wide age range (Feld & Straus, 1989) have been rather consistent in finding desistance rates of around 50% for males over a 1-year period. For the OYS sample, using a similar dichotomous measure, we found desistance rates of 51% for the young men and 38% for the young women partners from late adolescence to young adulthood. Around 30% of those who reported not engaging in physical aggression toward a partner in late adolescence reported engaging in such aggression in young adulthood, which suggests that a rather large proportion of individuals may engage in such behavior at least occasionally during their romantic relationships. These findings also indicate that dichotomous scores may be of rather limited value in identifying individuals and couples who are at risk for more severe problems with physical violence in their relationship. Frequency and severity are important dimensions not captured by such scores.

A major implication of the developmental-contextual theoretical perspective is that young men's aggression toward a partner may change with environmental changes. If aggression toward a partner was found to be as stable over time for men with new partners as for men with the same partner, but the aggression of the new women partners did not show significant association with that of the prior partners, this would be strong evidence that the aggression was entirely associated with something within the man (e.g., patriarchal dominance or antisocial behavior). If male aggression toward a partner is more stable over time for men with the same partner than with a different partner, this suggests that characteristics of the partner or the dyadic context and interaction play an influential role in the occurrence of such aggression.

Findings for stability in aggression toward a partner from late adolescence to young adulthood for the constructs of physical and psychological aggression, including reports by both partners and observational data, indicated that there was significant stability in both physical and psychological aggression toward a partner by *both* the young man and the woman if the couple remained intact over that period (Capaldi, Shortt, & Crosby, in press). If the young man was with a new partner, there was no significant association in the aggression construct or in reported aggression across this period. However, for observed aggression only, the young men's physical and psychological aggression in late adolescence significantly predicted his psychological aggression toward a new partner in young adulthood. Weight should be given to this latter finding in light of the fact that observational measures are a relatively objective measure that is not subject to self-report bias.

Further evidence for the dyadic nature of aggression was found in strong associations between the partners for change over time in both physical and psychological aggression within both same- and different-partner couples. Thus, the same-partner couples tended to move in the same direction in their level of aggression. An association of similar magnitude for the different-partner group likely indicated that if the new female partner had a greater or lesser level of aggression than the previous partner, the male partner would also move in that direction.

Overall, findings regarding change over time in aggression, along with findings from the developmental models, indicate that both individual differences in the young men's behavior and dyadic influences are factors in the stability of aggression over time in these young couples' relationships. Antisocial behavior indicates which adolescents are at risk, but such developmental risk is far from the full explanation of aggression toward a partner. Assortative partnering by antisocial behavior contributes further to risk. Aggression appears to be predominantly bidirectional, with the direction of change over time for both physical and psychological aggression toward a partner tending to be synchronous. A further important finding on this issue was that the young man's physical aggression toward a partner in young adulthood was just as strongly predicted by his female partner's late adolescent physical aggression as by his own. Along with the findings on risk for injury by partner if the young woman herself was frequently physically aggressive, this could indicate that male physical aggression in late adolescence and young adulthood is at least partially in response to a female partner's physical aggression.

Ethnicity and Culture

Very little work has been done evaluating ethnic or cultural group differences in aggression toward a partner. Studies that have been conducted suggest that African American youth may be at greatest risk and Asian-American youth at least risk (Foshee, 1996; O'Keefe, Brockopp, & Chew, 1986). In a review of the empirical data on dating violence prepared for the U.S. Department of Health and Human Services (Ringwalt, Bercuvitz, Graham, & Matheson, 1999), secondary data analyses were conducted using three nationally representative surveys (The National School-Based Youth Risk Behavior Survey, The National Health Interview Survey—Youth Supplement, and the National Longitudinal Study of Adolescent Health [Add Health]) to generate prevalence estimates and evaluate ethnic group differences in rates and correlates of partner aggression. Although each survey had questions about dating violence, only the AddHealth survey addressed this issue in some detail. Thus, the majority of conclusions drawn in the report are based on these data.

Similar to previous reports, data from all three surveys suggest slightly higher rates of both victimization and perpetration of physical violence among African American males and females. There were no ethnic group differences for reports of verbal aggression. For victimization, rates for females ranged from 18.4% for African American, 15.1% for Latino, and 18.1% for White youths. For males, rates ranged from 24% for African American, 17.1% for Latino, and 14.7% for White youths. For reports of perpetration of dating violence, rates for females ranged from 26.7% for African American, 25.7% for Latino, and 19.1% for White youth (Ringwalt et al., 1999). These rates were not broken down by gender.

For the CYDS, we found slightly higher rates for African American youth compared with Latino youth for both victimization and perpetration of aggression. These differences, however, were not significant. Among females, 53.3% of African American and 50% of Latino youth reported perpetrating physical aggression toward their partner; among males, 29.4% and 23.3%, respectively, reported physical aggression toward their partner. Thirty-five percent of African American females and 27% of Latino females reported being the victim of physical aggression from their partner. For males, 28.2% of African American and 26.7% of Latino youth reported victimization. Again, none of these differences were significant. It may be that the differences between these data and those reported previously actually reflect differences due to socioeconomic status (SES) or community level variation. The findings using the AddHealth data do not control for SES or differences in residence location, a point acknowledged by the authors. Thus, any ethnic group differences reported could be attributed to differences in socioeconomic level. The CYDS data are drawn from families living within similar types of urban communities. All of the communities are poor, with 20% to 40% of the population living below the poverty level, and experience high rates of community violence and other social problems (Gorman-Smith, Tolan, & Henry, 2000). Although there was some variation in economic level among these families, with Latino families having somewhat higher reported incomes, all were living at or below the poverty line within quite impoverished neighborhoods. Thus, the comparisons using CYDS data were made among youth from different ethnic groups, but who lived within a similar social environment. Although it is difficult to tease apart differences related to ethnicity versus those related to the social environment, this can only be done using adequate samples of persons from different ethnic backgrounds living within a similar social ecology. It may be that any differences in prevalence are more related to the social ecology than differences in ethnicity.

This is not to say that ethnicity is not important. Rather, ethnicity may not be the *most* important factor in understanding differences in prevalence. Meaningful ethnic group differences may have much more to do with predictors of risk, rather than ultimate level of the problem. For example, a previous study found differences in how family functioning related to differences in street violence among African American and Latino youth, although there were no differences in prevalence of violence between these two groups (Gorman-Smith, Tolan, Zelli, & Huesmann, 1996). For African American families, strong beliefs about the importance of family were related to decreased risk for violent delinquency. For Latino families, however, the opposite relation was found. Strong beliefs about the importance of family were related to increased risk for violence. One potential hypothesis to account for this difference may be related to acculturation and the accompanying cultural conflict about parenting and family between Latino parents and children (MacKune-Karrer, 1992; Szapocznik et al., 1986). For many Latino families, the acculturation process disrupts traditional family processes (Szapocznik, Kurtines, Santisteban, & Pantin, 1997; Szapocznik et al., 1986). Most of the Latino families in the CYDS are first- or second-generation Mexican Americans. It may be that generational differences occur among these families as native beliefs and values around parenting and family processes are in conflict with those supported in the current community. The substantial intergenerational differences in acculturation that develop in the family may either precipitate or exacerbate existing family problems (Szapocznik et al., 1986). Thus, ethnicity may be most important in aiding the understanding of risk and providing direction for prevention and intervention than in explaining prevalence.

PREVENTION

Findings from the OYS and CYDS studies indicate that interventions that may be helpful in preventing aggressive behavior toward female partners include: improving parenting skills to prevent the development of antisocial and delinquent behaviors, and limiting time spent with deviant peers in adolescence. Furthermore, attempting to counter and prevent hostile attitudes and statements about the opposite sex—especially about girls and young women —among antisocial males may also aid in preventing aggression toward a partner. To this extent, the male adolescent-peer group may be an important prevention target. Findings also indicate that women's behavior, including their antisocial behavior and aggression toward a partner, are important, but little acknowledged or understood aspects of intimate aggression, and of the intergenerational transmission of aggression.

Intervention and prevention programs throughout the country are based on the Western feminist model, with treatment of aggression focusing almost exclusively on men. Batterer interventions with men generally have poor attendance rates and poor outcomes regarding reduction or desistance in aggression (Hamby, 1998). Interventions for girls and women tend to focus on education, on gender socialization, safety planning, raising self-esteem, empowerment, and encouragement to leave a violent male partner (Hamby, 1998). Findings from the developmental studies reported here suggest that a major change in emphasis is needed in prevention programs for young couples and in treatment programs for at least a substantial proportion of couples. There are some programs that have successfully used couples' interventions for physical aggression (e.g., O'Leary, 1996).

Although some general youth violence prevention programs include dating violence as part of the intervention (Farrell, Meyer, Kung, & Sullivan, 2001), few programs exist that focus exclusively on prevention of adolescent partner aggression. The Safe Dates Project is one such program that was designed to test the effects of a program on the primary and secondary prevention of dating violence among adolescents in the Grades 8 and 9 (Foshee et al., 1996, 1998, 2000). The program was designed to decrease the occurrence of dating violence by (a) changing norms associated with dating violence, (b) decreasing gender stereotyping, and (c) improving conflict-management skills. In addition, for those who may already have experienced aggression in their dating relationship, program activities encouraged victims and perpetrators to seek help by addressing cognitive factors associated with help seeking. The intervention was multidimensional and included both school and community activities. The school activities included (a) a theatre production performed by peers, (b) a 10-session (45 minutes each) curriculum, and (c) a poster contest. The community activities included (a) special services for adolescents in violent relationships (e.g., crisis line, support groups, materials for parents) and (b) community service provider training. Treatment adolescents were exposed to school and community activities and control adolescents were exposed to community activities only. Thus, the effects of the school activities over and above the effects of the community activities were evaluated.

At 1-month follow-up, there were significant differences between treatment and control schools for both behavioral outcomes and some of the hypothesized mediating variables. At follow-up, there was 25% less psychological abuse perpetration, 60% less sexual violence perpetration, and 60% less physical violence perpetrated against the current dating partner in treatment schools than in control schools. In addition, school activities had effects on several of the proposed mediating variables, including dating violence norms, gender stereotyping, and awareness of services. For those students already experiencing violence in their relationships, there was 27% less psychological abuse perpetration in treatment than in control schools and 61% less sexual violence perpetration. Although students reported greater awareness of services, there were no differences in actual help seeking between treatment and control groups. There was also no difference in victimization. One explanation for this may be that many were dating people who were not in the study, with 75% of the girls dating older partners and 75% of the boys dating younger partners. Despite these initial promising findings, however, only the effects on mediating variables were found at 1-year follow-up.

The findings presented in this chapter suggest that prevention should be a high priority. There is evidence that preventive interventions focused especially on dating aggression can have some immediate impact, but it may be that more sustained efforts are needed for longer term effects. Following from the findings reported in this chapter regarding dyadic aggression, it is also likely that both partners needed to be involved in the intervention for it to be effective. Preventive interventions should focus on the role of *both* young men and young women in the emergence and escalation of physical and psychological aggression that can be damaging to the well-being of *both* partners and to the relationship. Findings regarding the surprisingly similar levels of injury and fear of partner for men and women suggest that the impact on men of women's physical aggression should not be dismissed by researchers and mental health professionals as practically nonexistent, as has been largely the case. Prevention programs for adolescents should stress nonviolence by both males and females, and include nonaggressive problem solving as well as de-escalation techniques. For treatment purposes, couples should be screened for the presence of mutual aggression, and the intervention for such couples should focus on both partners. For safety purposes, men who show histories of particularly severe and repeated physical aggression toward a partner may need to be treated separately. A well-designed intervention for mutual couple aggression could encompass the behavior of both young men and women, although placing a special responsibility on men, due to the higher likelihood of severe injury to women found in several studies. The evidence for the OYS was that engagement in frequent physical aggression toward a partner by some young women resulted in serious impacts on their male partners and higher risk for injury by male partners for these women themselves. The implication is that we are doing adolescent girls and young women a disservice by failing to recognize that they can have problems with physical aggression toward a partner. We are not providing them with adequate services to change their behavior, establish less conflictual intimate relationships, and avoid physical aggression and injury.

REFERENCES

Achenbach, T. M. (1991). *Manual for Teacher's Report Form and 1991 profile.* Burlington, VT: University of Vermont.
Aldarondo, E. (1996). Cessation and persistence of wife assault: A longitudinal analysis. *American Journal of Orthopsychiatry, 66,* 141–151.
Andrews, J. A., Foster, S. L., Capaldi, D., & Hops, H. (2000). Adolescent and family predictors of physical aggression, communication, and satisfaction in young adult couples: A prospective analysis. *Journal of Consulting and Clinical Psychology, 68,* 195–208.
Archer, J. (1994). Introduction. In J. Archer (Ed.), *Male violence* (pp. 1–20). London and New York: Routledge.
Archer, J. (2000). Sex differences in aggression between heterosexual partners: A meta-analytic review. *Psychological Bulletin, 126,* 651–680.
Bergman, L. (1992). Dating violence among high school students. *Social Work, 37,* 21–27.
Blumstein, A., Cohen, J., Roth, J. A., & Visher, C. A. (Eds.). (1986). *Criminal careers and career criminals* (Vol. 1). Washington, DC: National Academy Press.
Burcky, W., Reuterman, N., & Kopsky, S. (1988). Dating violence among high school students. *School Counselor, 35*(5), 353–358.
Burke, L. K., & Follingstad, D. R. (1999). Violence in lesbian and gay relationships: Theory, prevalence, and correlational factors. *Clinical Psychology Review, 19,* 487–512.
Cantos, A. L., Neidig, P. H., & O'Leary, K. D. (1994). Injuries of women and men in a treatment program for domestic violence. *Journal of Family Violence, 9,* 113–124.
Capaldi, D. M., Chamberlain, P., Fetrow, R. A., & Wilson, J. (1997). Conducting ecologically valid prevention research: Recruiting and retaining a "whole village" in multimethod, multiagent studies. *American Journal of Community Psychology, 25,* 471–492.

Capaldi, D. M., & Clark, S. (1998). Prospective family predictors of aggression toward female partners for at-risk young men. *Developmental Psychology, 34,* 1175–1188.

Capaldi, D. M., & Crosby, L. (1997). Observed and reported psychological and physical aggression in young, at-risk couples. *Social Development, 6,* 184–206.

Capaldi, D. M., DeGarmo, D. S., Patterson, G. R., & Forgatch, M. S. (2002). Contextual risk across the early life span and association with antisocial behavior. In J. B. Reid, G. R. Patterson, & J. Snyder (Eds.), *Antisocial behavior in children: A developmental analysis and model for intervention* (pp. 123–145). Washington, DC: American Psychological Association.

Capaldi, D. M., Dishion, T. J., Stoolmiller, M., & Yoerger, K. (2001). The contribution of male adolescent friendships to aggression toward female partners in young adulthood. *Developmental Psychology, 37,* 61–73.

Capaldi, D. M., & Owen, L. (2001). Physical aggression in a community sample of at-risk, young couples: Gender comparisons for frequency, injury, and fear. *Journal of Family Psychology, 15,* 425–440.

Capaldi, D. M., & Patterson, G. R. (1987). An approach to the problem of recruitment and retention rates for longitudinal research. *Behavioral Assessment, 9,* 169–177.

Capaldi, D. M., & Shortt, J. W. (in press). Understanding conduct problems in adolescence from a life-span perspective. In G. R. Adams & M. Berzonsky (Eds.), *Handbook of adolescence.* Oxford, UK: Blackwell Publishers Ltd.

Capaldi, D. M., Shortt, J. W., & Crosby, L. (in press). Physical and psychological aggression in at-risk young couples: Stability and change in young adulthood. *Merrill-Palmer Quarterly.*

Carlson, B. E. (1987). Dating violence: A research review and comparison with spouse abuse. *Social Casework: The Journal of Contemporary Social Work, 68,* 16–23.

Cate, R. M., Henton, J. M., Koval, J., Christopher, F. S., & Lloyd, S. (1982). Premarital abuse: A social psychological perspective. *Journal of Family Issues, 3,* 79–90.

Collins, W. A., Maccoby, E. E., Steinberg, L., Hetherington, E. M., & Bornstein, M. H. (2000). Contemporary research on parenting: A case for nature and nurture. *American Psychologist, 55,* 218–232.

Cordova, J. V., Jacobson, N. S., Gottman, J. M., Rushe, R., & Cox, G. (1993). Negative reciprocity and communication in couples with a violent husband. *Journal of Abnormal Psychology, 104,* 559–564.

Dishion, T. J., Andrews, D. W., & Crosby, L. (1995). Antisocial boys and their friends in adolescence: Relationship characteristics, quality and interactional processes. *Child Development, 66,* 139–151.

Dishion, T. J., Patterson, G. R., & Griesler, P. C. (1994). Peer adaptation in the development of antisocial behavior: A confluence model. In L. R. Huesmann (Ed.), *Aggressive behavior: Current perspectives* (pp. 61–95). New York: Plenum Press.

Dishion, T. J., Spracklen, K. M., Andrews, D. W., & Patterson, G. R. (1996). Deviancy training in male adolescent friendships. *Behavior Therapy, 27,* 373–390.

Dobash, R. P., & Dobash, R. (1979). *Violence against wives.* New York: The Free Press.

Dobash, R. P., Dobash, R. E., Wilson, M., & Daly, M. (1992). The myth of sexual symmetry in marital violence. *Social Problems, 39,* 71–91.

Doumas, D., Margolin, G., & John, R. S. (1994). The intergenerational transmission of aggression across three generations. *Journal of Family Violence, 9,* 157–175.

Dutton, D. G. (1994). Patriarchy and wife assault: The ecological fallacy. *Violence and Victims, 9,* 167–182.

Dutton, D. G., & Painter, S. L. (1993). Emotional attachments in abusive relationships: A test of traumatic bonding theory. *Violence and Victims, 8,* 105–120.

Egeland, B. (1993). A history of abuse is a major risk factor for abusing the next generation. In R. J. Gelles & D. R. Loseke (Eds.), *Current controversies on family violence* (pp. 197–208). Newbury Park, CA: Sage.

Elliott, D. S., Huizinga, D., & Morse, B. J. (1985). *The dynamics of delinquent behaviors: A National Survey Progress Report.* Boulder, CO: Institute of Behavioral Sciences, University of Colorado.

Fagan, J., & Browne, A. (1994). Violence between spouses and intimates: Physical aggression between women and men in intimate relationships. In A. J. Reiss & J. A. Roth (Eds.), *Understanding and preventing violence: Social influences* (Vol. 3, pp. 115–292). Washington, DC: National Academy Press.

Farrell, A. D., Meyer, A. L., Kung, E. M., and Sullivan, T. N. (2001). Development and evaluation of school-based violence prevention programs. *Journal of Clinical Child Psychology, 30,* 207–220.

Feld, S. L., & Straus, M. A. (1989). Escalation and desistance of wife assault in marriage. *Criminology, 27,* 141–161.

Felson, R. B. (1996). Big people hit little people: Sex differences in physical power and interpersonal violence. *Criminology, 34,* 433–451.

Follingstad, D. R., Rutledge, L. L., Berg, B. J., Hause, E. S., & Polek, D. S. (1990). The role of emotional abuse in physically abusive relationships. *Journal of Family Violence, 5,* 107–120.

Foshee, V. A., Bauman, K. E., Arriaga, X. B., Helms, R. W., Koch, G. G., & Linder, G. F. (1998). An evaluation of safe dates, an adolescent dating violence prevention program. *American Journal of Public Health, 88,* 45–50.

Foshee, V. A., Bauman, K. E., Greene, W. F., Koch G. G, Linder, G. F., & MacDougall, J. E. (2000). The Safe Dates program: 1-year follow-up results. *American Journal of Public Health, 90,* 1619–1622.

Foshee, V. A., Linder, G. F., Bauman, K. E., Langwick, S.A., Arriaga, X. B., Heath, J. L., McMahon, P. M., & Bangdiwala, S. (1996). The Safe Dates Project: Theoretical basis, evaluation design, and selected baseline findings. *American Journal of Preventive Medicine, 12* (Suppl. 5), 39–47.

Foshee, V. A. (1996). Gender differences in adolescent dating prevalence, types, and injuries. *Health Education Research, 11,* 275–286.

Gelles, R. J., & Harrop, J. W. (1989). Violence, battering, and psychological distress among women. *Journal of Interpersonal Violence, 4,* 400–420.

Gelles, R. J., & Straus, M. A. (1988). *Intimate violence: The causes and consequences of abuse in the American family.* New York: Simon and Schuster.

Giordano, P. C., Millhollin, T. J., Cernkovich, S. A., Pugh, M. D., & Rudolph, J. L. (1999). Delinquency, identity, and women's involvement in relationship violence. *Criminology, 27,* 17–40.

Gorman-Smith, D., Tolan, P. H., & Henry, D. B. (1997, November). *Violence toward partners: Both partners involved.* Paper presented at the annual meeting of the American Society of Criminology, Chicago, IL.

Gorman-Smith, D., Tolan, P. H., & Henry, D. B. (2000). A developmental-ecological model of the relation of family functioning to patterns of delinquency. *Journal of Quantitative Criminology, 16,* 169–198.

Gorman-Smith, D., Tolan, P. H., & Henry, D. B. (2003a). *Intergenerational transmission of violence: Parenting as a mediator.* Unpublished manuscript.

Gorman-Smith, D., Tolan, P. H., & Henry, D. B. (2003b). *Patterns of coupling among late adolescent youth: Pathways to risk.* Unpublished manuscript.

Gorman-Smith, D., Tolan, P., H., Zelli, A., & Huesmann, L. R. (1996). The relation of family functioning to violence among inner-city minority youths. *Journal of Family Psychology. 10,* 115–129.

Gottman, J. M., Jacobson, N. S., Rushe, R. H., Wu Shortt, J., Babcock, J., La Taillade, J. J., & Waltz, J. (1995). The relationship between heart rate reactivity, emotionally aggressive behavior, and general violence in batterers. *Journal of Family Psychology, 9,* 227–248.

Gray, H. M., & Foshee, M. (1997). Adolescent dating violence: Differences between one-sided and mutually violence profiles. *Journal of Interpersonal Violence, 12,* 126–141.

Greenley, J. R., & Mechanic, D. (1976). Social selection in seeking help for psychological problems. *Health and Social Behavior, 17,* 249–262.

Greenley, J. R., Mechanic, D., & Cleary, P. (1987). Seeking help for psychological problems: A replication and extension. *Medical Care, 25*(12), 1113–1128.

Hamby, S. L. (1998). Partner violence: Prevention and intervention. In J. L. Jasinski, L. M. Williams, & D. Finkelhor (Eds.), *Partner violence: A comprehensive review of 20 years of research* (pp. 210–258). Thousand Oaks, CA: Sage.

Henton, J. M., Cate, R. M., Koval, J., Lloyd, S., & Christopher, F. S. (1983). Romance and violence in dating relationships. *Journal of Family Issues, 4,* 467–482.

Heyman, R. E., Slep, A. M. S., Capaldi, D. M., Eddy, J. M., & Stoolmiller, M. (1999, April). *Physical aggression in couples' relationships: Toward understanding violent acts and their impacts.* Summary of the Raymond and Rosalie Weiss Foundation Think Tank on Aggression in Couples, Oregon Social Learning Center, Eugene, OR.

Holtzworth-Munroe, A., & Stuart, G. L. (1994). Typologies of male batterers: Three subtypes and the differences among them. *Psychological Bulletin, 116,* 476–597.

Jacobson, N. S., Gottman, J. M., Waltz, J., Rushe, R., Babcock, J., & Holtzworth-Munroe, A. (1994). Affect, verbal content, and psychophysiology in the arguments of couples with a violent husband. *Journal of Consulting and Clinical Psychology, 62,* 982–988.

Jaffe, P. G., Sudermann, M., & Reitzel, D. (1992). Working with children and adolescents to end the cycle of violence: A social learning approach to intervention and prevention programs. In R. De V. Peters & R. J. McMahon (Eds.), *Aggression and violence throughout the life span* (pp. 83–99). Newbury Park, CA: Sage.

Jezl, D. R., Molidor, C. E., & Wright, T. L. (1996). Physical, sexual, and psychological abuse in high school dating relationships: Prevalence rates and self-esteem issues. *Child and Adolescent Social Work Journal, 13,* 69–87.

Johnson, M. P. (1995). Patriarchal terrorism and common couple violence: Two forms of violence against women. *Journal of Marriage and the Family, 57,* 283–294.

Kalmus, J. (1984). The intergenerational transmission of marital aggression. *Journal of Marriage and the Family, 52,* 11–19.

Kaufman, J., & Zigler, E. (1993). The intergenerational transmission of abuse is overstated. In R. J. Gelles & D. R. Loseke (Eds.), *Current controversies on family violence* (pp. 209–221). Newbury Park, CA: Sage.

Kellam, S. G. (1990). Developmental epidemiological framework for family research on depression and aggression. In G. R. Patterson (Ed.), *Depression and aggression in family interaction* (pp. 11–48). Hillsdale, NJ: Lawrence Erlbaum Associates.

Kelly, H. A. (1994). Rule of thumb and the folklaw of the husband's stick. *Journal of Legal Education, 44,* 341–365.

Kim, H. K., & Capaldi, D. M. (2003). *Association of antisocial behavior and depressive symptoms between partners: Risk for aggression in romantic relationships.* Unpublished manuscript.

Krueger, R. F., Moffitt, T. E., Caspi, A., Bleske, A., & Silva, P. A. (1998). Assortative mating for antisocial behavior: Developmental and methodological implications. *Behavior Genetics, 28,* 173–186.

Kurz, D. (1993). Physical assaults by husbands: A major social problem. In R. J. Gelles & D. R. Loseke (Eds.), *Current controversies on family violence* (pp. 88–103). Newbury Park, CA: Sage.

Lackey, C., & Williams, K. R. (1995). Social bonding and the cessation of partner violence across generations. *Journal of Marriage and the Family, 57,* 295–305.

Laner, M. R., & Thompson, J. (1982). Abuse and aggression in courting couples. *Deviant Behavior, 3,* 229–244.

Maccoby, E. E. (1980). *Social development: Psychological growth and the parent–child relationship.* New York: Harcourt, Brace, and Jovanovich.

MacKune-Karrer, B. (1992). Unifying diverse parameters: The multicultural metaframework. In D. Breunlin, R. C. Schwarz, & B. MacKune-Karrer, *Metaframeworks: Transcending the models of family therapy* (pp. 193–236). San Francisco, CA: Jossey Bass.

Magdol, L., Moffitt, T. E., Caspi, A., Newman, D. L., Fagan, J., & Silva, P. A. (1997). Gender differences in partner violence in a birth cohort of 21-year-olds: Bridging the gap between clinical and epidemiological approaches. *Journal of Consulting and Clinical Psychology, 65,* 68–78.

Makepeace, J. A. (1981). Courtship violence among college students. *Family Relations, 39,* 97–102.

Malone, J., O'Leary, K. D., & Tyree, A. (1989). Generalization and containment: Different effects of past aggression for husbands and wives. *Journal of Marriage and the Family, 51,* 687–697.

Margolin, G., John, R. S., & Gleberman, L. (1988). Affective responses to conflictual discussions in violent and nonviolent couples. *Journal of Consulting and Clinical Psychology, 56,* 24–33.

Martin, B. (1990). The transmission of relationship difficulties from one generation to the next. *Journal of Youth and Adolescence, 19,* 181–199.

Martin, D. (1976). *Battered wives.* San Francisco: Glide Publications.

McLaughlin, I. G., Leonard, K. E., & Senchak, M. (1992). Prevalence and distribution of premarital aggression among couples applying for a marriage license. *Journal of Family Violence, 7,* 309–319.

Merikangas, K. R. (1982). Assortative mating for psychiatric disorders and psychological traits. *Archives of General Psychiatry, 39,* 1173–1180.

Mihalic, S. W., Elliott, D. A., & Menard, S. (1994). Continuities in marital violence. *Journal of Family Violence, 9,* 195–225.

Moffitt, T. E., & Caspi, A. (1999). *Findings about partner violence from the Dunedin multidisciplinary health and development study* (NCJ 170018). Washington, DC: U. S. Department of Justice.

O'Keefe, N. K., Brockopp, K., & Chew, E. (1986). Teen dating violence. *Social Work, 31,* 465–468.

O'Leary, K. D. (1996). Physical aggression in intimate relationships can be treated within a marital context under certain circumstances. *Journal of Interpersonal Violence, 13,* 450–455.

O'Leary, K., Barling, J., Arias, I., Rosenbaum, A., Malone, J., & Tyree, A. (1989). Prevalence and stability of physical aggression between spouses: A longitudinal analysis. *Journal of Consulting and Clinical Psychology, 57,* 263–268.

Patterson, G. R., & Forgatch, M. S. (1995). Predicting future clinical adjustment from treatment outcome and process variables. *Psychological Assessment, 7,* 275–285.

Patterson, G. R., Reid, J. B., & Dishion, T. J. (1992). *A social learning approach: IV. Antisocial boys.* Eugene, OR: Castalia Publishing.

Ringwalt, C., Bercuvitz, D., Graham, P., & Matheson, J. L. (1999). *Prevention of abusive intimate relationships among adolescents: Vol. 1. Summary of study findings.* Washington, DC: U.S. Department of Health and Human Services.

Roscoe, B., & Kelsey, T. (1986). Dating violence among high school students. *Psychology: A Quarterly Journal of Human Behavior, 23,* 53–59.

Rosenbaum, A., & O'Leary, K. D. (1981). Marital violence: Characteristics of abusive couples. *Journal of Consulting and Clinical Psychology, 49,* 63–71.

Simons, R. L., & Johnson, C. (1998). An examination of competing explanations for the intergenerational transmission of domestic violence. In Y. Danieli (Ed.), *International handbook of the Plenum series on stress and coping* (pp. 553–570). New York: Plenum.

Simons, R. L., Wu, C., Johnson, C., & Conger, R. D. (1995). A test of various perspectives on the intergenerational transmission of domestic violence. *Criminology, 33,* 141–172.

Stets, J. E. (1991). Psychological aggression in dating relationships: The role of interpersonal control. *Journal of Family Violence, 6,* 97–114.

Stets, J. E., & Straus, M. A. (1990). Gender differences in reporting marital violence and its medical and psychological consequences. In M. A. Straus & R. J. Gelles (Eds.), *Physical violence in American families: Risk factors and adaptations to violence in 8,145 families* (pp. 151–166). New Brunswick, NJ: Transaction Publishers.

Straus, M. A. (1976). Sexual inequality, cultural norms, and wife-beating. In E. C. Viano (Ed.), *Victims and society* (pp. 543–559). Washington, DC: Visage.

Straus, M. A. (1990). Measuring intrafamily conflict and violence: The conflict tactics scales. In M. A. Straus & R. J. Gelles (Eds.), *Physical violence in American families: Risk factors and adaptations to violence in 8,145 families* (pp. 29–47). New Brunswick, NJ: Transactions.

Straus, M. A. (1993). Physical assaults by wives: A major social problem. In R. J. Gelles & D. R. Loseke (Eds.), *Current controversies on family violence* (pp. 67–87). Newbury Park, CA: Sage.

Straus, M. A. (1994). State-to-state differences in social inequality and social bonds in relation to assaults on wives in the United States. *Journal of Comparative Family Studies, 25,* 7–24.

Straus, M. A. (1999). The controversy over domestic violence by women: A methodological, theoretical, and sociology of science analysis. In X. B. Arriaga & S. Oskamp (Eds.), *Violence in intimate relationships* (pp. 17–44). Thousand Oaks, CA: Sage.

Straus, M. A., & Gelles, R. J. (1986). Societal change and change in family violence from 1975 to 1985 as revealed by two national surveys. *Journal of Marriage and the Family, 48,* 465–478.

Straus, M. A., Gelles, R. J., & Steinmetz, S. K. (1980). *Behind closed doors: Violence in the American family.* Garden City, NY: Anchor/Doubleday.

Sugarman, D. B., & Hotaling G. T. (1989). Dating violence: Prevalence, context, and risk markers. In M. A. Pirog-Good & J. E. Stets (Eds.), *Violence in dating relationships: Emerging social issues* (pp. 3–22). New York: Praeger.

Symons, P. Y., Groer, M. W., Kepler-Youngblood, P., & Slater, V. (1994). Prevalence and predictors of adolescent dating violence. *Journal of Child and Adolescent Psychiatry Nursing, 7,* 14–23.

Szapocznik, J., Kurtines, W., Santisteban, D. A., & Pantin, H. (1997). The evolution of structural ecosystemic theory for working with Latino families. In J. G. Garcia & M. S. Zea (Eds.), *Psychological interventions and research with Latino populations* (pp. 166–190). Boston, MA: Allyn and Bacon.

Szapocznik, J., Rio, A., Perez,-Vidal, A., Kurtines, W., Hervis, O., & Santisteban, D. (1986). Bicultural effectiveness training (BET): An experimental test of an intervention modality for families experiencing intergenerational/intercultural conflict. *Hispanic Journal of Behavioral Science, 8,* 303–330.

Tolan, P. H., Gorman-Smith, D., & Henry, D. B. (in press). The developmental-ecology of influences on urban youth violence: Community neighborhoods, parenting, and deviant peers. *Developmental Psychology.*

Walker, L. E. (1984). *The battered women syndrome.* New York: Springer.

West, C. M. (1998). Leaving a second closet: Outing partner violence in same-sex couples. In J. L. Jasinski, L. M. Williams, & D. Finkelhor (Eds.), *Partner violence: A comprehensive review of 20 years of research* (pp. 163–183). Thousand Oaks, CA: Sage.

White, J. W., Smith, P. H., Koss, M. P., & Figueredo, A. J. (2000). Intimate partner aggression— What have we learned? Comment on Archer (2000). *Psychological Bulletin, 126,* 690–696.

Widom, C. S. (1989). The cycle of violence. *Science, 244,* 160–165.

11

Health Behaviors and Reproductive Health Risk Within Adolescent Sexual Dyads

J. Dennis Fortenberry
Indiana University School of Medicine

INTRODUCTION

From a clinical and public health perspective, the visible tracks of adolescent romantic relationships are the untoward consequences of sex marking obscure developmental trails toward a monogamous maturity expected by social traditions. These consequences—sexually transmitted diseases (STD) and unplanned pregnancy—are major causes of morbidity within adolescence. Rates of STD such as gonorrhea and chlamydia are as high or higher among 15–19-year-olds than among any other age group (Division of STD Prevention, 2002). Although most infections due to human immunodeficiency virus (HIV) occur in young adults, risk behaviors for this sexually transmitted infection typically begin during adolescence. In terms of unplanned pregnancy among adolescents, approximately 1 million occur each year. About 56% end with a live birth, 30% with an abortion, and 14% by miscarriage (Henshaw, 1999). Romantic partnerships are often integral to the sexual relationships that are key proximal factors to these adverse health events.

Romantic partnerships unfold within the context of increasing importance of friends (both same-sex and opposite-sex) as sources of support, shared values, companionship, and status (Buhrmester & Furman, 1987). Friends tend to share membership in cliques and other collectives defined on the basis of shared interests, intimacy, and activities (Brown, 1990). Romantic partnerships share many of the identity and affiliation functions of other types of friend relationships.

Friends resemble each other in terms of behaviors as well as attitudes and interests. Both similarity and socialization processes contribute to relative concordance of health-related behaviors within adolescent friendship dyads (Fisher & Bauman, 1988; Kandel, 1985). *Similarity* refers to a process of

279

assortative dyad formation whereby individuals select friends based on one or more shared characteristic. *Socialization* refers to the process of adapting attitudes, values, and behaviors that are in accord with those of important persons (Kandel, 1978). Although a subject of some disagreement within the research literature, both processes appear to contribute to behavioral concordance within adolescent friendship dyads.

A large body of research literature documents the importance of friends in the initiation and maintenance of behaviors with important consequences to health. Cigarette smoking, alcohol use, and drug use are consistently shown to be present at similar levels within adolescent friendship dyads (Curran, Stice, & Chassin, 1997; Downs, 1987; Hundleby & Mercer, 1987). Early initiation of sexual activity is associated with perception of peer norms endorsing sexual behavior and with perception of high levels of sexual experience among peers (Kinsman, Romer, Furstenberg, & Schwarz, 1998; Whitbeck, Conger, & Kao, 1993). Perceptions about friends' behaviors may serve as a source of efficacy expectations that influence both behavioral intentions and outcome expectations (Bandura, 1995). If romantic partnerships represent an extension of adolescent friend and peer relationships (Connolly & Goldberg, 1999), then similarity of health-related behaviors of members of a dyad might be expected based on the concept of selection as a basis for pair formation. Alternatively, romantic dyads could attain similarity as a result of mutual adoption of specific behaviors, especially if partners are key sources of companionship and social support (Fortenberry & Zimet, 1999; Laursen & Williams, 1997).

The importance of similarity of health-related behaviors within adolescent romantic dyads is increased because of the within-person clustering of health-related behaviors. Clustering of health-harming problem behaviors is a well-established characteristic of adolescent development (Jessor & Jessor, 1977). This clustering has sufficient robustness and magnitude to suggest a "lifestyle" that involves consistent engagement in problem behaviors (Elliott, 1993). Problem behaviors are defined by the norms of conventional society as undesirable. Problem behaviors usually elicit social and legal responses intended as prevention, control, or punishment. Adolescent problem behaviors include delinquency, alcohol use, use of marijuana and other drugs, and early initiation of sexual intercourse. A single common factor reflecting general psychosocial unconventionality may explain this behavioral covariation (Donovan & Jessor, 1985; Donovan, Jessor, & Costa, 1988).

Friends are important sources of influence for engagement in health-harming problem behaviors. Adolescents' perceptions of friends' behaviors are related to intentions to try substances or become sexually active (Hundleby & Mercer, 1987; Whitbeck et al., 1993). This is true even though the actual level of behavior by the friends' reports is often substantially lower.

First coitus during early adolescence, for example, is associated with greater friends' models for problem behaviors, irrespective of perceptions of friends' sexual activity (Costa, Jessor, Donovan, & Fortenberry, 1995). Relatively early initiation of sexual intercourse is also associated with younger age at initiation of dating. If networks of friends and peers form the basis from which dating and romantic partners are chosen, then substantial similarity in behaviors may be expected.

Friends may serve as direct influences on behavior by introducing a new behavior to the uninitiated. A *social contagion* model proposes that "experienced" adolescents "transmit" behaviors to inexperienced friends and peers. This model has been useful for explaining initial cigarette use, alcohol use, and sexual experience (Bowser, 1992; Rodgers & Rowe, 1993; Rowe, Chassin, Presson, Edwards, & Sherman, 1992; Rowe & Rodgers, 1991). The degree to which a dyad member introduces another dyad member to a new behavior, however, is not well understood.

The intra-individual clustering of health-protective behaviors is much less well described compared to health-harming behaviors. Health-protective behaviors are those relevant to maintaining physical health. Exercise, healthful dietary practices, seatbelt use, and dental hygiene are examples. Like problem behaviors, health-protective behaviors cluster, although these relations are typically weaker than those described for problem behaviors (Donovan, Jessor, & Costa, 1993; Elliott, 1993; Hays, Stacy, & DiMatteo, 1984; Kulbok, Earls, & Montgomery, 1988).

Transmission of health-protective behaviors within adolescent dyads could occur by means similar to the social contagion model just described. However, most health-protective behaviors, such as healthy dietary practices or seatbelt use, are more likely influenced by parental care-giving or modeling (Rossow & Rise, 1994). Friend influence is more likely to reinforce these existing behaviors than to serve as initiation (Maron et al., 1986; Wichstrom, 1994). Contraceptive and STD-prevention behavior is an important exception to this premise. Friends are important sources of contraceptive information but also often provide direct assistance in obtaining needed contraceptive or STD diagnostic services (Fortenberry, 1997a; Holmbeck, Waters, & Brookman, 1990).

Clustering of health-risk and health-protective behaviors within adolescent dyads is additionally important because of potential relationships to sexual and contraceptive behaviors. Coital experiences beginning during early adolescence are associated with greater involvement in health-risk behaviors such as alcohol and drug use (Costa et al., 1995). Rapid accrual of a large number of sexual partners is also associated with increased use of alcohol and other drugs as well as with delinquent behaviors (Fortenberry, 1997b; Richter, Valois, McKeown, & Vincent, 1993; Uitenbroek, 1994).

Contraceptive behavior is a central issue of adolescent sexual behavior because of its role in preventing the untoward outcomes of sexual activity. However, the structure of relations between contraceptive behaviors and other health-harming and health-protective behaviors is unclear. Failure to use contraception is associated with substance use and other risk behaviors (Fortenberry, 1995). Other studies have shown that consistent contraceptive use is associated with seatbelt use and healthy dietary practices.

To address this issue more directly, my colleagues and I examined three alternative models of the relations of contraceptive behavior to health-risk (alcohol use, drug use, violence, and delinquent behaviors) and health-protective behaviors (attention to healthy diet, exercise, seatbelt use, and dental hygiene). Participants were a multi-ethnic sample of males and females in tenth, eleventh, and twelfth grades. The alternative models assessed contraceptive behavior as a health-harming behavior, as a health-protective behavior, and as a behavior with structural relations to both health-harming and health-protective behaviors. As expected, two second-order factors representing health-protection and health-risk behaviors were negatively correlated. The best fit of data was provided by a model relating contraceptive use to health-protective behaviors (Fortenberry, Costa, Jessor, & Donovan, 1997).

The covariation of health-related behaviors (including contraceptive behaviors), the behavioral similarities between friends, and the importance of friend and peer networks in choice of romantic partners suggests the possibility that adolescent romantic dyads also share substantial similarity—by selection or by influence—for health-related behaviors. In any case, adolescent dyads could be expected to be characterized as relatively health-risk or health-protective, based on each member's antecedent behaviors. Dyad characteristics could then have important repercussions for individual health, especially in terms of STD and pregnancy prevention.

This chapter addresses three questions: (a) what are the similarities in health-protective behaviors within adolescent sexual dyads; (b) what are the similarities in health-harming behaviors within adolescent sexual dyads; and (c) is relative level of dyad-specific health-protection and health-risk associated with key reproductive health behaviors such as condom and contraceptive use? These questions were addressed in a small sample of sexual dyads enrolled in a study of sexual behavior and sexually transmitted diseases.

Methods

This study is part of a project evaluating factors associated with repeated bacterial and protozoan sexually transmitted diseases. Subjects were members of 39 heterosexual dyads (ages 13–25) attending a metropolitan sexually transmitted diseases clinic or one of three community adolescent health clinics. Index subjects were eligible for entry if they were treated for *Neisseria gonorrhoeae, Chlamydia trachomatis, Trichomonas vaginalis,* or non-gonococcal urethritis. Sexual partners were invited to participate by the index subject. Index subject enrollment and data collection typically took place during the same clinic visit. Enrollment of partners was completed within 2 weeks of index subject enrollment. All study instruments were completed independently by each dyad member.

Data were collected using a self-administered questionnaire and a structured interview administered by trained research assistants. The questionnaire assessed involvement in health-protective and health-harming behaviors, usually for the previous 2 months. The interview was designed to obtain information about each of the four most recent partners during the previous 2 months. Partners were identified by initials or first name. The questionnaire required about 20 minutes for completion; the interview required an additional 20–25 minutes for completion. Each subject provided written informed consent, but the requirement for parental consent was waived in order to maintain confidentiality regarding sexually transmitted infections. The study was approved by the institutional review board of Indiana University/Purdue University at Indianapolis.

Measures

Questionnaire and face-to-face interview items assessed demographic variables and health-protective and health-risk behaviors. Demographic variables included age, race, parental education and address. Addresses were used to identify the median household income (based on 1990 U.S. census) of the census tracts where the dyad members resided. Addresses were also used to calculate linear distances (in miles) between the residences of dyad members.

Measurement of Health-Protective Behaviors

Three health-protective behaviors were chosen to reflect domains of importance to adolescent health and well-being. *Seatbelt use* included two items (Cronbach's alpha = 0.90) addressing frequency of seatbelt use for car travel for short distances and for highway travel. Five response options were "Never," "Hardly ever," "Sometimes," "Most of the time," and "Always." *Attention to Diet* included four items (alpha = 0.84) reflecting the amount of attention given to limiting salt, choosing fruit instead of candy for snacks, reducing fat intake, and choosing baked or broiled rather than fried foods. Response options were "None," "Some," and "A lot." *Exercise Frequency* included two items (alpha = 0.89) the number of days per week of any type of vigorous exercise and the frequency each week of exercise lasting 20 minutes or more. Response alternatives for each item were "None," "One day," "Two days," "Nearly every day," and "Every day."

Measurement of Health-Risk Behaviors

Four health-risk behaviors were chosen to represent widely evaluated domains of problem behavior that have direct implications for health. *Cigarette Use* was a single item addressing the number of cigarettes smoked on an average day. Response options were "None," "Less than half a pack a day," "Half a pack to one pack a day," "1 to 2 packs a day," and "2 packs a day or more." *Alcohol Use* consisted of three items (alpha = 0.81) reflecting the frequency of any alcohol use in the previous 2 months, the usual amount of alcohol intake at each drinking episode, and frequency of five or more drinks at a single sitting. Response options for frequency were "Not at all," "2–3 times a months," "Once a week," "2–5 times a week," and "Every day." Response options for usual intake were "No alcohol intake in past two months," "One drink," "Two drinks," "3–5 drinks," "6 or more drinks of beer, glasses of wine or drinks of liquor." *Marijuana Use* consisted of two items (alpha = 0.79) assessing recent (past 2 months) and lifetime use of marijuana. Response options for recent use were "Never," "Once," "A few times," "About once a week," and "About every day." Lifetime marijuana use alternatives were "Never," "Once," "A few times," "Pretty often," and "Very often." *Violence* consisted of four items (alpha = 0.72) reflecting frequency of fist-fighting, slapping/hitting someone, carrying a weapon and participating in a gang fight (in the past 2 months). Response alternatives were "Never," "Once," "Twice," and "3 times or more." Violence between partners was not assessed. For all items and scales, higher scores reflect more involvement with the specified behavior.

Measurement of Reproductive Health Behaviors

Three dependent variables were chosen to represent behaviors thought to be associated with risk of adverse outcomes of sexual activity. Reproductive health variables included condom use at last coitus; hormonal contraceptive use (past 2 months) and alcohol/drug use before coitus. *Condom Use at Last Coitus* was used to reflect both pregnancy and STD prevention behaviors. The most appropriate measure for condom use is controversial but use at last coitus generally is highly correlated with other measures of frequency of use (Sheeran & Abraham, 1994). Condom use was assessed for the last coitus with the specific partner also participating in the project. Male dyad member's report of condom use at last coitus was taken to represent dyad condom use with the rationale that such behavior is more salient to men. Based on similar reasoning, *Hormonal Contraceptive Use* was operationalized as the female dyad member's report of use of oral contraceptive pills or depo-medroxyprogesterone as a contraceptive method in the past 2 months. Participants responded to a list of contraceptive options including oral contraceptives, depo-medroxyprogesterone, sub-dermal contraceptive implants (Norplant), condoms, spermicidal jelly/foam, diaphragm and intrauterine devices (IUD). Hormonal contraceptive use was coded "No" if neither oral contraceptives or depo-medroxyprogesterone were identified and "Yes" if one or both was marked. None of the female dyad members reported use of Norplant or IUD. No attempt was made to evaluate the reliability of these self-reports (e.g., by medical chart review). However, other research demonstrates substantial reliability of self-reported contraceptive use for the immediate past (Hunter et al., 1997). *Substance Use at Last Coitus* was assessed because of a widespread belief that alcohol or drug use associated with coitus increases risk of STD and unplanned pregnancy (Fortenberry, 1995). For this item, a report by either partner was coded as "Yes."

Statistical analyses were conducted using McNemar's test, paired t-test, and Spearman or Pearson correlation (Kashy & Kenny, 2000).

RESULTS

Both dyad members were African American for 19/21 dyads; two dyads were mixed-race (African American/White), and the both dyad members were White in the remaining 18 dyads. About 47% of the dyads reported the same address and presumably lived together. The median distance between residences of couples not living together was 3.3 miles. Between-gender comparisons of demographics, health-protection items and health-risk items are in Table 11.1. Male dyad members were (on average) 2 years older than female dyad members, and ages of dyad members were not significantly correlated. Maternal education was equivalent to approximately twelfth grade for both male and female dyad members. Paternal education level was somewhat higher but data were missing for four male dyad members and four female dyad members. Median household income for the census tracts of residence was higher for male dyad members than for female dyad members; however, these were significantly correlated. Overall, these data agree with other reports of substantial within-dyad similarity in socio-demographic background among adolescent sexual dyads (Ford & Norris, 1997).

Between-gender, within-dyad comparisons of scales and individual items for health protective behaviors are also in Table 11.1. Female dyad members

TABLE 11.1
Within-Dyad Comparisons—Sociodemographic
and Health-Related Variables

Socio-Demographic Measures	Males	Females	Correlation[4]
Age	19.3 (2.4)	17.5 (2.2)*	0.23
Mother's Education	4.2 (1.4)	4.2 (1.5)	0.29**
Father's Education	5.3 (2.0)	4.6 (2.1)	0.22
Median Household Income ($)	25,027 (8,621)	22,646 (7,791)*	0.73*

Health-Protective Behaviors	Males	Females	Correlation[4]
Seatbelt Use[1]	**5.4 (3.0)**	**7.0 (2.7)***	**0.33***
Streets	2.4 (1.6)	3.3 (1.4)*	0.29**
Highway	3.1 (1.6)	3.7 (1.4)*	0.27**
Attention to diet[2]	**4.9 (1.7)**	**5.3 (1.5)**	**0.34***
Reducing salt	1.6 (0.6)	1.7 (0.7)	0.07
Reducing fat	1.5 (0.7)	1.8 (0.8)**	0.01
Including fruits/vegetables	1.9 (0.8)	1.9 (0.7)	0.13
Baked/broiled foods	1.8 (0.7)	1.9 (0.7)	0.04
Exercise[1]	**6.0 (2.8)**	**4.6 (2.4)***	**0.56***
Frequency	3.0 (1.4)	2.4 (1.3)*	0.50*
Duration	3.0 (1.5)	2.3 (1.3)*	0.55*

Health-Harming Behaviors	Males	Females	Correlation[4]
Cigarette Use[1]	**2.2 (1.1)**	**2.1 (1.3)**	**0.63***
Alcohol Use[1]	**5.5 (2.6)**	**3.8 (2.2)***	**0.52***
Frequency	2.5 (1.3)	1.6 (0.8)*	0.38*
Quantity	3.0 (1.6)	2.2 (1.5)*	0.51*
5 or more drinks (binge)	2.9 (1.4)	2.7 (1.8)	0.23
Marijuana Use[1]	**6.7 (2.3)**	**5.6 (2.4)***	**0.27****
Lifetime Use	3.8 (1.1)	3.2 (1.2)*	−0.03
Use—past 2 months	3.0 (1.5)	2.5 (1.4)**	0.31**
Violence[3]	**6.0 (2.9)**	**6.0 (2.7)**	**0.09**
Fist-fighting	1.4 (0.9)	1.5 (0.9)	0.31**
Slapped or hit someone	1.7 (1.0)	2.0 (1.3)	0.24
Carried a weapon	1.6 (1.1)	1.5 (1.0)	0.10
In a gang-fight	1.3 (0.8)	1.1 (0.2)**	0.29**

Note. Numbers are means and (standard deviation).
*Male/female difference. $p < 0.05$ by paired t-test. **$p < 0.1$ by paired t-test.
[1]Items have 5 response options.
[2]Items have 3 response options.
[3]Items have 4 response options.
[4]Pearson Correlation coefficients.

reported higher levels of seatbelt use for both street and highway travel. Within-dyad correlation of seatbelt use was 0.33. Female dyad members reported slightly higher levels of attention to a healthy diet but this difference did not achieve statistical significance. However, within-dyad correlation of attention to diet was 0.34. Male dyad members reported significantly higher exercise frequency and greater frequency of vigorous exercise. Within-dyad correlation of exercise was 0.56.

In general, these data show—at least at the level of specific behaviors—a substantial degree of within-dyad similarity in health-protective behaviors, even when a significant between-gender difference in level of engagement in the behavior is noted.

In terms of health-harming behaviors, male dyad members reported significantly greater frequency and quantity of alcohol use, although there were no within-dyad differences in terms of frequency of intake of five or more drinks at a single drinking episode. Both lifetime and recent marijuana use was greater for male than for female dyad members. No within-dyad differences were noted for cigarette use. Involvement in violence was also similar within dyads.

The within-dyad scores for the multi-item scales of health-protection (seatbelt use, attention to diet, exercise) and health-risk (alcohol use, marijuana use, violence) are also shown in Table 11.1 (in bold). In general, female dyad members reported greater involvement in health-protection and less involvement in health-risk than male dyad members. The within-dyad concordance was also substantial. Seatbelt use, attention to diet, exercise, alcohol use, and marijuana use showed modest within-dyad positive correlation. Thus, even though there are gender differences in levels of health-protection and health-risk, substantial relative behavioral similarity is found within adolescent sexual relationships. The exception to this general finding was violence involvement. Males and females reported similar levels of these behaviors, but there was little within-dyad relationship in level of involvement.

Evidence for a within-dyad health lifestyle was examined using one overall index of health-protection and one index of health-risk for each dyad member. The indices were created by summing t-score transformations of each health-protection scale (seatbelt use, attention to diet, exercise) and each health-risk scale (cigarette smoking, alcohol use, marijuana use, violence). Average score for the Health Protection Index for both dyad males and dyad females was 30.0. This lack of difference reflects the greater exercise participation of dyad males and the greater use of seatbelts of dyad females. Average score for the Health Risk Index was 20.4 for dyad males and 17.5 for dyad females. This significant difference reflects the greater involvement of males with alcohol and marijuana use.

The within-dyad correlations for both Health Protection and for Health Risk indices were significant and substantial. The correlation for within-dyad health-protection was 0.65; the correlation for within-dyad health risk was 0.32. There was little evidence of a more pervasive ordering of protection and risk. In other words, within-dyad health protection was uncorrelated to within-dyad health-risk. This suggests the possibility that some dyads are characterized as having relatively high involvement in health protection as well as in health-risk behaviors. Some dyads may have low involvement in both domains of health behavior while others are mixed.

In order to explore this issue in more detail, a summary index of dyad health was created to shift analytic attention to the dyad as the unit of analysis rather than the relations of within-dyad individual self-reports. For each dyad member, an overall health score was created by subtracting the health-risk index score from the health-protection index score. These individual health scores were divided into low risk and high risk based on the median. Dyad-risk was created based on overall health (low risk or high risk) of both dyad members. Dyads were characterized as High Risk (2 members at high risk; 12 dyads); Mixed Risk (1 member at high risk; 15 dyads); and Low Risk (2 members at low risk; 12 dyads). Dependent variables were condom use at last coitus (no/ yes), hormonal contraceptive use (past 2 months; no/yes), and substance use at last coitus (no/yes).

Relationship duration, lifetime and recent sexual partners, coital frequency in the past 2 months, condom use at last coitus, hormonal contraceptive use, and substance use at last coitus are shown in Table 11.2. Most of the dyads were in relatively enduring relationships. However, these were not necessarily

TABLE 11.2
Sexual and Condom Use Behaviors With Adolescent Dyads

	Males	Females	
	Mean (SD)	Mean (SD)	Correlation
Months since first sex with partner	15.1 (16.2)	13.6 (14.9)*	0.96*
Number of partners, past 2 months	1.6 (1.0)	1.2 (0.8)*	0.53*
Number of partners, lifetime	17.7 (18.0)	9.9 (13.0)*	0.02
Coital frequency, past 2 months	39.0 (41.1)	29.5 (34.9)	0.40*
Condom use, last coitus w/ partner			
No	31 (85)	31 (85)	
Yes	8 (15)	8 (15)	

Note. Pearson correlation coefficients. $*p < 0.05$ by paired t-test.

TABLE 11.3
Reproductive Health Risk Within Adolescent Dyads—
by Dyad Health Status

	High Risk[1] N= 12 (%)	Mixed Risk N= 15 (%)	Low Risk N= 12 (%)
Condom use, last coitus	2 (17)	1 (7)	5 (42)**
Contraceptive use	2 (17)	9 (60)	5 (42)*
Substance use with coitus	12 (100)	7 (47)	6 (50)**

[1]High Risk—both members with high health risk; Mixed Risk—one member with high health risk; Low Risk—both members with low health risk.

$*p < .05. **p < .10.$

exclusive relationships as seen by the average number of partners in the past 2 months. Within-dyad reports of lifetime sexual partners were uncorrelated, supporting the idea that disassortive pair formation in terms of sexual experience may influence sexually transmitted diseases risk (Ford & Norris, 2000; Laumann & Youm, 1999).

Health behaviors and reproductive risk are in Table 11.3. Condom use at last coitus was reported by 8/39 (21%) male dyad members. Among High Risk dyads, 2/12 (17%) reported condom use at last coitus compared to 1/15 (7%) and 5/12 (42%) Mixed Risk and Low Risk dyads, respectively ($p < 0.10$).

Hormonal contraceptive use was reported by 16/39 (41%) female dyad members. Two of twelve (17%) female members of High Risk dyads reported contraceptive use compared to 9/15 (60%) and 5/12 (42%) of Mixed Risk and Low Risk dyad members ($p < 0.10$).

Substance use at last coitus was reported by 25/39 (64%) dyads. Among High Risk dyads, 12/12 (100%) reported substance use at last coitus compared to 7/15 (47%) and 6/12 (50%) for Mixed Risk and Low Risk dyads ($p < 0.05$).

Adolescent sexual dyads differ in level of engagement in health-protective and health-risk behaviors. Risky sexual behaviors such as condom non-use, contraceptive non-use and substance associated coitus are most common within dyads characterized by relatively low engagement in health-protection and relatively high engagement in health-risk behaviors. These behaviors are least frequent within dyads with high health protection and relatively low engagement in health-risk. Mixed Risk dyads tend either to fall between Low Risk and High Risk dyads or to most resemble Low Risk dyads. This suggests a protective influence of the low risk dyad member on overall dyad sexual risk behavior.

DISCUSSION

The analyses presented here asked three related questions about the nature of health-related behaviors within adolescent sexual relationships. The first question addressed within-dyad similarities and differences in health-protective behaviors. We found significant gender differences in the level engagement in various health-protective behaviors. In general, these gender differences are consistent with those reported by other studies of adolescent health-protective behaviors: more involvement in exercise by males and greater attention to safety and diet by females (Donovan et al., 1993). Despite these general differences, dyad members resemble each other in terms of relative level of engagement in these behaviors. Moreover, some adolescent dyads can be characterized as relatively low in health-protection. The influence on long-term health of membership in a dyad low in health-protective behaviors is unknown. For behaviors such as diet and exercise, adolescent sexual dyads may be too evanescent to be associated with adverse health outcomes. For behaviors such as seatbelt use and condom use, on the other hand, such dyads could experience an immediate health outcome with lifelong or fatal consequences to a dyad member.

There is no evidence from the data to clarify the source of within-dyad similarity in health-protective behaviors. While substantial research addresses similarity of health-harming problem behaviors as well as the relative contribution of selection and recruitment, much less is said about health-protective behaviors. Jessor and colleagues argued that engagement in health-protective behaviors constitutes an orientation toward psychosocial conventionality (Costa, Jessor, & Donovan, 1989; Costa, Jessor, Fortenberry, & Donovan, 1996; Donovan et al., 1993). Psychosocial conventionality is suggested by greater attention to traditional values, attitudes, and roles and is often represented by higher levels of affiliation with parents, schools, religion, and community (Jessor, 1991). These factors protect against development of health-risk behaviors as well as encourage health-protective behaviors (Jessor, Van Den Bos, Vanderryn, Costa, & Turbin, 1995; Resnick et al., 1997).

Within-dyad similarity in terms of health-protective behaviors may originate in shared standards for health-related behaviors that contribute to initial dyad formation. Behaviors are an observable marker for attitudes and values that may be valued as characteristics of potential partners (McGuirl & Wiederman, 2000; Regan, 1998). Behavioral similarities could be based in the reciprocal reward provided by consensual validation (Klohnen & Mendelsohn, 1998).

On the other hand, dyad members have substantial opportunities to influence the other's behavior. Health-protective behaviors such as riding in a car, healthy eating, and exercising have important social functions in addition to their utilitarian importance for health. Dyad members may actively encourage or discourage healthy behavior in their partner based on their own beliefs and behaviors (Sieving, Perry, & Williams, 2000). Along the lines of *self-efficacy theory*, a dyad partner could provide a source of efficacy beliefs for behaviors even if there is no direct influence (Bandura, 1995).

In answer to the second question, we found evidence for substantial within-dyad similarity in terms of health-harming behaviors. These data are similar to those obtained from adult marriage partners: not only are spouses' smoking habits highly correlated but other health-harming behaviors are also more common in marriage dyads with at least one cigarette smoker even if the other partner is a non-smoker (Inaba et al., 1998). Other studies show substantial similarity for cardiovascular risk factors that include both relative inattention to diet as well as cigarette smoking (Brenn, 1997; Wood, Roberts, & Campbell, 1997). The degree to which a dyad member influences his or her partner to reduce health-risk behaviors is less clear. Among adolescents, friends and sex partners are infrequently considered as potential sources of pro-social influence (Brown, 1990).

The observation that no gender differences were seen in levels of cigarette use and the substantial within-dyad correlation of smoking involvement may be an especially important example of the importance of understanding dyad health characteristics. If non-smoking dyad members provide a degree of mutual protection against cigarette use, substantial health benefits are possible. Likewise, two smoking dyad members may find quitting more difficult since some aspects of the relationship may depend on the joint validation of a shared, proscribed behavior (Wakefield, Reid, Roberts, Mullins, & Gillies, 1998).

The third question asked whether the relative level of dyad-specific health-protection and health-risk is associated with reproductive health behaviors such as condom and contraceptive use. Condom use in particular is a cooperative behavior that may reflect dyad rather than individual characteristics (Kashima, Gallois, & McCarnish, 1993). The level of dyad-specific health-protection relative to health-risk was associated with condom and hormonal contraceptive use, and with substance-associated coitus. Dyads characterized as high risk (because both members were high risk) were less likely to use condoms at last coitus and were also less likely to use a reliable form of contraception. Use of alcohol or drugs before sex—which may serve as a marker for risky sex (Fortenberry, 1995)—was more common among high-risk dyads. Earlier research suggests that condom use covaries with health-protective behaviors (Fortenberry et al., 1997). Data from the analyses presented here suggest that dyad health characteristics are associated with a shared behavior of both dyad members, that is, sexual intercourse with a condom.

The data presented here represent a small number of highly selected dyads from similar social and economic environments. The participants were in middle- and late adolescence. These are periods of greatest risk for the adverse outcomes of adolescent romantic and sexual relationships. However, sexual relationships of early adolescents—when they occur—are especially risky and should be addressed in subsequent research. Approximately half of the dyads shared a residence, suggesting a sample of dyads somewhat more stable than might be expected in a more general population of adolescents. Most importantly, at least one member of each dyad had a sexually transmitted disease at enrollment. The importance of STD for adolescents emphasizes the importance of study of these dyads. However, the data cannot be generalized to a broader sample of lower risk adolescent dyads. Obviously, data from larger, more representative samples of adolescent dyads are desirable. Such dyad studies—especially with longitudinal designs—are very difficult to conduct. Data from the National Longitudinal Study of Adolescent Health (Add Health) should fill many current gaps (Udry & Bearman, 1998). However, these data are still in preparation.

If confirmed, these findings have several implications for adolescent health practice and research. Clinicians may need to give greater attention to partner characteristics and the extent to which they reflect the relative health protection and/or risk of an individual. Inquiry about partners and spouses is encouraged for clinicians caring for adult patients (Wood et al., 1997). It may be time to extend such attention to adolescents. Clinical efforts to prevent sexually transmitted diseases and unwanted or mistimed pregnancy are likely to be especially sensitive to dyad characteristics. Interventions to prevent sexually transmitted diseases, for example, typically focus on skills required for correct condom use. Such interventions may be more successful in low-risk and mixed-risk dyads than in high-risk dyads. High-risk dyads may require additional attention to the larger domain of health risk behaviors in order to successfully influence STD risk behaviors. Clinicians should also bear in mind the health of children that are not uncommonly present within these adolescent dyads. The health of these children reflects the health environment in which they are reared (Rossow & Rise, 1994). Inquiry into parental health behaviors may inform understanding of their children's health behaviors and provide a focus for intervention at a family level.

Adequate paradigms for research about adolescent romantic and sexual dyads should be developed and evaluated. As noted earlier, the Add Health study represents substantial progress in this direction. Such data should allow questions about the extent of continuity in health-related characteristics of subsequent sexual dyads and about potential long-term influences on health.

The phrase "it takes two to tango" reflects the widespread social recognition that coitus is a single activity requiring the coordinated behavior of two people. Recognition of the importance of sexual partners within the areas of adolescent sexual behavior, sexually transmitted diseases, and pregnancy is likewise a commonplace understanding. However, quite a lot more than sex is going on within adolescent sexual dyads. Understanding this may improve efforts to enhance health and prevent illness that may reverberate in the life course well beyond the weeks and months of a youthful relationship.

ACKNOWLEDGMENT

This chapter was supported in part by a grant from the National Institute of Allergy and Infectious Diseases (U19 AI31494) to the Midwest STD Cooperative Research Center.

REFERENCES

Bandura, A. (1995). Exercise of personal and collective efficacy in changing societies. In A. Bandura (Ed.), *Self-efficacy in changing societies* (pp. 1–45). New York: Cambridge University Press.

Bowser, B. P. (1992). African-American culture and AIDS preventions: From barrier to ally. *Western Journal of Medicine, 157*, 286–289.

Brenn, T. (1997). Adult family members and their resemblance of coronary heart disease risk factors: The Cardiovascular Disease Study in Finnmark. *European Journal of Epidemiology, 13*, 623–630.

Brown, B. B. (1990). Peer groups and peer cultures. In S. S. Feldman & G. R. Elliott (Eds.), *At the threshold: The developing adolescent* (pp. 171–196). Cambridge, MA: Harvard University Press.

Buhrmester, D., & Furman, W. (1987). The development of companionship and intimacy. *Child Development, 58*, 1101–1113.

Connolly, J., & Goldberg, A. (1999). Romantic relationships in adolescence: The role of friends and peers in their emergence and development. In W. Furman, B. B. Brown, & C. Feiring (Eds.), *The development of romantic relationships in adolescence* (pp. 266–290). New York: Cambridge University Press.

Costa, F. M., Jessor, R., & Donovan, J. E. (1989). Value on health and adolescent conventionality: A construct validation of a new measure in problem-behavior theory. *Journal of Applied Social Psychology, 19*, 841–861.

Costa, F. M., Jessor, R., Donovan, J. E., & Fortenberry, J. D. (1995). Early initiation of sexual intercourse: The influence of psychosocial unconventionality. *Journal of Research on Adolescence, 5*, 93–121.

Costa, F. M., Jessor, R., Fortenberry, J. D., & Donovan, J. E. (1996). Psychosocial conventionality, health orientation, and contraceptive use in adolescence. *Journal of Adolescent Health, 18*, 404–416.

Curran, P. J., Stice, E., & Chassin, L. (1997). The relation between adolescent alcohol use and peer alcohol use: A longitudinal random coefficients model. *Journal of Consulting and Clinical Psychology, 65,* 130–140.

Division of STD Prevention. (2002). *Sexually Transmitted Diseases Surveillance, 2001.* Atlanta: Centers for Disease Control and Prevention.

Donovan, J. E., & Jessor, R. (1985). Structure of problem behavior in adolescence and young adulthood. *Journal of Consulting and Clinical Psychology, 53,* 890–904.

Donovan, J. E., Jessor, R., & Costa, F. M. (1988). Syndrome of problem behavior in adolescence: A replication. *Journal of Consulting and Clinical Psychology, 56,* 762- 765.

Donovan, J. E., Jessor, R., & Costa, F. M. (1993). Structure of health-enhancing behavior in adolescence: A latent-variable approach. *Journal of Health and Social Behavior, 34,* 346–362.

Downs, W. R. (1987). A panel study of normative structure, adolescent alcohol use and peer alcohol use. *Journal of Studies on Alcohol, 48,* 167–175.

Elliott, D. S. (1993). Health-enhancing and health-compromising lifestyles. In S. G. Millstein, A. C. Petersen, & E. O. Nightingale (Eds.), *Promoting the health of adolescents: New directions for the twenty-first century* (pp. 119–145). New York: Oxford University Press.

Fisher, L. A., & Bauman, K. E. (1988). Influence and selection in the friend-adolescent relationship: Findings from studies of adolescent smoking and drinking. *Journal of Applied Social Psychology, 18,* 289–314.

Ford, K., & Norris, A. (1997). Sexual networks of African-American and Hispanic youth. *Sexually Transmitted Diseases, 24,* 327–333.

Ford, K., & Norris, A. (2000). Patterns of union formation among urban minority youth in the United States. *Archives of Sexual Behavior, 29,* 177–188.

Fortenberry, J. D. (1995). Adolescent substance use and sexually transmitted diseases risk: A review. *Journal of Adolescent Health, 16,* 304–308.

Fortenberry, J. D. (1997a). Health care-seeking behaviors related to sexually transmitted diseases among adolescents. *American Journal of Public Health, 87,* 417–420.

Fortenberry, J. D. (1997b). Number of sexual partners and adolescent health lifestyle: Use of the AMA's *Guidelines for Adolescent Preventive Services* to address a basic research question. *Archives of Pediatrics and Adolescent Medicine, 151,* 1139- 1143.

Fortenberry, J. D., Costa, F. M., Jessor, R., & Donovan, J. E. (1997). Contraceptive behavior and adolescent lifestyles: A structural modeling approach. *Journal of Research on Adolescence, 7,* 307–329.

Fortenberry, J. D., & Zimet, G. D. (1999). Received social support for sexually transmitted disease-related care-seeking among adolescents. *Journal of Adolescent Health, 25,* 174–178.

Hays, R., Stacy, A. W., & DiMatteo, M. R. (1984). Covariation among health-related behaviors. *Addictive Behaviors, 9,* 315–318.

Henshaw, S. K. (1999). *U.S. teenage pregnancy statistics with comparative statistics for women aged 20–24.* New York: The Alan Guttmacher Institute.

Holmbeck, G. N., Waters, K. A., & Brookman, R. R. (1990). Psychosocial correlates of sexually transmitted diseases and sexual activity in black adolescent females. *Journal of Adolescent Research, 5,* 431–438.

Hundleby, J. D., & Mercer, G. W. (1987). Family and friends as social environments and their relationship to young adolescents' use of alcohol, tobacco, and marijuana. *Journal of Marriage and the Family, 49,* 151–164.

Hunter, D. J., Manson, J. E., Colditz, G. A., Chasan-Taber, L., Troy, E., Stampfer, M. J., Speizer, F. E., & Willett, W. C. (1997). Reproducibility of oral contraceptive histories and validity of hormone composition reported in a cohort of U.S. women. *Contraception, 56,* 373–378.

Inaba, S., Kurisu, Y., Nagata, C., Takatsuka, N., Kawakami, N., & Shimizu, H. (1998). Associations of individuals' health-related behavior with their own or their spouses' smoking status. *Journal of Epidemiology, 8,* 42–46.

Jessor, R. (1991). Risk behavior in adolescence: A psychosocial framework for understanding and action. *Journal of Adolescent Health, 12,* 597–605.

Jessor, R., & Jessor, S. L. (1977). *Problem behavior and psychosocial development: A longitudinal study of youth.* New York: Academic Press.

Jessor, R., Van Den Bos, J., Vanderryn, J., Costa, F. M., & Turbin, M. S. (1995). Protective factors in adolescent problem behavior: Moderator effects and developmental change. *Developmental Psychology, 31,* 923–933.

Kandel, D. B. (1978). Homophily, selection, and socialization in adolescent friendships. *American Journal of Sociology, 84,* 427–436.

Kandel, D. B. (1985). On processes of peer influences in adolescent drug use: A developmental perspective. *Advances in alcohol and substance abuse, 4,* 139–163. New York: Haworth Press.

Kashima, Y., Gallois, C., & McCarnish, M. (1993). The theory of reasoned action and cooperative behavior—It takes 2 to use a condom. *British Journal of Social Psychology, 32,* 227–239.

Kashy, D. A., & Kenny, D. A. (2000). The analysis of data from dyads and groups. In H. T. Reis & C. M. Judd (Eds.), *Handbook of research methods in social and personality psychology* (pp. 451–477). New York: Cambridge University Press.

Kinsman, S. B., Romer, D., Furstenberg, F. F., & Schwarz, D. F. (1998). Early sexual initiation: The role of peer norms. *Pediatrics, 102,* 1185–1192.

Klohnen, E. C., & Mendelsohn, G. A. (1998). Partner selection for personality characteristics: A couple-centered approach. *Personality and Social Psychology Bulletin, 24,* 268–278.

Kulbok, P. P., Earls, F. J., & Montgomery, A. C. (1988). Life style and patterns of health and social behavior in high-risk adolescents. *Advances in Nursing Science, 11,* 22- 35.

Laumann, E. O., & Youm, Y. (1999). Racial/ethnic group differences in the prevalence of sexually transmitted diseases in the United States: A network explanation. *Sexually Transmitted Diseases, 26,* 250–261.

Laursen, B., & Williams, V. A. (1997). Perceptions of interdependence and closeness in family and peer relationships among adolescents with and without romantic partners. *New Directions for Child Development, 78,* 3–20.

Maron, D. J., Telch, M. J., Killen, J. D., Vranzian, K. M., Saylor, K. E., & Robinson, T. N. (1986). Correlates of seat-belt use by adolescents: Implications for health promotion. *Preventive Medicine, 15,* 614–623.

McGuirl, K. E., & Wiederman, M. W. (2000). Characteristics of ideal sex partners: Gender differences and perceptions of the preferences of the other gender. *Journal of Sex and Marital Therapy, 26,* 1153–1159.

Regan, P. C. (1998). What if you can't get what you want? Willingness to compromise ideal mate selection standards as a function of sex, mate value, and relationship context. *Personality and Social Psychology Bulletin, 24,* 1294–1303.

Resnick, M. D., Bearman, P. S., Blum, R. W., Bauman, K. E., Harris, K. M., Jones, J. L., Tabor, J., Beuhring, T., Sieving, R. E., Shew, M., Ireland, M., Bearinger, L. H., & Udry, J. R. (1997). Protecting adolescents from harm: Findings from the National Longitudinal Study on Adolescent Health. *Journal of the American Medical Association, 278,* 823–832.

Richter, D. L., Valois, R. F., McKeown, R. E., & Vincent, M. L. (1993). Correlates of condom use and number of sexual partners among high school adolescents. *Journal of School Health, 63,* 91–99.

Rodgers, J. L., & Rowe, D. C. (1993). Social contagion and adolescent sexual behavior: A developmental EMOSA model. *Psychological Review, 100,* 479–510.

Rossow, I., & Rise, J. (1994). Concordance of parental and adolescent health behaviors. *Social Science and Medicine, 38,* 1299–1305.

Rowe, D. C., Chassin, L., Presson, C. C., Edwards, D., & Sherman, S. J. (1992). An "epidemic" model of adolescent cigarette smoking. *Journal of Applied Social Psychology, 22,* 261–285.

Rowe, D. C., & Rodgers, J. L. (1991). Adolescent smoking and drinking: Are they "epidemics"? *Journal of Studies on Alcohol, 52,* 110–117.

Sheeran, P., & Abraham, C. (1994). Measurement of condom use in 72 studies of HIV-preventive behaviour: A critical review. *Patient Education and Counseling, 24,* 199- 216.

Sieving, R. E., Perry, C. L., & Williams, C. L. (2000). Do friendships change behaviors, or do behaviors change friendships? Examining paths of influence in young adolescents' alcohol use. *Journal of Adolescent Health, 26,* 27–35.

Udry, J. R., & Bearman, P. S. (1998). New methods for new research on adolescent sexual behavior. In R. Jessor (Ed.), *New perspectives on adolescent risk behavior* (pp. 241–269). New York: Cambridge University Press.

Uitenbroek, D. G. (1994). The relationships between sexual behavior and health lifestyle. *AIDS Care, 6,* 237–246.

Wakefield, M., Reid, Y., Roberts, L., Mullins, R., & Gillies, P. (1998). Smoking and smoking cessation among men whose partners are pregnant: A qualitative study. *Social Science & Medicine, 47,* 657–664.

Whitbeck, L. B., Conger, R. D., & Kao, M.-Y. (1993). The influence of parental support, depressed affect, and peers on the sexual behaviors of adolescent girls. *Journal of Family Issues, 14,* 261–278.

Wichstrom, L. (1994). Predictors of Norwegian adolescents' sunbathing and use of sunscreen. *Health Psychology, 13*(5), 412–420.

Wood, D. A., Roberts, T. L., & Campbell, M. (1997). Women married to men with myocardial infarction are at increased risk of coronary heart disease. *Journal of Cardiovascular Risk, 4,* 7–11.

12

Romantic Relations
Among Adolescent Parents

Paul Florsheim
University of Utah

David Moore
University of Puget Sound

Chuck Edgington
Oklahoma State University

Between 1985 and 1995, approximately 11% of young women between the ages of 15 and 19 became pregnant. About half of these women decided to continue the pregnancy and keep their children (Ventura, Mosher, Curtin, Abma, & Henshaw, 2000). Although adolescent pregnancy and childbirth usually occurs within the context of an intimate relationship, there has been remarkably little research on the relationship between adolescent mothers and their partners (Coley & Chase-Lansdale, 1999; Florsheim, Moore, Zollinger, MacDonald, & Sumida, 1999; Lamb & Elster, 1985; Marsiglio & Cohan, 1997). Perhaps it is assumed that because the relationship between an adolescent mother and her partner is likely to be unstable, it is less consequential to the process of parenting. However, it could be argued that the unstable nature of these relationships only heightens their importance (Whiteside & Becker, 2000). That is, adolescent mothers and fathers who experience serious relationship problems may have a more difficult adjustment to parenthood, either because they lack the benefits of a supportive partner, or because relational distress interferes with parental functioning (Cutrona, Hessling, Bacon, & Russell, 1998; Gee & Rhodes, 1999; Nitz, Ketterlinus, & Brandt, 1995). The basic premise of this chapter is that because the process of raising a child is intensely interpersonal, we need to better understand the relationships that develop between pregnant and parenting teenagers and their coparenting partners (Belsky & Hsieh, 1998; Brunelli, Wasserman, Rauh, & Alvarado, 1995; Osofsky & Culp, 1993; Osofsky, Osofsky & Diamond, 1988).

The chapter is organized around three goals. First, using data from a longitudinal study of adolescent mothers and their partners, we examine whether the quality of a young expectant couple's relationship is relevant to how each parent adjusts to the first year of parenthood. For the purposes of this chapter we defined "the adjustment to parenthood" in terms of (a) the parent's level of stress associated with parenting tasks and roles and (b) the status of the couple's relationship 1 year following childbirth. Second, we describe the interpersonal functioning of expectant adolescent couples, focusing on the association between each partner's subjective appraisal of the relationship and his or her observed interpersonal behavior. More specifically, we clarify the relationship between how young expectant parents feel about each other and how they behave toward one another. Finally, based on findings from the Young Parenthood Project, we discuss some general guidelines for intervention efforts designed to improve the relationships of expectant adolescent couples.

ADOLESCENT ROMANCE, TEEN PREGNANCY, AND THE TRANSITION TO PARENTHOOD

The transition to parenthood among married adults is often experienced as a rewarding but difficult process characterized by rapid changes in a couple's relationship and new sources of stress (Cowan & Cowan, 2000; Cox, Paley, Payne & Burchinal, 1999; Levy-Shiff, 1999; Lindahl, Clements, & Markman, 1998; Osofsky & Culp, 1993). However, the stress and disequilibrium associated with the advent of parenthood may also be an impetus for positive growth and the development of new interpersonal skills (Antonucci & Mikus, 1988; Cowan & Cowan, 2000). Although many new parents report feeling strained by the experience of parenthood, few admit regret.

Research on social support and parenting has demonstrated that the quality of a young parent's primary relationships—the core of his or her social network—plays an important role in how the transition to parenthood transpires (Cummings & O'Reilly, 1997; Gottleib & Pancer, 1988; Rhodes, Ebert, & Meyers, 1994). A conflict-ridden or unsupportive social network can have a negative impact on a new parent's experience of parenthood and his/her behavior as a parent (Belsky, 1984; Cox et al., 1999; Gottlieb & Pancer, 1988). On the other hand, a highly supportive social network can facilitate the psychological well-being and behavioral functioning of a new parent (Belsky & Hsieh, 1998; Cox et al., 1999; Crockenberg, 1987; Cummings & O'Reilly, 1997; Cutrona, 1984; McHale & Rasmussen, 1998; Katz & Gottman, 1996; Shapiro et al., 2000).

An important component of a parent's social network is the quality of his or her relationship with the co-parenting partner. Based on research with adults, there is ample evidence that the quality of relations between co-parents is highly relevant to the process of parenting (Cowan & Cowan, 2000; Cox, Paley, Payne & Burchinal, 1999; Katz & Gottman, 1996; McHale, Keursten-Hogan, Lauretti, & Rasmussen, 2000; Stocker & Youngblade, 1999). For example, Katz and Gottman (1996) found that hostility in the marital relationship was related to higher rates of negative paternal behavior, and husband withdrawal was related to negative maternal functioning, including high rates of intrusiveness and criticism in the parent–child relationship. Research with adult couples has also indicated that the way a couple communicates and the way each partner feels about the other is related to the long-term prognosis of their relationship. For example, Gottman and colleagues (Carrere & Gottman, 1999; Gottman, Coan, Carrere, & Swanson, 1998) have demonstrated that one partner's feelings about the other influences how he or she will interpret and respond to his or her partner's communications. Conversely, how a couple engages (behaviorally) with one another is likely to influence how both partners feel about their relationship. The complex interplay between subjective experience and interpersonal behavior is relevant to the course and outcome of a couple's relationship. Couples who communicate less effectively are more likely to become divorced or become engaged in a persistently conflict-ridden and unsatisfying relationship (Gottman et al., 1998).

Although much can be learned from research on adult couples making the transition to parenthood, what we know about adult couples may not be directly applicable to the adjustment of adolescent coparenting couples. There are several differences between adult and adolescent parents that suggest that adolescent couples may approach parenthood with a somewhat different set of interpersonal challenges.

First, the event of a teen pregnancy is often unexpected, which may contribute to a high level of stress between co-parents because one or both may feel unready or unwilling to assume the task of childrearing. Second, because adolescents tend to be less interpersonally skilled than adults, expectant adolescents are less than fully equipped to meet the interpersonal challenges of parenthood and the responsibilities associated with a coparenting relationship (Brooks-Gunn & Chase-Lansdale, 1995; Crockenberg, 1987; Culp, Appelbaum, Osofsky, & Levy, 1988; East & Felice, 1996). Third, adolescent coparenting couples are less likely than adult coparenting couples to be living in the same household or married, even when they remain romantically involved. The living arrangements of young parenting couples pose a somewhat unique set of challenges to their functioning as coparents, often contributing to strain in their relations. For example, coparenting couples who are not cohabiting are less able to coordinate childrearing tasks. Fourth, adolescent couples are more likely than adult couples to become disengaged from one another. Although many young fathers plan to remain actively involved in childrearing, a large proportion of them becomes decreasingly involved over time (East & Felice, 1996; Furstenberg & Harris, 1993; Lerman, 1993; Marsiglio & Cohan, 1997).

Currently, most of what we know about the relationship between pregnant adolescents and their partners is based on the self-reports of pregnant and parenting adolescents (Coley & Chase-Lansdale, 1999; Crockenberg, 1987; Cutrona et al., 1998). Research based on maternal reports indicates that the quality of a young mother's relationship with her partner can be an important component of how she adjusts to motherhood. Several recent studies have indicated that young mothers who described their relationship with their partners as stable and supportive were less depressed than adolescent mothers who reported negative coparenting relationships (Cutrona et al., 1998; East & Felice, 1996; Gee & Rhodes, 1999). However, there is also evidence that how a young mother feels about her relationship with her child's father is related to the quantity of his involvement with his child (Cutrona et al., 1998). This finding suggests that while some mothers are disappointed in their partners because they are less involved as parents, others may prevent their fathers from becoming involved because they are dissatisfied with the relationship. It is often assumed that absent fathers choose to disengage from their children. However, it seems equally possible that some young mothers may choose to cut off contact with their child's fathers when their romantic liaison ends.

Unfortunately, we have very little first-hand information about how expectant fathers feel about their relationships with their partners or how these relationships affect their adjustment to parenthood. There is some evidence, based on a study of adolescent mothers and their partners, that the quality of a young father's relationship with his partner is closely linked to the quality of his relationship with his child (Lamb & Elster, 1985). Related to these findings, Florsheim and colleagues (Florsheim et al., 1999; Moore & Florsheim, 2001) found that expectant fathers who expressed more hostile behavior toward their partners were also more likely to engage in low rates of nurturing behavior. Generally, these findings suggest that how successfully a young couple negotiates their relationship with each other is likely to impact on the quality and quantity of paternal engagement and the psychological well-being of the young mother.

If we accept the premise that the quality of a young parent's relationship with his or her partner is relevant to how well he or she will function as a parent, then it is important to develop a better understanding of these relationships. Educators and clinicians who have contact with pregnant adolescents and their partners need concrete, useful information that will (a) help them distinguish between healthy and unhealthy relationships and (b) help them provide guidance to couples who are seeking to improve the quality of their relationships. It seems likely that knowing more about how young parents jointly negotiate the transition to parenthood would help us to develop programs designed to facilitate positive parental functioning among both mothers and fathers.

METHODS

Study Participants

Participants in the study were selected from The Young Parenthood Project, which is a longitudinal study of adolescent mothers and their partners making the transition to parenthood (Total N at Time 1 = 178 couples). Inclusion criteria for the study required that female participants be between the ages of 14 and 19, expecting their first child, and willing to meet with us in the company of their partner. Male participants were required to be between 14 and 24 years of age. Couples were recruited through public high schools, agencies providing social and educational services to pregnant teens, and clinics specializing in prenatal services for pregnant teens. Couples participating in this study self-identified as either African American (n = 102), Latino (n = 45), White (n = 21) or mixed (n = 10). Three couples were removed from the analysis because they had missing data.

The mean age of expectant fathers was 18.4 (SD = 2.1) and for expectant mothers was 16.4 (SD = 1.4). The socio-economic status of study participants was calculated using Hollingshead's Four-Factor Index of Social Status (Hollingshead, 1975).[1] The mean SES of the sample (based primarily on information about parents' occupation and education) was in the low to lower middle

---

[1] Assessing the socioeconomic status of adolescents is difficult for several reasons. Many adolescents live with one parent but receive some degree of financial support from the other, and some are in the process of becoming less financially dependent on their parents. Thus, it is often difficult to judge who is primarily responsible for an adolescent's financial well-being. Moreover, most adolescents are unable to accurately report their parent's income. Because of these difficulties, we elected to use the Hollingshead four factor index (Hollingshead, 1975) to provide a rough estimate of adolescent fathers' socio-economic status (Edwards-Hewitt & Gray, 1996).

More specifically, we used the mean Hollingshead SES scores (based on gender, marital status, education and job) of up to three persons, including the participant, the participant's father or stepfather, and the participant's mother or stepmother. Decisions about whom to include in determining SES scores were made on a case-by-case basis. For example, if a participant worked full-time, lived with his mother, and received no support from his father, father's education and occupation scores were not included when calculating his SES score.

class range. A total of 18% of the participants were classified at the lowest end of the Hollingshead Scale (i.e., unemployed or unskilled laborers or menial service workers). Thirty-seven percent were classified as lower middle class (i.e., machine operators and semi-skilled workers), 32% were classified in the middle-class range, and 13% were classified in the upper middle-class range. Most of the participants (69%) were living with one or both parents at the time of the first interview.

Of the expectant mothers, 87.4% were enrolled in high school at the time of recruitment. Of the expectant fathers, 71.2% were either enrolled in high school or graduated. Of the expectant mothers, 15.7% were working (full or part-time), compared to 60.9% of the expectant fathers. The mean length of time the couples had known one another (romantically or otherwise) was 26.5 months. Only eight (4.4%) of the couples were married at Time 1, but 41 (23%) were living together, often with one partner's parent. Female participants were 5.2 months into their pregnancy at the time of the first interview.

The recruitment rate for this study was approximately 50%. Many pregnant teens who were asked to participate in this study declined because they were not in contact with the father of their child, and many others indicated that the father was unwilling to participate. We were concerned that our sampling strategy, which depended on a young father's willingness to be interviewed, had led to the recruitment of an atypical sample of young parents. In an effort to address this concern, we collected data from a small group ($n = 19$) of pregnant adolescents, whose partners refused to participate in this study. The pregnant adolescents in this subgroup indicated that their partners were still involved but would not come in for the interview. Comparisons (t-tests) were made between this subsample of pregnant adolescents and the pregnant adolescents whose partners did participate with respect to age, socioeconomic status, length of relationship with partner, quality of relationship with partner at Time 1, and parenting stress at the Time 2 follow-up. No significant differences were found.

Procedures

After obtaining informed consent and parental consent for all teens under the age of 18, couples were separated and individually administered an interview designed to gather demographic information including age, ethnicity, socioeconomic status, employment status, level of education achieved, living situation, and length of relationship with partner. Following the interview, couples engaged in a 10-minute videotaped conflict task in which they were asked to discuss and resolve a recent conflict or disagreement and to try to come to some resolution on the issue. After explaining the task, the interviewers left the room to allow the adolescents to talk privately. The researcher followed a standard protocol and asked the couples to try to interact with each other as they normally do. Finally, participants were asked to fill out a series of questionnaires focusing on their relationships. Data collection occurred in one of the study offices (located in a public high school and a YWCA), the participants' school, or one of the participants' homes, depending on their stated preference at the time of the recruitment.

Participants were contacted for follow-up when their baby was between 12 and 15 months old. At this second wave of data collection, adolescent parents who agreed to participate were again interviewed and administered questionnaires, focusing on the adjustment to parenthood. Participants also filled out questionnaire measures again at the Time 2 follow-up. The rate of attrition between Times 1 and 2 was 15.8% for young mothers and 29.3% for young fathers. However, the attrition for fathers who were still involved in parenting was 19.3%. That is, the higher attrition rate among fathers (compared to mothers) is partly attributable to those fathers who became disengaged from their children. Participants were paid $40 each ($80 as a couple) for their participation at Time 1 and $30 each for their participation at follow-up.

Measures

Relationship Satisfaction. The Quality of Relationship Inventory (QRI; Pierce, 1996) was used to assess participants' self-reported relations with their partners. The QRI is a 25-item self-report measure designed to assess level of support, conflict and depth in dyadic relationships. The support subscale assesses the extent to which a respondent feels emotionally supported by a selected other. The conflict subscale assesses the extent to which a respondent experiences his or her significant other as an ongoing source of conflict. The depth subscale assesses the extent to which a person feels emotionally invested in the relationship. The QRI consists of questions such as "To what extent can you trust this person not to hurt your feelings?" and "To what extent can you count on this person to help if you were in a crisis situation, even if he or she had to go out of his or her way to help you?" Items are rated on a 4-point scale ranging from "not at all" to "a lot." Higher scores on the QRI indicate more positive appraisals of the relationship.

For the purposes of this study, we combined the three subscale scores into a total QRI score intended to reflect the overall quality of the relationship. The QRI has been found to have high internal consistency, test–retest reliability, and high levels of construct, convergent, predictive, and discriminate validity (Pierce, 1996; Pierce, Sarason, & Sarason, 1997; Pierce, Sarason, Sarason,

TABLE 12.1

Quality of Relationship Inventory Scores among Relationship Satisfaction Groups

	All Couples N = 178 Mean (SD)	Both Partners Low n = 40 Mean (SD)	Expectant Mother Low, Expectant Father High n = 17 Mean (SD)	Expectant Mother High, Expectant Father Low n = 33 Mean (SD)	Both Partners High n = 88 Mean (SD)
			Relationship Satisfaction Groups		
Quality of Relationship Scores at Time 1					
Expectant mothers	77.46 (12.71)	62.20 (10.26)	66.53 (10.04)	83.21 (4.83)	85.54 (5.91)
Expectant fathers	76.43 (11.21)	64.15 (6.93)	80.35 (8.84)	67.93 (5.18)	85.00 (5.79)

Solky-Butzel, & Nagle, 1997). The internal consistency of the QRI for this sample was good (alpha = .87).

QRI partner scores obtained for this study ranged from a low of 37 to a high of 99, indicating a wide range of feelings about the quality of these relationships. To prepare the QRI data for the analysis of group differences, couples were divided into four relatively distinct groups based on their reported level of relationship satisfaction (a lower satisfaction group, two mixed satisfaction groups and a higher satisfaction group). The criterion for inclusion in the lower satisfaction group (Group 1) was that both partners have a QRI score below 75. The criterion for inclusion in the mixed satisfaction groups (Groups 2 and 3) was that one partner have a QRI score below 75 and the other have a QRI score above 75. In Group 2, the expectant fathers had lower scores and the expectant mothers had higher scores and in Group 3 the expectant mothers had lower scores and the expectant fathers had higher scores. The criterion for inclusion in the higher satisfaction group (Group 4) was that both partners had QRI scores above 75. QRI cutoff scores were based on the fact that a score of 75 indicates that a participant reported the relationship to be relatively low in conflict, relatively high in support and depth (personal communication with Gregory Pierce in January, 2001).[2] A summarization of raw QRI scores for couples in each of the four groups is presented in Table 12.1.

Interpersonal Behavior.   At Time 1 (prior to childbirth), couples participated in a 10-minute videotaped conflict task in which they were asked to discuss and resolve a recent conflict or disagreement. These videotaped interactions were then coded using the Structural Analysis of Social Behavior (SASB; Benjamin, 1974). The SASB is a circumplex-based model of interpersonal relations and their intrapsychic representations developed by Benjamin (1974). The SASB coding scheme measures three aspects of behavior: the focus (self, other, or intrapsychic), the degree of affiliation (warmth vs. hostility), and degree of interdependence (control vs. autonomy-granting and submissiveness vs. assertiveness).[3]

---

[2]To help confirm the validity of these groups, we conducted a cluster analysis following the procedures recommended by Aldenderfer and Blashfeld (1984), dividing the sample into four groups of couples based on QRI scores. We obtained results that were largely consistent with those outlined in Table 12.1 (Cohen's Kappa = .55; $p < .001$). That is, the four groups included 72 couples for whom both partners had scores above 75, 18 couples for whom both partners had scores below 75, 27 couples for whom the male partner had a score above 75 and the female had a score below 75, and 54 couples for whom the male partner had a score below 75, and the female had a score above 75.

[3]A more full description of the SASB model can be found in Seefeldt, Florsheim, and Benjamin (chap. 7, this volume) or Florsheim and Benjamin (2001).

The process of SASB-coding a unit of interpersonal behavior involves three steps. First, the coder decides whether a behavior is self-focused, other-focused, or both self- and other-focused. Once the focus of the behavior has been determined, its degree of interdependence is rated on a scale ranging from highly enmeshed to highly differentiated. Finally, the degree of affiliation is rated on a scale ranging from extremely hostile to extremely warm. Based on these three coding decisions, a more specific categorical code is assigned to each behavior. These categorical codes differentiate between various combinations of hostility, warmth, control, autonomy, and submissiveness and are described in more detail in Table 12.2.

For the purposes of this study, we used the SASB-Composite Observational Coding Scheme (Moore & Florsheim, 1999), which is based on the same principles as the original microanalytic SASB coding scheme (Florsheim & Benjamin, 2001; Humphrey & Benjamin, 1989). However, there are two primary differences between the composite and micro-analytic coding schemes. First, rather than assign a code to each specific "speech act," composite coders assign frequency scores (ranging from 0 to 7) to every 2-minute interval of interaction. Frequency scores are based on tallies of specific SASB codes. The second difference between the composite and micro-analytic systems is that in addition to estimating the frequency of specific codes over each 2-minute period, composite coders provide intensity scores. Intensity refers to the strength with which an interpersonal message is conveyed. Intensity scores, which range from 1 to 3, are intended to allow for a greater degree of behavioral specificity when assigning composite scores.

Videotaped discussion tasks were rated by coders who had received a minimum of 75 hours of training in the original SASB system and an additional 20 hours of training with SASB-Composite. All coders attained a criterion level of reliability with both the original SASB coding scheme (Cohen's weighted kappa > 0.7) and SASB-Composite (Intraclass correlation > .80). Inter-rater reliability (assessed by intraclass correlation) ranged from 0.80 to 0.95, with a mean of 0.90. Intraclass correlation is designed to assess for the rate of agreement between two or more raters on a continuous scale or interval data, while controlling for any systematic bias among raters (Shrout & Fleiss, 1979; Streiner, 1995)

The SASB model has been widely used in clinical research (Benjamin, 1994; 1996), and the SASB observational coding scheme has been previously found to have good discriminant and construct validity (Benjamin, 1996; Florsheim, Tolan, & Gorman-Smith, 1996; Florsheim & Benjamin, 2001). Although the composite system has been less extensively used than the micro-system, initial results suggest that it functions similarly to the micro-analytic system (Florsheim et al., 1999; Moore & Florsheim, 2001).

TABLE 12.2
Descriptions of Other-Focused and Self-Focused SASB-Cluster Codes

SASB Code	Description	Example
1-1: Emancipate	Neutral autonomy-giving, which includes letting another "be their own person," express their own identity, feelings, or beliefs. This form of behavior is neutral on the affiliative dimension, communicating little warmth or hostility.	"Do whatever you want, it's totally up to you"
1-2: Affirm	Warm autonomy-granting, communicating empathy and understanding of another's experience; includes actively listening and validating the other's perspective or opinion.	"I understand how you must feel."
1-3: Active Love	Extreme warmth, which is neither particularly autonomy-giving nor controlling. This behavior often involves initiating affection.	"I love you."
1-4: Nurture	Warm, caring control, which may involve taking care of, protecting, teaching, or guiding another person.	"Would you like some help with that?"
1-5: Control	Behavior that is controlling or monitoring and which conveys little warmth or hostility. This type of behavior may include telling another person what to do or how to think.	"Do as I say"
1-6: Blame	Hostile control. This form of behavior communicates criticism or condescension toward another person.	"You never get anything right."
1-7: Attack	Extremely hostile behavior, which is neither particularly autonomy-giving or controlling. This form of behavior involves destroying or threatening another person (physically or verbally).	"I hate you."
1-8: Ignore	Hostile autonomy-giving behavior, which may involve abandoning, neglecting, or ignoring another person.	"Get lost!"
2-1: Separate	Neutral autonomy-taking behavior, which may involve acting independently and asserting one's own ideas and beliefs. As neutral on the affiliation dimension, this form of behavior is neither particularly warm or hostile.	"I'm going to do things my way."
2-2: Disclose	Warm autonomy-taking; characterized as a friendly, open sharing of ideas, experiences, and feelings with another.	"I'm feeling frightened right now"

(Continued)

TABLE 12.2 *(Continued)*

SASB Code	Description	Example
2-3: Reactive Love	Extreme warmth which is neither autonomy-taking nor submissive. Involves responding to the other's approach in a receptive, loving, and joyful manner. This communicates enjoyment in being close to the other.	"I love you too."
2-4: Trust	Warm submissiveness; involves willingly receiving help or learning from another person. This behavior is classically "child-like."	"Would you help me with this?"
2-5: Submit	Submissiveness which is neither warm nor hostile and This type of submissiveness usually involves giving in, yielding, or complying with expectations.	"Yes, ma'am."
2-6: Sulk	Hostile submissiveness, which might include whining, "poor me" statements, defensive self-justification, resentful compliance, and "scurrying" to appease another person.	(In a whiny, defensive tone) "Fine . . . I'll do what you say—just like I always do!"
2-7: Protest	Extreme hostility, which is neither autonomy-taking nor deferring. This type of behavior communicates fear, hate, and/or disgust towards another, and may include an attempt to escape from or fight off a perceived attacker.	"I feel disgusted by you."
2-8: Wall off	Hostile autonomy-taking, which may involve shutting others out, isolating oneself, or withdrawing from an interaction.	"Bug off"; Nonresponse

Note. The descriptions of these codes are based on summaries found in Humphrey and Benjamin's (1989) SASB observational coding manual.

Parenting Stress. The Parenting Stress Index (PSI; Abidin, 1990) was used to assess the level of parenting stress among young mothers and fathers at follow-up (1 year after childbirth). The PSI is a widely used, well validated self-report measure that requires respondents to rate the relevance of 101 statements to their personal experience or current life situation on a five-point Likert scale. Examples of the statements include: "My child is not able to do as much as I expected" and "I feel trapped by my responsibilities as a parent." The PSI is designed to assess stress in the parent domain (stress related to being a parent) and stress in the child domain (stress related to a child's difficulties). The Parent Domain scale consists of seven subscales, including depression, attachment, role restriction, sense of competence, social isolation, relation with partner, and health. The Child Domain scale consists of six subscales, including adaptability, acceptability, demandingness, mood, distractibility/hyperactivity, and reinforcement of parent. Previous research has indicated that global PSI scores represent a clinically meaningful index of a parent's adjustment to parenthood (Abidin, 1992; Bigras, LaFreniere, & Dumas, 1996). A global PSI score was derived from the combination of these subscales. The alpha reliability coefficient for the PSI global score was .87.

Relationship Status. At the 1-year follow-up, young parents (both males and females) were asked whether their partner was involved in co-parenting, whether they were romantically involved, and whether they were cohabiting. Each couple's relationship status was classified as *disengaged* (the father was not at all involved with his partner or his child), *coparenting but not romantically involved* (the couple shared some responsibility for parenting their child but were not romantically involved), *romantically involved but not cohabiting* or *romantically involved and cohabitating*. In this study, we defined co-parenting more broadly than other researchers,[4] allowing for a great deal of variability in parental involvement. For example, while some "co-parenting" fathers shared equally in parenting, others were minimally involved in parenting, seeing their child two or three times a month.

Due to evidence from pilot data that mothers and fathers may report discrepancies in their level of involvement and concerns raised by other researchers that fathers may be prone to exaggerate their own level of involvement (Coley & Morris, 2002), maternal reports were used when disagreements arose. Because more mothers than fathers participated in the follow-up, we relied on mother reports of relationship status when fathers were not available. There were participants ($n = 17$) who did not complete the follow-up interviews and questionnaires, but whom we were able to contact by phone

---

[4]In the adult literature, co-parenting is generally defined in terms of the how couples coordinate their efforts to raise their children (Margolin, Gordis, & John, 2001). For example, McHale, Keursten-Hogan, Lauretti, and Rasmussen (2000) studied co-parenting by examining how couples engage with one another while parenting their children. Most of the research on co-parenting has focused on married couples and recent researchers have pressed the point that the co-parenting relationship is different from the marital relationship (Margolin et al., 2001; McHale et al., 2000). However, the concept of co-parenting between adolescent parents requires a broader, looser definition. Most adolescent parents neither marry nor live together, and many do not remain romantically involved with their partners, but continue to be involved, at least peripherally, with their children. In this study, we defined the co-parenting relationship as an arrangement that involves at least a minimal level of coordinated behavior. In this context, the mother and father may rarely (or never) engage with the child as a team, but would nonetheless consider themselves to be co-parents, in the sense that there is some degree of shared responsibility for parenting.

and gather information regarding their relationship status from either one or both partners.

RESULTS

Demographic Variables, Relationship Functioning, and the Adjustment to Parenthood

A series of analyses were run to test for associations between demographic variables (age, gender, length of relationship, ethnicity, and socioeconomic status), relationship variables (satisfaction at Time 1, interpersonal behavior at Time 1, couple involvement at follow-up) and parenting stress at follow-up. First, analysis of variance (ANOVA) was used to test for demographic differences among the four relationship satisfaction groups (lower satisfaction group, the higher satisfaction group, and the two mixed satisfaction groups). Results indicated there were no demographic differences between the four satisfaction groups with respect to age, ethnicity, socio-economic status, school status, work status, or length of relationship with partner (in months).

Next, analyses were run to assess the relationship between age, gender, ethnicity, socio-economic status and SASB coded behavior scores. Ethnic and gender based differences in SASB scores were examined using a repeated measures MANOVA with the couple's ethnicity as the between group factor and gender as the within group factor. The main effect for ethnicity was significant, $F(39, 492) = 2.01$; $p < .01$. More specifically, results indicated that compared to African American couples, Latino couples were more *Nurturing*, $F(3, 174) = 3.54$; $p < .05$, more *Trusting*, $F(3, 174) = 5.46$; $p < .01$, more *Submissive*, $F(3, 174) = 3.62$; $p < .05$, and less *Walling off*, $F(3, 174) = 2.74$; $p < .05$.

The main effect for gender was also significant, $F(13, 162) = 5.53$; $p < .001$. More specifically, compared to their partners, expectant mothers were more *Blaming*, $F(1, 174) = 4.63$; $p < .05$, more *Trusting*, $F(1, 174) = 5.46$; $p < .01$, more *Loving*, $F(1, 174) = 8.85$; $p < .01$, more *Sulking*, $F(1, 174) = 18.61$; $p < .001$, less *Separating*, $F(1, 174) = 18.86$; $p < .001$, and less *Ignoring*, $F(1, 174) = 4.11$; $p < .05$.

Next, analyses were run to assess for the effect of demographic factors on a couple's relationship status at follow-up. Chi square results indicated that ethnicity was associated with relationship status at follow-up, $\chi^2 (9, 162) = 30.95$; $p < .01$. Post hoc analyses indicated that White and Latino couples were more likely than African American couples to be cohabiting at follow-up. However, African American couples were neither more likely to be disengaged nor less likely to be co-parenting. Analyses indicated that demographic variables were unrelated to variations in parenting stress.

Interpersonal Behavior and Relationship Satisfaction

A second set of analyses were designed to examine the effect of satisfaction group membership on SASB coded interpersonal behavior. Repeated measures MANCOVA was used to examine whether there were differences among the four satisfaction groups on SASB-coded interpersonal behaviors. In this analysis, satisfaction group membership was included as the between-groups factor and gender was included as the within-group factor. The repeated measures technique was used to control for the relatively high level of interdependence between couples' interaction data. Ethnicity (dummy coded) was included as a covariate.

Results indicated a main effect for satisfaction group membership, $F(39, 476) = 1.47$; $p < .05$, and a main effect for the interaction between gender and satisfaction group, $F(39, 476) = 2.02$; $p < .01$, on SASB coded behavior. Post hoc univariate analyses of differences among the four satisfaction groups indicated that couples in the high relationship satisfaction group were more *Nurturing*, less *Controlling*, less *Blaming*, less *Walling off*, less *Ignoring*, and less *Sulky* than couples in the low relationship satisfaction group. Couples in the low relationship satisfaction group were more *Walling-off* than couples in both the high satisfaction group and couples in which expectant fathers were more satisfied than expectant mothers.

Post hoc examination of significant interactions between gender and satisfaction group membership indicated that expectant mothers whose partners reported relatively lower levels of relationships satisfaction tended to be more *Controlling* and more *Sulking* than expectant mothers with more satisfied partners. Also, expectant fathers who were less satisfied than their relationships were more *Walling off* than the expectant fathers who we more satisfied with their relationships. These results are summarized in Table 12.3.

Relationship Variables and Adjustment to Parenthood

A final set of analyses was designed to examine the effect of relationship variables (Relationship Satisfaction and SASB scores) on Parenting Stress Index (PSI) scores and Relationship Status at follow-up (when the child was 12–15 months old). Analysis of Covariance, with ethnic status as the covariate (ANCOVA) was used to examine whether satisfaction group membership was related to parenting stress. ANCOVA results indicated a main effect for relationship satisfaction group membership on father's PSI scores, $F(3, 118) = 4.98$;

TABLE 12.3
Effects of Gender and Relationship Satisfaction on SASB Coded Interpersonal Behavior

Relationship Satisfaction Groups based on QRI scores

SASB Codes	Both Partners Low (BPL; n = 40) Father M (SD)	Mother M (SD)	Expectant Mother Low, Expectant Father High (EML; n = 17) Father M (SD)	Mother M (SD)	Expectant Mother High, Expectant Father Low (EFL; n = 33) Father M (SD)	Mother M (SD)	Both Partners High (BPH; n = 88) Father M (SD)	Mother M (SD)	Significant Group Differences at (p < .05,) Based on Post Hoc Analyses (Tukey's HSB) Couple Type	Gender X Couple Type
Affirm	6.72 (5.48)	5.78 (3.93)	5.21 (2.23)	7.14 (4.26)	7.07 (3.71)	6.43 (4.37)	8.25 (4.18)	7.56 (4.51)		
Loving Approach	1.11 (2.00)	0.61 (1.64)	1.21 (1.97)	0.86 (1.23)	1.97 (2.72)	0.50 (1.04)	2.27 (3.35)	1.27 (2.10)		EFL Females > EFL Males
Nurture	9.17 (6.38)	7.47 (6.39)	13.79 (5.44)	10.71 (6.59)	11.17 (8.12)	10.03 (6.45)	12.94 (6.61)	11.87 (7.88)	BPL < BPH	
Control	21.64 (8.42)	20.36 (9.45)	16.57 (7.98)	19.50 (9.18)	16.37 (8.19)	21.03 (8.77)	15.89 (9.33)	17.41 (8.43)	BPL > BPH	
Blame	8.83 (8.04)	10.31 (6.97)	2.93 (3.79)	7.86 (6.62)	4.33 (5.18)	7.07 (7.43)	4.79 (6.13)	6.34 (6.84)	BPL > BPH	
Ignore	3.89 (4.97)	2.22 (2.79)	0.86 (2.21)	1.29 (1.68)	2.77 (4.29)	1.67 (2.59)	1.44 (2.72)	0.80 (1.41)	BPL > BPH	
Assert	18.44 (6.11)	15.44 (6.67)	21.71 (4.70)	15.14 (6.96)	21.83 (5.84)	16.90 (6.07)	19.94 (6.87)	17.75 (5.49)		
Disclose	2.06 (2.96)	1.83 (2.41)	4.43 (4.38)	2.71 (3.10)	3.87 (4.09)	3.60 (3.93)	4.00 (4.49)	3.42 (4.16)	BPL < BPH	
Loving Response	1.06 (2.12)	1.53 (2.24)	1.64 (2.76)	1.71 (2.37)	1.47 (2.75)	2.60 (3.95)	2.10 (2.58)	3.61 (3.92)	BPL < BPH	
Trust	4.69 (4.79)	8.42 (5.27)	6.50 (3.98)	8.43 (4.93)	6.40 (4.60)	7.87 (6.27)	6.94 (5.12)	8.69 (5.51)		
Submit	1.75 (3.24)	3.50 (3.78)	3.36 (4.03)	3.50 (3.90)	3.10 (5.11)	1.93 (2.55)	2.35 (3.03)	3.14 (4.31)		
Sulk	6.31 (5.92)	12.47 (10.47)	3.00 (4.00)	7.07 (6.27)	3.40 (4.40)	7.50 (6.31)	4.69 (7.06)	6.21 (7.51)	BPL > BPH	BPL Females > BPL Males
Wall Off	6.19 (6.17)	7.94 (9.02)	2.93 (4.08)	2.64 (3.20)	5.43 (7.34)	2.63 (3.17)	2.31 (3.10)	2.61 (3.69)	BPL > BPH; BPL > EML	EFL Males > EFL Females

$p < .001$, but not mother's PSI scores, $F(3,154 = 2.14; p = 0.1$. Post hoc analysis indicated that fathers in the high satisfaction group and fathers in one of the mixed satisfaction groups (with fathers reporting higher satisfaction) had lower PSI scores (were less stressed) than fathers in the low relationship satisfaction group and fathers in the other mixed satisfaction group (with fathers reporting lower satisfaction). Relationship satisfaction was unrelated to mothers self reported parenting stress. Chi Square analysis results revealed a significant relationship between satisfaction group membership at Time 1 and relationship status at follow-up, χ^2 (9, 162) = 21.98; $p < .01$. As indicated in Table 12.4, couples in the high satisfaction group were most likely to be romantically involved and cohabiting at follow-up.

Zero order Pearson correlations were used to examine the relationship between SASB coded behavior scores and parenting stress scores (separately for fathers and mothers). Results indicated that fathers who were more *Nurturing* or *Affirming* toward their partners at Time 1 had lower PSI scores at follow-up ($r = -0.232$ and $r = -0.197$, respectively; $p < .05$). Fathers who were more *Walling off* toward their partners at Time 1 had higher PSI scores at Time 2 ($r = 0.301$; $p < .05$). However, after controlling for chance findings based on the large number of tests run, these results would not be considered statistically significant, and should be regarded as preliminary. Results of analyses run to examine the relationship between SASB coded interpersonal behavior and relationship status at Time 2 (repeated measures MANOVA) indicated that relationship status at the Time 2 follow-up was not related to interpersonal behavior at Time 1.

DISCUSSION

The study presented in this chapter was designed to (a) clarify the relationship between how a young expectant couple feels about each other (their relationship satisfaction) and how they behave toward one another and (b) examine the association between relationship factors and the adjustment to parenthood, defined in terms of couples involvement and parenting stress.

Results outlined herein reveal similarities and differences in the interpersonal behavior of the couples classified in the higher, mixed, and lower satisfaction groups. First, with respect to similarities, we found that the young men and young women in all four groups of couples were highly oriented toward controlling their partners *and* maintaining their own autonomy in relation to their partners (20% of the observed behavior was coded as *Controlling* and 21% was coded as *Separating*). The high rate of assertive or autonomy-taking behavior observed among couples may be related to a normative tendency

TABLE 12.4

Relationship Satisfaction Groups, Parenting Stress, and Relationship Status

	All Couples	Both Partners Low (BPL)	Expectant Mother Low, Expectant Father High (EML)	Expectant Mother High, Expectant Father Low (EFL)	Both Partners High (BPH)	Significant Group Differences ($p < .05$; Tukey's HSB)
			Relationship Satisfaction Groups			
Parenting Stress Index Scores at Follow-up (presented as means and standard deviations)						
Mothers' scores	228.44 (38.14)	232.78 (40.87)	234.75 (35.45)	237.80 (40.63)	220.87 (35.51)	
n at follow-up	150	34	16	30	70	
Fathers' scores	232.91 (36.12)	250.00 (30.50)	219.33 (35.00)	254.80 (22.00)	220.23 (36.50)	BLS, EFLS > BHS
n at follow-up	126	25	12	25	64	
Relationship Status at Follow-up (presented in terms of the number and percentage of couples in each category)						
Disengaged	23 (14.2%)	11 (6.8%)	4 (2.5%)	2 (1.2%)	6 (3.7%)	
Co-parenting only	23 (14.2%)	8 (4.9%)	2 (1.2%)	4 (2.5%)	9 (5.6%)	
Romantically involved co-parenting, but not cohabiting	62 (38.3%)	12 (7.4%)	8 (4.9%)	12 (7.4%)	30 (18.5%)	
Co-parenting and cohabiting	54 (33.3%)	6 (3.7%)	2 (1.2%)	14 (8.6%)	32 (19.8%)	

among adolescents to seek autonomy, while the high rate of controlling behavior may be responsive to the pressures associated with their expectancy status. That is, the impending birth of a child may lead both expectant mothers and fathers to become more possessive of their mates and more intent on maintaining a stable, secure interpersonal environment for their child (Moore & Florsheim, 2001).

We also observed several differences in the behaviors of couples in the higher and lower satisfaction groups, indicating a high level of consistency between how young expectant couples felt about their relationship and how they engaged with one another. For example, couples in the lower satisfaction group were more *Ignoring* and more *Walling off* than couples in the higher satisfaction group, indicating that they were generally more disengaged from one another. They were also more *Blaming* and *Sulky*, which indicates that when they do become engaged they tend to do so in a way that is characteristically hostile. These observations suggest that the lower satisfaction couples are more likely to engage in complementary patterns of hostile engagement and disengagement.

Couples in the higher satisfaction group were observed to engage in some hostile behavior, but much less frequently than couples in the lower satisfaction group. Moreover, the couples in the higher satisfaction group were generally more disclosing, nurturing and loving, exhibiting a pattern of behavior that seems comparable with what Gottman has referred to as "Positive Sentiment Override" (Carrere & Gottman, 1999). Positive Sentiment Override occurs when one partner, who has positive feelings about the other responds more warmly than expected to problems that arise in the relationship. Conversely, partners who feel emotionally disconnected from one another or have generally negative feelings about their relationship are more likely to perceive their partner as hostile and/or to initiate hostile communications. Gottman and colleagues have found that couples who expressed negative sentiments about their partnership *and* engaged in negative behaviors toward one another were at high risk for relationship dissolution (Carrere & Gottman, 1999; Gottman et al., 1998). Based on the findings outlined above, it seems reasonable to assume that the couples who we classified in the lower satisfaction group may be similarly disposed. For example, couples who felt positively about the relationship (as indicted by high QRI scores) tended to respond to their partners complaints with acceptance and understanding. Whereas couples who felt less satisfied tended to become defensive (sulky) or mutually accusatory (blaming).

It is not really possible to say whether the couples in the lower satisfaction group were less warm and more hostile because they were less satisfied, or whether they were less satisfied because they were less warm and more hostile.

Whatever the cause of a couple's satisfaction or dissatisfaction, how they feel about one another *and* how they treat one another is, by most accounts, of critical importance to the psychological well being of their children (Cox et al., 1999; Fincham, 1998; Katz & Gottman, 1996).

Moreover, our findings suggest that if *one* partner is satisfied with the quality of the relationship (or at least perceives the other in a generally positive light) those feelings may have an "overriding" positive impact on the quality of the couple's interpersonal behavior. This suggests that attempting to provide therapy to a couple in which at least one partner is invested in the relationship is likely to be much less difficult than treating a couple in which both partners are marginally invested and/or dissatisfied.

Several gender-based differences in interpersonal behavior were observed among the participants in this study. Most notably, the expectant mothers were more likely than their partners to engage in submissive behaviors (both warm and hostile) and controlling behaviors. By contrast, expectant fathers were more autonomy-seeking. These gender-based behavioral differences may be partly related to the expectancy status and age of our participants. That is, the event of an unexpected pregnancy may leave some young women feeling vulnerable and anxious about their partner's level of commitment. Some respond to this situation by becoming more dependent, whereas other become demanding. However, it seems likely that these differences also reflect status based differences between men and women which encourage men to be more autonomous and assertive in the context of their heterosexual relations and encourage women to be more deferential (Eagly, Wood, & Diekman, 2000; Pasley, Kerpelman, & Guilbert, 2001). The results based on the interaction between gender and satisfaction group membership further elaborate these general gender-based differences. That is, the tendency for expectant mothers to become controlling and expectant fathers to become autonomy seeking is related to their respective levels of satisfaction with their relationship.

Results just outlined also suggest that the quality of the relationship between a young father and his partner was significantly related to his adjustment to parenthood. Most notably, expectant fathers who were engaged in satisfying relationships with their partners (at Time 1) were more likely to remain romantically involved with their partners through the first year of co-parenting. Conversely, expectant fathers in relationships rated as low in satisfaction were more likely to become disengaged from their partners and children. Moreover, young fathers who reported higher levels of relationship satisfaction were more likely to report lower levels of parenting stress compared to fathers who reported lower levels of relationship satisfaction. These results seem to indicate that how a young couple feels about their relationship is likely to have an impact on how the transition to parenthood unfolds, particularly for the young father.

ISSUES FOR CLINICIANS WORKING WITH ADOLESCENT PARENTING COUPLES

It is difficult for many adult couples to respectfully negotiate serious problems in their marriage associated with parenthood (Cowan & Cowan, 2000; Katz & Gottman, 1997; Osofsky & Culp, 1993). This process is likely to be more difficult for adolescent parents, who are often less interpersonally skilled and less developmentally equipped to handle the responsibility of childrearing than adults. Yet, the ways in which a young couple negotiates the dissolution of their romantic relationship and redefines the terms of their co-parenting relationship is often critical to the long-term development of their child (Katz & Gottman, 1997; Lee, 1997; Roye & Balk, 1996; Whiteside & Becker; 2000). So what can clinicians and educators do to help resolve relationship problems between adolescent co-parenting couples? Although more research is needed to fully address this question, it is possible to provide a short set of guidelines.

Given the developmental status of these couples and the fact that many adolescent pregnancies are unplanned, encouraging a couple to marry or stay together may be counterproductive (Wakschlag & Hans, 2000). Nonetheless, a young couple's ability to communicate effectively will help them negotiate changes in their romantic relationship while preserving a warm, nurturing environment for their child (Katz & Gottman, 1996). Thus, it may be useful to develop educational programs designed to help young expectant couples learn to positively negotiate current disagreements in anticipation of the fact that they will encounter a great deal of interpersonal strain in the ensuing months. Such programs could be linked to publicly funded educational and clinical services provided to pregnant teenagers.

The task of helping adolescent couples negotiate a shift in the status of their relationship may be particularly challenging for those expectant couples who approach parenthood already expressing dissatisfaction with the quality of their relationship. Yet, these couples are at high risk for developing serious problems in the adjustment to parenthood and are most in need of help. It seems likely that some of the negative behavior evident in these couples is a by-product of their relatively unhappy relationship. However, it also seems likely that some of the adolescents in these relationships may have a history of interpersonal problems.

In recent years, marriage theorists and marital therapists have emphasized the role of acceptance as a primary agent of change (Jacobson & Christensen, 1996). Related to this, interpersonally oriented theorists and therapists have argued that interventions are most likely to be effective when they can accommodate to the client's interpersonal profile. For example, it may be easier to help a young father learn to be warm and respectful when he attempts to control his partner than it is to get him to stop trying to control her altogether (Moore & Florsheim, 2001).

The findings reported in this chapter suggest that adolescent couples who are not satisfied with their relationship might benefit from an intensive intervention designed to "warm up" their interactions while preserving the core dynamic of the relationship. Such a program might teach one partner to (a) accept the other's efforts to control or separate without trying to undermine, invalidate, or challenge his or her basic interpersonal position and (b) express his or her own need for separateness and control more warmly. Our findings and the findings of other research groups (Cox et al., 1999) suggest that an interpersonally oriented intervention designed to increase the expression of warmth between expectant couples may help facilitate a more positive adjustment to parenthood, particularly among young fathers.

Understanding the interpersonal functioning of expectant and parenting adolescents is important because parenting is a fundamentally interpersonal process. In summary, it is important to underscore the need for more research on the relationships between pregnant adolescents and their partners, particularly research focusing on how these relationships change during the transition to parenthood. However, there is also a rather urgent need to provide much needed services to those couples who lack the requisite skills to negotiate this transition. In the study described in this chapter, we have tried to describe the romantic relationship of adolescent coparenting couples in a way that clinicians working with adolescent parents will find informative and useful.

ACKNOWLEDGMENTS

This research was supported by a grant from the Adolescent Family Life Program, The Office of Population Affairs, The Department of Health and Human Services (Grant #APR 000965-01-1); a grant from the Robert Woods Johnson Foundation; and funds provided by the University of Utah. We would like to express our appreciation to the research assistants who worked so hard to gather the data for this study and the participants who shared their experiences with us.

REFERENCES

Abidin, R. (1990). *Parenting Stress Index manual* (3rd ed.). Charlottesville, VA: Pediatric Psychology Press.

Abidin, R. R. (1992). The determinants of parenting behavior. *Journal of Clinical Child Psychology, 24,* 407–412.

Aldenderfer, R. K., & Blashfeld, M. S. (1984). *Cluster analysis.* Sage University paper series on Quantitative Applications in the Social Sciences, 07-044. Newbury Park, CA: Sage Publications.

Antonucci, T. C., & Mikus, K. (1988). The power of parenthood: Personality and attitudinal changes during the transition to parenthood. In G. Y. Michaels & W. A. Goldberg (Eds.), *The transition to parenthood: Current theory and research. Cambridge studies in social and emotional development* (pp. 62–84). New York: Cambridge University Press.

Belsky, J. (1984). The determinants of parenting: A process model. *Child Development, 55,* 83–96.

Belsky, J., & Hsieh, K. H. (1998). Patterns of marital change during the early childhood years: Parent personality, coparenting, and division-of-labor correlates. *Journal of Family Psychology, 12,* 511–528.

Benjamin, L. S. (1974). Structural Analysis of Social Behavior. *Psychological Review, 81,* 392–425.

Benjamin, L. S. (1994). SASB: A bridge between personality theory and clinical psychology. *Psychological Inquiry, 5,* 273–316.

Benjamin, L. S. (1996). *Interpersonal diagnosis and treatment of personality disorders* (2nd ed.). New York: Guilford Press.

Bigras, M., LaFreniere, P., & Dumas, J. (1996). Discriminant validity of the parent and child scales of the parenting stress index. *Early Education and Development, 7,* 167–178.

Brooks-Gunn, J., & Chase-Lansdale, P. L. (1995). Adolescent parenthood. In M. H. Bornstein (Ed.), *Handbook of parenting: Vol. 3. Status and social conditions of parenting* (pp. 113–149). Mahwah, NJ: Lawrence Erlbaum Associates.

Brunelli, S. A., Wasserman, G. A., Rauh, V. A., & Alvarado, L. E. (1995). Mothers' reports of paternal support: Associations with maternal child-rearing attitudes. *Merrill-Palmer Quarterly, 41*(2), 152–171.

Carrere, S., & Gottman, J. (1999). Predicting the future of marriages. In E. M. Hetherington (Ed.), *Coping with divorce, single parenting, and remarriage: A risk and resiliency perspective* (pp. 3–22). Mahwah, NJ: Lawrence Erlbaum Associates.

Coley, R. L., & Chase-Lansdale, P. L. (1999). Stability and change in paternal involvement among urban African American fathers. *Journal of Family Psychology, 13*(3), 416–435.

Coley, R. L., & Morris, J. E. (2002). Comparing father and mother reports of father involvement among low-income minority families. *Journal of Marriage and the Family, 64,* 982–997.

Cowan, C. P., & Cowan, P. A. (2000). *When partners become parents: The big life change for couples.* New York: Basic Books.

Cox, M. J., Paley, B., Payne, C. C., & Burchinal, M. (1999). The transition to parenthood: Marital conflict and withdrawal and parent–infant interactions. In M. J. Cox & J. Brooks-Gunn (Eds.), *Conflict and cohesion in families: Causes and consequences* (pp.87–104). Mahwah, NJ: Lawrence Erlbaum Associates.

Crockenberg, S. B. (1987). Predictors and correlates of anger toward and punitive control of toddlers by adolescent mothers. *Child Development, 58*(4), 964–975.

Culp, R. E., Appelbaum, M. I., Osofsky, J. D., & Levy, J. A. (1988). Adolescent and older mothers: Comparison between prenatal maternal variables and newborn interaction measures. *Infant Behavior and Development, 11*(3), 353–362.

Cummings, E. M. & O'Reilly, A. W. (1997). Fathers in family context: Effects of marital quality of child adjustment. In M. E. Lamb (Ed.), *The role of the father in child development* (3rd ed., pp. 49–65). New York: Wiley & Sons.

Cutrona, C. E. (1984). Social support and stress in the transition to parenthood. *Journal of Abnormal Psychology, 93*(4), 378–390.

Cutrona, C. E., Hessling, R. M., Bacon, P. L., & Russell, D. W. (1998). Predictors and correlates of continuing involvement with the baby's father among adolescent mothers. *Journal of Family Psychology, 12*(3), 369–387.

Eagly, A. H., Wood, W., & Diekman, A. B. (2000). Social role theory of sex differences and similarities: A current appraisal. In T. Eckes & H. M. Trautner (Eds.), *The developmental social psychology of gender* (pp. 123–174). Mahwah, NJ: Lawrence Erlbaum Associates.

East, P. L., & Felice, M. E. (1996). *Adolescent pregnancy and parenting: Findings from a racially diverse sample.* Mahwah, NJ: Lawrence Erlbaum Associates.

Edwards-Hewitt, T., & Gray, J. (1996). Comparison of measures of socioeconomic status between ethnic groups. *Psychological Reports, 77,* 699–722.

Fincham, F. D. (1998). Child development and marital relations. *Child Development, 69*(2), 543–574.

Florsheim, P., & Benjamin, L. S. (2001). The Structural Analysis of Social Behavior Coding Scheme. In P. K. Kerig & M. Lindahl (Eds.), *Family observational coding schemes: Resources for systemic research* (pp. 127–150). Hillsdale, NJ: Lawrence Erlbaum Associates.

Florsheim, P., Moore, D., Zollinger, L., MacDonald, J., & Sumida, E. (1999). The transition to parenthood among adolescent fathers and their partners: Does antisocial behavior predict problems in parenting? *Applied Developmental Science, 3,* 178–191.

Florsheim, P., Tolan, P. H., & Gorman-Smith, D. (1996). Family processes and risk for externalizing behavior problems among African-American and Hispanic boys. *Journal of Consulting and Clinical Psychology, 64,* 1222–1230.

Furstenberg, F. F., & Harris, K. (1993). When and why fathers matter: Impacts of father involvement on the children of adolescent mothers. In R. Lerman & T. Ooms (Eds.), *Young and unwed fathers: Changing roles and emerging policies* (pp. 117–138). Philadelphia: Temple University Press.

Gee, C. B., & Rhodes, J. E. (1999). Postpartum transitions in adolescent mothers' romantic and maternal relationships. *Merrill Palmer Quarterly, 45,* 512–532.

Gottlieb, B. H., & Pancer, S. M. (1988). Social networks and the transition to parenthood. In G. Y. Michaels & W. A. Goldberg (Eds.), *The transition to parenthood: Current theory and research. Cambridge studies in social and emotional development* (pp. 235–269). New York: Cambridge University Press.

Gottman, J. M., Coan, J., Carrere, S., & Swanson, C. (1998). Predicting happiness and stability from newlywed interactions. *Journal of Marriage and the Family, 60,* 5–22.

Hollingshead, A. B. (1975). *Four-Factor Index of Social Status.* Unpublished manuscript. Yale University, New Haven, CT.

Humphrey, L. L., & Benjamin, L. S. (1989). *An observational coding system for use with Structural Analysis of Social Behavior: The training manual.* Northwestern Medical School, Chicago, IL.

Jacobson, N. S., & Christensen, A. (1996). *Integrative couple therapy: Promoting acceptance and change.* New York: W. W. Norton & Co.

Katz, L. F., & Gottman, J. M. (1997). Buffering children from marital conflict and dissolution. *Journal of Clinical Child Psychology, 26*(2), 157–171.

Katz, L. R., & Gottman, J. M. (1996). Spillover effects of marital conflict: In search of parenting and coparenting mechanisms. In J. P. McHale & P. A. Cowan (Eds.), *Understanding how family-level dynamics affect children's development: Studies of two-parent families. New directions for child development* (pp. 57–76) San Francisco: Jossey Bass Inc.

Lamb, M., & Elster, A. (1985). Adolescent mother–infant–father relationships. *Developmental Psychology, 21,* 768–773.

Lee, M. Y. (1997). Post-divorce interparental conflict, children's contact with both parents, children's emotional processes, and children's behavioral adjustment. *Journal of Divorce and Remarriage, 27*(3–4), 61–82.

Lerman, R. (1993). A national profile of young unwed fathers. In R. Lerman & P. Ooms (Eds.), *Young unwed fathers: Changing roles and emerging policies* (pp. 27–51). Philadelphia, PA: Temple University Press.

Levy-Shiff, R. (1999). Fathers' cognitive appraisals, coping strategies, and support resources as correlates of adjustment to parenthood. *Journal of Family Psychology, 13,* 554–567.

Lindahl, K., Clements, M., & Markman, H. (1998). The development of marriage: A 9-year perspective. In T. N. Bradbury (Ed.), *The developmental course of marital dysfunction* (pp. 205–236). New York: Cambridge University Press.

Margolin, G., Gordis, E. G., & John, R. S. (2001). Coparenting: A link between marital conflict and parenting in two-parent families. *Journal of Family Psychology, 15,* 3–21.

Marsiglio, W., & Cohan, M. (1997). Young fathers and child development. In M. E. Lamb (Ed.), *The role of the father in child development* (3rd ed., pp. 227–244). New York: Wiley & Sons.

McHale, J. P., Keursten-Hogan, R., Lauretti, A., & Rasmussen, J. L. (2000). Parental reports of coparenting and observed coparenting behavior during the toddler period. *Journal of Family Psychology, 14,* 220–236.

McHale, J. P., & Rasmussen, J. L. (1998). Coparental and family group-level dynamics during infancy: Early family precursors of child and family functioning during preschool. *Development and Psychopathology, 10*(1), 39–59.

Moore, D. R., & Florsheim, P. (1999). *Structural Analysis of Social Behavior—Composite Observational Coding Scheme.* Unpublished manuscript, University of Utah, Salt Lake City, UT.

Moore, D. R., & Florsheim, P. (2001). Interpersonal processes and psychopathology among expectant and nonexpectant adolescent couples. *Journal of Consulting and Clinical Psychology, 69,* 101–113.

Nitz, K., Ketterlinus, R., & Brandt, L. (1995). The role of stress, social support, and family environment in adolescent mothers' parenting. *Journal of Adolescent Research, 10,* 358–382.

Osofsky, J. D., & Culp, R. (1993). A relationship perspective on the transition to parenthood. In G. H. Pollock & S. I. Greenspan (Eds.), *The course of life, Vol. 5: Early adulthood* (pp. 75–98). Madison, CT: International Universities Press.

Osofsky, J. D., Osofsky, H. J., & Diamond, M. O. (1988). The transition to parenthood: Special tasks and risk factors for adolescent parents. In G. Y. Michaels & W. A. Goldberg (Eds.), *The transition to parenthood: Current theory and research. Cambridge studies in social and emotional development* (pp. 209–232). New York: Cambridge University Press.

Pasley, K., Kerpelman, J., & Guilbert, D. E. (2001). Gendered conflict, identity disruption, and marital instability: Expanding Gottman's model [Special issue]. *Journal of Social and Personal Relationships, 18*(1), 5–27.

Pierce, G. R., (1996). The Quality of Relationships Inventory: Assessing the interpersonal context of social support. In B. R. Burleson & T. L. Albrecht (Eds.), *Communication of social support: Messages interactions, relationships, and community* (pp. 247–264) Thousand Oaks, CA: Sage Publications.

Pierce, G. R., Sarason, I. G., & Sarason, B. R. (1997). Assessing the quality of personal relationships. *Journal of Social and Personal Relationships, 14*(3), 339–356.

Pierce, G., Sarason, I., Sarason, B., Solky-Butzel, J., & Nagle, L. (1997). Assessing the quality of personal relationships. *Journal of Social and Personal Relationships, 14*(3), 339–356.

Rhodes, J. E., Ebert, L. & Meyers, A. B. (1994). Social support, relationship problems and the psychological functioning of young African-American mothers. *Journal of Social and Personal Relationships, 11*, 587–599.

Roye, C. F., & Balk, S. J. (1996). The relationship of partner–partner support to outcomes for teenage mothers and their children: A review. *Journal of Adolescent Health, 19*, 86–93.

Shapiro, A. F., Gottman, J. M., & Carrere, S. (2000). The baby and the marriage: Identifying factors that buffer against decline in marital satisfaction after the first baby arrives. *Journal of Famliy Psychology, 14*(1), 59–70.

Shrout, P. E., & Fleiss, J. L. (1979). Intraclass correlations: Uses in assessing rater reliability. *Psychological Bulletin, 86*, 420–428.

Stocker, C. M., & Youngblade, L. (1999). Marital conflict and parental hostility: Links with children's sibling and peer relationships. *Journal of Family Psychology, 13*, 598–609.

Streiner, D. L. (1995). Learning how to differ: Agreement and reliability statistics in psychiatry. *Canadian Journal of Psychiatry, 40*, 60–66.

Ventura, S. J., Mosher, W. D., Curtin, S. C., Abma, J. C., & Henshaw, S. (2000). *Trends in pregnancy rates for the United States, 1976–1979: An update. National Vital Statistics Report, 49(9).* Hyattsville, MD: National Center for Health Statistics.

Wakschlag, L. S., & Hans, S. L. (2000). Early parenthood in context: Implications for development and intervention. In C. Zeanah (Ed.), *Handbook of infant mental health* (2nd ed., pp. 129–144). New York: Guilford Press.

Whiteside, M. F., & Becker, B. J. (2000). Parental factors and the young child's postdivorce adjustment: A meta-analysis with implications for parenting arrangements. *Journal of Family Psychology, 14*, 5–26.

III

COMMENTARY AND SUMMARY

13

Are Adolescent
Same-Sex Romantic Relationships
on Our Radar Screen?

Ritch C. Savin-Williams
Cornell University

SIGNIFICANCE OF SAME-SEX
ROMANTIC RELATIONSHIPS

Same-sex relationships have been stigmatized or ignored by social scientists, perhaps because they violate the cultural imperative to procreate and because they depart from sex-role expectations. Yet, romantic relationships are at least as developmentally significant to an adolescent who is attracted to same-sex individuals as they are to an adolescent who is attracted to different-sex individuals. Diamond (chap. 4, this volume) notes, "The average sexual-minority youth spends far more time ruminating about love and romance than about suicide, hate crimes, or homelessness, and they have nowhere to turn with their concerns." When considering the multiple transitions that occur during adolescence for healthy development, love does not discriminate based on sexual orientation or the object of one's infatuation.

My task is to review how the present volume covers romantic relationships that include two adolescents of the same sex. A previous book on adolescent romantic relationships (Furman, Brown, & Feiring, 1999) integrates information about same-sex relationships in several chapters and includes a separate chapter discussing reasons investigators should be inclusive of sexual orientation issues. Given that most contributors in the present volume appear familiar with this collection and, therefore, the arguments about why same-sex romantic relationships ought not be ignored, and because several contributors are innovative thinkers, willing to set agendas, I anticipate that this volume will realize an inclusive approach to romantic relationships.

LEVELS OF SENSITIVITY TO SAME-SEX ROMANTIC RELATIONSHIPS

A limitation to the inclusion of same-sex relationships, noted by several authors, is that insufficient data have been collected on adolescent same-sex romantic relationships. As with other areas of inquiry, when data are restricted to a particular sex, age, ethnicity, or social class, extrapolation from existing research is indicated to suggest possible associations. Thus, although data on same-sex attracted adolescents are not plentiful, one could reference the much larger literature on adult same-sex couples. In evaluating the present chapters, the issue is not whether extensive data exist—because they do not—but the authors' use of strategies that are regularly applied when discussing adolescent heterosexual romantic relationships: borrowing from the adult literature or expanding the focus to related literatures, usually information drawn from peer group and friendship literatures.

To assist the reader in evaluating the sensitivity of the chapters in the present volume to these issues, I appraise them on a five-level scale, from least to most desirable:

Level One
- No mention of same-sex romantic relationships, despite the availability of relevant data and writings.
- Heterocentric assumptions are explicitly or implicitly made.

Level Two
- Acknowledgement that same-sex romantic relationships exist, usually in the introduction.
- Statement that the topic will not be covered, with either no or a false reason provided, usually reflecting an ignorance of relevant data and writings.
- Heterocentric assumptions are explicitly or implicitly made.

Level Three
- Acknowledgement that same-sex romantic relationships exist, usually in the introduction.
- Statement or discussion that the topic will not be covered, with a fair and reasonable explanation of why this decision was made.
- Heterocentric assumptions are reduced to a minimum.

Level Four
- Separate section addressing same-sex romantic relationships.
- Rationale given for including this separate section.
- Non-heterocentric language is used.

- Information is accurate and current (if not, subtract one half level).

Level Five

- Discussion of same-sex romantic relationships is integrated.
- Discussion of the ways in which same-sex romantic relationships are similar to and different from heterosexual ones.
- Non-heterocentric language is used.
- Information is accurate and current (if not, subtract one half level).

LEVELS APPLIED TO THE PRESENT BOOK CHAPTERS

Level One: Five Chapters

Nearly half of all chapters fail to acknowledge the existence of same-sex romantic relationships, with no justification provided about why they are omitted. All examples and case histories are of boy-girl pairings. Yet, issues of pregnancy, STDs, HIV, condom use, domestic violence, maltreatment, parenting, couple conflict, and substance abuse affect same-sex oriented adolescents and their romantic relationships as well. If researchers believe that no data exist on these topics, then they might have been the "first" to provide them. In reality, however, data on same-sex attracted individuals exist on all topics discussed in these five chapters. In part, this lapse in coverage might have been driven by the fact that the authors' own research methodology inquires only about heterosexual adolescents or relationships.

Heterocentric language and assumptions thrive in these chapters. One is left wondering whether every relationship is heterosexual. Sex is often defined as sexual intercourse (penile-vaginal activities) and "normative" dating only involves girls with boys. Heterosocial interactions are considered critical to healthy sexual and dating development. Adolescents move "normally" from same-sex cliques to mixed-sex groupings to heterosexual dating. Females always have boyfriends and never girlfriends. References are frequently made to heterosexually married couples, but not to same-sex domestic partners. The parenting partner of a mother never appears to be another female. Authors want to facilitate positive parental interactions among a mother and a father but not, apparently, among two mothers or two fathers.

Level Two: Three Chapters

One quarter of the chapters minimally acknowledge the existence of adolescent same-sex oriented romantic relationships, and then announced that they are excluded. These chapters correctly note that relatively little research has been conducted on same-sex experiences during adolescence, but they do not reference existing data or research of adult same-sex couples, as they did to better understand heterosexual adolescent couples.

One chapter escapes Level One classification because its authors include data on non-heterosexual youths in a footnote. They note that no "substantive conclusions" were altered when they statistically controlled for sexual orientation and thus the authors decide "not to present detailed analyses involving sexual orientation." Another chapter determines that same-sex adolescent couples are "not within the scope of this chapter." A third chapter ignores relevant research on sexual orientation and puberty, brain organization, hormones, sport participation, age of sexual experiences, and HIV. Even when sexual-minority adolescents do not vary from heterosexual youths, these lack of differences could be noted to challenge existing stereotypes.

Level Three: No Chapters

Level Four: Two Chapters

Within this "acceptable" level are two chapters that (unsatisfactorily) attempt to address adolescent same-sex romantic relationships. Although heterocentric assumptions are generally kept to a minimum, they do occasionally infiltrate the text. For example, sexual behaviors are not necessarily "precursors to sexual intercourse" for sexual-minority youths.

Furman and Shaffer argue in their introduction that little is known about gay, lesbian, and bisexual adolescent relationships. Although they include a paragraph late in their chapter summarizing several relevant research findings, unfortunately, several of these are outdated—age of awareness of same-sex attractions now averages third or fourth grades and youths are now almost routinely engaging in same-sex couplings (Savin-Williams, 1998; Savin-Williams & Diamond, 2000). More significantly, data on sexual-minority youths that address many of the issues they raise about heterosexual romantic relationships are not cited, even those that would have been useful facilitating an understanding about how romantic relationships obstruct or enhance adolescent identity development. The provocative questions broached by Furman and Shaffer are not of limited relevance to the experience of growing up heterosexual, but have equal significance for same-sex attracted youths, depending, in part, on their own consolidation and acceptance of their sexual desires:

- Romantic relationships can be a particular source of conflict and tension within families when the relationship is with a same-sex peer.

- Same-sex attracted adolescents who face particular interpersonal and familial difficulties because of their sexuality might seek romantic relationships earlier during adolescence to help them cope with feelings of isolation and rejection from peers and family members.
- Ex-partners might be more likely to become a part of a same-sex attracted youth's friendship network because of their common minority status.
- Parents might be more stressed that their child is in a same-sex romantic relationship because it means she/he is *really* gay. Or, they may be happy that their child is in a committed relationship because it reduces the likelihood of engaging in dangerous sex and of growing old alone. Same-sex romantic relationships may thus be a mixed blessing to parents.
- Dating someone of the same sex may not raise, but lower, one's peer group standing because the "gayness" is too visible, and thus too real, for homophobic peers.
- It may be less important to same-sex attracted youths that their body is maturing "in reproductive capacities." They may be less likely to view puberty as establishing a reproductive agenda.
- Similarly, an emphasis on sexual intercourse as the "ultimate" sex act might alienate same-sex attracted youths in terms of the sexual experiences that are of greatest importance to them in their sexual development.
- Casual or committed romantic relationships might not be the primary context for sexual behavior and learning about sexuality for some gay and bisexual *males*. Many do not have their first sexual experience with someone with whom they are going steady or know well. The opposite is true for same-sex attracted females.

To progress to Level Five, more than a brief, separate paragraph on "gay youth" is necessary. Rather, when a specific issue is discussed for heterosexual romantic relationships then a mention about its possible relevance for same-sex romantic relationships might be warranted. Even when findings are similar across sexual orientations, it could be important to document this if by so doing incorrect assumptions (e.g., gay boys are more gay than boys) are challenged. Discussing same-sex relations might also be particularly significant if it helps an author reinforce or exemplify a point—such as noting diverse patterns of growing up, highlighting dyadic sex composition, and re-examining assumptions about adolescent development.

Carver, Joyner, and Udry have collected rare and potentially highly significant data on same-sex romantic relationships. My major reservation is that the data are too seldom used to enlighten the reader about these relationships. The authors acknowledge that "an exclusive focus on opposite-sex romantic relationships fails to adequately capture the experiences of sexual-minority youth." This crucial and insightful point does not, unfortunately, adequately guide their data analyses. Their findings on same-sex romantic relationships are confined to a three-paragraph section, rather than distributed throughout the chapter when the relevant topic emerges. This organization emphasizes the uniqueness of same-sex attracted youths at the expense of their similarity to heterosexual youths.

By contrast, Carver and associates cover variations by sex, age, and race in both separate (uniqueness) and integrated (commonality) sections throughout the text, thus providing an excellent model for how data on same-sex attracted youth should be discussed. They frequently note racial, age, and sex differences in relationship stability, homogamy, content, commitment, intimacy, and first sex, but not differences by sexual orientation. Data tables do not include distinct entries for same-sex romantic relationships. For example, in terms of "relationship homogamy," Carver and associates observe that romantic partners resemble one another on a variety of characteristics, including attractiveness, education, race, religion, and height. Given the authors' interest in sex differences within romantic relationships, same-sex romantic relationship would appear to be an ideal testing model (homogamous for sex). Unlike heterosexual male adolescents, gay and bisexual male adolescents continue to prefer older partners. Why? Are they "acting" like girls? Same-sex attracted girls prefer same-age partners—unlike both heterosexual boys and girls and gay boys. Why? Although some sexual-minority youths date heterosexually during adolescence to test or hide their attractions or identity, as the authors point out, are there other reasons? Perhaps they date the other sex because they are genuinely attracted to her or him and thus are expressing their true sexuality (consider bisexuals).

In terms of the stability of same-sex romantic relationships, if "girls have more experience than boys with intimate relationships," would not one thus predict that when romantic relationships consist of two girls, then they would be particularly long lasting? Yet, they are not. Perhaps there is less stability in same-sex romantic relationships because they receive less support and encouragement—which implies that social approval might trump sex composition when it comes to stability. Or, if adolescent boys have only a singular same-sex romantic relationship or it is with an older partner, then perhaps it is because in most high schools there are few choices in partner selection. They stay together longer and choose older partners than their peers because they have fewer options than do heterosexual youths. The adult literature on same-sex couples can provide possible answers.

Many youths in Carver's sample with same-sex romantic *attractions* do not report same-sex romantic *relationships*—perhaps because they have few opportunities to date a same-sex other or are too frightened to do so. Less clear is why so few of those with a same-sex romantic relationship report a romantic attraction to a same-sex partner. It might be less threatening to admit to a gay behavior (same-sex romantic relationship) than to say one is romantically attracted to same-sex persons, which is tantamount to "admitting" one is lesbian, gay, or bisexual—a seemingly more permanent and consequential self-definition. Or, perhaps, many of these youths are not primarily or essentially lesbian, gay, or bisexual. After all, if same-sex attracted youth can and do become romantically attracted to a different sex, then why cannot heterosexuals also fall in love with same-sex others? It is unfortunate that the authors do not raise the same question for heterosexuals—whether those with heterosexual romantic relationships are the same ones who are romantically attracted to a different-sex individual.

Level Five: One Chapter

Welsh, Grello, and Harper nicely summarize the major points of this commentary: "Further, by focusing exclusively on heterosexual intercourse as the definition of sexuality, the current research literature fails to capture the diversity of sexual behaviors experienced by heterosexual as well as gay and lesbian adolescents and the mental health implications of these behaviors." Their chapter is closest in this volume to capturing how best to address the lives of youths with same-sex attractions—integration of research findings from both the adolescent and adult literatures as particular issues are discussed. My primary reservations are that they could have done this more frequently and that it would have been helpful to highlight the unique stresses faced by same-sex romantic couples in a separate section.

The first two thirds of their chapter provides a general overview of adolescent romantic relationships, noting age and sex differences, but not sexual orientation differences. This is not a tragic flaw, although the distinctiveness of same-sex relations would be of interest. More importantly, the language of Welsh and colleagues is inclusive and does not negate same-sex relations: "adolescent couple members," "interactions with their romantic partners," "partners' behaviors," and "committed relationships" apply regardless of the sex composition of the couple. Only when they cite research that applies specifically to mixed-sex couples do they use terms such as "heterosexual" adolescents' relationships to clearly distinguish them from "gay" adolescents' relationships.

Welsh and colleagues note differences between heterosexual and gay males on infidelity attitudes. Gay males are more permissive because they "may not hold the strong value about the wrongfulness of the behavior." Although this might be a valid observation (which needs elaboration), this unique "value" may be changing as same-sex romantic relationships are more often recognized and honored in adolescent peer culture. As a result, same-sex couples may increasingly appear similar to heterosexual pairings—going to proms, promising fidelity, sharing jewelry, fighting, and making up. On another point, a purported finding independent of sexual orientation noted by the authors might disguise a sexual orientation difference. The authors rightly recognize that termination of an intense relationship is traumatic for both gay and heterosexual youths. However, although the latter *often have* multiple sources of support, the former do not, which can prolong and intensify the trauma. Other points in need of expansion include the unique stressors faced by same-sex couples, the applicability of romantic stage models to same-sex relationships, the variable motivators for sexual behavior among same-sex attracted youths, and the implications of research results on same-sex attracted youths and their romantic relationships for program planning, education, and intervention. Finally, a discussion of the heterocentric and homophobic views of a number of "pioneers" of adolescent development that Welsh and colleagues cite would have been appreciated. Both Dunphy and Sullivan assume that same-sex chumships "naturally" and "necessarily" evolve into mixed-sex dating if they are to contribute to healthy development. Furthermore, Erikson (1968) views homosexuality as a negative identity because it prevents a synthesis of production, procreation, and creation of the primary unit (family).

Diamond Chapter

I applaud Diamond's positions regarding the romantic landscape of same-sex attracted youths. Too often researchers "simply extrapolate from research on heterosexual youths and switch the gender labels" without recognizing the "full range of variation in sexual-minority youths' sexual and affectional desires for same-sex and other-sex partners." In addition, researchers might assume that adolescent girls in same-sex relationships will act like adolescent boys, and vice versa. This can indeed be true. For example, lesbians are more similar to heterosexual men than women in their de-emphasis on their partner's status and gay men to heterosexual women than men in giving importance to emotional rather than sexual commitment (Bailey, Gaulin, Agyei, & Gladue, 1994). However, although this might be true in particular domains, more often sex trumps sexual orientation in terms of relational qualities. The same researchers report that gay men are more likely than lesbians to express interest in uncommitted sex and gay women are less likely than gay men to emphasize their partner's physical attractiveness—similar to heterosexuals of their respective sex.

Furthermore, as Diamond argues, all too often the unique situation of those with "ambiguous, late-appearing, or bisexual attractions during adolescence" is ignored. The gay/straight paradigm is an inadequate advancement from the purely heterosexual perspective because it disregards the many youths who by their identity and the nature of their romances do not fall into one of these two categories. A significant number of adolescents desire to explore intimate relationships with both sexes without the pressure to "decide" which way to identify. Their mixed-sex relationships might well demonstrate an openness and curiosity that are healthy resolutions to the complexity of sexual and relational attractions during adolescence.

PARTING THOUGHTS

The inclusion of marginalized groups has been conspicuously absent in psychological research. Consequently, the culturally "different" are subject to discrimination and prejudice in the scientific literature (Fukuyama & Ferguson, 2000). As the chapter authors exemplify, developmental researchers seldom investigate same-sex romances, whether desired and consummated by teenagers who identify as lesbian, gay, or bisexual or by those who reject sexual labels or identify as heterosexual. It is not that social and behavioral scientists deny that such relationships exist—they are too obvious within the contexts of adolescent culture to disavow—as much as they *ignore* same-sex couples. In the process, investigators present, by default, a myth of the "normalcy" of heterosexual relationships. I agree with my colleagues Don Barr and LeNorman Strong (1989) that when we do not respect the behavior of those who differ from ourselves, we are co-conspirators in privileging the status quo and the existing power structure. Although many social scientist advocate a liberal philosophy, Barr and Strong argue, "If we judge their commitment by looking at what they do instead of what they say, we might well question their sincerity" (p. 85). By omitting any reference to same-sex relationships, social scientists perpetuate a cycle of empowerment to heterosexuals. By their silence, social scientists provide privilege to the norm, the acceptable, and oppression to those who do not conform.

By contrast, Diamond makes a case for appreciating sexual diversity in order to further draw researchers out of the "dark ages" of adolescent research in which "youths were uniformly presumed heterosexual, and the very existence of sexual-minority adolescents was never acknowledged." When a significant, natural aspect of their lives is disregarded by "experts," teens who do not conform to traditional notions of heterosexual identity, behavior, and attractions suffer chilling effects:

- The silence and secrecy of their romantic relationships are fortified, thus increasing shame and decreasing self-regard.
- False notions of that which is "normal" and, by default, that which is abnormal or deviant, are reinforced.
- Categorization, stereotyping, exploitation, devaluation, and loss of humanity that typically plague sexual-minority youths and others who are assigned "out-group" status (Staub, 1989) are fortified.
- The complexity of integrating multiple social identities and coping with multiple forms of oppression can be so unnerving that stress, depression, anxiety, and isolation result. The self is diminished relative to the perceived "norm."
- Erroneous or no information is distributed to health care providers, educators, policy makers, parents, and others who care for adolescents.

Although "scant," *some* data are available about adolescents' same-sex romantic relations. This deficient representation should not, however, justify its further submersion and exclusion. Furthermore, insight can be gleaned from the adult literature. Social science investigators have explored the initiation, duration, and termination of lesbian and gay romantic relationships; the purpose and meaning of being in a committed same-sex relationship to individual participants; and the support provided by same-sex communities to same-sex couples. Whether the topic is the distribution of power, domestic violence, effects on children, sexual behavior, sex differences, sex roles, or prevalence, social scientists have investigated adult same-sex couples.

So why is there silence surrounding adolescent same-sex relationships? One explanation is provided by Tracy and colleagues who note the difficulty of soliciting a sufficient sample of same-sex romantic relationships when so few adolescents volunteer having them; only about 1% of their sample claimed a bisexual or homosexual identity. However, the seemingly low prevalence of same-sex romantic relationships is further compounded when they are overlooked or disregarded. Most social scientists never offer the possibility in their research that such relationships exist. Words ("sexual intercourse") and assumptions (when adolescents report "dating" then they must be referencing heterosexuality) convey heterosexual expectations. Research designs rarely request the sex of the dating partner. Not surprisingly, some sexual-minority youths buy into these heterocentric expectations, having sex and dating both heterosexually and homosexually yet only reporting the former. Despite difficulties sampling same-sex couples, scientists have not necessarily ignored other low-occurring adolescent phenomena, such as hard drug use, giftedness, sexual abuse, and early maturation. Prevalence rate should not be—and seldom is—the sole criterion for determining what is investigated.

Rather than ignoring same-sex attracted youths, scientists should find innovative ways to recruit them for research projects. One strategy to overcome their reticence to volunteer or to identify themselves is to avoid heterocentric sampling techniques or research instruments. The Add Health data set presented by Carver and associates in the present volume asks not about sexual identity, which often carries considerable baggage for same-sex attracted youths, but inquires about romantic attractions with both girls and boys. As a result, their population of non-heterosexual youths is not the usually reported 1% to 2% of the total sample, but over 5%. The process of asking about both same- and mixed-sex relationships communicates that multiple kinds of couplings are normal and creates an environment in which youths with alternative relationships are more likely to fully participate in our research and programs.

A second explanation for the omission is that authors felt relieved from the responsibility of including same-sex relationships in their review because they assumed that Diamond would adequately address the topic. Perhaps authors were unfamiliar with the relevant literatures and thus did not know what to cover. Perhaps authors concluded that they needed to limit the scope of their chapter and excluding same-sex romantic relationships was an expedient manner to accomplish this goal. It is difficult to be all-inclusive. With ethnicity, sex, social class, region, disabilities, cohort, and many other groupings demanding space, some measure of comprehension had to be sacrificed. Forced to choose, authors might have ignored a phenomenon that has little importance or relevance for their lives.

I suspect that the greatest motivation for remaining silent is the discomfort or uneasiness that many scholars feel with homosexuality and same-sex attractions, especially among pre-adults. Adolescents are often judged to be too young to know if their sexual orientation is other than heterosexual, and for adolescents to "choose" a same-sex relationship feels to these scholars to be childish, narcissistic, or imprudent—at best, a passing phase. Other scholars' moral creeds may dictate the undesirability of such relationships and to research them is tantamount to legitimizing that which they believe to be blasphemous. Finally, authors' uneasiness may be due to their perception that funding agencies, research partners (e.g., schools, community agencies), human subject committees, university departments, and colleagues will be uncomfortable with the topic. The net effect is that researchers feel that the perceived consequences are not worth the risk. I cannot document these sources of discomfort; it is my subjective reading of the situation. However, I do know that the "collective silence" among scientists has contributed to yet another research project, adolescent textbook, and think piece that does not consider "alternative" adolescent sexual relationships.

Regardless of the reason for the neglect, it is relatively easy to read this book, skip the Diamond chapter, and conclude that all romantic relationships are heterosexual. I do not attribute malice to chapter writers, merely short-sightedness. However, as the result of their disregard, it is difficult to be optimistic about the future. Disclaimers that same-sex romantic relationships are not addressed because little research exists appear disingenuous and inconsistent with the treatment of poorly researched domains of heterosexual lives, an insupportable excuse to restrict focus exclusively on heterosexual romantic relationships. This is disheartening because it is not exclusively heterosexual youths who rely on romantic relationships to provide "healthy, developmentally appropriate" experiences that are critical for social support, companionship, and social competencies that "will help them sustain nurturing, intimate ties over the life span" (Diamond, chap. 4, this volume). Some of us will continue to make the case for inclusion, hoping to lower resistance and place same-sex romantic relationships on researchers' radar screens.

REFERENCES

Bailey, J. M., Gaulin, S., Agyei, Y., & Gladue, B. A. (1994). Effects of gender and sexual orientation on evolutionarily relevant aspects of human mating psychology. *Journal of Personality and Social Psychology, 66,* 1081–1093.

Barr, D. J., & Strong, L. J. (1989, Spring). Embracing multi-culturalism: The existing contradictions. *National Association of Student Personnel Administrators,* pp. 85–90.

Erikson, E. H. (1968). *Identity: Youth and crisis.* New York: W. W. Norton.

Fukuyama, M. A., & Ferguson, A. D. (2000). Lesbian, gay, and bisexual people of color: Understanding cultural complexity and managing multiple oppressions. In R. M. Perez, K. A. DeBord, & K. J. Bieschke (Eds.), *Handbook of counseling and psychotherapy with lesbian, gay, and bisexual clients* (pp. 81–105). Washington, DC: American Psychological Association.

Furman, W., Brown, B. B., & Feiring, C. (Eds.) (1999). *The development of romantic relationships in adolescence.* New York: Cambridge University Press.

Savin-Williams, R. C. (1998). *". . . and then I became gay." Young men's stories.* New York: Routledge.

Savin-Williams, R. C., & Diamond, L. M. (2000). Sexual identity trajectories among sexual-minority youths: Gender comparisons. *Archives of Sexual Behavior, 29,* 419–440.

Staub, E. (1989). *The roots of evil: The origins of genocide and other group violence.* Cambridge, UK: Cambridge University Press.

14

A Marital Process Perspective
of Adolescent Romantic Relationships

Amber Tabares
John M. Gottman
University of Washington

In this review we are commenting on the chapters in this volume from the context of our research on marital processes. We use our experience in observational research of married couples to outline important areas of study needed in adolescent romantic couple research. We also tackle the developmental themes of identity formation and intimacy that are addressed by several of the authors in this volume and discuss how these areas are recognized within the context of marital relationships and how they might be represented in adolescent romantic relationships.

An important goal of our work in marital relationships has been to understand the processes functioning within marital communication. Through the study of these processes we have come to understand particular structures of marital communication including the significance of daily interactions, the ability of partners to accept influence from their spouse, the impact of negative emotions during conflict, and how couples try to repair negativity. Through observational research we have identified both effective and harmful patterns of communication within marital interactions and have started using this knowledge to develop interventions.

As a field, we are still in the process of discovery with regard to adolescent romantic relationships, and we have yet to identify many critical patterns of communication or emotional expression used by adolescents in these relationships. Many of the authors in this volume agree that extensive research is required to understand adolescent romantic relationships, with particular emphasis on how these relationships develop across the stages of adolescence. We suggest that an important method for understanding these changes is to identify specific patterns of interaction that occur in adolescent dating couples. An example of a study that took this approach is seen in the Young Parenthood

Project conducted by Florsheim, Moore, and Edgington (chap. 12, this volume). They used observational methods to measure interpersonal behavior during conflict and related these observations to relationship satisfaction and later parental stress outcomes. Their study took advantage of a procedure for observing couples' interactions, typically seen in studies of adult couples, to identify significant patterns of interaction in the relationships between pregnant teens and their partners. Similarly, our goal in this chapter is to use the marital communication patterns that we have discovered through our observational research to illustrate the approaches that are needed to gain a better understanding of the processes of adolescent romantic relationships described in this volume.

Currently there is a drive to identify the effect of adolescent romantic relationships on developmental processes and to specifically understand the links between these dating relationships and other social behaviors. These links are often determined by examining correlations between occurrences of specific behaviors and incidences of adolescent dating. For example, literature on early-maturing teens looks at the correlations between their romantic relationships and psychopathological behavior. In comparing adolescents with early-timing of sexual activity versus late-timing of sexual activity, for example, the early-timing group has poorer psychosocial adjustment, including higher levels of depression and lower self-esteem than the late-timing groups (Bingham & Crockett, 1996). While Bingham and Crockett suggest that these patterns of psychosocial development point to individual trajectories of development, as relationship researchers we should be thinking about how these patterns affect the developmental trajectory of romantic relationships. Researchers should consider the types of romantic relationships in which these adolescents are involved and how they might contribute to, or explain, negative behavioral outcomes. These studies, in which outcomes are related to occurrences of romantic relationships, are necessary for mapping the place of adolescent romantic relationships within development. The next step should be to recognize these relationships as units and use observational methods to fully understand the specific behavioral processes involved in these couples' interactions in order to learn about which specific mechanisms are effecting outcomes and how satisfied and unsatisfied adolescent romantic couples can be characterized.

ADOLESCENT THEMES

Identity formation is central to adolescent development. Identity develops as adolescents struggle to find a balance between autonomy and connectedness. This struggle is seen most clearly as adolescents begin to shift from seeing their parents as a primary source of support to seeing their peers as a greater support system. As children grow into adolescence they start spending less time with their parents and more time with their peers (Burhmester & Furman, 1986). They begin to increase closeness in their relationships with peers and develop their first romantic relationships. At this time new experiences are an opportunity for learning about oneself and there may be no experience more important to the development of identity than the development of close relationships. These relationships are critical because patterns of interaction that are learned may lay the groundwork for communication skills used in all future partnerships including marital relationships. Adolescents use their relationships as mechanisms for understanding themselves and others. They experiment with alternative selves by being very different in different relationships. Thus, a child may try the persona of "outlaw" in one relationship and "community leader" in another, and "rescuer-helper" in another. Some of these personas will be short adventures and be discarded as not fitting the desired emerging self the adolescent is building, while others may feel more right and fitting.

Findings from the Florsheim, Moore, and Edgington study (chap. 12, this volume) addressed issues of adolescent identity and autonomy. The study involved asking pregnant teens and their parents to discuss an area of disagreement for 10 minutes on videotape. Using the Structural Analysis of Behavior (SASB) partners' interactions were assessed for focus of a behavior, affiliation, and interdependence (see Florsheim et al. for details). The parental dyads were grouped by relationship satisfaction using the Quality of Relationship Inventory (QRI). Couples were categorized as low, high, or mixed relationship satisfaction based on each partner's scores on the QRI. The mixed group consisted of couples in which one partner had scored high on the QRI and the other partner had scored low. In a comparison across groups, Florsheim and colleagues found that regardless of satisfaction group, all partners tended to get high SASB scores for controlling behaviors toward their partner and maintaining their own autonomy. These adolescents seem to be establishing roles within their relationship that preserve independence in the face of early parenthood. These findings suggest that issues of identity and autonomy may play a significant role in the relationships of pregnant teens and their partners. The study illustrates the significance of observational research in understanding processes within adolescent romantic relationships that may demonstrate adolescent developmental trends, such as the quest for autonomy.

Adolescents also begin to use their peer relationships and romantic relationships as primary sources of emotional support (Berndt, 1996). In doing so, studies should consider that the nature of these relationships evolves over time. It is in romantic relationships that adolescents begin to learn about their own needs versus those of others and about who they are as individuals. They begin to learn more about those who are important in their lives and compare themselves to dating partners and close friends. They start to learn about the type of relationship they are comfortable with and the types of emotional interactions they like in a partnership, which in the future will help them understand when a relationship is going well. As Shulman describes in his chapter, the balance between emotional closeness and autonomy determines both patterns of conflict within relationships and relationship quality. Finding the right balance is a process of self-discovery.

Strong emotions arise within the context of close friendships and romantic relationships. These emotions are peak experiences for the adolescent, the source of the very high highs and the very low lows. Discovering the right level of emotionality in relationships is another source of self-discovery as is learning to negotiate responses to these new emotional reactions. Close peer and romantic relationships start to become more intimate. Adolescents may begin learning to identify their emotions, and then intimate friendships begin to be characterized by open, self-disclosures of personal information (Berndt, 1996). In these intimate interactions, adolescents learn about themselves and their partner or close friend. They may come to realize that they are more comfortable expressing certain emotions and may share these in their intimate friendships and romantic relationships. Others may realize they prefer to remain more private with emotions in their relationships. Many close friendships and some romantic relationships developed in adolescence last through adulthood. As relationships develop, adolescents build loyalties and gain skills at maintaining intimacy and getting over hard times. Early romantic relationships and close friendships can be a great training ground for intimacy in future marital relationships or committed partnerships.

In our marital intervention studies we have discovered the importance of intimacy and friendship within the marriage and what makes a "Sound Marital House" (Gottman, 1999). The marital friendship lays the foundation for a healthy marriage and is the best defense against developing negative patterns that cause corrosion in the marriage. The pinnacle of the marital friendship, or the top of the marital house, is the Shared Meaning System. This is the place in which spouses hold the thoughts, metaphors, and stories about their marriage. They create a sense of shared purpose, shared interaction rituals, and shared values, roles, and life goals. They share a similar view of central symbols, like the home, love, and spirituality.

At the base of the Sound Marital House are Love Maps, which reflect each spouse's awareness of the other's world. Couples with a sound marriage know one another and create a system for updating that knowledge. In their daily interactions they communicate interest, understanding, and solidarity. The next level of the Sound Marital House is the Fondness and Admiration system. Spouses are able to display vulnerability, respect, empathy, and affection toward one another. Some of the aspects from each level of the Sound Marital House have been observed in couples' responses to our Oral History Interview (OHI). The OHI asks couples to use stories to discuss the history of their relationship including memories of how they met, what led them to marriage, adjustments to being married, and good and bad times within the marriage. In this interview couples describe their shared values and illustrate their overall fondness and affection toward one another or their level of disillusionment in the marriage (Buehlman & Gottman, 1996). All of these elements in the Sound Marital House create a system by which spouses are able to honor one another's dreams. The ability to create high levels of intimacy in the Sound Marital House is affected by the dynamics within the marriage and by each individual's previous experiences. It is probable that through observational work of adolescent romantic relationships and intimate friendships, we will gain an understanding of how adolescents develop the skills necessary for creating intimacy in future relationships.

A focus of our interventions is teaching couples how to create the different levels of the Sound Marital House in order to make the marriage effective as a safe place to share dreams and make aspirations come true (Gottman, 1999). Adolescents in close friendships, and especially romantic relationships, are developing their own stories about their relationships. As adolescents begin to form new romantic relationships, they may find that each new romantic involvement is different and each partnership they form could be categorized differently. A focus for adolescents is the development of their own identity, and different types of relationships serve to show how they fit as individuals in their romantic partnership. In these new experiences with romantic partners they are developing their relationship preferences.

It is important for us to use observational research to discover the types of patterns within adolescent relationships that would enable us to characterize different kinds of couples, as seen in the Shulman and Knafo study of adolescent close friendships (see p. 124, this volume). Using the Card-Sort Problem-Solving Procedure, Shulman and Knafo (1997) measured cooperation and problem solving between close friends and adolescent romantic partners. Participants were given a set of cards that could be sorted in two ways. They were told to sort the cards anyway they liked in as many piles as they chose. Participants underwent two sorting tasks, in the first they were asked to sort independently, in the second, they were allowed to consult while sorting. Three consistent friendship types were found in both the close friendships and romantic relationships: interdependent, disengaged, and consensus-sensitive dyads. Interdependent friends sought solutions in which the individual and dyad were respected, disengaged dyads expressed independence and did not use information from their partner, and consensus-sensitive dyads chose to suppress independent opinion in favor of complete agreement.

In this study, strategies used by pairs of adolescents illustrated types of couples based on the varying degrees of cooperation seen in the dyads. This observational study also found that these couple types were consistent across time but that conceptualizations of friendship changed across development. Qualitative differences in patterns of behavior were discovered in close friend relationships versus romantic relationships. It would be important to understand what these couple types mean for the development of future romantic relationships and how ideas about relationships change as adolescents develop. There may be similar types of patterns specific to dysfunctional couples that would enable us to develop pertinent interventions.

EMOTION, CONFLICT, AND THE FOUR HORSEMEN

Understanding the nature of dysfunction in relationships usually begins with a focus on conflict, both by clinicians and researchers. In the study of adolescent romantic relationships, conflict may be a particularly useful tool for observing emotional reactions. Shulman (chap. 5, this volume) proposes that adolescent conflicts emerge as "adolescents face dilemmas of balancing conflicting needs of self and the other" (p. 115). When faced with addressing these differing needs, Shulman says they use negative emotions to help interpret interactions before the partnership has developed into a lasting relationship. In these cases they are learning to identify and interpret their own negative emotions, leading to a greater development of personal identity. To know the truth behind this premise it is essential for us to use observational methods to study adolescent conflict interactions and to assess emotional expression.

Conflict interactions paint a picture of communication patterns couples have developed and of emotional expression between partners. Therefore one logical starting block for the study of adolescent romantic relationships is learning about conflict. The aim of the Shulman chapter is to discover the role of conflict within the context of adolescent romantic relationships. In other words, Shulman sees the occurrence of conflict as a factor that contributes to explaining the significance of adolescent romantic relationships in development. While this perspective allows us to view the possible meaning of conflict in adolescent romantic relationships, we do not learn about specific processes adolescent romantic partners use to interact during emotionally salient conversations. We can gain more information about adolescents in their romantic relationships by measuring patterns of behavior within conflict. These patterns can demonstrate adolescents' emotional responses and show us different types of romantic relationships. Styles of communication between partners during conflict can shed light on what constitutes a happy or successful adolescent romantic relationship.

Conflict gives us insight into patterns of emotional expression. These patterns are especially important in adolescence because emotions are central to the adolescent experience. Furman and Shaffer discussed Wilson-Shockley's (1995) findings that adolescent romantic relationships are the primary source of strong positive and strong negative emotions. Welsh, Grello, and Harper posit that romantic relationships are connected to the rise in adolescent depression. How adolescents cope with these negative emotions within their romantic relationships is virtually unknown. Conflicts tend to be emotionally charged situations. By conducting observational studies of conflict in adolescent romantic relationships, ways in which adolescents express emotion and ways in which different types of couples handle conflict can be determined. Florsheim, Moore, and Edgington (chap. 12, this volume) found differences in behaviors displayed during conflicts between satisfied and unsatisfied adolescent parental dyads. Couples in the lower satisfaction group were more disengaged toward their partner and exhibited more hostile behavior than couples in the higher satisfaction group. High satisfaction couples demonstrated the same type of hostile behavior, such as blaming and sulking during conflict, but they did so for shorter periods of time than the lower satisfaction couples. Higher satisfaction couples also demonstrated more disclosing, nurturing, and loving behaviors than lower satisfaction couples. Based on this knowledge, Florsheim et al. suggest the usefulness of educating adolescent parenting couples about positive ways to negotiate conflict to help them in their adjustment to parenthood. Couples' behaviors during conflict can be used to develop interventions to prevent the negative outcomes of serious relationship dysfunction both in adolescence and adulthood.

Specific communication patterns between adolescent peers have shed light on associations to later aggression toward romantic partners, as seen in the chapter by Capaldi and Gorman-Smith. Their findings indicate that, "friendships between antisocial male adolescents are likely to include expression of mutual hostile talk about women that may then undermine the quality of intimate relationships with women" (chap. 10, p. 258). They found that interactions between these friends predicted later strategies used during conflict in romantic relationships. These findings highlight the significance of studying specific interaction patterns through observational study. Once a better grasp of the character of conflicts in adolescent romantic relationships is obtained, we may be better able to determine the role these conflicts satisfy.

In marital research, a major factor in predicting divorce has been the identification of specific affects displayed during marital conflicts through observational coding. Gottman and Levenson (2000) found a group of couples that
tend to get divorced in the first 7 years of marriage. This group of "early
divorcers" was distinguished by the emotions they displayed during marital
interactions; namely, they exhibited high levels of negativity during conflict
discussions.

Four specific emotions were found to be characteristic of conflicts in the
group that divorced early. We called these the Four Horsemen of the Apoca-
lypse. The Four Horsemen were discovered using the Specific Affect (SPAFF)
observational coding system. The Four Horsemen are Criticism, Contempt,
Defensiveness, and Stonewalling. Criticism includes global complaining,
statements that include the words "you always" or "you never," and character
attacks. Criticism might sound like, "You never want to go dancing. You're just
not the type of person who can have fun." Contempt conveys disgust and disrespect between spouses. It is seen through sarcasm, mockery, insults, eye rolls,
and hostile humor. Contempt is used to belittle the partner, "Are you kidding
me? You are an idiot!" One spouse uses defensiveness as a response to a comment made by the other and includes An innocent victim posture (e.g., whining) or a righteous indignation posture, e.g., counter-attacks and blaming. In
all cases defensiveness denies responsibility for a problem. A defensive spouse
might respond to their spouse's complaints about housework by saying, "You
didn't clean either (counter-attack). Besides, I didn't do it because it was your
turn (blame)." The fourth of the Four Horsemen is Stonewalling. At this point
one spouse becomes overwhelmed by the conflict and withdraws by appearing
to not listen to the speaker at all; the listener effectively ignores the speaker.

Observation of conflict provides a detailed picture of behavior. Observational studies of couples' interactions offer a rich view of communication patterns that cannot be ascertained solely by means of self-report, especially when
emotional reactions are difficult to identify. It is vital that the field of relationship study become more observational in order to better identify noteworthy
patterns of interaction in romantic relationships. For adolescents, some of
these romantic experiences and emotional situations are so new it may be difficult to accurately recognize certain emotions during conflict. Couples can display several types of negative emotions during conflict. The SPAFF coding
system contains 14 possibilities for negative emotions that can be observed
during an interaction and 5 possibilities for positive emotions. In our studies
we have used these observed affects to identify certain emotions and communication patterns during conflict interactions that predict groups of couples
that will divorce. In his chapter, Shulman proposes that ways in which couples
resolve conflict can mark differences between relationships, but in our work on

marriage we find that the types of emotion delivered during conflict have been most effective at distinguishing between types of couples. This methodology can be extremely useful for understanding adolescent interactions in romantic relationships. The outcomes of these patterns would of course be different, but they might still identify meaningful aspects of adolescent romantic relationships. This, in turn, could help inform us on factors related to relationship quality and shed light on patterns that reveal developmental markers in adolescent romantic relationships, as seen in the Florsheim, Moore, and Edgington study of pregnant teens and their partners. It may be, for example, that studying affective patterns in interactions or conflict styles of adolescent romantic relationships may identify couple types that are typical at varying points in development.

Interpretation of various behaviors within relationships may be dependent on developmental stages. As described in chapter 10, by Capaldi and Gorman-Smith, even physical aggression may be interpreted differently in young couples versus adult couples. They posit that physical aggression may be a complex manner of establishing intimacy and serve a role in narrowing the distance between inexpert partners. The authors suggest a relationship between physical aggression and observed components of problem-solving interactions such as irritability, impulsivity, sexual ownership display, and sexual signaling (p. 266). Further observational study in this area could reveal connections between physical aggression and emotional displays during couples' interactions and might point to specific patterns that change across development.

COUPLE TYPES

Our work on conflict has also led us to discover three conflict styles, or couple types that work well for happily married couples. We call these couples *validators, volatiles,* and *avoiders.* Each type of couple approaches conflict differently and all three styles can be equally effective. Mismatches between these basic types predict divorce in marriages. In adolescence these mismatches may predict breakups, but they may also predict self-discovery. Adolescents are just beginning to develop these styles as they are learning about how to manage conflict with romantic partners. Clashes may arise as differences in conflict style for each partner begin to appear. In our marital work, we have found that these couple types are successful when both individuals have the same style for dealing with conflict.

Happily married couples exhibit three distinct conflict styles. *Validators* are couples who like to discuss their problems. They are very good friends and are skilled at validating their spouses' emotions and opinions. Validators have few disagreements, but when they do arise, each partner maintains respect for the other. They rarely raise their voice during disagreements and usually resolve their conflicts by compromising. *Volatile* couples have a style of conflict quite different from Validators. They approach conflict with a much higher level of intensity and disagreements are more explosive. Both partners passionately express both positive and negative emotions. The key to stability for Volatile couples is that their expressions of positive emotions balance their expression of negative emotions. The last couple conflict style belongs to *avoiders*. These couples avoid disagreements by accentuating the positive qualities of the marriage and ignoring complaints. When disagreements do surface, partners generally agree to disagree.

As mentioned, there is evidence indicating changes in the types of friendships developed in adolescence across time; from best friendships, to peer groups, to romantic relationships. Across each type of relationship there are varied levels of intimacy and it is likely that there are characteristic ways of interacting and handling conflict. Within adolescent romantic relationships, as in marriage, we may find couples who are emotionally engaged or couples who engage in conflict. In adolescence, individuals are starting to learn that there are different types of relationships and as these differences become more crystallized individuals begin to learn about their own identity and develop a personal outlook on relationships. It may be that types of romantic couples arise based on a developmental course. As adolescents acquire further social skills and personal needs, different interaction patterns may develop. Observational studies of interactions in adolescent romantic relationships will assist our knowledge of these behaviors.

COOPERATION AND ACCEPTING INFLUENCE

Through our observations of couples' conflict interactions we have also discovered a pattern for resolving disagreements used by happy, stable couples in which partners are able to accept influence from one another. Accepting influence describes each partner's willingness to yield at least some ground during an argument. For these couples, the goal is not to be the winner of the argument but to achieve a close and satisfying relationship (Driver, Tabares, Shapiro, Nahm, & Gottman, 2003). By accepting influence, one spouse is able to find some level of agreement with the other that does not feel like a complete surrender of the self; they learn to cooperate and work together as a couple.

Accepting influence from one's partner requires cooperation and a sense of self-identity. Accepting influence is extremely difficult for some spouses and part of the reason for this may be that the skills were never developed in ado-lescence. Shulman describes an observational study of adolescent romantic partners who were given the choice to cooperate or work individually on a joint task (Shulman, Levy-Shiff, Kedem, & Alon, 1997). They found that the majority of romantic partners cooperated with each other without imposing their own ideas and communicating respect for the ideas of the other. This is very similar to how we observe accepting influence in happily married couples. Perhaps the adolescents who are able to cooperate and respect the ides of their partner are likely the same individuals who later accept influence in their marriage.

The absence of accepting influence, particularly by husbands, is a factor that discriminates happily married couples from unhappily married couples and couples who later divorced (Driver et al., 2003). Coan, Gottman, Babcock, and Jacobsen (1997) described the relation between accepting influence and abuse. Husbands in abusive couples were found to not accept influence from their wives. Shulman et al. (1997) found some cases in which adolescent part-ners did not cooperate with each other, while others attempted to impose their own ideas in the task. Longitudinal research of these interactions would demonstrate whether these individuals later develop dysfunctional interaction patterns in their romantic relationships.

PERCEPTIONS AFFECTING RELATIONSHIPS AND REPAIR

In their discussion on depression and adolescent romantic relationships, Welsh, Grello, and Harper describe models of the development of adolescent relationships. These models discuss the influence of past relationships on current relationships and the importance of adolescent "views" as described by Furman and Wehner. They argue that qualities adolescents bring to the romantic relationship, including their views of romantic relationships, affect the way in which individuals view interactions within their current relation-ship. Florsheim, Moore, and Edgington describe "the complex interplay between subjective experience and interpersonal behavior [as] relevant to the course and outcome of a couple's relationship" (p. 299). Their study lends sup-port to the significance of perceptions in adolescent relationships because of the relationship they found between adolescents' reported satisfaction in the relationship and their behaviors during conflict.

In our work with married couples we also try to understand the filters through which spouses view their marriage. Individuals develop perceptions about relationships that affect how they interpret comments made by their partners and the choices they make when responding to each other. We have studied these perceptions in our observations of couples' repair attempts during conflict interactions. Repair attempts are interactions aimed at decreasing negative escalation during disagreements. They can occur at any time during a discussion of disagreement; they may occur during high levels of negativity in an effort to reduce mounting negativity, or they might occur early in a discussion as a way to prevent negativity. Some examples of repair attempts are apologies, humor, affection, and changing the subject. While these have been observed in marital conflict interactions, one can imagine how an adolescent might use these skills to prevent negative interactions with family or friends. These interactions are not necessarily related to the content of the argument but may simply provide a brief reprieve from it.

Our preliminary analysis indicates that happy couples use more repair attempts early in conversations to prevent negativity. Repair attempts are used in a variety of interactions. Types of repair interactions start as early as infancy, as described by Tronick and Gianino (1986), who studied repair in mother–infant interactions. Repairs may continue on a developmental path through adulthood, with parents and adolescents using repair attempts in their conflict interactions, and adolescents using these skills in romantic relationships and intimate friendships. Shulman noted, from the work of Caplan, Bennetto, and Weissberg (1991) that conflict within adolescent friendships revealed less coercion and negative affect than with family members, but that adolescents' use of "constructive negotiation strategies, as performed within their families, is related to the quality of their friendships" (p. 15). Further observational studies would give us meaningful information about the specific behaviors related to lower levels of negative affect and higher relationship quality in close friendships and romantic relationships.

We have come to understand that an important component of Repair Attempts is the partner's response to a repair and responses seem to be linked to individuals' perceptions of the relationship. Each partner's ability to respond in a positive way when a repair is made seems to indicate distinct patterns that differentiate between happy and unhappy couples. For example, one husband suddenly stopped in the middle of a heated debate, looked out the window and said, "It's really raining out there." At that point the wife could have made any number of responses to her husband's change of subject. This wife chose to respond positively by accepting the repair attempt, "Wow, you're right. I think we've had three inches in the past week." She could have reacted negatively by ignoring his comment and continuing with the disagreement, or reacting in a hostile manner, "What does that have to do with our discussion? Are you trying to ignore me?" In this example, the wife's positive response allowed for a brief respite from the disagreement. In our research, this is typical of how a spouse in a happy marriage might respond to a change of subject during an argument. This type of pattern might be seen in all types of adolescent relationships. How individuals in different types of dyads view their relationships, affects their ability to respond to repair attempts. Adolescent's views of relationships may explain the differences in patterns of conflict with friends versus family members. It may be that many adolescent dating partners avoid high levels of negative affect during disagreements by using repair interactions early in their interactions.

Further observational studies on adolescent communication patterns are necessary to understand the types of response patterns adolescent develop in their relationships. These responses may expose the effect of views adolescents hold about relationships; including how their needs fit with those of their partner, power imbalances, and their ideas of significant roles within the relationship. As described in chapter 8, adolescents' views of romantic relationships are correlated to perceptions of their interactions, but more evidence is still needed to comprehend this link. Still to understand are how these views affect communication patterns. Negative views of relationships or romantic partners may be linked to negative behavioral outcomes that could be addressed in interventions.

SUPPORT AND TURNING

Chapter 1 describes the importance of adolescent romantic relationships in terms of how they are related to other developmental contexts. Peer and family relationships are important markers of adolescent development. The placement of romantic relationships in terms of these markers is important, but it is also necessary to appreciate the qualities of communication and emotional expression in romantic relationships that set them apart from peer and family relationships.

The authors consider peer groups as a developmental starting ground for romantic relationships. They have found that, "over the course of adolescence [teenagers] increasingly turn to their peers for support" (p. 8). They spend less time with their families and more time with peers. While peer interactions increase in frequency, so do interactions with the opposite sex. Connolly, Furman, and Konarski (2000) have found that adolescents whose peer groups frequently include members of the opposite sex are more likely to develop romantic relationships. Therefore, there is some evidence of a linear developmental trajectory determining the course of adolescent relationships and a link in the effect of peer relationships on romantic relationships. Furman and Shaffer also discuss the influence of adolescent romantic relationships on peer groups in terms of changes to peer networks. From the perspective of investigating the effect of peer relationships on romantic relationships or vice versa, the focus is still on linkages between relationship types and not on the specific dynamics within romantic relationships. While considering the links between relationships in the family, peer, and romantic contexts, it is important to identify the characteristics of romantic relationships that make them different from other teen interactions.

Affiliative behavior may take on its own meaning within romantic relationships with unique effects. For adolescents, behaviors such as cooperation may be displayed in ways unique to their romantic relationships. As with marriage research, observing the patterns of behavior within romantic interactions will lend the most information to our understanding of the roles of adolescent romantic relationships in adolescent development. According to Furman and Shaffer, supportive behavior is an important element in relationships of various types across development. They found that support in relationships between adolescents and their parents was associated to supportive behavior with romantic partners. This linkage indicates the existence of a consistent behavior in relationships across development and adds meaning to the role of romantic relationships in adolescent development. But, adolescents would be better served by the increased use of observational methods to discover specific ways in which they maintain supportive behavior in their romantic partnerships.

From a marital perspective, supportive behavior is important in identifying specific patterns in marital relationships. Driver and Gottman (2001) have discovered affiliative types of behaviors to be important in couples' day-to-day lives; these daily interactions become a crucial component for marital success. These everyday interactions were observed in couples who were asked to come to an apartment laboratory and live as they would at home. They were allowed to bring anything from home that would help them feel comfortable and they were videotaped for twelve hours. To capture their everyday interactions the "Turning Toward" observational coding system was created (Driver, 1999). This system categorizes the ways in which couples initiate and respond to each other on a moment-to-moment basis. Invitations to interact are defined as "bids" and they include sharing of emotional support. Responses to bids ranged from low-level to enthusiastic and playful and were categorized as positive, "Turning Toward"; or negative, "Turning Away" and "Turning Against."

Bids for attention can be very unobtrusive comments. For example, a couple might be standing in line for movie tickets and the husband says, "Did you see that car?" At that point the wife has several choices for a response. She can ignore the comment and continue reading the movie times (turning away); she can get angry and say, "Aren't you suppose to be helping me pick a movie?" (turning against); or she can look at the car and comment on its appearance, "Wow, it's tiny" (turning toward). The type of response the wife makes to the husband's bid influences his further attempts to interact. Ignoring the interaction or responding in a negative way fosters distance and separation, while even a minor response helps promote emotional connection and friendship (Driver et al., 2003).

Observing these daily moments in couples enabled the differentiation of patterns in affiliative types of behavior between happy and unhappy couples. Driver and Gottman (2001) found that happy couples responded to 85% of bids with positive responses, rarely ignoring their partners. Sometimes these positive responses were enthusiastic, but sometimes they were just looks or smiles of acknowledgment. Another characteristic of happy couples was incidences of playful bidding. Playful bids were never seen in the daily interactions of unhappy couples. Playful bids included good-natured teasing with some physical sparring. Overall, eagerness to interact and positive responses seem to increase bidding and affiliative behavior, which increases friendship within the marriage.

In early romantic relationships Shulman sees conflict mainly serving as a means to dissolve the partnership. This being the case, the study of daily interactions outside of conflict may be a meaningful focus for understanding adolescent romantic relationships. How is it that adolescents bid for attention in their daily lives? Do they initiate affiliation differently across relationships? Do romantic partners and close friends respond to bids differently? It would be interesting to note whether adolescents bid in ways that are similar or different to our research on adults. For example, playful bids might be more common in adolescent romantic relationships across all types of couples. Differences in the subtlety of bids and responses may be found with adolescents initiating behavior more overtly.

Being able to observe these interactions in marriage has shed new light on some of the specific mechanisms of support and affiliation in daily marital interactions. The observational system helps us understand how spouses support one another and the types of daily interactions that are meaningful in terms of marital happiness. The Turning Toward coding system also has implications for couple's therapy. For example, Driver and Gottman (2001) found that couples who demonstrated playfulness and enthusiasm in their daily lives were better equipped to use humor and affection during marital conflict discussions. Are the skills required to initiate bids and respond positively to a partner's bids learned in adolescence? Previous experience in romantic relationships may cause individuals to develop beliefs about the appropriateness of initiating affiliation.

These are issues that could only be uncovered through the use of observational research. Through observation we have been able to reveal important processes of daily interaction that identify happy and unhappy couples, while gaining greater understanding of the dynamics of marital relationships. For adolescent romantic relationships it is still unclear how romantic partners support each other or how adolescent partners initiate interaction. It would be interesting to know whether these couples initiate interactions differently across relationship contexts and whether levels of affiliation between partners in romantic relationships change across adolescence. Another important question is whether bidding behavior or responses to bids are related to relationship quality in adolescent romantic relationships. In considering bids across relationship contexts it may be that bidding in family interactions, with parents and siblings, is related to their success in romantic relationships.

RESEARCH AGENDA FOR STUDYING ADOLESCENT ROMANTIC RELATIONSHIPS

We suggest taking an approach to studying adolescent romantic relationships that is similar to the approach to studying marriage. An approach that includes a combination of self-reports, semi-structured interviews, and observation in interactions would yield a multi-faceted view of adolescent romantic relationships.

Despite the importance of adolescent romantic relationships described by several of the authors in this volume there is much left to uncover. This unfortunately leaves the field relatively uninformed on how to assist adolescents. Adolescent romantic relationships serve to aid in the development of individuality and identity, they are sources of strong emotional experiences, and for some couples they can be the foundation for dysfunctional patterns leading to violence and abuse. As a result, gaining a clear picture of specific patterns of communication and expression within adolescent romantic couples is essential to developing interventions that can help adolescents negotiate these new relationships and develop healthy patterns of communication. Florsheim, Moore, and Edgington suggested an approach to assisting adolescents by developing interventions for pregnant teens and their partners aimed at increasing warmth and positivity in their conflict interactions while preserving couples' interpersonal dynamics.

Interviews would be a useful way to develop an understanding of adolescent perspectives of romantic relationships. Through interviews research can be informed about adolescent romantic relationships in the language of adolescents, without imposing our views of committed, adult relationships. Observational coding of our interviews of married couples have enabled us to measure marital quality in a more comprehensive way than from questionnaires alone. Through interviews, couples are able to speak openly, using evocative descriptions that give us glimpses of their shared meaning system. Contextual cues such as: facial expression, voice tone, and affect are also apparent during observational coding of interviews and these supplement the verbal narrative for coding. As in clinical work, these cues can be used by interviewers as guides to further exploration of areas with emotional content.

Interviews may reveal salient patterns of description that play a part in defining relationship quality of couples. An open-ended interview similar to the Oral History Interview (OHI) that we conduct in our lab with married couples may be a practical tool in the study of adolescent romantic relationships. Dimensions of the OHI enable us to gather information such as: couples' perceptions of their relationships, global affect toward their spouse and the relationship, expressivity, and closeness (Buehlman & Gottman, 1996). An interview that gets at dating partners perceptions of each other and their relationship both through verbal and non-verbal behaviors would begin to identify the roots of particular relationship patterns. This type of interview could also be aimed at defining family involvement and influence within the relationship. Interviews about emotions and emotional reactions to family and dating partners may provide necessary information for developing interventions for dating couples. These interviews can serve to detect target areas for prevention of dysfunctional adolescent relationships by illustrating situations in which adolescents are unable to regulate emotions.

Further observational studies of romantic couples' interactions are also a necessary course for future study. As described in this commentary and by researchers throughout this volume, observational research has demonstrated particular patterns that identify couple typologies whether the studies are of families, close friends, or romantic partners. The field needs to expand upon studies in which various types of interactions in romantic relationships may be observed. Salient behavior patterns could be discovered by observational studies of daily exchanges such as: conversations about the events of the day, interactions at lunchtime or in the hallways at school, or even on dates. Further observational studies examining conflict have the potential to yield information on adolescent responses in emotionally charged situations, both in romantic partnerships and in interactions with close family and friends.

Adolescents are at a critical period of development in which many do not possess the skills to adequately negotiate their own romantic relationships. It is critical that researchers understand the characteristics of a successful adolescent romantic relationship through observations of partner interactions. With further study in this area researchers will be able to develop ways to impart their observations of romantic relationships to adolescents in the form of educational and community programs.

REFERENCES

Berndt, T. J. (1996). Transitions in friendship and friends' influence. In J. A. Graber, J. Brooks-Gunn, & A. C. Petersen (Eds.), *Transitions in friendships through adolescence: interpersonal domains and contexts* (pp. 57–84). Mahwah, NJ: Lawrence Erlbaum Associates.

Bingham C. R., & Crockett, L. J. (1996). Longitudinal adjustment patterns of boys and girls experiencing early, middle, and late sexual intercourse. *Developmental Psychology, 32,* 647–658.

Buehlman, K. T., & Gottman, J. M. (1996). The Oral History Coding System. In J. Gottman (Ed.), *What predicts divorce: The measures* (pp. OH11–OH118). Hillsdale, NJ: Lawrence Erlbaum Associates.

Buhrmester, D., & Furman, W. (1986) The changing functions of friends in childhood: A Neo-Sullivanian perspective. In V. K. Derlega & B. A. Winstead (Eds.), *Friendship and social interaction* (pp. 41–62). New York: Springer-Verlag.

Caplan, M., Bennetto, L., & Weissberg, R. P. (1991). The role of interpersonal context in the assessment of social problem-solving skills. *Journal of Applied Developmental Psychology, 12,* 103–114.

Coan, J., Gottman, J. M., Babcock, J., & Jacobsen, N. (1997). Battering and the male reflection of influence from women. *Aggressive Behavior, 23*(5), 375–388.

Connnolly, J., Furman, W., & Konarski, R. (2000). The role of peers in the emergence of heterosexual romantic relationship in adolescence. *Child Development, 71,* 1395–1408.

Driver, J. L. (1999). *Bids and Turning Coding Manual.* Unpublished manuscript.

Driver, J. L., & Gottman, J. M. (2001). *Daily marital interactions during dinnertime in an apartment laboratory and positive affect during marital conflict among newlywed couples.* Manuscript submitted for publication.

Driver, J. L., Tabares, A., Shapiro, A., Nahm, E., & Gottman, J. M. (2003). Interactional patterns in marital success or failure: Gottman laboratory studies. In F. Walsh (Ed.), *Normal family processes: Growing diversity and complexity* (3rd ed., pp. 493–513). New York: Guilford Press.

Gottman, J. M. (1999). *The marriage clinic: A scientifically based marital therapy.* New York: W. W. Norton.

Gottman, J. M., & Levenson, R. W. (2000). The timing of divorce: Predicting when a couple will divorce over a 14-year period. *Journal of Marriage and the Family, 62*(3), 737–745.

Shulman S., & Knafo, D. (1997). Balancing closeness and individuality in adolescent close relationships. *International Journal of Behavioral Development, 21,* 687–702.

Shulman, S., Levy-Shiff, R., Kedem, P., & Alon, E. (1997). Intimate relationships among adolescent romantic partners and same-sex friends: Individual and systemic perspectives. In S. Shulman & W. A. Collins (Eds.), *Romantic relationships in adolescence: Developmental perspectives* (pp. 37–51). San Francisco: Jossey-Bass.

Tronick, E. Z., & Gianino, A. (1986). Interactive mismatch and repair: Challenges to the coping infant. *Zero-to-Three, 6*(3), 1–6.

Wilson-Shockley, S. (1995). *Gender differences in adolescent depression: The contribution of negative affect.* Unpublished master's thesis, University of Illinois at Urbana-Champaign.

15

The Joy of Romance:
Healthy Adolescent Relationships
as an Educational Agenda

Bonnie L. Barber
University of Arizona

Jacquelynne S. Eccles
University of Michigan

The diversity of topics covered in this volume on adolescent romantic relationships and sexuality highlights the increasing complexity with which we view
these topics. Covering different perspectives and approaches, the authors
highlight three broad themes of importance to educators and educational policy makers: (a) romance and sex are normative, important elements of adolescent development; (b) as we think about adolescent partnerships, we need to
consider how individual differences interact with relationship contexts to
either foster or undermine positive development and healthy growth; and
(c) gender and gendered development are critically important components of
romantic relationships and sexuality. That these themes are so salient in this
book reflects a shift from the consideration of sexuality in adolescence as a
deviant or risky behavior to the emergence of more complex frameworks that
focus on the quality and diversity of adolescent romantic and sexual experiences. Until recently, research on adolescent sexuality has been focused on
problematic aspects—pregnancy, STDs, and failure to use contraception
(Koch, 1993). The authors in this volume have provided a rich and multifaceted view of adolescent romantic relations and sexuality, illustrating the need
for educational programs and policies that are responsive to the characteristics
of the youth they target. This theme was also highlighted in Andrew Collins's
2002 presidential address at the biennial meeting of the Society for Research
on Adolescence (Collins, 2002).

IMPORTANCE OF ROMANTIC
RELATIONSHIPS

The chapters illustrate the prevalence of romantic relationships in adolescence, and the key role they play in development. According to Carver, Joyner, and Udry (chap. 2, this volume) two thirds of adolescents experience some form of a romantic relationship over an 18-month period. The exact nature of these experiences varies across age, with older adolescents reporting both more stable, intimate relationships and more abusive relationships. In light of the normative nature of romantic relationships, a number of developmental consequences of these partnerships are discussed throughout this volume, including identity formation, relationship skill building, emotional maturation, and achievement socialization.

In discussing the developmental importance of romantic relationships, several authors in this volume highlighted *identity formation* (Diamond, chap. 4; Furman & Shaffer, chap. 1; Tracy, Shaver, Albino, & Cooper, chap. 6; Welsh, Grello, & Harper, chap. 8). Adolescence is a time to reflect upon and try out different identities (Erikson, 1968). Amazingly little attention has been paid to the development of either a romantic or a sexual identity given the importance of these aspects of life for most adolescents and adults. In contrast, these themes pervade popular culture in all Western cultures. Several of the chapters suggest that such relationships are likely to play an important role in both the general affective and specific content dimensions of identity formation and consolidation. Positive experiences can lead to a positive romantic self-concept and view of the self as an attractive partner, which in turn should contribute to healthy global self-esteem during both adolescence and adulthood (Furman & Shaffer, chap. 1; Tracy et al., chap. 6). In contrast, negative experiences may result in current feelings of humiliation and shame as well as do long term damage to both general self-esteem and more specific aspects of confidence and values in the domains of romance, intimate partnerships, dating, and sexuality that can plague a person for the rest of his or her life (Tracy et al., chap. 6).

The role of romantic relationships are likely to be especially important for identity validation for sexual minority youth precisely because they are often forced in our culture to keep their sexual orientation secret even from their parents and sexual majority friends. Consequently, their romantic partners may be their only source of the types of emotional, intellectual, and sexual intimacy needed to help them work through the process of sexual and romantic partner identity formation and consolidation (Diamond, chap. 4).

This theme of self-definition and identity formation within the context of relationships suggests that adolescents who miss out on desired opportunities to have a romantic partner may suffer considerably in the identity consolidation process. Similarly, having to cope with this identity formation task in the absence of good scaffolding by supportive adults and well-functioning role models makes the task even more treacherous. Certainly, the media provides many models of less than optimal developmental pathways through these domains. There is amazingly little to counterbalance these images and role models.

Romantic relationships also provide a context in which *social competencies are both learned and tested.* In the context of secure romantic partnerships, adolescents receive training in intimacy and mutual affirmation (Tracy et al., chap. 6) as well as in communication and negotiation skills, and interpersonal conflict management skills (Shulman, chap. 5). Similarly, because romantic relationships are also a major source of strong positive and negative emotions, they also provide a context for learning emotion regulation skills (Larson, Clore, & Wood, 1999). Dating relationships typically provide challenges to emotional well-being, particularly with regard to issues related to infidelity and breakups (Welsh et al., chap. 8). As Diamond (chap. 4) points out, participating in romantic relationships during adolescence can facilitate acquiring the very skills needed to manage the heightened emotionality that is likely to accompany these partnerships throughout life.

The authors also draw attention to the role of romantic partners as *social influences* during adolescence. Unlike the prevalence of concern over the negative consequences of romantic relationships during this period in much of the existing rhetoric and research, the authors in this book provide a more balanced view. For example, although beginning dating, romantic relationships, and sex too early are predictive of lower achievement, Furman and Shaffer (chap. 1) point out the potential for positive, as well as negative, partner influence on career plans and aspirations, educational/vocational identity and both educational and occupational attainment. Having achievement-oriented friends during adolescence is predictive of higher educational attainment (Epstein, 1983; Stone, Barber, & Eccles, 2000). The same should be true for romantic partners. Having achievement-focused romantic partners should facilitate greater educational focus and school attachment. Although studies of adolescent partnerships on this point are scarce, Belansky (1994) reported that partner support at age 20 predicts educational attainment in young adulthood. Furthermore, emotionally healthy romantic partnerships in late adolescence often provide the turning point for youth who have been involved in very risky behaviors throughout most of their adolescent years (Horney, Osgood, & Marshall, 1995; Pickles & Rutter, 1991; Sampson & Laub, 1993). This is particularly true for males who have been heavily involved in criminal behavior. More work is badly needed on this topic.

In contrast, negative experiences related to sexuality during this period can have quite troubling consequences. Recent reports from the American Association of University Women (1993, 2001) suggest that sexual harassment is quite common in American schools. Increasing attention is being drawn to date rape during the adolescent and young adult years, and to victimization based on sexual orientation. These types of experiences have serious negative consequences for school achievement, high school completion, mental health, and general well-being (Hershberger & D'Augelli, 1995; Jozefowicz, Colarossi, Arbreton, Eccles, & Barber, 2000).

Given their importance and prevalence, romantic relationships should be a focus of educators. Well-designed curricula may help adolescents develop knowledge and interpersonal skills that improve their chances of experiencing positive relationships as well as help them benefit from the learning opportunities inherent in such relationships. In addition to facilitating healthy development, such curricula could help them learn the interpersonal skills and self-confidence necessary to extract themselves from risky romantic relationships. The challenge in developing and delivering a program or curriculum on sexuality and romantic relationship education is that a developmentally appropriate solution will vary across contexts and different groups of adolescents. We elaborate these points in the next section.

CONSIDERING THE INDIVIDUAL IN THE CONTEXT OF THE RELATIONSHIP

One of the clear messages of these chapters is that relationships are complex, and that a homogeneous conceptualization of "adolescent romantic relationships" is not realistic. Numerous factors, including individual differences, context effects, and the interaction of person and context characteristics need to be considered when planning for educational programs. Although this makes program delivery difficult, it is necessary if we want the interventions to be effective.

Individual Differences

The chapters emphasize that relationships are experienced differently, depending on the individual characteristics of those involved. Some of the characteristics raised in chapters include gender (addressed later), pubertal timing and hormone levels, sexual orientation, attachment style, and relationship expectations.

Pubertal Timing and Status

When designing educational programs for adolescents, it is crucial to consider the developmental level of the audience. Pubertal maturation is an obvious consideration for programs targeting sexual behavior and romantic relationships. Halpern (chap. 3, this volume) highlights that both pubertal status and relative timing have been linked to sexual activity. For boys, earlier pubertal development, and the higher testosterone levels accompanying that development, are related to earlier sexual behavior (Graber, Brooks-Gunn, & Galen, 1998). Hormone–behavior links are more complex for girls. Although relatively early puberty is associated with girls' earlier sexual activity, the relationship is more pronounced in certain life circumstances, such as in mixed-sex schools, and affiliation with older males (Halpern, chap. 3, this volume). Similarly, social control interacts with hormone levels for girls, with testosterone predicting sexual behavior only if the father is not present in the home.

Some of the most important work on the impact of pubertal timing and development during adolescence has been done by Stattin and Magnusson (1990), and this work is directly related to the issues discussed in this book. Stattin and Magnusson (1990) found that early maturing Swedish girls obtained less education and lower status jobs than their later maturing peers. They also married and became parents at a younger age than their later maturing peers. Why? Stattin and Magnusson argued that these girls were more likely to be pulled into a working class older male peer group because of their early sexual maturation. Once they were pulled into this peer group, their educational and marital trajectories were shaped by the needs and values of these males. Essentially, the young women's desire to be popular with older males made them vulnerable to the opportunities these older males were ready to offer. It is unlikely that these young women understood the long-term consequences of these early romantic choices. Educational programs could be designed to help them make better informed and more self-protective choices.

Sexual Orientation

As Diamond suggests, it is crucial to resist making assumptions about the sexual and romantic interests of students. Programs that focus exclusively on heterosexual attractions and sexuality ignore the interests and concerns of sexual minority youth. Furthermore, Diamond highlights the importance of individual differences among sexual minority youth, as some self-identify as having exclusively same-sex attractions, others are bisexual, and still others may be questioning their sexual identity. Experiences of sexual and romantic relationships will vary for these different groups, and educators must attend to their diverse expectations, goals, and circumstances in designing curricula and support opportunities.

Views of Relationships

Several chapters in the volume make it clear that educational programs for adolescents should consider students' previous relationship experiences and accompanying schemas for romantic involvement. Program content and format should address the diverse needs of those who have had early victimization experiences, relationship difficulties, of those who are characterized by insecure attachment styles or dependent depression, and of those who have grown up in violent and abusive families. Wekerle and Avgoustis (chap. 9, this volume) suggest that childhood maltreatment may influence one's working model of close relationships, and result in unmet dependency needs and fear of injury, loss, or abandonment. This relationship view is consistent with that of "dependently" depressed individuals described by Seefeldt, Florsheim, and Benjamin (chap. 7, this volume). The need for acceptance may compromise rejection-sensitive adolescents' judgment in selecting partners, and place them at risk for depression (girls) or abusiveness (boys) (Downey, Bonica, & Rincon, 1999). Such a relationship style may not be improved simply with better communication and problem-solving skills. Downey and colleagues (1999) suggested that rejection sensitivity can be modified by disconfirming experiences, such as having a supportive and accepting partner, but also acknowledge that the pool of potential adolescent partners may not have the full range of relational skills to scaffold such change. Programs designed to address the underlying insecurity may be effective in improving relationships for such individuals (Seefeldt et al., chap. 7, this volume).

Similarly, Tracy et al. (chap. 6, this volume) found that anxiously attached girls, compared to securely attached girls, reported more sexual experience and were more likely to say they had sex for fear of losing their partner. They recommend that for this group, an important program goal might be to learn the differences between love, sex, and security, and to consider healthy and unhealthy goals of relationships. Furthermore, Shulman (chap. 5) suggests that unrealistic expectations of one's partner, or previous unresolved conflict, may lead to difficulties in negotiating issues of self and other. It is especially important for educators to develop and deliver programs about healthy relationships for adolescents with negative dating and interpersonal behaviors and expectations, in order to reduce the likelihood of their negative patterns continuing into their adult relationships.

Social Contexts

Development of sexuality and relationship skills is embedded in the adolescents' changing ecological contexts (Bronfenbrenner, 1979), and the chapters in this volume highlight several contexts to consider in education efforts, particularly in the areas of relationship quality and partner characteristics. The heterogeneity of relationship contexts presents a challenge to educators, as optimal programs to help those in troubled or violent relationships may not be effective for enhancing healthy relationships among most youth.

Relationship Quality

A substantial number of adolescents report experiencing abusive behaviours within their relationships (see chaps. 10, 2, and 9, by Capaldi & Gorman-Smith; Carver et al.; and Wekerle & Avgoustis, respectively). The prevalence of dating violence among high school students results in a substantial number of youth who could benefit from prevention and intervention efforts, and suggests that schools would be an important venue for program delivery. However, it will be a challenge for educators to simultaneously intervene to meet the immediate needs of those in problematic, hostile relationships, and educate those who may be at risk of forming unhealthy relationships. Both are important goals.

Intimacy and support are key characteristics of romantic relationships. Satisfying relationships can translate to better adjustment to parenthood and less stress for young fathers (Florsheim, Moore, & Edgington, chap. 12, this volume). Given the importance of relationship quality for early parenting, educational programs targeting communication, problem solving, and negotiation skills in adolescence are likely not only to improve the interparental relationship, but also to benefit the development of their children. Thus, educators should pay particular attention to those expectant parents and adolescents at risk of becoming parents who are having relationship difficulties.

Partner characteristics are critically important. Fortenberry describes the within-dyad similarity in health harming and health protecting behavior. This assortative pairing has implications for partnership violence. Aggression is more likely in a couple when both partners are antisocial (Capaldi & Gorman-Smith), highlighting one of the challenges in intervention in schools with adolescent couples. Health promotion programs will be less successful for youth in these high-risk dyads if they only target one member of the couple. Such programs are unlikely to be successful precisely because the partner does not participate.

Person–Environment Interaction

Halpern reminds us that development involves biological factors that are related to, as well as interact with, social contexts and psychological processes. For example, as discussed earlier, Stattin and Magnusson (1990) found that early maturation in females lead some of these females into early dating with older male peers, which, in turn, put them on a life path leading to early marriage and lower educational attainment. Other person–enviroment interactions might result from the developmental mismatch experienced by many adolescents as they move from elementary school into middle school and then into high school. Both Eccles and her colleagues (e.g., Eccles et al., 1993) and Simmons and Blyth (1987) have shown that some youth, particularly low achieving youth and early developing girls, are at increased risk of declining school engagement and achievement following these school transitions. During the earlier adolescent years, these youth may be particularly susceptible to the negative influences of premature sexual and romantic relationships. School-based and out-of-school programs that provide both activities in which these youth can feel successful and valued and educational experiences related to managing their own sexual and romantic lives could be very important for these young people.

GENDER

Gender is a theme in several of the chapters. For example, Furman and Shaffer (chap. 1, this volume) discuss how the phenomenon of gender intensification (i.e., the increasing differentiation of expected gender roles for males and females) can be reinforced in romantic partnerships, or in the quest for a partner. An older study (see Algier & McCormick, 1983) illustrates this point very well. In this study, both male and female participants rated how they thought the other sex expected them to behave as well as how they actually wanted their dates to behave. Both males and females had much more gender-role stereotyped views of how they thought the opposite sex expected them to behave on a date than either gender actually indicated on the items assessing their own expectations about how they would like their dates to behave. These overly stereotyped expectations of what the other gender wants can lead both males and females to behave in an exaggerated sex-typed manner in the early stages of heterosexual dating. Educational programs that involve self-assessments about expectations and then shared discussion of how exaggerated each sex's views of the opposite sex's expectations are could help correct some of these gender stereotyped misperceptions and the associated inauthentic behavior on dates.

Closely related to the role of gender stereotypes in romantic relationships is the research on conflict reviewed by Shulman (chap. 5). Consistent with gender stereotypes, Shulman highlights research that indicates gender imbalances in power and influence in adolescent relationships, especially in regard to sexuality. Young women are more likely to be the one who "gives in" to a male partner's sexual advances because they believe this is expected in order to both maintain the relationship and to increase the level of emotional intimacy in the relationship. Educational programs that make both males and females aware of how gender role stereotypes influence this dance of intimacy might help both sexes overcome some of the pressures associated with adolescents' desire to both please their partners and to be seen by the partner as romantically competent.

Gender role stereotypes are also important in same-sex relationships, not because of a gender imbalance of power or roles, but because of the concordance of gender roles. As Diamond (chap. 4, this volume) points out, there is evidence that gender differences in relationship behavior can be magnified in same-sex partnerships. How are emotional intimacy and sexual initiation negotiated in the absence of differentiated gender role norms? The lack of social scripts for same-sex relationships can present both a challenge and an opportunity for sexual minority youth. Early dating experiences may occur in a context of uncertainty about how same-sex dating differs from opposite-sex dating (Diamond, Savin-Williams, & Dubé, 1999). Without the differentiated gender-role proscriptions of conventional opposite-sex romance scripts, gay and lesbian adolescents may have more freedom to interpret and express their roles within relationships based on their individual perspectives and desires.

We discussed another example of the ways in which gender is important earlier in conjunction with our discussion of the Stattin and Magnusson work (1990). The long-term consequences of gender stereotyped interactions in romantic relationships can be quite different for males and females. Often these consequences are more negative for females. For example, because teen mothers are still more likely to accept the responsibility for their children than teen fathers, the cost in terms of adult educational and occupational attainment of having a child during adolescence is usually greater for young women than young men (Furstenberg, Brooks-Gunn, & Morgan, 1987). Similarly, the likelihood of being pulled into an older and less achievement oriented peer group is much greater for early maturing girls than early maturing boys due to fact that older males are more likely to want to date younger females than older females are to want to date younger males. Finally, getting caught up in the traditional female romantic role is more likely to lead young women to lower their educational and occupational aspirations than getting caught up in the traditional male romantic role is for young men. In fact, getting caught up in this role may lead young men to adopt increased educational and occupational aspirations and engagement.

Taking a different perspective, Tracy et al. (chap. 6, this volume) point out that young women report experiencing more negative and fewer positive emotions than young men in their sexual experiences regardless of their attachment style. This finding is consistent with work reports from a large national study (Add Health) that found that girls are more vulnerable to the negative effects of romantic relationships than boys (Joyner & Udry, 2000). In this study, those adolescents, particularly those young women, who became romantically involved over the course of a year experienced greater increases in depression. The disadvantage for the young women was not limited to negative emotions—those young women who became romantically involved experienced decreases in their happiness as well.

The role of violence in dating and romantic relationships is another area in which gender and gender roles are very important. There is an ongoing debate in the domestic violence literature about the gender symmetry of relationship violence perpetration. On the one hand, there is evidence that men and women can be equally violent in intimate relationships, particularly during arguments in which one or both partners lash out physically at the other (Johnson & Ferraro, 2000). This type of relationship violence does not escalate, and has been called "common couple violence" by Johnson (2001). On the other hand, there is a heavily male type of violence ("intimate terrorism"), which is much more likely to escalate, consistent with the motive to control or subdue one's partner, rooted in patriarchal ideas about the relationships between men and women (Johnson & Ferraro, 2000). Intimate terrorism is less likely to be reciprocal, and is more likely to involve serious injury.

The distinction between types of violence makes it clear that there are likely to be multiple paths to relational violence, and education and intervention efforts may be differentially successful in preventing these types of violence. Johnson (2001) has suggested that for common couple violence, communication and anger management skills might be appropriate targets. We discuss this approach in the relationship skills section to follow. The suggestions are less clear for prevention of intimate terrorism. The man's attitude about controlling the female partner may be one area to consider. Capaldi and Gorman-Smith (chap. 10, this volume) describe findings indicating that adolescent males' hostile talk about girls and women predict partner aggression in young adulthood. One suggested intervention to prevent aggression toward female partners is to counter and prevent hostile attitudes and statements about girls and young women, particularly among antisocial males (Capaldi & Gorman-Smith).

AN EDUCATIONAL AGENDA

Taken together, the chapters on normative adolescent romantic relationships and sexual behavior illustrate that negotiating the pathway to successful adult relationships and sexuality involves adolescents' building relationship skills as well as developing romantic and sexual identities. Educators can facilitate the acquisition of these important emotional and interpersonal capabilities in at least three ways: interpersonal relationships skills programs, sexuality and relationship education, and opportunity provision for safe exploration of relationships for sexual minority youth.

Relationship Skill Programs

Destructive adolescent relationship patterns can set the stage for later family difficulties (Shulman, chap. 5, this volume), and are therefore important to target before the cycle is integrated into adolescents' schema of how relationships operate. Educational efforts targeting conflict resolution and negotiation should offer opportunities to improve communication in the context of disagreements, enhance interpersonal understanding, strengthen social skills, and monitor behavior (Shulman, chap. 5). Conflict management skills are a part of the Safe Dates Project (Capaldi & Gorman-Smith, chap. 10; Seefeldt et al., chap. 7), and together with changing social norms about dating violence and decreasing gender stereotyping, these program components predicted decreases in perpetration of psychological abuse, physical and sexual violence. Given the bidirectional violence Capaldi and Gorman-Smith (chap. 10) report in their sample, a decrease in perpetrating by one partner may result in lower levels of aggression in adolescent couples. However, they point out the need for a sustained effort over time with both partners.

Because effective relationship functioning requires both interpersonal skills and self-beliefs of efficacy to use those skills, programs should include educational modules that facilitate the consolidation of a sense of competence for all participants. Programs with such a focus should not only help to prevent aggression in adolescent relationships, but also promote such positive relationship qualities as communication and support. Such content might satisfy Furman and Shaffer's suggestion that we go beyond anatomy and contraception in sex education classes, and address relationship issues (chap. 1). Furthermore, a number of the chapters in this volume highlight the need for the content of all relationship education programs to be sensitive to the gender, sexual orientation, relationship context, attachment style, mental health, and developmental level of the students.

Sex Education

There are certainly structural barriers to the provision of developmentally appropriate and facilitative romantic and sex education. Some worry that frank discussions and provision of information will result in earlier sexual experimentation, despite the evidence to the contrary (Kirby, 2001; Russell & Andrews, in press). Conservative coalitions lobby educational policymakers to resist any discussions of sexuality with youth. Federal funding for education in the area of sexuality has been focused away from contraception with the proscriptions of the Personal Responsibilities and Work Opportunity Reconciliation Act of 1996 that provides millions of dollars each year for abstinence-only education, and bans the mention of contraceptives in those educational programs, except to describe their risks (Wilcox, 1999). Despite the lack of compelling evidence that this type of sex education is effective in changing behavior, President Bush has expanded the funding for teaching abstinence in his 2003 budget proposal, that would raise federal spending on "abstinence only" education by $33 million, to $135 million.

In 1999, a nationally representative survey of secondary school teachers found that 23% of sexuality education teachers taught abstinence as the only way to avoid pregnancy and STDs, up from 2% in 1988 (Darroch, Landry, & Singh, 2000). These numbers are consistent with a 1998 survey of public school district superintendents that showed that of the 69% of districts that have a policy to teach sexuality education, 14% cover abstinence as one option for adolescents in a broader program, 51% promote abstinence as the preferred option, and 35% teach abstinence as the only option outside of marriage (Landry, Kaeser, & Richards, 1999). The lack of sound education on contraception and prevention of STDs and HIV is not developmentally appropriate given the prevalence of sexually active adolescents, particularly in high schools. Furthermore, a review of nine of the fear-based, abstinence-only-until-marriage curricula, conducted by the Sexuality Information and Education Council of the United States (SIECUS, 2001) indicated that the programs reinforced stereotypical views about gender, placing primary responsibility for maintaining sexual limits on girls. Moreover, the focus on abstinence until marriage is heterosexist, and does not meet developmental needs of sexual minority youth.

Teachers were less likely in 1999 than in 1988 to say that sexuality education classes should cover sexual orientation in Grade 7 or earlier (39% in 1999 vs. 54% in 1988) or by the end of Grade 12 (78% in 1999 vs. 95% in 1988) (Darroch et al., 2000). The conservative shift in the teachers' beliefs is also reflected in their behavior—the proportion of sexuality education teachers covering sexual orientation decreased sharply from 1988 to 1999 (69% to 51%). Given that positive feelings about teachers play an important role in mediating the school troubles experienced by sexual minority youth (Russell, Seif, & Truong, 2001), these increasingly missed opportunities for teachers to be supportive and affirming are likely to contribute to further marginalization of sexual minority students.

These shortcomings in sexuality education are not new—they were well described in Fine's (1988) summary of her ethnographic study of sex education in which she described how the anti-sex rhetoric of public school sexuality education suppressed a discourse of female sexual desire and explicitly privileged married heterosexuality over other practices of sexuality. The most recent data suggest that the climate has worsened for young women and sexual minority students since Fine's report.

How can we do a better job preparing youth to develop self-understanding and make responsible decisions about such an important aspect of identity and experience? Welsh and colleagues recommend that school-based health education programs consider both the joys and the challenges of adolescent romantic relationships. In particular, to prevent depression, they suggest that curriculum include adaptive coping strategies for the especially difficult aspects of relationships including unreciprocated love, infidelity, and breaking up. A positive and affirming curriculum would go even further if it focused on helping adolescents to understand their sexuality and sexual identity, and emphasizing their role as active agents in their own sexual lives.

Opportunity Provision

Key to successful creation and consolidation of an identity is the opportunity to explore different roles and identities. Students with opposite sex attractions have many arenas in which to pursue such self-discovery in the domains of relationships and sexuality. As Diamond suggests, we also need contexts for sexual minority youth to explore their sexual identity—to discuss relationships and meet others who share their sexual orientations and to develop a supportive network of sexual minority peers. Russell (in press) has highlighted the importance of Gay–Straight Alliances in high schools, not only for providing support and advocacy for sexual minority youth in schools, but also for their educational efforts, not just for members, but for other students, teachers, and administrators. Such organizations may facilitate Diamond's goal that educators understand the diversity of sexual minority students and resist making assumptions about the romantic interests of all students.

Teacher Education and Preparation

Beyond direct educational efforts with the adolescents, it is important to consider the needs of those who teach and advise them. Educators and parents should also receive more normative information about teenagers' relationships (Furman), as well as guidance in how to deal with the emotions that may accompany adolescent relationships (Welsh et al., chap. 8). Teacher training in sex education may be another area to target, and SIECUS (National Guidelines Task Force, 1996) has recommended 36 topics on sexual health and responsibility in their *Guidelines for Comprehensive Sexuality Education: Kindergarten–12th Grade.*

This volume has highlighted the importance of romantic relationships and sexuality for adolescent development. The chapters provide compelling evidence to guide educational efforts for youth. Above all, they remind us of the importance of examining the developmental appropriateness of curricula offered to youth, and the limited likelihood of success if the needs of individuals are not considered.

ACKNOWLEDGMENTS

The writing of this chapter was funded by grants from the Spencer Foundation and the William T. Grant Foundation to Bonnie Barber and Jacquelynne Eccles. We are grateful to Jenifer McGuire, Stephen Russell, and Janine Zweig for their helpful advice and comments. The views expressed in this chapter are those of the authors.

REFERENCES

Algier, E. R., & McCormick, N. (1983). *Changing boundaries: Gender roles and sexual behavior.* Palo Alto, CA: Mayfield Press.

American Association of University Women. (1993). *Hostile hallways: The AAUW survey on sexual harassment in America's schools.* Washington, DC: Author.

American Association of University Women. (2001). *Hostile hallways: Bullying, easing, and sexual harassment in school.* Washington, DC: Author.

Belansky, E. S. (1994). *Predicting women's marital and family choices: Understanding the roles of self-concepts of ability, gender-role traditionality, peers, and values.* Unpublished dissertation, University of Colorado, Boulder, CO.

Bronfenbrenner, U. (1979). *The ecology of human development: Experiments by nature and design.* Cambridge, MA: Harvard University Press.

Collins, W. A. (2002, April). *More than myth: The developmental significance of romantic relationships during adolescence.* Presidential address delivered to the Society for Research on Adolescence, New Orleans.

Darroch, J. E., Landry, D. J., & Singh, S. (2000). Changing emphases in sexuality education in U.S. public secondary schools, 1988–1999. *Family Planning Perspectives, 32,* 204–211.

Diamond, L. M., Savin-Williams, & Dubé, E. M. (1999). Sex, dating, passionate friendships, and romance: Intimate peer relations among lesbian, gay, and bisexual adolescents. In W. Furman, B. Bradford Brown, & C. Feiring (Eds.), *The development of romantic relationships in adolescence* (pp. 175–210). Cambridge, UK: Cambridge University Press.

Downey, G., Bonica, C., & Rincon, C. (1999). Rejection sensitivity and adolescent romantic relationships. In W. Furman, B. B. Brown, & C. Feiring (Eds.), *The development of romantic relationships in adolescence* (pp. 148–174). Cambridge, UK: Cambridge University Press.

Eccles, J. S., Midgley, C., Wigfield, A., Miller Buchanan, C., Reuman, D. Flanagan, C., & Mac Iver, D., (1993). Development during adolescence: The impact of stage/environment fit on young adolescents' experiences in schools and in families. *American Psychologist, 48,* 90–101.

Epstein, J. (1983). The effect of friends on achievement and affective outcomes. In J. Epstein & N. Karwait (Eds.), *Friends in school* (pp. 177–200). New York: Academic Press.

Erikson, E. H. (1968). *Identity: Youth and crisis.* New York: Norton.

Fine, M. (1988). Sexuality, schooling, and adolescent females: The missing discourse of desire. *Harvard Educational Review, 58,* 29–53.

Furstenberg, F. F., Jr., Brooks-Gunn, J., & Morgan, S. P. (1987). *Adolescent mothers in later life.* Cambridge, UK: Cambridge University Press.

Graber, J. A., Brooks-Gunn, J., & Galen, B. R. (1998). Betwixt and between: Sexuality in the context of adolescent transitions. In R. Jessor (Ed.), *New perspectives on adolescent risk behavior.* Cambridge, UK: Cambridge University Press.

Hershberger, S. L., & D'Augelli, A. R. (1995). The impact of victimization on the mental health and suicidality of lesbian, gay, and bisexual youths. *Developmental Psychology, 31,* 65–74.

Horney, J., Osgood, D. W., & Marshall, I. H. (1995). Criminal careers in the short-term: Intra-individual variability in crime and its relation to local life circumstances. *American Sociological Review, 60,* 655–673.

Johnson, M. P. (2001). Conflict and control: Symmetry and asymmetry in domestic violence. In A. Booth, A. C. Crouter, & M. Clements (Eds.), *Couples in conflict* (pp. 95–104). Mahwah, NJ: Lawrence Erlbaum Associates.

Johnson, M. P., & Ferraro, K. (2000). Research on domestic violence in the 1990s: Making distinctions. *Journal of Marriage and the Family, 62,* 948–963.

Jozefowicz, D., Colarossi, L., Arbreton, A., Eccles, J., & Barber, B. (2000). Junior high school predictors of high school drop out, movement into alternative educational settings, and high school graduation: Implications for dropout prevention. *School of Social Work Journal, 25*(1), 30–44.

Joyner, K., & Udry, R. (2000). You don't bring me anything but down: Adolescent romance and depression. *Journal of Health and Social Behavior, 41,* 369–391.

Kirby, D. (2001). *Emerging answers: Research findings on programs to reduce teen pregnancy (Summary).* Washington, DC: National Campaign to Prevent Teen Pregnancy.

Koch, P. B. (1993). Promoting healthy sexual development during early adolescence. In R. Lerner (Ed.), *Early adolescence: Perspectives on research, policy, and intervention* (pp. 311–314). Hillsdale, NJ: Lawrence Erlbaum Associates.

Landry, D. J., Kaeser, L., & Richards, C. L. (1999). Abstinence promotion and the provision of information about contraception in public school district sexuality education policies. *Family Planning Perspectives, 31,* 280–286.

Larson, R. W., Clore, G. L., & Wood, G. A. (1999). The emotions of romantic relationships: Do they wreak havoc on adolescents? In W. Furman, B. B. Brown, & C. Feiring (Eds.), *The development of romantic relationships in adolescence* (pp. 19–49). Cambridge, UK: Cambridge University Press.

National Guidelines Task Force. (1996). *Guidelines for comprehensive sexuality education: Kindergarten–12th grade.* New York: Sexuality Information and Education Council of the United States.

Pickles, A., & Rutter, M. (1991). Statistical and conceptual models of "turning points" in developmental processes. In D. Magnusson, L. R. Bergman, G. Rudinger, & B. Torestad (Eds.), *Problems and methods in longitudinal research: Stability and change* (pp. 133–165). Cambridge, UK: Cambridge University Press.

Russell, S. T. (in press). Queer in America: Sexual minority youth and citizenship. *Applied Developmental Science.*

Russell, S. T., & Andrews, N. S. (in press). Adolescent sexuality and positive youth development. In D. Perkins, L. Borden, & K. Villarruel (Eds.), *Positive youth development: Beacons, challenges, and opportunities.*

Russell, S. T., Seif, H., & Truong, N. L. (2001). School outcomes of sexual minority youth in the United States: Evidence from a national study. *Journal of Adolescence, 24,* 111–127.

Sampson, R. J., & Laub, J. H. (1993). *Crime in the making: Pathways and turning point through life.* Cambridge, MA: Harvard University Press.

Sexuality Information and Education Council of the United States. (2001). Toward a sexually healthy America: Abstinence-only-until-marriage programs that try to keep our youth "scared chaste." New York: Author.

Simmons, R. G., & Blyth, D. A. (1987). *Moving into adolescence: The impact of pubertal change and school context.* Hawthorn, NY: Aldine de Gruyter.

Stattin, H., & Magnusson, D. (1990). *Pubertal maturation in female development.* Hillsdale, NJ: Lawrence Erlbaum Associates.

Stone, M. R., Barber, B. L., & Eccles, J. S. (2000, March). *Adolescent "crowd" clusters: An adolescent perspective on persons and patterns.* Paper presented at the biennial meeting of the Society for Research on Adolescence, Chicago, IL.

Wilcox, B. L. (1999). Sexual obsessions: Public policy and adolescent girls. In N. Johnson, M. Roberts, & J. Worrell (Eds.), *Beyond appearance: A new look at adolescent girls* (pp. 333–354). Washington, DC: American Psychological Association.

16

Adolescent Romantic and Sexual Behavior: What We Know and Where We Go From Here

Paul Florsheim

University of Utah

In my work as clinician with an exclusively adolescent clientele, romantic relations are a prominent theme. I regularly struggle with what I can say and do that will be useful and developmentally supportive. In a recent session with a 17-year-old gay adolescent who I see in an outpatient setting, we focused on his reluctance to become involved romantically or to even have male friends until he leaves home because he doesn't want to upset his mother, who knows and disapproves of his sexual orientation. On the same day, working with a group of adolescents in co-ed residential treatment for substance abuse, we (the group) focused on two members who had been surreptitiously kissing and touching in the laundry room for several weeks. With my outpatient client, I challenged him to consider that maybe he was using his mother as an excuse to avoid intimacy and to forestall dealing more concretely with what it means to be gay. With my group, I tried to gently suggest that the romantic relationship between the two group members was counter-therapeutic; that the young woman was looking for a domineering male to validate her and help her avoid feelings of despair and self-loathing, re-enacting old patterns established with previous men in her life. The young man was eager to accommodate her wishes.

In both situations, I would like to believe that my interventions were based on a solid understanding of clinical theory, the particular circumstances of my clients, and the role of romantic relations in adolescent developmental and psychopathological processes. Unfortunately, how I talk with my adolescent clients about their romantic relations is not well informed by research or clinical theory. I am not confident that I know how to best help my adolescent clients move forward in their interpersonal relations toward satisfying adult relationships, higher levels of intimacy, and more stable and enduring commitments.

The chapters included in this volume were selected to address romantic relations among developmentally normal and at-risk populations of adolescents. The effort to consider both typical and atypical populations together was intended to help clarify the distinction between normal or healthy and dysfunctional or maladaptive romantic relations. Although such distinctions are almost always imperfect and problematic, the effort to make them is necessary if we are to help adolescents develop the skills to make positive romantic relationships. I begin this chapter with a discussion of the difficulties involved in delineating healthy from dysfunctional romantic relations. In the second section, I outline some core themes covered by the authors contributing to this volume. In the last section, I discuss some of the practical (e.g., clinical and educational) implications of these cores themes.

DIFFERENTIATING BETWEEN HEALTHY AND DYSFUNCTIONAL ROMANTIC RELATIONSHIPS ISN'T GOING TO BE EASY

When it comes to adolescent romantic and sexual behavior, the question of what is normal or adaptive is not easy to answer for a variety of reasons. One difficulty is that our expectations about adult romance have changed over time, as indicated by the dramatic increases in divorce and out-of-wedlock childbirth over the past 40 years (Modell, 1989; Mott, 1993). It seems that these changes must have had a trickle-down effect on the romantic expectations and behaviors of adolescents, but the impact is not clear. If we assume that social norms and values pertaining to romantic relations are still in flux, it is likely that our children and their children will have different sets of standards for evaluating the quality of their romantic relationships. Such cohort effects seem like obstacles to those seeking to discover enduring principles for understanding and guiding psychological processes. However, the changing face of adolescent romance only underscores the importance (and the urgency) of collecting data that will allow us to track trends and fluctuations and determine their meaning and direction.

A *second* difficulty is that most dysfunctional relationships are likely to include some positive elements, and most healthy relations are likely to include some conflict and unhappiness. Although developmentalists currently regard adolescent romance as a normative, adaptive learning experience, it is often very painful (Collins, 2002; Welsh et al., chap. 8, this volume). As Shulman indicates in chapter 5, conflict in close relationships is expected and can help partners develop clearer boundaries, negotiate their respective roles, and learn to achieve a more individuated and perhaps more satisfying level of intimacy.

Thus, it is very difficult to tease apart negative emotions associated with a normative adolescent romance from psychological symptoms associated with a dysfunctional relationship, except in the extreme (Joyner & Udry, 2000).

When we consider romance from a developmental perspective, we can see that the process of learning how to engage in romantic and sexual relations unfolds over many years (Collins, Hennighausen, Schmit, & Sroufe, 1997; Conger, Cui, Bryant, & Elder, 2000; Moore, Driscoll, & Lindberg, 1998). From this perspective the finding that novices report more problems (regardless of their age at initiation) makes sense because they are struggling to master a new and particularly difficult developmental challenge (Cantor & Sanderson, 1998; Zimmer-Gombeck, Siebenbruner, & Collins, 2001). However, developmental theory also reminds us that some adolescents are better prepared to engage in this process than others. For example, adolescents who are particularly sensitive to rejection are more likely to experience relationship problems and distress associated with relationship problems than their less sensitive, more interpersonally resilient peers (Downey, Bonica, & Rincon, 1999; Welsh et al., chap. 8, this volume; Tracy et al., chap. 6, this volume).

A *third* difficulty in differentiating normal and abnormal romantic relations is that our current views of adolescent romantic relations are highly constrained by social and cultural expectations. In his commentary chapter, Savin-Williams (chap. 13., this volume) makes the point that most of the chapters in this volume rely too heavily on a heterocentric perspective on adolescent romance. There are several unfortunate consequences of remaining comfortably heterocentric in our thinking about adolescent sexuality. First, we know too little about what is normative among gay, lesbian, and bisexual youth. Second, we have overemphasized the pathological among sexual minority youth, coming close to pathologizing same-sex behavior in general. Third, we have failed to adequately address the phenomenon of same-sex behavior and same-sex longings among youth who identify themselves as heterosexuals, ignoring the sometimes fuzzy distinction between gay and straight. Finally, and perhaps most importantly from a clinical perspective, rigid definitions and expectations about sexuality can make life very difficult for those youth who are exploring their own. As Diamond suggests in chapter 4, our conceptual understanding of adolescent sexuality needs to catch up with the richness and diversity of our data on individual adolescent lives.

It is unfortunate that this volume is also quite ethnocentric. The chapters are based on samples drawn from Westernized industrialized nations (U.S., Israel, Canada), where views of adolescent romance are strongly influenced by somewhat contradictory messages conveyed through the popular media, including the following: (a) having a boyfriend or girlfriend is socially desirable; (b) premarital sex is probably wrong but expected and normative; (c) a healthy romantic relationship is based in love; (d) it is good to date around and not get too serious with any one partner; (e) men and women occupy very distinctive roles in romantic relations but ought to be treated as equal; and (f) beauty is closely associated with mate value. The relevance of these assumptions about adolescent romance to other cultural groups has not been adequately examined. While we tend to assume that "love" and "sexual longing" is a universal human trait that cuts across most cultures, there is some evidence that how love and sex are experienced and negotiated among adults varies across cultural contexts (Coates, 1999; Dion & Dion, 1996; Hatfield & Rapson, 1993; Jankowiak & Fischer, 1998).

The problem of not knowing much about cultural or subgroup variation in romantic and sexual relations is pertinent to the problem of distinguishing what is normal from what is abnormal. There is some evidence that cultural groups differ with respect to "the basics" of adolescent romantic and sexual relations, including the age of initiation, the importance attributed to love, and the nature of romantic commitment (Carver, Joyner, & Udry, chap. 2, this volume; Doherty, Hatfield, Thompson, & Choo, 1994; Doljanac & Zimmerman, 1998; Feldman, Turner, & Araujo, 1999; Hatfield & Rapson, 1993; Upchurch, Aneshensel, Mudgal, & McNeely, 2001; Wu & Thomson, 2001). However, much of the work on the diversity of romantic and sexual behaviors has tended to emphasize problematic trends in subpopulations. Currently, the field is just beginning to build a framework for understanding how distinctions between healthy and pathological romantic relationships are influenced by cultural values and/or social circumstances. Clearly, the need for more research in this area is necessary if we are to avoid imposing our own culturally bound expectations onto others (Dion & Dion, 1996).

A *fourth* difficulty in differentiating normal from abnormal romantic relations is that there are methodological gaps in our understanding of adolescent romance. For example, much of the research on adolescent romantic relationships is based on data collected from one partner rather than from the dyad (Tabares & Gottman, chap. 14, this volume). Although subjective reports are an important component of the assessment process, the health of a relationship cannot be adequately evaluated solely on the basis of individual perceptions. For example, a young man with a history of violence against women may not provide all the information needed to evaluate the quality of his romantic relations. This example underscores the necessity of addressing the tension between objectivity and subjectivity in the assessment of adolescent romance and developing strategies for interpreting discrepancies between partner reports (Furman, Brown, & Feiring, 1999).

Another reason for studying dyads is that when a problem between romantic partners occurs, it is often the outcome of a complex interpersonal process.

We need to develop a clearer understanding of how partners reinforce one another's problem behaviors (Capaldi & Gorman-Smith, chap. 10, this volume; Fortenberry, chap. 11, this volume). For example, the decision to have unprotected sex is influenced by the attitudes and beliefs of both partners. Also, when violence occurs between romantic partners, it is often reciprocal. These observations suggest that researchers must carefully consider how interpersonal processes might contribute to the occurrence of risky behavior. Future research on adolescent romance is likely to benefit from incorporating methodologies developed for studying dyads, such as those described by Tabares and Gottman (this volume, chap. 14) and Seefeldt, Florsheim, and Benjamin (this volume, chap. 7).

A *fifth* problem facing researchers who want to distinguish between normal and abnormal aspects of adolescent sexuality is the political delicacy of the topic. Most school districts throughout the country are likely to prohibit researchers from asking questions about sex and romance. The current zeitgeist regarding adolescent sexuality and sexual behavior presents a formidable obstacle for researchers who are interested in collecting data form normative populations from the school system. Nonetheless, the research described in this volume and other recent volumes (Furman et al., 1999; Shulman & Collins, 1997) demonstrates that conducting such research is possible, despite the political challenges that researchers will inevitably face.

CURRENT THEMES IN THE STUDY OF ADOLESCENT ROMANTIC BEHAVIOR

Romance Is a Normative Component of Adolescence

It is during adolescence that we become biologically and socially primed to engage in romantic and sexually behavior (Halpern, chap. 3, this volume). Although many adolescents do not begin dating until late adolescence, we have evidence that about half the population of 15-year-olds report being involved in a romantic relationship (Carver, chap. 2, this volume). By the age of 17, more than half of adolescents have had sexual intercourse (Moore et al., 1998). Chapter 2, written by Carver, Joyner, and Udry, provides valuable information about what adolescent romance looks like at different developmental stages, but more information is needed about the range of romantic and sexual experiences among adolescents. As Diamond suggested in chapter 4 (this volume), we are still at a phase in our understanding of adolescent romance where our assessments of what is normal or typical is over-determined by social and cultural norms and under-informed by data. Furthermore, the information we have about what is typical or "expectable" romantic or sexual behavior does not fully or directly address the question of what is healthy.

Tracey, Shaver, Albino, and Cooper (chap. 6) approach the issue of defining healthy sexual relations by describing the sexual relationships of psychologically healthy (securely attached) adolescents. In their study, they found that securely attached adolescents were no more or less likely than insecure adolescents to have romantic relationships or to describe themselves as "in love." However, the motivations of securely attached youth for engaging in sexual relations were different from those of insecurely attached youth. For example, the securely attached adolescents were more likely than the insecure adolescents to regard sex as a means of expressing feelings of love rather than a way to avoid abandonment. Securely attached adolescents also reported their sexual experiences as more positive, more passionate, less negative, and less aggressive.

Examining the romantic and sexual behavior of secure, psychologically healthy adolescents brings us closer to an understanding of what constitutes a healthy romantic relationship. Approaching the issue from a different angle, Furman and Shaffer (this volume, chap. 1) suggest that one way to evaluate the health of a romantic relationship is to ask whether it facilitates or inhibits other aspects of each partner's development. For example, it might be useful to ask whether the relationship promotes (or at least does not inhibit) achievement orientation and the development of more mature relations with parents. This perspective seems consistent with other developmentally based theories of romantic love (Collins, 2002; Conger et al., 2000; Taradash, Connolly, Pepler, Craig, & Costa, 2001). It also underscores the point that adolescent romance might be considered an important developmental milestone, marking a shift toward a greater emphasis on intimacy and pair bonding. Most adolescents become increasingly fixated on the particular goal of finding a romantic partner. Indeed, romance has become so integral to how we think about adolescence that one wonders if the adolescent who fails to become romantically involved is developmentally "off-track."

Adolescent Romance Does Not Exist in a Developmental Vacuum

When an adolescent becomes involved in a romantic relationship, the development of that relationship is generally (but not perfectly) consistent with the quality of that adolescent's developmental history (Brown, 1999; Conger et al., 2000; Furman & Shafer, this volume; Tracy et al., this volume). The quality of the adolescent's family relations (including attachment security) and peer relations predicts the quality of his or her romantic and sexual relations (Collins et al., 1997; Conger et al., 2000; Connolly, Furman, & Konarski, 2000). Adolescents who have experienced high levels of conflict or instability in family or peer relations are more likely to repeat this pattern in their romantic liaisons by engaging in aggressive relationships and/or being unable to form close or intimate bonds with romantic partners. There is also evidence that adolescents who have a history of psychological problems (such as depression, aggression) are likely to exhibit these problems within the context of their close relations, including romantic relations (Welsh et al., chap. 8, this volume; Capaldi & Gorman-Smith, chap. 10, this volume).

The continuity in the quality of close relations across the life span and the link between individual psychopathology and dysfunctional romantic relationships illustrates the ontogenetic principle of development (Werner & Kaplan, 1968). It also helps to explain the transmission of dysfunctional interpersonal patterns across generations because hostile relations between a co-parenting couple tend to spill over into hostile parent–child relations, which in turn predict the development of emotional and behavior problem in children, and so on (Katz & Gottman, 1996). This persistence of dysfunction across generations raises the important question of how the cycle of dysfunction can be broken, and new interpersonal information can be introduced into developmental systems.

Romantic Relations Can Be Transformative

Despite the fact that there is a high degree of consistency across an adolescent's relations with his or her family, peers, and romantic partners, there is some evidence that romantic relations may be transformative. A central thesis of the chapter by Furman and Shaffer (this volume, chap. 1) is that adolescent romantic relationships often play an important role in how adolescents manage critical developmental tasks. In this respect, romantic relations can function to either heighten or diminish risk factors. For example, if an adolescent becomes romantically involved with someone who engages in risky behavior, he or she is more likely to engage in similarly risky behavior, regardless of predisposing factors. However, the opposite may also be true—an adolescent who is predisposed to engage in risky behavior and who becomes romantically involved with a more emotionally stable and cautious partner may "settle down."

Adolescent romantic relationships play a potentially important role in the developmental life cycle by challenging precedents set by the individual's attachment history and providing opportunities to "try out" new interpersonal behaviors. Because families often operate as relatively closed systems, close relationships that develop during adolescence may fulfill an important function simply by providing the adolescent with new interpersonal information. More specifically, romantic relationships may serve as "points of contrast" for the adolescent, moderating the influence of early attachment relationships on the individual's interpersonal-developmental trajectory.

Related to this point, in her chapter on biological factors, Halpern (this volume, chap. 3) argues against a biological deterministic perspective of adolescent sexual behavior. Despite the evidence that an adolescent's biological status (such as testosterone levels or onset of puberty) is likely to influence his or her sexual behavior (such as age at first coitus), sexual encounters are socially negotiated events, clearly influenced by the biological, psychological, and social status of both partners. Thus, who we choose to be our partner and how we choose to engage with that person can moderate the link between biological predisposition and social and psychological outcome.

Sex and Romance Can Be Dangerous

Despite the normative and adaptive role of adolescent romantic relations, there are several very serious risks associated with adolescent romance (Davies & Windle, 2000; Davila, Steinberg, Kachadourian, Cobb, & Fincham, 2002; Kotchick, Shaffer, & Forehand, 2001; Moore & Chase-Lansdale, 2001; Neemann, Hubbard, & Masten, 1995; Whaley, 1999). There is evidence that adolescents who are heavily involved in dating have lower levels of academic achievement and tend to report higher rates of psychological symptoms, especially if they are young (13–14 years old). In some cases, relationship problems are directly related to the development serious psychological problems (Joyner & Udry, 2000; Welsh et al., chap. 8, this volume). As indicated by Welsh et al. (chap. 8, this volume), romance can contribute to the development of a depression or make matters worse for adolescents who are already depressed. However, in most cases the link between romance and psychological distress is reciprocal; vulnerable adolescents are more likely to experience relationship problems, which in turn can increase depressive symptoms. As Capaldi and Gorman-Smith indicate (this volume, chap. 10), there is recent evidence that adolescent romantic partners engage in relatively (and alarmingly) high rates of interpersonal violence which can have severe physical and psychological consequences (Silverman, Raj, Mucci, & Hathaway, 2001). Also, adolescents are more likely than adults to engage in unprotected sex, which puts them at greater risk for contracting sexually transmitted diseases and unplanned pregnancies (Fortenberry, Chap. 11, this volume; Florsheim, Moore, & Edgington, chap. 12, this volume).

The level of risk associated with any romantic liaison depends on a mix of factors, including the relationship history of each partner, each partner's level of psychological dysfunction, and the quality of the relationship itself (Neemann et al., 1995). For decades we have been invested in treating adolescent psychological dysfunction by either focusing on the individual client or on his or her family. The growing body of evidence on the links between romantic relationships and psychological well-being (and dysfunction) suggests that we should invest more heavily in treatments that focus on the adolescent's romantic relations as a primary target for prevention and intervention.

PRACTICAL IMPLICATIONS

While it would be unusual for a clinician to treat an adolescent couple, most clinicians who work with teens regularly address romantic relationship problems indirectly through issues that arise in individual and family therapy. Therefore, clinicians need to know how to help their adolescent clients develop the skills to have healthy romantic relationships and the judgment to know when and how to get out of an unhealthy relationship. Similarly, most teachers and parents deal with issues related to adolescent sexuality on a daily basis, and yet are likely to feel constrained in their capacity to provide guidance or successfully intervene when problems arise. Adults often feel stumped by problems and issues posed by adolescents. Ironically, several clinical researchers have noted that high school students are a particularly good age group for early intervention or prevention efforts because they tend to be open to influence (Kazdin, 1993; Wekerle & Wolfe, 1998). This suggests that if programs were developed and implemented, adolescents would be receptive. In this section, I address the issue of how clinicians, parents, and educators might help adolescents to have safe and healthy romantic and sexual relationships.

If romantic relationships can have a transformative effect on the health and well-being of adolescents, then it is hard to avoid the issue of how we—as members of the adult world—can help ensure that the transformation is positive (Collins, 2002). As we begin to develop a clearer understanding the distinction between healthy and dysfunctional romantic relations and sexual practices among adolescents, it seems likely that there will be increased pressure to translate this knowledge into action. The notion that youth approach romantic relations at varying levels of risk suggests that we will need to target particular groups of youth with focused interventions (Coie, Watt, West, & Hawkins, 1994). For example, it seems likely that most (if not all) youth could benefit from programs that address basic relationship skills, such as how to talk about potentially uncomfortable issues (such as having safe sex, not wanting to have sex, or wanting to break up) with a romantic partner (Arnold, Smith Harrison, & Springer, 2000; Nitz, 1999; Rotheram-Borus, O'Keefe, Kracker,

& Foo, 2000). A more focused approach, such as a program designed to address relationship violence might be of most benefit to youth who have a history of aggressive behavior or victimization. Similarly, youth who have a history of depression or attachment problems may benefit from programs that help them address specific interpersonal deficits such as rejection sensitivity, as discussed in Welsh et al. (this volume, chap. 8) and Tracy et al. (this volume, chap. 6).

In their commentary chapter, Barber and Eccles (chap. 15) refer to three basic approaches to supporting positive romantic and sexual behaviors among adolescents. These approaches include sexuality and relationship education, interpersonal skills programs, and opportunity provision for safe exploration of relationships for sexual minority youth. Education-oriented approaches assume (or hope) that if adolescents are provided with information about relationships and sex, they will be better able to make informed, intelligent decisions about their own relationships. Some education programs are designed to provide "the facts," whereas others focus on developing "positive" values and attitudes regarding romantic and sexual relations. For example, STD prevention programs tend to inform adolescents about how particular diseases are transmitted and what they can do to prevent transmission. Abstinence programs tend to be value-oriented in the sense that they advocate a particular type of lifestyle.

The clear benefit of educational approaches is that many adolescents do not have the knowledge base to make informed decisions. There is some evidence that education-based approaches work, particularly for low-risk or universal populations. For example, Basen-Engquist et al. (2001) examined the effectiveness of *Safer Choices*, which is an education-based program designed to prevent STD, HIV, and pregnancy. They found that youth attending schools in which the Safer Choices program was administered reported using safer sex practices than youth attending matched control schools that did not administer the program. Although the strength of these effects diminished over time, this study demonstrates the potentially positive impact of education programs administered through the public school system on the risk behavior of high school students.

Providing information and guidance to adolescents is certainly a legitimate and potentially effective approach to preventing problem behavior and promoting healthy behavior among adolescents. However, such an approach can be perceived by adolescents as patronizing, paternalistic, or marginally relevant to their particular circumstances (e.g., boring). Several chapter authors have underscored the importance of developing interventions designed to help adolescents acquire the interpersonal skills necessary to protect themselves against harm (physical abuse, sexually transmitted diseases) and to successfully manage relationship challenges when they arise (conflict, pregnancy). These types of programs are based on the principles of action-learning, relying on exercises and group discussions (Wolfe et al., 1996; Foshee et al., 2000). For example, Wolfe and his colleagues (Wolfe et al., 1996) developed an 18-week program designed to facilitate "action-learning" in which small groups of youth are led through a series of exercises by two group leaders. Youth participants are encouraged to express their own points of view, explore alternative perspectives, examine their own communication styles, discuss the distinction between healthy and unhealthy relationships, and practice relationship skills, such as assertiveness and empathic listening. Although the effectiveness of this program has not been tested, the program as described in the manual is clearly conceptualized, thoughtfully developed, and seems very promising.

Programs designed to facilitate the development of interpersonal skills, like the one described by Wolfe et al. (1996), are few and far between. This is unfortunate because the developmental research strongly suggests that such programs could be tremendously useful in addressing many of the prevailing risks associated with adolescent romance. For example, a skill-building approach that focused on what to do and say in the "heat of the moment" may help prevent unwanted sex and unwanted pregnancies. A relationship-focused program may help pregnant adolescents and their partners navigate a successful transition to parenthood (Florsheim, Moore, & Edgington, chap. 12, this volume). Most expectant adolescents approach parenthood unprepared for making a lifelong commitment and unable to communicate effectively with their partners about conflicts and concerns. A skill-based approach could help expectant adolescents learn to argue constructively and/or to cooperate as co-parents even if their romantic liaison dissolves.

Barber and Eccles also note the importance of creating and supporting contexts in which adolescents can safely explore sensitive issues such as sexual orientation and same-sex attractions. More concretely, they underscore the role of educators in promoting organizations such as Gay–Straight Alliances that help legitimize the issue and provide a structure and environment that encourages healthy exploration. The approach of targeting the naturally occurring contexts of adolescents has been successfully utilized by at least two programs designed to promote safety in sexual and romantic relationships. The promising results reported by Foshee et al.'s (2001) *Safe Dates* program and Basen-Engquist et al.'s (2001) *Safer Choices* program demonstrate that it is possible to facilitate a positive peer culture among high school students.

Related to the idea of providing adolescents with a safe context for exploration, it may also be useful for some programs to target the more intimate interpersonal contexts of adolescents. There are some existing programs designed to help parents and their adolescent children communicate more effectively about issues related to sex (Meschke, Zentall, & Bartholomae, 2000). These programs were developed in response to research indicating that (a) the quality of parent–child communication is related to adolescent sexual behavior and (b) many parents are quite uncomfortable talking to their children about sex and romantic relations. The focus of these programs is to facilitate a positive exchange between parent and child regarding these highly sensitive and potentially volatile issues, helping both the parent and the adolescent communicate more effectively with each other.

Each of these approaches (educational, skill building, relationship building, and opportunity provision) is potentially useful. The success of any given approach varies depending on the needs and circumstances of the targeted population. For example, while an educational approach may be very useful for some issues (such as preventing the spread of sexually transmitted disease), they may be less useful for other, more skill-based issues (such as the prevention of relationship violence). Clinicians, educators, and parents should carefully consider their goals before deciding how to approach their audience.

We still have a great deal to learn about how romantic relationships and sexual behavior can either facilitate or inhibit the development of adolescents. If we are to develop effective strategies for helping adolescents with their romantic relationships, we will need to further clarify the distinction between adaptive and dysfunctional romantic relations, how psychopathology influences the development of romantic relations, and how dysfunctional relations might influence the development of psychological symptoms. Furthermore, we will need to explore these issues among diverse groups of adolescents if we are to avoid overgeneralizing the relevance of our findings. Although we still have a long way to go before clinicians, educators, and policymakers can speak confidently about how to promote the development of healthy adolescent relationships and begin to effectively intervene when problems occur, the chapters included in this volume bring us closer to those goals.

REFERENCES

Arnold, E. M., Smith, T. E., Harrison, D. F., & Springer, D. W. (2000). Adolescents' knowledge and beliefs about pregnancy: The impact of "ENABL." *Adolescence, 35,* 485–498.

Basen-Engquist, K., Coyle, K. K., Parcel, G. S., Kirby, D., Bansprach, S. W., Carvajal, S. C., & Baumler, E. (2001). Schoolwide effects of multicomponent HIV, STD, and pregnancy prevention program for high school students. *Health Education and Behavior, 28,* 166–185.

Brown, B. B. (1999). "You're going out with *who?*" Peer group influences on adolescent romantic relationships. In W. Furman, B. B. Brown, & C. Feiring (Eds.), *The development of romantic relationships in adolescence* (pp. 291–329). New York: Cambridge University Press.

Cantor, N., & Sanderson, C. A. (1998). The functional regulation of adolescent dating relationships and sexual behavior: An interaction of goals, strategies, and situations. In J. Heckhausen, & C. S. Dweck (Eds.), *Motivation and self-regulation across the life span* (pp. 185–215). New York: Cambridge University Press.

Coates, D. L. (1999). The cultured and culturing aspects of romantic experience in adolescence. In W. Furman, B. B. Brown, & C. Feiring (Eds.), *The development of romantic relationships in adolescence* (pp. 330–363). New York: Cambridge University Press.

Coie, J., Watt, N. F., West, S. G., Hawkins, J. D. (1994). The science of prevention: A conceptual framework and some directions for a national research program. *American Psychologist, 48*, 1013–1022.

Collins, W. A. (2002, April). *More than myth: The developmental significance of romantic relationships during adolescence.* Presidential Address delivered to the Society for Research on Adolescence, New Orleans.

Collins, W. A., Hennighausen, K. H., Schmit, D. T., & Sroufe, L. A. (1997). Developmental precursors of romantic relationships: A longitudinal analysis. In S. Shulman & W. A. Collins (Eds.), *Romantic relationships in adolescence: Developmental perspectives* (pp. 69–84). San Francisco: Jossey-Bass.

Conger, R. D., Cui, M. K., Bryant, C. M., & Elder, G. H., Jr. (2000). Competence in early adult romantic relationships: A developmental perspective on family influences. *Journal of Personality and Social Psychology, 79*, 224–237.

Connolly, J. A., Furman, W., & Konarski, R. (2000). The role of peers in the emergence of heterosexual romantic relationships in adolescence. *Child Development, 71*, 1395–1408.

Davies, P. T., & Windle, M. (2000). Middle adolescents' dating pathways and psychosocial adjustment. *Merrill-Palmer Quarterly, 46*, 90–118.

Davila, J., Steinberg, S. J., Kachadourian, L., Cobb, R., & Fincham, F. (2002, April). Early romantic experiences and depressive symptoms: Emerging depressogenic patterns. In D. Welsh (Chair), *When love hurts: Adolescent romantic relationships and depressive symptoms.* Symposium at the conference of the Society for Research on Adolescence, New Orleans, LA.

Dion, K. K., & Dion, K. L. (1996). Cultural perspectives on romantic love. *Personal Relationships, 3*, 5–17.

Doherty, R. W., Hatfield, E., Thompson, K., & Choo, P. (1994). Cultural and ethnic influences on love and attachment. *Personal Relationships, 1*, 391–398.

Doljanac, R. F., & Zimmerman, M. A. (1998). Psychosocial factors and high-risk sexual behavior: Race differences among urban adolescents. *Journal of Behavioral Medicine, 21*, 451–467.

Downey, G., Bonica, C., & Rincon, C. (1999). Rejection sensitivity and adolescent romantic relationships. In W. Furman, B. B. Brown, & C. Feiring (Eds.), *The development of romantic relationships in adolescence* (pp. 148–174). New York: Cambridge University Press.

Feldman, S. S., Turner, R. A., & Araujo, K. (1999). Interpersonal context as an influence on sexual timetables of youths: Gender and ethnic effects. *Journal of Research on Adolescence, 9*, 25–52.

Foshee, V. A., Bauman, K. E., Greene, W. F., Koch, G. G., Linder, G. F., & MacDougall, J. E. (2000). The safe dates program: 1-year follow-up results. *American Journal of Public Health, 90*(10), 1619–1622.

Furman, W., Brown, B. B., & Feiring, C. (1999). Love is a many-splendored thing: Next steps for theory and research. In W. Furman, B. B. Brown, & C. Feiring (Eds.), *The development of romantic relationships in adolescence* (pp. 399–414). New York: Cambridge University Press.

Hatfield, E., & Rapson, R. L. (1993). Historical and cross-cultural perspectives on passionate love and sexual desire. *Annual Review of Sex Research, 4*, 67–97.

Jankowiak, W. R., & Fischer, E. F. (1998). A cross-cultural perspective on romantic love. In J. M.

Jenkins & K. Oatley (Eds.), *Human emotions: A reader* (pp. 55–62). Malden, MA: Blackwell Publishers.

Joyner, K., & Udry, J. R. (2000). You don't bring me anything but down: Adolescent romance and depression. *Journal of Health and Social Behavior, 41,* 369–391.

Katz, L. F., & Gottman, J. M. (1996). Spillover effects of marital conflict: In search of parenting and coparenting mechanisms. In J. P. McHale & P. Cowan (Eds.), *Understanding how family-level dynamics affect children's development: Studies of two-parent families* (pp. 57–76). San Francisco, CA: Jossey-Bass.

Kazdin, A. (1993). Adolescent mental health: Prevention and treatment programs. *American Psychologist, 48*(2), 127–141.

Kotchick, B. A., Shaffer, A., & Forehand, R. (2001). Adolescent sexual risk behavior: A multisystem perspective [Special issue]. *Clinical Psychology Review, 21,* 493–519.

Meschke, L. L., Zentall, S. R., & Bartholomae, S. (2000). Adolescent sexuality and parent–adolescent processes: Promoting healthy teen choices. *Family Relations: Interdisciplinary Journal of Applied Family Studies, 49,* 143–154.

Modell, J. (1989). *Into one's own: From youth to adulthood in the United States 1920–1975.* Berkeley, CA: University of California Press.

Moore, K. A., Driscoll, A. K., & Lindberg, L. D. (1998). *A statistical portrait of adolescent sex, contraception, and childbearing.* Washington, DC: National Campaign to Prevent Teen Pregnancy.

Moore, M. R., & Chase-Landsdale, P. L. (2001). Sexual intercourse and pregnancy among African American girls in high-poverty neighborhoods: The role of family and perceived community environment. *Journal of Marriage and Family, 63,* 1146–1157.

Mott, F. (1990). When is father really gone? Paternal–child contact in father absent homes. *Demography, 27,* 499–517.

Neemann, J., Hubbard, J., & Masten, A. S. (1995). The changing importance of romantic relationship involvement to competence from late childhood to late adolescence. *Development and Psychopathology, 7,* 727–750.

Nitz, K. (1999). Adolescent pregnancy prevention: A review of interventions and programs. *Clinical Psychology Review, 19,* 457–471.

Rotheram-Borus, M. J., O'Keefe, Z., Kracker, R., & Foo, H.-H. (2000). Prevention of HIV among adolescents. *Prevention Science, 1,* 15–30.

Shulman, S., & Collins, W. (Eds.). (1997). Romantic relationships in adolescence: Developmental perspectives. In W. Damon (Series Ed.), *New directions in child development* (No. 78). San Francisco: Jossey-Bass.

Silverman, J. G., Raj, A., Mucci, L. A., & Hathaway, J. E. (2001). Dating violence against adolescent girls and associated substance use, unhealthy weight control, sexual risk behavior, pregnancy, and suicidality [Special Issue]. *JAMA: Journal of the American Medical Association, 286,* 572–579.

Taradash, A., Connolly, J. A., Pepler, D., Craig, W., & Costa, M. (2001). The interpersonal context of romantic autonomy in adolescence. *Journal of Adolescence, 24,* 365–377.

Upchurch, D. M., Aneshensel, C. S., Mudgal, J., & McNeely, C. S. (2001). Sociocultural contexts of time to first sex among Hispanic adolescents. *Journal of Marriage and Family, 63,* 1158–1169.

Wekerle, C., & Wolfe, D. (1998). Windows for preventing child and partner abuse: Early childhood and adolescence. In P. K. Trickett & C. Schellenbach (Eds.), *Violence against children in the family and the community* (pp. 339–369). Washington, DC: American Psychological Association.

Werner, H., & Kaplan, B. (1963). *Symbol formation: An organismic-developmental approach to language and the expression of thought.* New York: Wiley.

Whaley, A. L. (1999). Preventing the high-risk sexual behavior of adolescents: Focus on HIV/AIDS transmission, unintended pregnancy, or both? *Journal of Adolescent Health, 24,* 376–382.

Wolfe, D. A., Wekerle, C., Gough, R., Reitzel-Jaffe, D., Grasley, C., Pittman, A. L., Lefebvre, L., & Stumpf, J. (1996). *The youth relationships manual: A group approach with adolescents for the prevention of woman abuse and the promotion of health relationships.* Thousand Oaks, CA: Sage Publications.

Wu, L. L., & Thomson, E. (2001). Race differences in family experience and early sexual initiation: Dynamic models of family structure and family change. *Journal of Marriage and Family, 63,* 682–696.

Zimmer-Gembeck, M. J., Siebenbruner, J., & Collins, W. A. (2001). Diverse aspects of dating: associations with psychosocial functioning from early to middle adolescence. *Journal of Adolescence, 24,* 313–336.

Author Index

A

Abbey, A., 231, 232, *235*
Abidin, R., 308, *318*
Abidin, R. R., 308, 309, *318*
Abma, J., 11, *18*
Abma, J. C., 11, *18,* 297, *322*
Abraham, C., 284, *296*
Achenbach, T. M., 253, *272*
Adams, G., 191, *207*
Adams, P. F., 28, 29, *52*
Adcock, A. G., 196, *206*
Adelson, J., 25, *53*
Agnew, C. R., 70, *79, 81*
Agostinelli, G., 199, *210*
Agyei, Y., 87, *102,* 332, *336*
Ainsworth, M. D. S., viii, *xii,* 139, *156,* 214, *235*
Akman, D., 216, *235*
Alapack, R. A., 109, *132*
Aldarondo, E., 266, *272*
Aldenderfer, R. K., 305, *319*
Alexander, E., 10, *18*
Alfano, M. S., 175, *182*
Algier, E. R., 362, *368*
Allen, J. P., 196, 197, *206, 209*
Allen, P. A., 110, 118, *131*
Allison, K. W., 51, *53*
Alon, E., 114, 117, *135,* 347, *354*
Alper, T. G., 96, *105*
Alvarado, L. E., 297, *319*
Anderson, D., 90, *102*
Anderson, D. A., 86, *102*
Anderson, E., 51, *52*
Andreoli-Mathie, V., 198, *210*
Andrews, D. W., 248, 256, *273*
Andrews, J. A., 170, *181,* 254, *272*
Andrews, N. S., 366, *370*

Aneshensel, C. S., 374, *384*
Antonucci, T. C., 298, *319*
Appel, A. E., 227, *235*
Appelbaum, M. I., 299, *319*
Appleman, D., 28, *54*
Araujo, K., 374, *383*
Arbreton, A., 358, *369*
Archer, J., 247, 249, *272*
Arends, E., 229, *237*
Arias, I., 266, *276*
Arnett, J. J., 137, *156*
Arnold, E. M., 379, *382*
Aro, H., 7, *18*
Arriaga, X. B., 119, *134,* 180, *182,* 220, 243, 270, *274*
Asai, M., 74, *82*
Asmussen, L., 137, *158,* 192, *209*
Astrom, M., 74, *83*
Attie, I., 25, 28, *54, 80*
Avery-Leaf, S., 223, 224, 226, *235, 236*
Avgoustis, E., 228, *235*
Ayduk, O., 175, *181*

B

Babcock, J., 259, 264, *275,* 347, *354*
Backlund, B. A., 171, *182,* 200, 204, *208*
Bacon, P. L., 297, 300, *320*
Bailey, J. M., 71, 79, 88, *102,* 332, *336*
Baker, S. W., 62, 65, *82*
Balach, L., 17, *18*
Balk, S. J., 317, *322*
Bandura, A.128, *131,* 217, *235,* 280, 291, *293*
Bangdiwala, S., 220, 243, 270, *274*
Bankston, C. L., 50, *56*
Bansprach, S. W., 380, 381, *382*
Barbee, A., 23, 25, 45, *56*

Barber, B., 358, *369*
Barber, B. L., 357, *370*
Barker, R. C., 65, *83*
Barling, J., 266, *276*
Barr, D. J., 333, *336*
Barth, R. J., 96, *103*
Bartholomae, S., 382, *384*
Bartholomew, K., 126, *131,* 137, 140, 148, 155, *156, 157, 159*
Bartle-Haring, S., 119, 128, *134*
Basen-Engquist, K., 380, 381, *382*
Baugher, M., 17, *18*
Bauman, K. E., viii, *xiii,* 180, *182,* 220, *237,* 243, 270, *274,* 279, 290, *294, 295,* 381, *383*
Baumeister, R. F., 88, *103,* 194, *206*
Baumler, E., 380, 381, *382*
Baumrind, D. A., 229, *235*
Baxter, L. A., 29, *52*
Beach, F. A., 60, *79*
Bearinger, L. H., 290, *295*
Bearman, P., 196, *206*
Bearman, P. S., viii, *xiii,* 30, 31, 290, 291, *295, 296*
Beck, A. T., 172, 173, 174, 175, 177, *181, 182*
Becker, B. J., 297, 317, *322*
Beebe, T. J., 229, 231, *237*
Beitchman, J. H., 216, *235*
Belansky, E. S., 357, *368*
Belin, T. R., 74, *82*
Bell, A., 200, *206*
Bell, J. J., 62, *82*
Bell, K. L.110, 118, *131*
Belmaker, R. H., 74, 75, 76, *80*
Belsky, J., 64, *82,* 297, 298, *319*
Bem, D. J., 88, *103*
Benazon, N. R., 175, *181*
Benes, F. M., 61, *79*
Benjamin, C., 62, *84*
Benjamin, J., 74, 75, 76, *79, 80*
Benjamin, L. S., x, *xii,* 164, 165, 172, 177, *181,* 305, 306, *319, 320*
Bennett, E. R., 74, *80*
Bennett, N. G., 25, *53*
Bennetto, L., 112, 119, *132,* 348, *354*
Benson, B., 24, 28, *55,* 90, *105,* 117, *134*
Bercheid, E., 128, *133*
Bercuvitz, D., 268, *277*

Berg, B. J., 252, 259, *274*
Berger, R. M., 86, *105*
Bergman, L., 224, *235,* 243, *272*
Berndt, T. J., 13, *18,* 96, *102,* 119, *131, 339, 340, 354*
Berry, E., 231, *236*
Bethke, T. M., 222, *235*
Beuhring, T., 290, *295*
Bidlingmaier, F., 59, *82*
Biemer, P., 200, *208*
Bigras, M., 309, *319*
Billy, J. O. G., 62, 66, *84*
Bingham, C. R., 197, *207,* 338, *354*
Birmaher, B., 163, 164, *181*
Bissonnette, V. L., 119, *134*
Bivens, L., 220, *238*
Blaine, D., 74, *80*
Blakemore, J. E. O., 25, *54*
Blasband, D., 198, *206*
Blashfeld, M. S., 305, *319*
Blass, R. B., 110, *131*
Blatt, S. J., 110, *131,* 172, 173, 174, 175, 177, *181,* 185, 186, 190, *209*
Blehar, M., 139, *156*
Bleske, A., 249, *275*
Block, J., 138, *156, 159*
Bloom, D. E., 25, *52*
Blos, P., viii, *xii,* 111, *131*
Blum, R. W., viii, *xiii,* 87, 93, *104,* 229, *236,* 290, *295*
Blumenthal, D. R., 218, *238*
Blumenthal, J., 60, *80*
Blumstein, A., *103,* 262, *272*
Blumstein, P., 91, 100, *103*
Blyth, D. A., 6, 9, *18,* 23, *55,* 57, *83, 362, 370*
Bonica, C., 69, 70, *80,* 126, 129, 130, 187, 189, 191, 195, 199, *207,* 360, *368,* 373, *383*
Bookwala, J., 225, *235*
Borgerhoff-Mulder, M., 64, *79*
Bornstein, M. H., 256, *273*
Boston, A., 119, 125, 126, *132*
Bouchard, T. J., Jr., 71, *79*
Bouchey, H. A., 3, 8, 10, 15, 17, *18, 20, 22*
Bowen, M., 129, 130, *131*
Bowlby, J., viii, *xii,* 138, *156,* 188, 205, *206,* 217, *235*
Bowser, B. P., 281, *293*

Bradbury, T. N., 122, *131*
Bramlett, M. D., 14, *18*
Brandt, L., 297, *321*
Brender, W. M., 12, *19*
Brene, S., 74, *82*
Brenn, T., 291, *293*
Brennan, K. A., 140, 141, 155, *157, 158*
Brent, D. A., 17, *18,* 163, 164, *181*
Briere, J., 231, *235*
Brinton, C., 25, *54,* 147, *158,* 201, *208*
Britto, P. R., 24, 1 *54,* 95, *208*
Brockopp, K., 222, *238,* 268, *276*
Bronfenbrenner, U., 361, *368*
Brookman, R. R., 281, *294*
Brooks, R. H., 9, *21,* 25, *55*
Brooks-Gunn, J., 24, 25, *54,* 58, 62, 63, 64,
    79, 80, 81, 195, 196, *208,* 299, *319,* 359,
    363, *368*
Brown, B., 85, *104*
Brown B. B., viii, *xii,* 8, *18,* 23, 25, 28, 29, *53,*
    54, 90, 91, 92, *103, 104,* 115, *131,* 279,
    291, *293,* 325, *336,* 374, 375, 376, *382,*
    383
Brown, L. M., 116, *132*
Browne, A., 231, *237,* 245, *274*
Bruckner, H., 196, *206*
Brunelli, S. A., 297, *319*
Bryant, C. M., 373, 375, 377, *383*
Buber, M., 112, *132*
Bucholz, K. K., 71, *80*
Buehlman, K. T., 341, 353, *354*
Buhrke, R. A., 96, *103*
Buhrmester, D., 6, 8, *18, 20,* 95, 96, *103,* 111,
    132, 279, 293, 339, *354*
Bui, K. T., 202, *206*
Bukowski, W. M., 12, *19,* 115, *134*
Bumpass, L. L., 27, *53*
Bunk, B. P., 202, *210*
Bunzow, J. R., 73, *84*
Burchinal, M., 298, 299, 316, 317, *319*
Burcky, W., 223, 224, 230, *236,* 249, *272*
Burke, L. K., 244, *272*
Burton, L. M., 51, *53*
Bush, D. M., 23, *55*
Buss, D. M., 26, *53*
Buster, M., 71, *83*
Butenandt, O., 59, *82*
Byrne, D., 147, *157*

C

Cairns, B. D., 63, *79*
Cairns, R. B., 57, 63, *79, 82,* 216, *236*
Caldwell, L. L., 6, *19*
Callahan, J. E., 222, 224, *239*
Camarena, P. M., 96, *103*
Campbell, B., viii, *xiii,* 62, 64, 67, 70, *81*
Campbell, M, 291, *296*
Campbell, S. M., 85, *106*
Cano, A., 223, *235*
Cantor, N., 373, *382*
Cantos, A. L., 250, *272*
Capaldi, D., 170, *181,* 254, *272, 275*
Capaldi, D. M., 9, *19,* 221, *235,* 245, 247,
    248, 249, 250, 251, 252, 253, 256,
    257, 259, 261, 262, 264, 267, *272,*
    273, 275
Caplan, M., 112, 119, *132,* 348, *354*
Caren, M. W., 73, *82*
Carlsmith, J. M., 58, *80*
Carlson, B. E., 227, *235,* 244, *273*
Carlson, E. A., 139, *159*
Carnelly, K. B., 140
Carnelley, K. B., *157*
Caron, M. G., 73, *82, 84*
Carrere, S., 299, 315, *319, 320, 322*
Carvajal, S. C., 380, 381, *382*
Carver, K. P., 43, 50, *53*
Cascardi, M., 223, 224, 226, *235, 236*
Caspi, A., 57, 62, 64, *79, 82,* 244, 245, 246,
    249, 254, *275, 276*
Cass, V., 100, *103*
Cassavia, E., 216, *235*
Castellanos, F. X., 60, *80*
Cate, R., 223, 224, 225, *237, 275*
Cate, R. M., 244, 245, *273*
Cauffman, E., 23, *53,* 198, 199, 200, *207*
Caughlin, J. P., 28, *54*
Cavanaugh, L. E., 149, *210*
Cernkovich, S. A., 254, *274*
Chamberlain, P., 252, *272*
Chandra, A., 11, *18*
Chandy, J. M., 229, *236*
Chang, F. M., 73, *79*
Chasan-Taber, L., 285, *294*
Chase-Lansdale, P. L., 5, 13, *19,* 297, 299,
    300, *319,* 378, *384*

Chassin, L., 280, 281, *294, 296*
Cherlin, A. J., 27, *53*
Chew, E., 222, 268, *238, 276*
Chinchilli, V. M., 69, *80*
Chiu, C., 71, 73, 75, *82*
Choo, P, 374, *383*
Chopak, J. S., 197, *207*
Christensen, A., 120, 128, *133,* 317, *320*
Christopher, F. S., 244, 245, *273, 275*
Christopher, J. S., 213, 218, *237*
Christopher, S., 223, 224, 225, *237*
Christopherson, C. R., 145, *158*
Cicchetti, D.185, *206*
Cimbalo, R. S., 95, *103*
Civelli, O., 73, *84*
Clark, C. L., 144, 155, 156, *157, 158, 181*
Clark, D. A., 173, 174
Clark, D. B., 229, *236*
Clark, S., 247, 248, 252, 253, 256, *273*
Clausen, J. A., 61, *79*
Claussen, A., 217, 226, *236*
Cleary, P. 261, *275*
Clements, M., 298, *321*
Cliquet, R. L., 64, *84*
Cloninger, C. R., 73, 75, *79, 79*
Clore, G. L., 69, *79,* 91, *105,* 116, *133,* 137, 138, *158,* 192, *209,* 357, *369*
Coan, J., 299, 315, *320,* 347, *354*
Coates, D. L., 24, *53,* 374, *383*
Coatsworth, J. D, 94, *105*
Cobb, R., 378, *383*
Coccaro, E., 73, 74, *80*
Cochran, S. D., 85, *106*
Coffrey, P., 217, *237*
Cohan, C. L., 122, *131*
Cohan, M., 122, 297, 300, *321*
Cohen, J., 262, *27y*
Cohen, K. M., 91, *103*
Cohen, S. F., 62, *82*
Coie, J., 379, *383*
Colarossi, L., 358, *369*
Colditz, G. A., 285, *294*
Cole, H. E., 119, *133*
Coleman, J., 25, *53*
Coleman, J. S., 93, *103*
Coley, R. L., 5, 13, *19,* 297, 300, 309, *319*
Collins, B. E., 70, *81*
Collins, C., 12, *19*

Collins, N. L., 140, 143, 144, 145, 148, 151, *157*
Collins, W., 375, *384*
Collins, W. A., xii, 6, *19, 21,* 23, 25, *53,* 110, 111, 128, *132,* 187, 188, *206,* 256, *273,* 355, *368,* 372, 373, 376, 379, *383, 385*
Comings, D. E., 71, 73, 74, 75, *80, 82*
Compas, B. E., 70, 185, *206*
Conger, R. D., 248, 255, *277,* 280, *296,* 373, 376, 377, *383*
Connolly, J., 28, *53,* 109, 110, 115, *132,* 191, *206,* 213, 222, *236,* 280, *293, 354*
Connolly, J. A., 4, 8, 9, 10, 17, *19,* 29, *53,* 89, 96, 101, *103, 236,* 376, 377, *383, 384*
Connor, J. K., 185, *206*
Conway, M., 69, *79*
Cook, S. W., 196, 200, 202, *207, 209*
Cooper, C. R., 111, *133*
Cooper, M. L., 143, 144, 145, 148, 151, *156*
Cordova, J. V., 251, *273*
Cornelius, J., 25, *54,* 147, *158,* 195, 201, *208*
Cornelius, J. S., 26, 50, *54*
Costa, F., 196, *208*
Costa, F. M., 280, 281, 282, 290, 291, *293, 294, 295*
Costa, M., 376, *384*
Costa, P. T., Jr., 74, *84*
Covington, S. S., 230, *236*
Cowan, C. P., 298, 299, 317, *319*
Cowan, P. A., 298, 299, 317, *319*
Cox, C. I, 119, *134*
Cox, G., 251, *273*
Cox, M. J., 298, 299, 316, 318, *319*
Coy, K. C., 6, *21*
Coyle, K. K., 380, 381, *382*
Coyne, J. C., 173, *181*
Craig, P. H., 25, *52*
Craig, W., *52,* 109, *132,* 213, 222, *235,* 376, *384*
Cram, F., 225, *237*
Creasey, G., 119, 125, 126, *132*
Crittenden, P., 217, 226, *236*
Crockenberg, S. B., 298, 299, 300, *319*
Crockett, L. J., 197, *207,* 338, *354*
Crosby, L., 9, *19,* 221, *236,* 245, 247, 249, 252, 256, 264, 267, *273*
Crowe, P. A., 6, 9, *21*

Csikszentmihalyi, M., 6, 8, 91, 193, *209*
Cui, M. K., 373, 376, 377, *383*
Cullari, S., 196, *207*
Culp, R., 297, 317, *321*
Culp, R. E., 299, *319*
Cummings, E. M., 298, *319*
Curran, P. J., 280, *294*
Curtin, S. C., 297, *322*
Cutrona, C. E., 297, 298, 300, *320*

D

D'Amico, E. J., 231, *237*
D'arcangelo, M. R, 69, *80*
D'Augelli, A. R., 12, *19*, 86, 90, 93, *103*, 358, *368*
Da Costa, G. A., 216, *235*
Dahl, R. E., 163, 164, *181*
Daly, M., 250, *273*
Darling, N., 6, *19*
Darroch, J. E., 366, *369*
Davies, P. T., 378, *383*
Davies, W. H., 229, *241*
Davila, J., 378, *383*
Davis, K. E., 16, *19*, 137, 140, 141, 154, 156, *157, 158*
Davis, M. H., 9, *20*
Day, J., 112, 113, *135*
de Gaston, J. F., 117, 131, *132*
De Visser, R., 221, *239*
DeFries, J. C., 71, *80*
DeGarmo, D. S., 248, *273*
DeJoy, D. M., 222, *235*
Dembo, R. M., 231, *236*
Demers, L. M., 69, *80*
Diamond, L., 85, 87, 89, 93, *103*
Diamond, L. M., 12, *19*, 24, 27, *53*, 87, 88, 89, 93, 95, 96, 99, 100, *103, 104, 106*, 328, *336*, 363, *368*
Diamond, M. O., 297, *321*
Diana, M. S., 9, *21*, 25, *55*
Dickson, J. W., 17, *20*, 196, 197, *207*
Diekman, A. B., 316, *320*
DiMatteo, M. R., 281, *294*
Dinwiddie, S. H., 71, *80*
Dion, K. K., 374, *383*
Dion, K. L., 374, *383*

Dishion, T. J., 171, *181,* 248, 251, 256, 257, *273, 276*
Dobash, R. E., 246, 250, *273*
Dobash, R. P., 246, 250, *273*
Doherty, R. W., 374, *383*
Doljanac, R. F., 374, *383*
Donovan, J. E., 196, *208,* 280, 281, 282, 290, 291, *293, 294*
Dornbusch, S. M., 58, *80*
Dosch, M. F., 213, *238*
Doughty, D., 71, *83*
Doumas, D., 248, *273*
Douvan, E., 25, *53*
Dowdy, B. B., 6, 7, *19*
Downey, G., 69, 70, *80,* 126, 127, 129, 130, *132,* 175, *181,* 187, 189, 191, 195, 199, *207,* 360, *368,* 373, *383*
Downs, W. R., 280, *294*
Driscoll, A. K., 373, 375, *384*
Driscoll, R, 16, *19*
Driver, J. L., 346, 347, 350, 351, *354*
Drumm, P., 25, *54*
Du, V., 73, *81*
Dubé, E. M., 12, *19*, 24, 27, *53,* 85, 89, 93, 95, 96, 97, *103, 104,* 363, *368*
Duckett, E., 137, *138*
Duke, P., 58, *80*
Dumas, J., 309, *319*
Dunne, M. P., 71, *80*
Dunner, M. P., 72, *79*
Dunphy, D. C., 29, *53,* 191, *207*
DuRant, R. H., 70, *83,* 221, *239*
Dusek, J. B., 138, *157*
Dutton, D. G., 140, 148, *157,* 247, 250, *273*
Dyk, P., 191, *207*

E

Eagly, A. H., 316, *320*
Earls, F., 216, *236*
Earls, F. J., 281, *295*
East, P. L., 299, 300, *320*
Eaton, Y. M., 201, *207*
Eaves, L. J., 71, *82*
Ebert, L., 298, *322*
Ebertz, L., 88, *104*
Ebstein, R. P., 74, 75, 76, *80*

Eccles, J., 358, *369*
Eccles, J. S., 357, 362, *368, 370*
Eddy, J. M., 249, *275*
Eder, D., 3, *19, 55*, 92, 93, *104*, 116, *135*
Edwards, D., 281, *296*
Edwards-Hewitt, T., 301, *320*
Egeland, B., 139, *159*, 248, *274*
Eggert, L. L., 29, *55*
Eggert, W., 74, *82*
Ehrhardt, A. A., 62, *82*
Ehrt-Wehle, R., 59, *82*
Eichorn, D., 62, 63, *79*
Eichorn, D. H., 61, *80*
Ekelund, J., 74, *80*
Elder, G. H., Jr., 373, 376, 377, *383*
Elicker, J., 129, *135*
Elliott, D. A., 266, *276*
Elliott, D. S, 245, 280, 281, *274, 294*
Ellis, A. M., 88, 230, *240*
Ellis, L., 87, *104*
Elster, A., 297, 300, *321*
Emans, S. J., 221, *239*
Epstein, J., 357, *368*
Epstein, N., 174, 175, 177, *181*
Ericsson, M., 74, *83*
Erikson, E. H., viii, *xii*, 4, 5, *19*, 23, *53*, 138, *157*, 191, *207*, 332, *336*, 356, *368*
Esterberg, K. G., 91, *104*
Evans, A. C., 60, *81*
Evans, C., *55*, 116, *135*
Eyler, A. E., 221, *237*
Eyre, S. L., 10, *19*
Eysenck, H. J., 71, *82*

F

Fagan, J., 247, 254, *274, 276*
Fagot, B. I., 95, *104*
Faiman, C., 59, *80*
Farrell, A. D., 270, *274*
Feeny, J. A., 196, *207*
Feeney, J. A., 138, 141, 144, *157*
Fehr, B., 201, 202, *210*
Feingold, A., 26, *55*, 95, *104*
Feiring, C., viii, *xii*, 5, 9, 17, *19, 22*, 24, 25, *53, 54*, 85, *104*, 109, 115, *131, 132*, 190, 191, 200, *207*, 213, 219, 221, *236, 237*, 325, *336*, 374, 375, *383*

Feld, S. L., 245, 264, 266, *274*
Feldman, J. F., 62, *82*
Feldman, S., 189, *207*
Feldman, S. S., 119, *132, 134*, 198, 199, 200, 374, *383*
Felice, M. E., 299, 300, *320*
Felmlee, D., 116, *132*, 201, 202, *210*
Felson, R. B., 262, *274*
Fendel, H., 59, *82*
Ferenz-Gillies, R., 119, *133*
Ferguson, A. D., 333, *336*
Ferraro, K., 364, *369*
Ferraro, K. J., 29, *54*
Fessenden, F., 17, *19*
Fetrow, R. A., 252, *272*
Field, W. J., 74, *83*
Figueredo, A. J., 250, *278*
Fincham, F., 378, *383*
Fincham, F. D., 316, *320*
Fine, M., 88, *104*, 367, *368*
Fine, M. A., 202, *207*
Finkelhor, D., 231, *237*
Finkelstein, J. W., 69, *80*
Fischer, C. T., 109, *132*
Fischer, E. F., 374, *383*
Fisher, L. A., 279, *294*
Fisher, W. A., 147, *157*
Fitzgerald, H. E., 229, *240*
Fitzpatrick, M. A., 124, *132*
Flaherty, J. F., 138, *157*
Flanagan, A. S., 17, *20*
Flanagan, C., 362, *368*
Flannery, D. J., 62, *80*
Fleeson, J., 125, 128, *135*
Fleiss, J. L., 306, *322*
Fleming, W. S., 119, *133*
Florian, V., 144, *158*
Florsheim, P., 170, *182*, 297, 300, 305, 306, 315, 318, *320, 321*
Follansbee, D. J., 111, *133*
Follingstad, D. R., 244, 252, 259, *272, 274*
Foo, H.-H., 380, *384*
Ford, K., 62, *84*, 285, 289, *294*
Forehand, R., 378, *384*
Foreyt, J. P., 74, *83*
Forgatch, M. S., 248, 251, *273, 276*
Fortenberry, J. D., 280, 281, 282, 285, 290, 291, *293, 294*
Foshee, M., 245, *275*

Foshee, V., 180, *182,* 223, 225, *237*
Foshee, V. A., 220, 225, *237,* 243, 268, 270, *274,* 381, *383*
Foster, S. L., 170, *181,* 254, *272*
Fraley, R. C., 137, 140, 141, 154, 155, 156, *157*
Franzoi, S. L., 9, *20*
Frazier, P. A, 200, 202, *207*
Freitas, A., 127, *132,* 175, *181*
Freitas, A. L., 175, *181*
Fremouw, W., 222, *238*
French, S. A., 87, 93, *104*
Frieze, I. H., 29, *55,* 225
Fromme, K., 231, *238*
Fukuyama, M. A., 333, *336*
Fulker, D. W., 71, *80*
Fulkerson, J. A., 229, 231, *237*
Fuqua, D. R., 95, *103*
Furman, W., viii, *xii,* 3, 6, 8, 9, 10, 11, 15, 17, *18, 19, 20, 22,* 23, 24, 25, 27, *54,* 85, 90, 96, *103, 104,* 111, 114, 115, 117, 125, 126, 128, *131, 132, 133,* 137, 156, *157,* 187, 188, 191, 195, 205, *206, 207,* 213, 214, *236, 237,* 279, 293, 325, 339, 349, *354,* 374, 375, 377, *383*
Furstenberg, F. F., 280, *295,* 300, *320, 336,* 363, *368*

G

Gabrielidis, C., 50, *54*
Gagnon, J. H., 27, 29, 32, *55,* 87, 93, 100, *105*
Gaillard, G. L., 70, *83*
Galen, B. R., 195, *208,* 359, *368*
Galliher, R. V., 116, 117, *133, 135,* 189, 197, 198, *207, 210*
Gallois, C., 291, *295*
Galotti, K. M., 27, *52*
Gamble, W., 119, *133*
Gargiulo, J., 25, 28, *54, 80*
Garmezy, N., 94, *105,* 216, *237*
Garnefski, N., 229, *237*
Garofalo, R., 87, 93, *104*
Gaulin, S., 332, *336*
Gavin, L., 8, *20*
Gecas, V., 4, *20*
Gee, C. B., 297, 300, *320*
Geffner, R., 231, *238*

Gelernter, J., 73, 74, *80*
Gelles, R. J., 243, 246, 247, 248, 250, *274,* 277
George, C., 226, *238*
Gershoni, R., 25, *55,* 96, *106,* 137, *159*
Gest, S. D., 94, *105*
Getreu, A., 231, *236*
Gianino, A., 348, *354*
Gibson, E., Jr., 13, *21*
Giedd, J. N., 60, *80*
Gillath, O., 140, *158*
Gillies, P., 291, *296*
Gilligan, C., 116, *132*
Gilmore, G. D., 213, *238*
Giordano, P. C., 254, *274*
Girgus, J. S., 185, 186, 201, *209*
Gladue, B. A., 88, *105,* 332, *336*
Glebermann, L., 251, 259, *276*
Glenn, N. D., 25, *54*
Glickman, A., 221, 226, *240*
Goldberg, A., 27, 109, 110, 115, *132,* 191, *206,* 213, 222, *236,* 280, *293*
Golden, C., 100 *105*
Goldman, D., 74, *82*
Goodman, E., 87, 93, *104*
Gordis, E. G., 309, *321*
Gorenflo, D., 221, *237*
Gorman J. M., *275*
Gorman-Smith, D., 251, 255, 259, 269, *274, 275, 278,* 230, *320*
Gotlib, I. H.168, 170, *182*
Gottleib, B. H., 298
Gottlieb, B. H., *320*
Gottlieb, G., 57, 72, *81*
Gottman, J., 299, 315, *319*
Gottman, J. M., 120, 123, 124, *133,* 169, 170, *182,* 251, 259, 264, *273, 275,* 298, 299, 315, 316, 317, *320, 322,* 340, 353, *354,* 344, 346, 347, 350, 351, *354,* 377, *384*
Gough, R., 234, 381, *385*
Gowen, L. K., 119, *132*
Graber, J., 64, *81*
Graber, J. A., 24, *54,* 195, 196, *208,* 359, *368*
Graef, R., 91, *105,* 193, *209*
Graham, P., 268, *277*
Gralen, S., 23, *55*
Grasley, C., 234, *340,* 381
Gray, D., 85., *105*
Gray, H. M., 223, 225, *237,* 245, *275*

Gray, J., 301, *320*
Gray, M. R., 24, *54,* 109, *133*
Grecas, V., 4, *20*
Green, R., 88, *105*
Greenberg, B. D., 74, *79*
Greene, W. F., 270, *274,* 381, *383*
Greenley, J. R., 261, *275*
Grello, C. M., 17, *20,* 171, 189, 196, 197, *207*
Griesler, P. C., 256, *273*
Grinder, R. E., 7, 13
Gritsendo, I., 74, *80*
Groer, M. W., 249, *277*
Groff, T. R., 62, 66, *84*
Gross, R. T., 58, *80*
Grotevant, H. D, 111, *133*
Guan, H. C., 73, *84*
Guilbert, D. E., 316, *321*
Gulley, B. L., 62, *80*
Gustavsson, J. P., 74, *82*

H

Haddock, C. K., 74, *83*
Hall, G. S., 137, *157*
Halpern, C. T., 13, *20,* 62, 62, 64, 67, 68, 70,
    72, 74, *81*
Hamby, S. L., 270, *275*
Hamer, D. H, 74., *79*
Hanis, C. L., 74, *83*
Hannett, C. A., 199, *210*
Hans, S. L., 317, *322*
Hansen, D. J., 213, 218, *237*
Hansen, G. L., 199, *208*
Hardy, J. B., 62, *84*
Harper, M. S., 17, *20,* 170, 189, 197, *208*
Harris, D. B., 57, *81*
Harris, K., 300, *320*
Harris, K. M., viii, *xiii,* 290, *295*
Harrison, D. F., 379, *382*
Harrison, P. A., 229, 231, *237*
Harrison, R., 174, 175, 177, *181*
Harrop, J. W., 250, *274*
Hart, M. M., 12, *19*
Harter, S., 4, 5, *20,* 138, *158*
Hartup, W. W., 7, *20,* 111, 112, 113, 122, *133*
Harvey, J. H., 128, *133*
Harvey, S. M., 196, *208*

Haslam, N., 172, 173, *182*
Hatfield, E., 25, *54,* 147, *158,* 195, 201, *208,*
    374, *383*
Hathaway, J. E., 17, *22,* 378, *384*
Hause, E. S., 252, 259, *274*
Hauser, S. T., 110, 111, 118, *131, 133*
Hawkins, D. L., 221, 226, 232, 233, *240*
Hawkins, J. D., 379, *383*
Hays, R., 196, 281, *294*
Hazan, C., 8, *20,* 23, *54,* 126, *133,* 137, 138,
    140, 141, 143, 156, *158, 159,* 163, *182,*
    196, *208*
Healey, J. M., 62, *82*
Heath, A. C., 71, *80*
Heath, J. L., 220, 243, *274*
Heavey, C. L., 120, *133*
Hegedus, A. M., 229, *236*
Helms, R. W., 180, *182,* 270, *274*
Helweg-Larsen, M., 70, *81*
Hendrick, C., 10, *20,* 71, *81*
Hendrick, S. S., 10, *20,* 71, *81*
Henning, K., 217, *237*
Hennighausen, K. H., 188, *206,* 373, 376,
    383
Henry, D. B., 251, 255, 259, 269, *274, 278*
Henshaw, S., 297, *322*
Henshaw, S. K., 279, *294*
Henton, J., 223, 224, 225, *237*
Henton, J. M., 244, 245, *273, 275*
Herman, J. L., 216, *237*
Hershberger, S. L., 90, 93, *103, 358, 368*
Hervis, O., 269, 270, *277*
Hessling, R. M., 297, 300, *320*
Hetherington, E. M., 73, *83,* 256, *273*
Heyman, R. E., 249, *275*
Higuchi, S., 74, *82*
Hill, C. A., 25, *54*
Hill, C. T., 27, *54,* 202, *206*
Hill, J., 5, 6, *20,* 111, *133*
Hill, J. P., 6, 9, *18*
Hill, S. Y., 74, *81*
Hinde, R. A., 115, 129, *133*
Hinden, B. R., 185, *206*
Hirsch, M. B., 62, *84*
Hirsch, S., 112, 113, *135*
Hirschi, R., 65, *81*
Hoffman, T. J., 221, *238*
Hoffman, V., 10, *19*

Hofman, J. E., 25, *55,* 96, *106,* 137, *159*
Hogarty, G. E, 60, *82*
Holden, G. W., 227, *235*
Hollingshead, A. B., 301, *320*
Holloway, C., 196, *211*
Holmbeck, G. N., 6, *20,* 111, *131,* 137, *158,*
    281, *294*
Holtzworth-Munroe, A., 259, 264, *275*
Homann, E., 172, *181*
Hood, J. E., 216, *235*
Hops, H., 170, *181,* 254, *272*
Horney, J., 357, *368*
Horowitz, L., 125, *131,* 155, *156*
Hotaling, G. T., 244, 249, *277*
Hoyt, D. R., 196, 197, *210*
Hsieh, K. H., 297, 298, *319*
Hubbard, J., 9, 13, *21,* 94, *106,* 131, *134,* 172,
    182, 219, *238,* 378, 379, *384*
Huesmann, L. R., 269, *275*
Huizinga, D., 245, *274*
Hull, E. M., 73, *81*
Humphrey, L. L., 306, *320*
Hundleby, J. D., 280, *294*
Hunter, D. J., 285, *294*
Huselid, R. F., 143, *157*
Huston, T. L., 16, *21,* 28, *54,* 128, *133*

I

Inaba, S., 291, *295*
Ireland, M., 290, *295*
Isensee, R, 85, *105*

J

Jaber, M., 73, *82*
Jackson, S., 171, *182*
Jackson, S. M., 225, *237*
Jacob, T., 168, 170, *182*
Jacobsen, N., 347, *354*
Jacobson, A. M., 111, *133*
Jacobson, K. C., 73, *81*
Jacobson, N. S., 251, 259, 264, *273, 275,* 317,
    320
Jacobvitz, D., 226, *238*
Jacoby, M., 221, *237*

Jaffe, K., 59, 140, *157*
Jaffe, P. G., 243, *275*
Jaffe, R. B., 59, *82*
James, S. E., 85, *105*
Jankowiak, W. R, 374, *383*
Jankowski, M. K., 217, *237*
Jarvelin, M. R., 74, *80*
Jeffries, N. O., 60, *80*
Jenkins, R. R., 62, *84*
Jennings, D., 58, *80*
Jensen, L., 117, 131, *132*
Jensen-Campbell, L. A., 117, 125, 129, *134*
Jessor, R, 74, 196, *208,* 280, 281, 282, 290,
    291, *293, 294, 295*
Jessor, S., 196, 197, *208*
Jessor, S. L., 280, *295*
Jezl, D. R., 29, *54,* 243, 251, *275*
John, R. S., 248, 251, 259, *273, 276,* 309, *321*
Johnson, A. M., 8, 10, 17, *19, 53,* 90, 96, 101,
    105, 236
Johnson, C., 247, 248, 254, 255, *277*
Johnson, M. P., 16, *21,* 27, 29, *54,* 260, 261,
    275, 364, *368*
Johnson, S. L., 168, 170, *182*
Jonson-Reid, M., 220, *238*
Joiner, T. E, 175, *182*
Jolley, J. M., 201, *207*
Jones, J., viii, *xiii,* 30, 31, *52*
Jones, J. L., 290, *295*
Jonsson, E. G., 74, *82*
Josselson, J., 109, 113, *133*
Jovanovic, V., 73, *84*
Joyce, P. R., 74, *83*
Joyner, K., 13, 17, *20,* 23, 25, 27, 38, *54,* 154,
    158, 193, 194, *208,* 364, *369,* 373, 378,
    384
Jozefowicz, D., 358, *369*

K

Kachadourian, L., 378, *383*
Kaczmarek, M. G., 171, *182,* 200, 204, *208*
Kaeser, L., 366, *369*
Kagan, J., 172, *182*
Kalmus, J., 248, *275*
Kanba, S., 74, *82*
Kandel, D. B., 5, *21,* 279, *295*

Kann, L., 28, *52*
Kantner, J., 62, *84*
Kao, G., 27, 38, *54*
Kao, M., 196, 197, *210*
Kao, M-Y, 280, *296*
Kaplan, B., 377, *385*
Karney, B. R., 122, *131*
Karpel, M., 112, *133*
Kashima, Y., 291, *295*
Kashy, D. A., 285, *295*
Kaslow, F., 173, *182*
Katz, E. C., 231, *237*
Katz, L. F., 317, *320, 377, 384*
Katz, L. R., 298, 299, 316, 317
Katz, M., 74, *80*
Kaufman, J., 163, 164, *181,* 248, *275*
Kawaguchi, M. C., 12, *22,* 116, 117, *133,*
    135, 189, 191, 197, 198, *207, 209, 210*
Kawakami, N., 291, *295*
Kazdin, A., 379, *384*
Kedem, P., 114, 117, *135,* 347, *354*
Keefe, K., 12, 13, *18*
Keefe, R. C., 26, 50, *54*
Kellam, S. G., 261, *275*
Kellogg, N. D., 221, *238*
Kelly, E. W., 23, *55*
Kelly, H. A., 247, *275*
Kelly, H. H., 128, *133*
Kelsey, T., 223, *239,* 250, *277*
Kennedy, D. R., 199, *210*
Kennedy, E., 112, *134*
Kennedy, J., 73, *84*
Kennedy, M. A., 74, *83*
Kenny, D. A., 285, *295*
Kenrick, D. T., 26, 50, *54*
Kepler-Youngblood, P., 249, *277*
Kerpelman, J., 316, *321*
Kershaw, K., 119, 125, 126, *132*
Keshavan, M. S., 60, *82*
Ketterlinus, R., 297, *321*
Keursten-Hogan, R., 299, 300, *321*
Khouri, H., 127, *132,* 175, *181*
Kidd, J. R., 73, *79*
Kidd, K. K, 73, *79*
Kiesler, D. J., 165, *182*
Killen, J. D., 281, *295*
Kim, H. K., 247, 259, *275*
Kim, K., 74, *83*
Kim, M., 175, *181*

Kincaid, S. B., 229, *241*
Kinder, B. N., 96, *102*
Kindermann, T. A., 13, *21*
King, P. K. 145, *158, 274*
Kinsman, S. B., 280, *295*
Kipnis, O., viii, *xiii*
Kirby, D., 366, *369,* 380, 381, *382*
Kirk, K. M., 71, *79*
Kirkpatrick, L. A, 140, 156, *158*
Klassen, A. D., 230, 231, *240*
Kliewer, W., 7, *19*
Klinkenberg, D., 92, 95, *105*
Klohnen, E. C., 290, *295*
Klotz, I., 74, *80*
Knafo, D., 124, *135,* 341, *354*
Knorr, D., 59, *82*
Kobak, R, 119., 126, *133,* 205, *208*
Koch, G. G., 180, *182, 209,* 270, *274,* 381, *383*
Koch, P. B., 196, 355, *369*
Kolko, D. J., 216, *238*
Konarski, R., 4, 9, *19,* 191, *206,* 213, *236,*
    349, *354,* 377, *383*
Kopsky, S., 224, 230, *236,* 249, *272*
Koss, M. P., 250, *278*
Kotchick, B. A., 398, *384*
Koval, J., 223, 224, 225, *237,* 244, 245, *273,*
    275
Kowalik, D. L., 170, *182*
Kozberg, S. F., 28, *54*
Kracker, R., 379, *384*
Krajewski, S. S., 213, *238*
Kranzler, H., 73, 74, *80*
Krueger, R. F., 249, *275*
Ku, L., viii, *xiii,* 29, *55*
Kulbok, P. P., 281, *295*
Kulin, H. E., 69, *80*
Kung, E. M., 270, *274*
Kunselman, S. J., 69, *80*
Kurdek, L. A., 85, 95, *105,* 200, *209*
Kurisu, Y., 291, *295*
Kurtines, W., 269, 270, *277*
Kurz, D., 245, *276*
Kuttler, A. F., 4, *21*

L

La Greca, A. M., 4, *21*
La Taillade, J. J., 259, *275*

Lackey, C., 248, *276*
LaFreniere, P., 309, *319*
LaGrand, L. E., *209*
Lamb, M., 297, 300, *321*
Land, D., 196, *206*
Landry, D. J., 366, *368, 369*
Laner, M. R., 244, *275*
Langer, L. M., 196, *211*
Langwick, S. A., 220, 243, 270, *274*
Larson, R., 6, 8, 9, *19, 21,* 91, *105,* 137, *158, 209*
Larson, R. W., 91, *105,* 116, *133,* 137, 138, 192, 193, 357, *369*
Laub, J. H., 357, *370*
Laumann, E. O., 25, 26, 29, 32, *54, 55,* 87, 93, 100, *105,* 289, *295*
Lauretti, A., 299, 309, *321*
Laursen, B., 6, 9, *21,* 110, 112, 113, 115, 117, 119, 121, 125, 129, 131, *132, 134, 135,* 280, *295*
Lavoie, F., 224, *239*
LaVoie, L., 231, *236*
Leadbeater, B. J., 185, 186, 189, *209*
Leary, T., 165, *182*
Lee, M. Y., 317, *321*
Lee, P. A., 59, *82*
Lefebvre, D. L., 216, *240*
Lefebvre, L., 170, 234, *240,* 381, *385*
Leitenberg, H., 217, *237*
Leonard, K. E., 243, *276*
Leonard, K. H., 119, 121, *134*
Lerman, R., 300, *321*
Lerner, R. M., 57, *82*
Leslie, L. A., 16, *21*
Lesnick, L., 229, *236*
Levenson, R. W., 120, 124, *133,* 344, *354*
Levine, M. P., 23, *55*
Levinger, G., 128, *133*
Levitt, M. Z., 163, *182*
Levitz-Jones, E., 191, *209*
Levy, J. A., 299, *319*
Levy-Shiff, R., 114, 117, *135,* 298, *321,* 348, *354*
Lewinsohn, P. M., 14, 17, *21, 170, 182,* 200, 201, *209*
Lewis, M., 213, 219, *237*
Lewis, R., 16, *21*
Lewis, S. F., 222, *238*

Li, F., 171, *181*
Li, L., 74, *79*
Liben, L. S., 69, *80*
Lichtermann, D., 74, *80*
Lindahl K., 298, *321*
Lindberg, L. D., viii, *xiii,* 29, *55,* 373, 375, *384*
Linder, G. F., 180, *182,* 220, *237,* 243, 270, *274,* 381, *383*
Linder, J., 74, *83*
Linnoila, M., 74, *82*
Lipetz, M. E., 16, *19*
Liu, H., 60, *80*
Livak, K. J., 73, *79*
Livson, N., 61, *82*
Lloyd, S., 223, 224, 225, *237,* 244, 245, *273, 275*
Locke, J., 74, *81*
Lorrain, D. S., 73, *81*
Lovald, B. E., 221, 226, *240*
Lucas, S., 96, *104*
Lumley, L. A., 73, *81*
Lundberg-Love, P., 231, *238*
Luster, T., 229, *238*
Lykken, D. T., 71, *79*
Lynch, M. T., 5, *20*
Lynch, T. R., 175, *182*
Lyons-Ruth, K., 226, *238*

M

Mac Iver, D., 362, *368*
Maccoby, E. E., 256, 266, *273, 276*
MacDonald, J., 64, *82,* 170, *182,* 297, *300,* 306, *320*
MacDougall, J. E., 270, *274,* 381, *383*
MacKune-Karrer, B., 269, *276*
Macmurray, J., 71, 73, 75, *82*
Madden, P. A. F., 71, 80
Magdol, L., 247, 254, *276*
Magnusson, D., 57, 62, 64, *82, 83,* 359, 362, 363, *370*
Main, M., 125, *134,* 226, *238*
Makepeace, J. A., 244, *276*
Makepeace, J. M ., 219, 222, *238*
Malamuth, N. M., 120, *133*
Malhotra, A. K., 74., *82*
Malone, J., 170, *183,* 217, *239,* 248, 266, *276*

Manki, H., 74, *82*
Manson, J. E., 285, *294*
Margolin, G., 248, 251, 259, *273,* 276, 309, *321*
Mark, E. W., 96, *105*
Markman, H., 298, *321*
Maron, D. J., 281, *295*
Marshall, I. H., 357, *368*
Marsiglio, W., 297, 300, *321*
Martin, B., 248, *276*
Martin, D., 246, *276*
Martin, J. A., 58, *80*
Martin, N. G., 71, 72, *79, 80, 82*
Mason, G. A., 67, *81*
Masten, A., 219, *238*
Masten, A. S., 9, 13, *21,* 94, *105, 106,* 131, *134,* 172, 182, 216, *237,* 378, 379, *384*
Masten, J., 217, *239*
Matheson, J. L., 268, *277*
Matuki, H., 74, *83*
Matuszewich, L., 73, *81*
Mays, V. M., 85, *106*
McAdams, D. P., 138, *158*
McAuslan, P., 231, 232, *235*
McCabe, S. B., 168, 170, *182*
McCarnish, M., 291, *295*
McClintock, E., 128, *133*
McCollam, T. L., 13, *21*
McCormick, N., 362, *368*
McDaniel, C. O., Jr., 23, *55*
McDonald, D. L., 23, *55*
McGee, R. A., 216, *238*
McGue, M., 71, *79*
McGuirl, K. E., 290, *295*
McHale, J. P., 298, 299, 309, *321*
McKee, S. A., 217, *240*
McKenney, J. P., 23, *55*
McKeown, R. E., 281, *295*
McLaughlin, I. G, 243, *276*
McMahon, P. M., 220, 243, 270, *274*
McNeely, C. S., 374, *384*
Mearns, J., 200, 201, *209*
Mechanic, D., 261, *275*
Menard, S., 266, *276*
Mendelsohn, G. A., 290, *295*
Mercer, G. W., 280, *294*
Mercier, L. R., 86, *105*
Mercy, J. A., 216, *236*

Merikangas, K. R., 249, *276*
Meschke, L. L., 382, *384*
Metalsky, G. I., 175, *182*
Metts, S., 201, 202, *210*
Meyer, A. L., 270, *274*
Meyer-Bahlburg, H. F. L., 62, *82*
Meyers, A. B., 298, *322*
Michael, R. T., 27, 29, 32, *55,* 87, 93, 100, *105*
Michaelis, B., 127, *132,* 175, *181*
Michaels, F., 87, 93, 100, *105*
Michaels, S., 27, 29, 32, *55*
Middleton, K., 140, 141, *158*
Midgley, A. R., 59, *82*
Midgley, C., 82, 362, *368*
Mihalic, S. W., 266, *276*
Mikulincer, M., 140, 144., 156, *158*
Mikus, K., 196, 207, 298, *319*
Milardo, R. M., 9, *21*
Miller Buchanan, C., 362, *368*
Miller, B. C., 24, 28, *55,* 90, *105,* 117, *134,* 145, *158*
Miller, E., 64, *82*
Miller, M., 196, 197, *210*
Miller, W. B., 71, 73, 75, *82, 83*
Millhollin, T. J., 254, *274*
Mills, A., 7, *21,* 25, *55*
Millstein, S. G., 10, *19*
Mineka, S., 175, *182*
Missale, C., 73, *82*
Mitchell, M. L., 201, *207*
Mizushima, H., 74, *82*
Modell, J., 372, *384*
Moffitt, T., 58, 64
Moffitt, T. E., 244, 245, 247, 249, 254, *275, 276*
Molidor, C., 224, 225, *238*
Mollidor, C. E., 29, *54,* 243, 251, *275*
Moneta, G., 137, *158*
Monroe, S. M., 14, 17, *21,* 170, *182,* 200, 201, *209*
Montgomery, A. C., 281, *295*
Montgomery, M. J., 195, 200, *209*
Moore, D., 170, *182,* 297, 300, 306, 315, 318, *320, 321*
Moore, K. A., 373, 375, *384*
Moore, M. R., 378, *384*
Morgan, S. P., 363, *368*
Morishima, A., 62, *82*

Moritz, G., 17, *18*
Morris, J. E., 309, *319*
Morris, N. M., 62, 66, *84*
Morse, B. J., 245, *274*
Morse, J. Q., 175, *182*
Moselle, K. A., 229, *235*
Moses, J., 73, *81*
Mosher, W., 11, *18*
Mosher, W. D., 14, *18*, 297, *322*
Moss, A. J., 28, *52*
Mott, F., 372, *384*
Mucci, L. A., 17, *22*, 378, *384*
Mudgal, J., 374, *384*
Muehlenhard, C. L., 196, *209*
Mueller, E., 214, *238*
Mulder, R. T., 74, *83*
Mulgrew, C. L., 73, 74, *80*
Mullins, R., 291, *296*
Muramatsu, T., 74, *82*
Murphy, B. C., 85, *105*
Murphy, C. M., 218, *238*
Murphy, D. L., 74, *79*

N

Naas, G., 25, *55*
Nagata, C., 291, *295*
Nagle, L., 305, *322*
Nagy, S., 196, *206*
Nahm, E., 346, 347, 351, *354*
Nangle, D., 213, 218, *237*
Nardi, P. M., 95, *105*
Nascimento, E., 187, *209*
Nash, S. R., 73, *82*
Nass, G., 9, *22*, 55
Neale, M. C., 87, *102*
Neemann, J., 9, 13, *21*, 94, *105, 106*, 131, *134*, 172, *182*, 219, *238*, 378, 379, *384*
Neiderhiser, J. M., 73, *83*
Neidig, P. H., 250, *272*
Neidt, H., 74, *82*
Neiswanger, K., 74, *81*
Nelson, B., 163, 164, *181*
Nelson, E., 198, *210*
Nemanov, L., 74, 75, 76, *80*
New, A., 73, 74, *80*
New, M. I., 62, *82*
Newman, D. L., 247, 254, *276*

Niederjohn, D. M., 191, *209*
Nilsson, T., 74, *83*
Nitz, K., 297, *321,* 379, *384*
Niznik, H. B., 73, *84*
Noam, G. G., 111, *133*
Noble, E. P., 74, *82*
Nolen-Hoeksema, S., 185, 186, 190, 201, *209*
Noller, P., 141, 144, *157*, 196, *207*
Norris, A., 285, 289, *294*
Nothen, M. M., 74, *82*
Novell, D. O., 95, *103*
Novick, O., 74, *80*

O

O'Beirne, H. A., 196, 197, *209*
O'Connor, T. G., 110, 118, *131*
O'Keefe, M., 223, 224, 225, 227, 232, *238*
O'Keefe, N. K., 222, 268, *276*
O'Keefe, Z., 379, *384*
O'Leary, K., *276*
O'Leary, K. D., 170, *182,* 217, 223, 224, 226, *235, 236, 239,* 247, 248, 250, 266, 270, 272, 276, 277
O'Reilly, A. W., 298, *319*
Obeidallah, D., 51, *53*
Offer, D., 137, *158*
Ohara, K., 73, *84*
Ono, Y., 74, *82*
Orlofsky, J., 191, *209*
Orlofsky, J. L., 113, 114, *134*
Osgood, D. W., 357, *368*
Osher, Y., 74, 75, 76, *80*
Osofsky, H. J., 297, *321*
Osofsky, J. D., 297, 298, 299, 317, *319, 321*
Otuka, Y., 74, *83*
Owen, L., 247, 250, 261, 262, 264, *273*
Owens, R. E., 86, *106*
Ozkaragoz, T. Z., 74, *82*

P

Painter, S. L., 250, *273*
Pakstis, A. J., 73, *79*
Paley, B., 298, 299, 316, 318, *319*
Pancer, S. M., 298, *320*

Pantin, H., 269, *277*
Papp, P., 116, *134*
Parcel, G. S., 380, 381, *382*
Parks, M. R., 29, *55*
Pasley, K., 316, *321*
Pasta, D. J., 71, 73, 75, *82*
Patterson, C., 74, *79*
Patterson, G. R., 248, 251, 256, *273, 276*
Patty, J., 141, 144, *157*
Paul, E. L., 27, *55*, 214, *239*
Paus, T., 60, *80*
Pawlby, S. J., 7, *21, 25, 55*
Payne, C. C., 298, 316, 318, *319*
Peirce, R. S., 143, *156*
Peltonen, L., 74, *80*
Pendergrast, R. A., 70, *83*
Peplau, L. A., 27, *54*, 85, 95, *106*, 128, *133*, 198, 202, *206*
Pepler, D., 109, *132*, 213, 222, *236*, 376, *384*
Perel, J., 163, 164, *181*
Perez-Vidal, A., 269, 270, *277*
Perper, J. A., 17, *18*
Perry, C. L., 291, *296*
Perry, D. G., 112, *134*
Perry, L. C., 112, *134*
Perry, T. B., 119, *131*
Peskin, H., 61, *82*
Petersen, A. C., 57, 62, 63, *79, 83,* 96, 196, *208*
Peterson, D. R., 128, *133*
Peterson, L., 11, *18*
Phillips, D., 126, *135*
Piccinino, L., 11, *18*
Pickles, A., 357, *370*
Pierce, G. R., 303, *321, 322*
Pietromonaco, P. R., 140, *157*
Pillard, R. C., 87, *102*
Pittman, A.-L., 221, 226, 234, *239, 240,* 381, *385*
Plaud, J. J., 230, 231, *240*
Pleck, J. H., viii, *xiii,* 29, *55*
Plomin, R., 72, 73, *83*
Poffenberger, T., 7, *21*
Poitras, M., 224, *239*
Polek, D. S., 252, 259, *274*
Pollack, K., 186, 187, *209*
Poon, L. W.138, *159*
Portes, A., 50, *55*

Poston, W. S., 74, *83*
Powers, S. I., 111, *133,* 186, 187, 190, *209*
Prager, K., 95, 96, 97, *103, 106*
Presson, C. C., 281, *296*
Priel, B., 74, *80*
Prinstein, M. J., 4, *21*
Propping, P., 74, *82*
Pryor, D. W., 87, 93, *106*
Przybeck, T. R., 73, 75, *79*
Pugh, M. D., 254, *274*
Putnam, S. K., 73, *81*

Q

Qian, Z., 26, *55*
Quinlan, D. M., 185, 186, 190, *209*
Quinton, D., 7, *21, 25, 55*

R

Rahhal, T. A, 138, *159*
Raj, A., 17, *22,* 378, *384*
Raj, M. H., 62, 66, *84*
Raley, R. K., 25, *55*
Rapoport, J. L., 60, *81*
Rapson, R. L., 195, *208,* 374, *383*
Rasmussen, J. L., 298, 299, 309, *321*
Rauh, V. A., 297, *319*
Read, S. J, .140, *157*
Reese-Weber, M., 119, 128, *134*
Regan, P. C., 95, *106,* 290, *295*
Reicher, H., 171, *183*
Reid, J. B., 251, *276*
Reid, Y., 291, *296*
Reider, E. E., 229, *240*
Reis, H. T., 96, *106,* 112, *134*
Reiss, D., 72, 73, *83,* 124
Reitzel, D., 243, *275*
Reitzel-Jaffe, D., 170, *183,* 216, 234, *240,* 381, *385*
Remafedi, G., 12, *21,* 87, 93, *104*
Resnick, M. D., viii, *xiii,* 87, 93, *104,* 229, *236,* 290, *295*
Reuman, D., 362, *368*
Reuterman, N., 223, 224, 230, *265,* 249, *272*
Rew, L., *239*

Rhode, P., 14, 170, *182*

Rhodes, J. E., 297, 298, 300, *320, 322*

Rholes, W. S., 126, *135*

Richards, C. L., 366, *369*

Richards, M., 91, *105*

Richards, M. H., 6, 9, *21,* 137, *158*

Richmond, J. B., 163, *182*

Richter, D. L., 281, *295*

Rincon, C., 69, 70, *80,* 126, 129, 130, 187,
189, *207,* 360, *368,* 373, *383*

Ringwalt, C., 268, *277*

Rio, A., 269, 270, *277*

Rise, J., 292, *296*

Ritchie, T. L., *82*

Roberts, L., 291, *296*

Roberts, L. J., 119, 121, 129, *134*

Roberts, T. L., 292, *296*

Robins, C. J., 175, *182*

Robins, R. W., 138, *156*

Robinson, S. W., 73, *82*

Robinson, T. N., 281, *295*

Robison, J. A., 173, *182*

Rodgers, J. L., 11, *21,* 71, *83,* 281, *296*

Rohde, P., 14, 17, *21,* 200, 201, *209*

Romer, D., 280, *295*

Rooney, W., 74, *82*

Roscoe, B., 9, *21,* 25, 55, 199, *210,* 222, 223,
224, *239,* 250, *276*

Rose, S., 29, *55,* 92, 95, 96, *105*

Rose, S. M., *106*

Rosenbaum, A., 247, 266, *276, 277*

Rosenberg, A., 58, *80*

Rosenthal, D. A., 221, *239*

Ross, L. T., 231, 232, *235*

Rossow, I., 281, 292, *296*

Rostosky, S. S., 11, *22,* 116, 117, *133, 135,*
197, 198, *207, 210*

Roth, C., 17, *18*

Roth, J. A., 262, *272*

Rotheram-Borus, M. J., 379, *384*

Rowe, D. C., 62, 71, 73, *80, 81, 83,* 281, *296*

Roye, C. F., 317, *322*

Rubin, D. C., 138, *159*

Rubin, Z., 27, *54*

Rubinstein, J. L, 119, *134*

Rudolph, J. L., 254, *274*

Rumbaut, R. G., 50, *55*

Rusbult, C. E., 119, *134,* 202, *210*

Rushe, R., 251, 264, *273, 275*

Rushe, R. H., 259, *275*

Russell, D. W., 297, 300, *320*

Russell, S. T., 366, 367, *370*

Rutledge, L. L., 252, 259, *273*

Rutter, M., 72, *83,* 216, *239,* 357, *370*

Ryan, K., 225, *275*

Ryan, N. D., 163, 164, *181*

Rybarik, M. F., 213, *238*

Rycoff, I., 112, 113, *135*

S

Sachar, T., 187, *209*

Sacher, J. A., 202, *207*

Sakamoto, K., 74, *83*

Sameroff, A., 216, *239*

Samet, N., 23, *55*

Sampson, R. J., 357, *370*

Sanderson, C. A., 373, *382*

Santisteban D. A., 269, *277*

Santisteban, D., 269, 270, *277*

Sarason, B. R., 303, *321, 322*

Sarason, I. G., 303, *321, 322*

Sarigiani, P. A., 96, *103*

Saunders, K., 140, 149, *157*

Savin-Williams, R. C., 12, *19, 21,* 24, 27, *53,*
85, 87, 89, 91, 93, 94, 99, 100, 102, *103,*
104, 106, 200, *210,* 328, *336,* 363, *368*

Saylor, K. E., 281, *295*

Schaefer, E. S., 165, *183*

Scharf, M. 109, 121, *135*

Schmeidler, J., 231, *236*

Schmit, D. T., 188, *206,* 373, 376, *383*

Schmitz, E., 195, *208*

Schoen, R., 26, *55*

Schoenborn, C. A., 28, *52*

Schonert-Reichl, K. A., 137, *158*

Schultz, L. H., 113, *134*

Schur, B. E., 230, *240*

Schwab, J., 69, *80*

Schwartz, P., 23, 25, 43, 56, 91, 101, *103*

Schwarz, N., 69, *79,* 280, *295*

Schweers, J., 17, *18*

Scott, K., 234, *240*

Scott, K. L., 226, *239*

Seal, D. W., 199, *210*

Sears, J. T., 12, *22*, 93, *106*
Sedvall, G. C., 74, *82*
Seeley, J. R., 14, 17, *21*, 170, *182*, 200, 201, *209*
Seeman, P., 73, *84*
Segal, N. L., 71, *79*
Segman, R., 74, 75, 76, *80*
Seif, H., 367, *370*
Seifer, R., 216, *239*
Seiffge-Krenke, I., 127, *134*
Seligman, M. E., 175, *183*
Selinger, M, 156, *158*
Sellman, J. D., 74, *83*
Selman, R. L., 110, 113, 115, 131, *134, 135*, 163, *182*
Senchak, M., 96, *106*, 243, *276*
Seymour, F. W., 225, *237*
Shaffer, A., 378, *384*
Shaffer, L., 8, 10, 11, 15, *20, 22*
Shaffer, L. A., 25, *54*
Shantz, C. U., 112, *135*
Shapiro, A., 298, *322*, 346, 347, 351, *354*
Sharabany, R., 25, *55*, 96, *106*, 137, *159*
Shaver, P., 23, *54*, 112, *134*, 196, *208*
Shaver, P. R., 71, *84*, 138, 140, 141, 143, 144, 145, 148, 151, 154, 155, 156, *157, 158, 159*, 163, *182*
Shedler, J., *159*
Sheeran, P., 284, *296*
Sheppard, W., 198, *209*
Sher, K. J., 231, *240*
Sherman, S. J., 281, *296*
Shew, M., viii, *xiii*, 290, *295*
Shimizu, H., 291, *295*
Shin, H., 32, *56*
Shortt, J. W., 245, 248, 264, 267, *273*
Shrier, L. A., 221, *239*
Shrout, P. E., 306, *322*
Shulman, S., viii, *xiii*, 109, 114, 117, 119, 121, 124, 129, *135*, 341, *354*, 347, 375, *384*
Siebenbruner, J., 373, *385*
Siever, L., 73, 74, *80*
Sieving, R. E., viii, *xiii*, 290, 291, *295, 296*
Silva, P., 64, *82*
Silva, P. A., 247, 249, 254, *275, 276*
Silverman, J. G., 17, *22*, 378, *384*
Silverman, N., 214, *238*

Simmons, R. G., 23, *55*, 58, *83*, 362, *370*
Simon, R. W., 25, *55*, 116, *135*
Simon, V. A., 8, 10, 15, 17, *20, 22*, 24, 27, *54*, 114, 115, 117, 125, 129, *132*
Simons, R. L., 247, 248, 254, 255, *277*
Simpson, J. A., 27, *55*, 126, *135*, 140, *159*, 196, 202, *206, 210*
Singh, S., 366, *368*
Sippola, L., 12, *19*
Skipper, J. K., 9, *22*, 25, *55*
Slade, A., 205, *210*
Slater, V., 249, *277*
Slep, A. M. S., 249, *275*
Slutske, W. S., 71, *80*
Small, S. A., 229, *238*
Smetana, J. G., 6, *22*, 111, *135*
Smith, A. M., 221, *239*
Smith, C., 225, *235*
Smith, E. A., 62, *84*
Smith, J. P., 220, 227, *239*
Smith, P. H., 250, *278*
Smith, T. E., 379, *382*
Smith-Slep, A.-M., 224, 226, *235*
Smolak, L., 23, *55*
Smollar, J., 6, 8, *22*
Solky-Butzel, J., 305, *322*
Solomon, B., 95, *106*
Sonenstein, F. L., viii, *xiii*, 11, *18*, 29, *55*
Sorell, G. T., 195, 200, *209*
Sparkes, R. S., 74, *82*
Speizer, F. E., 285, *294*
Spracklen, K. M., 171, *181*, 248, 256, *273*
Sprecher, S., 23, 25, 45, *53*, 196, 201, 202, *210, 211*
Sprigner, C., 196, *208*
Springer, D. W., 379, *382*
Spuhler, J. N., 25, *52*
Sroufe, L. A., 23, 125, 128, 129, *132, 135*, 139, *159*, 172, *183*, 187, 188, *206*, 373, 376, *383*
Stacy, A. W., 281, *294*
Stampfer, M. J., 285, *294*
Starzomski, A., 140, 148, *157*
Stattin, H., 57, 62, 64, *83*, 359, 362, 363, *370*
Staub, E., *336*
Steil, J. M., 116, *135*
Steinberg, L., 23, 24, *54*, 62, 64, *83*, 88, *106*, 109, *133*, 256, *273*

Steinberg, S. J., 53, 378, *383*
Steinmetz, S. K., 247, 248, *277*
Sternberg, R. J., 109, *135*
Stets, J. E., 245, 247, 263, *277*
Stewart, S. H., 229, *239*
Stice, E., 280, *294*
Stillwell, A. M., 195, *206*
Stocker, C. M., 299, *322*
Stone, C. P., 65, *83*
Stone, M. R., 357, *370*
Stoolmiller, M., 221, *235*, 250, 256, 257, *273*, *275*
Story, M., 87, 93, *104*
Stratham, D. J., 71, *80*
Straub, E., 334, *336*
Straus, M. A., 243, 244, 245, 246, 247, 248, 250, 261, 263, 264, 266, *274*, *277*
Streiner, D. L., 306, *322*
Strong, L. J., 333, *336*
Stuart, G. L., 259, *275*
Stumpf, J., 234, 381, *385*
Suchindran, C., 13, *20*, 62, 63, 64, 67, 68, *81*
Sudermann, M., 243, *275*
Sugarman, D. B., 244, 249, *277*
Sullivan, H. S., viii, *xiii*, 3, 15, *22*, 111, *135*, 191, *210*
Sullivan, P. F., 74, *83*
Sullivan, T. N., 270, *274*
Sumida, E., 170, *182*, 297, 300, 306, *320*
Surbey, M., 64, *83*
Surra, C. A., 9, *22*
Surrey, J. L., 230, *236*
Susman, E. J., 69, *80*
Svrakic, D. M., 73, 75, *79*
Swanson, C., 299, 315, *320*
Swarr, A., 6, 9, *21*
Sweet, J. A., 27, *53*
Symons, P. Y., 249, *277*
Szapocznik, J., 269, 270, *277*

T

Tabares, A., 346, 347, 351, *354*
Tabor, J., 290, *295*
Taipale, V., 7, *18*
Takatsuka, N. 291, *295*
Talbert, L. M., 66, *84*

Tanaka, A., 74, *83*
Taradash, A., 376, *384*
Taylor, B., 57, *83*
Taylor, E. R., 221, *238*
Taylor-Seehafer, M., *239*
Telch, M. J., 281, *295*
Tellegen, A., 94, *105*, 216, *237*
Thiel, K. S., 6, 9, *18*
Thompson, J., 244, *276*
Thompson, K., 374, *383*
Thompson, S., 3, *22*
Thompson, V., 70, *81*
Thomson, E., 374, *385*
Thorne, A., 138, *159*
Tolan, P. H., 251, 255, 259, 269, *274*, *275*, *278*, 306, *320*
Tolmacz, R., 144, *158*
Tolman, D. L., 88, *106*
Tolman, R. M., 224, 225, *238*
Tomitaka, M., 74, *83*
Tomitaka, S., 74, *83*
Toth, S. L., 185, *206*
Tourangeau, R., 32, *56*
Treister, L., 225, 227, *238*
Trinke, S. J., 137, 156, *159*
Troiden, R. R., 100, *106*
Tronick, E. Z., 348, *354*
Troy, E., 285, *294*
Truong, N. L., 367, *370*
Tubman, J. G., 197, *210*
Turbin, M. S., 290, *295*
Turner, C. F., viii, *xiii*, 29, *55*
Turner, R. A., 374, *383*
Tyree, A., 74, *82*, 170, *183*, 217, *239*, 248, 266, *276*

U

Udry, J. R., viii, *xiii*, 13, 17, *20*, 24, 30, 31, 43, 50, *52*, *53*, *54*, *56*, 58, 59, 60, 62, 63, 64, 65, 66, 67, 68, 70, 72, 78, *81*, *83*, *84*, 154, *158*, 193, 194, *208*, 290, 292, *295*, *296*, 364, *369*, 373, 378, *384*
Uhl, G. R., 74, *84*
Uitenbroek, D. G., 281, *296*
Umansky, R., 74, *80*
Upchurch, D. M., 374, *384*

V

Valois, R. F., 281, *295*
Van Cleave, E. F., 23, *55*
Van Den Bos, J., 290, *295*
Van Horn, M. L., 6, *19*
Van Tol, H. H. M., 73, *84*
Vandenbergh, D. J., 74, *84*
Vanderryn, J., 290, *295*
Vanni, D., 201, 202, *210*
Vasquez-Suson, K. A, 9., *20*
Veniegas, R. C., 85, *106*
Ventura, S. J., 297, *322*
Vicary, J. R., 197, *207*
Vickerman, R. C., 197, *210*
Vincent, M. L., 281, *295*
Virkkunen, M., 74, *82*
Visher, C. A., 262, *272*
Vranzian, K. M., 281, *295*

W

Wakefield, M., 291, *296*
Wakschlag, L. S., 317, *322*
Walker, L. E., 245, *278*
Wall, A.-M., 215, 217, 231, *240*
Wall, S., 139, *156*
Wallen, K., 59, *84*
Waller, J. G., 71, *84*, 155, *157*
Waltz, J., 264, *275*
Wang, J., 74, *84*
Warren, C. W., 28, *52*, 58
Warren, M., 64, *80*, *81*
Washburn, M., 231, *236*
Wasserman, G. A., 297, *319*
Waterman, A. S., 5, *22*
Waters, E., 139, *156*, *159*
Waters, K. A., 281, *294*
Watt, N. F., 379, *383*
Watts, W. D., 230, *240*
Weed, S., 117, 131, *132*
Wehner, E. A., 8, *20*, 90, *104*, 114, 125, 126, 128, *133*, 137, 156, *157*, 187, 188, 195, 205, *207*, 213, 214, *237*
Weinberg, M. S., 87, 93, *106*, 200, *206*
Weinfeld, N. S., 139, *159*
Weis, D. L., 196, *210*

Weisberg, R. P., 119
Weiss, B., 111, *133*
Weiss, R., 9, *22*
Weissberg, R. P., 112, *132*, 348, *354*
Wekerle, C., 170, 180, *182*, 215, 216, 217, 221, 223, 225, 226, 227, 228, 231, 232, 233, 234, *235*, *239*, *240*, 378, 381, *384*, *385*
Welsh, D. P., 11, 17, *20*, *22*, 116, 117, *133*, *135*, 171, 187, 189, 191, 196, 197, 198, *207*, *209*, *210*
Werner, H., 377, *385*
West, C. M., 244, *277*
West, S. G., 379, *383*
Westney, O. E., 62, *84*
Whaley, A. L., 378, *385*
Whitbeck, I. B., 196, 197, *210*
Whitbeck, L. B., 280, *296*
White, J. W., 250, *278*
White, K. M., 27, *55*, 214, *239*
White, L. A., 147, *157*
Whiteside, M. F., 297, 317, *322*
Wichstrom, L., 281, *296*
Widenmann, S., 29, *52*
Widom, C., 216, *240*
Widom, C. S., 248, *278*
Wiederman, M. W., 290, *295*
Wigfield, A., 362, *368*
Wilcox, B. L., 198, *210*, 366, *370*
Willett, W. C., 285, *294*
Williams, C. J., 87, 93, *106*
Williams, C. L., 291, *296*
Williams, J. G., 220, 227, *239*
Williams, K. R., 248, *276*
Williams, L., 231, *236*
Williams, T., 191, *206*
Williams, V. A., 6, 9, *21*, 280, *295*
Williamson, D. E., 163, 164, *181*
Wilsnack, R. W., 230, 231, *240*
Wilsnack, S. C., 230, 231, *240*
Wilson, J., 252, *272*
Wilson, M., 250, *273*
Wilson, S. K., 216, *238*
Wilson, W. J., 50, *56*
Wilson-Shockley, S., 3, *22*, 193, *211*, 343, *354*
Windle, M., 197, *210*, 378, *383*
Windle, R. C., 197, *210*

Winter, J. S. D., 59, *80*
Wintersteen, M. B., 17, 196, *207*
Wipprecht, G., 74, *81*
Wish, E. D., 231, *236*
Wissow, L. S., 87, 93, *104*
Wolf, R. C., 87, 93, *104*
Wolfe, D., 379, *384*
Wolfe, D. A., 17, *22,* 170, 180, *183,* 215, 216,
    217, 221, 223, 225, 226, 227, 228, 232,
    233, 234, *238, 239, 240,* 291, 381, *385*
Wood, D. A., 292, *296*
Wood, G. A., 91, *105,* 116, *133,* 137, 138,
    158, 192, *209,* 357, *369*
Wood, M. D., 231, *240*
Wood, W., 316, *320*
Woods, E. R., 87, 93, *104,* 221, *239*
Wooldredge, J., 26, *55*
Wotman, S. R., 195, *206*
Wright, T. L., 29, *54,* 243, 251, *275*
Wu Shortt, J., 259, *275*
Wu, C., 248, 255, *277*
Wu, H., 69, 73, 75, *82*
Wu, L. L, 374, *385*
Wunderlich, C., 221, *237*
Wynne, L. C., 112, 113, 114, 129, *135*

Y

Yagi, G., 74, *82*
Yoerger, K., 256, 257, *273*

Yoshimura, K., 74, *82*
Youm, Y, 289, *295*
Youmiss, J., 6, 8, *22*
Youngblade, L., 299, *322*

Z

Zabin, L. S., 62, *84*
Zani, B., 7, 9, *22*
Zeifman, D., 8, *20,* 137, 140, 141, 156, *158*
Zelli, A., 269, *275*
Zelnick, M., 62, *84*
Zentall, S. R., 382, *384*
Zezza, N., 74, *81*
Zhang, X., 74, *82*
Zhou, M., 50, *56*
Zhu, G., 72, *79*
Zigler, E., 248, *275*
Zijdenbos, A., 60, *80*
Zimet, G. D., 280, *294*
Zimmer-Gembeck, M. J., 6, 9, *22,* 373,
    385
Zimmerman, M. A., 374, *383*
Zimmerman, R. S., 196, *211*
Zollinger, L., 170, *182,* 297, 300, 306, *320*
Zonderman, A. B., 74, *84*
Zucker, K. J., 216, *235*
Zucker, R. A., 229, *241*
Zuckerman, M., 73, *84*
Zuroff, D. C., 172, *181*

Subject Index

A

Abuse, *see* child maltreatment, victimization
Academic achievement, 7, 13
Adolescent romance
 as developmental process, 5, 110, 116–131, 138, 171–172, 190–205, 213, 218–222, 337–338, 341, 345, 363, 373, 376–378
Adolescent romantic relationships, *see* Romantic relationships in adolescence
Add Health Study, *see* National Longitudinal Study of Adolescent Health
Adolescent fathers, *see* Adolescent parenthood
Adolescent mothers, *see* Adolescent parenthood
Adolescent parenthood, xi, 13, 28, 71, 297–318
 adjustment to, 298, 316
 clinical implications, 317–318
 cohabitation, 299, 309, 314
 coparenting, 297–301, 304–305, 309–311, 314–316
 father participation, 300, 316–317
 interpersonal behavior, 298–299, 310–315
 gender differences in, 310–312, 316
 research methodology issues, 301
 romantic relationships, 298–301, 309–312
 social support, 298–299, 314
 stress, 308–309, 313–314
Adolescent pregnancy, xi, 12, 279, 297–299
Adolescent marriage, 14
Affiliation, 9, 110–112
African-Americans, 25–26, 36–48, 285, 310
 cohabitation, 25, 26, 285
 marriage, 25–26
Age differences, *see* Age effects
Age effects (and romantic relations), 24–25,
28, 32–38, 45–47, 148, 213–215, 219–221
Aggression, *see* Violence in adolescent romance
Alcohol use, *see* Substance use
Ambivalence
 and adolescent romance, 7
Androgens, 59–60
Antisocial behavior, 170, 248, 254–258
Anxiety, 141–142
Asian-Americans, 33, 35, 39, 48, 50
Assortive mating, 23, 26, 40, 129, 258–259, 265, 361
Attachment, x, 8, 23, 125–126, 137–156, 163, 187–190, 214–218, 376
Autonomy, *see* Individuation

B

Behavioral genetics, 27
Biological models, 57
Biological processes, ix, 57–78
 cortisol, 70
 myelination, 60, 61
 physiological reaction to novelty, 70
 prenatal androgen exposure, 60
 related to sexual development, 60
Biosocial models, 61, 362, 378
Bisexuality, 88, 98, *see* Sexual minority youth
Brain structures related to sexual behavior, 60
Breakups, 14, 200–204

C

Case examples, 121–125, 164, 176–178, 214, 371

Casual sex, 71
Chicago Youth Development Study (CYDS),
      244, 252–253, 270
Child maltreatment, 213–220, 227–228, 248,
      255
Clinical implications of adolescent romance,
      xi, 5, 130, 155, 98–100, 202–205, 317–
      318, 371, 379
Cognitive processes, 188–189
Cohabitation, 245
Cohesion, 124
Cohort effects and romantic relations, 372
Commitment, 28, 43–44, 115
Communication skills, 111, see Interpersonal
      skills
Conflict, ix, 110–128
Conflict Tactics Scale (CTS), 250
Contexts for sexual development, 11, 12, 138
Contextual factors and romantic relations, 17,
      29, 40, 43, 48–50
Contraceptive use, 281–282, 288–289
Corrective emotional experiences, 15
Cortisol, 70
Couple types, 124, 169, 342, 345–351
Cultural and romantic relations, 373–374,
      see Ethnicity

                              D

Dating, 137–156, 218–220, 221–233; see
      Romantic relationships in adolescents
Depression, x, 14, 172–178, 185–194
   biopsychosocial model of, 187
   gender differences, 186–187
   interpersonal styles, 186–187, 190
   in marriage, 175
   screening for, 204
   and sexual behavior, 196–198
   types of, 172–178
Developmental processes
   discontinuity in, 58
   early adolescence, 4, 24
   identity, 3, 4, 5, 337–340, 356
   interpersonal skills, 27, 179, 340
   late adolescence, 4, 24
   middle adolescence, 4, 24
   peers relations, 3

   processes of, 14
   relatedness and autonomy, 23, 24
   sexuality, 3, 10
   transitions in, 58, 192
Developmental systems model, 72, 76
Developmental tasks, 3, 57, 180
Developmental trajectories, 87, 89, 91–92, 95,
      97, 100, 102
Diabetes, 127
Diagnostic and Statistical Manual of Mental
      Disorders, IV (DSM-IV), 173
Dopamine, 72–76
Double standards, 10
Drug use, see Substance use
Dyadic influences, 70, 128–129, 267–268,
      286–293, 374

                              E

Early adolescence, 4, 24
Early starters, 7, 13, 338
Education and health 203
Educational approaches, xii, 14, 203, 358–
      361, 364–368, 380–381
Emotions, 3, 9, 12, 93, 137, 142–150, 153,
      192–202, 342–345
Empathy, 27
Estrogen, 60, 69
Ethnicity, 33–51, 310
   African-Americans, 25–26, 36–48, 285,
      310
   Asian-Americans, 33, 35, 39, 48, 50
   Latinos, 33, 36–48, 310
Evolutionary theory, 26

                              F

Family relationships, 6, 29, 118–119, 128, 137
   attachment figures, 8
   and conflict, 6, 7
   and effects on romantic relations, 16
   individuation, 6
   support, 8
   torn loyalties, 7
   transformations, 6
Fels Longitudinal Study, 61

Freud, 57
Friendship, 10, 29, 111–113, *see* peer relations

G

Gay, lesbian, and bisexual, *see* Sexual minority
    youth
Gay-straight alliances, 367, 381
Gender differences, 116–117, 194, 362–364
    depression, 186–187
    expectations about romance, 5
    health behaviors 286–290
    interpersonal behavior differences, 310–
        312, 316
    partner selection, 38, 50
    prevalence of romantic relations, 34, 49
    role identity, 5
    sexual behavior, 45, 66, 148, 150
    sexual minority youth, 93, 95–97
    sexuality, 45, 66, 148, 150
    violence, 262–265, 268
Genetic factors, 58, 70–72, 74, 77
Goodness of fit model of, 63
Gonad development, 60

H

Health behaviors, 3, 24, 279–293
    contraceptive use, 281–282, 288–289
    dyadic influences on, 286–293
    education, 203, 267, 292–293, *see*
        Prevention
    gender differences in, 286–290
    measurement of health behaviors, 283–
        289
    risk behaviors, 280–284, 289–293
    prevention of risk, 292–293
    sexual behavior, 288–293
Health education, 203, 267, 292–293, 358–
    361, 364–368; *see* prevention
Healthy relationships, promoting, 348, 351,
    357, 376
Homosexuality, *see* Sexual minority youth
Hormones, 58–60, 65–67, 77
Human immunodeficiency virus (HIV),
    279

I

Identity, 3–5, 91, 99–100, 337–340, 356
Individual differences, 4, 15, 17, 109, 154, 358
Individuation, 111, 114, 118, 130, 186, 339
Infatuation, 115, 194–195
Infidelity, 198–200
Intercourse, 11, 28, 45, 58
Interpersonal processes
    measurement of, 164–180, 305–308
Interpersonal skills, 27, 111, 120–125, 179,
    340, 346–352, 365, 381
Interracial relationships, 26, 38–39, 50
Intervention, *see* Clinical implications of
    adolescent romance
Intimacy, 12, 28, 43–45, 90, 93–95, 97, 109,
    113–114, 142, 191, 337

J

Juvenile delinquency, *see* Antisocial behavior

L

Late adolescence, 4, 24
Latinos, 33, 36–48, 310
Lesbians, *see* Sexual minority youth
Love, 11, 142

M

Marital interaction, x, xii, 337–354
    couple types, *see* Romantic relationships in
        adolescence
    divorce prediction, 344
    marital intervention, xii, 341–342
    observation methods, 350–353
    perception of, 347–348
    relationship repair, 347–349
    Specific Affect Observational Coding
        System (SPAFF), 344
Marital process, *see* Marital interaction
Marital relationships, *see* Marital interaction
Mate selection, 26, 38, 40, 129
Media influences, 373

Menarche, 59, 64
Methodological issues, 30, 34–36, 165–170, 249–252, 301, 374–375
  health behaviors, 283–289
  interpersonal processes, 164–180, 305–308
  observation methods, 350–353
  sexual behavior, 145–147
Middle adolescence, 4, 24
Minority groups, *see* Ethnicity, Sexual minority youth

N

National Family Violence Survey (NFVS), 244
National Longitudinal Study of Adolescent Health (Add Health Study), 24, 30–51, 292–293, 364
National Longitudinal Survey of Youth (NLSY), 71
Negotiation, 110–112, 117, 131
Neuroendocrine system, 59
Nonshared environmental factors, 71
Norms, 23–51
Number of partners, 11, 288

O

Oral History Interview (OHI), 341, 353
Oregon Youth Study (OYS), 244, 251–252, 270

P

Pair-bonding, 23, 27
Partner effects, 70
Partner differences
  age, 36–38
Parent–child relations, 6, 111, 128
Parenting, 297–301, 304–305, 309–311, 314–316
Partner similarities, 9, 281–282
Peer groups, 8–9, 24, 280–282
Peer pressure, 196–197
Peer relations, 3, 8–9, 29, 92, 94, 96–97, 101–102, 256–258, 280–282, 349–350

Pregnancy, *see* Adolescent pregnancy
Prevention, 179–181, 270–272, 292–293, 364, 380–382, *see* Clinical implications of adolescent romance
  Youth Relationships Project (YRP), 234
  Safe Dates Program, 180, 270–271, 365, 381
  Safer Choices Program, 380
Psychological disorders, *see* Psychopathology
Psychopathology, x, 163–165
  antisocial behavior, 170, 248, 254–258
  depression, 14, 185–194
    biopsychosocial model of, 187
    gender differences, 186–187
    interpersonal styles, 186–187, 190
    in marriage, 175
    screening for, 204
    and sexual behavior, 196–198
    types of, 172–178
  prevention of, 179–181
  and romantic relationships, 163–165, 170–172
Puberty, 57
  androgen, 59–60
  bidirectional models of, 57
  biological model of, 57
  body fat, 65
  coactional processes, 58, 72
  developmental systems model of, 57, 72
  estrogen, 60, 69
  Fels Longitudinal Study of, 61
  Freudian model of, 57
  genetics and, 58, 72
  gonad development, 60
  hormonal changes in, 58–60, 65–68
  interactional model of, 58
  mediational effects model, 58
  menarche, 59, 64
  neuroendocrine system, 59
  off-time model of, 63
  psychological effects of, 59
  secondary sex characteristics, 60, 65
  sexual interest, 69
  sexual readiness, 60, 63
  social contextual factors in, 62, 64, 67, 68
  stage termination model of, 63
  status, 61–62, 359
  testosterone, 59, 63, 65–69

timing of, 58, 61, 62, 359
Public Policy, 77–88

Q

Quality of Relationship Inventory (QRI),
    303–305

R

Racial differences, 25, 29, 38, 44–46, 49–51,
    310
  African Americans, 25–26, 36–48, 285,
    310
  age at first intercourse, 29
  Asian Americans, 33, 35, 39, 48, 50
  interpersonal behavior, 310
  Latinos, 33, 36–48, 310
  partner selection, 38
  relationship violence, 268–270
  romantic relationships, 373
  sexual behavior, 46, 221
Rape, 223–224, 230–231, 358
Reciprocity, 50, 220–223, 245, 261–262
Rejection sensitivity, 69–70, 126–127
Relationship continuity, see Relationship
    stability
Relationship duration, see Relationship
    stability
Relationship repair, 347–351
Relationship stability, 10, 27, 40–43, 50, 115,
    219
Risk behaviors, xi, 14, 16, 219, 279–293, 338,
    378
Romantic relationships in adolescence, 4–5,
    110, 116–131, 138, 171–172, 190–205,
    213, 218–222, 337–338, 341, 345, 363,
    373, 376–378
  adolescent parents, 297–318
  affiliation, 9, 110–112
  age effects, 24, 25, 32–38, 213–215, 219–
    220
  aggression, see violence
  attachment, 8, 125–126, 137–156, 187–
    190, 214–218, 376
  autonomy, see relatedness; Individuation

biosocial approaches, 61, 362, 378
breakups, 14, 200–204
  and career choice, 13
  case examples, 121–125, 164, 176–178,
    214, 371
  catalyst for change, 13
  child maltreatment as risk factor in, 213–
    220, 227–228, 248, 255
  cognitive processes in, 188–189
  cohabitation, 245
  cohort effects, 372
  commitment, 28, 43–44
  communication skills, see interpersonal
    skills
  conflict in, 109–131, 343
  context for sexual development, 11, 12, 138
  contextual factors of, 17, 29, 40, 43, 48–50
  corrective emotional experiences, 15
  couple types, 124, 169, 342, 345–351
  cultural expectations, 373–374
  dysfunction in, 163–181, 342, 361, 372
  educational approaches, 203, 358–361,
    364–368
  emotions, 192–202, 342–345
  evolutionary theory and, 26
  family formation, 23
  family relations, 6, 29, 118–119, 128, 137
  friendships, 10, 29, 111–113
  gender differences in, 116–117, 194
  gender role, 362–364
  genetic factors, 70
  healthy relationships, see normative role of
  individual differences in, 15, 17, 109, 154,
    358
  infidelity, 198–200
  interpersonal skills, 111, 120–125, 346–
    352, 365, 381
  interracial relationships, 26, 38–39, 50
  intimacy, 28, 43–45, 109, 113–114, 191,
    337
  media influences on, 373
  models of, 187–190
  negative experiences, 4, 116, 342, 358
  negotiation, 110–112, 117, 131
  normative role of, 356–357, 372–376
  pair-bonding, 23, 27
  parent–child relations, 6, 111, 128
  parents' marriage and implications on, 15

Romantic relationships in adolescence
    (continued)
  partner similarities, 9, 281–282
  peer relations, 8, 9, 29, 256–258, 349–350
  pregnancy, *see* Adolescent pregnancy
  prevalence of, 32, 34
  racial differences, 25, 38, 49–51
  reciprocity in, 50, 220–223, 245, 261–262
  relatedness, 111, 114, 118, 130, 186, 339
  research on, 25, 34, 143–153
    methodological issues, 30, 34–36, 165–
      170, 374–375
  risks of, 14,16, 219, 338, 378
  scripts, 29
  seriousness of, 14
  sexual behavior, 45–46, 142, 148–153,
    284–285, 288–289, *see* sexual behavior
    (as main heading)
  social connectedness, 48–49
  social learning theory, 217–218, 249
  stages of, 115, 191–202, 213
  stability, 10, 27, 40–43, 50, 115, 219
  status achievement, 9
  stressors associated with, 192–194
  support, 7, 10, 339, 349–350
  violence in, 17, 29, 47, 49–50, 170, 213–
    235, 243–272, 343, 361
    Conflict Tactics Scale (CTS), 250
    definitions of, 249–251
    dyadic influences, 267–268, 374
    ethnicity and culture effects, 268–270
    gender differences, 262–265, 268
    injury rates, 262–265
    methodological issues, 249–252
    models of, 253–257, 259–270
    prevention of, 180, 270–272, 364, 380–
      382
    socioeconomic status (SES) and, 269
    stability of, 266–268
    theories of, 246–249

S

Safer Choices Program, 380
Safe Dates Program, 180, 270–271, 365, 381
Same-sex attractions, 87–89, *see* Sexual
    minority youth

Same-sex experimentation, 99
Same-sex relations, *see* Sexual minority youth
SASB, *see* Structural Analysis of Social
    Behavior
Self-assertion, 111
Self-concept, 4–5
Self-definition, 138, 356
Self-discovery, 340
Self-esteem (self-worth), 4–5, 90
Self-representation, 4–5
Self-respect, 5
Serotonin, 75–77
Sex education, 14, 203, 358–361, 364–368
Sexual behavior, 148–153, 284–285; 288–289
  age effects, 45–47, 148, 220–221
  biological processes, *see* Puberty
  biosocial approaches, 61, 77
  body schemas, 12
  casual sex, 71
  coactional processes, 58, 72
  contraceptive use, 281–282, 288–289
  decision making, 196–197
  developmental processes, 10, 196–198
  developmental systems model, 72, 76
  dopamine, 72–75
  double standards, 10
  drive, *see* motivations for
  early starters, 7, 13, 338
  education about, 14, 359, 365–368
  emotions, 12, 142, 149–150, 153
  gender differences, 45, 66, 148, 150
  genetic factors, 70–72, 74, 77
  health behaviors, *see* Health
  hormones, 58–60, 65–67, 77
  initiation, 62, 63, 67, 149–151, 288
  intercourse, 11, 28, 45, 58
  intimacy, 12, 28, 142
  love, 11, 142
  motivations for, 149, 153
  nonshared environmental factors, 71
  number of partners, 11, 288
  orientation, 12, 24, 144
  partner effects, 70
  peer pressure, 196–197
  "petting," 29, 45
  public policy, 77–78
  rape, *see* victimization
  reproduction, *see* Adolescent pregnancy

research on, 25, 61, 66, 143–153
romantic relations as context, 23, 138, 196
serotonin, 75–77
social moderators, 66, 74
social norms, 12
temperament, 69, 70
victimization, 17, 29, 148, 196, 221, 224, 231
Sexual confusion, 98–99
Sexual decision making, 196–197
Sexual initiation, 62, 63, 67
Sexual interest, 69
Sexual minority youth, ix, 4, 12, 27, 40, 50, 85–86, 325, 363
    bisexuality, 88, 98
    childhood experiences, 94
    clinical implications, 98–100
    confusion, 98–99
    developmental trajectories, 87, 89, 91–92, 95, 97, 100, 102
    disclosure of orientation, 86
    diversity, 98, 333
    education, 359, 363, 367
    emotions, 93
    femininity, 95, 97
    gay-straight alliances, 367, 381
    gender composition effects, 95
    gender differences, 93, 95–97
    identity, 91, 99–100
    interpersonal training opportunities, 96
    intimacy, 90, 93–95, 97
    isolation, 101
    love and sex, 87, 92–93
    masculinity, 95, 97
    mental health, 85
    normative pressures, 93
    peer relations, 92, 94, 96–97, 101–102
    relational concerns of, 89, 92
    sensitivity in research, 327–336
    role of counselors and educators, 100–101
    romantic relations, 92, 102, 325–336
    safe contexts for, 90, 99
    same sex attraction, 87–89, see Sexual minority youth
    same-sex experimentation, 99
    self-esteem of, 90
    sexual orientation, 359
    sexual questioning, 99–100
    social competence, 94, 97
    social support, 90, 93–94, 101
    stereotype, 87
    stigmas, 89–90, 94–95
Sexual orientation, 359
Sexual questioning, 99–100
Sexual transition, 68
Sexuality, see Sexual behavior, Sexual minority youth
Sexually transmitted diseases (STDs), xi, 28, 78, 279–283, 292, 366
    Human immunodeficiency virus (HIV), 279
Social competence, 94, 97, 357
Social context, 4
Social control theory, 65, 67
Social learning theory, 217–218, 249
Social support, 90, 93–94, 101
Socioeconomic status (SES), 269, 301
Sound Marital House, 340–341
Specific Affect Observational Coding System (SPAFF), 344
Stage termination model of, 63
Storm and stress, 137
Structural Analysis of Social Behavior (SASB), x, 164–180, 305–308, 311, 339
Substance use, 7, 142, 151, 291
    and aggression, 232–233
    and child maltreatment, 229–230
    and sexual behavior, 231–233, 289, 291
Systems models, 57, 72, 76, 112, 129

T

Teacher, 368
Temperament, 69, 70
Testosterone, 59, 63, 65–69
Teenage parenthood, see Adolescent parenthood
Teenage pregnancy, see Adolescent pregnancy

V

Victimization, 17, 29, 148, 196, 221, 224, 231
Violence in adolescent romance, xi, 17, 29,

Violence in adolescent romance *(continued)*
47, 49–50, 170, 213–235, 243–272, 343,
361
definitions of, 249–251
dyadic influences, 267–268, 374
ethnicity and culture effects, 268–270
gender differences, 262–265, 268
injury rates, 262–265
methodological issues, 249–252
models of, 253–257, 259–270
prevention of, 180, 270–272, 364, 380–382

socioeconomic status (SES) and, 269
stability of, 266–268
theories of, 246–249

Y

Young Parenthood Project (YPP), 301–316,
337–338
Youth Relationships Project (YRP), 234